RECORD OF YOGA

II

Sri Aurobindo

Record of Yoga

II

Sri Aurobindo Ashram
Pondicherry

First edition 2001
Third impression 2005

II

Rs. 270.00
(Soft cover) ISBN 81-7058-652-6

Published by Sri Aurobindo Ashram Publication Department,
Pondicherry - 605 002
Website: http://sabda.sriaurobindoashram.org
Printed at Sri Aurobindo Ashram Press, Pondicherry
PRINTED IN INDIA

CONTENTS

Part Two (continued)
Record of Yoga 1912–1920

1 January–27 February 1915	779
22 April–26 August 1915	830
19 February–20 March 1916	909
9 January–14 February 1917	919
15 February–31 March 1917	958
15 August–28 September 1917	994
14–28 February 1918	1021
3–27 March 1918	1033
20 April–20 May 1918	1038
21 May–1 July 1918	1083
24 June–14 July 1919	1095
15–26 July 1919	1125
27 July–13 August 1919	1147
14 August–24 September 1919	1169
1–29 February 1920	1184
1 March–10 April 1920	1200
7–26 June 1920	1225
17–19 October 1920	1239

Part Three
Record of Yoga 1926–1927

December 1926–6 January 1927	1245
7 January–1 February 1927	1249
7–22 April 1927	1265
24–31 October 1927	1271

CONTENTS

Part Four
Materials Written by Sri Aurobindo Related Directly to
Record of Yoga, c. 1910–1931

Undated Record and Record-related Notes,
   c. 1910–1914 — 1277
Sortileges of May and June 1912 — 1285
Undated Notes, c. November 1912 — 1287
Draft Programme of 3 December 1912 — 1289
Undated or Partly Dated Script, 1912–1913 — 1290
Sortilege of 15 March [1913] — 1311
Accounts of 31 May–15 June 1913 — 1312
Record Notes, 13 and 15 September 1913 — 1317
Vedic Experience, 14 and 15 December 1913 — 1319
Undated Notes, c. 1914 — 1321
Notes on Images Seen in March 1914 — 1323
Undated Script, c. 1920 — 1336
Undated Notes, c. December 1926 — 1337
Undated Notes, c. January 1927 — 1344
Notes on Physical Transformation, c. January 1927 — 1345
Diagrams, c. January 1927 — 1349
Miscellaneous Notations, c. February–April 1927 — 1352
Record of Drishti, 30 July 1927 — 1353
Undated Script, c. 1927 — 1354
Undated Script, c. 1927–1928 — 1356
Notes on Prophetic Vision, 1929 — 1358
Diagrams, c. 1931 — 1359
Undated Script Jottings — 1361

Part Five
Automatic Writing

"The Scribblings", c. 1907 — 1367
Yogic Sadhan — 1371
Automatic Writings, c. 1914 (First Set) — 1400
Automatic Writings, c. 1914 (Second Set) — 1404

CONTENTS

Automatic Writing, c. 1920   1410
Automatic Writings, c. 1920   1411

Appendixes
Material from Disciples' Notebooks

Miscellaneous Notes, c. 1914   1453
Sapta Chatusthaya — Scribal Version   1467

Note on the Texts   1485

There is still the same siege of the Asiddhi. Tamasic udasinata is always forbidding; but faith & Hasya are seriously breached. The Abhasan has also been successfully attacked in the physical prana, although it remains intact in the mentality (chitta).

There is finality of the perception of the triloka (three worlds), in the forces & powers that constitute it.

There is finality in the perception of the brihat satyam, without finality in the ritam. Satyam means truth of being, in thought, force, tendency, etc, not truth of fact in actual substantiality.

The finality of illuminated thought & vision is being prepared. When it is complete, there will be no farther asiddhi in the first two chatusthayas. Knowledge is the condition of perfection. The lower powers err, aiming at perfection without knowledge, & pursue & exaggerate perfection.

There is finality in the telepathic perceptions, satyam, of forces, tendencies, thoughts etc, but it is not yet brihat. Brihat is being prepared.

There is finality in the fundamental unity of the will. Wherever it is applied, it is a force to be reckoned with, although not yet a force that always prevails.

=

Yesterday closed the period of prevalent asiddhi. Today begins the period, for October, of siddhi prevailing in spite of Asiddhi. Seen in the Asiddhi, therefore, an uninterrupted progression of the Siddhi.

=

Record entry of 7 October 1914

January.

During December the advance has been chiefly in the third and sixth chatusthayas.

In the first, Asiddhi has been reduced to an occasional physical depression of the sukham which does not affect the being generally but only the nervous & physical layers of the physical consciousness. As a rule the full samata operates.

Positive Ananda is sometimes deficient. Asiddhi does not bring revolt, but only a temporary failing of positive Ananda and a depression of force and faith.

Everything being now seen as the play of the Lilamaya Krishna, revolt is no longer possible. It is also seen that all forces, all experiences act & occur, succeed & fail in pursuance of his self-fulfilment in the world. It is only in the relations of the Lilamaya with the Jiva that there is a defect, positive harmony proceeding by ignorance, uncertainty, some unfaith.

This renders itself by a defect of the second chatusthaya. Faith in the Yogasiddhi does not really falter except in relation to the Saundaryam. An increasing rapidity & sureness & safety, (dhananam satih), is acknowledged. But the decisive knowledge & effectivity being insufficient, faith in the entire rapidity is insufficient, faith in the Kriti grows, but is troubled by doubts.

Hence, the Ishwarabhava cannot fix itself & brings with it a

The Record for 1–6 January 1915 was kept in the notebook in use since 29–30 September 1914. Between 2 and 23 January an "intermediate record" was kept in another notebook. There are entries for 2–6 January in both records; these contain some repetitions. — Ed.

general laxity of the Virya and Devibhava. Nevertheless the faith & the Ishwarabhava grow steadily.

In the third chatusthaya satyam brihat has extended itself to the trikaldrishti, telepathy & tapas-siddhi, but have not yet been converted into the full ritam. Ritam is being organised, but is self-constructive rather than transcendently decisive. Therefore it lacks mastery & selfconfidence and fullness.

The defect is in tapas-siddhi. There is the play of forces, the acceptance of all forces, the effectivity of tapas in the end. But the balance wavers continually; the tapas effects itself through a struggle of mutual adaptation on the level of this action, not by union with a mastering will that transcends the action.

This defect is dependent on a defect in KrishnaKali relation & related to the defect of the faith & Ishwarabhava.

Swapna Samadhi has conquered all its difficulties and has now only to organise itself finally for steady manifestation and definite ritam and utility. In jagrat there is manifestation of all sorts of forms, but not yet a victorious hold of stable clearness on the Akasha.

Sharira is still in full struggle to manifest & organise itself.

Ananda has arranged all its terms, but cannot yet deploy them in a sure & normal continuity. Recurrence is established varying in frequency & stability in the different terms, but continuity is still prevented.

Arogya advances slowly. It has got rid of the permanence of certain affections & of all but the last remnants of their recurrence, but it is not yet sure of the non-return of rogas that have been expelled but not destroyed, — as instanced by the eye-affection. Assimilation still repeats the old see-saw between excessive consolidation and jalya-tejomaya dissolution. The Will for right assimilation does not succeed. The chakra makes advances in certain details, but not any organised advance. Will is effective slowly or swiftly in temporary movements.

Utthapana has abandoned the attempt at self-fulfilment by tapasya. But the exclusion of defect of anima by Will is not yet sufficiently advanced to replace tapasya.

Saundarya is still held back. The body is prevented from

obeying the Will. There is only a predominant, but slow and uncertain advance in some details. .

Kalikrishna is manifest & established in the completed Brahmadarshana; but there is need of smarana still. As soon as there is smarana, there is complete darshana, but emerging out of the incomplete darshana in which Ananda is involved, not dominant & Krishna concealed by the extended Brahman.

In the person Kali is organised in the Maheshwari-Mahaluxmi-Mahasaraswati combination, the second element as yet insufficient, but the dominant Mahakali is occasional only, the normal bhava being the contained and dominated Mahakali.

This again is due to the gulf that still remains between the Purusha & the Shakti. The Purusha is the dominant Krishna, bala, Balarama-Aniruddha; but the Prakriti does not always feel the fullness of the tertiary dasya & the actual presence of the bhava of madhura-dasya. Hence the Ishwara is recognised, but the Devi is not yet Ishwari by expressing the dominant will of the Ishwara.

Hence karma is not yet manageable. Sahitya is powerful & effective, but hampered by the sluggish response of the physical instrument. Dharma grows in strength, but is not yet easy & sure except in certain persons & movements & there not with sufficient force. Kriti is struggling slowly to emerge, but is still enveloped.

Kama is growing continually in bhava, but awaits the Sharira-siddhi.

Shuddhi-Mukti-Bhukti are imperfect only by the imperfect physical response. Siddhi moves forward steadily & surely, but is not yet victorious.

For January the development of ritam, the entire union of KrishnaKali in the madhura dasya, the organisation for life & action of the three first chatusthayas & the fullness & force of the completed chatusthayas seem to be indicated.

The struggle is now in Sharira and Karma. Ananda is assured, but its organisation has to be completed by continuity. Arogya has to conquer the obstacles to perfect sati & victorious fulfilment. Utthapana has to conquer defect of anima. Saundarya has to break down the wall of physical inadaptability. It is not clear how much of this can be done in the month of January.

The progress possible in Karma is still more obscure. . A great development in Sahitya & Dharma is possible. Kriti is enveloped in doubt. Kama waits on Sharira.

Probably the resistance will finally break down, if not completely, in January February.

Jan 1ˢᵗ

The day begins with a struggle as a result of which it is decided that no sadhana is necessary for the development of the ritam. The attempt at direct sadhana results in a return of old conditions and old defects.
≡

T³ [trikaldrishti, telepathy and tapas-siddhi] is now proceeding normally. The main movement is towards the substitution of Ishwarabhava in the tapas-siddhi for the attitude of effort and aim of the Devi.
≡

In Rupa also the old tendency to compel by tratak imperfect figures to become perfect, is from today abandoned. The imperfect figure is only an indication of the Drishti working upon the physical akasha to open it to the physical vision. . The Drishti will do its own work unaided by trataka.
≡

Ananda also must be left to perfect itself.
≡

Sadhan is still needed in the rest of Sharira, but sadhan only of the discerning Will.
≡

Lipi
   By the faith

Trikaldrishti
Vague intimation that S [Saurin] & others would return about 11.30 pm. They came at 11.22 —
≡

Ananda

Shuddha Ananda with Kama & Premananda inherent in it is beginning to dominate Chidghana-Ahaituka.

Rupa

Stable rupa partially distinct at night. Perfect rupa with initial stability occurs occasionally.

=

KrishnaKali

The Ishwara is beginning finally to dominate all the action. There is always tertiary dasya, but it is generally void of the madhura. The madhura is now about to establish itself as the normal bhava.

This is evident in the darshana of external objects and there it comes automatically. It is less easy in the internal darshana.

Kali is now everywhere revealed in the bhava of the madhura dasi dominated by Krishna & ministering to his bhoga.

This bhava is becoming by a secondary motion more normal in the internal darshana —

=

T^3

The decisive trikaldrishti is becoming more frequent & better justified in its frequency

=

Kriti

Kriti is manifesting tongues of potentiality, but at present it is action without any certain result.

Samadhi

In swapna samadhi lipi is still subject to a certain incoherence, ordinarily. Coherence of phrases is common.

St. [Sortilege]
1. The airship
2 Matches
3 safety.

=

Sharira

Ananda was recurrent, not continuous. There was frequently a physical obstruction.

Arogya also does not advance beyond the point already attained.

There was no utthapana

=

Samadhi

Samadhi at night was unproductive.

Dream was confused and entirely occupied with present associations.

=

Siddhi

The movement just now has reverted to the condition of obscured and disaggregated progress with preparation behind the veil.

Doubt of the Kriti has taken a somewhat acute form, although there is a struggling faith which refuses to retire.

Doubt of the Yoga-siddhi can no longer be reestablished. There is only uncertainty of the rapidity.

=

The ritam is steadily advancing under all.

Jan 2.

T^3

The ritam of telepathy is now becoming more & more marked and decisive. That of trikaldrishti is still hampered by hasty tapasic decisions. But these are converting themselves into excess of statement rather than misstatement.

The element of misstatement especially survives in the combination of Trikaldrishti & Tapas-siddhi.

=

The Tapas siddhi is now in a period of recoil. 80° acts seldom or not at all; long & obstinate resistances, contrary movements are the rule.

=

Utthapana

Arms, one hour. Easy; but afterwards there was some heaviness in the shoulder-muscles.

=

The Asiddhi is associated with an attempt of the Dwayavin consciousness to reassert itself and support an activity of the tamasic dhriti in the physical consciousness opposed to the constant manifestation of the Siddhi. The success has been to create a cleft between the divine consciousness & the physical by which the latter sees all things as the Brahman in the many, but not the Many as the One.

There is an alternation between this division & the integral consciousness.

Rupa

Jagrat Rupa of all kinds, except the perfect, with an initial stability, just before the eyes, emerging from pranic akasha.

=

Utthapana

Right leg, horizontal, recumbent on side, 20 minutes. At the end strong defect of anima, – always recurrent defect.

Saundarya

A certain gain has been effected in one of the features, but this is not accompanied by any general movement.

St.

   1 Forget me not   (nityasmarana)
   2 The New Way   (ie of the entire dasyam; by this the nitya-
                                  smarana will come)

=

Trikaldrishti

   1. The hold of the asiddhi passes away today
   2. 4 days of progressive siddhi.

Ananda

The physical Anandas again became active.

Lipi

1. light
2 destiny belongs to the Ishwari
3 entire stability of the lipi has to be reinstated　(fulfilled)
4. tapas siddhi
5 faith in the entire rapidity is about to be justified
6 fortnightly attack of the Asiddhi.
7. This is the entirety of the faith in the Yogasiddhi.

Jan 3ᵈ

The decisive Trikaldrishti is now regularising itself, putting away to each side of it the tapasic and tamasic insistences.

This involves a certain putting aside of the Tapas siddhi of tapasic aishwarya vashita, which has to give place to the self-knowing divine Aishwarya-Ishita-Vashita.

The Tapasic stress reveals itself more and more as a force working for a future effect in opposition to resistances (tamasic stress) and mistaken in its idea of time and circumstance because of absorption in the sureness of its own fulfilment. The tamasic stress is more in harmony with present time and circumstance, but mistakes present for future non-fulfilment. —
=

The day was chiefly given to work for the Review.
=

Utthapana half hour. At first dullness, afterwards force of the laghima.
=

Lipi active in sthapatya & manifesting page in single & double word, vivid & legible, but not entirely fixed.
=

At night activity of the tejomaya rupa in Swapnasamadhi.
=

Verification of distant telepathy.
=

Jan 4th

The morning devoted to work for the Review

=

Vijnana

T^3 continues to progress. Many combinations which come automatically in the unillumined mentality, prove to be right in every detail. This is a definite beginning of the ritam.

Tapasic stress justifies itself more & more as a promise of the future. But though the examples are many & striking, the fulfilment is either not invariable or does not always present itself to the observation.

=

80° does not now occur, but on the other hand there are instances of the almost immediate effectivity (70°) even where there is a previous opposite tendency & intention. Not yet, however, where the intention is strong and fixed, except rarely.

=

Stable dense rupa & dense developed (less stable) came frequently in jagrat antardrishta.

In swapnasamadhi there are now frequent instances of true scene, event & conversation of this world. Combinations are becoming more frequent & firm. But as yet there is not the use of samadhi for life-utilities.

=

Anandamaya Ishwaradarshan in all is now normal, but not usually intense.

=

Sharira

In Arogya there is something of a setback.

=

Physical Ananda can no longer be annulled. It can only be obstructed by a strong pressure.

=

The hair continues to be thin in front and especially on the left side. It is in the lower layer that the Asiddhi is obstinate.

=

Suddhananda is now fixed behind the Chidghana & Ahaituka. Prema & subjective Kama Anandas are as a result normalising themselves.

=

There is no indication as yet of any decisive movement in the Karma.

=

Utthapana of the arms one hour, laghima effective but burdened by [subsequent][1] reaction of the defect of anima.

=

Vijnana

80° acted twice in succession once for exact detail of aishwaryam, once after failure of aishwaryam for general effectivity of ishita

Swapnasamadhi continues at the same level wavering between imperfect and more perfect organisation.

=

Sharira

Denial of Arogya was a little stronger & one of the gains was temporarily abrogated.

=

Ananda sometimes obstructed, always impeded, yet maintains itself.

Jan 5th

In the morning a strong obstruction to the Ishwaradarshana preventing the physical consciousness from enjoying the light of the Affirmations even though aware of their actuality behind the denial.

This obstruction contains in itself a more entire, ready & solid participation in the siddhi by the whole conscious existence. The subconscious is being rapidly trained by the force of its obstructed aspiration towards the light.

---

[1] *MS* subagent

The response to the Asiddhi proceeds from the subconscious; as the source of these responses, it is being purified from them and fortified for the response to the Siddhi—

In the waking mind the obstruction creates a conclusion of un-faith in the rapidity of the Siddhi &, consequently, in the importance of the karma.

The element of error in the satyam is temporarily emphasised in order that the resultant truth may be more sure and self-assured.
=

St.

1. एति प्र होता व्रतमस्य मायया ऊर्ध्वां दधानः शुचिपेशसं धियं।

Agni, the divine force, precedes the present movement of action by the concealed creative & formative Maya of the Master of the Yoga holding in himself a thought pure in form of vision & exalted to the Vijnana. This is the sense of the present obstruction & its eventualities.

2. Any person must be able to trace his past, present and future.

Sharira

Ananda oppressed at night & in the morning acted from time to time during the day.
=

Utthapana

1. The utthapana of the arms failed because of the denial by physical heaviness.

2. Left leg, horizontal 27 minutes. Strong *laghu mahima*, strong defect of anima with *kampana*, finally prevailing. Intervals of pure anandamaya anima after the tremblings.

3. Back. One minute and a half. Mahat laghima, defect of anima.

Samadhi

Jagrat

1. A river with islands, chhayamaya but clear—occasionally dense

2. The same with a house on a small island in the middle, at first lit by a lamp which was afterwards extinguished

3. Objects, stable; one dense (the reel of thread[)].

Swapna

Scenes, objects, activities. Brief stability

Lipi, legible only in detached sentences of an illegible page or tract.

=

Trikaldrishti

The four days of steady (obstructed, not rapid) progress are over. The Lilamaya Ishwara darshana is confirmed.

Jan 6th

Today, the obstruction to the Lilamaya darshana is less powerful, though equally obstinate. It is put aside easily, but obscures the plenitude.

=

Satyam is again recovering its elasticity & throwing off the obstruction. Ritam is still obstructed, but not entirely. Tapas siddhi meets constantly the obstruction & immediate denial, though there are instances to the contrary.

[Here begins the "intermediate record" of 2–23 January.]

Jan 2$\underline{d}$
=

The continued oppression of the Siddhi is met by an equally effective repression of the attempted *Asamata*. The attempt to reintroduce *duhkha* and Ashanti has definitely failed.

—

For some time the force of the kshatriya viryam has been suspended. It will now be restored to its firm activity.
=

In the saundarya the attempt to denude the head of the fresh growth of hair has failed. The thickness has not returned. There the two powers of youth and age are evenly balanced. With regard to the whitening, the new growth is black; it is only the old hair that keeps up the appearance of age.
=

The remodelling of the nose has not proceeded far, but a certain definite advantage has been gained.
=

With regard to other features the resistance of the Prithivi continues.
=

St.
1. Forget me not —   (nityasmarana[)]
2. The New Way (ie of the entire dasyam, — by this the nitya-
                                    smarana will come.)
=

Telepathic Tr. [Trikaldrishti]
=

The hold of the Asiddhi passes away today.

Ananda
Ananda (kama) has been intense & continuous &, instead of being discouraged, assisted by manasa abhyasa.
Tivra shows a sufficient strength of spontaneity for a beginning of the new method.

None of the other Anandas is, separately, very active.

=

Script

There is as yet not sufficient certainty in the guidance. Its details of time & arrangement seem sometimes to be contradicted by the event. This defect is about to be removed.

=

Lipi

1 This is the entirety of the faith in the Yogasiddhi.
2. fortnightly attack of Asiddhi
3 light.
4 destiny belongs to the Ishwari.
5 entire stability of the lipi has to be reinstated.
6 tapas-siddhi.
7 faith in the entire rapidity is about to be justified.

=

5 has been already fulfilled. Stable lipi of two lines has manifested with a greater sureness & vividness than before.

=

Ananda of raudra & vaidyuta are again active, as also vishaya —

Samadhi

The restoration of activity, but not as yet any new development.

=

Vijnana

Activity was restored after an interval of the play of unilluminated mental forces. But it is not as yet a well-organised activity. The illumination is opposed and insufficient except at times.

Script.

The main movement and utility of the last two days has been to deepen samata (nati and rasagrahanam) and to strengthen the general force of tertiary dasya.

The elements of bhoga & udasina nati must be so combined as to unite into a secure and full sama Ananda.

Tertiary dasya is only complete when anandamaya nati is complete

=

Anandamaya nati is the condition of madhura dasya and madhura dasya of the full vijnanasiddhi.

But it must be the madhura dasya of Mahakali-Mahasaraswati, not of the merely passive Mahasaraswati.

=

Trikaldrishti-Vani
4 days of progressive siddhi.

Jan 3^d

The decisive Trikaldrishti[2] is now regularising itself, putting away to each side of it the tapasic and tamasic insistences.

This involves a certain putting aside of the Tapas-siddhi of tapasic aishwarya-vashita, which has to give place to self-knowing divine Aishwarya-Ishita-Vashita.

=

The morning has been given to sahitya for the Review; as also part of the afternoon.

=

The process with the first two Chatusthayas continues, as well as the progressive normalisation of the Krishna Kali consciousness in all vessels. The Anandam Brahma is already normalised.[3]

=

The Tapasic stress reveals itself more & more as a force working for a future effect in opposition to resistances (tamasic stress) and mistaken in its idea of time & circumstance because of absorption in the idea of its own fulfilment. The tamasic stress is more in harmony with present time and circumstance, but mistakes present for future nonfulfilment.

=

Activity of the tejomaya rupa in swapnasamadhi.

---

2 NB. An error. This was telepathic and not real trikaldrishti, called decisive only because the prevision and the event happened to agree. [*Sri Aurobindo's note*]
3 Errors. Both were imperfect and temporary. [*Sri Aurobindo's note*]

Jan 4ᵗʰ

Morning devoted to Sahitya for the Review.

=

T^3 continues to progress, many combinations coming automatically in the unillumined mentality, proving to be right in every detail.

=

The siddhi is now regulating itself in the new way. But the normal movement has not yet established itself in three members of the Sharira & in the Kriti.

=

The two trikaldrishtis of the second [January] have justified themselves. Moreover the full movement of the Asiddhi only lasted for three days at the most. There has been some relic of it for these two days also— But these will now pass away.

=

In Vijnana only jagrat rupa is giving real trouble. The rest is all moving forward very steadily in spite of the obstruction deliberately & massively opposed to it.

=

The Asiddhi of Samata is condemned to be now purely physical.

=

Two quickly successive instances of 80°, one of aishwarya in detail, the other of ishita in general movement.

=

The contradiction of the Sharira has now to be removed, first in the Arogya & Utthapana, then in the Saundarya.

Jan 5ᵗʰ

This record is not to replace the other,[4] but to supply another element.

=

---

4 I.e., the record written in the other notebook, which was temporarily abandoned after the sixth. —Ed.

The obstruction now offered is to the conscious use of the Affirmations. They are all present in act, but the physical consciousness is prevented from enjoying their light.

This obstruction serves eventually the end of a more entire & solid participation in the siddhi by the whole conscious existence; for the subconscious is being trained through the aspiration towards the light. It is from the subconscious that the responses to the Asiddhi proceed, & the source of these responses is being fortified and purified. But the waking mind derives from the sense of obstruction a conclusion of unfaith in the rapidity of the Siddhi and the importance of the Karma.

=

The element of error of the satyam is therefore emphasised this morning.

=

St

एति प्र होता व्रतमस्य मायया ऊर्ध्वां दधानः शुचिपेशसं धियं ।

Agni, the force of activity, precedes the present action by the concealed creative & formative Wisdom of the Master of the Yoga holding in himself a thought pure in form of vision & exalted to the Vijnana.

=

The denial of the Lilamaya Ishwaradarshan made strongly this morning, is again rectified.

=

The withholding of the Madhura Dasya bhava has now to be rectified.

=

The Ananda oppressed at night and in the morning, is again restored to its activity.

=

Jagrat samadhi.
  Landscape
1. A river with islands, chhayamaya, but quite clear.
2. The same river with a house on a small island in the middle; the house at first lit by a lamp, but this went out.
3. Objects (stable); one dense (the reel of thread).

Note – 1. became dense at times.

Some sukshma-shabda (vak).

Swapna-samadhi

Scenes, objects; actions. Brief stability.

≡

Utthapana

Left leg, horizontal, 27 minutes.

Strong laghu mahima; strong defect of anima with tremblings only succeeded in prevailing after 25 minutes. Intervals of pure anandamaya anima after the tremblings.

—

Back; 1 minute 30 seconds. Mahat laghima did not fail, but defect of anima prevailed.

=

Script.

The four days, as was perceived by the telepathic trikaldrishti, were of steady progress against obstruction as opposed to rapid progress.

The progress has been especially in Ishwaradarshana & telepathy.

It must now extend itself to tapas & trikaldrishti, – though in the latter also there has been progress.

The struggle in the Sharira must continue.

In the Karma there will be some progress.

=

St

Any person must be able to trace his past, present and future.

=

Script

The failure of faith in the Kriti and the rapidity was inevitable at this stage, since the forces that oppose are allowed to justify their denial in appearance at most points.

Yet it is evident that the great force of Aishwarya Ishita continues, only it works against a stubborn resistance which prevents rapid result and rapid progress.

In reality the Ishwaradarshan has been rapidly effected; it is easy, it is normal; only it is still liable to forcible interruption &

obstruction. The difficulty is no longer in the Siddhi asserting itself, but for the Asiddhi to prevent the self-assertion even by massing all its force on the point.

In the other movements the rapidity is veiled by the opposition

=

The rapidity will manifest in spite of the obstruction.
The Kriti will fulfil itself in spite of the denial.
The Sharira will prevail in spite of the struggle.

Jan 6.
St.

But lo he speaketh boldly & they say nothing unto him. Do the rulers know indeed that this is the very Christ?

=

The revival of the Satyam is a preliminary to the larger assertion of the ritam.

=

In the thought the ritam is restored. It has to be restored in the trikaldrishti in an enlarged movement.

=

Sudden & strong attack of the old kind of Asamata, leaving vibrations behind in the outer parts of the physical heart & mind. –

=

The day has been for the most part dull and inactive. This inactivity is a preparation for a greater passivity of the instrument and a more intense normality of the tertiary dasya & yantrabhava.

=

Samadhi

As yet obscured in its more effective parts, but active in all.

=

Passivity is still being perfected; the straining of the consciousness for the result is being systematically discouraged.

As the darshana of the Lilamaya Ishwara has become normal, so the madhura-dasya bhava in its full intensity must become normal.

Jan 7<u>th</u>

The passivity has now to be tested by action.

=

The References point both to the idea of the continual progression in the Yoga, not stopping short with an imperfect result.

=

Lipi

1. telos trikaldrishti tapassiddhi.

=

The physical passivity is now complete; that of the mind & heart must follow.

=

Samadhi
Jagrat Antardrishta
   1. Stable developed forms (books, reel)
   2. Human group.
Swapna
   Activity of organised drishti.. (not the most perfectly organised).

=

In the afternoon there was a return of Asiddhi, but the Ishwara persists in the enforcement of the Madhura Dasya. This will now be harmonised with the Tapas, the latter being delivered from the shadow of the independent ego.

=

The trikaldrishti is acting with the ritam on broad lines, in large questions akin to the jnana. The application in time & immediate circumstance does not yet take place.

=

Dream very coherent; a whole story read in dream lipi.

Jan 8<u>th</u>

The struggle between Siddhi & Asiddhi continues. At first sight obstructive Asiddhi seems to have replaced positive Asiddhi and to hold the field.

It is now suggested that this will endure till the fortnight is complete, 14th January, but there is also a suggestion that this formation will be contradicted.

The necessary realisation which it is so difficult to establish as a normally working practical view applied to every little detail of thought, feeling, action & event is that of the undivided Ishwara, who is at once fulfiller & opponent, Deva & Vritra. It is the relics of the Dwayavin consciousness that are the strength of the remnants of subjective Asiddhi.

=

Trikaldrishti is now active, both telepathic & decisive, but without ritam of time & exact arrangement of circumstance.

Nevertheless this ritam also is becoming much more frequent. There is an attempt to make the telepathic or mental trikaldrishti one with the decisive or veiled vijnanamaya. The completeness of the satyam of telepathy & telepathic trikaldrishti is becoming more & more absolute. The ritam lingers because of continued misapplication in time, circumstance, eventuality.

This is due chiefly to the tapasic suggestion at the right side of the head near the ear, false knowledge of false sruti, which is substantially true, but erroneous in circumstance. There are other elements, tamasic suggestion etc, but these are less important.

Tapasic suggestion more & more frequently fulfils itself in the end, though baffled at the moment. Tamasic suggestion fulfils itself chiefly at the moment, though still often in the finality.

Tapas is at present depressed and occurs as a rule only in the finality, but often ends in an adverse movement.

=

Ananda also is depressed, Arogya does not advance, Utthapana makes no appreciable progress, Saundarya is immobilised. —

Karma likewise is for the most part obstructed.

=

With the remanifestation of the intense Kamananda a progress is visible in Vaidyuta which now flows through the body with a great intensity, distinctness & spontaneity. Tivra is also manifesting greater intensity & vishaya is acquiring it.

=

Utthapana

Arms — about one hour. Some heaviness

Left leg — 10 minutes.

=

Trikaldrishti progresses. Many instances of decisive trikal-drishti of the nature of Chit-Tapas.

=

Some activity of Tapas-siddhi & Jagrat-rupa.

=

Samadhi

Jagrat Ant.

Perfect forms, but on the borders of sleep

Swapna

Reading of successive lipi.

Long continued action & rupa with intervals of eclipse.

Jan 9th

मह्रे नो अद्य बोधयोषो राये दिवित्मती

यथा चिन्रो अबोधय: सत्यश्रवसि वाय्ये

सुजाते अश्वसूनृते ।

The Sortileges are always appropriate; they are not always immediately fulfilled in their entirety. The reference given describes the movement towards which the Siddhi is directed, as yesterday's, अग्ने ऋतस्यासि क्षयो वामस्य भूरे: gave the preliminary movement begun yesterday, not finished.

Lipi.

1. Yes, it is already finished in the verity of the ideality

(on background)

(but has to be realised in the physical consciousness)

2. ἴσθι . . ἶνα μαθης θηρ. — (Chitralipi)

θηρ = पशु = the physical consciousness.

Ideality is accomplished, but has to be imposed on the whole physical consciousness. The siddhi of the mental & nervous dominating the physical are already complete, but they are veiled by Krishna as Vritra in order that they may not interfere with the enlightenment of the isolated physical consciousness.

3. good Tuesday (chitra) —
ie this movement will be complete by Tuesday.
4. perfect effectivity in the sahitya siddhi — (savalambana)
=

In the sahitya siddhi ineffectivity lingers in the form of a physical obstruction which prevents the inspired action of the vak. It can always be overcome, but its interference must be eliminated.
=

Utthapana
Left leg. — horiz. 30 minutes — attacks of an-anima ineffective, discontinued by will, not from necessity.
=

Samadhi
The same action of the samadhi continues
In ant [antardrishta] jagrat dense & developed rupa (book, shoe).
Some activity in bahirdarshi of rupa on the background.
=

Frequency of ritam in trikaldrishti is now normalised, but is not entirely complete and therefore not invariable.
=

It appears as if stable rupa on background in bahirdarshi were now established, but it is still far from perfect.
=

Stable clear rupa of all kinds, but imperfect in force of distinctness & lifelikeness is established in both antardrishta & bahirdarshi. Its development of perfection has to be awaited.
=

Therefore the vijnana continues to develop in spite of all obstruction with a limited & indecisive rapidity.
=

Ishwaradarshana is passing through the stage of Vritratwa after its final emergence. It is there but often concealed by the Vritra effort to restore the old bhavas of the darshana with a view to entire denial of all darshana. But this is now impossible.

Jagrad Rupa — Bahirdarshi   At night
  Akasha

Inkstand, — carriage & horses, house, & other objects; none of these, except the first, when it is dense or developed, is entirely distinct.

Human figures, groups, landscapes, scenes. — the same characteristic —

Very crude images of bird, butterfly & beast.

=

Kamananda, long intermittent, has become again spontaneously continuous. It so remained in act or tendency throughout the evening and till midnight.

=

Today Kavya was resumed.

=

Arogya continues to be subject to the Asiddhi.

=

The slight gain made in Saundarya is now being disputed by the Asiddhi. It is no longer apparent.

=

Swapnasamadhi inactive at night. Dream confused.

=

Exact instance of time trikaldrishti, S [Saurin] waking & rising at 3 pm instead of 4.30 pm. In other instances the time was only rough & approximate & hesitated between different alternatives (eg 8.15 & 8.30).

Jan 10th

प्रप्र पूष्णस्तुविजातस्य शस्यते महित्वमस्य तवसो न तंदते स्तोत्रमस्य न तंदते ।

अर्चामि सुन्नयन्नहमंत्यूतिं मयोभुवं ।

विश्वस्य यो मन आयुयुवे मखो देव आयुयुवे मखः ॥

That is, the growth of the Vijnana in many forms increases, its *mahattwa* is not destroyed by the opposition.

It increases close about & within the adhara bringing with it the Ananda; it is becoming more & more illuminated in the physical consciousness which increases in peace & joy.

It is applying itself unperceived to the minds of all and overcoming the opposition of the littleness, besieging the mentality of the world with the Truth.

=

All this is justified by the observed facts.

=

There is entire satyam and almost entire ritam & brihat of the jnana & the telepathy in relation to outward event; decisive trikaldrishti is yet defective owing to defect of tapas siddhi and prakamya vyapti is not yet normally brihat, although it has all the necessary capacities.

=

For the rest T³ is moving forward in the mass towards inevitable fulfilment.

=

Lipi

1. Tapas-siddhi   entirety of tapas-siddhi

(Tapas has to become one with knowledge in order that there may be entire tapas-siddhi).

=

Utthapana

Arms. morning — half an hour. heaviness & pranic fatigue eliminated

Afternoon, half an hour, force & ananda, but reaction at moment of cessation.

=

Kavya.

=

Tapas-siddhi & lipi in work of formation, nothing final or definite.

=

Arogya still refractory.

=

Lipi —

2 sahitya-siddhi.

3 rupa-siddhi in the light

4 delight. .

=

Kamananda has recovered its tendency of continuity. The other shariranandas manifest from time to time.

=

The madhura dasya is attaining continuity, but the mere dasya is still too dominant over the madhura. This is a defect that from tonight will begin to disappear.

The one real obstacle is insufficient sraddha in rapidity & in kriti.

=

Sahityasiddhi is now assured in all its parts. The physical opposition, it will be found, is disintegrated. Only the remnants of it remain.

Ritam of trikaldrishti is more & more emerging; only it is not yet applied to important things in a large & definitive fashion.

Telepathy of thought & feeling is recovering distinctness, but is not yet sufficiently confident of its ritam.

=

The Mahakali-Mahasaraswati consciousness with the Mahaluxmi colour is finally taking form, but has not yet sufficient force of Mahakali.

=

For today in the Script, a progress in jagrad rupa antardrishta, in tapas-siddhi and in lipi was specially indicated. These indications often denote a movement of tendency rather than of definite or immediate fulfilment.

Lipi is visibly arranging the page behind the veil and shadows out from time to time, in front of it the reflection of its concealed movement. This it did yesterday, the large page appearing, but unvivid and therefore illegible. In front, entire vividness & stability of the long single line was reasserted, less vividness & stability of the double line, still less of the triple. The lipi still keeps the tendency to dissolve when it has been read. This is the chief obstacle to progress. Only sthapatya lipi has conquered it. Chitra sometimes prevails. Akasha tries to prevail.

In antardrishta there is the same movement of lipi less pronounced in its partial success.

Tapas-siddhi seems to be preparing its movement rather than to be actually advancing.

=

The dasya of Mahakali-Mahasaraswati with the Mahalakshmi tinge is now affirmed.

=

Whenever the Mahakali consciousness has been affirmed in Mahasaraswati, it has had too strong a tendency to overwhelm both Mahasaraswati and Maheshwari & assert the violent Asuric Kali bhava. For this reason the combination Mahasaraswati-Maheshwari has been constantly strengthened against this assertion & each time it has thus been strengthened, it has absorbed more & more of the Kalibhava which it denied.

Tonight the combination Mahalaxmi-Mahakali was effected & held steady against the Asuric Kali tendency which it then took into itself. By this action the perfect harmony was established; for Mahalaxmi has always asserted itself in the Maheshwari-Mahasaraswati formula, that is to say, with the right continent and the right pratistha. All that has now to be effected is the strengthening of the Kali tejas & virya till it reaches the right intensity without disturbing the other elements of the harmony. The intensification is already proceeding.

The result is the divinised Asuro-Rakshasi Kali with the Pisachi, Pramatheswari & Pashavi contained in the Rakshasi element. Mahalaxmi-Mahasaraswati brings with it the Gandharvi element.

The smooth development is now possible because the dasya is now complete and is taking the madhura into itself. The bhava is firmly founded on jnana & state of being & the Ishwara is being felt in all thought, feeling & action. The distinction between Ishwara and Prakriti is not yet merged in the unity + difference, but the Prakriti is subordinate & more conscious of being a form of the Ishwara.

Mahalaxmi brings with her bhakti & prema, the stable permanence of which was so long denied.

Jan 11th

The growth of ritam in the trikaldrishti continues, but still works chiefly on the material of the telepathy.

There is also a movement towards ritam of the impulsions which is not yet complete, but their satyam is now pronounced.

=

Sraddha in the guidance is now becoming absolute, but is still only partly illumined by knowledge of the exact drift of the guidance. Nevertheless, the exact sense & utility of each movement, whether overtly favourable or apparently adverse is more & more understood.

The sraddha is limited also by the doubt of the rapidity & of the kriti. In the vijnana & subjectivity generally the doubt of rapidity is giving way to comprehension of an increasing swiftness & sureness in the development; but in sharira & kriti the view is still blind. It is certain that something will be done, but the way & the extent is withheld from the knowledge. It only appears as a speculative formation.

=

Samata is almost entirely free from reactions of positive depression. There is only a shadow of depression & impatience due to defect of tapas-siddhi.

Sraddha in exact tapas-siddhi once accomplished there will be no farther defect of the first two chatusthayas.

=

The completion of the third is therefore the practical assurance of the whole Yoga-siddhi. The rest is only a matter of Time.

=

Jan 12th

The progress is now rather in thought & sahitya; in the rest there is more of preparation.

=

The force of the Kamic chakra & the sahaituka kamananda is increasing, but the Arogya is not sufficient.

=

There is a constant application of tests to the samata; but except momentary touches of depression & impatience, there is no result. The sama Ananda increases constantly & the only shadow over it is that of the recurrent unfaith.

=

On the other hand Shakti is affected by non-fulfilment and Asraddha. Tapatya continues, but fitfully where there is not the faith and without assured Ananda.

=

The Siddhi seems to move towards the Ananda of a purely disinterested and instrumental Tapatya not depending on faith in the results. But this brings a certain indifference to the Tapas-siddhi which cannot be final.

=

Jagrat rupa is at last manifesting really stable forms of all kinds that are at the same time clear, vivid & complete.

4 footed animal forms, long withheld by return of asiddhi, today manifest freely, but at first had no stability. They have already however begun to assume stability, though the movement is not yet successfully accomplished.

All this is in crude & with trataka, just in front of the eyes in a thick pranic akasha.

The figures at first ran swiftly away to the right, but they can now be kept floating before the eyes.

Both these results, reappearance & initial stability of four-footed animal forms and the cessation of the fugitive movement, are instances of almost instantaneous effectivity of tapas.

=

Lipi continues to develop fixity of single line and legibility of the multiple line.

=

The advance of rupa has come at a moment when a long obstruction made it appear impossible to push forward this siddhi.

It was followed by an outburst of successful tapassiddhi after a long period of ineffectivity. In the course of two minutes there were six or seven instances of aishwarya siddhi swiftly effective against which all resistance was helpless.

=

Utthapana of arms one hour, not yet free from slight defect of anima.

Of legs for eight minutes, medial position, strong & successful oppression of the laghima.

=

Bahirdarshi rupa at night began to repeat the movement of the day.

=

A certain movement of Kriti, but not of any great importance in itself.

=

Dream & samadhi continue in the same condition, the first subject to confusion, the second somewhat inactive, but capable of stability.

Jan 13th

First stable page lipi — chitra — Not legible at once, though very vivid. Legible line [ ]5 by line. But the preceding lines once read remained firm & could be re-read. Some seven or ten lines with fairly long phrases (about 7 words), a phrase to each line.

=

Tapas-siddhi continues.

=

The force of the Ananda of event increases, although the surface nirananda (negative rather than positive) still continues.

=

The faith increases slowly. The rapidity now manifested is a relative rapidity, a rapidity of gradual progression, not a positive and masterful rapidity. The body, the physical consciousness, the physical akash, the physical world are being moulded to the siddhi, but present still a tamasic resistance which reproduces mechanically

---

5 MS &

the old forms of asiddhi. Hence the inability to advance with a positive rapidity.

=

There are other signs of a revived effectivity of Tapas-siddhi, but as yet it is not decisively extended to Kriti or to Sharira.

=

Utthapana   Arms one hour. Defect of anima a little more heavy than the day before.

=

Samadhi—

Long sleep. Struggle to conquer the tamasic nidra, only slightly successful.

=

The physical consciousness attempts to escape from the continued action of the Vijnana, not from hostility, but from tamas, indolence & addiction to easy & accustomed methods.

=

Telepathy of thought frequently occurs, but in a scattered form. It is not well-organised in the ritam.

=

The whole action now is one of adjustment occurring automatically, like a machine that is gradually putting itself to rights. . —

=

The attempt to conquer tamasic nidra continued. At night it was largely successful. There was a sense of samadhi rather than of nidra in the sushupti.

Swapna samadhi was rich in its activity & jagrat forms of considerable beauty (sea-scapes) appeared; but the more perfectly organised samadhi was not active.

Dream developed a great accuracy & considerable coherence of successive scenes & incidents, but the names & human images belonged to present ego & its associations.

=

In Arogya there is a struggle with revived form of old malady. Assimilation does not advance.

Saundarya is also stationary.

=

There seems to be a promise of recovered rapid realisation; but as yet there is no realisation.

Jan 14ᵗʰ

After a struggle with resistance the effective tapas-siddhi began to work as yesterday.

There are exceptions to its action of which the trikaldrishti becomes aware at the moment of tapatya. But this awareness is sometimes contradicted by a tapasic movement.

═

Utthapana. Arms, half hour. Defect of anima stronger, stiffness.

═

Return of Asamata in the forms of impatience, disbelief & duhkha. This came as usual from the unfulfilled promise of the Tapas & a violent repression of the siddhi. It is a direct denial of the suggestion made yesterday that the Samata is at last about to accomplish a complete finality and that rapid advance was about to return.

═

The period of asiddhi has now covered a whole fortnight, although for the most part (ie except in the body & in the rupa samadhi) it has taken the part more of an arrested siddhi than of any positive recoil. There have been movements of recoil, as in the samata today.

═

Darshana has gone back sometimes for a moment to the perception of the mere man in the Sarvam Brahman; but its normal pitch is now the Anandam J. A S [Jnanam Anantam Sarvam] Brahman as represented by the individual limited mental consciousness.

The Darshana of KrishnaKali is no longer normal.

═

It is now, however, manifesting again holding in itself both the double Personality & the bhava of Purusha enjoying Prakriti.

Stable scene & movements in scene in the jagrad antardrishta.

═

Serious & unforeseen blow to the Kriti, received without any reaction except incertitude & loss of faith in the Kriti or rather admission of the possibility of being entirely misled in the conception of the future.

=

At night perfect swapnasamadhi.

Intense, distinct & vivid vishayas, touch, hearing, taste, smell frequently repeated and well combined with rupa, with incident & with each other.

Perfect stability of rupa continued into the jagrat antardarshi.

Perfect coherent conversation

Rich activity of forms, scenes & incidents.

=

The only defects that remain are insufficient prolongation of the continuities, inapplicability to use in life and imperfect memory after the samadhi is over.

=

Jagrad rupa & vishaya are now the only parts of the Vijnana which are not well advanced; though none are yet finally perfect in their ordinary action, except pure jnana.

=

Sharira & Kriti continue to be backward, & this backwardness exercises its reactionary effect on the other chatusthayas.

=

Nevertheless now that the first three chatusthayas & the sixth are taking form, the power can be more concentrated on these so that the final question may be more rapidly fought out

Jan 15th

Clear & stable rupa on the background are now beginning to appear in bahirdarshi.

=

The period of dominant asiddhi seems to be over, since the obstruction in vijnana has proved ineffective. But the obstruction in Sharira & Kriti remains.

=

By the removal of the artificial obstruction of Asiddhi the Krishna Kali consciousness of the Anandamaya Purusha has been immediately normalised in all things & beings.

The sense of being in all things & all things being in oneself has returned.

The Devi envisages herself as the Ishwari though in conflict with her present world-form in order to purify & uplift it.

=

Lipi—

1   The object is faith in the tapas-siddhi.

2   Myself testing the opposition.

3   Honestly hopeful siddhi

4   The enthusiastic faith is still obstructed by the unfaith in the tapas-siddhi of the Kriti.

=

Utthapana

Arms one hour, stiffness more pronounced, but defect of anima less effective.

=

Kamananda which had been dulled becomes once more active.

=

Animal forms appear on the background & attempt to be stable, also objects, but the latter especially are not fine or correct in their outlines.

All kinds of forms & combinations are now so appearing as chhayas on the wall

Stable clearness has heralded but as yet failed to establish itself.

=

In jagrad antardarshi entirely stable forms attended sometimes by entirely & long continuous action are now well-established & begin to be various, but are surrounded by an atmosphere of dimness which makes them appear entirely crude though otherwise complete & even quite perfect & definite in form.

It is noticeable that continuous action here has a far better hold of the akasha & is far more firmly held by the vision than in swapnasamadhi.

=

Perfect rupas begin to reappear in the bahirdarshi, but they are still momentary.

=

Sukshma Vak is again attempting to manifest in the bahirdarshi —

=

A struggle over the Tapas-siddhi continues —

=

Perfect rupa in bahirdarshi at night also, but momentary —

=

Tamasic nidra took again some hold, but not a strong hold. Dream was confused. The higher parts of samadhi did not appear.

=

On the whole a day of progress.

=

Jan 16th
Tapas-siddhi is still active, but usually against strong resistance. 80° is long suspended.

=

Dream & samadhi are still under the shadow of the tamasic nidra; there was only one new outbreak, the inscription in antardarshi, *novae suae patriae percipere*. The first two words were slightly deformed "nuovae suoae". This inscription responded to nothing in the waking mind and was of the nature of Sruti.

=

Darshana varies between the perception of the lower Purusha in the individual, Anandamaya Brahmamaya, occupying Prakriti, & of the Lilamaya embracing & occupying all individuals.
The latter is the normal perception, but slides back into the inferior view. The darshana of Krishnakali is replaced by the darshana of Purusha-Prakriti.

=

The Ishwaribhava has again given place to the Devibhava with the Kali force quiescent and almost absent.

=

There has therefore been no definite progress during the day, although certain signs for the Kriti are good.
=

Utthapana
Arms — half hour. interrupted (diminished defect of anima)
Neck 10 minutes (strong defect of anima)
=

Samadhi
Obstruction of tamasic nidra.

Jan 17th

(1) तत्त्वंपदार्थौ तृतीयेऽध्याये निरूपितौ यद्यपि तथाऽपि त्वंपदार्थो नात्यन्तं निरूपितस्तदर्थमयं पञ्चमोऽध्याय आरभ्यते। धातुः प्रसादोपायस्तत्र चतुर्थेऽध्याये निरूपितः।
=

The nature & the person have been formed in the [   ][6] first three chatusthayas, but not being sufficient the fifth is now being pressed. The means of purification of the matter is being pursued in the fourth.

(2) स एष संप्रसादोऽस्माच्छरीरात्समुत्थाय परं ज्योतिरुपसंपद्य स्वेन रूपेणाभिसंपद्यते।
This is the means. (ततो न रोगादिभयमित्याह)

(3) प्रथमयोगप्रवृत्तेश्चिह्नानि दर्शयति—लघुत्वमित्यादि

(4) शिवां गिरित्रं तां कुरु मा हिंसीः पुरुषं जगत्।
=

The vijnana is gradually reasserting the Affirmations, but against a strong opposition.
=

This month has been a reassertion of the Dwayavin consciousness ending in the possession of a world unity in which two forces of the same Being are at strife, both directed by the Ishwara.
=

The attitude of continual struggle with the adverse forces is

6 *MS* the

being established in the consciousness. Tapatya is constant against a heavy obstruction.

=

St.

विश्वस्यैकं परिवेष्टितारमीशं तं ज्ञात्वाऽमृता भवंति ।

That is, the surrounding consciousness has to be normally felt as the Lord and not only as the continent & material & determining substance. This consciousness of the Lord is resisted by the Asiddhi; all the rest is well established in the Darshana.

=

80° is again manifesting itself.

Exact fulfilment is also manifesting itself.

Both, however, are as yet exceptions to the general rule of strong & often successful resistance.

=

Ananda is once more occupying the system.

=

The different physical Anandas are again at work in entire spontaneity & with strong intensity.

=

Utthapana of the arms, half an hour vertical, strong denial of Anima; afterwards, medial between horizontal & vertical, half an hour. In the latter laghima is exceedingly strong; but there is a subsequent reaction in the shoulders.

=

Utthapana of legs; medial, 6 minutes only.

Of left leg, horizontal, 15 minutes.

=

Swapna-samadhi

Two visions of actualities, living people, existing scenes.

=

The recovering Arogya was again attacked and pushed back. With the exception of Ananda, Sharira generally fails to advance. Ananda itself is only recovered, not advanced —

=

Madhura dasya is restored.

Vani is free & dominant.

Jan 18th

A new formation can be felt, marked for the moment by a great intensifying of Mahaluxmi and a mergence in her of Mahakali—

=

Lipi—
1. Rapidly telepathy is growing definite
2. There is a little result in the immediate futurity; in the remote there is the period of great results.

=

The satyam is restored, but still lacks the definitive & decisive ritam. It is a satyam of telepathy, not of the pure trikaldrishti.

There is a similar satyam, without definitive ritam, of the Tapas.

The satyam has a firmer ritam than before, but it is a ritam of telepathy & of manomaya forces, not vijnanamaya.

=

Utthapana of the arms—one hour & a half—increased laghima besieged by defect of anima.

=

Utthapana of legs, medial, 10 minutes.
Left leg, horizontal, 18 minutes—
Neck, 5 minutes.

=

Madhura dasya is well-established, but there is no action of Mahakali.

=

There is however a movement towards the fusion of the Mahakali & Mahaluxmi bhavas in the Anandamaya Tapas & Premamaya Virodha.

=

Jan 19th

There is no rapid or definite progress except in Darshana, where the Ishwaradarshana has become normal & the consciousness even when pulled back for a time to the simple Brahmadarshana, reverts naturally to the Siddhi.

The vivid personality of Krishna Kali is not yet normal in

the darshana, but Purusha-Prakriti comes easily & is always there implied.

It is noticeable that as in former times the morning brings a reversion to the asiddhi. Today the reversion is determined and powerful.

Its main object now is to prevent the ritam in the knowledge & tapas by besieging the mind with the agitated struggle & errors of the nervous & physical mentality.

=

Utthapana.

Arms. 1 hour 45 minutes. Afterwards strong reaction in left shoulder

Back — ten minutes

Neck — half an hour.

=

Karma of scholastic work has been begun with some initial steadiness (study of Rig Veda).

=

The poise of the Siddhi was restored during the morning, but the force of it is absent.

Utthapana increased.

General Ananda has become settled.

At the same time there is a lassitude with regard to the Kriti.

The Tapas is more firm on Sharira.

Jan 20th

Utthapana.

Legs 15 minutes — defective still, though improved

Arms 2 hours — pranic defect in the first hour, strong reaction after cessation, strain manifested in muscles of the back & loins. Laghima effective, but not mahat.

=

The consciousness of the cosmic Purusha-Prakriti confirms itself always; but belongs to an inferior plane, not to the Vijnana or the Ananda. There is no satisfaction to the Will or to the Mahakali element.

=

The same state of the Siddhi continues.

=

Work on the Veda continues.

Jan 21ˢᵗ

The samata continually deepens.

=

Utthapana —
Arms 1 hour and a half.

=

No definite progress, but the Ishwaradarshana deepens & fortifies itself.

Jan 22ᵈ

Samata is now very strong & has converted itself into a more or less dense Ananda.

=

Ishwaradarshana is also very strong & spontaneous. A little smarana is now all that is needed.

=

The same process of deepening & final basing is in process with regard to the Shakti. Along with this movement Mahakali is again emerging out of Maheshwari-Mahaluxmi-Mahasaraswati.

=

Rupa in jagrad is resuming activity after a long dullness. There is no disposition in the nature towards personal tapas of the Will, but only towards tapas of the action in the body.

St.
महे नो [अद्य बोधयोषो]⁷ राये दिवित्मती

=

Lipi again active in the Swapnasamadhi, but only partially coherent.

=

---

⁷ *MS* अद्योषो बोधय

Utthapana. Arms 1 hour.

Work for the Review.

The activity of Vijnana is re-forming, but not yet in possession.

Jan 23ᵈ
Utthapana.
Arms – 1 hour 25 minutes.
Neck – 35 minutes.

In the struggle between Arogya & Roga the latter had re-affirmed itself in the blood with great vehemence. It seems now to be again subsiding under the pressure of the Aishwarya.

यज्ञस्य वो रथ्यं विश्पतिं विशां होतारमक्तोरतिथिं विभावसुं।
शोचञ्छुष्कासु हरिणीषु जर्भुरद्दूषा केतुर्यजतो [द्यामशायत]⁸ ॥

The Mahakali element increases in the energy, but has yet no faith in the result of its thought or its action. It maintains udasinata & nati, but not an active attitude of tapatya.

The swapnasamadhi again became active, but jagrat state of the mind in swapna is not very firm.

Veda continues.

The Vijnana acts sometimes, but it is still usually the unenlightened physical consciousness which is dominant.

---

⁸ *MS* द्यामवाशयत्

[Here resumes the notebook set aside on 6 January]

Jan 24th

The intermediate record has been kept in a separate book (2d to 23d).

Throughout the month there has been an encroachment by Asiddhi on Siddhi which became strongest between the 16th & 23d

The result has been an entire confirmation of samata & sama Ananda, followed by a revival of Shakti on the basis of entire samata and, now commencing[,] a revival of Vijnana on the same basis.

=

The defect of last year's siddhi was the survival of a Tapas & Tapatya which responded too eagerly to sakama suggestions from outside. For this reason it was necessary to obscure the siddhi in order to assure entire titiksha, udasinata and nati of all favourable or adverse results, pleasant or unpleasant experiences. Especially, the Ananda of success & failure, truth & falsehood has been secured against the constant denial opposed to them by this recoil.

=

On the other hand a temporary abandonment of Tapatya and Mahakali bhava and an all-prevailing incertitude amounting to ill-faith was brought back by the necessities of this movement.

Arogya has been thrown back violently & Sharira generally retarded.

=

The Ishwaradarshan is now securely normalised with the Krishna Kali Ananda, Guna & Jnana as its contents.

This is the first chatusthaya (Brahma) entirely satisfactory in its finality. Only intensity of bhava and fullness of detail have to be added, but this depends partly on the progress in other chatusthayas.

=

Samata is also final, but still vibrates sometimes momentarily to the touch of tamasic asamata.

=

Shakti is not final for want of faith, but force of madhura dasya has greatly increased.

=

The Affirmations of the Anandamaya Ishwara, the madhura dasya & the submission to all bhoga are now ready for their perfection.

Those of the Anandamaya as continent & Ananda as base follow upon these, but the free & joyous Tapas & Prakasha as base depend upon the fullness of the Ritam & Satya Brihat Affirmations.

=

The two other Affirmations are still held back.

=

For the results in Vijnana, Sharira & Kriti it is necessary to await the emergence of these siddhis.

=

In Swapnasamadhi the full hold of stability & continuity on the Akasha; but not the full play of the jagrat in swapna.

Jan 25th
Utthapana. Arms ¾ hour; interrupted.

=

The energy is now more fixed upon action than on Yoga-siddhi. Work before which soon wearied out the body is now being pursued with tenacity and lines of effort that seemed formerly to be constantly broken & lead to nothing begin to prepare their fulfilment.

=

The Veda is taken up in two parts — Vamadeva's hymns on which notes are being taken from Sayana & the Ninth Book which is being copied and annotated.

=

The work of the Review must now be systematised as also the preparation of a statement of the Yoga —

=

The rest of the siddhi does not advance, but the first & sixth chatusthayas are maintained.

=

Sharira

The advance in Arogya has again been checked.

=

Ananda cannot normalise continuity because of the check to Arogya.

=

There is no progress in Saundarya.

=

Jan 28th

The last two days have been chiefly occupied with work & the Vijnana has been left inactive for the most part except in its dispersed action.

A slight depression in the superficial Samata is observable this morning; but the Vijnana is reviving its activity.

Ishwaradarshana remains firm.

The difficulty now experienced is with regard to the Tapas. The mind is unwilling to accept the effort of imperfect Tapas & no other manifests. There is also an entire uncertainty with regard to the Kriti & all things concerning the life & the life-work.

=

St.

इमं नु मायिनं हुव इंद्रमीशानमोजसा ।
मरुत्वंतं न [वृज्ञसे]⁹ ।
अयमिंद्रो मरुत्सखा वि वृत्रस्याभिनच्छिरः ।
वज्रेण शतपर्वणा ॥

=

By this it seems to be indicated that the mental activity of the Tapas has to be admitted and used to destroy the obstruction.

=

⁹ MS ओजसे

At present there are all sorts of brilliant formations of the nervous mentality which seem to have no sanction from the luminous mind

=

The action of the Vijnana is being resumed where it left off. There is occasional 80° but ordinarily resistance and imperfect result or delayed result, sometimes no apparent result.

What is now being attempted is the sustained and even obstinate action of the Tapas without regard to result and into this action the introduction of the united power & knowledge.

=

Utthapana

Arms. an hour and a half.

=

Samadhi

During the last few days samadhi & coherent dream have asserted themselves partially, with all their right circumstances & gains (except the jagrat); but there is still a dominant *Ashasti*, if not so strong an *abhisastih*.

=

Sharira

In Arogya at present the struggle seems to be turning again in favour of the siddhi.

=

Physical energy is more consistent but directed chiefly towards the support of brain work.

=

Vijnana

Aishwarya works again in immediate surroundings, but is not more advanced in effectuality.

=

There is this time no sudden & powerful revival of the Siddhi, but only a slow movement of recovered activity.

The finality, however, is greater in everything connected with the subjectivity.

Jan 29th

एवा नो अग्ने अमृतेषु पूर्व्य धीष्पीपाय बृहद्दिवेषु मानुषा।
दुहाना धेनुर्वृजनेषु कारवे त्मना शतिनं पुरुरूपमिषणि॥
वयमग्ने अर्वता वा सुवीर्यं ब्रह्मणा वा चितयेमा जनानति।
अस्माकं द्युम्नमधि पञ्च कृष्टिषु उच्चा स्वर्ण शुशुचीत दुष्टरं।

Script

Although the opposition seems to be strong, the force of the siddhi is stronger. It has already asserted itself entirely in the first, mainly in the second, entirely in the sixth chatusthaya. Except for deficient faith in the life, which is really a deficient knowledge, it holds the subjectivity. It has now to conquer the subjective-objective and this it is steadily doing in spite of all reverses & retardations.

=

The power on the immediate surroundings showed itself throughout the morning extremely effective in spite of all resistance sometimes compelling results subjectively, sometimes, where the subjective object resisted by the creation of circumstances which physically induced or compelled the necessary action. There was only one instance of failure.

=

Utthapana

Arms — 1 hr. 15 minutes —
Legs — 5 minutes only.

=

Samadhi.

Swapna Samadhi is trying to get rid of the Ashasti

Jan 30th

The Dyumna or luminous power (rajas, rochana) is established in the Bhuvar, it is now being established in the Divah. The energy is ready in the active nervous power and in the soul-thought (suviryam arvatá . . brahmaná) although manifest chiefly in the work of knowledge, thought, writing etc, not in the things of Prithivi, the objective world. It is here that the mental thought

(धीर्मानुषा) nourished by the ideal (बृहद्दिवेषु) is yielding its full results.

—

अनश्वासो ये पवयोऽरथा इंद्रेषिता अभ्यवर्तंत दस्यून् ॥
प्र ते पूर्वाणि करणानि वोचं प्र नूतना मघवन्या चकर्थ ।
शक्तीवो यद्द्विभरा रोदसी उभे जयन्नपो मनवे दानुचित्राः ॥

=

The activity is now great in the intuitional field of the intellect, but concentrated chiefly on the Veda etc.

=

The first line refers to the recent passive activity of the Aishwarya from which the nervous force & anandamaya movement (aswa and ratha) have been excluded in order that they may be replaced now by the right aswa & ratha. This is the new action for Indra who with the Shakti in him is to conquer the opposition & bring in the varied bright activity of the *swarvatir apah*.

=

This is already being done today, the activity of the luminous mind being extended beyond the jnana & literary work to the trikaldrishti, but as yet insecurely & incompletely.

Feb. 1st
    1. The Reference of the 29th repeated.
    2. Finally in the third Rik.

=

The day has chiefly been devoted to work of Sahitya & Veda. A great capacity for large quantities of work swiftly done is being now manifested.

There is an attempt also at the primary utthapana in the shape of diminished sleep and the rejection from the physical system of fatigue and exhaustion; but this applies at present only to brainwork, not to physical activity.

=

In samadhi there is a strong tendency to the development of sukshma Vak, but as yet this is normal only in isolated sentences and when there is concentration in the jagrat or without concentration in the swapnasamadhi.

=

The Kriti is not yet favourable in exterior results & circumstances, only a difficult defence of the Sati.

=

Each part of the Kriti has its own difficulties and when these are brought forward & seem to be accumulated in an unsurmountable obstruction, the faith falters or is eclipsed.

=

Samata remains undisturbed, only there is still uneasiness & occasionally a subtle depression in the bodily consciousness, but much less palpable than formerly.

=

Feb 2ᵈ
    Utthapana   Arms 1 hour.

The vijnanamaya plane manifests in the thought & trikaldrishti, but as yet there is no constant well formed action.

=

Swapna samadhi is sometimes active, but here also it is only a scattered activity of details. In jagrad there is no activity except of imperfect figures except in chitra & sthapatya.

=

The progress of Sharira has long been discontinued.

=

In jagrat samadhi vak is acquiring greater force and perfect rupa, unstable, is more frequent.

=

Poetry resumed with more power.

=

There is a pause before the deficient parts of the third chatusthaya declare themselves & until they declare themselves, the organised action of the chatusthaya cannot manifest itself.

=

The powers of obstruction, always, are not broken, but merely pushed backward. Rapidity, so often promised and on the point of realisation, is still unrealised.

=

Feb 3^d

There is a general increase of the siddhi in the vijnana, but not as yet anything decisive.

=

In swapna samadhi there is a movement towards utility, but nothing as yet of any value.

=

There is some relaxation in the physical force of the body for work

Feb 4th 5th

The same condition continues

=

Utthapana of arms daily for an hour or two.

=

The struggle in Arogya continues.

=

Kriti is still undecided.

=

Samadhi fluctuates; jagrat is mostly inactive, but vak becomes more & more spontaneous & sthula.

=

Karma of sahitya is alone pronouncedly active. Veda, poetry, Aphorisms.

Feb 6th

1. ἐπισχερω. Successively, in order, thence, afterwards.
2 We can begin then with this concentration and a constant consecrating of ourselves. . . For the first movement.

The concentration indicated is a movement no longer of personal effort, but of a sort of will from below evoking an action from above.

The result is a slow redevelopment of the beginnings of organised Vijnana.

[*Half a page left blank.*]

Feb 25th

The record has been suspended because of an almost entire suspension of all progress in which the hostile forces have seemed to take possession and only the literary & intellectual activity has continued to progress. In this field the perceptive intuition & creative interpretation grow in force.

Roga has been very powerful & violent.

Sharira has been practically suspended.

Kriti is a struggle in which minor points are gained, the great lost or left undecided or even if won are not decisive.

The one definite advance is in antardrishta where forms & vak are now perfect and sometimes stable, but this is when they come spontaneously, not when they are commanded.

Nevertheless there is progress, as now appears. First, the personal effort, view etc are more & more merged in the All. Action & thought & perception come more & more out of the All. Self is more and more identified with the All & proceeds out of it in its becomings rather than stands separate within it.

Secondly, telepathy & intuition are far more developed than before. Decisive intuition is fortified though not yet dominant.

Thirdly, the power of work without choice, steady, nishkama, proceeding out of Sat & Tapas of Sat is infinitely increased.

Feb 27th

The atmosphere of the Asiddhi still hangs heavy upon the system. Roga persists though the tide is receding. Sraddha finds no food to grow upon.

स सुतः पीतये वृषा सोमः पवित्रे अर्षति
विघ्नन् रक्षांसि देवयुः ।

The opposition is now no longer from Vritra, Vala, the Dwayavins, but from the Nidah & the Rakshas, – in reality however from the Rakshas giving the others their opportunity.

=

After a long interruption Kamananda is beginning again to be active.

=

In Samadhi the antardrishta and swapna are both perfect, except (1) for lack of long continued samadhi, (2) for lack of life utility.

=

22 APRIL – 26 AUGUST 1915

April 22d(?)[1]

1. The vision (in Samadhi) of the Theosophical Path on the table, fulfilled next day. Suggestion of importance—fulfilled by solution of the Vedic Rishi-idea by example of Bodhi-sattwas in Japan.
2. The waking drishti of the cigarette on the table. Suggestion of certain fulfilment by exceptional means. Found on floor.

April 24th

Anandam Brahma confirmed in its final generality.

Renewal of the Anandas all contained together in the Suddha.

Firm general definition of Karma.

First entirely spontaneous & prolonged intensity of Vaidyuta (yesterday).

April 25th

Krishna Kali in all beings confirmed in its final generality—still obstructed in the animal. Afterwards extended to this field as well.

Kamananda made persistent (predicted during the last few days)

Telepathy justified in its general satyam and accepted—trikaldrishti in telepathy, but obstructed.

Beginnings of final organisation of knowledge parts of the Vijnana.

General prevalence of Aishwarya-Vashita, against resistance, after lapse of time. As yet, no general perfection in detail. The field is still limited.

Other Anandas continue to grow.

---

[1] *The question mark was put by Sri Aurobindo.* — Ed.

Rupa etc still strives to emerge into distinctness, stability & variety.

Growth of the Kali permanence.

The second chatusthaya increases in power.

Tertiary dasya emphasised in action & thought.

3.[2] Telepathic trikaldrishti of movements of the child in the opposite house.

April 26th

Krishna-Kali now generalising itself at its lowest pitch. It alternates with the Anandam Brahma also at a low pitch, in the terms of the material Avidya. It is still as a rule more at the back of things than at the front.

The organisation of the Knowledge by illumination proceeds. Lipi & Rupa are included.

Lipi
1. Build desolated Europe into a city of God.
2 Eyes in the splanchna. (the pranic sense).

April 27 –

Prakriti Purusha well established in the Ananda Brahman.

Kamananda obstructed yesterday but not entirely discontinued in the body. Strong pressure for the Ananda from the Sukshma. Continuous under adverse circumstances.

All the physical anandas have for the time being slackened in frequency.

Organisation of vijnana continues against steady obstruction.

Prolonged rupa-vishaya (crow flying about in sky), chhaya, but not merely image, – saprana image left in the ether. True rupa vishaya of insects & birds in the Akasha (Prana akasha) are now common, but not detailed.

---

2 *Numbering continued from 22(?) April. — Ed.*

April 29.

The Krishna Kali as the all containing one (An. Br [Anantam or Anandam Brahma]) & everything as its expression in the terms of Purusha Prakriti.

The Ishwara begins to take final possession.

Truth continues to grow in the trikaldrishti telepathy, effectivity in the power. Rupa advances, but is still seriously obstructed.

April 30

Krishna Kali in all, but not in the intensity.

An established sama-ananda in harmony with the ish, but not as yet with its full forceful activity.

The harmonising with the unequal reactions of the more forceful activity has begun — they are brought & taken up by the Ananda which has entered into them.

April 30 —

Trikaldrishti has suddenly increased enormously in truth, but it has still its basis in the telepathy, and subject to the stress of error.

May 1st

The day is the close of one week of progress, steady and often rapid —

Samata

Universal *samata* has been finally confirmed and the reactions of *asamata* imposed from outside are now taken up by the Ananda.

In the body there are still movements & reactions of discomfort & *nirananda*, but these also are now being taken up. Even the pain of burning is pursued by the Ananda and generally accompanied by it. *Bhukti* is therefore on the point of accomplishment in generality. It remains to give it its destined intensity.

The reactions contradicting titiksha, nati, udasinata thus persist & are being purposely brought forward in order to be transformed. They can no longer prevail in their own kind.

Shakti

There is also a generalisation of Shakti. Sraddha is now confirmed except in the Karma where it still fluctuates and is environed by doubt. The doubt is no longer absolute. *Kalyanasraddha* has increased in the chitta.

The growth of knowledge, Ananda Brahman & Krishna has firmly based the Samatachatusthaya. The growth of power, Krishna-Kali & Sraddha has prepared the final basis of the Shakti-chatusthaya; but the power is not yet sufficient to assure the full sraddha and *devibhava (daivi prakriti)*.

Dasya is tertiary, but not always of the full intensity of its third tertiary form. D^3 is established, but not D^{33}, except as a frequent exception.

Brahman.

The generality of Sarvam Brahma, replaced by Sarvam Anantam, is now replaced by Sarvam Anantam Jnanam with the Anandam subdued but present in all the three. It is now in course of being replaced by the Krishna-darshana in the Jnanam Anandam; the Narayana-Vishnu Bhava persists, but as a past habit. The intensity of the Krishna-Narayana is now taking its place.

Karma.

Krishna-Kali bhava is growing to the point of the firm epiphany. Subjective kama is assured & the full subjective Ananda based on the Shuddha is present either in the subdued status or the intense movement. The oppositions of the subjective Vishaya-nirananda are being finally eliminated & exist only as external vibrations in the external mind. They are attended by the *viparita* Ananda.

Karma yet awaits the full power. In intellectual (intuitive) work it is now only combated by the remnants of the physical resistance; but in all else it is still bound & to a certain extent afflicted.

Vijnana.

All its parts, except Aishwarya-traya & Samadhi are in the hands of the Master, directly. The instrumental usurpation persists, but is no longer effective.

Telepathy is now mahat, except in thought-vyapti & thought-prakamya. Satyam is established, but ritam is still imperfect.

Trikaldrishti is now acquiring the satyam & has greatly improved in the ritam. The Chit-Tapas combination is beginning to prevail.

Aishwarya-traya & Samadhi have to be liberated in this month & essentially in its first week.

Sharira

All the physical Anandas are frequent & much more prolonged than ever before, but not yet permanent in continuity, only permanent in recurrence.

Vaidyuta (*ahaituka*) now manifests frequently, physical Vishaya *ahaituka* less frequently, but sahaituka is well-established.

Arogya grows in force, but has not yet expelled the habitual reactions.

Utthapana is suspended, but increases subjectively.

In Saundarya there is no appreciable advance.

———

The stress is now on Vijnana (especially trikaldrishti); it is growing in Aishwarya-traya and rupa. In the Sharira it is on Ananda & in a less degree on arogya; but it seeks to extend itself to the two deficient members.

Lipi
1. Yeast of bliss
2. Yeast of life 〉 yeast, that is the inchoate ferment
3 Yeast of trikaldrishti
4 pragmatic telepathy
5 taste.
6 glad of bliss — ie the system & all its environment consenting to the Ananda. This is now done
7 glad of Ares　in the force & struggle harmonised with the Ananda. This is now undertaken.
8 toil
9 [*no notation*]

References

1. enimvero . . certainly, but indeed . . enisus . . eniteo. (as an event) enitesco (as a habit) — enitor, enixe, enixus —

— connected with lipi 8. and indicating the struggle & luminous emergence now transferred from the person to the environing Prakriti.

2 eno —
    enodate. enodatio — } confirming (1) from another standpoint & throwing light on Vedic images in the hymns to the Aswins (Kaksh[ivan]) read yesterday & today.

=

Lipi, rupa etc are now taking the pragmatic turn more decidedly; but this is not yet extended to the telepathy.

=

May 2$^{\underline{d}}$

In the morning a general reduction to the lowest terms, with the object of taking up the apparent contradictions & turning them to siddhi.

=

Aishwarya traya increases in force & produces more rapid & exact results in the field of exercise, but is still subject to the obstruction & contradiction. In the karma it is still weak

=

Trikaldrishti grows in mahattwa of the satyam ritam, chiefly in its telepathic basis

=

Lipi

1. In the infinity youth; (not yet in the finite).

The adverse movement continues throughout the day, — reactions which are not taken up by the Ananda, voices, thoughts, suggestions which are not taken up by the Ishwara nor proceed from him, absence normally of the Krishnadarshana replaced by the Saguna-Nirguna Brahman, impaired Ananda of the vishaya of sight, failing faith, absence of udasinata & nati etc. Trikaldrishti, aishwarya etc act, but are no longer dominant.

=

Evening

The siddhi is now remanifesting, but with a residue of the Asiddhi. The main asiddhi is the reaction of Sushna Kayava, with the bhrista tavishi.

May 3ᵈ

    Lipi — 1. Yeast of love

           2   Yeast of difficulties   (general ferment of the opposi-
                            tion still left opposing the progress).

    1. Universal Prema is now becoming fixed & spontaneous, ie not needing the aid of the mind's attention to the object

=

The Rupa has been largely eclipsed for some time; it is now undergoing a fresh movement towards manifestation; but the obstruction is not yet conquered.

=

After a long struggle the covering consciousness has once more been removed & the Krishna Kali once more occupies all manifesting freely in all often with the intensity & directly, or else with the disguise of the form & mentality.

=

Vijnana strives to perfect itself; but is still pursued by the error of stress.

=

Dream is once more coherent & better organised.

=

Perfect organisation of *lipi*, thought & *sukshma vak* in jagrad antardrishta and swapnasamadhi.

May 4ᵗʰ

    The Kalikrishna darshana is now generalising itself more firmly.

    In the health, the struggle continues. One long persistent roga is now in the last stage of dying recurrences. Another that threatened to be chronic (the eyes) is being successfully attacked at its roots. Feverish exhaustion attempts to recur daily, but is expelled after a short struggle; nevertheless it lingers in the environing akasha. Two only are still in the persistent stage of recurrence.

Reference

सखायः सं वः सम्यंचमिषं – स्तोमंत्राग्नये – वर्षिष्ठाय क्षितीनामूर्जो नप्त्रे सहस्वते ।

This is now beginning to manifest & attempting to generalise itself.

===

Organisation of the vijnana of knowledge proceeds.

===

The sense of the universe in myself and all energies & activities even the most adverse has been restored & is now constant.

===

Great extension of effective Vashita working in harmony with an almost perfect ritam of the telepathy & trikaldrishti.

===

Samadhi continues to organise itself. The things of the pranic & mental worlds are now distinguished, lipi & vak grow in co-herence & organisation, there is a beginning of free rupa in the antardrishta.

===

Exact fulfilment in aishwarya vashita is again becoming fre-quent, but the deflecting resistance & to some extent the entire obstruction have still a power which though much diminished struggles to remain. The Shakti is now being led to apply itself with determination to the karma.

===

The सम्यक् इष् was first brought forward in the morning; it is now established in the action. The Agni is being developed ऊर्जो नप्ता सहस्वान्

===

Rupa became active, but did not increase to the full point attained in the past.

May 5 —
   Rf. [Reference]   Nulli visa cito decurrit tramite virgo —
=

There is no fresh advance, but only the yeast of what has been already accomplished combating the difficulties of farther progress. This difficulty of farther progress is a principle of retardation that has now to be destroyed as it is no longer useful for the purpose of [conservation].[3] The shakti can now dispense with such aids.
=

The struggle over the unfinished parts of the vijnana continues. It has not advanced appreciably beyond yesterday's limit, but is obviously preparing an advance. Meanwhile the sama Ananda etc are being strengthened.
=

Strong discomfort is being given & constantly met with the assumption of the discomfort by the ananda.. It is not as yet entirely transmuted.
=

Faith in the Karma fluctuates, but is normally much stronger than before.

May 6 —
   The Aishwarya-Vashita is less effective today, on the other hand the Trikaldrishti-telepathy increases.
=

Force of rupa increases, but slowly & against great obstruction.
=

Lipi
Transitional character of opposition struggle   (ie it is becom-
                                  ing more & more defensive).
=

No definite advance during the day.
=

Samadhi advances in all respects, but not yet victoriously.

---

[3] *MS* conversation

May 7.

The Krishna Darshana after going through several fluctuations has added to the darshana of the Continent & constituent which are now sufficiently fixed & that of the inhabitant which fluctuates the darshana of the identical (atmaivabhud bhutani). It is when the inhabitant, continent[,] constituent & identical unite that there is the full intensity.

=

Lipi.
1. for yeast of bliss — (to confirm it entirely the samata is being tested)
2 yeast of pain   (this is now being given to generalise the raudrananda).
3 for yeast of life.

=

Kamananda very intense for a time; now frequently recurrent, but usually subdued. The intensity, however, also recurs.

=

May 8th

The Siddhi is now restored in the Aishwarya, although not yet in entire force.

=

This time the disturbance of the Samata by the Asiddhi has been slight & quite inconsiderable.

=

The Trikaldrishti progresses always in spite of apparent setbacks.

=

Kamananda grows slowly in force, as also Samadhi.

=

May 9th

The fluctuations of the Vijnana chatusthaya continue, especially with regard to Aishwarya, rupa lipi and samadhi. This afternoon there is a general cloud of tamas.

May 10th

A day of advance, but not of decisive advance.

Telepathy has grown stronger & surer.

Trikaldrishti is restored almost entirely, *aishwaryatraya* partially..

Rupa advances, but does not yet break the barrier to stability.

Samadhi is depressed.

=

The work in process is chiefly a work of general basing.

May 11th

भुवत्कण्वे वृषा द्युम्नी आहुतः क्रंददश्रो गविष्टिषु—

At first aishwarya traya depressed by the resistance, then it assumed for some time the upper hand compelling the result against direct resistance sometimes immediately & entirely, always at least partially in the end. This movement clearly reveals the fact that the physical Akasha-shakti is now on its defence maintaining its freedom with difficulty & no longer assured of its empire.

May 12

Since yesterday the organisation of the Vijnana has become normalised, 1. in script, 2, in vangmaya thought, 3 in vani (today) 4. in perceptive thought. 5 in aishwarya traya. In the last two there is still positive defect, owing to the imperfection of the aishwarya which brings with it the struggle of the Will against the Akasha-Shakti and throws back on (4) the shadow of the excessive stress of will-thought.

Aishwarya traya today is working more evenly, though with less precise force. Ishita is becoming more prominent. The shadow of personal will is steadily losing force of insistence & giving place to the Master-will.

The personal relation with the Master manifests, not again to be suspended; it brings the madhura dasya, the delight in all things & the understanding of all experience & movements of event in the terms of the divine Will

Krishna darshana depressed & put in the background for the last two days but not suspended is once more general as the continent & as the all. It is only deficient as the Inhabitant.

Rupa increases always in force, samadhi is depressed.

Trikaldrishti gains always in ritam, thought-telepathy increases

Kamananda depressed for the last two days, but not suspended, is again active & sometimes intense.

Afternoon

Crude rupa in all forms presented both primary & secondary stability.

Developed rupa increased stability to the remote or indirect vision, but does not yet endure before the fixed gaze, except primarily in the type form of the reel.

In this movement aishwarya ishita was throughout the agent.

Krishnadarshana now embraces whole groups in a great & sometimes with the first intensity.. In the intensity it is not yet general.

Primary utthapana is being enforced, but is still not entirely dominant.

Rf—

पूर्वीरस्य निष्षिधो मर्त्येषु पुरू वसूनि पृथिवी बिभर्ति ।
इंद्राय द्यावो ओषधीरुतापो रयिं रक्षंति जीरयो वनानि ॥

The Rf in the morning to all the gods setting Agni to work (पनयंत) in his activities has been fulfilled.

The confusion of Knowledge Thought by Will Thought became very violent in the evening, but could not entirely annul even the decisive trikaldrishti; the telepathic maintained its satyam, but could not preserve the constant or always central use of its ritam. Subsequently, there was a reversion to the better harmony.

=

May 13th

Kamananda still active, with touches of intensity, sometimes in samadhi.

In the morning perfect telepathy & trikaldrishti. Aishwaryatraya sometimes in full force, but usually baffled by the resistance.

Gandhadrishti developing since yesterday was this morning full, varied, vivid & sthula. Rasadrishti also became active, but usually comes as a result or a part of gandha; not however always. It is sometimes associated with sparsha half-evolved from sukshma to sthula. Sparsha except in the old established touches is chiefly vivid sukshma. Shabda is infrequent & more sukshma than sthula. Darshana is poor and intermittent.

Samadhi has not yet recovered its activity and coherence.

Rupa is active, developed forms frequent, sometimes thickly frequent, but not stable.

Manusha sparsha has been experienced indirectly, on the cigar held between the fingers, not on the body itself.

Activity of the Rupa at night. At first free crude, akasha, & beginnings of free crude sadhara; also first stable dense & developed. Afterwards resistance brought in to spoil the forms.

Aishwarya of rain successful.

May 14th

The force of the aishwaryatraya is greatly increased.

There is a movement towards the completion of the satyam in the vijnana.

There is also an incipient movement of more complete ritam.

The bhava in the Ishwara is entirely confirmed; it is now being perfected in the Balaram-Aniruddha type, preparatory to the Sri Krishna-Rudra (the Asura).

The habit of relapse in the Krishnadarshana is being attacked.

=

Kamananda these two days has been constant with intermittences, but not continuous. This evening it has once more the tendency of continuity.

Rupa improves always, but does not yet confirm stability except in the crude.

Samadhi is beginning to reorganise itself.

Gandha is varied, but not so frequent & rich as yesterday. Aswada is also obstructed, though occasionally it manifests.

—

Samadhi is partly reorganised. Vangmaya thought is thoroughly established & continues in a stream even in the sushupta swapna, when memory, reason, mental attention are all absent. It was combined with lipi, perceptive thought & shabda (vak).

At night organised samadhi. Continuity of drishya, primary frequent, sometimes incipient secondary.

May 15

Organised samadhi in the morning.

Kamananda seems now to be settled in the system, as a constantly recurrent experience throughout the day and a permanent tendency. The other Anandas are still intermittent.

In the subjective Ahaituka is constant, Chidghana, frequent, Prema recurrent, Shuddha occasional.

The whole Vijnanachatusthaya is now on a line of fixed progress towards perfection. Sharira & Karmachatusthaya alone remain.

=

In the later part of the day a reaction and suspension of the progress.

May 16.

The reaction continues. Nothing is precisely lost except for a diminution of the Sraddha; but the forward impulse has ceased & in sharira & karma the adverse forces seem to be triumphant.

Asamata of satyasatya which hitherto gave such acute trouble has disappeared. Asamata of siddhi asiddhi has revived and is the sole asamata remaining; but it is neither absorbing, nor violent. It is being rapidly killed.

May 17

The reaction has deepened & injured without suspending the action of the Vijnana. The satyam is no longer perfect; the stress of suggestion & intellectual perception has revived. The Aishwarya traya acts less surely on the surroundings. Rupa is no longer active.

This morning the satyam is recovering tone & the aishwarya traya recovering force.

Krishnadarshana of a certain intensity is now general in spite of a constant effort in the Akasha Prakriti to pull it back to the mere Saguna Brahma or Narayanadarshana.

The Ishwara is now manifest in the Vani & as the master of all the thought & action; the dasyam is becoming entirely complete & personal. As yet it is the Balarama-Aniruddha Bhava with Aniruddha prominent.

Rupa revived, but not in full force.

Kamananda in spite of adverse circumstances.

Gandha frequent & varied.

May 18 —

Krishnadarshana seems to be invincibly established.

There is a tendency to the full restoration of the action of the Siddhi. This is most evident in the Aishwarya-cum-trikaldrishti, & in the three subjective chatusthayas & in Krishna Kali.

The new movement has not yet begun except in the first chatusthaya & the second & sixth where it is a completion and a preparation rather than an initiation.

Vak, jagrat, manifests, but with difficulty.

May 19th

All the subjective Anandas are confirmed, not in the intensity, but in their synthesis, from Suddha to subjective Kama.

Udasinata, Nati, Titiksha are finally established in their unabridged completeness & synthesis. The positive bhoga of Asiddhi is being enforced. This has been hitherto the one imperfection of the first chatusthaya & the point at which the Asamata always broke in. It was done chiefly through the impatience of Asatyam. That impatience is now killed. Without this basis the impatience of Asiddhi could not last.

Krishna Darshana resists all attacks.

Gandha continues, though less frequent.

Physical samata and Ananda of pain & discomfort are also

being finally confirmed. Touches which formerly overcame the Titiksha, are now anandamaya.

Kamananda continues intermittently against oppression.

The other siddhis are obstructed in act, but none actually abridged in fact.

The relation of the Dasya grows constantly in force.

The Sraddha is attempting to override its difficulties.

Vijnana is considerably obstructed and the movement towards the ritam seems temporarily to have receded and lost part of its force.

Rupa & Samadhi are comparatively ineffective

Karma & Sharira fluctuate.

Krishna-Kali is preparing its finality.

The sense of the Self everywhere & all energies as the Self's is returning to activity.

=

On the whole the Suddhi, Mukti, Bhukti are nearing final completion & the purely subjective siddhi. Only in the subjective-objective siddhi the victory is still delayed & in the objective the adverse forces still hold most of the ground except in the physical Ananda, where victory is now assured.

May 20 –

Dasyam is now becoming all-pervading and intense

Sraddha Bhagavati is almost complete; sraddha swashaktyam is still deficient. The sraddha bhagavati is hampered by the inability to have complete confidence in the Vani; all vanis are now being taken up by the Ishwara.

=

The siddhi has now to take a new turn. Basing itself on the complete Dasya, Sraddha & Ananda it has to acquire intensity in all that is possessed, sureness in the Vijnana, rapidity in the Sharira & Karma. The Seven Affirmations have to be finally completed & then the two that remain.

The state of these Affirmations may again be stated:

1. The universal sense of the Anandamaya Lilamaya Krishna

in the Brahmadrishti has become the continent of the conscious activity in knowledge & is becoming the continent of the conscious activity in Will.

2. Affirmation has almost entirely replaced rejection & denial, but not entirely.

3. Brihat of the satyam is affirmed as the basis of the development of the ritam, but is not yet free from attack

4. Ananda is now entirely confirmed as the base, free & joyous Tapas is in course of being established and in a less degree free & joyous Prakasha as the special instruments.

—

5. The Personality of Krishna is present in the consciousness governing all the activities, but sometimes there comes the veil of the Prakriti.

6. Dasya of Madhura & tertiary dasya confirmed entirely, but not yet in full intensity.

7 Acceptance of bhoga as a slave & instrument of the Lover only now entirely & finally accomplished. Intensity has yet to be given.

—

8. Siddhi on the basis of the largeness in the five worlds is prepared, but not yet accomplished

9. Time, Space & Circumstance still appear as determinative, not yet as instrumental factors.

—

Intensity is now being brought into the Suddha-Chidghana-Ahaituka-Prema Ananda and prepared in the Madhura Dasya which is becoming Saumya-Raudra. For the present the Saumya predominates, with the Raudra as a background. In the Sraddha there is greater intensity (answering to yesterday's lipi, "enthusiastic faith") but not yet certainty in the Karma and Vijnana.

To the tratak the moving clouds of the pranic akasha are visible, sometimes a star, living specks, birds or insects.

There is the old struggle between the decisive vijnana & the perception of actual possibilities; but the consciousness still dwells in the triloka. Vijnana & Ananda occupy it or are in the background, – they are not yet the habitation, *kshaya.*

Aishwarya continues to fluctuate, sometimes triumphant, sometimes resisted successfully in moving objects; in stationary objects (prani, not sthavara) resisted usually with success. In inanimate objects there is now often success of the aishwarya..... Resistance is almost invariable, but often it is rapidly overcome

—

Kamananda is once more dominant.

—

Reference –

शोध: Purification .. rectification .. acquittal of debts .. retaliation.

—

At night foiled attack on the samananda.

—

Movement towards the intensity of the madhura dasya accompanied with a stronger sense of the Ishwara not as Mechanist, but as Natha & Bhokta.

May 21st
    Rf   1   The haven must be reached.
            2   Not soon is God's delight in us completed, nor with one life we end. Termless in us are our spirits seated and termless joy intend.
            3. The heavens of the Three have beings bright (Sarvalokadrishti)

—

The subjective Ananda has made a sudden stride forward towards great intensity in all its parts.

The vangmaya has now risen from the effective-adequate to the illuminative & inspirational substance & form. This was preceded by a slow movement of the transformation of unharmonised satyam to harmonised ritam, which as a result of the rise has become rapid. The perceptive thought is becoming luminous & vijnanamaya in the vijnana instead of vijnanamaya in the manas.

Aishwaryavashita has also become much more forceful. Ishita tends to the same force, but is not yet so decisive.

Rupa-samadhi are still obstructed in their attempt to progress.

In aishwarya immediate decisive effects almost without resistance are now frequent; effect against resistance is more common in the ishita.

Trikaldrishti is following the same rapid forward movement. Decisive trikaldrishti, once more active, is aiming at exactness of place, time, circumstance.

Lipi
1) 15 . . 25 (ie 1915 – 1925 for the external purification & rectification).
2) solarithm (a new mathematical figure)
3) perfect disponibility of the lipi

The Aishwarya-Vashita is almost all-victorious this morning upon things in motion; only the insufficiency of the Ishita gives a hold to the resistance. Things in station feel the force, but resist successfully the exact fulfilment.

Where there is fixed intention with rapid movement, the Power does not as yet prevail. Fixed tendency, generally, is still an imperfectly mastered obstacle.

Rupa & samadhi are again active; the first in the crude with an imperfect deliverance of the form & a difficulty of the quadruped form, but with a greater hold on the akasha; the second imperfectly organised in rupa & vishaya, fluctuating in lipi, but perfect in thought, vangmaya & perceptive.

Samadhi
1. Conversation. "in emergency". (political. IO [India Office] & India)

2 "At such a distance we find that we can do nothing" and a figure in dhoti.

3 a conversation in French on a gnomic Greek poet, perfect in form although derivative in substance, indicating fresh discoveries of lost Greek poets. (N.B. The discovery of Bhasa's plays was fore-

seen a year or two before it happened. Saumilla's have also been promised).

=

The force of Tapas on the Roga increases. Chronic false cough has been expelled. The eruptional tendency is almost eliminated. Assimilation imperfection still resists as also the functional defect.

The resistance of living things in station is now overcome. Success is more usual than failure and exact fulfilment is frequent and striking. There are also now cases of immediate triumph over fixed intention in rapid movement.

It remains to give full intensity & universality to the power of the Tapas, raising it all round to the 80°, so that the resistance may disappear and Time, Place & Circumstance become instrumental instead of determinative. It is to this result that the siddhi now turns.

=

Effective tapas has to be imposed on the body & on the life (karma). Siddhi is effected in the first two chatusthayas & in the sixth & in three parts of the general (seventh) chatusthaya, & in the subjective half of the fifth, so far as is possible without dominance of the Tapas-Prakasha in the fourth & effective half of the fifth. In the third the successful & victorious march of the siddhi in all its four (five) members is now assured. Sharira & Karma-Kama remain.

=

The Siddhi at night showed signs of resuming the stability of the dense & developed; but the movement was not carried forward.

May 22^{d}

In swapnasamadhi successive scenes coherently connected together, but in themselves fleeting, though absolutely perfect. In jagrat antardrishta a scene of the manasa loka, (affective), coherent, well designed, but dim.

The vak of the thought maintains the level it had acquired and yet prepares a more ample & varied form. That it does this without

sinking into a more backward state, is a sign that the old rhythm of
[   ]⁴ progress & relapse is passing away; a movement anandamaya
anarvan is beginning

The Tapas is less in possession this morning; its directions are
more often refused or, when obeyed, usually more imperfectly. The
trikaldrishti is more confused by the will-thought

Krishnadarshana has for some time drawn back into a fuller
Ananda Brahma Saguna-Nirguna with the Narayan & Vishnu
bhavas contained & the Lilamaya without the all-pervading
expressed Krishna Nama in the rupa.

The violent attack of the old Asiddhi has failed after producing a few fugitive vibrations,—an effigies of incipient asamata &
non-vijnana.

The struggle between Kamananda and its obstruction is now
becoming constant.

=

Decisive trikaldrishti, independent of telepathy, increases in
force, frequency & certainty; but it works in the midst of a mass of
telepathies acting in the manas which tend indeed more & more to
reveal their satyam of tendency or actual possibility, but continue to
throw a shadow of confusion on the trikaldrishti. The Knowledge is
still farther confused by the anrita will-thought, which is a stressed
perception of tendency or actual possibility in the physical or subconscious that does not manifest in event, although it sometimes
manifests in conscious tendency.

Knowledge & Tapas are this morning acting again in the manas
& not in the vijnana; therefore there is no general ritam; only
a ritam disengaging itself with difficulty from the brihat of the
unregulated mental satyam. This constitutes a relapse.

=

The vibrations of asamata of asiddhi continue & amount to a
breaking in on the siddhi of the fourth chatusthaya. As usual, there
was a false security that this lapse would not again happen. There
is also a shadow of the asamata of asatya.

=

⁴ MS of

KrishnaKali Darshana is once more intense and more all-pervading than it was hitherto. There is an obstacle to the intensity of the darshana in the bird form and a general obstruction to the pervasiveness of the greater intensity & even a shadow of obstruction lingering about the intensity attained.

=

After a long struggle lasting till 3.30 pm the siddhi has again been resumed, but the vijnana has not yet been entirely recovered in all the movements, nor the complete Ananda in the manas. The delight of the vishayas has remained firm throughout in all its parts. It is the ananda of the physical Manas in asiddhi that has failed.

The intensity of the Ananda is, however, insufficient in a certain thin layer of vishaya sensation chiefly felt in the taste of insipid food, of vulgar & insipid faces, of coarse & discordant sound etc.

=

Samadhi has been afflicted by incoherencies of vishaya etc without losing what it had gained. What has not yet been gained, is being made prominent.

=

The Krishna-Kali-Darshana after a period of higher intensity has fallen back again into a lower degree of the Saguna-Nirguna dominated by Vishnu-Narayana with the Ananda in the background. The Asiddhi is still powerful.. Suddha & Prema Ananda have also become depressed, though not denied.

=

The Shuddha Prema is now being restored independently of the Krishna-Darshana.

=

Continuance of entire asamata in the evening—including rejection of nati. Resumed suspension of the progress of the siddhi.

The degree of the raudra up to which pain can be made subject to titiksha and converted into Ananda has immensely risen & is being rapidly & constantly heightened.

=

There is a reinforcement of the roga which had almost been eliminated, but as yet its materialisation is insignificant in force and extent.

None of the physical siddhis is yet decisively victorious in any of its parts.

=

The confusions & ill-results of the lapse continued even into the night. The refusal of the Jiva to participate in the effort of the Siddhi prevented the movement towards resumption of siddhi from taking definite shape. [Ritam][5] was challenged even in the script and vangmaya thought & therefore all confidence refused to any form of thought or knowledge. Samadhi at night was barren. All thoughts & suggestions from whatever source or through whatever instrument were contradictory & confused; the reconciling ritam was excluded in obedience to the asraddha.

=

The result of these movements in an increased siddhi cannot be apparent till the morrow.

=

May 23.

The siddhi is being remanifested, but with a successiveness which makes it appear like rapid rebuilding. The intensity of the dasya & the sraddha have not, however, been restored. In most movements the power of the siddhi emerges increased in range or intensity or in both.

The Aishwarya-Vashita has not yet the general force to which it temporarily rose, but it produces very often rapid effects in detail of a temporary or sometimes a final decisiveness, while its power of prolonged pressure has not decreased & that of the ishita has increased.

The unalloyed Ananda of defeat has not yet been restored.

The distinction is now being clearly drawn of trikaldrishtis certain of [themselves],[6] formed in the nature of knowledge & infallibly fulfilled and drishtis hesitating or else insisting & assuming a spurious certainty, formed in the nature of twilit & obscure force, dual, balanced or pursued by their opposites, representing a clash of forces & often or usually baffled of their result. The former are

[5] MS Anrita
[6] MS itself

growing in frequency. There is also an intermediate drishti, in which the certain emerges out of the uncertain, the pure trikaldrishti out of the telepathic, but without the clear luminosity of the spontaneous sureness.

There is a pressure of movement towards the harmony of knowledge & force (Prakasha-Tapas), but it is as yet vague & ill defined, a large & obscure fluctuation & inchoate formation.

=

During the afternoon a confusion of Asiddhi without yesterday's violences. The Ananda of defeat has not been restored and the attempt of the system to replace it by indifference or akriya udasinata in defeat is being constantly thwarted.

The relation with the Ishwara has also not been restored. The script, vani, thought are no longer regarded as entirely in his possession; full dasya sometimes returns, but with a reserve, & is then again disturbed. Sraddha is absent, except when the vijnana is in play.

May 24.

Samadhi failed to preserve the incipient organisation already realised. There was, however, a movement to remanifest the lost stability of rupa & continuity of active drishya, but the continuity achieved was only of the manasic drishta and the stability had no sufficient hold on the akasha.

=

The siddhi is now restored with a more direct presence of the Ishwara in the thought and script and a more intimate prabhutwa in the dasya by the diminution of the role and insistence of the instrumental ganas. Only the intensity of the Sraddha is lowered by the exclusion of the hasty tapasic element in the enthusiastic faith. The faith is now deficient in enthusiasm & entirety, because it is deficient in certainty.

=

The Krishnadarshan is now full of the Saguna Brahman with the contents of the Trinity & often descends into the Saguna

Brahman. At other times it rises to the KrishnaKali. Usually it is divided between the two.

=

Sraddha has not yet been restored.

Trikaldrishti works with some fullness, but not sufficient certitude. Tapas is temporarily depressed in order to give more scope for the *udasina prakasha*.

=

There is no decisive forward movement anywhere else.

Sahitya has been recommenced.

=

Samananda of siddhi asiddhi is still infirm in the prana.

May 25th

There is today greater strength of the Sama Ananda & the Asraddha is less aggressive.

Aishwarya is stronger in exact movement of things in station, less powerful over things in motion. The general effectivity is still depressed. Satyam of telepathy always increases in largeness.

Trikaldrishti is becoming more & more accurate in general fact and even in perception of general order of circumstance, but is much astray in time & place & therefore in exact order of circumstance.

Rupa grows always behind the veil rather than in front of it and slowly against a still prevailing obstruction.

Samadhi is gradually reestablishing continuity of active drishya.

=

Sparsha is now beginning to be sthula in other directions than in the falling of water drops on the body etc, but it is a very sukshma sthula. It is chiefly as indicated often in the lipi on the lips that it makes itself felt.

Gandha persists, but more sparely & sparsely than at first

Rasa is infrequent & seldom decided.

Chakshusha in the habitual forms of the Akasha.

Sravana is the most backward.

=

A reaction in which the tapasic powers that helped the siddhi are thrown out from the centre and appear in the environment as confused suggestions & will-forces that no longer command the light.

=

May 26th

The Siddhi is now in a period of transitional reaction.

=

Frequent coherent conversations in the Samadhi; better organisation of rupa; incipient organisation of lipi.

=

Satyam brihat very pronounced; resumed action of ritam in the satyam.

=

In the evening attempt of the sukshma vak to manifest more freely & fully

=

May 27th

Attempted movement towards the complete satyam-ritam of the trikaldrishti, broken down by a fresh reaction.

Aishwarya depressed.

Kamananda persists, but is slight & broken during the last two or three days.

=

The chief movement has been the emergence of the fixed Mahakali temperament with fixity in the struggle and yuddhalipsa and the rejection of the tamasic Mahasaraswati temperament which draws back from apparently useless struggle & desires either an easy progress or acquiescence in an imposed immobility.

—

May 28th

Reemergence of the siddhi. Trikaldrishti & Tapas now act combined, but the trikaldrishti is surer than the Tapas. There is also a growing combination of the telepathic and the decisive trikaldrishti. None of these movements are yet perfect.

=

Kamananda shows a tendency to recover force.
=

The Ishwara is still obscured.
=

May 29th

The Siddhi is now restored in all but the Aishwarya-traya &
the Rupa-Samadhi.
=

Among the Vishayas gandha alone persists & gandharasa. The
others have fallen back to a lower degree

May 30th

The Krishna-darshana is reestablished in its first intensity; the
difficulty of the unbeautiful face concealing the Sarva-sundara is
conquered in fact, though it attempts to return & does recur as a
reminiscent experience. The second intensity is now more frequent
and more secure as founded on a firmer foundation of the first
intensity.

Preliminary—	Krishna *sensed* behind the disguise
1st intensity—	Krishna *seen* behind the human mask.
2^d	Krishna seen in the human being
3^d	The human being seen in Krishna
Consummation.	The human being = Krishna.

The same rule holds with all things and beings

The samata holds against all things except complete asraddha
of the Karma; it then becomes udasinata on the surface as soon as
it has recovered from the positive depression.
=

In the second chatusthaya sraddha and consequently ishwarabhava & attahasya are still subject the first to depression, the second
to rejection from the front and non-emergence. The last two indeed
are seldom present.
=

Vijnana improves in trikaldrishti, but is there subject to violent
return of the falsifying will-thought due to baffled Tapas.
=

Rupasamadhi goes through a constant process of construction, demolition, reconstruction or manifestation, repression & gradual remanifestation.

=

Kamananda is now daily recurrent, but its intensity & continuity fluctuate. The other Sharira Anandas are intermittent.

Arogya grows slowly, but is not manifest in the two deficient points (teeth and the central function).

Utthapana & Saundarya are depressed or repressed.

=

The Krishnadarshan now varies between all intensities of itself and even all stages. Sometimes it lapses into the ordinary vision with the Brahman behind it.

The Dwaya consciousness which has long re-usurped this mind was again removed this morning, but still hangs about the mentality.

Aiswarya traya manifests sometimes, but is usually ineffective.

=

The rupa-samadhi attempts to progress, but as yet without any decisive success.

=

Gandha is now frequent & spontaneous. Sparsha is limited to the habitual touches, but capable of a surprising intensity & long after-effect in the contact.

May 31st

Another strong effort to organise swapna-samadhi by bringing coherence into vak, lipi, thought, successive rupa and connecting them together. A partial success.

=

The struggle is again over the vijnana. Aishwarya & trikaldrishti fluctuate, sometimes combining, sometimes acting against each other and at others both sinking into entire imbecility broken only by detailed & isolated successes.

=

The movements of thought occasionally move all in the vijnana or are vijnanamaya, but this is followed immediately by a collapse.

=

Physical touches of asamata persist.

=

Lapse of the Krishnadarshana; attempt to enforce the darshana of the Trinity, the Brahman or the mere Nara.

=

Repetition of the movements of the crises with Knowledge & Ananda combating & seizing on the disturbances, obscurities and painful reactions. The success of the movement has not been complete.

=

Trikaldrishti is telepathic, mental & non-luminous; it has a satyam which attempts & often succeeds in a non-luminous arrangement of the ritam.

=

Satyam of vijnana is well-established and does not fail during the asiddhi. It is the brihat ritam that fails & so much so as sometimes entirely to disaggregate even the particular ritam.

=

Exact trikaldrishti of time (by the watch or in the order of other measuring circumstances) has begun definitely yesterday and is continued today.

June 1st

Samata

The hope or idea expressed on the 1st May has had to be modified. Asamata is still capable of returning in its own kind; the tendency to turn it into Ananda is not yet victorious, although it prevailed till almost the end of May. In the body the growth of the bhukti continues without any sensible reaction.

Shakti

The same condition of things continues. Sraddha in karma came for a time only to be destroyed again. There is again a certain doubt even about full Yoga-siddhi. Devibhava is deficient, because of deficient power and sraddha.

Brahman

Full Krishnadarshana came, but is now subject to reactions of all the old bhavas.

Karma

Little has been altered. Krishna Kali remains, but is hampered by insufficiency of sraddha, power and general Krishnadarshana.

Vijnana.

Satyam is well-established even in trikaldrishti. Ritam began to be brihat, but has been thrown back.

Telepathy of thought is still deficient.

Aishwarya-Traya & Samadhi after a rapid movement are again hampered & successfully confined.

Sharira.

Stronger in the first two members; but vaidyuta is infrequent
==

Today sravana became acute & distinct, but only in one or two sounds. Gandha persists & a subtle rasa.
==

June 2$^{\underline{d}}$

Dasya has attained an extraordinary completeness in the tertiary form. Along with the dasya is the restoration of the perfect samata. But the Mahakali bhava (Singhabahini) is diminished and not always present. Nevertheless it is more normal now than the others.
==

KrishnaKali is now almost absolute.
==

The physical Anandas (sahaituka) continue to gain in force & normality. The ahaituka anandas are once more frequently recurrent. Raudra today is very frequent & prolonged. Sahaituka raudra is especially growing in force, intensity and above all normality.
==

The Will has once more abandoned the tapasic insistence on rapidity and immediate results.
==

Ananda of defeat & failure is restored; sraddha in karma is still depressed and partly withheld.

=

The lipi "intensity of delight" often repeated recently is now being fulfilled.

=

Gandha seems well-established; sravana (vak) is attempting to normalise itself.

=

Samadhi is again organising itself (swapna).

Emergence of the sukshma vak in various degrees of evolution, half-involved, evolved; half-audible; audible but unintelligible; intelligible in part, the rest to the mind; intelligible to the hearing.

June 3.

Rf.

1. Therefore saith the Lord concerning the prophets that make my people err, that bite with their teeth and cry, Peace.

2. Shall I count them pure with the wicked balances and the bag of deceitful weights?

=

Instances of exact fulfilment even by things in station are becoming suddenly very frequent, but the resistance is concentrated and obstinate. It is exceptional to have the 80° force or anything approaching to it.

The general power of the Aishwarya has increased.

Trikaldrishti of time continues to occur, but there is a wavering sometimes between possible general appreciations of time, sometimes of the exact minute or a falling short by a minute or two, eg. 11.22 (the right time) & 11.23 (a possibility), 11.35 instead of $11.34\frac{1}{2}$ (right time) or 11.27 instead of 11.34.

=

After the morning reaction of the Asiddhi. First two chatusthayas attacked & momentarily touched. Sraddha farther shaken especially in Saundaryam & Utthapana of the Sharira and consequently in Karmachatusthaya.

Ananda remains firm & all the 2^d [chatusthaya] except sraddha
Satyam of trikaldrishti etc without ritam, except isolated or
fragmentary movements. Vijnana obstructed.

Today asiddhi in the hair and progressive denudation.

Sharira is at [present]^7 obstructed & attacked. Karma likewise.
=

Attempt to fix the *sraddha swashaktyam*

June 4.

The state of obstruction continues; but it contains only a slight
amount of disruption.

Lipi.
1. Today — finality
2 finality of the delight
3 totality of the delight
=

Vaidyuta is again manifesting itself spontaneously.
=

The sense of the universe = self is growing in force and permanence, although strongly besieged by the dwaya consciousness. All
energies are now felt to be in oneself.

Along with this realisation comes the Ishwarabhava and attahasya. The hasya is also manifesting itself. The sense of the transcendent Krishna maintains the dasya.
=

The Aishwarya is again active and powerful.
=

There is sraddha, but not immediate or particular, only of
general and final result. There is still doubt as to the karma of the
life.
=

Krishnadarshana is once more general.
=

7 *MS* presented

Extreme intensity and sthulatwa of sukshma rasa (bitter). Other tastes, eg lemon, are less well defined in the sthula, though in themselves quite distinct.

June 5.

A day of no appreciable advance or recoil. The Krishna-darshana is attempting to fix itself & eliminate its denial by the less complete bhavas.

The denial of Arogya is still dominant in certain points and affects others where it was supposed to have been done with & expelled practically, if not in seed.

A proof of Tapas-shakti in Kriti

June 6.

The Krishnadarshan progresses greatly in fixity of its general presence, but is not yet free from temporary denial. There is, however, in essence no farther obstacle to the Darshanas; the obstacle is only a tamasic dhriti habit in the memory.

=

The first chatusthaya resists successfully the attempts at disruption, which are now losing all force; the second increases in Ishwarabhava & Yuddhalipsa. Sraddha is still deficient

=

Vijnana is obstinately resisted, especially in Trikaldrishti, Aishwarya & Samadhi. These sometimes fall back entirely, sometimes manifest a sudden completeness always just short of perfection. The struggle is over (1) perfection; (2) constant action; (3) organisation. Separately each element is there in something like perfection; they cannot be securely put together—the moment they are combined, a furious assault of the disruptive forces scatters them again and a fragmentary action takes place.

=

Sharira makes no definite progress. Daily recurrence of Kamananda is moving towards all day recurrence and a sort of incipient continuity; but this is not yet accomplished. Arogya is strongly combated. Saundarya recedes rather than advances. There is no progress of utthapana; the little that had been made is suspended.

=

In Karma KrishnaKali stands, although the first is not yet securely centralised; Karma Kama move forward or otherwise with the Vijnana.

=

Four assertions

1. Vijnana organised and in constant action within June — perfection perfectly organised afterwards

2. Sharira delivered & made sure to faith in all its members within June

3 Life begins to be developed under control of Ishwara

4. The seeds of these things to be laid down now within a few minutes.

=

The last assertion fulfilled.

=

June 7 —

Krishnadarshana remains constant even when the other bhavas (the Three, the Four etc) seem to occupy the whole front; they are superficial and cannot blot out the Lilamaya even when they seem to exclude him from the organised object.

=

Samadhi this morning (swapna) crept forward one step towards greater hold of the thing sensed on the akasha.

For a moment Samata was broken; afterwards the movements of the old crises repeated themselves mechanically without producing asamata.

=

Crisis continual throughout the afternoon. Samata suffered, but only in the prana of the physical being with an occasional reaction in its mind. Towards evening promise of the foundation of the first assertion made yesterday.

=

The vangmaya and script firmly established in their constant

(not incessant[)] action;[8] anandamaya, vijnanamaya, with the inevitable style in the vak of the thought, possessed by the Ishwara
even when an instrumental or interceptive devata comes to the
front. The vani also established, anandamaya.

The other instruments of the Vijnana are being prepared for
their finality of right & constant action.

=

Perfect action of vangmaya thought organised along with
other instruments (not perfect) in swapnasamadhi & antardrishta,
whether jagrat-swapna, swapna or sushupta-swapna.

=

Stability of rupa increases & variety increases in the swapnasamadhi.

June 8th

Vijnana continues to progress.

=

Intelligibility, authority & stability of the lipi make considerable progress.

=

Action of certainty in the trikaldrishti is increasing.

=

Lipi, "rapid ideality in telepathy" in the swapna, — fulfilled in
the progress of the siddhi.

=

Intense Krishnadarshana is becoming more firmly general.

=

Afternoon

A firm use of accurate and active telepathy, not yet entirely full
nor entirely ritam, of vijnanamaya rita perception and of incipient
positive and certain Trikaldrishti is now added to the action of
vijnana which is meant to be constant. The trikaldrishti is not
merely telepathic, but often pure vision. This movement however
is not yet luminous, & in the whole knowledge, except in jnana,
there is only at best a subdued light.

8 MS (not incessant action);

Krishnadarshana is again general although still sometimes obstructed, but successfully only in regard to certain classes of animals.

=

Ref.

Like long lost knowledge speeding back
In sudden swelling flights she fills my mind
With bliss intoxicant,

Lipi —

exhaustive lipi.

=

Some progress of trikaldrishti & tapas [attempted],[9] but marred afterwards by the irruption of the will-thought, destroying the ritam and adversely affecting the samata. For a time the trikaldrishti was admirable.

June 9th

Krishnadarshana rose to generality (with one defect), in human beings, of the third intensity, then collapsed, then reasserted itself.

=

The movement of the vijnana continues.

The trikaldrishti is attempting a greater wideness of the satyam ritam; aishwarya a stronger and more firmly & generally effective movement.

=

Lipi —

1. *perfect ideality of the trikaldrishti.*   movement towards
                                                fulfilment
2. *resurgence of life.*
3 *brilliant blaze.*   fulfilled
4. *oceanic drishti*   in course of fulfilment

=

⎯⎯⎯⎯⎯⎯

[9] *MS* attended

Strong threat against the kriti . . a general adverse wave against the kriti.

=

Instances of "exhaustive lipi".

=

Krishnadarshana in the third intensity is now perfectly generalised with regard to the human being; the defect in regard to animals is being remedied.

=

Satyam of the trikaldrishti manifests with something of the ritam.

=

Attempt to bring forward the primary utthapana ($6\frac{1}{2}$ hours; not continuous, but in three portions of $3\frac{1}{2}$, $1\frac{1}{2}$, $1\frac{1}{2}$ with intervals of 1 hour and $1\frac{1}{2}$ hours). Process of turning physical strain into electric ananda, raudra and force.

=

June 10th

Satyam of trikaldrishti and telepathy combining; ritam is yet very imperfect.

Satyam of Tapas is trying to establish itself.

There is also an attempt of Jagrat samadhi to evolve again & break out from behind the curtain. Samadhi perception of sukshma sparsha (a bird hitting against a tower) is one of the elements.

=

Reaction in the afternoon, throwing back Krishnadarshana into the unfixed and fluid state ranging from non-vision or veiled vision to the third intensity.

The Vijnana generally was attacked by the intellectuality

Nevertheless its progress still continues, — a progress of inchoate preparation rather than of decisive results.

=

Farther development of taste (sukshma rasa) predicted yesterday in the lipi.

=

Abhyasa of primary utthapana, 3 hours, 1 hour, 3 hours, $1\frac{1}{2}$

hour = $8\frac{1}{2}$ hours, with intervals of 1 hour, 2 hours, 3 hours. In the morning a reaction of weariness from yesterday's abhyasa —

June 11 —
The same state as yesterday.
=

Samadhi tends to grow; there is once more some application to life.

In the rest of the vijnana there is battle and preparation.
=

In the Sharira the Asiddhi has slightly the upper hand in Ananda & Arogya; entirely in Saundarya.

Practice of pr. utth. [primary utthapana] $11\frac{1}{2}$ hours (5 hours 10 minutes, 3 hours 20 minutes and 3 hours with intervals of 15 minutes and 30 minutes) up to 7.7 pm. After 9.40 half an hour = 12 hours. Result, no weariness, but considerable stiffness in muscles of the legs & pain of the soles of the feet. Elsewhere only slight reaction. Stiffness induces weakness physically not pranic —
=

The satyam of the telepathy-trikaldrishti with a great completeness but an imperfect ritam is now acting constantly.
=

The Tapas became very forcible & obstinate against a great and obstinate resistance and almost always gained its point in the general result; particular result also comes to be more & more subject to the force from day to day.
=

Kamananda was depressed & only occasionally recurrent.
=

The siddhi is moving to the union of chit & tapas.
=

There is now the attempt to fulfil the ninth Affirmation by overcoming the condition of Time. This is closely connected with the affirmation of the eighth principle, action on all the five planes at once which also tends to manifest.

June 12 —

Steady advance in Aishwarya-traya.

The Aishwarya-ishita-vashita now acts with a very frequent effectivity in exact detail, a still more frequent partial effectivity in detail and a habitual effectivity in general result on things in station.

=

Ishwarabhava & Yuddhalipsa increase. Sraddha tends to increase.

=

Rupa-Samadhi grows constantly, but the decisive line has not yet been passed.

=

Strong, frequent, prolonged, varied & perfectly materialised intense gandha in the evening (scents etc). Gandha has for some time been constant.

Taste tries to become more varied, but except in two or three aswadas is insufficiently materialised.

=

Intense vaidyuta ananda in palm of hand as result of slight contact with a chair by the side of the hand; prolonged, compelling movement of the fingers & recurrent in long continuity, gradually diminished in continuity & intensity. For half an hour. Vaidyuta Ananda fully established, sahaituka and ahaituka. (Afterwards felt in the rest of the body.) It extended from the palm to the whole arm, then with less intensity to the left arm; accompanied by raudra and by tivra in palm and armpit. Another touch brought a separate stream, the two acting together for a short time. All this justifies the most vivid imaginations of the Alipur jail.

=

Strong kamananda, continuous or recurrent for greater part of the day; free from asana; intense & continuous in walking, intense but not continuous in standing, more of body in sitting.

=

Retrogression in arogya (incipient cold; gathered power of skin-irritation)

=

P. utth $10\frac{1}{2}$ hours (3.45 + 2.15 + 3 + $1\frac{1}{2}$ with intervals of $\frac{1}{4}$, $\frac{3}{4}$ and $3\frac{1}{2}$ hours)

June 13 –

The "first assertion" is now to a great degree fulfilled.[10] All the parts and instruments of the Vijnana are in constant action and more or less organised. "Constant" is not "continual". There are periods of disorganisation and broken action, even of quiescence or mere mental action, – although the latter survival is decreasing in force and frequency.

Thought and script are frequent and normally vijnanamaya, but too often possessed by *ganas* who try to veil the Iswara. Perceptive thought is more often pulled down into the mentality, but still it rises again into the luminous action. *Trikaldrishti* is constant; though often disorganised. *Aishwarya-traya* is constant, though often broken and even confined to isolated effects.

Samadhi (swapna) is now organised; there is stable scene & movement, continuous action, combination, but it does not go beyond a brief stability & continuity. *Samadhi jagrat* is not yet delivered from the obstruction. This is the only absolute defect of the organised vijnana, but even here there is incipient organisation.
=

The contradictions of the Samata have now *ananda* behind or in them, except when the ananda also is expressly overpowered.

Sraddha & devibhava waver, but are founded, – though not yet complete.

Brahman is complete, but not yet quite securely Lilamaya in the Ishwara. The defect however is occasional & slight.

Krishna-Kali is constant, but not yet quite continuous.
=

All the physical Anandas ahaituka & sahaituka have progressed greatly.

Utthapana is attempting to emerge. In primary utthapana weariness, stiffness, pain can all be got rid of or rendered ineffective

---

[10] *See the entry of 6 June, page 863.* — Ed.

by the Tapas, but the exhaustion of the store of Pranic energy in the *annakosha* still persists as a habit & the resultant weakness tends to bring back these reactions. These are, however, very rapidly cast off. . The secondary & tertiary utthapanas are not now in action.

In Arogya there is still the dominant recurrence of the habitual fragments of roga and the persistence of the two that are yet unbroken. Cold is attempting to return.

Saundarya is still unable to break its shell.

＝

Karma & Kama await the growth of the Aishwarya & the Sharira. The life & its work [are][11] still under the menace of the Enemy & deprived of their instruments and equipment.

＝

During the day 9 hours primary utthapana, but with greater breaks & less force of utthapana.

＝

The relapse from the Arogya increases rather than diminishes.

＝

On the other hand Sharira Ananda of all kinds grows more spontaneous, frequent, intense and prolonged.

＝

A crisis during the day lowering the sraddha and the force.

＝

No definite progress in the Vijnana which has been thrown back into the "yeast" of a confused and obscured action with the perceptive thought and tapastraya trying to form out of it.

＝

June 14—

Some increase in the organisation of swapna samadhi. In the afternoon lipi of swapna samadhi again began to come right.

＝

Continuation of relapse & crisis till the middle of the afternoon—＝

---

[11] MS is

Krishnadarshana, relapsed for these two or three days, is again active in its various intensities, but sometimes lapses into the Brahman.

=

Force of aishwarya traya increased a little, but the resistance still prevails over the attempt to apply it in all cases.

=

Taste developed strongly, so that always in the swallow there is some kind of taste sukshma or sthula. Taste of sweetness entirely sthula & intense lasted for many minutes. Gandha is frequent, often entirely *niradhara* — *Shabda* tries to develop.

=

The rule of not sitting or lying except when necessary, but always walking or standing is being observed and in this way almost the whole day has passed. Standing restores the declining force & thus a continuous spell of 4 hours in the afternoon has been done without any serious difficulty. Whole period of primary utthapana $4\frac{1}{4} + 1\frac{1}{4} + 4 + \frac{1}{2}$ hours with intervals of $\frac{1}{4}$, $\frac{1}{2}$ & 4.

=

Sleep 12.30 to 7.15.

=

June 15 —

Pr. utthapana 15 hours ($4\frac{3}{4} + 7\frac{1}{4} + 3$ with intervals of $\frac{1}{4}$ and $2\frac{1}{4}$ hours). Today practically 12 hours were done without a break. The reaction became powerful at times towards the end, but always lightened. Standing is sufficient without other rest for restoration, but sometimes the restoration of strength comes while walking.

=

A great advance in certainty of trikaldrishti and some in Aishwarya. The basis of perfect organisation of the knowledge has been laid.

=

Arogya is still affected by the persistence of the attack.

=

Karma is also suffering.

=

In the Vijnana it is evident that Will & Thought are drawing towards each other preparatory to union. At times they coincide entirely, but not yet in a well-organised fashion. Something of the tapasic stress still survives in the will affecting the thought. Something of the passive inertness and absence of power still lingers in the thought divorced from will

=

Vishaya has not yet definitely advanced, although shabda seems to be preparing, & there are pure sukshma movements in the others.

=

Samadhi is almost stationary in swapna; in jagrat dense forms of a certain stability imperfectly manifested in the darkness.

=

There is no advance in Saundarya.

=

In Krishnadarshana the vision of everything as a form of Krishna Kali seems fixed. Darshana of Krishna Kali ranges between the various intensities down to non-intensity.

=

Ananda is firmer, as the remnants of responsibility & desire have been diminished, the former to vanishing-point; but sraddha is not restored. There is sraddha in Yoga-siddhi minus Saundarya, imperfect in all Sharira except Ananda, but none in Karma.

=

The 16th will be a day of progress.
Sleep 6 hours.

June 16—
An enormous progress in Krishnadarshana, which has fixed itself rapidly, first in the mere darshana, then in the first intensity, then in the third where it varies between the first & third in the third. The first in the third is Sarvamaya, the second is Anantagunamaya and the third is Anandamaya Krishna.

A great intensity of 3^3 Kd [Krishnadarshana] in things, sounds etc.

=

The vijnana made considerable progress in trikaldrishti. The will also began to become more easily identical with knowledge. But there is still the difficulty of accommodating the transvolutive will & perception with the evolutive will and perception.

=

In rupasamadhi no definite progress.
Vishaya is depressed.

=

Anandamaya Samata made considerable progress towards undisturbed perfection. There is some attempt at backsliding in the invulnerability of the physical ananda

=

Ten hours pr. utth. but much broken. Reaction prevails

=

Arogya struggles to regain its ascendency, but it is not yet accomplished

=

Sleep about 6 hours.

=

June 17—
The Krishnadarshana is now almost fixed in the third degree of the third intensity, but the lower degrees still tend to return sometimes into predominance.

=

The entire *vijnanising* of the mentality proceeds rapidly, but the Tapas today is less potently effective. There is a movement, however, towards the entirety of the vijnana organisation.

=

In *swapnasamadhi* stability is both stronger and more frequent.
Jagrat samadhi is still preparing more behind the veil than in front of it.

=

In the second chatusthaya Ishwarabhava grows & declines along with the intensity of effective Tapas. Sraddha follows the same fluctuations.

=

The Ishwara is now manifest behind all thought & vani, sometimes both behind and in it.

=

Sharira is still subject to struggle.

Utthapana is under the influence of the reaction which is now strong & persistent; the weariness & weakness recur, but only in the annakosha & its pranic environment, not in the pranashakti proper. Stiffness & pain also recur, but are not persistent.

Ananda (sharira) is less active & vishaya depressed or obstructed.

Karma is obstructed, but the Tapas maintains itself & produces slight positive & much negative result.

=

A great advance in the combination of knowledge and tapas
Lipi . . *"figurative fashioning tapas"*

=

Pr utt. $7\frac{1}{2}$ hours.

=

Sleep 5 hours — swapnasamadhi $1\frac{1}{2}$

June 18 —

The Krishnadarshan fluctuates and admits new combinations, but with a general fixity of the third intensity which only occasionally gives way. The intensity is imperfect with regard to animals.

=

The disorganised mentality is again active & all parts of the Siddhi depressed.

=

Lipi increases in regular activity.
    (Lipi — *regularity of the lipi*)

=

June 19 —

The Mahakali-Mahasaraswati consciousness with the Maheshwari *pratistha* & the Mahaluxmi colouring is now being firmly & finally established.

=

A similar finality of Krishna Kali is in process of final foundation.

=

The revolt of the evolutive tendency non-central to the adhara is the cause of the relapse of these last two days and the break of the unity in the universal consciousness. As usual the relapse has synchronised with the reappearance of the Mahakali energy.

=

Anandamaya samata has been superficially disturbed, but tends always to hold its own.

=

Sraddha is affected with regard to karma and rapidity, but the lapse is much less complete than on any former occasion of the same magnitude.

=

Lipi.
The last attack on the telepathy trikaldrishti.

=

Growth of the balabhava and manifestation of the KrishnaKali relation, the latter element in perfection, the former in imperfection.

=

Free recurrence of the sharira Anandas, depressed for some time, is now reviving.

=

A good part of the sleep turned into Samadhi.

June 20 –
The Krishna relation is now established with perfection of the Krishnabhava.

=

Experiment has shown that the Kamananda is much stronger than it ever was before, reviving almost immediately from what formerly depressed it for a day or for half a day. Moreover it is beginning to manifest in the body and no longer only at its own centre.

=

Greater activity of the sukshmavak.

=

June 21

The Krishna-Kali relation is fixed & confirmed.

=

The Krishnadarshana which had gone back to the Anantaguna is now recovering the Anandamaya, the third degree of the third intensity.

=

The Sharira Anandas are again on the increase, more intense, more recurrent, tending to the continual recurrence & even to the continuous.

=

Satyam of combined telepathy, trikaldrishti, tapas is again active with greater force, but ritam is imperfect.

Strong increase of sukshmavak: it is not however entirely developed from the material envelope (Vritra).

=

Manasik rupa has for some time been occasionally active; manasik sparsha, sravana, etc are also occasionally active and not only in the form of imperfectly materialised vishayas, but as pure *manasa*.

=

The premananda which was long involved, has reemerged to the surface & is both general and particular.

The suddhananda also, which was contained & almost suppressed in the ahaituka + chidghana, has reemerged. With it the full intensity of the third degree of Krishnadarshana is reemerging.

=

Vishayas of smell & taste are again becoming active with the first force.

June 22 –

An uprush of a material layer full of the asiddhi.

Chidananda emerges with Sadananda behind it giving the

ananda of the material oneness (substance) & of the all-life in its vital activity (prana).

=

The vijnana obscured during the last two days reemerges with the decisive Will-Knowledge.

=

Siddhi of Kriti, but not yet decisive.

=

June 23 –

There is a movement towards the settled intensity of the Anandas, subjective & objective, but the material environment resists strongly & obstinately.

=

Certainty of trikaldrishti, telepathic and pure, is very strong in the general result, but the *anritam* prevails in the detail. The movement is towards such a correction of the physical mentality that it shall record faithfully the *ritam* even when not illumined, but this movement is as yet unsuccessful except in moments of concentration.

=

The struggle in the Arogya continues. There is nowhere complete deliverance, but there is an increasing effectivity of the Will on the body in respect of Roga. In Utthapana & Saundarya the Will is depressed, held down and sometimes overcome.

=

There is a general repression of the Siddhi by the physical nature, but through it all the Siddhi progresses.

June 24 –

General intensity of premananda with occasional high intensity.

=

The shuddhananda increases.

=

Intense revelational-inspirational thought is manifesting in the

vangmaya. Vijnana is active illuminating the perceptive thought &
thought suggestions.

=

Rupa has for some days been increasing in intensity in the
jagrat (perfect developed & dense) but has only an initial stability
or none. Crude jagrat rupa has receded and seems dissolving rather
than forming.

The Krishnadarshana is fixed, but depressed, at the lowest
intensity possible to the complete darshana, except in occasional
instances or moments of concentration. There is now a movement
to recover & fix the general intensity beyond relapse.

The work now being done is to fix all gains in the lowest
physical consciousness so that they may be always secure and
not only present during periods, however long, of concentration,
illumination or exaltation.

=

Tivra is beginning to generalise its intense recurrence throughout the body. Vaidyuta is also seeking to pervade the body and with
less force kama and vishaya.

=

Rupasamadhi is growing by little jets of progress in the midst
of an obstructing physical consciousness.

=

Trikaldrishti grows constantly in force, but fluctuates in completeness and especially in ritam.

=

Intensity of premananda fails now only because of the inability
of the prana to hold it. The prana is accustomed only to calmness
or to an equable ananda.

=

Kriti wavers in the balance & progresses only in little points.

=

The vishayas are depressed in their recurrence.

=

The defective parts of the second chatusthaya grow in strength.

June 25th

Vishaya is now the strongest pervasive Ananda in the body. The others are becoming continually recurrent at points & more disposed to pervasiveness. Pervasive Kama is the most backward.

=

The second chatusthaya is now fixed in its lesser completeness & intensity. The greater awaits the full organisation of vijnana.

=

Ananda is now complete & organised, the subjective & the physical; only the continuity in intensity has to be acquired. Continuity is beginning in all the physical anandas.

=

Trikaldrishti & tapas increase in force, but the organisation is once more inchoate preparing a stronger harmony.

=

Krishnadarshana is moving steadily towards its full & fixed intensity.

=

There is now a strong movement to replace the remnants of the intellectuality altogether by the ideality. It has already made some progress.

=

Crude akasha rupa of a certain stability & variety seems now to be established in the jagrat. Crude dense is also frequent.

=

Ananda Brahman came to the front; this was followed by a lapse into Jnanam Brahma. Afterwards Anandamaya Ishwara took its place.

=

Continuity of Sharira Ananda still needs smarana; recurrence is almost free from the necessity.

=

The Vijnana movement was obstructed & receded again in the afternoon.

=

Drishti of sukshma rain etc.

June 26th

Yesterday's lipi—175 = 17 + 5 and 1 + 7 + 5—In accordance with the first Ananda Brahman & some progress in Samadhi. In accordance with the latter progress in vijnana, sharira ananda and drishti of other planes.

=

17 + 5. Lilamaya Ananda Brahman with full fivefold subjective Ananda perfectly organised.

=

115. 11 + 5 preparing (Kalibhava on five planes). The action of the divine Prakriti must centre in the Vijnana and flow from it and work itself out through a passive receptive channel of mind, a passive enjoying Prana, a passive instrumental body.

=

The Seven Affirmations.

The three Krishna affirmations are now unalterably established in the being, but are sometimes pale to the consciousness

The four Brahma affirmations are fixed, but for their full action await the Ritam of the vijnana

The two Prakriti affirmations, Time & the five worlds, are in course of being established.

=

June 27th

The day has been devoted to the farther confirmation
    (1) of the Ananda Brahman;
    (2) of the 1st chatusthaya in sama Ananda; especially Ananda of failure
    (3) of the 2^d, especially in sraddha
    (4) of the combination of Ishwarabhava & (3)
    (5) of the vijnana organisation.

The only true resistance now is in the physical obstacle [affecting]¹² especially (1) samadhi, (2) three members of the Sharira, especially Saundarya, in a less degree utthapana, in a still less degree Arogya, (3) Karma

=

---

¹² MS effecting

At night repeated coherent swapna.

June 28th

Organisation of samadhi has entered into the deepest sushupta swapna; but is not yet more than initial, conversations of three or four sentences, brief complex actions, short stabilities, rapid but not long continued thought, vangmaya & perceptive etc.

=

For the rest the established siddhis are growing stronger, especially telepathy & trikaldrishti, but there is a thick veil and siege of the environing manastattwa through which the vijnanamaya action has to break.

=

Lipi.
1. large interesting results.
2 pursue all the business ‖ of the aishwarya, telepathy, tri-
            (double line lipi)   kaldrishti

=

Double line lipi in akasha & sadhara (chitra) is becoming gradually frequent.

June 29th

Great progress in organisation of tapas, telepathy, trikaldrishti.

=

The swapnasamadhi organisation progresses & confirms itself on a surer base.

=

There seems to be some beginning of a freer movement in the jagrad rupa.

=

June 30th

Swapnasamadhi very strong in all but stability of rupa and long continuity. Rupa in jagrat continues to attempt a freer breaking through the veil.

=

On the whole the vijnana may be said to have been well organised, but not perfectly in the month of June.
=

The Sharira has been delivered only in Ananda, not in Arogya etc; nevertheless there is a foundation of firm faith in the Sharira, but it wavers on the surface with regard to tertiary utthapana and saundarya.
=

The Iswara leads the life, but not yet to any definite result.

July —

June has been the period of four powerful finalities —

1. *Anandamaya Samata*

The first chatusthaya is delivered from the external attacks of the nirananda and asamata. Only a slight vibration is left combating the Ananda of failure, but this is itself becoming Anandamaya of the duality and is kept only to found a particular vibration of the pure Ananda.

2. *Daivi Prakriti*

The daivi prakriti and the fundamental sraddha are founded firmly and the Mahakali energy has occupied the Mahasaraswati frame, covered the Maheshwari pratistha, assumed the Mahaluxmi colouring and made its fiercer working compatible with the *anandamaya samata*. This movement is not yet touched to the final perfection and the *ishwarabhava* and *sraddha* are still insufficient and fluctuate on the surface. But the former defect is likely to disappear during the month. The latter depends on the imperfection of the *vijnana* and will disappear as the Tapas increases in its effectiveness.

3. *Brahman & Krishna Kali*

The Anandam Brahma is now fixed in the vision of all things and only occasionally goes back for a moment into the Anantam Jnanam Brahma. Along with this finality there is also the finality of the *Lilamaya darshana* in all existences; there is no longer the sharp distinction which confined the strong darshana to that which is *urjasvi*, the beautiful, young, noble or emphatic in character or to the human being. The siddhi however needs a more unwavering firmness and a more delightful intensity. These come to it sometimes, but are not yet part of the normal vision.

Krishnakali has been fixed in the consciousness finally. The Ishwara governs the action, thought etc entirely, but not yet with an invariable prominence. He is *vibhu*, but not always immediately & directly prabhu. Still the vangmaya, script & vani belong to him directly; only the perceptive thought & feeling are still indirectly possessed except in their extraordinary moments.

4. *Organised vijnana*

Vijnana is organised in all its parts. Tapas, telepathy, trikal-drishti work together, but while telepathy is *brihat* and almost entirely and spontaneously *ritam*, trikaldrishti though always active, has often to wait for or acquire its *ritam* out of the mass of the possibilities. The *ritam* however plays a large part and grows continually. Tapas is effective sometimes as will-thought against resistance, sometimes as Chit-Tapas. It is not yet entirely chit-tapas and therefore not in possession of the *samrajya*.

Samadhi is still crude & unstable in the jagrat, and in the swapna still brief and often attacked by confusion and dislocation, but all the necessary elements are present and work more and more together.

=

The perfection of the first three siddhis may be expected in July as well as a much greater perfection of the fourth.

=

Deficiencies

Sharira is the field of the main conflict; the Arogya is subject to constant attack which takes the form of habitual fragmentary roga. Utthapana after making a great stride (primary) fell back & is suspended. Saundarya has been unable to manifest in the head and *jara* attacks chiefly in the hair. In the *bhava* there is eternal youth.

=

Karma makes little visible headway. It waits on the growth of the effective Tapas. It is attacked chiefly in equipment and freedom.

=

Physical Ananda

All the physical anandas are daily active and even have an initial combination and organisation. This is the one physical siddhi which is liberated from complete obstruction and ready for finality.

July 1 —
Lipi —
    1. sahitya-siddhi
        trikaldrishti tapas telepathy　　　ie the right combination
        της ὑγιειης　　　　　　　　　ie the substitution of the healthy
                          Prakriti for the rogamaya.
           Lointain　　　　　　　　ie distant telepathy etc.
(ie these are the things that must now be brought to perfection)
    2. telepathy
    3 trikaldrishti-siddhi.

=

In accordance with lipi 2. there was a great extension of telepathy of thought, the motions of thought in one physically near being followed with a great and constant, though not invariable exactness and proved by the subsequent action; the working was by a sort of combined mental prakamya and vyapti, prakamya predominating, — neither of them yet luminous, — manomaya, not vijnanamaya.

=

In accordance with lipi 3. there was a swift movement of ritam in trikaldrishti at the same time. This has yet to [be] perfected and extended to the distant (*lointain* of lipi 1); for in the distant there is still mainly the surge of possibilities, telepathy not trikaldrishti.

=

Sahitya-siddhi seems to be moving towards the recovery of the lost Mahalakshmi colouring in the style. (lipi 1).

Throughout the day a violent struggle between the Arogya-prakriti & the Rogasharira. The latter has manifested for some days in bad forms of assimilation and incipient cold, and now in incipient fever. The latter has been defied in all respects except not bathing & so far has been unable to make itself felt except in a fluctuating recurrent heat and occasional tendency to weakness. The weakness however makes no difference either to intellectual work or to physical exertion. This is the struggle to establish the Arogyasharira (lipi 1. της ὑγιειης)

=

The lipi "trikaldrishti tapas telepathy" is not yet in visible course of fulfilment, but there are incipient movements.

July 2$^{\underline{d}}$
Lipi

> to full effectivity hereafter in the telepathy trikaldrishti tapas
>   together.

It is becoming more clear that the life has been directly taken in control by the Ishwara

=

Reference.
1. प्र सोमस्य पवमानस्योर्मंय इन्द्रस्य यंति जठरं सुपेशस:
2 it is the glow of life, its finest breath

=

Developments in the jagrad rupa showing that the definite foundation has really begun (akasha, sadhara)

=

The struggle in the Arogya continues.

July 3$^{\underline{d}}$
Sudden advance in several directions.

=

The fixed general tertiary intensity of the Krishnadarshana in the third degree has been suddenly established, free from all subjection to forms and circumstances. All fluctuations are in different degrees of *purohiti* of the Ishwara.

=

Vijnanamaya satyam of the jnana (complete) as opposed to manomaya satyam and, with less completeness & nearness, of the trikaldrishti in surrounding movements has been suddenly established

There is ritam of the jnana, only partially of the trikaldrishti & force.

=

Satyam of the force is preparing.

=

Ishwarabhava & sraddha have taken a step forward.

=

Thought, vangmaya, vani have all been entirely possessed by the Ishwara; the other voices & suggestions are being either taken up by him or turned into sukshma vak. This latter movement is assured, but has not yet the final definite completeness.

=

Personal relation of Ishwara & the jiva (prakriti) is now complete though not yet forceful in its central characteristic (rudra-bhava).

=

The ritam of telepathy-trikaldrishti-tapas has now to be fixed.

=

Lipi—
   1) 12   2) 13   3) great results.

=

Strong emergence of the shuddhananda involved in the chidghana-ahaituka; also of the subjective prema-kama. They are not entirely fixed in generality in their intense forms.

Since yesterday the gandha has again recovered its intensity & variety and is today beginning to become frequent. There is a movement of recovery in the rasa, great intensity in habitual sparshas & preparation of variety involved in indeterminate sparsha, incipient certainty & considerable intensity in sravana (chiefly in habitual sounds), spasmodic recurrence of darshana.

=

Trikaldrishti of things distant in space & time is beginning to be generalised (telepathy was already working & occasional trikaldrishti); but as yet there is no certainty, as there is still the siege of possibilities. Ritam is not yet certified to the intelligence. Lipi is beginning to work again on these things and rupasamadhi is preparing to follow.

=

In the afternoon the siddhi receded from the morning's intensity and in the evening there was even some touch of the reaction contradictory of samata usually associated with the Mahakali rajasic activity.

=

There is a considerable attempt of jagrat rupa to advance in all parts, but the success is not yet manifest.

At the same time the tendency to use even imperfect rupas for purposes of vijnana increases and seems to help the attempt.

=

July 4 —
   Ref.

ut sûryo brihad archinshi açret, puru viçwâ janimâ
                                           mânushânâm
samo divo dadrishe rochamânah, kratwâ kr'itah sukr'itah
                                           kartr'ibhir bhût.
sa sûryah prati puro na ud gâ, ebhih stomebhih etaçebhir evaih
pra no mitrâya varun'âya vocho, anâgaso aryamn'e agnaye
                                           cha
vi nah sahasram çurudho radantu, r'itavâno varun'o mitro
                                           agnih
yachchhantu chandrâ upamam no arkam, â nah kâmam
                                           pupurantu stavânâh—

Lipi
   1. light to be manifested entirely telepathy trikaldrishti tapas.

The suddhananda as the result of yesterday's movement is fixed, dominating the Chidghana and *sajosha* with the subjective premakama, but not yet in its invariable intensity—

=

Yesterday's general attack is being overcome— It failed to create a crisis.

=

The fivefold plane is being manifested in thought etc (puru viçvâ janima manushânam) with the illumined mind as the centre (samo divo dadrishe rochamâno) & the *brihad archis* of the vijnana as the source.

The five *purah* are being manifested even to the rupadrishti. The vijnana (surya) has yet to ascend into all. The completion of this movement will establish the eighth Affirmation (of the nine, ebhih stomebhih), see May 20. The three Krishna affirmations are almost perfect. The four Satya-Ananda affirmations await for their perfection the free Tapas & Prakasha.

=

The dominance of the Vijnana has been restored, but it has to be consciously related to its roots in the Ananda. As foreseen in the jail the Ishwara is seated in the Ananda; the Ishwara + Jiva in the Vijnana.

Development of samadhi continues—

1 Jagrat Antardrishta—Any image willed comes after a time, always recognisable, but not always clear in outline or distinct.

2 Jagrat bahirdarshi—Images on the background independent of the will, a few distinct & stable, others clear, constant but shifting, not very distinct, others changing & fleeting.

3 Swapna. Combinations of vision, speech, action.

July 5th

Strong opposition and attack.

=

Ananda (sharira) continues to be constant in recurrence, sometimes continual in recurrence (especially tivra & kama) with an occasional continuity (especially kama). The anandas (vaidyuta, vishaya, raudra) are often pervasive. Pervasive kama & tivra also occur, but with less force & hold.

=

Samadhi continues slowly to develop.

=

Vijnana of trikaldrishti, telepathy, tapas is much obstructed

July 6th

Again a day of obstruction and struggle. Sharira is especially obstructed and the positive Asiddhi seems to prevail at some points.

=

The day devoted chiefly to sahitya (poetry).

Continuities of kamananda.

July 7th

The decisive trikaldrishti has during these few days acted only fragmentarily or dimly at a distance. Telepathy & its stresses have governed the field. Tapas has been with difficulty effective, often ineffective —

Kamananda is increasing against obstruction its force of continuity; but there is a tendency in the body to insist only on one continuous ananda at a time.

Last night pain of strained nerve in the knee joint turned to Ananda, but imperfectly owing to jugupsa.

July 8th

The vijnana siddhi touched bottom-point & then suddenly rose again. It appears that the final elimination of temperamental stress is being now engineered & that this was the principal object of the retrogression.

Sama Ananda has stood firm, except for rare touches; the second chatusthaya & the Mahakali bhava have been strengthened, even the ishwarabhava & the temperamental sraddha (in the heart) although the intellectual mind has been shaken.

Krishnadarshana increases in the tertiary Anandamaya sense through all fluctuations.

Sharira & Karmasiddhi have been obstructed & retarded; but the vijnana has been the chief sufferer.

July 9th – 10th

Indefinite progress at various points

Telepathy, trik. tap. [trikaldrishti, tapas] are recovering force in their combination, but telepathy always predominates —

July 11th

The first part of the month has passed in the usual relapse into a confused and inchoate condition of the siddhi marked by a partial and temporary dissolution of what had just been gained, some amelioration & confirmation of previous gains and the vague beginning of a fresh advance.

It is indicated that there will now be a steady movement forward.

=

The right form of the Krishnadarshana seems now to be fixed — the Ananda-Purusha Krishna containing the Ananda Brahman which contains the Ananda Purusha as the Jiva — the Shuddha Ananda containing the Chidghana & Ahaituka and giving rise to the PremaKama. The right harmony in intensity of the three elements is not yet fixed.

—

Daivabhava of Mahakali is fixed. The Maheshwari Pratistha is submerged, but the Mahalaxmi-Mahasaraswati continent is still too strong for the right intensity of the Mahakali inhabitant to fix itself.

=

In Samata there is still a tendency to return of depression by non-faith in Siddhi.

=

The Pranic deficiencies of Ananda have yet to be mended; the indriyas are now fixed in the subjective vishaya & the buddhi in chidghana of vishaya, but the prana is not yet free from the memories of *virodha* in *bhoga*, eg in bad food, certain reminiscences of repulsion in sound, smell, sight, mental vishaya. These are however shadows that fall from the external auric shell and are rejected by the Prakriti when not compelled to respond.

=

Tapas-telepathy-trikaldrishti are now successfully combined and strong; but imperfection of trikaldrishti has to be mended before there can be perfection of tapas.

=

Jagrat rupa is once more seeking perfection in the crude.

=

Sudden development of the antardrishta; many scenes, stable, but marred by a constant "flottement" of the images—eg a sea against a rock, landscapes, in one a small cottage in the night, a fight in process, long continued flashes from & against the window from which first a light shone, figures behind watching a man on horse-back wading through a wide expanse of water, also long-continued etc.

=

Tapas & trikaldrishti are gaining in general force of fulfilment, but they act mentally not with the light.

=

July 12th

Lipi.

1. Easy delight faith aiswarya result
2 energetic faith
3 tejas.

for the fulfilment of the harmonised T³

Perfect T³ as the result of the above combination; it cannot yet be steadily applied because of defect of energy in the physical prana and of faith in the physical mind.

It is indicated by the Vani that telepathy must become trikaldrishti and trikaldrishti turn into Tapas = Chit-Tapas.

Already the perfect examples of telepathy turned trikaldrishti are being given, long, continuous, many movemented, exact in each detail.

=

Dream is once more attempting to turn itself into swapna samadhi

=

Telepathic trikaldrishti is now acting with almost entire perfection, only slightly marred by tapasic stress. Tapas is increasing in effectuality. All this in the mentality, not in vijnana.

The resistance of thing in statu to the exact movement willed is now often overcome.

=

Lipi.

4. to the entire liberation of the tapas in the physical siddhi
5. to the authority of the lipi.

(Both these are in the future – in preparation)

=

After a long discontinuance of some months secondary uttha-pana has been resumed. Laghima-mahima are very strong, defect of anima persists.

=

Lipi

6. third chatusthaya perfected
7. finality of the Krishnadarshana.

=

Exact trikaldrishti of time.

July 13th

A day of struggle. The T³ is attacked and underwent some relapse, but in the perfection gained, not in its continued activity, except for some temporary failure in the activity of the tapas. Telepathy is sometimes clouded by will-thought masquerading as telepathy.

=

Samadhi is obstructed and does not make any advance. It is continually being suspended (ie thrown back to a former imperfection) in swapna and antardrishta

=

Vijnana is almost suspended, except for an occasional action. The mentality is being exercised in non luminous reception & action according to a concealed vijnana behind. The attempt is to make it mechanically right in all its movements.

=

Sharira makes no sensible advance.

=

Ananda Brahman containing Ananta-Jnana = Suddha Ananda containing Chidghana seems to be fixed, but it is still capable of following to the greatest point of depression consistent with non-evanescence.

=

In pain even when intolerable there seems always now to be a basis and content of Ananda; it is only the skin, as it were, of the contact that still preserves the memory of mere pain. This is at least true up to a certain & a high degree of intensity.

=

The pranic nirananda of the vishaya is in course of disappearing; it is already immensely extenuated; eg in tasteless food, disagreeable sounds, bad smells, ugly or vulgar forms, uncomfortable contacts.

=

Nirananda of event is now entirely physical & in.posed by force from outside.

Lipi

1. justice for the $\begin{smallmatrix}\text{tapas}\\\text{youth}\end{smallmatrix}$ — georgos   justice ἐγγυς —

2. youth.   tapas.   youth
                       κλεινος

3. the divine Indian dynasty (Ch. Vsa?)[13]

=

The Dasya is constantly increasing in an all-embracing intensity. Madhura which has often fluctuated since May 26, but has always been behind the veil when not present or insistent in front, will now be always in front. Bhoga of the slave & instrument is also now complete. The presence of the Ishwara has often been veiled by his manomaya personalities & *ganas*, but is now to occupy the directing centre in the Ananda tattwa. The triple Krishna affirmation is therefore perfected.

July 14ᵗʰ 15ᵗʰ

Again an apparently stationary condition.

The Ishwara remains, the forward action seems to be opposed & inhibited.

Literary work is now done more rapidly.

---

13 *Ch. Vsa = Chandra Vaṁśa. The question mark is Sri Aurobindo's. — Ed.*

July 16th 17th, 18th

The lapse into mentality with a disorganisation of the vijnana in T^3, preparing a farther discarding of the imperfections in the previous organisation, eg – stress of telepathy, stress of tapas, division of trikaldrishti from tapas.

The Samadhi advances dully enlarging itself, but shadowy, not luminous or in possession of itself.

July 19th

Development of swapna samadhi. Pages of lipi; but the power to read coherently is still withheld; coherent parts of sentences are frequent but mixed with parts of other sentences. Rupa, Vishaya & event are oftenest shadowy, but all kinds occur and there is occasional stability & continuity. Thought in Samadhi is fragmentary or suspended.

Telepathy & trikaldrishti of tendencies & "contingent certainties" is greatly extended. Tapas is slowly recovering itself. Positive trikaldrishti is discouraged and tapas no longer sure of itself.

Lipi
1 perfect inability to digest in the pristine fashion
2 perfect telepathy.

July 20th 21st

Slow recovery of the organised vijnana.

Mechanical unillumined trikaldrishti of exact time (3 times in one evening).

[*Here a third of a page left blank.*]

July 31st

July has been throughout a month of Asiddhi; retardation, suspension of activities gained has been its leading characteristic. All that is unripe in the siddhi has manifested itself, – all the error and false leading.

Samata is established except in regard to siddhi of result where continued asiddhi brings an occasional positive depression and vague touches not of asanti but of suffering & shadows of the old revolt against the leading. On the other hand complete samananda of siddhi asiddhi is obviously preparing & has become more normal than asamata.

=

In shakti faith is depressed, in siddhi of physical yoga, in siddhi of karma, in siddhi of rapidity and in God & self-power. It is doubted whether the leading is directly divine, — whether the leader of the yoga is the Master of all. Mahakali-shakti is depressed in its Mahakali bhava.

=

The third chatusthaya is entirely clouded; its action is disorganised & only mental, though constant. The satyam has gained, the ritam only occasionally manifests itself except in fragments. Power is slow & uncertain in its effectivity. Samadhi does not advance, but keeps beating against a wall of aggression.

=

Sharira is in all points obstructed & in most thrown back.

=

Karma gets no sure foundation; only sahitya progresses. Asiddhi prevails in kriti.

=

In Brahmadarshana jnana is strong, Ananda Brahman vague & often only implicit. Krishnadarshana is no longer intense; although it is laying its foundations more solidly.

≡

A general physical lassitude & indifference of the will prevails.

≡

August 1ˢᵗ

रदत् पथो वरुणः सूर्याय प्राणाँसि समुद्रिया नदीनाम् ।
सर्गो न सृष्टो अर्वतीऋँतायञ्चकार महीरवनीरहभ्यः ॥

1 Wideness & purity of the Soul. (Varuna)
2 Has to cut out paths for the Vijnana in the mind.
3 Along those paths must be the flow of the higher existence.
4 The Tapasic impulsions and will-thought have to [be] turned into truth of Vijnana.
5. So all the activities or streams of the existence have to be made vast for the dawns of the Vijnana by the rapid movement of the wideness & purity.

=

Sukshma gandha recurred after a long time with intensity and frequency.

=

Vijnana is attempting once more to organise itself, better & more soundly than before. There is especially a perception of the relative truth of the physical, mental & vital satyam & ritam, with the absolute truth of the vijnana behind it.

Ritam increases slowly but steadily in the trikaldrishti & telepathy.

—

August 2ᵈ

Chiefly, a preparation of finality in the Anandamaya Ishwara-darshana.

Formerly the Brahmadarshan was of the impersonal Sarvam Anantam Jnanam Anandam, centred either in the Sarvam or Anantam or Jnanam or at the highest in the Anandam. Now this is a past state that recurs; it is the Personal in & embracing the Impersonal that is now the more normal, but this is most often in the Jnanam. From yesterday it begins to be more fixedly, more recurrently, for a longer time in the Anandam.

=

At the same time the second chatusthaya with the Mahakali bhava tends to fix itself. There is sraddha in the struggle & power of battle, not yet firm sraddha in the result.

The main point is that the maintenance of Mahakali bhava no longer depends on successful manifestation of power. Formerly with insuccess it fell back to Maheshwari-Mahasaraswati, recently to M.M with quiescent Mahakali. At present it wavers between M^3 with predominant Mahakali & insufficient Mahaluxmi colouring and M^4 with insufficient Mahakali force. In the latter case Maheshwari pratistha tends to be hidden, as is intended, in Mahakali intensity of the prana, but the intensity ceases in the general Tapas. In the latter there is intensity of tapas, but the pratistha appears & emphasises itself so as to support the tapas & prevent a relapse into the rajasic Kali. In the former there is a harmony and the intended harmony, but with insufficient sense of power.

This has now to be remedied.

=

Vijnana & Sharira continue as before; but in Vijnana there is the foreshadowing of victory, Sharira still dwells in the shadow of defeat. In Karma there is nothing decisive.

Aug 3.

एवा वंदस्व वरुणं बृहंतं नमस्या धीरममृतस्य गोपां ।
इमां धियं शिक्षमाणस्य देव [क्रतुं दक्षं]^{14} वरुण सं शिशाधि

Yesterday sukshma gandha only in the evening, today active with the taste. Neither free.

=

A movement of the vijnana by which the central vani, script, thought (vangmaya) separate themselves from the indirect and apocryphal and assure themselves more firmly to the faith

=

This movement proceeds along with a[n] increasing firmness in the foundation of the Mahakali bhava and a definite assurance of the finality of the Ananda.

=

It is not yet clearly fixed for the intellect that the Master of the Yoga is the Master of the World, but it is fixed for the faith;

---

^{14} *MS* दक्षं क्रतुं

& this is clear that it is the Swarat of the system accepting the conditions he has created for the work of development and not at once manifesting his full power and knowledge. It had already been indicated that this was his method—a progressive unveiling out of the satyam and anritam of the human creature. The same rule would then apply to him as Master of the World, Samrat,— but there the mastery is not yet so wide & absolute, the evolution has not proceeded so far and is therefore not so evident.

Aug 4.

Faith today seems to be completely founded & formed except in the detail and in the rapidity, but faith in the detail is preparing. It remains to be seen whether what has been formed can again be shaken.

—

In the Vijnana a preparation of farther advance towards (1) certainty of trikaldrishti-telepathy, (2) more general effectivity of tapas, (3) firm foundation of samadhi which has again been obscured & depressed. In the kriti there is again some effectivity, no longer merely of detail; in the sharira as yet no advance.

=

Lipi

1. act realise begin (in strong letters, but not sharply distinct)
2. rely on the aishwarya
3 delight. (ie in the action & result).

=

There has been as yet no definite success in the directions indicated, only a general strengthening which does not visibly go beyond the actual results already obtained. The fluctuations of the vijnana still continue.

=

There is a tendency towards renewed activity in the Sharira especially in Ananda which has become sparse and sluggish. It has to be remembered in order to come.

Aug 5—

A great advance towards certainty of the Ritam in the trikal-drishti.

At the same time there has come a rush of the will-thought attempting to establish itself as the effective thought with the knowledge thought contained in it. This is the same movement which formerly followed any considerable advance of the siddhi,—a rush of Mahakali pravritti, with confidence in the immediate fulfilment of the hope, desire etc in the rajasic being and a subsequent recoil of disillusionment, disappointment and loss of faith.

At present, however, the will-thought is much more normally effective than it ever was before; but it is not yet entirely effective and seldom immediately effective. Its enlightenment is imperfect & even when it is right, it is still half obscure of the nature of right-Force but not of Light or luminous right force. It is not *kratum sachetasam*, but only *prajavat, suvitam*.

The harmony of the will-thought & knowledge-thought must be the next step, leading to their entire oneness.

=

Some slight advance, but not yet quite firm in the *jagrad antardrishta*. Perfect forms initially stable.

=

Constant movement towards settled perfection for several days in the Brahma and Krishnadarshana.

Aug 6.

Movement towards harmony of the will-thought & knowledge-thought. Greater effectiveness of the will-thought.

=

Increasing frequency of the pure inspired & revelatory vijnana.

=

The whole process of the Yoga is now concentrated towards the perfection of the vijnana (samadhi excepted) and the perfection of the Krishnadarshana. In the former the entire perception by sanyama of the mental state of the object is now frequent, but the entire perception of the thought has to be added: the right (rita) perception of the trikaldrishti in that which is near in place & time is gained and frequent, but the perception of that which is far in time & place is inadequate. There is also the lapse into the intellectual perception visited by vijnana from the general vijnanamaya perception suffered by the intellectual & sensational mind. These defects have to be remedied.

In the Krishnadarshana, the difficulty of the entire perception of all forms as entirely Krishna is still only occasional & the siddhi which has progressed rapidly oscillates back into the lower stages from and through which it has progressed. The Shakti is aiming at the final removal of these defects.

=

The movement of the Samadhi is again suspended.

=

Sharira still continues in the same state of obstruction.

=

Ananda (kama) in sharira tries to move again towards normal continuity, the others towards normal recurrence.

Aug 7 –

The Krishnadarshana has surmounted several of its difficulties. Formerly the adult vulgar & hirsute masculine face did not at once throw back the idea of Krishna. Now all faces at once reflect him. There was also a division between the Krishna in human form & the formless & universal Krishna. Either the first was intensely sensed & the latter became merely Brahman or the latter was seen & the human form became a mask of Brahman + guna etc. This is now in type surmounted; but the Siddhi goes back to this stage firmly in order to bridge over the division by proceeding from the universal to the individual and no longer from the individual to the universal. In all probability this movement will be complete today.

=

The tapas is becoming extraordinarily effective both in general movement & in exact movement whether of things in statu or things in motu. But it is only occasionally effective immediately

& without resistance. Therefore for things in motu the perfect movement is delay[ed], others contrary or imperfect intervening, or there is a failure of the occasion. In the latter case either the failure is definitive or the object returns to the same place & executes the movement or some other comes & executes it in its place. For things in motu, the movement is often executed, but in another place & time than was first indicated, after one or more contrary or imperfect movements; sometimes it is done immediately, sometimes in the same place but after delay or return.

Nevertheless the end of resistance is within sight for things near in time & place

=

Vani has assumed the entire *madhura dasya* relation which is beginning to affirm itself definitively; with it comes the full sense of the Lila and the *attahasya*.

The intermediate vani now makes no difference.

This siddhi is extending itself to the script & vangmaya.

At the same time the perceptive thought is becoming more powerful in trikaldrishti.

=

Tivra Ananda is becoming much more intense and tends to unite itself with madhura.

Raudra is becoming frequently spontaneous (without smarana).

The perfect spontaneity of all the sharira Anandas must be assured before there can be fixed recurrence and continuity.

=

The entire Krishnadarshana, individual in universal, universal in individual and both the same, is now accomplished. It has yet to be given such force & consistency as to eliminate all relapse and to be raised to higher intensities.

=

Farther combination of the instruments of the vijnana; especially script begins to work simultaneously with vangmaya which is getting rid of sthula sabda.

=

Renewed activity of samadhi in all parts, but with insufficiently firm hold on the akasha. There is sometimes perfect combination, but no stability and lipi in swapna has not recovered its coherence.

Aug 8ᵗʰ
  1. Dieu sorti de l'école
  2. fonder l'enseignement morale.

There is again a point of arrest, farther progress attempting to realise itself, a passive obstruction resisting.

In the tapas & knowledge the movement is toward immediate effectiveness of the tapas and automatic accuracy in detail of the knowledge. This is sometimes entirely realised, but immediately afterwards contradicted.

In Krishnadarshana it is the intensity.

In rupa it is the fixity & perfection of the rupa in all its variety.

Finally, the effective control of the body & of all outward result by the Will

=

The activity of Samadhi continued – stability and firm continuity, but not very prolonged. Occasional coherence of lipi in Swapna.

=

On the whole, however, the day has been one of arrest. The Tapas etc fell back slightly and the force of the Mahakali bhava; at the same time there was no forcible retrogression.

=

Kriti continues to be slight & limited, but it works.

=

It is felt that another advance is being prepared.

Aug 9ᵗʰ
  The day chiefly occupied with Sahitya.

=

Spontaneous gandhadrishti shows a tendency to regularise itself.

Sukshma vak is also developing in its spontaneity.
=

The more subtle form of the vangmaya is already established; the script unsupported by vangmaya is also developing.
=

There is a suspension of organised vijnanamaya perception; but trikaldrishti of exact time is repeating itself. It is telepathic in its suggestion, rather than vijnanamaya; but it is trikaldrishti, not telepathy.
=

Sukshma vak tends now to develop sentences and is growing rich in implicit voices.

All drishti is attempting to break down the veils that have so long confined it. Sparsha is much stronger than before, but does not get beyond the habitual touches. The barriers still prevail in rupa.

Since writing, however, three or four dense & developed forms have appeared stable straight under the eyes.
=

Rupa in swapna samadhi is growing in habitual intensity, but there is still the influence of the chhaya over all, though all is not now chhayamaya.
=

Aug 10th

तममृक्षंत वाजिनमुपस्थे अदितेरधि विप्रासो अण्व्या धिया.

That is to say, the suspension of the vijnana action is for the purification of the Pranic Force in the vast of the infinite consciousness by the right action of the pure mind.
=

Great stability in profound swapna-samadhi.
Repeated coherence & samadhi character of swapna.
=

During the day no sensible advance. Occasionally it is shown that the siddhi has not really retrograded.
=

The movement is towards a more complete possession by

the Ananda & Vijnana & the elevation of vijnana thought and perception to the pure drishti & sruti.

But the obstruction seeks to draw it back to the intellectuality.

This obstruction is being used as a means for the necessary transformation; it allows the habit of the inferior activity of vijnana to be weakened by suspension.

==

There is also an assertion that the decisive effectivity of the tapas is to be evolved.

==

Aug 11th – 12th

Dream & samadhi united at the borderline.

—

There is now definitely a new period of obstruction & of attempt at relapse; hostile attack is evident & not merely the pause of transition. Even the Samata has been slightly touched.

==

In the Krishnadarshan all that has now to be done is to exhaust the force of the habit of relapse which allows the opposition to affect the consciousness attained & throw it back to the simple Brahmadarshan or even the mere Sarvam & Ananta or Jnana or else to the inferior stages of the Krishnadarshana. This reversion seems now to be merely mechanical & to happen only because it has happened in the past and can still be forced on the consciousness in the present.

==

The loss of faith in the Sharira & Karma is still possible & brings with it brief touches of Asamata with all the old symptoms & reversions to the mere Mahasaraswati type. All these are forced upon the system by long and persistent violence & with great difficulty and are not natural to it, much less normal.

==

Yet the suspension of the Vijnana is not real, but only an appearance fastened onto the mind by sheer force. The coverlid is held on by sheer force & whenever contrary force is applied, it is lifted.

Aug 13th 14th

Progress chiefly in samadhi, confirmation of one or two stable dense & developed rupas, coherence of dream etc; but nothing very strongly decided.

—

The adverse current prevails in sharira and kriti and is not yet removed in the rest of the siddhi. The most discouraging fact is the return, however slight & transient, of the circumstances of the Asamata, ashanti, asukham which seemed to have been definitely excluded. Although no lodgment was effected, the attack itself contradicts this elementary & initial finality. The hope of rapidity in the rest of the siddhi has now to be postponed indefinitely.

=

Krishnadarshana is also successfully resisted & kept fluctuating between its inferior degrees & those of the Brahmadarshana.

=

Seven days have been given to almost entire asiddhi & almost the whole of July. None of the instruments of Vijnana can yet be firmly & wholly trusted, since they all seem to give themselves to the intrusion of inferior powers.

=

Physical Ananda is infrequent and the vishayas again rare & sluggish.

=

Aug 15th 16th

विहि होत्रा अवीता: [विपो न रायो]¹⁵ अर्थ: —

=

The Siddhi is again dominant in the vijnana, but the element of mental error remains, though subordinated, & the element of tapasic ineffectivity.

The higher energies of the vijnana are trying to manifest, होत्रा अवीता: Repeatedly indications that seem to be contradicted or in constant course of contradiction & the corresponding tapas fulfil themselves victoriously; but the fulfilment is not always perfect.

=

---

15 MS रायो न विपो

There is as yet no firm possession of the Vijnana and the realisations acquired sometimes descend and take possession, sometimes stand back & allow the old conditions to play in front of them, sometimes seem to be almost entirely obscured.

=

At present a process is going on with the mind in which that is at the mercy of mental suggestions and all that is true is carried on from above automatically, the mind being only a channel and not participating except very slightly & wrongly.

=

Later on (16th morning) entire return of the siddhi (tapas-telepathy-trikaldrishti-lipi).

=

Ananda sharira is again becoming normally active. The whole poise of the siddhi has been restored and the beginnings of a new organisation manifest.

Aug 26th

The last nine or ten days have been a period of uncertainty and confused labour; the main result has been to confirm the satyam entirely in knowledge thought & will thought on both the two planes of nervous & pure mental mind, but not yet in the intuitive mind; for satyam of intuitive mind = ritam.

Tapas effectiveness varies between all the different degrees from postponed or deflected effectivity to 80°

Telepathy is in the same condition, active, but not well-organised.

Samadhi is obstructed.

=

Krishnadarshana is firm in the Jnanam Brahma, but Anandam Brahma is not yet sufficiently brought forward, — therefore the full intensity is ordinarily absent.

=

Sharira is still denied.

=

Kriti is stronger than before, but very partial.

=

यदुत्तमे मरुतो मध्यमे वा यद्वावमे सुभगासो दिवि ष्ठ
अतो नो रुद्रा उत वा न्वस्याग्ने वित्ताद्धविषो यद्यजाम॥
अग्निश्च यन्मरुतो विश्ववेदसो दिवो वहध्वे उत्तरादधि ष्णुभिः
ते मंदसाना धुनयो रिशादसो वामं धत्त यजमानाय सुन्वते॥

This is an indication that the satyam (and ananda) are to be extended to the highest or intuitive mind as well as the two others. It has begun to be fulfilled to a certain extent.
=

Gandha seems now to be fixed in recurrence, but it is sometimes rare, sometimes more frequent. Rasa also comes, but less firm & intense & often as a result of gandha. The others are frequently suspended & do not attain to any new variety or freedom.
=

Raudrananda has increased, especially in the agneya-sparsha.
=

19 FEBRUARY – 20 MARCH 1916

February 1916

In the interval since August there has been a period of long torpor and inertia followed by a period of more steady advance.

Samata chatusthaya is complete as well as the positive bhukti; only touches of asamata now occur, chiefly in the form of momentary depression though touches of uneasiness also sometimes but rarely occur. For the most part samata, shanti, are untouched, sukham occasionally, hasyam is sometimes clouded, but not seriously or positively.

The viryam is complete, except in touches of a-shaurya; only *nyunata*, not positive defect of contradiction is manifest in the other elements. Tertiary dasyam is complete & firmly established, but not always forceful. Shakti is deficient in the body, in the rest complete, but not forceful, and sometimes touched. Aishwaryabhava and sraddha (swashaktyam) are improved, but not yet firm, except for the sraddha in yoga-siddhi, minus *shârira*. There is no sraddha in adesh-siddhi.

Brahma chatusthaya is now complete, constant in Sarvam, Anantam, Jnanam; established but not always intense in Anandam. The Person is manifest in all, but not always vividly and there is still a divorce between the individual & the All in personality, no longer in the impersonality.

Sharira makes no evident progress, except in the frequency of the Anandas; kama and tivra especially are established, but not always operative.

Jnana is firm, as also telepathy except that of thought; trikaldrishti and tapas-siddhi are drawing towards a first initial perfection; the instruments are developed, but not frequently active;

Samadhi is slowly developing a firm basis in swapna, but has been thrown back in Jagrat.

——

Feb [Saturday Feb 19th]

Bath fixed first after 11, then at 11.20, (the intellect tried to fix 11); actually at 11.19. The exact time was fixed about half an hour before fulfilment, the approximate time about an hour before.

═

The tapas-siddhi has been steadily increasing in general force. The rule of resistance is no longer so absolute. Very often the exact movement is fulfilled again and again without resistance or with a minimum of resistance; but where the object is stationary at first, there is usually resistance. Eg. a squirrel on opposite ledge, suggested to mount on parapet, afterwards perceived that it was not to be at that spot (A), but might be farther on (B); seen that it would go on to the turn of the ledge; went on beyond to the end whence it attempted to descend. Stopped by will which suggested and trikaldrishti affirmed that it should mount the parapet suddenly; was compelled to do so by arrival of crow. This movement was twice willed, foreseen and fulfilled. Afterwards it went near position A, on the ledge, then frightened by a crow on the other side, fled to B exact and mounted in accordance with the original suggestion. This example and many others show that trikaldrishti and tapas, so long enemies, are beginning to unite and coalesce.

═

S's [Saurin's] return seen at either 9.15 or 9.30. The intellect first leaned to the latter, but after willing for the former, the ideality approved 9.15 (by the watch, by the right time 9.24), although the intellect still doubted. S came at 9.16.

═

In the evening two drishtis of a watch pointing to 11.50 and 2.57; the first indicated by the thought as the time at which S. would come upstairs tonight, the second connected with teatime tomorrow. S came at nearly 11.40 by the watch which must have been about 11.50 by the right time

Sunday—

S rose in the afternoon at 2.55 by the watch (right time 3.16) and went to make tea a minute afterwards; this agrees with the watch-dristi 2.57 last night: there is a minute's difference which may be due to wrong observation, since the watch-rupa was diminutive & the exact minute could only approximately given. It is to be noted, however, that the two drishtis seem to have referred to different time-pieces.

=

Aishwarya increased in force. Formerly the object of the will would execute four or five evolutions & then escape entirely from the will-force. Today after the first escape it only deviated for a moment & that in obedience to a previous suggestion not maintained and subsequently still obeyed others, though not so perfectly as in the first five or six evolutions.

Sunday.

Feb. [20]

It is noticeable that [there][1] are now no longer long gaps of time in which a brief play of tapas and trikaldrishti gives place to confusion of knowledge and entire barrenness of effectivity in the will. The telepathic knowledge is always active and increases marvellously in correctness, although it is still troubled by a certain amount of false stress and false distribution but very much less than formerly; trikaldrishti is constantly active although it does not yet securely lead, but it is becoming frequent and active.

Tapas sometimes fails entirely for a few minutes, afterwards it rights enough. It always produces some effect slight or great, immediate or subsequent, in the object willed or other object not willed, perceptible in act or only just perceptible in tendency: but accurate result is now becoming frequent, though not yet continuously active. All this however, does not entirely apply outside the field of ordinary exercise of the will & knowledge.

Rupa in jagrat is growing, but slowly and with relapses, not

[1] MS they

into long suspension as formerly, but into inferior activity. The
vishayas are yet very rudimentary; gandha is the most advanced.

Tuesday 22ᵈ February.

Final confirmation of satyam of telepathy, followed by a great
confusion of ritam owing to the insurgence of the mental and pranic
environing suggestions. The precise place of these was, however,
made clearer by the experience.

—

The Krishnadarshana (personal) generalised firmly in all existences, a little defective in animals. This darshana formerly depended on strong perception of the Ananda Brahman coupled with
strong perception of the Lilamaya. It is now automatic, even when
Ananda Brahman is depressed and sense of Lila not prominent.
Only the invariability & intensity have now to be confirmed and the
perfect union of Krishnakali bhava and the now complete Brahma
chatusthaya will be founded.

—

The right interpretation of lipi and the lekha (sortilege) is now
automatic.

=

The swapnasamadhi has now definitely advanced. Formerly
the drishya there was evanescent, disappearing as soon as manifest,
or else permanent only so long as the waking mind in sleep did
not turn its eye upon the thing seen and it was only watched by
the dream mind above. Now drishyas are common which remain
before the swapna-jagrat eye long firm and constant in the *sthana*
though not for very long in the *karma*. Transient drishyas are also
more frequently lifelike & not shadowy. Lipi is more frequently
coherent.

Thursday 24ᵗʰ

The vijnana overpowered for two days is returning to activity.

Meal fixed by trikaldrishti after 12 and bath with some hesitation at 11.55. (fixed about 11.) Bath at 11.55 (called at 11.54) and
dinner at 12.5 to 12.10. Trikaldrishti (apara) continually justified
in movements of birds etc.

Development of a powerful self-fulfilling force which is sure beforehand of its result, yet is not trikaldrishti, but still fulfils irresistibly; only it is only in general movements & does not apply victoriously in sthana or exact circumstance, but only in kala. It is not knowledge but sasraddha shakti — not the doubtfully effective rajasic tapastya but true tapatya. This however does not come at will.

Lipi. *perfection of delight.*

Friday.

Two strong telepathies in the evening

1. Bh. [Bharati] will not come, combated by a weaker telepathic suggestion of coming. Bh did not come, as he does daily

2. At 9.18 (by watch) strong suggestion that S [Saurin] would come immediately, combated by suggestion of mind trying to fix 9.30. Assurance that it was before 9.30 and indeed immediate. Mind compromised saying "Now probably, but at least before 9.30". S came at 9.20.

Constant growth of firm-founded general satya in the telepathy, trying to convert itself to ritam.

Saturday.

Satya of telepathy becomes more & more ritam; general satya of trikaldrishti preparing.

Growth of the more intense Vishayananda of the mind in all the objects of sense.

Growth of Krishna Kali bhava in the Brahma darshana

Thursday

March 2

In the evening telepathic trikaldrishti that N [Nolini] will come soon after 8.30, M [Moni] soon after 9.0, S [Saurin] soon after 9.30. N came at 8.35, M at 9.8, S at 9.35. The approximate time after was also correct.

Friday.
  March 3
    The telepathic trikaldrishti has now an element of certainty in general results distinguishing it from the mere telepathy; the latter also tries to represent itself as trikaldrishti, but is not accepted as before without the certainty.

    All the siddhis are going through evolutions of recoil and advance. Firm and strong sama ananda is secure except in the case of strong and massed baffling of siddhi. Hasyam is beginning to take a stronger hold on the system.

    Time of bath given correctly as after 12. and then as 12.10. (first mistaken for dinner-time); ready at 12.10, called at 12.11

Sunday
  March 5
    The Krishna-consciousness is now perfectly normal and universal, though not as yet seated on the plane of the Vijnana or Ananda, but only on the mental. Smarana is still necessary, though not invariably.

    The dividing line between the Nara and Narottama is removed. General Satyam of trikaldrishti is adding itself to satyam of telepathy in the immediate time, place and event; ritam is as yet only in its initial stage.

    All siddhi, except in the first chatusthaya, is subject to temporary denial in its later acquisitions.
=
    Instances of immediate or exact fulfilment of tapas begin to become more normal; eg, a kite near the window pursued by crow; knowledge-will that crow should strike three times rapidly, then fly away; immediately & exactly fulfilled. Crow on bar under balcony opposite; willed to go one side, then return, then fly away from a particular spot; first two fulfilled immediately, the last after hesitating and moving several times to one side and another.

    [*Here one page left blank.*]

Tuesday. Mar [7][2]

The satyam of thought, telepathy and trikaldrishti is attempting to arrange itself in the terms of the ritam, but as yet only succeeds occasionally in the type. There is the old struggle between the intellectuality to keep the truth for itself & become intuitive mind of the intelligence and the ideality to replace the intellectuality and establish the pure intuitive mind or the vijnana itself. For the present the intellectuality prevails; but tends to lose its hold of both satyam and ritam in the struggle.

Wednesday. March [8][3]

The Krishnadarshana is again subject to fluctuations. It has descended into the Anantam & the Jnanam; but the Chidghana is now more normally informed & encompassed by the Ananda and perceives the Narottama in the Nara. Sometimes however it is more Anantam than Jnanam and then sees merely the Nara with only an implicit Ananda and the Chidghana prayas.

All is now being turned into Ananda in the mind & body. The old reactions returned for a long time in the morning, but were forced to be anandamaya, as are all discomfortable sensations in the body. Nor can they now disturb the calm of the being, but only suspend the hasyam with a minor contradiction of the sukham making itself an ananda of asukham & ashivam.

Monday. Mar. [13][4]

वाङ्मनःकर्मभिः पत्यौ व्यभिचारो यथा न मे (स्यात्) – तथा विश्वंभरे देवि मामंतर्धातुमर्हसि॥ विश्वंभरा देवी = Aditi, अनंताभेदमयी चिच्छक्तिः तस्या एवांतः प्रतिष्ठां दातु –

A new brihattwa, deepening, intensifying and unification of

---

2 MS 6 *From this point until the entry for "Monday. 19th March" the days of the week do not agree with the days of the month in the calendar for 1916. The days of the week appear to be correct, as many of the days of the month were added afterwards in a different ink. – Ed.*
3 MS 7
4 MS 12

Titiksha, Udasinata & Nati with each other and all three with unified rasa, bhoga & ananda.

Intense chidghana is moving up into shuddhananda & the sense of a faery beauty in all things, even the most ugly. The downward movement of pure shuddhananda embracing chidghana and ahaituka is suspended. Sakama premananda and saprema kamananda are being unified, more firmly generalised & normalised.

After several days cessation the trikaldrishti is being again worked over, for a more positive satyam. The first movement is a greater certainty of the final result, but this is still by suggestion to the intellect or in the intellect. The difficulty is still to distinguish always, though it can now generally be done, the ideal suggestion from the intellectual certainty which cannot be securely trusted.

There is also an attempt to fix ritam of detail; this is still done in the old way, by unillumined suggestion to the intellect. Eg re the bath; fixed as after 11.30. Times fixed 11.35, 11.30 for unknown stages, 11.38 for being called to bathe: then 11.30 was fixed for S [Saurin] getting up from under the tap, 11.35 for M's [Moni's] finishing the actual bathing. 11.38 & 11.30 came out exactly to the second, but there was some doubt about 11.35 as the exact time was not noticed. At $11.35\frac{3}{4}$ M had left the tap and was drying himself.

Usually tapas is eventually successful in the immediate environment — but the tapas is no longer personally used; it comes of itself.

Since yesterday script and vangmaya are constantly in the type of vijnana with *prakasha*, *asu* and *ananda*, and Vani, less securely, in the type of pure ananda containing vijnana.

Reference carries with it a great clearness, appositeness and sure fulfilment.
=

Sometimes there is wrong application or combination of time and circumstance. Eg. 7.8 was given and taken as the time when Bh. [Bharati] would come; but at 7.8., the servant went out, Bh. came at 7.27. Afterwards indeed 7.25 or thereabouts was given, but it was thought by the intellect Bh would not come, although the ideality had given its decision that he would.

10.5 given by rupa of watch; decided to be time at which dinner would be finished, for it was already foretold that S would come early (he came about 9.15); when the watch was seen two or three minutes after finishing dinner, it was exactly 10.5.

=

9.40 and 7.50 given by rupa of watch.

Tuesday [14][5] March

9.40 doubly fulfilled, in the morning as the time when work on Veda (Bengali) was resumed (unforeseen), in the night as time of meal (foreseen), the first exact, the latter probably approximate, the watch not being immediately consulted —

Friday [17][6] March

After a crisis of anrita of intellectuality in which the unreliability of intellectual suggestions was insisted upon, there being no means of detecting whether they are ideal or merely telepathic, the Yogasiddhi is resumed on other lines.

Krishnadarshana fluctuates again for more confirmed normality of what has already been gained.

Rupa is slowly developing, but still without stability of perfect forms; samadhi fluctuates.

Samata is not yet entirely immune, but hasya has become entirely normal. Asamata is now usually anandamaya and only caused by strong nonfulfilment of yogasiddhi.

In the second chatusthaya, the only positive fluctuation is in sraddha and ishwarabhava and in the externalities of dehashakti.

Sunday. [19][7] March

In fixing time of Bh's coming two suggestions came 7.45 and 7.55. At 7.44 the servant went; at 7.55. Bh came.

[5] MS 13
[6] MS 16
[7] MS 18

Note —

Only these exact correspondences of time are at present being recorded; the numerous fulfilled telepathies, trikaldrishtis etc which occur each day are not [set][8] down.

Monday. [20th][9] March

Known by telepathy & telepathic trikaldrishti that Bh [Bharati] would not come; still 7.30 suggested — nothing external happened, only the beginning of an internal movement.

8.20 suggested for N's [Nolini's] coming. N came at 8.20 exact (by the watch)

Telepathy that N. would not come to read Greek; justified.

Will for S [Saurin] & M [Moni] to come at 9: they came at 9.3.

[8] MS sent
[9] MS 19th

Jan 9th 1917.

Re. [Reference]

य ओहते रक्षसो देववीतावचक्रेभिस्तं मरुतो नि यात।
यो वः शर्मीं शशमानस्य निंदात् तुच्छयान्कामान् करते सिष्विदानः॥

"The Rakshasas who rush to the attack in the birth of the godheads,
— O Thought-gods,[1] him assail in your wheelless cars who confines
your work when man seeks his self-expression and with sweat of
effort creates little fragmentary desires."

This corresponds to the actual state of the siddhi. *Samata* is
conquered; only vague unsubstantial touches of asamata can now
trouble the outer physical skin of the *pranakosha*. Shakti on the basis of dasya is well founded, though still imperfect in the application
of *sraddha* through uncertainty of knowledge & will and therefore
imperfect also in *aishwarya* of *devibhava*. But the third chatusthaya
is held back in order to get rid of the last fragments of the ghost
of desire which prevent the free identification of the effortless will
with the cosmic Will and to get rid also of the defect of the thought
which the Rakshasa still tries to limit to the stumbling movements
of the intellect.

Telepathy is now strong and spontaneous in its satyam, but
the ritam is imperfect because of the persistence of the intellectual overstress, false choice, false valuation, false interpretation.
Trikaldrishti is gradually strengthening itself, but is still occasional
and uncertain because usually rendered by the physical mind intellectually and not ideally.

Re परिष्कृतस्य रसिन इयमासुतिश्चारुर्मंदाय पत्यते

---

[1] *In the manuscript, "Thought-gods" is written above "Maruts", which is not can-*
celled. — Ed.

The Ananda purified felt a little afterwards flowing through the sukshma body like a sweet and delightful wine (juice of grapes).

Jan 10

Sensitiveness of pranic body; intense pranic and emotional & sensational telepathy, brihattara; also development of sense-thought telepathy in the mind & some vague pure thought telepathy. Strength of sanyama

Valuative vartamanadrishti becoming more & more ritam. Immediate trikaldrishti strong, but still more tentative than decisive.

Ref.

अग्निस्तुविश्रवस्तमं तुविब्रह्माणमुत्तमं ।
अतूर्तं श्रावयत्पतिं पुत्रं ददाति दाशुषे ॥

Not immediate future. श्रावयत्पतिं indicates vijnanamaya realisation of the Ishwara.

While rejecting suggestion of fifth chatusthaya, fourth member —

द॰ प्रियो भूत्वा परमं सुखमश्नुते

Distant future, questioned by mind. In answer

कृणुष्व पाजः प्रसितिं च पृथ्वीं याहि राजेवाऽमवानिभेन । तृष्वीमनु प्रसितिं द्रूणानो अस्तासि विध्य रक्षसस्तपिष्ठैः ॥

That is by rapidity of development of the divine Will and its destruction of the opposing powers, the thing may be realised even in this life.

Jan 11th

Both perceptive (ideal) thought & vangmaya as well as coherent lipi are constant in samadhi, seated, even at great depths which formerly brought sleep. Now sleep is put back and only slightly, occasionally and for a moment or two overcomes the swapna-sushupti or supta-swapna. It remains to be seen whether this great advance is firmly consolidated & whether or how far it will extend to samadhi, lying down, daytime. Night is still given to sleep, & until yesterday it prevailed always after a time in the daytime recumbence.

Re योंऽतःसुखोंऽतरारामस्तथांतज्योतिरेव यः ।
स योगी ब्रह्मनिर्वाणं ब्रह्मभूतोऽधिगच्छति ॥
लभंते ब्रह्मनिर्वाणमृषयः क्षीणकल्मषाः ।
छिन्नद्वैधा यतात्मानः सर्वभूतहिते रताः ॥

Doubt is being destroyed by the growth of the ideality, samata and dasya perfected have got rid of egoistic desire and its attendant stains, the Ishwara is governing the being; therefore the time has come to establish the inner joy and light, in itself entirely, the joy of things being merely its outflowing & not at all dependent on things. With this will come the completion of the brahmabhava by the dissolution of the remnants of mentality & the power to begin the karma. Thus *atmarati* & *brahmabhava* are already established, but still besieged by old habits of mind & therefore still imperfect.

Jan 12th

Stability, spontaneity, legibility of the lipi. When legibility is imperfect, spontaneity suffers[,] the mind interfering to catch the unexpressed or decipher the illegible portions. Stability also is then diminished.

There is some revival of intellectual confusion preparing a larger ideality.

Jan 13th

The battle to transform the telepathy into ideal thought and perception continues.

There is a distinct advance towards the universalisation of chidghana-shuddhananda & the sense of universal divine beauty in place of shuddha ahaituka ananda and the sense of natural beauty. If this is established, the अंतःसुखोंऽतरारामः will be complete.

The chidghana is now firmly prominent in the ahaituka in place of the nirvijnana ahaituka, even in human figures & faces where it was or tended to be absent. For some time chidghana has been perfect in things and present in animals.

Jan 16ᵗʰ

After two days of struggle & obscuration in which the Asamata pressed upon and into the consciousness owing to the revival of rajasic struggle, there is a triumph of the Ananda, cosmic, possessing the whole being, though it is still besieged from outside in the physical Prana by the resuscitated Asamata. This is connected with defect of Aiswarya & sraddha in the perfect siddhi.

Brahmadarshana has become again & more firmly Ananda-brahmadarshana and is now being refilled with Krishna-Kali-darshana.

At the same time madhura dasya is restored with intensity.

The last remnants of the personal egoistic attitude are being attacked and persistently and rapidly removed to be replaced by the divine & cosmic ego, for whose will, enjoyment, knowledge, power the mind, life & body are to exist & not at all for the separate individual will & enjoyment.

Antahsukha & antararama are therefore well founded, but antarjyotih is only beginning. It cannot be complete except by complete conversion of *manas* into *vijnana*.

Jan 20ᵗʰ

The last few days have seen

(1) Strong confirmation of the first chatusthay in its completeness. There is now little opposition. Only the intensity of the sama ananda has to be increased and an occasional recurrence of vague disappointment prevented from returning.

(2) Increased strength of second chatusthaya especially of *sraddha bhagavati*, *devibhava* and confirmed *dasya*. In the latter madhura has to be increased. Aishwarya has to be encouraged & devibhava to be less Maheshwari-Mahasaraswati with more in it of Mahakali. The Mahalakshmi colour comes with the positive *ananda* & *madhura*, fades with the sinking back towards mere *shanti* and general *samata* & *sukha*. The rest awaits the development of the third chatusthaya.

(3) Great extension of perception of satyam in telepathy, which is preparing to embrace sensational & mental telepathy

and telepathic trikaldrishti. Tapas is increasing towards *brihat* effectiveness, but is not yet ideal (*vijnanamaya*). It awaits the development of pure trikaldrishti unified with pure will.

(4) A struggle in the fourth chatusthaya *arogya*. The opposition still prevails, though more hard put to it to maintain itself.

(5) Considerable extension of lipi.

(6) Increase of KrishnaKali, but not in the perfect form. *Karma* has suffered a return to the deadlock.

The instruments of vijnana are becoming more directly the Ishwara's.

अंतःसुख & अंतराराम being assured, अंतज्योतिः is increasing. Agni is massing strength (कृणुष्व पाजः) in order to create a wide & swift movement (पृथ्वीं प्रसितिं & तृष्वीं प्रसितिं). But the principal action still needed is that of the Maruts रक्षसो नि यात.

Jan 21ˢᵗ

The lipi is still developing though hampered by the mental eagerness of the environment which seeks to anticipate and reproduce its own ideas in the lipi. The lipi is slower when not pressed, but more spontaneous, stable, vividly legible.

Spontaneous, stable, legible jyotirmaya lipi: also tejomaya. Varnamaya comes but with less ease. Dhumramaya and agnimaya are least spontaneous.

    Script in the morning
    "Today third chatusthaya"
    "Lipi, script, thought, vani"
    "Samadhi
    Tapas-siddhi"

In the first part, the programme commenced its own fulfilment at once. A great flood of ideality in all these members is pushing out the siege of the intellect. At every point the ideality shows its superior truth in giving the light, the right relation to fact of any part, fraction, aspect of the thought, which the intellect has bungled.

The inspiration is fixing itself into all the instruments of the vijnana, even the perceptive thought.

Interpretation of the rupas (sadhara) has begun

Script. "Believe luminously"—that is by the ideality, in spite of the apparent resistance and nonfulfilment. This is now coming into force and the belief justifies itself by the eventual fulfilment; the light is also seeking to embrace more perfectly the details of the resistance and the fulfilment.

In consequence tapassiddhi is becoming larger in its movement and more frequently & powerfully effective, often immediate or nearly immediate, sometimes exact in circumstance.

In the afternoon samadhi made a general forward movement towards

(1) activity of ideal thought, perceptive as well as vangmaya. Hitherto vangmaya alone was partly ideal

(2) coherent & consecutive lipi, thought, narrative

(3) continuous drishya combined with sravana and sparsha.

(4) removal of mere *shama* in samadhi, replacement by shama + tapas + prakasha.

The motion is large, but not as yet entirely victorious. Especially is there resistance in the drishya etc.

On the whole the movement is that of the कृणुष्व पाज:, the पृथ्वी तृष्वी प्रसिति of Agni, the अंतज्र्योति: added to अंत:सुख & अंतराराम.

Intimation in the lipi several times repeated that this movement of the ideality will come to a head on Tuesday

Jan 22d Monday

For the first time today the Ishwara is the sakshi, and not the Jiva. At the same time the Ishwara jnata, bharta, anumanta, karta is being rapidly strengthened,[2]—(the karta from this moment after being added[)]. There is still a downward tendency of the mental powers trying to insist on the jiva in these capacities, but it is losing force.

Ideality of style & substance is constantly increasing in the vijnana instruments, especially the perceptive thought, in spite of

---

[2] *The word "karta" was added between the lines, apparently when this point of the sentence had been reached. Sri Aurobindo explained the insertion in the next phrase.—Ed.*

the tamasic resistance of the old mentality in its general sanskara.

Script

Ideality in (telepathy), trikaldrishti, tapas

Samadhi.

(1) is being already fulfilled; first as indicated in the trikaldrishti-tapas; that is to say will & knowledge are combining, preparatory to unification; afterwards in all three[3]

Lipi. "future telepathy turns to trikaldrishti" This is being gradually fulfilled.

The tendency of the mind to carry on one thing at a time, insisting tamasically on the impossibility of doing all at a time in the siddhi of the ideality, is being constantly contradicted and corrected.

Ideal intellectuality is receding out of the system under pressure of intellectual ideality and that is constantly turning itself into ideal ideality, predominantly of the srauta kind (inspiration).

It is found more & more that every impulse, suggestion etc in the sadhan has its utility for its own purpose, but for that utility to be perceived and appreciated, the truth and limits and relation of each has to be ideally perceived. This is now being done more & more.

All this action is principally in the "school", not yet applied to life at large.

=

Antarjyoti may now be considered as established. Brahmabhava is growing, but has to be made more vivid & steady.

The पाज:, पृथ्वी प्रसिति & तृष्वी प्रसिति are founded. What is left is the destruction of the limiting Rakshasas and the royal march of Agni. यो . . तुच्छयान्कामान् करते सिष्विदान:, that Rakshasa is being destroyed rapidly. The निद:— यो शर्मीं शश्मानस्य निंदात् has lost much of his field, but still holds the body & the karma and is not quite driven out of the ideality.

=

---

3 *Apparently the script first came: "Ideality in trikaldrishti, tapas", the word "telepathy" being added later. The parentheses around and the caret below "telepathy" in Sri Aurobindo's transcription of the script appear to be his way of representing this sequence.* — Ed.

In Samadhi the activity of ideal thought perceptive and vang-maya is becoming quite normal, continuous, coherent in all the lighter layers & even in the middle depth. It is penetrating into deep samadhi. The real struggle continues to be in the jagrat

Ideal activity has now become normal in all depths of the mental samadhi. There is as yet no jagrat in vijnana-samadhi.

Rupa-drishya manifests coherently only in brief scenes of a few seconds' occurrence; the deeper the samadhi, the richer the power of vision, although this [   ]^4 is not invariably the rule. Lipi and reading ditto. They are coherent, easily, only in swapna & sushupta, but in sentences only. It is at night that they begin to be long and yet coherent.

In jagrat antardarshi a little impression has been made, but it is nothing firm or definite. . It is here, in jagrat, that siddhi has been most deceptive in the past. The results have always been stolen by the Rakshasas.

=

Script

More progress. First in jagrat samadhi. Next in ideality of t^3. Thirdly, in physical siddhi. Some progress in vishaya. Today.

In jagrat rupas of all kinds begin to reappear with a greater general tendency to siddhi.

T^3 increases in ideality, broadly; nothing definitely new.

In physical siddhi the tivra & vishaya are taken up again and carried forward with greater generality & spontaneous intensity.

———

Jan 23$^{\underline{d}}$ Tuesday.

Script—

The t^3 has to formulate itself in the ideality

Jagrat develops farther.

Vishaya improves

Sraddha swashaktyam, aishwaryabhava and devibhava have to found themselves firmly.

———

4 *MS* this

T^3 is faulty in detail. To mend that fault must be the next movement of the third chatusthaya.

———

Brahmabhava is now vivid & steady. To Brahmabhava has been added & united = Brahmatmabhava. To this there is attempting to unite itself Ishwarabhava, but here there is a difficulty. . "Each body is the body of God" lipi realises itself with vividness, but not steadily. Each mentality the mind of God in spite of *anishabhava* less vividly, less steadily. The sense of the Spirit = Deva presiding over mind and body comes only occasionally.

Ananda Brahma has been for many days in suspension in favour of Manas Brahman. It is now returning sometimes with, sometimes without vijnanananda.

———

Sraddha swashaktyam (subject by dasya to sraddha bhagavati) is founded, — so too Devi bhava of the Dasi-Ishwari (Mahakali-Mahasaraswati) and as a result a qualified daiva aishwaryabhava

—

T^3 is formulating itself; but there is confusion owing to misplacement of detail by intellectual tapas. This is removed in general thought, where ideal tapas has almost replaced intellectual, but not in the application of t^3 to objects even in the "school-field".

———

Rupa in jagrat is now often clear and complete in crude, ghana crude & occasionally in perfect developed crude. It includes all the four main forms — animal, man, object, scene or group. But it is perfect & stable only in the bird form which has been chosen for the type owing to the preoccupation with the flight & movement of birds in the vicinity during the exercise of t^3.

—

Vishaya last night began to remanifest, but without any distinct improvement except in sravana. There was, however, the perfect & vivid sense, sukshma-sthula, of the sparsha of object with object, eg the moth knocking itself or moving on the window-pane or resting on the wall.

＝

The पृथु पाज: is now accomplished, but it is not as yet

sufficiently full of driving force to follow an entirely तृष्वी प्रसिति. Still the rapidity in the third chatusthaya is great; it has to be perfect.

==

Touch is developing itself more strongly in the sukshmabodha, and the result-sensation is often felt in the sthula; but the contact-sensation is only occasionally & very imperfectly sthula, except in the two or three familiar touches, especially that of water.

Taste is recovering its force, but has yet no [   ]⁵ stability except in the vaguer touches. Gandha is redeveloping.

—

See towards end of book⁶

Jan 23ᵈ 1917. Tuesday. (continued)
The Devibhava has now been fully defined —

क. शौर्यमुग्रता युद्धलिप्साट्टहास्यं
ई शांति: विशालता ऐक्यलिप्सा आत्मप्रसाद:
ल प्रेम भावसमृद्धि: सौंदर्यलिप्सा स्नेहहास्यं
स. दास्यं बुद्धिचातुर्यं कर्मलिप्सा प्रीति:

Common to the four दया ईश्वरभाव: सर्वकर्मसामर्थ्यं

The last three bhavas, ई ल स [i.e., Maheshwari, Mahalakshmi and Mahasaraswati], are now complete; the first is there except अट्टहास्यं, but not steady nor well combined with the rest.

The afternoon has passed in a massive resistance to the recent siddhi, which has developed Ananda in battle, resistance & temporary defeat. The Devibhava has triumphed over the resistance.

Sukshmabodha of sparsha continues to develop.

==

The mental-pranic tejas (rajasic) has been absorbed into tapas; the intellectual tapas is being now excluded & its action

⁵ MS no
⁶ *In the manuscript, thirty pages of previously written notes on the Veda intervene between the first and second parts of the entry of 23 January.* — Ed.

transformed into ideal tapas. This can only be completed by identification of the three members of t^3.

==

Varna in the lipi, – blue, green and red as well as the usual black, blue black & occasional brown & yellow. Varna, chhaya, tejas, jyoti, agni, are now all manifest with perfection in crude rupa of the three kinds. Developed crude is becoming common, though not so common as dense crude.

Jan 24th

Sahaituka Tivra now increases instead of diminishing by repeated sparsha. The old rule of decrease is not entirely abolished, but the new of increase has been established.

The body still tends to sink back from ahaituka tivra etc and only to feel it, except rarely, when remembered and willed. But each time it revives activity, it revives with greater intensity, though not with greater continuity.

In Arogya, the habit of disease is still violently strong. New disease does not come, but the old maladies persist by irrational, causeless habit & do not lose hold. Cold formerly could not materialise; this time it materialised for two days, but though really cured in two or three, the inert habit of certain of its reactions has continued, decreasingly, for 7. The two chief maladies on the other hand persist not decreasingly, but always with recurrence of force. Breast pain on the other hand is subject to the will, though not utterly abolished.

The physical siddhi is still the chief stronghold of intense and massed resistance by the opposing forces.

==

After an obscuration, lasting all yesterday afternoon & evening & partly this early morning – intended to get rid of intellectual tapas by isolating it, showing its futility when unenlightened & unsupported by the vijnana – t^3 is reviving, still largely telepathic, but more easily converted to ideal terms.

==

Chitra is now being perfected in richness & variety; some are marvellous in the perfection of every detail.

Rupa (crude) is increasing in variety & frequency and manifesting sadhara, but is usually imperfect in stability, vividness or finish. Prakasha and chhaya, a little vague, are commonest.

Jan 25th

Some advance in samadhi.

The movement of ideal thought entered well into the deepest manasik sushupti, but it is not yet at home and in possession there, as it is in swapna and antardarshi jagrat. Still a kind of jagrat in sushupti is becoming more common, though not yet well-sustained.

Coherent dream, which has almost ceased to have its dream element and rather reproduces some truth not yet grasped in its circumstances, is becoming common in daytime. At night it is less common.

Lipi fluctuates in the manasik sushupti.

Long continued stable rupa drishya and long coherent action in it, is increasing in frequency and firmness. But it is usually a little vague in its outlines & always shadowy in its substance. The vivid & the tejomaya are less stable.

Antardarshi tends to advance in rupadrishya but very slowly.

Jan 26th

Lipi fluent with a perfect legibility, but not vivid, and a spontaneity often anticipated by the thought. It is vivid only in brevity.

Vaidyuta is now common and even normal in association with tivra. Raudra is increasing in frequency & force and is also associated though less firmly with tivra & vaidyuta; it is also entering into tivra.[7]

The opposition to the Ananda-vijnana-darshana of living faces & figures (mostly faces) is breaking down; ananda is even intense; but the vijnana is still oppressed by manomaya.

---

[7] *Sri Aurobindo may have intended to write "vishaya" instead of one of the two apparently redundant occurrences of "tivra" in this sentence. —Ed.*

T^3 is recovering its force and increasing in light, knowledge and effectuality, but is still far from perfect in arrangement of detail and in certainty of result. Telepathy is still too predominant and intellectual tapasbuddhi still distorts the decisive perception

Script.
T^3 developed into trikaldrishti-tapassiddhi
Vishaya
Samadhi
Physical siddhi. Anandas
Fifth chatusthaya. Krishnakali
$=$

T^3 has begun to develop into T^2 [trikaldrishti-tapassiddhi], very crudely.
Vishaya has increased in sparsha (brihat sukshmabodha and strong sthula resultant feeling)
Samadhi in stability of clear rupa-drishya in motion. The slow advance of antardarshi continues.
Krishnakali has reestablished its force, increased with an entire hold of Ananda-vijnana.
The Anandas continue to grow slowly.

Jan 27th
Script
$T^3 = T^2$
Samadhi especially jagrat and rupadrishya
KK [KrishnaKali] – madhura dasya.
Physical siddhi – Anandas.
$=$

T^3 is progressively becoming T^2, but trikaldrishti is stronger than tapassiddhi, although the latter increases steadily in largeness and force, the will becoming more and more impersonal.
Madhura dasya of the KrishnaKali relation is well-established. It is now repelling all return of the nirananda relation as of that of the mere dasya.
Vishaya is crudely active in three, afflicted in two vishayas; but in the latter when it acts, it is sufficiently sthula.

The working of turning all pain and discomfort into raudra ananda is proceeding. Much sharper and stronger touches than before have become anandamaya.

=

Rupadrishya in jagrat at night developed all kinds of clear, perfect & stable forms; some of these were dense or developed or turned from crude to dense and developed.

Samadhi continues to gain in force, variety, stability, continuity of rupadrishya; but is not yet perfectly secure in these qualities. The penetration of manasik sushupti by the ideal thought & perception continues; it is only in the deepest sushupta that nidra or its swapna easily arrives.

Ananda Brahman with vijnanananda in the shuddha continues to grow in hold & force; in the mental darshana vijnana elements tend to become more pronounced.

Physical ananda slowly develops.

Jan 28th Sunday.

There is considerable assault of the intellectuality. Still tapas grows in effectuality and the element of certainty in trikaldrishti remains constant, though it cannot yet grow firmly.

Activity of vishaya & rupadrishya.

Jan 29th

Progress considerable in samadhi, richness of drishya — occasional perfect stability attained in rupa (swapna-samadhi) and frequency of relative stability — frequency and greater firmness of continuous drishya: perfect combination of rupa, shabda, sparsha — the speech as well as sound proceeding from rupa and not merely associated with it. Persistence of continuous event with vague or shadowy rupa, — eg. cutting meat etc. This is even in antardarshi. Substantial progress in antardarshi; fixity of progress made in crude rupa in bahirdarshi.

Physical raudrananda (sahaituka) now normal and general, all touches of discomfort & pain bring their ananda, except in sudden

& strong bahyasparsha of pain; even there the after effects tend to be anandamaya.

Tapas-siddhi against roga is getting stronger, though still not decisive.

Krishna growing stronger in personal Krishna Kali. Kali now normal, old bhava of personality almost entirely destroyed. All the instruments of vijnana are becoming the Ishwara's entirely. Madhuradasya increases.

T^2 still hampered & obscured, but developing.

Samananda hardly at all interfered with; when amangalabodha comes, it is anandamaya; the place of the amangala as a step of the mangalya is usually understood at once.

In second chatusthaya, aishwarya, Mahakali bhava, sraddha swashaktyam, daihik shakti still imperfect, – the rest satisfactory. Daya very strong. Mahalakshmi colour, once quite absent or almost quite, is now very deep. Dasyam is almost absolute, except in certain remnant movements of the intellectual suggestions.

Karma is now stationary, with slight advantage to the hostile forces.

Premananda is beginning to be general & strong, though more ahaituka than sahaituka. It manifests and relapses, then manifests again, but is on the point of becoming normal.

Jan 30 –

Third chatusthaya is now complete, though imperfect. It is most advanced in jnana where it is almost perfect in its more luminous movements.

Script

Today a great movement forwards intended in T^2, samadhi and for breaking of the obstacle in vishaya and rupadrishya.

=

Certainty in T^2 is now becoming rapidly general & normal; but it is only in the main event, not in the details surrounding it which are supplied by telepathic trikaldrishti which [is][8] uncertain

[8] *MS* in

but usually correct, though with certain lowerings & fluctuations, misses and overstresses. The certainty also arises out of telepathic perception & is in its own nature telepathic, that is the certainty that the tapas in Nature will effect the thing seen as the event. There is not yet, except exceptionally, action of pure trikaldrishti or united or identical action of the ideal knowledge & will. With the increase of certainty, the tapasbuddhi is becoming regulated, the tapassiddhi more effective and the sraddha in effectuality increases according to the frequent directions or predictions in the lipi "telepathy, trikaldrishti and tapassiddhi" and "enthusiastic faith in the light, knowledge and effectuality."

=

The degree of pain intensity from bahyaspars at which ananda is possible has been sensibly raised, so much that it promises even complete siddhi of every touch short of those which break, cut, rack or crush the body

=

All the fundamental tastes are established, the bitter, sour, astringent in strength, spontaneity & solidity, frequency & persistence, the sweet rare & less strong except in one touch, the rest intense, but less solid & spontaneous, fairly frequent but not persistent.

Tratak brought the old forms in the pranic air[,] dark & brilliant living spots, shadows of real winged things, & insects & butterflies seen in the body, the first vividly, the second shadowily, but both without detail

—

In Samadhi a movement towards generalisation of the ideality in the depths of mental sushupti—ideal perception, vangmaya, lipi, etc. The jagrat chaitanya has to take possession & sushupti to be shifted upwards out of the mentality.

=

Activity in vishayas, but not yet breaking of the obstacles.

=

Some initial successes, not decisive, in bringing stable developed & dense into jagrat bahirdarshi.

=

All this activity is being indicated in spite of a massed assault
& obstruction which tries to destroy results obtained and prevent
fresh results.
=

Jan 31.
The same programme
T^2 advances; its chief difficulty is to get rid of the intellectual
tapasbuddhi. Mental tejas seems to be definitely taken up into the
tapas.
Premananda continues to develop itself. It is including in itself
by intensity and the spiritual embrace of the physical the shuddha
kamananda

Feb 1.

A higher ideality is now manifesting in the jnanam and takes
up a large part of the thought
T^2 is developing, but still greatly hampered by overstress of
telepathy and tejomaya intellectual tapasbuddhi
A great advance in Samadhi. . The last two days there was the
attempt to normalise the ideal consciousness in manasic sushupti
of the deepest kind, but this was only successful in fragments. Today coherent, continuous and even, in the lighter stages, unceasing
ideal thought vangmaya and perceptive, continuous statement and
speech, continuous action with almost perfectly stable rupa were
brought firmly in and for the most [part] normalised in the deepest
sushupti except perhaps in one layer of strong nidra. Dream is
becoming entirely coherent vision and dream vision is acquiring
the force of real vision. Lipi written before the eyes is coherent
even in sushupti; lipi already written is still incoherent. All this is
in daytime and is only trying to begin in the night
Lipi (antardarshi) is beginning to manifest in long, almost interminable lines and in three lines at a time, but is still in these
circumstances almost illegible from faintness.
The ideality is now more revelatory than inspirational.
The spontaneity of lipi is being made absolute and anticipation by the mind discouraged, other words being substituted

for those fixed by the mind when it escapes from control and anticipates.

Feb. 2

Brief incursion of asukham and ashanti after ineffectual touches during the last two days—announced by lipi—"grief" day before yesterday. A certain violence in it, but no power of stability—rejected by centre of being in the mind & prana & by its bulk: chief effect in surface of prana, touch in heart & mind momentarily forceful, but ineffectual. . Return of T^3 during last two days ending in confusion of T^2

=

In the afternoon again a stronger outbreak of asukham & ashanti with all the old circumstances of revolt against the method of the sadhana and the self-assertion of the Jiva, his refusal of anumati.

=

No progress in samadhi except a stronger tendency to read the written lipi coherently.

Rupa moves in the old rut of crude, usually crude crude, with occasional unstable perfect or half stable imperfect rupas.

=

In the evening a firm foundation of the higher ideality in script, vangmaya and less completely in the perceptive thought, where it is still ill disengaged from the mentality. But the revelation, revelatory inspiration, revelatory intuition, revelatory judgment were all displayed.

Feb 3.

There is a confirmation of the last night's work and the habit of refusal of all that is not reduced to the terms of the higher ideality. This siddhi is extended to the lipi and is being prepared in the tapas.

The Mahakali bhava has taken possession and is being combined with the Mahalaxmi colour.

Ananda is beginning to take possession of the prana and body. It has long been in possession of the chitta and mentality.

The higher perceptive ideality is not yet confirmed owing to deficiency of T^2.

R[eference]

इत्था सोम इन्मदे ब्रह्मा चकार वर्धनं ।
शविष्ठ वज्रिन्नोजसा पृथिव्या [निः शशा अहिं]⁹ अर्चन्नु स्वराज्यं ।

This indicates the possession of the knowledge by the Ananda and the summing up of the work of the Maruts in the revelation of the Indra godhead, divine Mind of vijnana destroying the obstacles summed up in the one Vritra-force

The पाजः of Agni is attempting to become universal and ideal.

═

No definite advance in Samadhi, but wakefulness of the Purusha in mental samadhi is more विभु and has more पाजः and dream was also more attacked by the inner wakefulness, यो सुप्तेषु जागर्ति –

═

Mental, moral, pranic certainties are being reduced to their proper position, deprived of their certainty and shown to be merely probabilities & expectant forces, so that the ground may be clear for the generalisation of ideal certainty. Tapas-siddhi is now at the 50° and there fairly sure of itself and general.

═

The whole mental consciousness is now beginning to be pervaded by a sense of substantial light (jyotih) and the body with a sense of the flowing of a wine, an ecstatic subtle liquor of delight, Soma. The sense of will as a fire, Agni, is sometimes present.

─

There is a strong movement in jagrat rupadrishya towards the development of the dense & developed on the former large scale, but with greater firmness and permanence. As yet however there are only scattered signs, the few developed and perfect or dense & perfect rupas that come being momentary or only having a second's stability in the pranic akasha.

═

---

⁹ *MS* अहिं निः शशा

Great progress, sudden in its definition, though long prepared in tivra ananda. First intensity has much more than doubled its normal force and tends to be decupled. Secondly, the law of the deadening or diminution of tivra by repetition of touch whether slow or rapid, is giving way & may be said to have given way to the law of increase by repetition. The old rule struggles to survive but is suppressed. The tivra maintains itself, if oppressed recovers, usually increases. The law of increase is not yet very strong, but it is born as a law & not, as before, only as an occasional phenomenon and then an often oppressed tendency.

=

Higher ideality has made its way into the perceptive thought in the midst of a general luminous play of inspirational intellectualised ideality (श्रवांसि — मनीषा:). It is now seeking to confirm & generalise itself. Indra is destroying Vritra on the earth, — in the physicality of the mind.

It is attempting to extend itself to all trikaldrishti.

Telepathic trikaldrishti of time

1. The three young men will come before nine; or at least two. vague in detail.

N [Nolini] & M [Moni] came at 8.45

2. N will come before 9.

Uncertain when he came, either just before 9 or just after; within 9.5 at latest.

3. Someone will come at 9.10.

Sn. [Saurin] came at 9.10

4 9.20 named as time of meal — changed to 9.10 by my watch, which is ten minutes slow.

Meal at 9.20 (9.10) or a minute or two earlier — usually at 9.30 or after, rarely so early as 9.20

5. 9.25 (by my watch = 9.35) named — first associated with S's coming, afterwards with finishing of meal. Meal finished at 9.25 exact

Feb. 4.

Script.

Today the higher reality will grow and be confirmed in its possession. The rupadrishya will make a great stride forward by the night. Lipi will advance. T^2 will begin to confirm itself. Kamananda will increase steadily in force from today. The battle for the health will continue. More force will come to the saundarya.

=

In the afternoon a strong attack of the old mentality, accepted yet rejected by the Purusha, which helped finally to put the intellectual movements in their right place.

=

The higher ideality is now at the back of the perceptive thought and will as of all other instruments. Wherever it gives the sanction as a sort of Will-Knowledge, though with more force in it than light because of a certain veil between it in its source and its manifestation in the mind, the thought or will infallibly fulfils itself. The rest has to be regulated and put in its place; for now the truth behind each thought & will is perceived, but not at once in its right relation to the rest and result.

For a while trikaldrishti was almost absolutely perfect, but without certainty.

=

Thespesia.

1. Lipi. feast.

At first misunderstood, afterwards understood rightly, but not with certainty – In the afternoon, long after, the Mahomedan came to arrange for pullao in the evening.

2 Yesterday, prevision of karana this evening. No intention in any mind, yet fulfilled by afternoon event.

3 Today, prevision of the same tomorrow. Contrary to all custom and intention arranged for by event and impulse in every mind but one, although resisted in act by myself. These incidents are decisive of a trikaldrishti which is no longer telepathic or uncertain.

=

Rupadrishya developed force of full dense & developed, but only in the type figure of the bird. In the rest a general tendency to display of the unstable or else imperfect dense & developed. Samadhi is only labouring to confirm and generalise its past gains.

═

Lipi is taking possession of the material trikaldrishti.

═

Kamananda is continually growing in force, but not yet free from dependence on hetu.

═

The will to saundarya is increasing, but as yet without any definite visible result. The habitual rogas still assert their force of persistence and recurrence though not with the old sovereign force.

═

On the whole T^2 is at last firmly founded.

═

R. [Reference]
यद्वाहिष्ठं तदग्नये बृहदर्च विभावसो —

That is to say, the general light in the mentality has to be turned into a large illumination of ideal knowledge which will be a firm support for the ideal will.

═

Prediction. Things — objectivity.

That is, the subjective-objective being now on the road to siddhi, the battle will be more henceforth for the control of things and objects, the bodily, prithivi.

Feb 5.

Script.

"The ideality must be confirmed against such attacks as yesterday's which must rapidly be made impossible

"There must be definite and steady progress in the Shuddha-Ananda-sarva-sundara-darshana on the Ananda-vijnana basis."

═

In the morning sudden efflorescence of a perfect shuddha anandamaya-vijnanamaya vision of universal beauty. Every detail is seen in its perfect, divine sense and faery loveliness and in its place in the whole and the divine symmetry of the whole based on its "brihat" Idea, even in what appears to the mind [un]symmetrical. This was realised in things yesterday, today in faces, figures, actions, etc. It is not yet stable, but strong and returns in spite of the force that depresses the vision and attempts to return to the diffuse mental view of things. In the mental view the general shuddha ananda is ahaituka, even when it is full of feature; in this it is self-existent, yet contains all hetu, guna, rasa = Ananda with vijnana in its embrace.

=

Script

T^2

Ideality in all the instruments

Samadhi

Rupadrishya

Ananda

—

Ideality enlarged its hold on the perceptive thought & intensified its action in the other instruments.

T^2 also developed

=

Trikaldrishti of time

1. 8.5 for first arrival. Incorrect by the watch.
   L arrived at 8.10.
2. Arrival at 8.25
   N & M arrived at 8.25
3. 8.55. Mistaken for time of arrival of Ns.

As it happened, we sat down exactly at 8.55.

General forecast of lateness today justified.

—

Samadhi strengthened itself considerably in continuity, stability, force of manifestation. Rich tejomay scenes appeared. Lipi became firmer. Written lipi & dream reading improved.

=

In jagrat rupadrishya is getting rid gradually of the method of fluid and fluctuating creation of images out of a confused blur of material. In antardarshi trailokyadrishti is attempting to emerge.

=

In Ananda raudra alone made some definite advance.

Feb. 6

Ideality is more and more overcoming the intellectuality which has lost all selfconfidence and only persists when it thinks itself the ideality or inspired by the ideality. This confirms recent lipi — "servant of ideality"

Samadhi confirmed its movement. It is trying to become complete. In jagrat there is still the obstacle and the same movement.

=

Jagrat bahirdarshi is slowly developing force and precision

Trikaldrishti still uncertain among the telepathies, sometimes almost entirely, rarely entirely accurate in all details, usually right in many points, overstressed & therefore wrong in others. — eg

1. Crow running along ledge — telepathic suggestion of its flying up to the parapet, though it ran the contrary way & then returned with constant impulse to fly downwards into the road.

2 Perception that it would not fly downward — fulfilled in spite of repeated impulsions & repeated uncertainty. It flew onto parapet fulfilling (1).

3. Perception that it would fly away in frontal direction. Fulfilled after much uncertainty & hesitation of telepathic perception and with a first movement sideward, justifying the uncertainty

=

Samadhi develops coherency [of] dream reading and dream-event.

=

Attempt to develop primary utthapana. Concentration on physical siddhi — not yet effective.

Feb 7. Wednesday.

Ideality taking up all telepathies; but this brought confusion of telepathic stress, — tejas & tapas — into trikaldrishti tapassiddhi. Though rejected, they insisted.

=

Samadhi is beginning to move towards fullness[,] firmness & sureness

=

Yesterday's time tri.

1. N will come early, take dinner and go out. N came about 8.20 and went just after 9.35 – the latter time seen, but not quite accurately placed; it was considered that he would finish his meal then; he finished at 9.33, went up at 9.35.

2. Ns would come second – he came at about 9 – (a little before) – time wrongly placed by a few minutes.

3. S at 9.5 – he came at 9.3

4. 9.25 & 9.30 named for S's coming and finishing dinner. Both happened at 9.30.

Hour begins to be seen by rupa of watch-hands, eg 11.45 for going to bed.

=

Wednesday's

Much less accurate; nevertheless generally correct.

=

Samadhi developed perfect coherence of dream. What has now to be got rid of is the presence of present personalities & namarupa in dream vision of past & future events.

Absolute stability of chhayamaya rupa. Tejomaya perfect but unstable. Trailokyadrishti begins to develop.

Feb 8.

Continuance of telepathic insistence in the morning. Confidence of intellectuality as representative of ideality destroyed; desire to pose as ideality practically destroyed except as a mechanical past habit. In the afternoon ideality resumed its expansion, completing more largely what it had begun before the interruption [–] the taking up of telepathy & putting it in its right place for T^2.

=

In jagrat bahirdarshi stable developed & dense are beginning to manifest spontaneously in type rupa; perfect rupa (life) manifested, also in the type rupa, with the power but not the fact of stability.

=

Coherent lipi is founding itself in the samadhi, both ready written and consecutive. Reading remains.

Tejomaya is beginning to develop.

Perceptive ideal thought is taking firm hold of mental sushupti. Results perceived before commencing samadhi.

In vishaya and antardarshi the obstruction remains quite unbroken.

=

The highest ideality is manifesting through the veil.

=

The normal intensity of tivra is greatly increasing. Two new movements are beginning to define themselves, (1) a prolongation of tivra after cessation of touch, by repeated recurrence, not yet by continuity; (2) simultaneous tivra and raudra. Also there is a visible preparation of general tivra-sthiti.

=

Time.

No accuracy.

(1) General perception that all but one would come early; between 8.30 & 9. Three & L came at 8.35.

(2) Perception of early meal—9.5 or 9.10. Meal at 9.5

—

Samadhi

Dream coherence; lipi; attempt at coherent dream reading

—

Feb 9

Attack of old intellectuality and asamata throughout the day. Confused progress.

=

Ananda intensifies in vaidyuta, kama, raudra. Intensity is becoming normal. Kama much resisted.

=

Energetic tapas for removal of chronic ailments. It seems to be dominating in one direction; in the others doubtful. No progress as to chakra-shakti.

Samadhi again overpowered by nidra, still attempts to generalise chaitanya of the vijnanamaya in the mental sushupti and arrive at brihat. Jagrat relapses.

=

The secret or one secret of incoherent lipi etc in swapna is now found to be false combination. The thought is now able sometimes to correct the combination; by correction perfect coherence emerges.

=

There is still a fluctuation between the deadening of ananda by constant sparsha and the increasing by constant or repeated sparsha; the former intervenes, the latter begins, recurs and tends eventually to prevail. It is stronger in the tivra than in the other anandas.

=

Time.

=

(1) At 9 – some will come between 9. & 9.15 by watch
M came before 9.10.
(2) At 9.10. N will come separately from S. and next
N came at 9.13
(3) At 9.13. Ns. will come at 9.25. dinner 9.30 perhaps 9.35 (without regard to watch)
Ns came at 9.26 by clock below; dinner at 9.36.
(4) After 9.30 – S will come close on 10. S. came at 9.55 or thereabouts.
Clock vision. 10.19, direction, not prediction. . fulfilled.

=

Samadhi resisted – confirmed some of its gains, but with less force. However, combination of sparsha and drishti perfectly & repeatedly emphasised; also dream-reading and continuity of drishya in action.

Feb 10

Result of yesterday's attack – telepathy & mental tapas deprived of all force of certainty. Telepathy correct when seen as force, intention, what is trying to fulfil itself. When sanctioned from above, then fulfilled. The sanction is sometimes perceived; but there are also mental sanctions which only give an added force for fulfilment, but not certainty or else force for subsequent fulfilment. Even the higher sanction is not to be considered absolute, unless it is the luminously ideal sanction.

=

Therefore mental certainty is abrogated and non-existent. Ideal certainty is temporarily suspended

=

The instruments, except perceptive thought, are free now from the remnants of intellectuality.

=

There are three planes of ideality. The third or lowest regards the intellect, corrects and fulfils it. The first is absolutely independent. The second is intermediate.

=

Samadhi reaffirmed most of its gains against massed and violent obstruction; but with an inferior force of vividness and largeness. Obstruction successful against lipi and tejomaya drisya. Dream-reading of printed book began. Afterward lipi reaffirmed in jagrat antardarshi.

=

Script.
The difficulty of certainty arises from the refusal to affirm more than from the haste to affirm wrongly. Affirm and correct.

=

This being done, knowledge with Tapas proved to be invariably right in main issue; telepathy (knowledge without tapas) of details sometimes certain and correct, sometimes uncertain.

=

Violent tapas, long forbidden because rajasic or mental, is now being applied with success.

The ideal Tapas-knowledge is being more widely applied but the incertainty of the untransformed telepathies creates a strong obstacle to its ideal use.

=

Rupadrishya emphasises developed, dense and perfect, but only in the type.

=

What is called riot of the lipi develops, this time without the old effort and confusion or with only a shadow of it. It is not yet perfect, being often stable, but illegible or legible but unstable

=

Contacts now create kamananda response as well as the other anandas. . Kamananda is trying to generalise itself (ahaituka) in the body. The movement is as yet occasional only.

=

Various complete rupas even to the most developed manifest at night with great spontaneity but with no stability. The stable are always imperfect and incomplete, usually crude, sometimes dense, never developed.

=

There is a general growth of ideality taking up the telepathies[,] revealing their truth, their right relations and limits, correcting the errors of the mind's valuations and interpretations.

=

Samadhi, reaffirms continuity of action; stability of chhaya-maya forms and scenes, variety; begins to develop more stable though less brilliant tejomaya; continues dream coherence but is still subject to the obstruct[ive] attempt at limitation and dislodgment from its gains.

=

Antardarshi yesterday developed variety of forms, some of them perfect, stable, in status and motion, complete; though mostly crude. (reel, dense; bed, [?crude] in status, birds in motion magnified, in status, book, etc). Today violently obstructed and sterile.

Feb 11. Sunday.
Telepathy, brihat, confused in ritam, though greatly increased in ritam; entirely satyam in the sense of being true in essence, though misapplied in fact. Tapas has still an effect perturbing to the ritam by its mental overstress. .

=

Telepathy = trikaldrishti steadily increases, but tapasic over-stress of will in the suggested thought prevents as yet entire amalgamation of tapas = trikaldrishti, which is meant by T^2. The illumination of Tapas is, however, progressing, though with a more hampered movement.

=

Tapas is now being used for primary utthapana & the nature & laws of primary utthapana are being developed in the thought and initially brought in the body, though constantly borne down by the normal physical nature.

The nature of it is liberation from exhaustion, weariness, strain and all their results.

The laws are

(1) Standing, however long, shall be effectively as much a rest from motion as [sitting][10] or lying down.

(2) Lying down as a rest shall cease to be indispensable.

(3) The greater and more prolonged the motion, the greater the increase of force for continued motion.

It is evident that if the last is accomplished, the first will be unnecessary and the second will be fulfilled.

At present stiffness as an after result is reduced to a minimum, but muscular pain and sense of strain after persistent exercise of muscles in walking (especially in shoulders & neck) persist. Immediate exhaustion can be very rapidly cast out, but accumulative effect is still painful.

The general pranic force increases by sadhana, but the body is affected and through the body the most physical part of the pranakosha.

=

Lipi "Telepathy is the effective trikaldrishti." That is what is seen by the foreseeing & willing knowledge becomes effective force, feeling, impulse, etc and is perceived by the Manas. That is telepathy. What is foreseen is also forewilled—thus sight & will in the Knowledge coincide.

[10] MS standing

What was seen by the manas, is now beginning to be seen by the ideal mind into which the manas is being withdrawn or changed.

=

The tapas is moving towards its self-harmonising with the supreme Will in the matter of Time both as to final result and detail of stages in the evolution of the result.

=

Accumulative fatigue is being massed and emphasised in order to be exhausted more rapidly and attacked more completely by the Tapas.

The exhaustion felt was very great, so much that the body insisted on the need of recumbence to ease the back, but a few minutes afterwards – after half an hour's sitting – all had gone, activity returned, wine of anandamaya tapas was felt in the body and the tables were rearranged, dusted and motion kept up for an hour and a quarter with return of pain in the shoulder and neck and with unease in the physical nerve matter, but without the sense of dominating fatigue, rather of dominating vigour. Nor is there now any inclination in the Prana to rest.

=

All thought (not trikaldrishti), even what was formerly the discursory vagabondage of the mind, is becoming luminous, ideal and true in its limits.

Raudra Ananda is developing. Sharp & long-running muscular pain three times repeated, which would formerly have been felt as torture, was entirely anandamaya; the sharp pain in the neck-muscles is also being transformed. The prolonged contact of heat (the burning terrace floor at noon) was yesterday borne and turned into ananda-pain.

=

Time – Seen that the three would come late, long after 11 and the dinner be late, after 12. Came at 11.40 – dinner at 12.30.

Sharp hunger conquered, but not abolished, nor actually turned into anandamaya bubhuksha; but this movement seems to be beginning.

Continued walking, half an hour; pain in neck-muscles suddenly abolished, though left in subtle form and power of revival.
Afterwards it attempted to develop in the legs and partly succeeded;
when tapas is withdrawn, fatigue declares itself.

Rupasiddhi is successfully developing variety in the crude.
Formerly only a few types came with difficulty or easily only by
repetition – the woman, the horse, the man on horseback or driving,
sometimes groups of men [and] women, two horses and riders – the
bird (crow or sparrow), butterfly or moth, one or two objects, a
hill with figures or a building on it. Now many kinds of fourfooted
animals, birds, insects, moths of various forms and hues. Others
seem to be coming, fish, variety of objects, not yet variety of scenes
& human figures.

After swapna samadhi this has increased; already, all sorts of
fourfooted beasts – the thing most resisted till now – while variety
of figures (boys, a man's face and head with hat) has begun, variety
of scenes is trying to manifest; old forms which were vague (horse
with carriage) are now becoming clear and complete. These shapes
have usually little stability, swift variation, a trend to momentary
precision. Sometimes they are precise and have an initial stability,
sometimes more stability with precision and perfect completeness,
but this is rare. Now however an attempt to combine precision,
completeness and stability with the variety has begun.

Samadhi

Antardarshi. A certain variety of forms, but not clear & perfect
as day before yesterday, except one or two, and not stable. Riot of
varied lipi, not organised, but trying to organise itself.

Swapna. All perfect in swapna except richness of scenes &
images. Coherent lipi, perceptive & vangmaya thought.

Sushupti. Fluctuates between confusion and coherence.

Dream-speech, narrative with lipi, lipi, etc.

It is notable that in daytime nidra is usually entirely absent,
except for an occasional fleeting touch which today did not come.
Even at night sushupti is beginning to replace nidra. In place of the

sense of being asleep or the memory of it, there is the sense and memory of sushupti, full of shanti, ghana chaitanya and now of incipient ananda.

Pages for reading are being presented with more firmness, not yet with much success.

In jagrat bahirdarshi variety of scenes is beginning eg a house above a ghat, the ghat very clear, the house sufficiently & coloured; a bridge over a stream, a boy upon it not sufficiently clear and vivid; a temple and ghat and road—the same & high bank of a river. Other scenes longer and more detailed, but vague.

Variety of human figures increased, women, children, young men, boys (youth & beauty predominate) in various postures, groups, scenes, action. Variety of birds and insects and fish is developing. A great variety of buildings of all forms and structures, chiefly in colour, when not in prakasha.

Thus the poverty of the crude rupa seems to be at an end.

Raudra ananda is increasing greatly in frequency, intensity and even in prolonged intensity. Vaidyuta also tends to develop. Vishaya is strong and general, but in intensity tends to pass into the others.

Prolonged intensity of pain (internal, ahaituka and sahaituka) no longer overpowers the ananda; it increases it, merges into it or turns into it. Also pain is now seldom separate from the ananda; it does not come and cause it whether at the moment of the touch or after the touch has seized it, but is amalgamated with it. It is either anandamaya pain or pain-ananda or pure raudra ananda. Even in strong pain from outside touches, eg burning, this tends to be the rule. The old separation is only an occasional survival. Discomfort is following the same rule, but has not gone so far towards absorption.

Strong attack on the siddhi. Results

(1) Violent reaction against primary utthapana, but the utthapana was forcefully depressed in the body, not abolished even in the physical prana; and revived and resumed work though with a wounded force.

(2) Reaction in arogya. One of the chronic rogas which was on the point of abolition, reasserted tendencies of recurrence, but with a minimum force producing very slight material results. Another which was being depressed, revived, but still with less force than in former reaffirmations.

(3) Temporary return of phantasy and ideal intellectuality in perceptive thought, quickly removed. A quite momentary touch in one or two of the vijnana instruments, immediately gone.

(4) A shadow upon the faith, ineffective in the faith of siddhi. Faith of karma is still immature and uncertain.

(5) Obstruction of the lipi, samadhi, rupasiddhi, only partially effective.
=

Variety of scenes, mountains, valleys, river banks, oceans, with human figures, ships etc, but all vague, pallid and indistinct, though the objects are recognisable. Initial movement to variety of objects. All this in the crude, mostly crude crude, sometimes dense crude.
=

Samadhi. First combination of absolute stability of perfect scene with absolutely firm continuity of action in clearly seen perfect rupa. A street of picturesque houses, a woman in blue walking down the street to the end, joined at the end by a woman in green.

Second complete scene; a richly furnished room; only momentarily stable.

This marks a great advance in rupa power, for this combination has always been successfully resisted; either the scene was shifting and unstable and vague or if stable and clear, void of action and motion.
=

Feb 12.

Continued effect of yesterday's denial of utthapana. Strong sweat in the heat of the sun to get rid of toxic matter generated by fatigue. N.B. Usually, exposure to heat produces no such sweat or very little. The utthapana-shakti persists in spite of denial; it does not, as it formerly used, collapse and acknowledge defeat, except apparently for an hour or less.

=

The attack on growing arogya also continues. Sensitiveness to cold and discomfort returned.

=

Ideality is taking hold of the interpretation of lipi; only the intellectual atmosphere still surrounds it. This, according to the lipi, is to be removed by tonight.

Ideality is also taking firm hold of telepathy in connection with trikaldrishti. All telepathy of the kind is now correctly understood in substance; the sole disturbing factor is the remnants of the mental tendency to fix event by the mind choosing one of the possibilities or tendencies or intentions thus seen as *the* event. Often this is done correctly, the possibility being properly valued, but then the method breaks down. If this can be removed, there will be no farther positive obstacle to correct certainty in the trikaldrishti; though some negative obstacles will remain.

All this is in the field of exercise, not yet applied to life and the world at large.

=

Tapasic mind action, = will stress in the knowledge or effective mind action is being idealised and taught the truth within it and its limits as well as its possibilities.

=

Intensity of self caused sahaituka tivra is greatly increasing. In the physical Ananda all the movements recorded are being more generalised and normalised, but most of them are not perfectly general and most fluctuate, sometimes manifest, sometimes are suspended.

=

In Antardarshi lipi developed, but its abundance cannot yet organise itself without the help of the interpretation which is becoming ideal in the antardarshi as well as in the bahirdarshi, in samadhi as well as in waking.

Rupa became more vivid in antardarshi with groups and a long though interrupted stability of scene, but instability of human

figures. It would be easy to develop a great variety of vague, imperfect, instable figures, but both in inner and outer jagrat vision
this is being rejected and combined precision, stability and variety
is being insistently demanded.

=

Rupas of yesterday, of all kinds, but a few or one or two of
each, in spite of the obsession of the akasha by the type rupa, which
again appeared strongly in all forms, except the perfect or lifelike.
The higher forms appear freely only after long watching of the
living object. Stability + precision is not yet satisfactory (outside
type rupa) except in one or two forms.

=

Source of ideal certainty has appeared, tapas-light, and is
beginning to group round it[s] certainty telepathies of the stages
and their tendencies. The movement is as yet kachcha. It was
interrupted by a violent, rather brief attack of mental tapas
which left the telepathy much freer than before from false incidence. Brief physical touches of asamata, strong but without
body. The attempt is now to abandon all tapas except the ideal
will-knowledge.

=

Physical asiddhi continues, but the siddhi also, though over-
weighted, persists.

=

Free play of crude rupa on larger dimensions, at night, in
artificial light, combining precision and stability, though in various
degrees, with variety; all kinds of forms, but quadrupeds few and
human figures only in the old form. Greater variety of objects,
utensils chiefly. Scenes not yet developed in this kind.

Some stable dense forms bear the gaze and remain complete;
one of them turns to developed. Till now complete dense & developed forms were unstable.

=

Samadhi failed both afternoon and night, except for play of
ideal thought in swapna and jagrat (afternoon).

Feb 13.

Temporary suspension of ideality, for a certain development of first two chatusthayas amounting to forceful samata and combination of ugrata and dasya. Caused by a circumstance throwing life siddhi into doubt. This endured till nearly noon when the ideality began again to play. It has firmly acquired certain elements of certainty of event, but for the most part it is composed of certainties of ideal telepathy.

Thought telepathy is beginning to take shape and justify itself in a less scattered fashion, more habitually and organically.

=

The habit of evolving rupas out of a confused blur of material, one changing into another before it was well formed, most not developing properly, many only hinting themselves, others confused together, is being again discouraged. Only figures which present precision first, then precision + stability are accepted. Variety is at the same time being demanded. As the result of yesterday's crude progress, the delineation of entirely perfect stable crude figures is gaining strength, frequency and variety.

=

Antardarshi is at last taking into itself the bahirdarshi gains; but stability & precision are not yet properly combined, neither being quite perfect in itself. Variety is great and scenes and colours are more vividly depicted.

It is noticeable that the physical light still makes a difference; when the room is open, the atmosphere of the antardarshi is luminous and the forms & scenes tejomaya and vivid; when two of the windows are closed, it is chhayamaya and the scenes and forms vague and chhayamaya though vaster, more full of unseen details.

At first samadhi was [?received] by the lower nature but the Will as Shakti (now manifest as the Ishwari in the Samadhi) insisted and prolonged samadhi with important results followed

(1) Ideal thought is now at ease in all realms of the mental samadhi, fluent, coherent, dealing even in the sushupti largely, consecutively, powerfully, grasping and solving problems the waking mind had missed. This is done though there is nothing awake in the mind except the inactive Sat-Purusha who hardly

even watches, is merely bharta. All is done by the supreme Shakti from above.

At first the ideal thought failed and broke off in sushupti owing to nidra, but the Shakti insisting, the thought resumed, *without coming back to swapna,* in the sushupti itself. Still in the deepest depth of all, there is still a little difficulty in eliminating nidra.

(2) Recently, the samadhi has developed the power of being in sushupti and yet receiving clear sense knowledge of the waking world — limited to one or two sounds etc — without for that ceasing to be sushupta. Today this developed into a triple Samadhi, the Ishwari sushupta, full there of ideal thought and absorbed consciousness, yet aware of another swapna consciousness open to a second plane of action and another conscious without living in it of things in the outer world

(3) Consciousness of the supramental Ishwari, the Shakti of which the mental Jiva is a mental personality

The Akasha still resists the rupadrishti. It can no longer persist long in denying forms to the eye; but it still perseveres ordinarily in the blur method and is more ready to give precision than stability. It yields free variety of forms only when quick succession is allowed and complete precision is not demanded, and even then with a certain reluctance, a preference of forms that have been often repeated, a tendency to deny those, eg quadrupeds, which it has been in the habit of denying.

Formerly, the principle was to form by mental-physical pressure images out of akashic material, the material being of seven kinds, — chhaya, dhuma, tejas, jyoti, varna, agni, prakasha. The result was a blur of material shaping itself into forms. A second method was sudden manifestation of form partial or complete out of other akashas into the physical.

The second is now preferred. Mental and physical pressure are abandoned except when they recur involuntarily as a habit. Ideal will only is used.

=

Depression of the physical in the evening in the mental shama. Quiescence of all progress.

Feb 14th

Recoil of the siddhi, owing to perception of *anrita* in what professed to be the *ritam*; this comes by excessive and therefore wrong affirmation. Attempt henceforth neither to overstress affirmation nor to linger in negation. Right affirmation of the truth in or behind all thought and perception is the secret. But the difficulty must not be underrated, nor achievement too easily announced.

=

There is greater spontaneity with a certain amount of variety, precision, stability in the rupa. But the stability is less than the precision, the variety comes still with difficulty. The terrestrial akasha is overborne, but not yet conquered and possessed.

Antardarshi still lingers amid difficulties. Scenes and objects come, but without clarity of precision or clear stability or ease of variety.

In Samadhi yesterday's experience reaffirmed, but with a less powerful grasp on the sushupti. On the other hand, the triple Samadhi has developed. Not only are sushupti, swapna and jagrat simultaneous, but the sushupta purusha or shakti not only observes, but judges the jagrat experiences and, initially at least, the swapna perceptions.

=

Telepathy grows in brihat & satyam in the field of exercise, but ritam is a little discouraged.

=

Samadhi (sitting) of a lighter kind than in the afternoon, but the same type and a strengthening of the jagrat in conjunct[ion] with sushupti or swapna or both; swapna stronger, sushupti lighter. Attempt to regularise firmly lipi, etc. in sushupti. At night rich and brilliant (jyotirmaya) rupadrishya in swapna of sushupti.

Record of Yoga
Feb 1917

Feb 15

Programme laid down in script on 14th

(1) Today T^2 combination of knowledge-tapas

From 15th to 28th perfectioning of knowledge-tapas

(2) Today. Spontaneity of rupa-drishya with tendency to precision + variety + stability.

From 15th to 28th perfectioning of spontaneous precision-variety-stability.

(3) Today – breaking down of habit of relapse in samadhi

Completion of elimination of relapse and normalising of the elements of the samadhi

(4) Vishaya.

Breaking down of the obstacle. Evolution of general, spontaneous and varied vishaya.

These for the third chatusthaya

For the fourth

(1) Ananda.

Today; commence regularising kamananda.

From 15th to 28th regularising of kamananda – the others to arise out of it and it to arise out of others. They will also be generalised separately

(2) Arogya.

Elimination of blood-asuddhi confirmed. The stomach to be regulated.

(3) Utthapana

The battle of the primary utthapana to proceed towards victory.

(4) Saundarya

The obstacle to youth and saundarya to be more vigorously and successfully attacked.

=

T^2.

The shakti continues the elimination of mental stress in the telepathies.

(1) That which is perceived by mental prakamya vyapti is tendency, impulsion, intention, force etc. The mental tapas tries to turn it into fact without knowing whether, how, when, to what extent it is destined. The telepathy must simply observe without willing; but it must observe the force for fulfilment as well as the fact of intention etc.

(2) That which mental tapas wills, mental intelligence hopes, believes, is certain will happen — when it does not unduly negate. Mental tapas, awaiting its elimination and transformation into ideal tapas, has to feel itself only as a force and await fulfilment or nonfulfilment.

(3) However often or even invariably mental tapas or telepathy may be fulfilled, it must not be trusted; but simply observed. Only ideal knowledge-will must be trusted. .

This is what is now being brought into actuality.

=

Kamananda

Regularity commenced yesterday in customary posture, but not perfect. This morning regularised without regard to posture, sitting, walking, standing, but of varying intensity, sometimes intense, sometimes almost nil, though always potentially present and manifest as potentiality

=

Rupadrishya.

Only a small number of images come with a little difficulty, others, eg, quadrupeds, with great difficulty and no completeness or no stability. The whole represents a small variety, though of all kinds, and all the other abundance of images brought out during a moment of siddhi do not emerge, except a few, rarely.

=

T²

T² is now aiming at the development of ideal certainty, not only in the field of exercise, but in life, and with application to time and circumstance. It has already begun, but enveloped still with a confused mist of groping mentality.
=

K.A.

Kamananda continues striving against a suspensive obstruction which sometimes overpowers it and against the absence of smarana.
=

Phantasy is being brought forward in order to be destroyed.
=

Lipi.

Lipi is much more organised and now often vividly legible and stable.
=

Samadhi.

Keeps its gains and is attempting as yet without success to remanifest the perfection of its other constituents and perfect those which were still deficient.
=

Tapas.

Ishita is growing visibly in force, but is still too mental. Aishwarya is nearer ideality.

K.A

Kamananda recovered force at night and remained steady.
=

Samadhi.

Strong, frequent, almost generalised stability and continuity, but chhayamaya, often vague, sometimes with great force of outline and detail, but always shadowy. Attempt to read perfectly stable printed page in very minute type; only one brief sentence suddenly magnified and legible. Tejomaya still unstable and infrequent. .

Feb. 16. Friday.

Lipi continues with a tendency to fix itself, but is yet resisted by the physical akasha.

The lipi is rapidly organising itself. First it has come sparingly making itself precise. Here there are two movements. In one suggestion, no longer intellectual, but ideal, helps the lipi to manifest, but it is then legible, yet not vivid, with a relative stability and only becomes vivid and stable by repetition; but it comes swiftly and writes itself out fluently. In the other movement it comes of itself, without assistance of suggestion, but slowly, sparingly; it is then usually very vivid, legible, spontaneous, stable — not with a long stability, but sufficient to be clearly read and held.

Subsequently there has come, with the assistance of suggestion, with all the characteristics of the first movement, [?   ] but are imperfectly realised to vividness. Now it is emphasising this tendency and preparing to reject entirely the help of the suggestion. By suggestion is meant now the ideal mind's perception of what the lipi is going to write or intends in its sense, but has not yet written.

=

K.A.

Kamananda is not so vivid as yesterday, but has a greater natural persistence in trying to manifest itself uninterruptedly. In this it does not yet succeed.

=

Arogya

The battle of the arogya still continues; the force of health increases and the tapas for health, but the undominated roga tendencies still hold the body against it. The one dominated attacks sometimes with energy, but its physical results are scattered and feeble.

The main struggle now is over the digestion and assimilation where there has been a setback.

=

Sharira

The other physical siddhis are in the same state as before, except that there seems to be some return of primary utthapana and dissipation of the physical depression of fatigue.

=

Samadhi

Samadhi in the afternoon has been rich and successful.

(1) Antardarshi; a great freedom and variety of rupa, chiefly human groups and sometimes scenes, brilliant, tejomay, often coloured, but extremely unstable in a floating varnamaya atmosphere. Scenes of the heavens of mental ananda.

(2) In swapna and sushupti all the elements, but not free in their manifestation, except continuity and stability of chhayamaya. Tejomaya has begun to be stable as chhayamaya tejomaya or tejomaya chhayamaya. At a higher level of tejas, it is sometimes stable, but only when the consciousness is not turned upon it; then it fades into the shadowy tejomaya.

Lipi in all three stages, but not copious; three kinds (1) self-writing, (2) written, (3) printed.

=

T^2

T^2 continues to idealise the telepathies, but more to justify them even intellectually by reducing them to their right proportions. It is noticeable that mental tapas-telepathy is now much more frequently and often much more rapidly effectual. It seems even as if the time obstacle were beginning to come under control.

=

Vijnana

A great rush of ideality, jyotirmaya, higher, highest as well as lower taking up and transfiguring the intellect remnants into the light of truth. Mostly timeless idealities, in jnana, not yet except slightly in trikaldrishti and then without reference to time.

=

Darshana

The Anandamaya darshana has been steadily increasing and generalising itself, but more often contains vijnana of mentality than the vijnana-ananda proper. This however is also increasing in force and frequency and is general enough, though not yet universal in objects. It is still in human figures that the vision of the vijnanamaya sarva-saundarya finds still a difficulty in manifesting or, if manifested, in ascending into the shuddha ananda without losing itself.

$=$

Rupa.

Rupa enforced variation in images seen in a relative darkness – on the terrace.

Feb 17.

Obstruction in the third chatusthaya. Negative sadhana.

$=$

Samadhi.

At first strong and persistent *nidra*, but with elements of samadhi enforcing themselves in the midst of the *nidra*

Afterwards samadhi.

(1) Ideal perceptive thought attained to the same abundance, fluency, continuity, power even in deepest sushupti as the vangmaya had already attained. Neither now needs to descend from the higher to the deeper states; both can act freely and initially even in the deepest.

(2) Power of physical action even in the deep sushupti. The particular action was writing with the hand what occurs in the thought. At first the consciousness dwelt on the thought and the action was mechanical; afterwards it dwelt on both the thought and the action united, continuous, unbroken

(3) Coherence in deepest sushupti even of the reading, lipi, dream speech, dream narrative. Concordance of successive scenes.

(4) Visions of chhayaloka, with light on incoherence of thought and action, visual hallucination etc. (eg. cat prolonged in leaping on table by persistence of sukshma image, pail of water about to be thrown on a table with books etc)

Ananda

Kamananda afflicted with frequent discontinuity.

Raudra touch anandamaya even when intolerable (extreme heat of terrace floor to the feet).

$=$

Rupa.

First, refusal of images, then persistence of blur unable to take shape, then inconstancy of images changing into each other, sometimes before complete formation. All these are being discouraged by failure.

The tendency to variety of images, less or more various, partly or entirely precise, initially stable or unstable seems to be now fixed in the physical akasha. The type still persists in usurping the place of the others, but with less force.

=

T^2

T^2 deals still with telepathies removing from even the most positive all decisive certainty.

=

Arogya

Asiddhi of the digestive process is still in possession.

=

Rupa

Greater freedom of dense rupas sometimes lifelike in the daylit atmosphere.

Samadhi

Great dream coherence. Only in dream reading is the incoherence still dominant.

Feb 18.
T^2

T^2 is now taking up telepathies on a larger scale and more rapidly. The siddhi attempted is to receive mental telepathies rapidly in great number without attaching to any one of them a decisive certainty or seeking for their fulfilment, secondly, to accept every telepathy and discover rapidly its ideal truth and exclude the mental error associated with it.

=

Rupa

Rupa is attempting to develop spontaneous and perfectly precise and complete images with variety. The tendency to frequency of dense, even developed images, sometimes lifelike, but unstable except when sadhara, continues.

=

Devibhava

Mahakalibhava seems to be now normal and the reversion to Mahaluxmi-Mahasaraswati empty of it, is rare. But there is variation between raw Mahakali bhava too ugra and saumya Mahakali with Mahaluxmi colour. Maheshwari, normally, is quite covered and a *pratistha* only.

=

Kamananda seems to be recovering force of continuity and even of intensity, though not the full force.

=

Samadhi.

(1) Antardarshi. Chhayamaya scenes, a railway line by a precipice, a train speeding up and back far out of sight, a path among mountains or moors or between two precipices with a cavalcade going, a two horsed carriage advancing, a horseman turning to fight, groups on foot, etc. Mountain scenes. A lake with a boat and a woman; the same with bird or a fish leaping. All vague and shadowy and yet every image clear enough to be recognizable; often a shoot of shadowy distinctness.

(2) Coherency of dream reading insisted on and constantly enforced, though still with a certain effort and difficulty. Lipi very coherent and continuous in nidra; so too dream thought, as opposed to ideal thought, dream speech, all dream connections.

=

Rupa.

The blur habit seems now to be definitely going out; the tendency of image formation overpowers it and is dominant; but the habit of rapidly inconstant, incongruous, ill combined or only partially successful formations still persists. Also, the customary incapacities, eg of formation of quadrupeds, try to persist; though it is often overpowered, it makes itself felt.

Still, the variety with sufficient precision for a recognition of the object is established. Even variety with perfect precision and completeness, natural and without effort, is frequent; stability

combined with these though comparatively rare, is still not absolutely infrequent.

=

T^2

Sudden development of tapas siddhi; exact place and manner
of movement was manifested repeatedly, and even three rapidly
successive times in the same object, without resistance, only a pause,
very brief. This is 80° power of tapas. The fourth time there was
resistance and wrong place (direction) but right manner and upshot.

There is again an attempt to combine telepathy with ideal
certainty, largely but not entirely successful.

Samadhi.

There is now a struggle to create the same general rule of
coherence and continuity at night in the sleep, as in the daytime, in
the involuntary as in the willed samadhi.

=

Kamananda stronger today, but discouraged in the evening

=

Feb 19 Monday.
Ananda.

Sparsha now as a rule creates a triple Ananda, tivra-vishaya-
kama, one or other sometimes predominating and leading, or else
all three equal and practically simultaneous. Sometimes one tends
to overpower the others.

=

Arogya.

The struggle in the Arogya continues to be immediately adverse
to the siddhi. Physically depression returns persistently, the old roga
that had been abolished returns slightly, the asiddhi of digestion still
continues.

=

Samadhi

Afflicted by nidra. Some development of tejomaya.

=

T².

T² pursues its work of taking up the telepathies. Some development of distant telepathies, the object being far or unseen.

=

K.A.

Kamananda strong in recurrence, not yet continuous throughout the day; but it seems to have overcome the old habit of long suspension. It is now only depressed or suppressed for short periods, within the day itself.

Feb 20th. Tuesday.

A certain inactivity of the siddhi or lessened activity during the last two days — partly owing to preoccupation with "Arya". At the same time there is a great increase of certainty and accuracy in the idealised telepathies and a slow but steady growth of force of effectuality in tapas.

=

Lipi is almost free from the aid of suggestions and manifests itself more or less vividly, usually in a stable legibility fluent or strong; but not with freedom in its perfection. Fluent, it tends still to be a little indistinct.

=

Samadhi infructuous, afternoon and night, except for some development of tejomaya

=

Rupa struggles to develop variety in the stable precise (crude) but is also strongly obstructed.

=

Kamananda less strong; persistent with a dull largeness rather than intensity in asana.

=

Physical depression has the upper hand of the primary utthapana.

=

The struggle in arogya sadhana continues.

=

The whole physical siddhi is for the time being more or less held up as were the other chatusthayas at the same stage.

=

Ananda darshana progresses slowly towards normalising of the global ananda, but as yet attains no finality of the movement.

=

The fifth chatusthaya is also obstructed. In all obstruction, however, there is now some sense of progress prepared.

Feb 21st

The movement towards generalisation of ideality continues. The movement is towards elimination of the critical intellect, the mind of doubt, and its replacing by the ideal judgment.

=

Obstruction of third chatusthaya has been strong for the last three days. Nothing fresh achieved. A strong preparation of advance in Brahmachatusthaya.

=

Kamananda continues, but less continuous. It is strong only in asana. There is some tendency to the renewal of advance in other anandas which are in no way thrown back, but a little quiescent.

Arogya in the half-abolished affection seems to be getting the upper hand. It is still oppressed by the old habitual inequalities in the assimilation, though for the time less intensely. The other members of the physical siddhi are obstructed or depressed.

=

Nothing in samadhi except in bahirdarshi jagrat greater tendency to freedom of unstable dense & developed, solitary intrusion of dense into antardarshi which otherwise is oppressed in lipi, no advance in swapna-sushupti, but less force of nidra.

=

Purification of tapas is proceeding; the tendency is to get rid of the remnants of tapastya and tapatya.

Feb 22^{d}

Some activity of samadhi in the early morning. Coherence of reading and lipi is here the one siddhi most often distressed.

=

Attack of the old breast pain; at first only in sukshma (pranic) parts, ineffectually touching from time to time the surface of the annakosha. This for a long time. Then a physical attack unprecedentedly rapid in its repetitions of intense pain. Ananda (raudra) maintained itself with difficulty, sometimes overborne but always repossessing the pain. The attack very soon cast out; formerly it would have lasted an hour. Remnants, dull, are still left in recurrence or more often the attempt to recur.

=

Fear of disease and death is practically abolished; touches only come from outside. The physical shrinking from intense pain is still able to affirm itself in a subdued, but effective fashion. The prana is touched by it, but not the mind.

=

Complete unification of all the anandas of darshana on their mental basis. Frequent affirmation of chidghana, intense or less intense. Its universalisation may now shortly be expected, since no images or objects, faces or figures can now be successfully free from it.

=

Rupa is remanifesting with a greater tendency to dense crude and dense Prakasha of the seven kinds. Hitherto in the last movement of the siddhi Prakasha has almost monopolised the field of the crude rupa. Now real chhaya has begun again to manifest.

Stable and precise rupa is increasing its force of manifestation. There are notable scenes of a vividness and ensemble superior to almost anything previously manifested in the jagrat without adhara. Others are less vivid & stable, but all have the tendency.

Samadhi remanifests in almost all its features, but with some difficulty and still without sufficient force. Nidra is almost absent, but deep sushupti is refused.

Antardarshi has begun again to manifest with a greater unful-filled promise of abundance but not yet freely, except in chhaya-maya landscapes. One alone was tejomaya.

=

T^2 is still mostly quiescent.

=

Roga is attacking in a curious fashion suddenly, without im-mediate cause, through the sukshma, usually between sleep and waking; it vanishes as abruptly, without evident reason, except the pressure of the will, but leaving behind it slight vestiges. This is the old attempt to reinforce a malady which still has force of recurrence and make it chronic. In the morning it was breast-pain, in the afternoon cough and cold.

23^d–24th

T^2 develops the perfect ideality of the telepathies into stuff of trikaldrishti.

=

Otherwise things remain in status quo or obstructed,—espe-cially samadhi.

Feb. 25th

The idealisation of the telepathies is finally confirmed. The intellectual are now only a mechanical survival and when they occur make no attempt to know, but passively record suggestions as suggestions. It is only when will is applied, that they recur to their old nature of seeking to anticipate fulfilment or non-fulfilment.

Renewed activity of the samadhi. Preparation for conscious vijnana-samadhi. Continuity of action and stability of scene are now firmly established.

A great lessening of the physical asiddhi in its generality, though in certain directions it is still felt heavily.

Vishaya is still heavily obstructed and practically inactive ex-cept occasionally in gandha.

Feb. 26th Monday.

Kamananda powerful and repeatedly intense and increased in force of continuity.

=

No other noteworthy movement. There is the repression of activities in order that a new movement free from the old defects may emerge.

=

Activity of samadhi at night – rupa-drishya.

Feb 27th Tuesday.

The play of the higher ideality is renewed. The movement now imposed is the removal of the direct source of the action and its plane to the level of the higher idealities. The intellect-regarding vijnana must take a lower place as part of this higher movement.

=

Absolute passivity of the lower being is demanded in order that all action and all siddhi may be conducted openly by the Ishwara from the higher nature.

=

Kamananda tested, momentarily depressed, survives the test and continues its previous action.

Feb 28.

Continued purification from the independent action of the lower nature. Preparation of a new movement in which it will fall into its place as part of the ideal nature.

Meanwhile, suspension of the illumined higher action, in order that the lower, deprived of the light, may learn to be passive & not seek to substitute itself, as if it could make up for the deficiency, but wait always for the higher to remanifest. This impulse of the lower to act when the higher withholds itself, is now the one strong positive obstacle in T^2. Its removal marks the turning-point of the siddhi.

Mar 1 Thursday

Large play of ideality in jnana. All thought or thought-suggestion taken up into the ideality and its ideal truth luminously revealed. As yet this is only the action of the higher ideality acting on the intellect through the lower vijnana, not yet on its own plane.

The light does not yet become in the same way brihat in the T^2.

Samadhi of all kinds is more or less in abeyance or active only in crudities or reduced to the type.

In the physical siddhi Kamananda goes on preparing its normality: there is flux and reflux, but no absolute suspension. The other anandas act occasionally.

The nirananda ahaituka and sahaituka (asiddhi & asraddha) is being taken up by Ananda so as to ensure final finality of positive samata.

Mar 2. Friday.

The large ideality playing on mind and mental suggestion is taking up all telepathies and showing their ideal truth by discernment of their form & limits; so also, though less largely all tapas. The principle of faultless certainty of trikaldrishti (future and, to a less extent, present) is being sought for, but is not yet perfectly found.

Telepathy of pranic & mental thought & feeling in animals is being founded in the brihat, not prakamya-vyapti of human thought & feeling & impulse, which is still only sought in the isolated and spasmodic fashion of the past.

The suspension in the rest of the third chatusthaya continues.

Samadhi active but quite incoherent, assailed by nidra.

Mar. 3

The lipi is once more active, entirely independent of suggestion even when attacked by it; but still obstructed in its physical manifestation. Legible, but not always vivid or stable.

Increased general intensity of tivra and of visvasparsha in kama + tivra.

=

Return of samadhi, but not yet in its full force of continuity or coherence.

=

At night coherence of the Samadhi in dream-reading and dream-thought.

=

Vishaya (gandha & rasa) begins to remanifest.

=

Some remanifestation of rupa in antardarshi and bahirdarshi.

=

Thought-telepathy (animals).

=

Mahakali bhava now firmly founded and in possession. Harmony of the four bhavas not yet developed on the new basis of Mahakali Mahasaraswati.

Mar 4.

Stability and vivid legibility of the unsuggested lipi is developing against the obstruction.

=

The Maheswari bhava concealed as pratistha in Mahalakshmi-Mahasaraswati has again risen, though it can no longer possess; it has to be concealed again in the Mahakali-Mahasaraswati with the Mahalakshmi colour.

=

Tapas is recovering its old effectualities which had fallen into disuse; but they are now only material for the larger effectuality, not, as once, an object in themselves.

=

There is in the kshetra a sort of rough and imperfect tapas-siddhi now fairly generalised. The main object is roughly attained, but not, except exceptionally, in the details and always with difficulty. The siddhi does not rise above the 50° or 60° limit in its general power. In life there is only khanda-siddhi, the attainment of partial effects which do not assure the success of the main object, and even this though much more frequent & general than before, is yet far from being quite general. Always there is some effect, but not always effectuality.

=

The development of the lipi continues and is almost in possession of the akasha.

=

Tendencies of redevelopment in samadhi and rupasiddhi

Mar 5. Monday.

Lipi is becoming rapidly stronger in vividness, stability and a certain relative abundance.

=

Almost entire recovery of swapna and sushupta samadhi. Example of perfect stability and continuity of action in tejomaya, shadowy but distinct and generally increased force of both in tejomaya. Movement towards idealisation of the samadhi

=

Greatly increased general force of effectuality of tapas-siddhi even in exact result, but always within limits of the 50° or 60° power and still in the kshetra. As yet the final combination of T^3 into T^2 lingers and is mastered by the obstruction.

=

Mar 6.

Samadhi in the early morning. Perfect coherence of ideal thought (vangmaya) in deep sushupti. The lapse of memory persists, but was powerfully overcome and the lost memory restored in the samadhi itself.

=

Telepathies & tapasbuddhi are being more largely taken up into the brihat satyam of the ideality preparing the brihad ritam.

=

Unity of action in lipi, reference, T^3 and other instruments of the vijnana is being established.

=

Tapas continues to increase in force, but is still far from being master of the akasha.

=

Samadhi in afternoon. Lipi in sushupti incoherent except when the ideal consciousness was present and either saw coherent lipi or evolved coherence out of confusion by disengaging the words from each other and adding what was incomplete. But all else tended to be coherent even when the ideal consciousness was not present.

At the end all sushupti and swapna became possessed by the ideal consciousness.

Images related to life upon earth.

=

Sukshma sparsha revived, but as yet it fails to pass into the sthula except in the accustomed touches.

=

Lipi developed independent fluency with some diminution of legibility and much of stability. It occasionally follows the ideal suggestions, but is usually independent or else affirms its independence by substituting other words when the thought has divined too soon the word that was coming.

=

The passage of T³ into T² continues.

=

Strong & intense kamananda recurrent throughout the day. Intensity of tivra and vishaya.

—

Manifestation of the gods as agents of the ideal action, especially Surya in charge of the ideal vangmaya thought (recalling the last 15 August)—less directly Indra behind the perception, Agni behind the will. Mental images of the four Shaktis on the lower & middle planes of the ideality.

=

Traigunyasiddhi in type; shama full of prakasha and tapas, prakasha full of shama and tapas, tapas full of shama and prakasha.

=

Devibhava complete and strong, in type, not yet in action. Reemergence of one of the talents, — chitra.

Mar 7.

An attack of the intellectualities begun yesterday, continues. Still the devibhava is confirmed. It tends to bring also the sraddha bhagavati swashaktyam cha and as a result the sraddha in the complete siddhi, also a great physical energy into the body.

=

The attack of the intellectualities continues and there is no progress in the third chatusthaya.

=

Samadhi confined to an attempt to convert dream into samadhi, not as yet successful except in a minor degree

One prophetic image in yesterday's samadhi was justified today by the physical fact.

=

Samata severely tested has this time held good in spite of one or two adverse touches; the second chatusthaya (faith, devibhava) sometimes gives way, but reasserts itself swiftly. . The lower nature still resists the new devibhava and attempts to go back to the old sense of limitation and essential incapacity.

=

The devibhava is taking into itself Surya, Soma, Agni, Indra and seeking to unify them.

=

As a result, partly, of the unsuccessful attack sama ananda is greatly strengthened & is increasing rapidly in force. It is finally overcoming the dwaita of siddhi & asiddhi, as it did the dwaita of mangala and amangala.

Premananda remanifesting with the sense of self as all things and the Ishwara as all beings for its basis.

Mar 8.

The Premananda is combining its elements — (1) self = Ishwara; prakriti self all things and all beings. Therefore all the prakriti of

Ishwara one with myself (2) the beauty of the Ishwara – shuddha governing chidghana with ahaituka involved in it – (3) relations of brotherhood, love, motherhood & childhood, sakhya, madhura, vatsalya united into one composite bhava. It includes also guru-shishya, sakhya-vaira etc. Others are preparing to enter into the composite bhava.

=

The united action of the ideality, transforming virodha, is being prepared.

=

The shuddha-vijnanananda is now generalising itself success-fully and firmly. It lives sometimes in the mental, sometimes in the vijnana plane; in the first shuddha predominates with vijnana subordinate to ahaituka; in the latter sometimes shuddha some-times vijnana predominates. The tendency is for vijnana to be a prominent term of shuddha with ahaituka involved as a subordinate term.

=

Dasya vaira of Mahakali. The Energy serves all, but enforces on them with more or less violence the higher in place of the lower aims of their being; thus it is often in vaira or virodha with their lower desires which it yet accepts as part of its system and as material of its work.

The sixth chatusthaya of Sarvam Anantam Jnanam Anandam Brahma is now complete in itself. Its completeness of contents de-pends on the perfection of the third, fourth and fifth chatusthayas. Subjective bhukti may be now considered complete as well as sub-jective mukti. Subjective shuddhi is only defective in as much as the intellectual mentality still resists complete elimination by trans-formation into the ideality; but the separation & distinction of the two in knowledge is now complete. The full transformation is rather siddhi than shuddhi. Therefore only siddhi remains of the four elements of the seventh chatusthaya.

Physical shuddhi, mukti, bhukti though far advanced is not yet absolute, nor can be except by initial siddhi of the fourth chatusthaya.

=

The siddhi of the three chatusthayas still to be completed depends on the glory and power (sri) of the ideality perfecting itself and taking full possession not only of the mental being, but of the body and the life. The negative states are being replaced by the positive; quiescence by shama-tapas-prakasha, the human poise by the divine, the Brahmi by the Aishwari sthiti.

=

No advance in samadhi

=

The play of the old telepathies and tapas-telepathies continues with a view to their loss of all decisive force and reduction to their proper proportions. Meanwhile the action of higher ideality in T^2 is suspended. It is in force only in the jnana.

The direction is now for the ideality to act wherever it is free, jnana-perception, vangmaya, lipi, reference etc and not to wait suspended for the T^2. This it is already beginning to do

=

The alternations between the higher and the lower devibhava continue. The higher has at present too much of the Maheshwara in it, being dominated by Surya.

=

There is an increasing attempt at control of the speech by the ideality.

=

The power of the ideality is definitely emerging out of the state of subjection to the circle of the physical mentality. For some time it has acted in this field and upon it from above, dealing with the facts and the ideas open to the lower mind, the knowledge beyond its ken being presented to it as suggestions, not as light possessed by the mind. A higher action is now beginning to outline itself, not, as before, as something beyond the normal, but as the normal action of the new vijnana-buddhi.

=

Mar 9.

Three ideal planes—one observing the facts of the manifest world, the second the facts and the forces, possibilities etc out of which the facts emerge, the third & highest both these and the certainties, prefigured in the truth, which both possibilities and realised facts figure out in the succession of time. The lower knows the higher as the thing behind to which it refers back for the source of its activities; the higher looks down to the lower as its own fulfilment.

—

Suddha vijnanananda is becoming more and more confirmed, brilliant and intense on the vijnana plane. It is becoming also full of the devibhava and is preparing to base the full Krishna Kali darshana.

—

Devibhava grows in firmness and intensity and is preparing to expel the habit of reversion by the full illumination of the lower bhava and the removal of the division between para and apara.

—

Kamananda severely tried for the last few days has persisted in spite of depression and may now be considered as firmly established against all dependence on condition and attempt at temporary expulsion. It is still however capable of temporary depression, never now amounting to entire suppression, and subject to rise and fall of intensity, to lesser or greater power of recurrence and continuity. It also varies with the asana, tending to be quiescent in the others except by smarana or uddipana. These are the defects that have yet to be conquered.

—

The other anandas seem to be awaiting the complete victory of the kamananda. Only the sahaituka tivra advances steadily, though without any marked rapidities and subject to temporary quiescences. It is still not free from the fault of the cessation of the nervous response after constant stimulation. For a time the response maintains itself, may even become more intense, afterwards it becomes neutral or changes to vishaya, raudra or vaidyuta.

—

The energy of the Shakti is more and more changing from saumya to raudra. The Mahakali bhava has therefore taken full possession of the centre of energy, though it still fluctuates and has not taken its final character.

Mar 10.

At present the attack of the old against the new is the general feature of the sadhana. An attack in the first place on the siddhi of the third chatusthaya, obstruction and inefficiency, with the view of breaking down the recent gains of the first and second, and thus bring the system back to the poise of the old intellectual mentality of the limited human poise. While there is no definite breaking down, there is a certain success in restoring old touches of the asamata that had been expelled—touches of the asukham (predicted by lipi, "grief".)

=

The traigunya-siddhi is especially denied. Shama alone seems perfect; tapas and prakasha fall back into mental rajas & sattwa when there is an attempt to particularise their actions.

=

Devibhava also now tends to sink to the lower condition by separation from the higher and, when joined to it, the poise is still in the lower rather than in the higher nature. There is a denial of ishwarabhava and sraddha in which the knowledge of the buddhi is resisted and tends to be overcome by the sense of deficiency & nonfulfilment acting on the pranic temperament.

=

Absolute finality, therefore, is still to seek in the first two chatusthayas.

=

Samadhi of the three avasthas; freer play of ideal thought, vangmaya and perceptive, the latter first free, afterwards obstructed.

For some time there have been sudden attacks on the health during samadhi which could not be successful during the waking. This is because a certain physical depression or even disintegration seems to take place in samadhi which is not possible when the tapas is concentrated on the physical world as the mental. Although this has been greatly reduced, it is still sufficient to leave the room open for attacks, eg yesterday of violent nausea, a thing easily dominated and dismissed if it comes in the waking state, today, of pain near the muladhara which refused to be turned into ananda although it could [not] prevent some ananda from being associated with it, though much submerged or rather overweighed and oppressed.

Almost all the recent gains of the siddhi have been temporarily denied by the results of the attack; but they have a stronger & swifter tendency to revive, even though they are not entirely reestablished

The siddhi begins to recover from the attack.

Mar. 11.

The main necessity is the full illumination of the tapas which remains on the lower level and for this the return to the direct dasya, but dasya to the vijnanamaya anandamaya Ishwara.

For some days the sense of the immediate presence of the Ishwara has been withheld and all has been done by the Prakriti. Now the presence is being restored and with it the intensity of dasya, but not the entirely immediate presence. The Prakriti still stands between.

Kamananda oppressed yesterday, though always present in sensible tendency, is recovering itself, in action at first, not yet in intensity.

The tapas-siddhi is losing its exclusive insistence on the particular result, accepting as its own the opposite energies and their results. Yet at the same time it is increasing its power of general and particular result.

The Chitshakti is insisting on a more universally vivid sense of all beings and objects as the anandamaya Ishwara manifesting himself in various forms. This is resisted by the mentality which is accustomed to see Brahman in all and all in Brahman and, with a less facile readiness, Brahman as all, but not all as the Ishwara. Notably, it makes more resistance as to beings than as to objects; in the latter the shuddha-chidghana-ananda is more habitually seen than in beings.

The difficulty of the tapassiddhi is still to combine it with trikaldrishti. The aspect[s] of will and idea in the telepathic mind, —tapas and jnana,—are being now gradually harmonised; but the decisive trikaldrishti and the decisive tapas do not come together.

=

Samadhi is recovering its force, but as yet no new progress has been made.

=

A considerable advance has been made towards the firm normalisation of the chidghana ananda in objects.

=

Samadhi continues to progress towards complete recovery of its force, but is not as yet in firm possession of itself.

Mar 12.

The universalising of the Ishwara-darshana is extended to beings as well as objects. When the ananda-darshana falls back into the mentality, it tends to be replaced by the Brahma-darshana; when it remains in the vijnana, it is firm. There is now a tendency to have the Ishwara vision in the mentality even, but only as a circumstance of the Brahma vision. In the vijnana the two become one, Brahma (Akshara and Kshara) being only aspects of the Ishwara.

=

Samadhi is now in possession of itself. It moved forward in three directions (1) The enforcement of the ideal consciousness as basis of vijnana-samadhi. (2) The insistence against lapse of memory. (3) The insistence on coherency everywhere.

In addition there was a manifestation of chhayamaya tejas & varna, scenes shadowy but full of beauty, subdued brilliance, rich colour and the faery atmosphere of the ananda.

=

The insistence throughout the day has been on the fifth chatusthaya + Ishwara, ie on the Ananda Brahman merging into the Anandamaya Purusha (Krishna-Kali).

=

For days the rupadrishya has been disorganised. The mental

stress and formation is being eliminated. Meanwhile the old round of breaking up and rebuilding the broken siddhi is feebly occupying the atmosphere.

=

Samadhi at night confirms the day action.

=

Kavya for the last two days. Chitra daily, crude but with the automatic movement and growing norm.

March 13. Tuesday.

The suddha chidghana is now the normal basis of the ananda-darshana for objects, the attempt at reversion to mental shuddha still surviving, but feebly. The same holds good for animal forms, but with more strength in the reversion. It is only in the human figure (chiefly the face) that the reversion is still strong; but here too the sarvasaundarya of shuddha chidghana is gaining rapidly in strength and becoming normal. The strength of reversion here is due to the fact that there is a standard of divine beauty to which the actual form does not correspond.

=

The movement now is to strengthen sraddha so that there may be no room for any lapse, even slight, in the first two chatusthayas.

In the first there is still a deficiency in ananda of asiddhi and in the shuddha chidghana ananda of the vishayas, taste, sound etc — especially taste. Rasagrahana is there, but not invariable bhoga — owing to the pranic resistance — and therefore not the full, vivid and satisfying ananda.

=

Kamananda is recovering intensity. There is strong obstructive resistance to the physical siddhi, also to the karma-siddhi.

=

The chief obstacle to the ananda of asiddhi is that when it comes entirely, it tends to bring acquiescence in asiddhi: but the true bhava is ananda in and acceptance of asiddhi as a step towards siddhi. The other therefore is not allowed to establish itself, while the true bhava is as yet obstructed; its basis is not yet properly laid.

The movement now is to the fixing of that basis.

=

The progress in samadhi continued. Free chhayamaya of all kinds, though seldom at once the stability and the force of presentation. Lapse of memory minimised in sushupti in the perceptive thought (mainly ideal) as well as the vangmaya.

=

Today the ananda has begun to overbear the resistance of prana in the taste. In hearing, smell and touch, there is always the bhoga of ananda, not merely the rasagrahana. The only defect is defect of the chidghana, for the shuddha is always there though often only mental shuddha. But in the taste there is frequently denial of ananda or neutrality.

Lipi is rapidly normalising itself in the vivid legibility with an initial perfection of stability. The suggestion is again allowed to play a part in removing the obstruction, but it is always an interpretation of unmanifest lipi rather than a former of uncreated lipi. The lipi is largely spontaneous.

=

The telepathy is beginning to indicate in itself its spontaneous ritam; similarly the ideality even when it manifests in a thick veil or a thick atmosphere of mentality.

=

Some insistence on a spontaneously retentive memory, but the amnesia is still dominant; memory is more active, but retains its usual or capriciously selective character.

=

The insistence on ananda in the taste continues.

=

There is a covert struggle between sleep and the shakti that tries to overcome it. The physical reaction of diminished sleep, is still the stronger, even when the total amount of sleep is the same and the diminution is only of the night sleep. eg. tonight 5 hours (from 2 to 7) after 2 hours in the daytime, making the sufficient quantity of 7 hours. It is true that the day sleep was mostly samadhi and only a brief nidra. . As yet samadhi is not a substitute for nidra; the body is rather adversely than favourably affected by it. The opposite tendency is present, in state of preparation, but not yet effective.

=

Dream is no longer samadhi-like. It is again incoherent.

=

Samadhi at night very slight, mostly rupa-drishya in sushupti

Mar 14
 Script.
 "Today T² and lipi
 "Confirmation of the first two chatusthayas and the (fifth + sixth) Brahmamaya Ishwara.
 "Completion of the Ananda (subjective)

—

 "First the shuddha chidghana in the chidghana, on that basis the Brahmamaya Ishwara."

=

This was immediately fulfilled. The chidghana darshana is being founded firmly in the chidghana consciousness, with a firm delineation of vijnanamaya form in all things. The shuddha is shuddha of chidghana, and the premature tendency to insist on the shuddha of ananda is being postponed. The first result was to have shuddha-chidghana of forms, but shuddha ananda with strong envelope of mentality in the surrounding Brahman. Immediately, however, the vijnana Brahman manifested in the containing Purusha, taking possession of the Akasha in place of the Manas Brahman.

The Brahmamaya Ishwara at once came in and associated itself firmly with this vijnanananda darshana.

This is the basis for the next step of the siddhi and has to be made inviolable before the final step can be successfully taken.

All vishaya is being subjected to this chidghana ananda sense of things.

The manasic sense in the darshana still hangs about, but it no longer dominates.

=

In T^2 the difficulty is still in the tendency of the telepathy to attempt the decision of the event. Left to itself in the mentality, it now speedily drops this tendency; but when the telepathy is idealised the resulting brilliance and positiveness gives it the false idea of decisiveness; it tries to supplement the ideal telepathy by the intellectual decision or determining choice. This is the secret of most of the intellectual error of brilliant minds. The ideal telepathy only gives the idea of intentions, forces, facts, possibilities surrounding the moment of time. Decisive certainty belongs only to the trikaldrishti. Therefore the final purification for T^2 consists in the discharging of the false foreseeing certainty of the intellect which tries to attend the ideal suggestions.

=

In the morning sudden attack of the external (exiled) mentality on the sraddha & sukham (samata). At first touching the buddhi, it failed to take possession of it. It only reproduced a mechanical repetition of some of its old movements on the prana and sense-mind by a purely physical touch. Striving constantly to recur, it failed to endure.

=

In Samadhi much interference of nidra, but at the same time the ideality is taking hold of it and undermining incoherence. The grasp of ideal perceptive thought in mental sushupti is increasing. Especially lipi in all the four states is gaining fluency, legibility, cohesion, stronger in swapna than in antardrishti, in both than in sushupti.

=

Lipi has now accomplished fluency in perfect legible stability. The result has only to be thoroughly confirmed, deepened and released from minor defects, the survivals of the older imperfection. The stability is essential, it does not as yet remain long fixed in the akasha; but there is no tendency to vanish as soon as it is manifested or, as before, even in the act of manifestation. The tendency is to remain as long as is necessary.

=

Chidghana in the human figure is being constantly pulled back into the mentality and constantly reasserted. This is now the only serious defect, but the affirmation is stronger than the denial.

=

Telepathies combined with tapas siddhi which begins to have the light of the trikaldrishti in the telepathies.

=

The first two chatusthayas recover their norm in the evening.

=

Brief manifestation of variety of crude rupa (in the darkness of the terrace). Only relative precision + stability.

Mar 15.

Manifestation of perfect stability of "readymade" sentences, rushing into the physical akasha from behind and holding it before the suggestion can interfere. This is now increasing. This stability is vivid and often vichitra in its lettering, that is in varna, jyoti etc as well as chhaya.

=

The combination of telepathies and tapas-siddhi continues, but the element of trikaldrishti in the telepathies is not yet precise; uncertainty predominates.

=

Besides the developing elements of the three first chatusthayas and the Ananda + Ishwara, the Script indicates Vishayas and Rupa-drishya as part of the day's progress.

=

The Ananda Ishwara manifests itself with greater force and perfection of chidghana than yesterday. The human figure has come into the line with the rest. Only in the human face the tendency to reversion has some strength, but it is daily diminishing.

=

Some drishyarupa.

=

Most of the afternoon & evening taken up with kavya.

=

Vishaya hardly noticeable – gandha

Mar 16.

Lipi is now confirmed in legible stability with a fair amount of fluency. The legibility is usually vivid.

=

Trikaldrishti begins to increase in the telepathy + tapasbuddhi.

=

Ananda now goes back to the manasa chidghana and not to the mere ahaituka or shuddha in manasa. There is a tendency to greater intensity of this subjective ananda.

=

More rupadrishya, but imperfect.

=

In Samadhi antardarshi is more frequent but slight.

=

Vishaya of rasa.

Kamananda discouraged for these two days begins to revive. Tivra is always intense with smarana, but tends otherwise to sleep.

=

Strong adverse movement in karma.

Mar 17.

The Ishwaradarshana has made a rapid bound to the shuddha Ananda possessing the chidghana, with the sense of the absolute universal beauty with the variety of feature. The chidghana gives a centrality and perfect harmony to the variety and reveals the spiritual law of each form of beauty, the guna and the swabhava, the thing it expresses. The Ananda is sometimes intense, sometimes moderate, sometimes goes back to the manasa shuddha chidghana; but the trend to intensity prevails.

=

Energy of tapas-siddhi is increasing, but there is still the division from trikaldrishti, the three elements of T^3 acting separately and not taken up into the union in duality of T^2

=

Sense (physical) and delight of touch in the contact of objects outside oneself, even at a distance, has long been developing,— mostly behind the veil with manifestations in front—and is now thinking of universalising itself. The sense is sometimes subtle physical, sometimes sthula.

=

Lipi confirms fluency in legible stability, but its free manifestation is forcefully obstructed.

=

Successful samadhi. Lipi in sushupti often coherent; otherwise resolved by ideal thought into some form of coherence; only occasionally left to incoherence. Increasing force of rupadrishya; present also, but more successfully resisted in antardarshi. The obstruction to samadhi is obstinate and strong.

Mar 18.

The rudra energy which has long been attempting to seize the system, has now laid hold.

=

Lipi
"Do not limit the rapidity possible to the Shakti."
"Do not admit defeat."
The last means obviously definite defeat; for actual adverse result has to be admitted. Script—"There must be a constant insistence, but an illumined insistence"

—

Script.
"From today the third chatusthaya has to be pushed on, the denials of the first and second energetically refused.
"Today the foundation of the rudra energy has been successfully laid and the Maheshwari in Mahakali once dominated (taken in as pratistha) will be perfected."
The Maheshwari already taken in as pratistha was Maheshwari in Mahasaraswati, the other sometimes manifest is Maheshwari in Mahalakshmi. Once in Ch. [Chandernagore] Maheshwari herself was manifest. This is the last stage of the pratistha preparation. It is connected with the union of aishwarya-ishita-vashita with trikaldrishti and prakamyavyapti.

=

For the last few days a revolution in Russia with Michael brought to the throne as Czar has been telepathically suggested to the mind. This is half-fulfilled by today's news.

Reference.

"The result will be that Prakriti will lose her power of reflecting herself in the Brahman" ie the lower Prakriti which interferes with the ideality. The higher is simply the consciousness and will of the Ishwara.

=

Samadhi

Force of distinct variety in rupa-drishya of Antardarshi. Great power of suppression of incoherence in the sushupta.

=

The sarvasaundarya of the Ananda chidghana is growing more and more, although it is not as yet secure against relapse.

Mar 20.

The sarva-saundarya increases in its hold. It tends to lose the vividness of its prema-kama elements and of the Ishwaradarshana, but easily recovers them.

=

The external asamata now is failing in its touch on the mind as well as on the buddhi; it touches only the physical sheath and affects the physical prana, but by evanescent touches, even when it is allowed to act without any attempt at expulsion.

=

There is an attempt of the asiddhi to confuse the Devibhava and sraddha which that draws back a little to see how the asiddhi works when the system is left to itself.

All these are the vestiges of the old mentality which come athwart the ideality without actually replacing it.

=

Samadhi oppressed by nidra.

=

There are constant returns of the physical asamata, never assuming the assent of the buddhi and the mind, but touching,

sometimes settling for a while on the physical emotionalism.
=

The main work today has been the persistent and rapid discouragement of all tapatya whether of will to determine event or of will [to] determine knowledge or of will to secure results or enjoyments. Tapatya is intellectual, mental, rajasic will. In order to do this almost all will and almost all favourable result or inner activity has to be stopped, except such as is purely passive.
=

In the evening a movement outlined itself that has been for some time preparing, that of correct self-telepathies, telepathies perceiving at once their own substance of truth. This gives no surety of trikaldrishti, but only actualised fact of event, state, tendency, intention etc correctly conceived or rather felt & seen.
=

The old time-trikaldrishti, long discontinued, revives with its old imperfections.
1. M's [Moni's] return at about 8.55.
2 N's [Nolini's] return approaching
3 S's [Saurin's] early return and meal at about 9.15 and 9.25 but only the times came right, the two events being wrongly placed, S's return at 9.25, the meal at 9.15 or 9.25.

Mar 21.
Most of the day given to work for Arya. Negative condition in the siddhi. Asiddhi emphasised, as far as it will go, in all the chatusthayas. Some play of ideality in the evening.

Mar 22
Out of the inhibition and asiddhi there is being created a new luminously mechanical ideal substratum of thought and action —jnana tapas—combined which replaces gradually the old half-intelligent action or thought, habitual, instinctive etc which rose out of the subconscient or was determined by the subconscient. This rises out of the realised *sat* in the mental, vital, physical *prakriti* (pradhana elementalised) and is therefore satyam. It is not yet ritam,

but prepares to be. It will be brihat by the large assimilation of the circumconscient under the law of the ideality.

Physical tamas has been for some days dominant. It is now being violently thrown off to be replaced by the dasya-tapas guided by an inherent, though largely involved shama-prakasha. The reactions of a sort of unreal, yet actualised physical weakness are fighting against this new type of action, — new, because formerly, when it came, it contained an element of rajas.

Ashanti is becoming more & more purely physical. It contains a sort of mechanical asamata and asukham. .

The resistance to the light of the ideality still continues. There is a physical repression of the thought when it tries to rise into the jyotih. The diminishing of the asamata into the pure physical touch continues.

Mar 25

The last two days given chiefly to Arya and poetry. No marked incident in the sadhana.

Today samadhi is recovering its activity after a temporary cessation.

Mar 30–31.

Revival of the active sadhana.

=

The chidghana shuddha is now perfectly founded, normalised & universalised. Only its status varies.

The Ishwara-darshana is equally founded and universalised. But there are two experiences of it, one in which it is only present to the observation as the material of consciousness, but does not come home to the mind, the other in which it is vivid and the very nature of the soul's view of things.

The Ishwara is not as often before Krishna or Kali, Purusha and Prakriti, in the individual, but the Lilamaya impartially in all, Krishna with Kali in the purusha, Kali with Krishna in the *stri*.

The prema-kama is normalising itself in the same way, – in two ways separately, first as essential stuff of the ananda; secondly, as essential result of the chidghana shuddha and its revelation of universal saundarya. This is not yet quite firm and complete.

=

For some time samata and dasyam were isolated from shakti, in order that the last power of attack of asamata might be removed. It now touches from outside without any hold on the buddhi or the manas and a very weak clutch at the prana, as a sort of mild physical depression in the prana dependent on defect of sraddha in the karma. The velleities of ashanti, revolt (absence of nati) etc which the external Nature would force on the individual, have no power left to form themselves, the aid of buddhi and manas being refused.

=

The active side is now being revived. Absolutely perfect reference, telepathy perfect in satyam of substance, perfect too in ritam of arrangement when it does not attempt to develop trikaldrishti and tapas; occasionally perfect trikaldrishti. Tapas is still tainted with the habit of effort and struggle; trikaldrishti with the false tapasic stress in its telepathic parts.

Aug 15th 1917. Wednesday.

The siddhi has reached a fresh turning-point.

The first chatusthaya is firm, complete, universal – except for occasional and quite momentary touches which have no power to fix themselves in the consciousness or outlast their moment or acquire intensity, – except, again, rarely in the failure of samadhi. But this is quite exceptional. Even the earth of the system (called in lipi, γη, territoriality) is subjected to the law of the samata. Only the positive ananda is still weak in [siddhi].[1]

The second chatusthaya is complete, fixed, universal; but there are defects, principally in devibhava (*ishwari bhâva, sarvakarmasâmarthyam,*) in *sraddha swashaktyâm* and most in *daihiki shakti.* All needs to take on a greater intensity, but all are founded, all firm except these three, but all have their points of weakness. Eg. *dasyam* is not yet normally tertiary of the third degree.

Defects in the first two chatusthayas are really not self-existent, but the result of insufficiency in the third, the vijnana. Here all hitherto has been preparation. Gnana is well advanced, T^2 only founded, samadhi is still subject to mentality and incoherence, the physical basis is undeveloped; but all have acquired their crude material. Lipi is specially forward. All the stages of the ideality are customary.

The fourth chatusthaya is developed only in Ananda. Arogya is prepared but still subject to fragmentary denial, in all but the [. . .] roga which still persists. Utthapana is thrown backward, Saundarya only developed in psychic youth and a few preparatory movements of the physical change.

Krishna Kali are both developed, but not perfect. Karma kama are psychically progressing, physically held back.

[1] *MS* asiddhi.

Brahmadarshana is complete as continent, incomplete in contents.

Shuddhi, mukti, bhukti are well-advanced psychically, strong with fragmentary defects physically. Siddhi depends on the perfection of the still imperfect chatusthayas.

———

Aug 15th to 20th
Arogya.

Attack of roga, — attempt at cold and fever. Slight cold and eye-affection; the former unable to materialise entirely, the latter materialised successfully after three days' struggle, but not with the same force as formerly. Strong on 17th and 18th, slight since. The disease was made an occasion for the exercise of the tapas-siddhi on the mental level, where the effect is never more than partial when used against strong resistance.

=

T².

During these days the telepathic mentality has been entirely and firmly idealised on its own level in the perception of force, tendency, possibility, and entire satyam thus secured. Even when the ideality is removed, the satyam remains as an unillumined perception. The movement towards ritam (T²) is being resumed.

The stress on forces = mental tapas. This tapas has begun to be idealised and is already of the nature of a half-illumined balance of force-action. The satyam of the mental tapas is not so sure or not so illumined ordinarily as the satyam of the mental perception.

Samadhi.

Strong play of rich and perfect chhayamaya. There is a lack of stability and continuity; but these are firm in the obscure chhayamaya, sufficient in the half tejomaya chhayamaya without richness and variety. This rich and perfect but unstable play of rupa occurs sometimes in the jagrat antardrishta, — though more often various than rich and perfect. It is trying to emerge even in the bahirdrishta.

Vishaya.

Vishaya develops only in the sukshma, not in the sukshma sthula where it is still held up.

=

Aug 20th Monday.
Ananda.

Ananda is stationary in kama and tivra, preparing for a fresh advance. Vaidyuta has attained to occasional fullness in body and in length of pervasion. The basis of raudra is being farther perfected.

=

The rule of decrease by repetition is more and more giving way to the increasing power of the rule of greater intensification. Orgiastic tivra direct from the touch, after it has ceased, and subsequent sympathetic tivra orgiasm elsewhere have begun to show themselves. Sometimes repetition produces variations from intense tivra to intense vaidyuta and back

Orgiastic kamananda stream in pervasive non-orgiastic kamananda. The orgiastic tends to suppress and replace the pervasive, but sometimes the latter persists circumferentially in the body or is even increased. Simultaneously increasing orgiasm of both has to be developed.

Vaidyuta tends to grow constantly, to be pervasive and to be ahaituka as well as sahaituka.

=

Tivra touch continued in the same place for five minutes; constantly disappearing into vishaya or lessened, but always recurring and increasing though with [necessity]² of smarana or smarana + tapas. After slight discontinuity more intense than before. This begins or presages the final victory of the law of increasing intensity. After complete cessation orgiastic tivra, continued briefly and often repeated.

Aug 21st Tuesday
Dasya

Tertiary *dasya* in the third degree is now being more regularly

---

2 *MS* necessary

enforced in the movements of the body, even the slightest. The remnants of the secondary degree are being swallowed up into the third

The same control is now to be enforced and is being enforced in the script, *vâni* and *vângmaya*. The dasya is now thoroughly introduced into the *îswarîbhâva*. Also into all bhoga. The firmness of this siddhi has to be firmly guarded.

The introduction of the *dasya* into the perceptive thought seems more difficult, but it is being easily done in the *jnana*. The test will be in the *trikaldrishti-tapas*. All responsibility for action, physical, vital, mental must be left entirely to the Iswara, the Shakti is only an instrument and the Jiva their meeting-place.

All traces of the *asamata*, now only the occasional recurrence of an old habit, must be finally removed. This can be done by bringing forward the delight in the *asiddhi*.

Brahma

Strong *Ishwaradarshana sarvabhuteshu*, followed by *jyotih* of the *Anantam (Jnanam) Brahma* in things. This was preceded half an hour ago by the *lipi* 15, several times repeated, the number of the *Anantam* in the enumeration of the siddhis which compose the last five *chatusthayas*.

1. *jnanam*, 2 *trikaldrishti*, 3 *rupa-siddhi*, 4 *tapas* 5 *samadhi*
6 *arogya*, 7 *ananda*, 8 *utthapana*, 9 *saundarya*
10 *Krishna*, 11 *Kali*, 12 *karma*, 13 *kama*
14 *Sarvam Brahma*, 15 *Anantam*, 16 *Jnanam*, 17 *Anandam*
18 *suddhi*, 19 *mukti*, 20 *bhukti*, 21 *siddhi*.

This *jyotih* is not yet to be free from interruption and diminution, but it is founded and from henceforth bound to increase. It is *jyoti* not *tejas*, ideal light, not the mental. It is now trying to ally itself entirely with the *Jnanam* and *Anandam Brahma*. . These manifest usually each with a separate intensity in which the three others disappear from view; henceforth the quadruple intensity has set out to create its united effulgence.

Aug 22ᵈ Wednesday.

The *siddhis* established yesterday stand, except in *vismriti*, in which they are not so much denied as either unnoticed or in suspense. The tertiary *dasya* seems to be absolutely firm in the body, script, *vani*, and only suspended by *vismriti* in the perceptive jnana and in the *vangmaya* for the change which is being operated. This change is the transference of the thought from the control of the inferior *devatas* to that of the *Jiva-Prakriti* receiving it direct from the Ishwara. The perceptive thought is being similarly transferred. Thought is to occur henceforth in the *vijnana* of the *Jiva*; not as suggestion, but as thought in action and the thought of the *Ishwara* in origin.

At present the perceptive thought is becoming impersonally *vijnanamaya* with a vague sense of the *Ishwara* behind. In telepathic *trikaldrishti*, when it is not *vijnanamaya*, its nature and descent as *manasic* suggestion from the mind-world through the *rajas* of the pranic is more and more often perceived in its fullness. This is the false *trikaldrishti*, which is in reality no more than telepathic suggestion of possibility. These suggestions come either from above or from around, from the mind and life-planes of the earth; in reality the latter derive rapidly from the former except when there is exchange on the earth plane itself; even then the derivation is eventually the same.

Brahman.

The *jyotih* of *Jnanam Anantam* is now taking into itself the *Anandam*.

=

Lipi— September, the physical siddhi begins its perfection.

       tejorashi. (yesterday) fulfilled today in the flow of ideality into the perceptive thought.

Vijnana

The real trikaldrishti is slowly growing over the telepathic basis, but combated always by the mental doubt. Lipi — "It is fashioning itself gradually in spite of the intellectuality; first, it has to take itself up into the ideality." "Together the effective telepathy

and the trikaldrishti." "Telepathy tapassiddhi."
==

Rupasiddhi and samadhi are resisted, sometimes growing, sometimes falling back.
==

Trikaldrishti is increasing as indicated in the lipi, in spite of a mass of intellectual suggestions of the old type; out of it emerge three elements, (1) the ineffectual suggestion which falls away, (2) effective telepathy, ie telepathy tapas sometimes dropping into pure tapas without foresight sometimes into foresight with an involved tapas, (3) trikaldrishti proper, but insufficient[ly] illumined and uncertain of itself. Only when there is illumination, is the trikaldrishti sure of itself and its fulfilment.
==

The pranic suggestions which amount only to rajasic imagination are being finally discouraged.
==

Some activity of vishaya in smell and taste. The latter is stronger in sukshma than in sukshma-sthula, but there is some sign in the latter of progress from the crude basic states to the dense and developed, which have hitherto appeared only in the madhura.

Aug 23 Thursday.
T²

Lipi, "perfect telepathies siddhi." Perfection implies liberation from false stress and, positively, accurate limitation and accurate extent. This has begun to develop, but is yet imperfect. The necessary condition of perfection is that the mentality should cease all attempts to determine the *trikaldrishti* and leave that entirely to the ideality.

The force of tapas increases but as this works as telepathy tapas and increases only the effective telepathy, it makes the distinction of telepathy, ie mental perception of present fact, force and tendency, from *trikaldrishti*, as perception of present and future (the past has so far been mostly left alone), more difficult; for a constantly effective telepathy tapas easily masks as *trikaldrishti*, until an occasional failure shows the mistake. All this would not occur if the highest ideality were at work for T^2, but at present it is only the lower ideality working on the mental perceptions

The satyam of the telepathy is now extremely perfect, the ritam more perfect than it has ever been before; sometimes the perfection is entire. But all this is as yet in the field of vision where truth and error can be tested by immediate result. The telebuddhi and telesiddhi on which the lipi has been for some time insisting, is as yet imperfect and very limited.

—

Renewed action of samadhi with an increased general hold of the ideality in thought, vangmaya, lipi. Rupa, dialogue, reading etc have made no definite progress

Aug 24 Friday.

Entire perfection of stability and solidity in lipi with an almost perfect freedom in manifestation. There is only a slight obstruction still sensible in the akash, but this is sufficient to compel a return to the less perfect lipi. Until a siddhi has become entirely the nature of the system and environment, according as it is purely subjective or subjective-objective, it is not perfectly possessed and is liable either to temporary loss or diminution. A siddhi maintained by force or by habitual exercise is imperfectly possessed; it must be held entirely by nature, as easy as breathing or thinking.

—

Rupasamadhi is again obstructed; the obstruction is now evidently artificial, maintained by a pressure upon the nature of the terrestrial *sattwa* which is ready to yield the coherent *vijnanamaya samadhi* in its full abundance.

—

In all subjective movements and those subjective-objective in which the subjective element predominates and the personality alone is concerned, the obstruction of the γη is similarly artificial, not belonging to the earth nature itself, but to the Patala nature into which the old powers have been exiled but from the borders of which they still maintain their opposition.

The ideality is therefore obstructed in its progress only by this opposition; the real obstruction is only in the fourth and fifth chatusthayas.

Saturday 25.th August.

Lipi more emphasised in its perfection, especially stability which is now practically universal; the solidity varies and the legibility is sometimes partial to the eye, and sometimes still at first the lipi is stable only, or solid also, but there has to be tapas to bring out the legibility. Sometimes it is incomplete, part of a sentence, or else words are omitted; sometimes it becomes coherent, instead of appearing formed, coherent and [complete][3] at one leap of emergence into the akasha. But the latter is now common, and all defects disappear at the first touch of tapas

In tivra the law of increase grows yet stronger, interruption decreases, intensity tends to be maintained. But at present if left alone, the general impressionability to tivra sinks often into a sort of subdued half quiescence and the intensity reawakens only after the first touch or the first few touches.

Samadhi varies, sometimes yielding to the obstruction, sometimes reemerging. Only the ideality of thought, vangmaya, lipi maintains itself and seems to be firmly established. Dream is commonest, comes very readily and is vivid, bordering on samadhi in its aping of coherence, vividness of rupa, dialogue etc, force of presentation. It is not however really coherent, as it was sometimes, but fanciful and extravagant in its details and connections. The nearness of a siddhi artificially withheld is however strongly felt. Rupa remains obstructed.

Sunday August 26.th

The siddhis already established are now being taken up and carried to their completion on a higher plane.

Vangmaya is being taken up into the Ananda of the vijnana level, where it is no longer the thought of the Jivaprakriti with

---

[3] MS complement

the Ishwara as the origin of the thought, but the thought of the Ishwara in the Shakti who is the medium and the instrument of the thinking. This has been done perfectly in the type; it has yet to be universalised.

A similar process is taking place with the perceptive thought and has been done less strongly and perfectly in the type, but its perfection and universalisation cannot proceed so far because the ideal perceptive thought still carries in itself an element of mentality and therefore more easily descends into mental thinking than it ascends into pure ideal thinking.

In the script to the presence of the Ishwara is being added the personality of the Ishwara and his relation of madhuradasya containing all his other relations with the Jiva-Shakti.

T^2 is still unidealised, but is pressing towards idealisation.

Lipi is rapidly universalising perfection of form and light in the thought-interpretation.

The containing Brahmadarshana is preparing to fix itself in the Ananda with the Jnana Ananta as content and Sarva as base.

Physical siddhi

In the physical siddhi *kamananda* pervasive and orgiastic is becoming more easy and natural in all positions, but needs and indeed is almost entirely dependent on *smarana* and sometimes on smarana + tapas: but the need of *tapas* is being gradually rejected. It is no longer entirely dependent on excitation of the centre by *sparsha*.

Ahaituka tivra has been for a long time less common, but it has a greater intensity and force for insistence when it comes and comes, besides, more easily everywhere.

There is the same increase of intensity in *vaidyuta* and *vishaya*, and also in the former a greater ease and normality in arrival, development and extension. But it needs *smarana* or *smarana* and *tapas*, more commonly both, in the ahaituka and in the *sahaituka* current, *smarana* only — and not always — in the intense *sahaituka* touch.

The other three members of the physical siddhi have made no definite advance and are except in certain directions subject to relapse.

=

Karma (subjective), though often and increasingly effective, is subject to great opposition, obstruction and reaction. *Kama* at present is not being pressed.

=

Samadhi

The other parts of *samadhi* not yet idealised, began to be taken hold of by the *vijnâna* in the afternoon, except the reading and rupa; all at the same time increased in coherence. At night the reading also was taken hold of, powerfully, both in its coherence and in its incoherence. Mentality now reigns only in *swapna*, although it still strives to persist also in *swapna-samâdhi*; but *swapna* is increasing in coherence. Even when interrupted, it tends to be resumed at the same point or to return to the same subject; this even happens after a long diversion to another subject. It is still, however, a sort of fragmentary coherence. The ideality also works in a fragmentary fashion, except in vangmaya

Tapas

Lipi, "sixty seventy". 60 degrees rising to 70 degrees of *tapas* effectiveness is being enforced in type and has set out to generalise itself. Hitherto *tapas* effect was all haphazard and incoherent, often strong, seldom perfect, frequently weak or nil, always partial except in details, never or hardly ever final except in certain broad effects after much difficulty

Aug 27 Monday.

60° to 70° effectiveness is becoming more general; though 50° and less persist and 80° occasionally occurs, but rarely. The 60° is sometimes in swiftness of overcoming resistance, sometimes in amount of effect, which is often not perfect, but only partial, a $\frac{3}{5}$ or $\frac{4}{5}$ effect, — especially in *tapas* of exact circumstance; — sometimes in both respects there is only this partial success.

Extension of *kâmânanda* proceeds against obstruction.

Much action of Samadhi in the direction of strengthening the ideality, but all is still fragmentary. The incoherent reading tends to be turned into coherence or replaced by coherent reading or

else taken as it is and interpreted in its scattered parts. Increase of
coherence is the rule.

Tuesday Aug 28.

The telepathy-*tapassiddhi* is becoming again idealised in the
sense of being seen in its right limits of the satyam in the light of
the vijnana; the *tapas-siddhi* is also acquiring more force with 60°–
70° as the average force, though it falls below and goes above, the
latter more often than the former, because of the renewed strength
of obstruction. T^2 is in abeyance. A similar process of idealisation, more advanced and luminous, is being applied to the mental
deformations of the *jnâna*.

Violent attack of the asiddhi chiefly on the first and third
chatusthayas, but to a certain extent in all six. The old method
of forcing undelight in asiddhi on the system from without
through the pranic physicality aided by intellectual suggestions
and throwing it out from within by the tapas and the buddhi.
Pranic manas in its physicality is still compelled to respond, with
a slight or evanescent response in its emotivity, but not in its
buddhi which does not recognise the undelight as belonging to the
system. The freedom of the buddhi from undelight is stronger for
the attack; moreover the restoration of the ananda is becoming
ahaituka or depends on the tapas and no longer on the buddhi.
The habit of return of physical depression is also being eliminated, as well as the remnants of susceptibility to the suggestion
of desire. Complete asiddhi is contemplated without revolt or
depression.

There is now commencing an attempt to establish a more lasting stability in the lipi so that several lines may be manifested
simultaneously—this has already been done often enough in type,
but vanishingly,—with a firm hold on the akasha.

In the evening a preparation of farther progress towards the
complete taking over of the whole action of the consciousness by
the Ishwara.

Wednesday Aug 29<u>th</u>

Continuation of yesterday's last movement. No definite advance, except that even the telepathy, trikaldrishti and tapas are being taken up by the Ishwara.

=

The taking over of the whole ideality by the Ishwara is now complete; only the recurrence of the old movements has to be eliminated.

Samadhi.

Strong original lipi of the highest ideality in the *samâdhi*, (*antardarshi* and *swapna-samadhi*). *Rupa* is active and abundant, but not stable in *antardarshi*; obstructed, but sometimes luxuriant in certain *chhâyâmaya* forms in *swapna samâdhi*. Brief dialogue in *sthula sukshma* word in swapna, coherent but not continuous or perfect. Reading, sukshma dialogue etc vary again from coherence to absolute incoherence. Thought of all kinds is much stronger in the ideality.

At a very deep level of samadhi neighboring on the sushupti the old defects still remain, but dream has less hold.

=

Telepathy and trikaldrishti are now beginning to shake off some of their imperfections, but the latter is still very hampered and limited. *Lipi.* "perfect telepathy trikaldrishti" (yesterday) today, "perfect telepathy, perfect trikaldrishti". The perfection realised is necessarily only in type. It is now attempting to extend itself into the large and perfect satyam ritam. This attempt made formerly on the mental, is now being done on the *vijnâna* level.

=

Ambulant orgiastic kamananda

Aug 30 – Thursday.

Ishwarabhava in the Brahmadarshana seems now to be fixed in its universality, sometimes subdued, sometimes intense; but it varies from the mental to the *vijnanamaya* and Ananda levels and is generally upon the mental. It is only by tapas and smarana that it returns to the higher planes. The subjective *prema-kamananda* is also now absent, except by *smarana*.

Aug 31 Friday.
  Ananda
    Steady progress in the *tivra*.
    Orgiastic *kamananda* is becoming more frequent and progressing towards normality, although still dependent on *smarana* and liable to obstruction. Ambulatory ananda is developing very fast, stationary is beginning to make itself normal, the sedentary without regard to *asana* shows sign also of following suit. The necessity of tapas is disappearing, smarana alone is required, except when the obstruction tries to recover strength; the normal readiness of the physical system for the Ananda may be considered as established.
    Arogya is still obstructed, subject to relapse and unable to make any large advance.
    Saundarya is also obstructed. Only psychological *yauvana* has become almost normal, varying in force and age, but never now settling into *vârdhakya*.

    =

    The pervasive kamananda is now orgiastic in its nature, even when subdued in its force and insufficiently sthula in its hold. The ananda has now taken hold of all positions, recumbent and loose sedentary as well as ambulant, sistory and close sedentary. It is rapidly increasing in intensity, continuity and power of self-repetition. It has even occurred once or twice without *smarana*. This is the beginning of the "vertiginous rapidity" predicted today in lipi of samadhi.

    =

    In samadhi reading more firmly gripped by the lipi. Vishaya in samadhi, separated or combined, taste, sound, touch, sight, —smell is rare and unready,—occur often in great intensity, but intermittently. They are not yet a standing feature of vision in swapnasamadhi.

1st Saturday.

Telesiddhi (karma)

Telesiddhi takes place frequently in fragments; large, decisive or final success is rare except in telesiddhi of some propinquity. In the main matters the obstruction and opposition are in the mass, though hampered, still successful.

=

Ananda

The kamananda seems now to be firmly established as a normal dharma of the body. Continuity and intensity have to be normalised. There is continuity with smarana; continuity without smarana has to be established. Intensity increases with the continuity. Ananda wave by strong *sparsha* on any part of the body is now being taken up; it is kama with admixture of tivra, vaidyuta, raudra. It is at first dependent on smarana and tapas; but in fact the latter is being eliminated; the ananda now as a general rule develops best and most readily when there is smarana without pressure of tapas; the latter, at least if too direct, is even something of an obstacle. Practically this ananda wave by touch has been established in its universality, but the siddhi has now to be entirely confirmed. All this development has taken place in the course of five minutes or so, with the vertiginous rapidity.

Ananda of acute discomfort has for some time been developing and is now preparing to be confirmed and perfected.

=

In samadhi stronger grip of observing ideality on narrative and dialogue.

Tapas is now more frequently effective (60°–80°) in the environment (not life) on general event; it has begun to work more frequently also in exact circumstantial effect but against great obstruction and with more frequent failure than success. This is on the mental level, by itself, or in conjunction with telepathies, without trikaldrishti.

=

Obstruction is being offered to the new ananda siddhis; they lower the readiness, frequency, continuity and intensity, but do not succeed in altogether suspending; meanwhile independence of the *ahaituka* pervasion and normality of the short *sahaituka* wave are increasing.

—

Strength of ideal lipi in the samadhi.

Sept 2. Sunday.

Obstruction in all the siddhis and attempt to enforce relapse yesterday and today. In the first it is unsuccessful except for fleeting and increasingly unsubstantial touches. In the second it lowers the force of tertiary dasya in the third degree and keeps in abeyance the ishwarabhava and the intenser sraddha. In the third it forces back the ideality and keeps up the dead play of the disjointed intellectual mentality, as well as the direct sense of the Ishwara control. In the fourth it tries to keep up the old stereotyped rule of denial of siddhi after a day of exceptional siddhi in the kamananda and enforce *vismriti* on the body; it is only partially successful[;] it diminishes and interrupts but cannot suspend.

—

The process of changing separated telepathy and tapas into united T^2 is being given a new turn. This is to give always the decisive event first as at once trikaldrishti and tapas, and attend afterwards to the movements which try to contradict the decreed and foreseen result and those which help with the aids and modifications of the opposing forces to bring it about. For the latter purpose it is being attempted to universalise the ideal light in the telepathies. The difficulty is always to distinguish the real finality from something that imitates it and to seize the right measure of the telepathies. The force of possession of the telepathies by the ideality is as yet insufficient, the interference of the mentality yet too frequent to allow of this invariable certainty.

Sept 3 Monday

The movement of T^2 continues. To idealise the decisive T^2 entirely and to enforce *ritam* on the *satyam* of the telepathies are the two requisite preliminaries for perfection. The latter is the more difficult of the two processes.

—

Lipi is confirmed in the ideality; it is now attempting to raise itself into the highest ideality.

=

Attempt at *lipi-trikaldrishti*, but as yet distant prediction without detail of circumstance or time.

The lipi now varies from the lower idealities to the three forms of the highest vijnana.

=

Movement of T^2 continues to be prepared; but as yet with no decisive result. Only the satyam becomes more pronounced.

=

Samadhi is stationary, persisting in its present gains, but also in the obstacles

Sept 4 Tuesday

In Samadhi the tejomaya is reappearing, chiefly in the chhaya-maya environment, clear, perfect, but only with an instantaneous stability, although a tendency of increased stability is not altogether absent. The chhayamaya is now capable at all stages of a great stability which is not infrequent, but still even in the chhayamaya stability is not the rule; instability prevails.

—

Lipi is now full of the highest vijnana light and usually or almost invariably belongs to that plane in its substance and status and increasingly in its style.

=

Thought also has followed the same development, but it is not as yet so advanced in the universality of the highest and most luminous vijnana.

=

T^2 is attempting to follow. The illumined satyam of the telepathies is now the rule, the darker movement is the exception and is immediately replaced by the light of the vijnanamaya interpretation. But the tapas is not equally illuminated in its satyam. With the increase of *satyam*, *ritam* also increases. Still *vijnānamaya* T^2 is the exception, T^3 is still the rule.

Wednesday. Sept 5.

Tapas effectivity in the environment tends towards greater normality of 70°, greater frequency of 80°, but this tendency is not yet well established. This effectivity however does not extend to exact detail of circumstance in which asiddhi both of will and eventual knowledge is the rule, siddhi the rare exception. Telepathy of contributory force, tendency, intention, impulse etc is sufficiently exact, though not always sufficiently complete.

Contributory tapas is becoming illumined in the same way as telepathy, in its *satyam* and increasingly in its *ritam*. But decisive tapas like decisive vision and even more is still unillumined or insufficiently illumined.

On the whole the vijnanamaya is now well-grounded and the rule of the being, but very far from perfection.

===

Tivra seems to have gone slightly back, but this is only the emergence of tendencies which had been held down by the energy of the tapas, not quite eliminated, though diminished and depressed. The habit of fluctuation from greater to less and from less to greater response has to be got rid of. Moreover the intimacy of the response has to be secured, that is to say, the inherent excitability of the physical system responding immediately to the sparsha by an intimate and intense thrill. At present this excitability is lost by prolonged excitation and replaced by an unsteady communicated excitability. Moreover the necessity of tapas has to be eliminated and smarana made sufficient. In kamananda this necessity is already recognised, and the advance is therefore retarded in order to get it satisfied

===

There is now increasing frequency of tapas-siddhi in exact circumstance, often sustained, varying from 70°, 75°, to 80°, but also sinking to 60°. Below 60° the normal, though not invariable rule is asiddhi. Delay of fulfilment brings often inexactitude in place as well as time or even incompleteness of the effect.

Thursday Sept. 6.
The lipi is now fixed normally in the highest ideality.

=

Kamananda has resumed its action of continuity. It is noticeable that pressure of tapas is eliminated, although an original act
of tapas-memory is still sometimes used to set it in action. Smarana
is still necessary except sometimes in the most habituated asanas.
There is some indication of the future substitution of a partial or
side attention for smarana, but this is not yet anything more than
an unrealised intention in the system.

=

Rupa is active to some extent in the jagrat, but there is no
ascertainable progress.

Friday Sept 7.
There is a more settled ritam in the telepathy and tapas working
in the unillumined or partially illumined mentality. The increase
in effectivity of tapas seems now to be settled and normal. The
development of this movement continued throughout the day has
been the one feature of its siddhi. Also the return of the Ishwara
control

Saturday Sept 8
The substitution of the necessity of half-attention for the necessity of smarana in orgiastic kamananda is taking place; it is already
strongly established in the type. At first it was only sufficient for
the sustaining of the ananda, not for its inception after cessation
or its assertion against obstruction; but the sufficiency of the half-
attention for initiating or renewing the ananda is now established.
All this is in type; much has to be done before it can be universalised.
In the end even this will not be necessary. The old habit of applying
tapas survives in a fragmentary fashion, but is no longer accepted
or efficient, except in *smarana-tapas*.

=

The Ishwara control is now firmly universalised in vani, script
and vangmaya, with whatever survival of *gana* participation; it is

not yet universalised in perceptive thought, still less in T². That is being prepared.

⸗

The excentric waves and currents of kamananda are following rapidly the same development as the main or central surge; they have to come to depend first on smarana without tapas — though at first with an implied tapas in it, — then on a half-attention, while the removal of even this necessity is being already prepared. Here too maintenance without full smarana is easier and more frequent than inception or even renewal.

These excentric currents are often ahaituka, that is, not created as before only by actual sparsha. There are signs that *ahaituka tivra* will also be soon prepared for normality. At present it is still dependent — except in the three main locations where half-smarana is already sufficient, — on the full *smarana* and usually on *smaranatapas*.

⸗

Vaidyuta is developing indistinctly along with the *tivra* and *kama*. Separate development of *vaidyuta* and *raudra* seems to have been postponed.

⸗

Intense continuous ahaituka tivra is being prepared and established in type in all the nine locative centres; it is already done in type in the seven main and is begun in the two subordinate centres. The discursive tivra, which once emerged, is now being encouraged to reappear. Note that there are three other subordinate centres of the third class in which the same preparation is being indicated.

The fault of incomplete pervasion in the ananda surge is being remedied in the type.

Sunday Sep. 9.

The force of greater ananda continuance seems definitely to have been established. Obstructive denial persists, but it is greatly weakened and half ineffective. It can only have a temporary strength as a result of discontinuance by *vismriti*.

—

So far it is only in Ananda that the prediction of September as the first month of strong physical siddhi is being fulfilled. In the rest obstructive denial or successful resistance are paramount, denial in 8 and 9, resistance in the Arogya.

=

The half smarana is now often reduced to a minimum of attention chiefly in the physical mind or even the mind of the body and the dependence of the Ananda on the attention begins to be replaced by the involuntary Ananda forcing the attention. But this is only occasionally. Usually greater or less smarana is required. If the mind is vacant, then the attention can sink to the minimum. If it is concentrated on any object or subject, the ananda either sinks and ceases or is kept in abeyance and resumed with full force on the cessation of the absorption.

A new circumstance is the pervasion of the pranic body by the ananda as well as, with a less forcefulness of sensation, the manasic body. In the latter, at the highest, it is pure *madhu* of the Soma.

All the anandas show signs of an increasing tendency to the orgiastic

Monday Sept 10.

A strong attempt by the artificial obstruction to renew its power of strongly suspending the Ananda; at times almost successful, it has decisively failed.

The ananda in the pranic body has now the power of taking possession of the physical.

=

Kamananda diminished in force of continuity and frequency, but not suspended. The obstruction is no longer able to suspend it strongly and imperatively as before. Its occasional control is becoming more and more artificial and its strength to obstruct more and more laboured. No longer intervals of suspension, but intervals of more difficult manifestation are the most it can impose.

Tuesday Sept 11.

Kamananda is gradually recovering its force and the greater pervasion is being insisted upon.

T^3 after a somewhat prolonged eclipse is once more idealising itself, but not with any great force.

Even in the lesser force of the Ananda the power of the involuntary Ananda is increasing; it often re-initiates suddenly the forgotten or oppressed orgiasm.

Wednesday Sept 12.

The lipi now perfectly founded in the highest ideality, is aiming at perfect fluidity on that level. It is easier in the chitra than in the akasha lipi, though even there there is some difficulty of immediate physical manifestation. In this difficulty are comprised all the formal defects that still remain in the lipi.

A certain lethargy of the vijnana action which has been dominant for some days, is now in process of being removed. It is noticeable that even the intellectual action is really a perfectly accurate action of the ideality except in T^3, but its perfection is only realised when the ideal perception, ketu, stands above to observe it. Even in T^3 the action would be perfect in its justice, if the remnant intellect judgment would not misinterpret and misemphasise it

Kamananda is increasing in the type its force of involuntary initiation and involuntary retention or repetition. The force hovers, it is true, on the borders between pure involuntariness and a minimum, hardly noticeable or even unnoticeable act of *smarana*.

=

Revival of samadhi activity. Very perfect ideality of thought, lipi, vangmaya. The lipi has suddenly taken on the full perfection of ideality already established in the jagrat as well as certain types of extreme formal perfection which used only to occur in the beginning, years ago, when the vital force of the sadhana was strong, but the ideal weak.

=

The lipi predicts the return of that vital force into the new ideal principle. At present vital force is often at a minimum due to the excessive force of shama which was necessary to purification. But as shama is now absolutely strong, tapas-force in vitality can be increased without perturbance.

=

The interregnum of non ideality was necessary to get rid of false certainty and the last insistences of the intellect trying to play the part of the ideality. These have now been immensely weakened, though not abolished. The intellectual action is now in T^3 becoming more and more just, even when quite unillumined. It is far however from having then a perfection of *ritam*.

Ahaituka tivra is taking on firmly the orgiastic character

Intense pain, other than burning, now often not only takes on the character of ananda but keeps it when prolonged. It is noticeable however that pointed, lancing pain is easier to deal with than the long-edged and the long-edged easier than the massed. Also the nervous is easier to transform than the gross physical produced by a physical object. The Nirananda element in certain forms of discomfort obstinately returns, even when their ananda has been frequently strong and complete in the type.

Thursday. Sept 13

In samadhi yesterday's gains repeated; in addition a stronger force of conscious ideality took possession of narrative, dialogue etc which attained to a firm, long, consecutive coherence hardly exampled before. Fragmentariness however still remains and relics of the dream mentalising touched the action at its best. Reading and rupa still remain to be developed in the ideality.

A movement in the samadhi, jagrat, swapna, etc to take possession of all activities by the highest idealities. But this is not yet a sustained movement

=

T^3 continues its development, and even in the unillumined action the growth of ritam is removing the distinction between telepathy and trikaldrishti. Tapas has still to take its proper place in the ritam which extends only to the two other members of T^3.

Friday. Sept 14.

Chiefly, the continuance of the movement by which the direct Ishwara control in the highest ideality is taking possession of the whole vijnana. The T^2 is still the least prepared for the change and its preparation is the main feature of the sadhana, apart from the movement of the Ananda.

Steady progress in the Brahmadarshana. It is confirmed in the Ananda mentality and is being lifted into the Ananda ideality. There is no longer any strong tendency of relapse into the mental *asundara* and *nirananda*.

Saturday. Sept 15

The poise of the Brahmadarshana in things has changed rapidly, suddenly from the vijnanamaya with Ananda in it to the Ananda full with vijnana. It is only in beings that the lower poises are still strong. It only needs the sense of the infinite Ananda in each thing to be added and the darshana will be completely founded. This is already being prepared and is partially active even in regard to persons.

T^3 has been rapidly prepared this morning for the ideal control. It is only when the physical brain relaxes into failure to respond or when there are too rapid suggestions from the external intellectuality that the ideal reception fails. Even the intellectual ideality is now losing all its credit, because of its failure to satisfy the needs of the siddhi, especially the ritam.

Great incoherence in the reading. The other powers of samadhi maintain their ideality or at least their coherence, though sometimes with an initial difficulty. In rupa and reading the sadhana is up against the curious phenomenon which seems insuperable in jagrat rupa, vishaya, and the physical siddhi other than ananda, the stereotyped difficulty, the action of the Vedic *Nidah*, which consists in the eternal repetition of the past movements of success and failure forming a circle which refuses to be broken. In all the siddhi this phenomenon has been active, but most obstinately in certain members of the sadhana. In others siddhi has arrived in spite of it, has been more forceful than the tendency to turn each step into a final step, but in others it has seemed powerless. This however can be only an appearance. The change must come.

Sunday Sept 16.

Ananda darshana moves between suddha ananda proper and the same in the *ananda vijnana* or *ananda manas*. Sometimes it falls back into vijnana or mentality. This falling back is due to the recoil from the attempt to realise the infinite Ananda not only in but behind each finite, for which the mentality is not ready and therefore falls back into some fine or coarse mental representation of the thing desired by the will and sometimes, but insecurely seized in the knowledge.

=

Brilliant jyotirmaya action of the vijnana working sometimes upon the stumblings of the intellectual T^3. This is the real *surya*, still hampered by the limited receptivity of the mind, but already presaging in type its opulence of plenary light.

=

Yesterday's lipi was "Today is the last day of the intellectuality in the telepathy trikaldrishti aishwarya; it will be the first day of the ideality"; that is the last day of acceptance of the intellectual T^3 as a means of knowledge-siddhi and will-siddhi. The remnants continue to force themselves on the mind, but do not receive acceptation from the Jiva-Prakriti.

Monday Sept 17

Remoulding of the stuff of mind so that all thought and will and feeling may be *vijnanamaya*, has set in in earnest. The progress is rapid; though not yet of the highest rapidity, still of a decisive rapidity.

Tuesday Sept 18. Wednesday 19.

The same movement with a tendency to relapse.

Thursday Sept [20][4]

Renewal of intensity of kamananda. This time full pervasion in the intensity is established. But the power of the obstruction

4 MS 19

to profit by the vismriti has to be removed. Activity of the other anandas was also in a sort of abeyance and is reviving.

———

The passive samata is much stronger than before; positive ananda in the asiddhi is not yet quite firm, therefore a vague depression is still able to touch the system. Sraddha is capable of suspension with regard to rapidity, to complete physical siddhi and to karma; the ishwarabhava also and the sense of direct Ishwara control.

———

Arogya does not visibly advance; the other physical siddhis are still subject almost entirely to the denial.

═══

Confirmation of the intense, all-pervasive Ananda in all positions. The strengthening of the separate current or wave so as to effectively universalise it, is beginning; but strong smarana with tapas in it is usually necessary.

Friday Sept [21][5]

Conversion of the passive samata, *titiksha, udasinata, nati,* into their positive forms of Ananda through *Ishwaraprema* and *dasya.* By this ananda in asiddhi will be perfected, since asiddhi will be the accomplishment of the will of the Ishwara, when decisive, of his temporary will and tortuous movement to siddhi when temporary.

═══

Dasyam completed by intensity and universality. The Ishwarabhava belongs to the Ishwara at present, the Shakti has only the Mahasaraswati *dâsîbhâva.* So also sraddha in the power of the Ishwara; not yet in swashakti as its expression. The sraddha is now in the accomplishment of the will of the Ishwara, whatever it may be, through this adhara; for the siddhi only in eventual accomplishment, except for a doubt of the *sharira siddhi* and of the extent of the *karma.*

———

[5] MS 20

With this the determining of the Kali-Krishna bhava in the personality; together, dasya of the Kali-prakriti as expressive of the Krishna-purusha both making the upper and lower sides of one personality. The Ishwara of the system, with the Ishwara of the worlds above, one in two *dhamas*.

=

Idealising of the telepathies and perceptive thought practically complete; tapas is being also taken up by the Ishwara entirely and idealised; unideal tapas is being rejected. Decisive Trikaldrishti rare

Saturday Sept. [22][6]

In sahaituka tivra, the law of increase has received a setback. Attention is necessary to maintain it if there is a rapid and prolonged excitation, and finally attention even with tapas becomes unavailing in some local sthanas; the sensibility seems for a time entirely to fail, although it revives after cessation. On the other hand the attempt on the contrary to make even attention unnecessary is being made and has an initial success. This method of enforcing strong advance out of temporary regression and denial, is noticeable in other parts of the sadhana. To a certain extent the defect in the tivra is being remedied

=

Premananda, long held in abeyance, is now again universalising itself, and this time firmly, as the subjective kama has universalised itself. It has two aspects, the prema within independent of the object, *ahaituka*, but ready to apply itself to all objects, and the prema awakened by the object, all objects, *sahaituka*.

=

Lipi is pressing for the immediate manifestation in fluidity of the ideal lipi. The territoriality resists, but the resistance is much weakened.

=

General flood of ideality, not yet perfectly clear and distinct in all its details or perfectly luminous in its hold.

[6] MS 21

Sunday. Sept [23].[7]

Fluidity of the immediate independent manifestation in the lipi is gaining great strength. It is now oftenest independent of the suggestion of words, but when delayed or incomplete in its manifestation, sometimes dependent on suggestion of substance.

Independent manifestation is secured; it must be universally immediate.

═══

Sahaituka raudrananda has increased in force and hold. Ananda of discomfort is not yet universalised. Ananda of pain still subject to limitation by degree, but much less than before.

Monday Sept [24].[8]

Lipi develops force of manifestation; but it does not yet get rid of the initial obstructiveness of the *parthiva akasha*

═══

There are times when the whole action of the mentality becomes vijnanamaya with a long continuity; afterwards there is a fall into a confused tamasic condition of the receiving brain, when the unredeemed physical mind tries to work; after a struggle the light of the vijnana reappears in whole or in part action.

Friday Sept [28].[9]

No definite movement during the last few days except the preparation of absolute spontaneity in the immediate manifestation of the lipi and an uncertain movement towards restoration of right activity in the samadhi. For the rest, the sadhana has been in a state of torpor and slight relapse. In arogya strong and persistent attack. In vijnana remnants of intellectual ideality at work — suspension for the most part of true ideality.

7 MS 22
8 MS 23
9 MS 27

Feb 14.

After a long interval, mainly end of December and January, devoted to poetry, there has been during February a steady Yogic activity.

Results.

(1) Siddhi of first chatusthaya finally complete. Momentary touches of asamata in asiddhi alone remain, but are being rapidly replaced by ananda, which is now not only the passive, but the active Brahmabhava occupying the whole conscious being.

(2) Second chatusthaya finally completed though still not quite perfect in devibhava (aishwaryabodha, attahasya). Dasya absolute except for some remnant of the habit of responsible effort in the will.

(3) Ananda Brahman complete. Brahmachatusthaya only now needs filling in; the uttama and the akshara are complete. The view of things, creatures etc as well as the sense of the containing Akasha is the Ananda view; = suddha, chidghana (vijnana), prema, kama. Some more perfect confirmation is all that is needed.

(4) Suddhi, mukti, bhukti complete except so far as they depend on the remainder of the unfinished siddhi. Subjectively they may be considered as complete; only the physical remains.

(5) Krishna Kali firmly established, but it has to be more developed.

(6) Vijnana is at last taking firm possession not only of Jnana, but of the telepathic mind. This movement is as complete today as it can be without the development of ideal T^2. T^3 has reached a certain relative completeness – not satisfactory – and is making towards the satisfactory completeness and perfection which will turn it finally into T^2. Thought telepathy is still weak and all is obstinately obstructed. Rupasiddhi and Samadhi are successfully

obstructed and get little play; what there is, is fragmentary and unsatisfactory.

(7) Physical Ananda is developing (ahaituka) against obstruction. Ahaituka kama promises to fix itself. Sahaituka tivra is well advanced, and only imperfect by a remnant of the habit of interruption when rapid continuous excitation takes place, but this interruption no longer amounts to a suspension, much less a relapse. The rest is slowly pushing its advance, but not yet with any large effect. Arogya is still in the struggle. Saundarya and utthapana still obstructed from manifestation except in details.

Feb 15

T^3 is definitely turning itself into vijnana. The final step must be to turn the intelligent mind from the recipient and judge which it is now into a channel, so that the ideality will no longer send its messages into the lower mind, but work in itself for itself, with itself as its own observer and judge. This is now being undertaken.

Hitherto it is the active activity of the intelligent mind which has had to be eliminated by a long progression of advances and relapses; now it is the passive activity which must also go. It is only in the tapas that the active activity still makes any noteworthy attempt to persist.

Lipi is now entirely idealised. It is attempting to stabilise perfectly its spontaneous legibilities. This stability is becoming more and more frequent, pronounced and ample; but when the tapas is not applied, the old confusion, indistinctness and evanescence still tend to predominate. The truth of the lipi is now continually being justified by results.

Trikaldrishti proper is developing (until now all has been really intelligent and telepathic); but all is being arranged first in the lower intuitional vijnana, not in the higher revelatory and inspirational ideality.

In physical siddhi Kamananda is progressing rapidly. Today for the first time there was settled unmoving ahaituka kamananda pervading the whole body, *somasya hradah*. This was at first only in the sitting posture, — owing to old habit it could not at first take hold while walking. But this also was confirmed in the afternoon;

but here there was a greater tendency to movement. Movement of ahaituka k. [kamananda] was established in the evening. All this depends still on smarana; but it tends to be constant and even when interrupted returns immediately at the call of smarana. The effect of the opposition is slight and transient. Sahaituka occurs now most frequently as a wave in the ahaituka.

Some action of rupasiddhi. The old forms are beginning to recur

Feb 16.

Full force of constant ahaituka kamananda, standing. The only defect now is the dependence on smarana. In the afternoon full ahaituka k. lying, in antardarshi, over the borders of samadhi, united with thought.

Lipi increases in legibility and stability in antardarshi, where confusion was formerly the law. It is noticeable that as the samadhi gets deeper, vividness and stability increase.

The interpretation of the lipi is now being done entirely by the vijnana; but definite trikaldrishti with time, circumstance etc is still to seek, except as regards the sadhana.

In T^3 there has been today a throw back to the intellectuality which is still attempting to judge what it receives and even indirectly to determine.

More old rupas tend to revive. Some weak hints of vishaya returning

Feb 17

The movement is now to get rid of the intellectual element altogether and allow only the intuitive vijnana to act.

Intense ahaituka ananda not dependent on smarana.

Script is now perfectly idealised, following in the footsteps of the vani.

Asmarana k. is now established; it is interrupted by exclusive thought-concentration, but is found again at once still in possession or else recovered at once, usually of itself without need of smarana, when the exclusive concentration ceases. This has now to be confirmed in complete continuity. It remains (1) to get rid of the interruption noted above, (2) to increase the intensities.

The lipi has reached a certain relative perfection of combined legibility[,] spontaneity and stability: but the old imperfect type still recurs where tapas is not applied. The sadhana has now to eliminate (1) confused or indistinct lipi; (2) incomplete expression. This done the rest is a matter of intensity of inspirational and revelatory speech, which is already beginning to become common.

Vijnana thought is now inspirational and revelatory as well as intuitional, but chiefly in the intuitional form.

The rule is established that there shall be first knowledge, then tapas in accordance with the will, reversing the former order in which tapas came first and then it was questioned whether it should be fulfilled.

Feb 18.

Confusion is being got rid of in the lipi; indistinctness remains. It is only in the imperfect lipis that these things exist, but even there confusion is rapidly disappearing. The habit of intuitional interpretation, especially of suggestive lipi where it is most difficult, is being confirmed. In express lipi it is becoming the rule.

Rupasiddhi is manifesting the perfect as well as the developed forms; but for the former the old defects persist, (1) side manifestation, (2) want of stability, (3) want of variety—for it is almost entirely in the type form, though with variety in that narrow limit.

Continuity and intensity of ahaituka k. increase, but not yet sufficiently to conquer the interruption of exclusive forgetfulness.

Tapas on the mental plane is being abandoned; trikaldrishti also must be abandoned. It is finally seen even by the intelligence that there can be here no absolute certainty of foresight or result, since it is the play of partial, conflicting and mutually self-adjusting tendencies, forces, ideas, impulses. The telepathy of these things and the understanding of them is becoming wider, subtler, more accurate, though far yet from being perfect and complete. Meanwhile T^3 is suspended. T^2 is postponed.

The hostile powers are attempting, as they are no longer able to prevent directly the continuity of the a. k. [ahaituka kamananda], to turn it into a neutral vishaya with extremities of acuteness turning to discomfort, so that this may be a cause for its discontinuance. But the effect has been only temporary.

Variety is returning to the rupa, but only, as before, in the crude forms.

Feb 19.

Samadhi after a long time recovered its activity. The ideal lipi chatusthaya is founded; vangmaya thought is freely active on all four states of the mentality; ideal perceptive thought has initiated itself in the three inner states as well as the one outer. The rest is still mental only; but there was the seed today for reading, narrative, dialogue. Rupa was active only in the vague chhayamaya. All this was done in a rush, by the exclusion, almost though not quite complete, of sleep. Henceforth sushupti must mean the Yogic sleep of the mind with wakefulness of the vijnana.

Lipi is advancing continuously and rapidly. It has become all intuitional lipi to the exclusion of the telepathic ideality – though prediction of material events may be an exception. It is becoming distinct in an orderly completeness, and now fluid in a legible and spontaneous legibility. This has not yet been universalised, but it is becoming a general rule.

Both sahaituka and ahaituka raudrananda are advancing. The burning touch is entirely anandamaya, except when it is so continued as to be intolerable, but even then in certain forms and up to a certain degree, a high degree, it remains anandamaya. There are signs of a similar progression, not yet so far advanced in the mârana –

Five forms of raudra – karshana, apakarshana, prakarshana, apikarshana, sankarshana

Strong relapse in T^2 still persists. Relapse means now stress, the attempt of the intelligence to attach certainty to the results of mental telepathy and tapas

Lipi is now seated in the antardarshi and bahirdarshi; but in the former it has still to conquer a natural tendency to instability, in the latter the large though now less insistent recurrence of the old imperfections.

Great strength of intuitional light in all the instruments of thought; imperfect only in T^2

Feb 20.

For the last two days ahaituka k. much subjected to violent suppression to its minimum point and easily interrupted, sahaituka obstructed. Smarana can always restore the former to action and generally but not always to intensity. It is mainly while walking that the adverse movement takes place. Nevertheless the intensity is increasing both in force and in general level and in power of sustained continuity. The habit of interruption is the one real difficulty in ahaituka k.

In rupa perfectly developed and perfect forms now show, especially the former, a certain power of stability, but they arise from long tratak on the living object as their excuse or starting-point, though not their real cause, and they are confined to the type form, chiefly in the three varieties most commonly watched.

A clear ideal (intuitional) trikaldrishti is now acting, but it has to be firmly distinguished from the less certain vision of the mental and pranic superplanes which sometimes come in its place and sometimes are mixed with it. Moreover it is isolated and gives only the general result without time, place or circumstance of intermediate event. Tapas siddhi is still manasic, but has greatly increased in force for general, and even though much less, for particular result. The power varies from $10°$ or $20°$ to $60°$. A higher force is rare, except in moving objects, where it sometimes reaches $80°$

Unity of Trikaldrishti (telepathic and intuitional) and tapas has been roughly accomplished. The siddhi is now attempting to get rid of the confusion which periodically overtakes the T^2 thought, owing to revival of intelligential turmoil and false stress.

Ahaituka k. is again continuous, ordinarily with a certain intensity. . the periods of exclusive forgetfulness find it still in the body; therefore it must be considered to have been there all along in a suppressed state.

In Samadhi the effects of yesterday were carried a little farther, in antardarshi and swapna of the lighter kind. Lipi especially made great progress to an easy, spontaneous and unsupported perfection which it realised, but cannot always maintain against the old faults of confused manifestation, instability and vagueness and dimness. Some initial ideality and coherence was manifested in reading, dialogue and narrative, but none of them were well sustained. Tejomaya rupa in chhayamaya atmosphere, but evanescent. Some stability in some chhayamaya rupas, but not of long duration.

In afternoon work.

Feb 21.

Spontaneous variety in crude rupa greater than ever before, but all in the crude crude. Perfect stability only in two or three type forms, but an initial stability is striving to fix itself in the others. The rupas are not yet always complete or perfect.

Vangmaya, vani, script suddenly taken up in full by the Ishwara.

Inspirational ideality begins in the lipi and is already as common as the intuitional. Lipi begins to justify its trikaldrishti—eg with regard to the situation in Roumania, viz that the principle had already been settled, to yield after a little velleity of resistance. It is notable that the telepathic interpretation of the situation was correct. The perfect lipi with well developed stability is becoming more normal.

The style of the thought vangmaya is becoming more and more illumined and inspirational.

The intuitional lipi is oftenest perfect with difficulty,—it has not except at its best an immediate stability, legibility, spontaneity; the inspirational has it normally; the slower manifestation is exceptional to it. It is even sometimes instantaneously perfect as if in the flash. It is now however taking up the intuitional lipi.

Free manifestation of chhayamaya rupa in swapna-samadhi at night; stable forms, scenes, etc, continuous action. Even in one case the supreme stability of vivid scene, but with a certain *chanchalya* of motion in the scene and appearing and disappearing of figures. Strong stability of reading in one case. It is to be noted that the old habitual difficulty of quadruped forms seems to have been overcome in all fields; wherever this has happened, there has come as a sign, as previously predicted in the lipi, the form of the Antelope.

For some time lipi kaushalya has been tending to develop: clear fiery and jyotirmaya lipi in antardarshi. In bahirdarshi tejomaya is common and dhumramaya occurs; varnamaya is rare and not varied in hue.

Feb 22.

The intelligence is being pushed aside as the judge and recipient; it still persists, but is being dominated. It is the intuitive mind that is taking its place, while in the thought etc it is mostly the ideality itself that is the judge and recipient.

Lipi trikaldrishti is now being constantly fulfilled.

After taking up telepathies into the intuitive mind and observing there all the relative uncertain certainties of the mental, vital and physical planes, so as to give them their right incidence and root out false stress, — a rapid summing up of the movement of the last few days, — the intuitional trikaldrishti has founded itself. The intellectual action with regard to T^3 is now only a habit-survival which must progressively be discouraged and eliminated.

In samadhi large masses of reading and a persistent attempt to decipher, but only brief clauses or phrases decipherable, separate or in the mass. These however, are becoming more common. Development is also proceeding in the other deficient parts.

Feb. 23.

The union of T^2 is becoming closer, but there is strong resistance to the development of the intuitional ideality. It is, however, progressing.

Full variety in crude rupa. The tendency to clear completeness and stability does not yet fix itself; and all is done against great obstruction.

Inspirational ideality entirely takes the place of intuitional in the vangmaya and establishes itself in the perceptive thought; only the lower telepathic thought is intuitional. The trikaldrishti is also now inspirational and tends to increase, but is still imitated and hampered in its development by false inspirational certainties of the mental, pranic and physical planes. This in the midst of a violent attack of the old intelligence.

Samadhi advances greatly. Long coherent narrative and reading and to a less extent dialogue, but still infirm and floating; the dream element predominates. Lipi is becoming more and more perfect in the antardarshi.

Some attempt to recover activity in the vishaya; still much obstructed as also rupa.

Shadow of athumia still prevents perfect continuity of the first chatusthaya, though it is unable to persist successfully. Purely in reference to siddhi and asiddhi.

Feb 24

Intuitional lipi of the inspirational type is giving way before the pure inspirational which is more perfect in substance and form. The inspired lipi has at its highest an element of direct revelatory sight

T^2 has been considerably extended, but there is still much that has to be taken up before it can be secure or complete in its extension.

Sahaituka Kama Ananda has for some time been reduced almost to nil, and ahaituka depressed so as only to be active on condition of attentive smarana and intense by tapas smarana. Ahaituka is now recovering its vina-smarana activity suspended only by exclusive concentration, and its intensity. Vaidyuta has been showing occasionally signs of development.

Perfect development of narrative and reading in Samadhi, coherent, long-continued and initially idealised. The old incoherence intervened only at the end and very slightly from time to time. Dialogue also, but on a lesser scale, yet with the same essential qualities. Long continuity is frequent in rupa of swapna samadhi but stability is rare, except sometimes a troubled and recurrent stability. Chhayamaya reigns. In antardarshi lipi alone is really active. Rupa is obstructed more even than in the jagrat.

Rupa and vishaya fail to advance beyond their former bounds, except that the type touches are frequently stable and long-continued and the general touch is coming out from sukshma just over the borders of sthula. The sthula effect of feeling is partly there, though the touch remains sukshma

Great force of delight in raudrananda even when pain is strongly present. There are exceptions.

Feb 25.

Farther elimination of the attempt to decide things by intelligential telepathy. As a result the inspirational thought and T^2 are growing stronger.

Vishaya is resuming development, touch on the lines already indicated, taste and sight resuming their old gains, but hearing and smell are still obstructed, the first almost entirely, the latter partially.

Kamananda varies between the sasmarana and vinasmarana; the first is still more usual. Sahaituka is slowly recovering.
=

Brief attack (10 minutes) of the old form of asiddhi modified.
=

The inspirational ideality has completely taken up the lipi, the perceptive thought, the vangmaya: even the intuitional thought or lipi is inspirational in its substance and manner. Only the T^2 and the phantasy still admit the intellectual thought. In the former however both telepathy and tapas are becoming inspirational. Interpretation of lipi is following the same course.

Great play of rupa in the evening of all kinds, but imperfect except in crude and in the rest only when seen indirectly or sadhara (sthapatya) etc or in type forms. Stability is yet unattained and variety in the perfect forms is only promising to develop.

Sudden lipi perfect in form is becoming frequent.

Feb 26.

The inspirational ideality continues to enlarge, in spite of a turmoil of recurrent intellectuality assailing the system from outside.

Idealising of samadhi continues. Long continuity of successive event increases in rupa, but stability is still only recurrent, except up to a certain point. There is much obstruction. In vishaya and rupa there are only small isolated gains; the obstruction prevents a secure basis being founded.

Shanti resisted all attacks today, sraddha faltered for a while. Dasya is deepening. Once hasya and sraddha are perfectly established, only the secure intensity of the chandibhava of devi will remain in the first two chatusthayas to be secured against all attack or temporary relapse. Dehashakti is however still subject to superficial failure; at bottom it remains.

Feb 27.

T^2 is now successfully taking up all the old T^3, this time with a certainty of rapid finality. The attempt to decide by other means than the inspirational vijnana, whether by knowledge or will, is not entirely eliminated, but is now far advanced, and prevails only in moments of forgetfulness. As yet it is only to the extent of the old T^3 which was far from complete that this success obtains, but it is extending itself to the whole range of possible intelligent thought and will, to complete the brihat satyam ritam. Beyond that, however, there is the highest T^2, absolute, which has yet to manifest.

The defects in the strength of I and II [*first and second chatusthayas*] are being rapidly dealt with, except in dehashakti.

Raudrananda is raised to a high degree, but not yet absolute. Above a certain point, the first impression is pain, though ananda immediately intervenes and takes possession. In subsequent effects pain mingles, but the tendency is for ananda to prevail. The general receptive attitude of the physical being is anandamaya and this is rapidly prevailing.

The intelligence has not only lost, but renounced its right to judge; but it is still involuntarily the recipient in the lower mental system and even by habit in the thought, except when the latter acts as if by a sort of force in the inspirational ideality. The ideal action has not yet become natural to the whole being. The result was a temporary inability to act subjectively, a sunk quietude. No disturbance of samata, nor of dasya, but some of sraddha

Rupasiddhi continues to prepare its advance. Intermittent recurrence of variety in the crude is the only siddhi as yet well established.

Feb 28.

The inspirational ideality has suddenly become natural to the system, especially in thought of all kinds. The defect lies still in vyapti which comes to the emotion, intelligence or vital feeling, and in decisive trikaldrishti which is sometimes ideal, sometimes mental. But this is being rapidly remedied.

Physical siddhi has for some time been left to itself and does not advance. It maintains itself, but with difficulty and lapses. Vina smarana Ananda especially has lost its hold and comes only intermittently after sasmarana.

3–27 MARCH 1918

March 1918

The month of February has been the month of the founding of the vijnana in the type; the month of March is marked out for its confirmation and primary completion in all parts of the third chatusthaya. April for the farther confirmation and a greater completeness.

March 3.

After two days of oppression by the environing Intelligence, the ideality is again busy defining its form in the lipi, ideative thought and vangmaya. First, there has been in the thought, including telepathic thought of trikaldrishti, the entire revelatory intuitional ideality in the bed of the intuitive mentality. It is now seeking to get rid of the intuitive mental response and become pure revelatory inspirational ideation, the highest point reached on Feb. 28 in type. The surrounding Intelligence tries still to preserve its habit of response; this is still the chief stumbling-block.

Lipi more easily confirms itself in the revelatory inspirational vijnana; the lower forms occur, but are there easily discouraged.

March 4

The decisive trikaldrishti has at last fixed itself in the revelatory intuitional type.

Perfect lipi, sudden, spontaneous, vividly legible, completely stable of a high revelatory inspirational ideality is now beginning to make itself entirely normal.

Letter in the samadhi perfect in form except for want of vivid distinctness, not stable enough to be slowly deciphered, but recurrent in variation

Premananda is becoming normal in the sarvadarshana.

March 5.

Telepathies of thoughts, intentions, impulses, tendencies which do not fulfil themselves are to be known and are now to be addressed to the idealised heart consciousness, — it is not yet idealised, — all positive fact of trikaldrishti is to be known by the vijnana buddhi

Mar 7.

The lipi now fixed in the inspirational or middle ideality is being firmly founded in the eight qualities, spontaneity, legibility, stability, rapidity, fluidity, completeness, light, justice. The lipi kaushalya is being finally developed and all forms occur with some initial frequency of recurrence except the pure varna. Jyotir is commonest, tejas and agni occasional; prakasha seems to have been abandoned.

Both forms of thought have replaced, when the ideality is active, the inferior by the middle or inspirational vijnana, which holds in itself revelation and has taken up intuition and viveka. Trikaldrishti is in course of transformation. The middle ideality has a surer certainty and lends itself less to the relapses of the intuitive intelligence.

Prema kamananda in the darshana have firmly combined with the shuddha. The full ananda only fails when the sarvasaundarya darshana is deficient or withheld.

Vishaya and rupa are again obstructed.

Certain and decisive trikaldrishti is enlarging itself rapidly; tapas-siddhi is coalescing with the ideal knowledge and pure telepathic tapas is being rapidly abandoned. It is in fact no longer admitted. T^3 has received its dismissal. It only continues to exist in chaotic fragments in the external suggestions which are no longer accepted. This is with regard to the buddhi, — but in the sense-mind intuitively intelligential telepathy still exists.

There are trikaldrishtic indications that March will be a month of the extension of the physical Ananda and that secure continuity in the Kamananda will be rapidly established. The movement has already begun.

Sudden intensification, with prolonged recurrence, of the sa-haituka vaidyuta, current through the body (arms and legs).

Mar 11

The revelatory has suddenly today substituted itself for the inspirational ideality, but it is at present the intuitional revelatory. It is taking up all the action of the ideality and enlightening and transforming the relics of the intelligential mentality.

=

There has been a struggle in the Kamananda. Persistent continuous recurrence seems to have been well established, though the enemy still struggles to bring about a long entire suspension; but secure continuity is not yet established.

Mar 15

The sadhana is going through what would formerly have been a relapse but is now a process of readjustment through the permission of the intellectual action trying to reestablish itself, but bringing about at each step a farther diminution of its power to return.

The first two chatusthayas are being steadily confirmed in their completeness and the touches of denial are being eliminated. The first is practically complete in its armour of passive samata, almost complete in the active. The second is feebly besieged at times, but the completion of the dasya and the chandibhava is evident. The latter is only deficient in hasya.

Continuity of ahaituka kamananda, when not suspended by exclusive vismarana, is confirmed. Sahaituka has been for long depressed and only occasional.

The Ananda in darshana is complete and consolidated in its combined action, but sometimes falls momentarily back into the mental form with one or two habits of dissociation, mostly omission of kamaprema; but this ordinarily, is instantaneously corrected with regard to living beings. The whole has still to be raised to a firmer intensity.

Kamananda continued through samadhi, light and double, only suspended by the deep and complete interiority. Other former incompatibilities initially conquered. A beginning has been made in overcoming the exclusive forgetfulness, but this is not yet confirmed.

Mar [*date not written*]
    The first chatusthaya is now entirely confirmed. Even if old touches of impatience, discomfort etc arrive from outside by strong habit to touch the surface of the physical mentality, they are at once stopped and either disappear or are transformed.

=

The second chatusthaya is now complete in all its circumstances with the one fault that the Kali element in the Devibhava, which is constant, is not steady; the ordinary condition is that of the Mahasaraswati with a strong Mahaluxmi colouring and submerged Maheshwari basis. This is full of shama ananda, but insufficient in tapas. It is the Mahakali element that carries the full tapas, ishwarabhava and attahasya of the lila; but when the Mahakali element is there, the Mahaluxmi colouring and ananda intensity diminishes; this defect is the cause of the unsteadiness. Tapas ananda has to take possession of shama ananda; Mahakali has to mould itself into the Mahasaraswati, and be the contained in that continent.

=

After a long period of lower working the revelatory ideality is taking possession. The old physical lethargy of the mind can no longer act; but in its place is the akartri-shama; into this the prakasha of the revelatory vijnana (drishti) is beginning to pour itself.

=

The ahaituka tivrananda is recurring after a long interval of rarity. It is now pervasive, more prolonged in persistence, occurs in all the members.

=

Lipi is enforcing itself in the eightfold qualities against the old etheric obstruction.

=

Ishwaradarshana has taken possession of the Anandadarshana. It dwells more normally in the Ananda than in the lapse to the mentality.

=

Although violently obstructed, vaidyuta ananda now occurs, more and more pervasive in its current.

=

For several days the ahaituka kamananda has been violently obstructed and persistently expelled, but it retains its ground, though often reduced to a minimum.

=

There is a continual alternation now between the Mahakali bhava and the Mahasaraswati for possession, the latter becoming more and more full of the former.

Mar 25. The Mahakali element has fixed itself. Eight days are given by the lipi, up to April 2, for its taking full possession of the bhava.

Mar 27. Only momentary and rare touches affect the first two chatusthayas. The one deficiency is an infirm faith in the full extent of the siddhi in the sharira and the life; the devi hasya is there, but not constant. The third chatusthaya is extending itself, but experiencing still at each step the lapse towards the mentality.

20 APRIL – 20 MAY 1918

Notebook of the Sadhana.

20th April 1918.

A manifest change has been the accomplishment of the Chandi personality in the Devibhava of the Prakriti. This bhava is in its nature Mahasaraswati, the Aniruddha-shakti. It has for its base Maheshwari; it is strongly coloured with Mahaluxmi. This combination was finally expressed in a strong and long-permanent personality, perfect in equality, intense in bliss, full of universal love and *madhurya*, but deficient in *virya* and *shakti*, ῥαθυμος. The advent of the Chandi bhava, effected in accordance with lipi and other prediction on the 2ᵈ, stabilised and completed in rudra force on the 15th, since then undergoing modifications and vicissitudes, has brought the completion of the Devibhava, not yet altogether perfect, but firm fundamentally. It is Mahasaraswati personality with the Mahakali bhava; the Mahaluxmi colour, a hidden Maheswari base (*pratishtha*).

Defects still existent. (1) Occasionally the ῥαθυμια of the Mahasaraswati gets the better of the *rudra tejas*; this is mostly when things are getting on well or when the samata in shama gets the better of the samata in tapas. This however is rare. Ordinarily samata in tapas is the temperament.

(2) The samata having lost its old base is disturbed from time to time. The excessive mental tapas and its reactions which used to come with the Kali bhava recur, though with less and less hold on the system; they come but they cannot remain. They rush upon the adhara from outside, but can only partially get their hands upon it and have to loose their hold. Nevertheless this is now the chief difficulty and the root of all the others.

(3) The ishwarabhava has come with the Chandi virya. It is in its perfection the aishwarya of the *Dasi* empowered by the Lover

and Master, the [real][1] aishwarya being his, the executive aishwarya hers. But the mind element often insists too much on the instrumental aishwarya acting through the mind in forgetfulness of its source. Then there is trouble and disturbance of samata.

(4) The hasyam of the first chatusthaya is developing the attahasyam of Mahakali into which is to be taken the jnana-hasyam, sneha-hasyam and kautuka-hasyam of the three other powers. But with defect of perfect *sraddha swashaktyam*, of perfect samata in tapas and of perfect ishwarabhava, this cannot take possession of the temperament.

(5) Sraddha has an occasional perfection when it is sraddha in the Bhagavan and in the shakti as his executive power; but in the absence or defect of ideal tapas-siddhi, this also wavers. General habit of sraddha prevails, but is crossed by the intellectual uncertainty as to the intention of the Ishwara.

(6) & (7) Resultant defect of Mahaluxmi colour (bliss and love) and resurgence to the surface of the Maheshwari to correct the defect of excessive mental tapas and asamata.

━━

Lipi predictions. Finality of the ideality from 15ᵗʰ July. (20ᵗʰ April).

> *The seagod in the ideality* (Varuna).
>
> Liberty in the idealities soon (21ˢᵗ April)
>
> January to July the ideality, July to January the physical siddhi. (3ᵈ May).
>
> The seagod in the telepathies, trikaldrishti, tapassiddhi. (May 4ᵗʰ)

The devihasyam which was formerly only in the buddhi and from thence affected the temperament, is now manifesting originally in the temperament. It is a compound of the four kinds of hasya or a combination of them. It has not yet occupied the place of the original colourless and featureless hasyam (ahaituka), but is preparing its occupation. Incidentally the ῥαθυμια of the Mahasaraswati is being taken up by the Mahakali,—it is an

---

[1] *MS* really

anandamaya titiksha-udasinata-nati — and will be converted into an element of the sama tapas (shamomaya tapas). Sraddha, ishwara-bhava etc are also taking their proper shape and the other elements of the shakti-chatusthaya are preparing a more perfect combination and fusion. All this, however, is not yet well accomplished or perfectly sure in its action.

21st April.

The akashic lipi is developing with an extraordinary swiftness. The lipis are manifesting in spite of a dull etheric resistance still left with a phenomenal rapidity and fluidity and an outflow of ideal justice and light in the substance and ordinarily, though not always, in the expression; also, with a great completeness. This is being done by the aid of the suggestions, but these are now not the intellectual, but the ideal suggestions. The resistance is to the rapidity in the completeness, but this is being overcome; and to the legibility; but the illegibility also is being overcome, though less perfectly; and to the spontaneity. Spontaneous lipi flows less readily, but this also is preparing to associate with itself the other qualities. Interpretation of the lipi is now really ideal with a spontaneous judgment (γνωρισις). There is still a habit of confusion when the mass of outflow is left to itself, but this is mainly in the chitra-lipi. This progress is in the bahirdarshi; lipi in the rest is still imperfectly developed. All this has been done in a few days.

22d April.

The development of the lipi and a certain development of the ideality — the sea-god in the ideality — is making itself common to bahirdarshi, antardarshi and swapna, but as yet with less force and ripeness of large action in the two last. In the jagrat there is an action of tapas which is at last quite freed from the personal element and perceives all its willings as actions of knowledge and has even begun to distinguish with a commencement of automatic fidelity those which will realise themselves from those which will remain as yet unfulfilled tendencies, impulses or intentions. What was formerly called the trikaldrishti was simply a telepathic stress which happened to come right, but had no sure principle or light of judgment and might easily turn to false stress. What is now coming, is an automatic fidelity to truth, a fidelity not of the telepathic stress in the intuitive intelligence, but of the intuitively revelatory judgment in the ideality. This is as yet very imperfect in its action and still involved in the intellectual telepathies.

25th April

After two or three days of a confused action, the intuitively revelatory judgment has disengaged itself and is extending its action. As yet it applies only to tapas and telepathies. As regards the latter it sometimes replaces them, that is, it takes them up idealised and accompanies them with the ideal judgment, so that they are entirely correct ideal and not doubtful mental telepathies, or it observes and judges them, or there is a mixed action. The latter has to be eliminated as an evident source or pratistha of error. With regard to the tapas, it is the impersonal perception of what has to happen, because that is what is being definitively willed in the ideal Vijnana; at present it is correct with the substance of the ideal Truth, but not often clearly luminous with the light of the ideal Truth. This is because it leans on what is being willed in the present, but does not go back to what stands as willed in the Eternal Idea. There is as yet much tendency to attendant intellectual hesitation and error of circumstance, where the fulfilment is not immediate, but this is being eliminated. The action of the ideal Truth as applied to present status of invisible objects is not yet developed beyond the telepathic action. What the ideal T^2 is now working on, is the present tendency and future action of visible objects.

30th April.

Completion of the Brahma-chatusthaya in the perception and sense of all things as the conscious body of the Purushottama. This was prepared by the *sors,*

रसोऽहमप्सु कौन्तेय प्रभास्मि शशिसूर्ययोः
प्रणवः सर्ववेदेषु शब्दः खे पौरुषं नृषु

followed by the sense of the Ishwara as the delight, *rasa*, in the flood of the being, अप्सु, the light of knowledge in the vijnana (sun) and mentality (moon), the word and the thought, the tapas. This led to the perception and sense of all substance of matter and consciousness, quality, force, thought, action etc as the Ishwara. Formerly these perceptions were of separate things (tattwas, elements) and temporary, though often of long duration, but now it is global, integral and steadfast. It rejects the remnants of the intellectual fragmentation and division which still come to deny its completeness.

Ananda of samata has proved sufficiently firm throughout the month. It is now combined firmly with the tapas; desire has perished, though tapatya still remains, but only as a minor element. Therefore the touches of asamata can get no hold, are entirely external and are cast out of the adhar automatically as soon as they enter. External, moreover, not of any near, but of a distantly watching, rather than environing mentality.

Tapas is now very strong; in the field of exercise the obstacle has no longer a genuine power of resistance, but only of persistence and this again persists only by a persistent recurrence which gives it after much difficulty the power for a time to reestablish itself rather than by a right of its own in the environment. This is even when the tapas is without knowledge of trikaldrishti. The movement has now begun which will turn Time from an obstacle with which the personal Tapas had to struggle into an instrument which the personal Tapas, become that of the transcendent will working upon the universal to modify it as well as through the universal, will use for the disposition of its results. This movement is as yet only initial; as it advances tapas and trikaldrishti will become entirely reconciled and identified. Trikaldrishti increases in frequency and has begun to carry with it the right perception of Time.

This development enables the Chandi in the devibhava to affirm its characteristic singhi element more firmly. The ishwarabhava and attahasya are preparing to grow upon the system.

The intellect is gradually fading out of the system, (lipi, euthanasia of the intellectuality) and the whole is becoming vijnana + intuitive mentality. Only a vague floating remnant of the real intellectuality is left; it acts most when faced with the obstacle in life.

All is being idealised in the samadhi, but the dialogue, narrative etc are still usually mental, swapnamaya, though much more sustained and coherent. Reading is still normally incoherent. All are occasionally ideal. Lipi is always ideal, but is less perfected in its eightfold quality and less free and spontaneously active in the antardarshi than in the bahirdarshi. Rupa and vishaya in the bahirdarshi are still unable to take firm hold of the etheric system.

On the whole the "liberty in the idealities" (lipi, 21st April) is working itself out, but does not cover the whole third chatusthaya and is nowhere quite absolute.

May

May 1st – Lipi predicted today perfect ideality and the beginning of physical delight; but it is only the seed of the perfect ideality and the definite beginning of physical delight in the tivra that the interpretation relying on the mental pre-sentiment admitted. It is this which has actually evolved, but as a beginning in both cases of a steadier final development, of the perfect ideality including T^2 and of the total physical delight in all five anandas.

May 4th Saturday

Yesterday the siddhi in the sahaituka tivra developed beyond all mistake an incipient finality of development. First, an universality of the tivra response to any touch however slight, and even a general mass response even to such habitual sparsha as the close pressure of the cloth at the loins usually unfelt and the loose pressure on the legs. This tivra contains the vishaya and develops the kama, as is now seen, today. This triple movement is preparing to become a law, but as yet sometimes the vishaya prevails over the tivra, sometimes the tivra alone remains, or else the vishaya is at once the kama without any intermediate tivra. The tendency however is for all vishaya to become tivra. At the same time an abundant ahaituka raudra is beginning to manifest even while the sahaituka is pressing to generalise itself. Vaidyuta comes with more difficulty owing to want of past habit in the body or insistence in the mental tapas, but when it is insisted on, is more assured and can have more mass than before. Kama has for a long time been most vehemently resisted and suppressed partly because it has been the most demanded by the mental tapas and has therefore attracted the mass of the physical opposition, partly because it is the most central and vital of all the Anandas. It is now pressing to remanifest more securely, but has not yet got rid of the suppression, though that is steadily becoming less effective. All this justifies the lipi "today total delight", the truth of which was doubted by the intelligence because to the mental perception the physical opposition to the kamananda seemed too strong to be surmounted.

The script set down yesterday. "The first week of May outlines the ritam in the satyam brihat. It prepares the totality of the physical delight. It prepares too the samadhi." All three predictions are being fulfilled with what has been called the enthusiastic, that is a sudden, vehement and anandamaya rapidity.

In the samadhi today continuous vangmaya and ideal ideation was established, the habit of fatigue in the physical mind which demanded cessation or intermission being denied its claim and dismissed. The habit of simultaneous action of the two which has hitherto been violently or obstinately resisted by the physical mind, was firmly founded and illustrated by a rich continuity of simultaneous action. Initially the habit of simultaneous manifestation of the lipi in the antardarshi and even in the *swapna*, where it has been the most difficult, was immediately afterwards founded, in the same stream of rapid progress. The lipi in the *antardarshi* is now assuming the same freedom and perfection of the eightfold quality as in the *bahirdarshi*, only it is still rather more resisted by the physical ether, its manifestation less free, prompt and fluid in completeness, its stability more initial and less definitive. Ideal ideation is driving out the dull habit of intellectual thought in the samadhi along with the physical fatigue; it has been busy with its electric needleplay modifying the physical mind, in its sukshma brain-stuff even when no definite ideation was at work.

The same movement has begun in the outward waking mind; it is extending first to a confident play of the ideal telepathy, that is what was the intelligence's perception of present intention, tendency, possibility etc. This is now firm in the satyam brihat, except for actual situation etc of objects where the tamasic darkness of the external intelligence opposes the action of a power which has already been established in the mental telepathy, but has yet to be established in the ideal. T^2 today is developing the play of the universal ideal perception and tapas and for the first time manifested the transcendent Tapas and idea which predestines and decides. This is evidently the first beginning of that perfection which, it has been declared, will be made final in July.

That this may be done so rapidly, the lethargy habit has to be abolished, as the lipi has predicted, that is, the demand of the physicality for cessation and intermission, its refusal to respond to the tapas and idea which was the real though hidden basis for the habit of long cessation and relapse which the sadhana has been struggling with and at last gradually eliminating, — recently quite rapidly, — during the last seven years. It is still strong in the physical sadhana; therefore there is there except in the Ananda, only a slow and laboured and intermittent progress, though in some directions still a steady progress, and in some respects only a defensive denial of farther active asiddhi relapse, in others a balance of relapse and reparation with a slight gain sometimes for the siddhi, sometimes for the asiddhi. It is in utthapana and saundarya that the asiddhi is strongest, in arogya the siddhi for the most part holds its own and even has had definite particular victories and advances; in Ananda it is hampered, but now on the verge of a general triumphant progress, even engaged in its actual inception.

In the evening some initial fulfilment of the lipi, "the seagod in the telepathies, trikaldrishti, tapassiddhi.", chiefly in the telepathies.

Activity in the remainder of the samadhi, increasing with some difficulty and a tendency to constant intermissions, is not yet idealised or well-combined, but it tends in that direction.

May 5.

There is a considerable increase in frequency of the transcendent idea-tapas but the rest of T^2 has been acting through the intelligence this morning therefore uncertainly and without clear light. The chief advance has been in effectivity of vashita for particular effect, but the movement, though not without strength is only initial.

The main cause of the descent has been a general physical lassitude which has been indulged to a certain extent. Fatigue has begun now to be excluded from the mind, the psychic prana and the prana upholding the action of the body and confined to the body and the physical prana directly involved in the body. Action of the body can go on in spite of the fatigue in the muscles, but the general effect of the latter can still throw a general effect on the upholding prana, not precisely of fatigue, but of lassitude in the *virya*. The only imperative effect is the reaction of muscular strain

Tivra has now established the rule of increase by excitation; but this modified by a continued habit of intermediate deadening or diminution of response. The rule — in continuous excitation — of response with interstices of deadening or diminution followed by renewed and in the end increased response is being supplanted by the habit of sustained response; but the substitution is not yet complete.

Prolongation of response after cessation of touch and repetition after cessation, the latter sometimes an often repeated and almost continuous repetition, is rapidly coming in; so also the habit of sympathetic response, after cessation.

Pervading vaidyuta has begun, but is not yet strong in its hold or intense. The intensity is however increasing.

Sahaituka tivra still generally demands *nistapas smarana*, passive attention; continuity usually requires *satapas smarana*. Ahaituka is trying to develop frequency of its *nihsmarana* action. With smarana it occurs spontaneously anywhere.

After strong obstruction in the daytime a great development in the night of swapna samadhi. The undeveloped movements develop fluidity and ease in coherency; especially reading firm, clear, legible, sufficiently stable, only once or twice incoherent, frequent, fluid. Only when presented in the mass and not in short sentences, was it still incoherent, illegible, quite unstable, but even here there was an attempt at improvement.

Dream is now normally consecutive and coherent, though not invariably. It still has, however, the nature of phantasy.

May 6th

Tapatya is being exiled steadily from the action of T^2. Tapatya is the straining to know and fulfil; it is not in itself desire, but the cause of desire in the prana and heart; desire being banished, tapatya has remained as an illegitimate prolongation and stress of what is received in the ideality, it is mental tapas, bringing false stress and falsification of values. Although not a cause of grief and disappointment like desire, it is a cause of false hope and false doubt and also of undue pravritti and undue nivritti of mental action and as a result of temperamental and physical action. It is being driven out by the establishment of the transcendent idea-will of which the universal tendencies and movements become the effective media and results. At first this tends to bring an excessive passivity of the instrumental Jiva, but this is a defect which is in the course of being remedied. Tapatya took up the communications of the idea will and personalised them into a mental effort, belief, hope in the instrumental Jiva. They have, where necessary, to be personalised but as part of the personality of the Ishwara creating in the Jiva ideal sraddha and pravritti.

The day has been one chiefly of obstruction, only minor progress made. Fluency with incoherence in the newly progressing parts of the samadhi. Tejomaya rupa is frequent in swapna samadhi, but it is instable or imperfectly stable, without hold on the chidakasha. Perfect rupa has once or twice manifested in antardarshi, usually it is only crude; but it is only momentary.

Ananda progresses distinctly only in the tivra; there is a general tendency to suppression.

May 7.

The defect that has to be got rid of throughout the ideality, is the descent of the vijnana into mind. This makes the intellect the receptive agency which creates a sort of receptive intellectual judgment, assent and denial, a cause of error and uncertainty. It prolongs the old defects, especially in T^2, the defect of taking (1) inactual possibilities, (2) actual tendencies and possibilities as definite trikaldrishti. The first is not frequent and has no imperative power, the second is still the chief cause of positive error, although it is less powerfully insistent than it was formerly. The removal of this defect begins today. It is prolonged by the *rhathumia*, the leaving things to take care of themselves instead of insisting by the ideal tapas upon perfection. It gives an undue force to the etheric resistance in the physicality and prevents the full liberation of the ideality to act largely and perfectly. When it is absent, there is an anandamaya certainty.

The script has laid down for May in the physical siddhi (May 5)

(1) primary utthapana, to be pressed steadily and laid down in the base;

(2) a distinct general advance in arogya;

(3) a struggle with old age and asaundarya;

(4) a complete fivefold physical ananda.

All these necessarily to be only an initial movement.

For today the script runs

"The liberation of the ideality is to be completed today within certain limits. T^2 will take a little more time; so will effectivity of tapas in rupasiddhi and vishaya."

Nothing is said here about the samadhi.

=

The liberation of the ideality is being effected by two movements;

(1) elimination of the intellectual response, involving a physical movement by which the thought ceases to descend into the area of the mental brain-stuff in the sukshma body environing the brain in the physical body and acts from the junction of the sukshma mind and the vijnana above the head, upon and above the sahasradala;

(2) substitution of the inspirational for the intuitional stuff in the ideality.

This has been done already in speech thought and ideation; it is still to be done in T², though there too it is done within certain limits. Rupasiddhi has begun today with a more ideal tapas, but as yet no definitive progress has been made in the forms. Rupasiddhi also has eight qualities to be perfected, — spontaneity, stability, vividness, rapidity, fluidity, completeness, variety, coherence, and a ninth, truth (ie, point, right relation, utility) corresponding to the "light" and "justice" in the lipi qualities.

Vishaya shows no tendency to develop beyond its persistent limitations.

There is no longer any difficulty about maintaining the ideal liberty in the speech thought, it is normal; there is still difficulty in the ideation, it is only becoming normal.

Lipi is perfect in sadhara and niradhara, normally; it is still difficult to maintain perfection or even to enforce it in the chitra lipi and sthapatya lipi. The absolute perfection comes most easily in the niradhara; but in none is there entire freedom from the resistance of the physical ether to the perfect manifestation. Some force of tapas is always required; left to itself the ether yields always ideal lipi, but in an imperfect form.

For the second week of May the script runs.

"The second week of May is more important than the first. What was begun in the first, will be made effective in the second, that is, free ideality, abundance and accuracy of T², evolution of physical ananda, idealisation of the samadhi. In addition rupasiddhi and vishaya will break the long obstruction which has prevented their evolution. Other results will outline themselves during the week."

Physical ananda is once more active; the kama is overcoming the obstruction and it is developing a new movement which shows that even in the physical movements there is such a thing as the ideal and the mental action. That is to say, the ananda hitherto manifested even if in its origin supramental, was supported by the intelligent mind or at the best by the intuitive mind, while what is now manifesting is ideal delight in the body. That was mixed in its character, modified by the lower physical reaction, this is pure and sovereign and has taken up the physical reaction into the ideality; it is self-existent even when sahaituka. The sparsha only awakens, it does not produce it. A similar distinction is prefigured in the arogya but is not as yet practically defined.

May 8

The first week of May has fulfilled the outline of progress laid down for it, a preparation within certain limits. It has effected a great liberation in speech thought, ideation and lipi and not only outlined, but laid down here the clear and strong ideal ritam in the satyam brihat, fixing it for the present mainly in the inspirational form or at the lowest in an intuitional form truly ideal and not intellectualised. Sometimes the old intellectualised form still recurs, but this is an exception without power or sanction in the nature. In T^2 it has done no more than prepare, but it has got [rid]² of desire in the tapas and diminished the force of tapatya: it has put the telepathies in their right place and tried to make the field clear for the real trikaldrishti; it has also laid down the right relation between the transcendent and the universal in this action of the ideality. But as yet the nature has not perfectly accommodated itself to the ideal law. The physicality persists in besieging the system with the old imperfect action. Lipi is fixed in the ideality, but has only established the formal perfection in the type frequently occurring, it has not as yet successfully universalised it, though for a time it seemed on the point of an almost complete success. The totality of the physical delight has been prepared, but not accomplished, except to a certain extent in the tivra. The samadhi has made great progress in the lipi, ideation and speech thought, which are all idealised and the [ ]³ first two well established in all depths of the samadhi, except for occasional touches of nidra bringing interruption and breaking of the thread; lipi occurs in all [*four states*], but not freely

---

2 MS ride
3 MS two

and firmly except in the antardarshi. Other elements now occur freely in swapna and have an initial ideality, but are not yet firm in it; rupa is less forward, but it has achieved frequency of tejomaya and an occasional initial stability in it. Formerly the stability and continuity was only in chhayamaya.

Script. Today, physical delight, T^2, ideality, vishaya, rupa. Physical delight, especially kamananda, progress, not final finality. T^2 very perfect, but certainly not yet universal. Ideality perfect. Vishaya insistence, rupa d[itt]o.

T^2 today has almost got rid of tapatya, but still has tapata, an uninsistent intellectual stress. When the decisive sight comes, it is exact so far as it goes, but does not come freely, nor is it either luminous or forcible.

Kamananda is redeveloping against a strong, but still weakened physical obstruction (from the environmental ether, not in the body), but it is still subject to the old difficulties, limitations and disabilities. It has not yet any force of pervasion or the massed intensity and enthusiasm of former accesses of kamananda.

This has come subsequently, a pronounced and pervasive ananda. At first proceeding from the centre to pervade the lower parts of the body and occupying, from thence rising to pervade the upper parts to the brain. It was only by application of tapas that the contrary movement was induced; but it is a noteworthy instance of the tendency of the physicality to make laws of imperfections which are in their origin only temporary movements and stages in the complete evolution, that the normalising of this latter movement and the full occupation by it is still resisted and is not so complete as that of the former. This kamananda is long continuous, but not entirely continuous; it has however already the habit of constant return. It can be continued into samadhi, but there tends to drop away.

In samadhi of all depths an abundant play of lipi is now established. It is ideal, almost but not entirely free, but not yet perfect in the eightfold quality. Reading is acquiring force, the other movements are less apt to come freely.

Insistence on vishaya has only brought isolated internal spar-sha in antardarshi and isolated combined drishti, sparsha and sravana in swapna samadhi. Insistence on rupa has only brought perfection of form in the type rupas. But the insistence has been only occasional.

In samadhi great wealth of reading, but with the established tendency to coherence a great bringing forward of the old tendency to incoherence. Rupa in swapna develops, but still not beyond the line already attained.

May 9.

Some difficulty is found in preventing even vangmaya thought from descending into the [intellectuality].[4] Still the pure inspira-tional is rapidly developing freedom and normality and the frequent descent tends to stop at intuitional ideality, without now the descent into the intellect and even this is now a secondary and no longer a chief movement.

It is noticeable that even what might be called the subconscient telepathy, — for that is what it was once, and it is still really that emerging to the surface of the sense mind, — is beginning to become idealised. This is a great step in advance and a promise of the total idealisation of the mind-stuff.

The inspirational ideality prevails more and more and has de-veloped rapidly a higher revelatory substance, but the divergence has brought an unease and want of ananda into the mental system. This has been used as a discouragement to the intellectual thought when it comes because it creates a positive physical unease, but this use is contrary to the ideal method all whose means must be anandamaya. The ideality does not need the reactions of the old mental method to assist its progress; it can go on more rapidly and satisfactorily without them by its perception of truth and its own force to fulfil it.

The inspirational vangmaya now descends more freely into the physical region of the intellect without descending psychologically,

4 MS ideality

— that is to say, it is not intellectualised or turned into intuitional thought, it remains the inspirational ideality. The ideation tries to follow the movements of the speech thought; but it is more backward and owing to its past habit of conversion into intellectual thought unable to effect the same progress as successfully.

It is noticeable that the difficulty is greater in samadhi than in the outward jagrat, which is also a reversion to a former state of things. Samadhi is now divided into two parts, the lighter forms in which the purusha is wakeful and ideality reigns, the deeper in which nidra reigns and the action is intellectual with much of the old incoherence. But now in this nidra the purusha is wakeful though in a swapnamaya fashion and the intellectuality is nearer to ideality and is sometimes idealised. It is on the point of conversion to the ideality. In this nidra kavya has suddenly made itself frequent.

Sparsha is increasing in swapna and even trying to enter into antardarshi

The ideation and speech thought have now effected the requisite conversion and the force of the ideality in them can be trusted to complete it and remove or transform the unconverted elements or tendencies that still remain. T^2 is now turning to make the same conversion and has begun it, but here the intellectual confusion and chaos of mental telepathies has been so great, though now partly cleared, that time is required to make the conversion equally effective.

The true revelatory thought has begun to manifest in the lipi, but with an absorbing inspirational form of itself or with a strong and too heavy intuitional tendency. The highest and subtlest form of it is not yet manifest

This revelatory thought has at once extended itself to the speech thought both in the jagrat and the antardarshi and swapna samadhis, and to a less extent to the ideation. Nowhere does it occupy the field, but it is already dominant everywhere.

Lipi now well established in antardarshi and swapna, even the deepest, is now insisting against great opposition on (1) perfectly free manifestation with no obstruction from the lethargy of the

ether, (2) perfect manifestation in possession of all its eight qualities.
It has already some initial success.

Reading in the swapna is becoming rapidly coherent, except
when it presents itself in masses; it is then illegible and the attempt
to read brings in incoherence.

May 10.

Script today fixes a large programme.

(1) The decisive conversion of T^2 fixed in all its parts
(2) Vishaya and rupa farther insisted on.
(3) Samadhi developing the undeveloped parts in a mass.
(4) Kamananda settled
(5) Ideality progressing in the revelatory thought.

T^2 at present has to deal with the following component situation.

1. The largest element to be dealt with is the old telepathic intellectual perceptions. These now are unable to insist on themselves
and are no longer false trikaldrishtis, but perceptions of thought,
tendency, intention, impulse, either belonging to the object or working on it from the environmental physical Virat or from the pranic
and mental planes. Yesterday the inspirational thought was busy
observing them and giving them their right place and scope. They
have to be replaced by the intuitional telepathies.

2. The next largest element is the intuitional perceptions which
are real[ly] telepathic, but which the intellect tried to represent by
overstress as definite trikaldrishti of future action. These are now
putting on their ritam and have begun to figure as accurate intuitions of present tendency etc and immediate or closely subsequent
future action. This telepathic trikaldrishti of the future, however,
can only be definitive if approved by the higher revelatory or inspirational ideality. Moreover they are vague about time and not
quite full in circumstance.

3. Blind or unluminous inspirational thought of trikaldrishti-
tapas, ie indicatory inspirations without farther discernment of
detail or aspect, limit or scope, and without light of the revelation.
To be entirely replaced by luminous revelatory trikaldrishti; this is
the main conversion.

4 Luminous inspirational perception of trikaldrishti-tapas. These have been few and disputed by mental perceptions which imitate them, seem to give an ideal sanction, but are really only the ideality's sanction to the telepathic tapas, that is to attempts, partial results, side results etc. This is the element that has to be converted into decisive revelation and to dominate.

Sors

इंदविंद्राय बृहते पवस्व सुमृळीको अनवद्यो रिशादः ।
भरा चंद्राणि गृणते वसूनि —

इंदु is the Ananda, both ideal and physical — इंद्र बृहत् the large ideality

The kamananda is now, for the time being at least, so fixed that it is present whenever the attention or any part of it is turned to the body. There have been three recurring stages always of this Ananda, (1) prevalent obstruction refusing the Ananda even to the tapas, except occasionally, (2) the obstruction broken down by satapas smarana, Ananda recurring but intermittent though with periods of continuity, (3) constant Ananda dependent on nistapas smarana, but varying in intensity, sometimes full, sometimes only an impression, not definite Ananda. What has to be developed is ni[h]smarana Ananda, that is enforcing itself on the sense in the body even without smarana. This is now acting in the sahaituka

The sahaituka creates a stronger deposit of ahaituka; but this tends to diminish and fade away. When this tendency ceases, the Ananda will be perfectly founded.

The strong intense sahaituka still leaves a doubt whether the body is capable of bearing and therefore holding its indefinite prolongation and increase. This *dharana-samarthya* also must be determined in order to ensure permanence. When it is fixed, Ananda will help to enforce perfect arogya on the body.

The transformation of all telepathy into intuitional ideality is proceeding rapidly. When it is completed, thought will be entirely idealised, an ideal mentality will replace the average imperfect mentality. But this intuition has now (1) an inspirational and a revelatory element within its limits, (2) a strong intellectual element and atmosphere. The latter has to be entirely eliminated, the former strengthened and made dominant.

The vaguer parts of roga, not those that still have a strong and definite hold on the body, are being brought forward, evidently for the ideal tapas to begin to deal with them. If this is done, the arogya as well as the Ananda will be brought within the field of the new ideal activity.

The elimination of the intellectual atmosphere of the telepathy has begun. It will take time, but the difficulty is not so great as at first appears or as past experience would lead one to think, for the mentality now pervading the body is intuitive and not intellectual-vital; the intellectual element and atmosphere are brought in from outside, from the environmental mind.

The concession given to the intellectuality, led to a renewed intellectual interruption, but this has been very rapidly remedied, and it has served its turn in establishing a real will in the intellectual devatas in the environmental mind to seek for their own idealisation instead of resisting the idealisation of the adhar.

Both smarana of kamananda and ni[h]smarana ahaituka and sahaituka are becoming easy and frequent in samadhi. Even some initial continuity has shown itself.

The Ananda has now only to overcome the tendencies of discontinuation to be fixed.

In Samadhi there was a massed development, in strong and firm type, of ideality in kavya, dialogue, narrative, reading etc; a first movement turning these from ideal phantasy into truth of a definite aim and utility in the purpose of the divine Yoga, at least in one first instance of combined reading and lipi (Indian News . . nerv. [. . .]); also a first instance of strong, though partial legibility in persistent mass lipi, with however the defect that its persistence did not amount to legible stability. Kavya developed remarkably, eg "What swoon has brought The key of many immortalities?" But the farther progress was hampered by the after effects of the intellectual reaction, as the thought-action in the intellect hampered the revelatory thought from acting.

The physical anandas no longer as a principle of action replace, prevent or interfere with each other, but all seem to help the kamananda. The kamananda suffers not only from the old defects of diminution and discontinuity, but from its other old defect of insufficiency in ambulando. There seems however to be on the whole a much greater force of continuity than on former occasions. The intensity of the morning's sahaituka has not been repeated. There is strong reaction of negative vaidyuta on the sukshma body affecting the sthula. Recurrent Ananda is now fixed in the system.

The inspirational ideality has now sunk to the secondary place, – a degradation of the revelatory in the intellectual region. Thus another part of the script programme has already been fulfilled.

In T^2 the telepathy has become inspirational idealistic in the intuitive mind; there is also a secondary trikaldrishti which reposes upon it and is therefore telepathic in its nature; the intellectual element occurs rarely and is rejected and dismissed. Part only of the script programme has been fulfilled under this head and that too not completely; still it is a decisive conversion and therefore so far the fulfilment is, verbally, complete. In addition a pure inspirational trikaldrishti, not telepathic, has begun to operate again. But these inspirations are only just enough illumined for their restricted work. They have a narrow discrimination, no revelation. They give only the particular result sometimes with a time element, but no accessories or attendant circumstances except when another inspirational or intuitional indication is added to eke out the first main indication. There is satyam and ritam of a sparse and narrow character, no brihat.

Tapatya is being destroyed along with the intellectual element; but there is tapata. All trikaldrishti now contains its own effective tapas, and separate tapas apart from trikaldrishti is rarely employed. It is being eliminated, except to some extent in the action of will on the body. Tapas comes in the trikaldrishti only as if a sort of subordinate accessory, although really in the ideality both are necessary to each other and essentially inherent in each other. But the subordination is kept up in order to get rid of tapata. Once that is removed, the way will be open for an equal unified idea-tapas in the T^2.

Revelation with a stronger discriminatory power is now entering into the pure trikaldrishti, but it acts oftenest by a descent into the intuitive mind. Time, place, circumstance, though now often correct, are still pursued by intellectual error and uncertainty.

In the evening and night strong intellectual obstruction which for the most part prevented any definitive progress. Still there was a notable advance in the development of revelatory thought.

Vishaya [ ]⁵ has only gained so far by insistence (1) a daily but isolated occurrence in swapna, (2) intensity of subtle sparsha in jagrat, antardarshi and bahirdarshi, (3) greater intensity of the type sparshas already in force

Rupa is still limited to tendency in the jagrat, to occasional frequency of established movements in swapna.

Great intensity of audition and mental vision of the personalities (devatas) that stand behind the action of the intuitive and intellectual mind and temperament in the sadhana. The truth of the developments thus seen is established by the subsequent result in the changes of the mentality.

Script.
"What will outline itself, will be
1. An advance in the arogya, a decisive advance
2. An advance in primary utthapana
3. An advance in saundarya.
Also the T^2 acting in life."

May 11.
Script programme
"Conversion of the thought-speech to the revelatory is already complete. Ideation is to be converted today; for that has only begun. T^2 has to be converted from the inspirational-intuitive to the revelatory inspirational

---

⁵ MS by insistence

"Kamananda to overcome several of its difficulties and to be sure of fixity.

"Vishaya and rupa farther to insist and develop.

"Samadhi to develop the idealities gained and to insist specially on rupa."

The thought speech is now revelatory in all its forms. Even when the inspirational and intuitive occur, they are revelatory in their substance. Lipi also is always revelatory in the same way. It is, it says, to develop T^2 and be the diary (journalier) of the trikaldrishti, telepathies, tapassiddhi.

Ideation is still afflicted ordinarily by the necessity of expressing itself, though ideal in substance, in the intuitive mind. Until this difficulty is overcome, its full conversion cannot take place.

Kamananda was oppressed in the latter part of the day yesterday; it is now recurrent rather than continuous.

Intense continuous kamananda; action of the nihsmarana sahaituka and in a less degree of the nihsmarana ahaituka. The Ananda has now only to strive with the forgetfulness in the body which tends to be quite effective only when supported by exclusive absorption in the mind. The Ananda in ambulando is maintained by nistapas smarana and in ahaituka partly by nihsmarana sahaituka, the latter sometimes of a fair intensity. Pervasiveness and an increase of force not yet amounting ordinarily to intensity were brought in successfully, even the fourfold wave movement.

Kamananda has attained power of continuity and easy maintenance by smarana in lighter swapna.

In Samadhi strong action of lipi even in the depths and frequent and strong sparsha. Play of rupa; instance of perfect rupa, but unstable.

The barrier has not yet been broken down in jagrat rupa. One definite development is the progressive elimination, by force of rejection, of what was once most common, rupa formed painfully out of chaotic material in the akasha. Spontaneity is now the rule; vividness has also begun to predominate; but stability is only initial, except in certain crude forms and even there it is very little more.

Only some incomplete forms have more stability. Completeness however is not yet perfectly established, though it is common; incomplete forms are frequent. Rapidity and fluidity increase, but are not perfect. Variety is growing strong in the type rupas, but other rupas for the most part come imperfectly and without any developed variety. Group coherence is very occasional. The two main things the will insists on, stability and variety in vivid completeness of the spontaneous developed or perfect figure only come, — if at all the first, — in the type forms. The main barrier remains erect.

In the afternoon much trouble of intellectual suggestion and obstruction, so that no new development came in the subsequent samadhi, except intensity and extension of lipi, speech-thought and ideation. Some mass lipi and reading, but no advance in coherent legibility. The rest was obstructed and occurred, if at all, feebly, and not often in the ideality.

The development of ideation was also much baffled and the two lines on which it proceeded rendered for a time doubtful and ineffective by intermixture or intervention of intellectuality. Now, however, the effect has become pronounced; 1st, conversion of intuition to the revelatory ideation, but with an intuitive burden and a tendency to drop towards mental intuition, 2dly revelatory inspiration, as demanded in the script programme for T^2, with a leaning also, very often, to excess of intuition; 3dly, though rare, revelatory ideation proper, a little broad and blurred in its light. By the development and liberation from defect of this process will come the complete conversion both of the ideation and of T^2.

Kamananda seems to be strong and fixed in a constant or frequent recurrence; it remains to be seen whether the old obstruction will again prevail to impose a long discontinuity or only the present tendency of brief discontinuity by *vismriti* will limit this siddhi.

Chitra rupa and sthapatya rupa are very strong, stronger even than at any previous time, although they have been well founded for several years. Rupa shows a tendency to variety, especially in the crude; but this cannot be entirely relied on as there has again and again been the same tendency, never leading to permanent siddhi;

it has always been undone, built itself up again, but each time with a diminution rather than a progress. The element of spontaneity however gives this time a greater chance of a final true initiation of progress.

Kamananda, though as usual less in the decline of the day, preserved its power of recurrence until sleep.

No definite progress in vishaya. There is some tendency of expansion of shabda in the sukshma voice.

Primary utthapana fluctuates from return of a certain strong exhaustion in the upholding prana, not the vital, but the physical, and an expulsion of the fatigue tendency, which then clings only by the habit of muscular strain exhausting temporarily the body's force for motion, but not the upholding prana. For some days the exhaustion has held sway, tonight the elimination was again resumed.

May 12.

Script gives, (1) T^2, to be pushed forward, – (2) conversion of ideation, to be enlarged and universalised, (3) kamananda, progress decisive, – (4) rupa, progress decisive, – (5) vishaya, insistence, – (6) action of ideality on health and primary utthapana. Add rapid development in things established, lipi, vangmaya, etc.

T^2 is now proceeding automatically in the idealisation of the telepathies which are to be converted from the mental to the intuitive ideal. It is dealing with all telepathies and fixing them decisively in their proper place.

Vangmaya is now to be noted in two movements, effulgent and refulgent; (1) effulgent, the pure vangmaya, vak leaping forth from the ideality with the ideation contained in it, (2) expressive of or responding to a previous ideation or else proceeding from a silent indefinite ideation to which it gives form and expression. The former tends to be always revelatory thought and to reject the inferior inspirational and intuitional forms; the latter is ordinar[il]y revelatory in the intuitional form or merely intuitional and can even sink to mental intuitive speech. Ideality is working upon this latter action to assimilate it to the effulgent revelatory speech.

Ideation is now usually full of revelatory substance and sometimes of revelatory light, but is obstructed in its form of manifestation by the old tendency to expression in the mentality. This is being indulged in order that the resisting intellect may be forced to change entirely into ideal substance of thought. It is the unconverted T^2 which is the main support of this obstruction.

The physical obstruction, taking advantage of suspension during the night, has tried to get rid of the kamananda, to disprove fixity. But the powers of fixity and pervasion have prevailed. They are now natural to the body, can do without tapas and, even when suppressed by the suspension, need only smarana to set them in action. To get rid of suspension by vismriti is now the task that lies before the Ananda. It is now no longer dependent on position, but self-acting in all positions, even in ambulando, where indeed it has a great power of spontaneity and pervasion. Nihsmarana ananda has also become self-acting.

Rupa develops variety in the quite crude forms, but the old defect of chaotic non-spontaneous formation with defect of rupa qualities is again strong in them, as in instability and want of variety in the spontaneous forms. These are the two rocks upon which the progress has always fatally stumbled, come to a halt and gone back.

Accuracy of intuitive telepathic trikaldrishti is now very strong and embraces detail, though here it is not always quite perfect in its choice. Confusion of stupefied intellect in the physical brain atmosphere is the one successful obstruction now remaining. When this occurs, the ideality has to break its way through to manifest.

In samadhi rupa shows a tendency to manifest in antardarshi, some of the forms with an initial, others with a greater stability, but all crude. Developed rupa in swapna once with a strong stability; chayamaya with a long continuance of chitras or action. The rest — reading sometimes very vivid and initially stable — ordinarily idealised, but their free action is not yet fixed in the samadhi.

Conversion of ideation into the revelatory-inspirational thought is now enlarging itself very rapidly and being applied to T^2. Decisive trikaldrishti is frequent, but it is usually telepathic or leans on the telepathic. The greater trikaldrishti awaits the development of the secondary ideality of which there are some precursor signs and instances. T^2 applied to internal movements is advanced, T^2 applied to objects in the field of exercise copious but weak, T^2 applied to life hardly yet in action, except for scattered instances.

Rupa developed some variety of fugitive perfect rupas in the evening; they do not emerge perfectly from the chidakasha.

The conversion of ideation has been founded, enlarged and developed a strong tendency of universalisation; T^2 has advanced, but is still obstructed. Kamananda has fixed recurrence and an initial power of nihsmarana. Rupa has a certain fixity of its will to progress. Vishaya made no progress. Ideality is acting on arogya and primary utthapana, but without any definite progress.

May 13.

T^2 is to be rapidly developed today; ideality to continue to universalise its action in the thought and its conversion of thought-speech to the revelatory form and substance; kamananda to develop sasmarana continuity and nihsmarana force, rupa and samadhi to compel their obstacles. Physical siddhi has to generalise its initial progress in its other members.

T^2 is busy with the telepathies. It is distinguishing two fields of telepathic knowledge. By identification (sanyama) with the physical plane of being, it feels accurately the tendencies etc that materialise in the object and determine its action; it can even see provisionally the presently future action to a certain extent, provided it does not miss the possibilities that are not yet in action, but may or will be in action. It can see which will prevail, provided no higher idea or will intervenes. Secondly, there are the forces of the lower mental and pranic planes. These it sees before they at all touch the physical; that they are true, it can see by feeling their reality and also because they translate themselves subsequently into intention, tendency, action, impulse, impression etc in the object observed. It is here that the danger of perversion by false stress is strongest, — though it occurs everywhere, — because the pranic especially have a vehement urge towards selffulfilment, the mental a strong intention to fulfil and belief in their success, and they convey this to the observing mind. But only a few can really act upon the object effectively and fulfil their aim. Their action is irregular; they often produce a subsequent partial effect or modify the immediate or subsequent action without fulfilling themselves as they had wished, or they fulfil themselves at other times, in another place, under other circumstances, even in other objects. Often the object first influenced escapes, but another which has come into the field of the influence is entirely affected; it is as if the powers acting in him took up and carried out the suggestion which the powers acting in the first had rejected. The powers of the higher mental and pranic planes fulfil themselves much more frequently, powerfully and [   ]⁶ they have more of the truth in them. But in all this there is no absolute certainty of future trikaldrishti, though prevision after prevision may be fulfilled with unvarying accuracy for a long time; still it is only even then a prevailing certainty, a mental and moral, not an absolute and ideal certainty. Moreover in all this there is a will attending the idea and the will in the observer may help or retard, make possible or prevent the fulfilment; because the powers hostile to a result take note and resist more strongly and if they are stronger, prevail, the powers favourable to it take advantage, strengthen themselves and if the observer's will is strong, they prevail. All this is now felt, seen, participated in by the intuitive-inspirational or less easily by the revelatory-inspirational perception in the being. The element of revelation however is now increasingly present in the first or else attends it in the accompanying ideation

The perception of all these things is becoming steadily more intense and satisfying, it is increasing in the quality of the satyam brihat and in the ritam of the satyam brihat. The pressure from above is for what is subconscient to be mentally or ideally

⁶ *MS* frequently,

seen and felt, and for the mental perception to be transformed
into the ideal or to be accompanied or enlightened by the ideal
thought.

Kamananda is [increasing][7] rapidly in sasmarana continuity,
but it still tends sometimes and the Ananda tends always to diminution of intensity by vismriti. The opposite tendency of increase by
continuity is not yet strong enough to get permanently the upper
hand. There is also the habit of discontinuity which though no
longer proper to the physical body is imposed on it by the mind of
the Akasha of the surrounding [physicality][8] and accepted through
force of past habit. The old sanskara of the body that the Ananda
must be discontinued to give it relief, exists also in that mind and
has its effect in bringing about discontinuity. The latter can be more
easily eliminated than the general habit of discontinuance, which
cannot be finally expelled except by the growth of the nihsmarana
action.

In Samadhi rupa played freely in swapna, occurring automatically with spontaneous fluidity, rapidity, vividness, usually with
completeness and with much variety every time, the moment the
verge of swapna was crossed; but it is still unstable. This play
carried itself also into the antardarshi, but there with a certain
inability to impress itself on the chittakasha; the rupas however
were in their nature of the developed kind. There is still a recurring
obstruction to the free play of all the members of the samadhi; the
etheric akasha holds them back, is forced, again withholds and has
again to be forced. Nevertheless reading manifested and narrative
by succession of images.

Sasmarana continuity seems now to be sufficiently established,
but nihsmarana is still too easily suppressed. The stress has now to
be more upon the overcoming of vismriti and its effects.

Script. "In kamananda the vismriti to be conquered in these
three days, not indeed entirely, but fundamentally.... Rupa and

7 MS increasingly
8 MS physically

samadhi will still take some time. The ideality to move strongly forward in thought and T^2."

The vismriti seems already to have been conquered in its effects and it is being now initially conquered in itself, that is, its force is being diminished and at times the Ananda persists against it enforcing itself and drawing back the mind to it instead of waiting for the mind to return from its preoccupation and then either reforming or renewing itself. Even when it waits, it does not now need to reform or renew, but is there all along and is simply felt again by the sense, like the water in which a swimmer is moving.

The movement in ideality and T^2 is preparing to set aside its remaining deficiencies.

May 14
    Script.
        (1) Kamananda, initial conquest of vismriti.
        (2) T^2, emergence of pure trikaldrishti, enlarging of the tapas element
        (3) Ideality; revelatory thought in the speech; farther conversion in the ideation.
        (4) Rupa and samadhi proceed with their development.
        (5) Vishaya to be strongly insisted on so as to break the barrier.

The initial conquest of vismriti is growing rapidly and irresistibly in strength. The obstruction is now falling back on the fear of the kamananda in the external physicality, its sense that the body will not be able to bear continuous or at least continuously intense kamananda. The only present justification is that the body does not feel quite at home with the grosser, too physical-vital, unidealised form which the ananda still tends too largely to take.

Rupa has now broken down two barriers, (1) the inability to proceed with its self-development which arose from a wrong attitude towards the processes actually employed and a haste to get done with imperfect movements; (2) denial of stability in perfection to all but very crude forms.

The development is proceeding steadily against every difficulty; all the old difficulties, presenting themselves as strongly as they can, are being overborne. Secondary initial stability as well as primary has been established in perfect, developed, dense and crude forms alike, but only in the type. Primary initial stability is when the object stands long enough for the eye as well as the mind to get a strong view and impression of it; it is momentary, of one moment. Secondary is when the object stands longer than is needed for this, lingers a moment or two and vanishes; it is a stability of two or three moments. Tertiary is when it stands for several moments. Final stability comes when the object stays as long as the will holds it.

The defect of the siddhi, the third barrier still unbroken is its lack of variety. Other forms come, but either they have not even the primary initial stability or, having it, yet they do not come so easily as the type, are not so complete or are in other ways deficient; and in the crude they tend always to be anticipated or replaced by the type. When this barrier breaks down, rupa in the jagrat will be able to develop rapidly its completeness, freedom and perfection.

Revelatory thought on the right level and in the inevitable style pure or the inevitable forms of the inspired, illuminative, effective and adequate styles is now well fixed, natural and normal, practically universalised in the original vangmaya. In the derivative it is beginning to triumph finally over the mental gravitation.

Vishaya is now reviving in gandha and taste.

The position of vishaya is complex and unequal. In gandha it has already been well developed, but it is subject to exceedingly long periods of obstruction and cessation and has then to be redeveloped by tapas. If this habit is overcome and sthula and sukshma gandhas well distinguished, there will be perfect siddhi. Crude primary tastes are similarly established, but here tapas is more easily effective and the distinction is clear; specific tastes occur, but not freely nor in great abundance; of substantial taste there is only an imperfect first movement. Sparsha is violently limited to a few habitual touches which are however well-developed, intensely sthula in their effect, capable of stability; very sukshma effect is more though not quite free, for its variety is limited. Shabda is still more baffled, even where established rare and obstructed and most confused of all by the sthula sounds of the material world. Darshana is only of the pranic akasha and two or three of its objects, and that too imperfectly developed.

Another attack from the external physical mind, but this was unable to take the old form of a lethargy of the tapas, relapse into inactive shama and prolonged cessation of the siddhi. It shaped into an upheaval of the lower ideal-intellectual confused-tapasic activity and an attempt to annul temporarily part of the gains of the ideality by a backsliding downwards of the active being. In kamananda it was unable to annul the conquest of the effects of vismriti, but succeeded in giving a fresh lease to the vismriti in itself, which was on the point of disappearing. The difficulties in the ideal conversion, which were disappearing, were also temporarily renewed. On the other hand the ideation gained and especially the perception of the causes, objects and utilities of the opposition movements were immediately seen; there was no disturbance of the samata, except for one or two flying touches.

Samadhi limited by the attack. But sthula shabda conversation in the swapna reached a rapid frequency not before realised, —ordinarily the dialogue is in sukshma shabda of the nature of thought overheard, though really it is speech. This was speech overheard, but in single sentences or single question and response, not connected dialogue.

Ideation has now effected initially its final conversion in the primary ideality. First, the revelatory intuition has begun to fall away and is now only an occasional and attendant lower activity (tertiary) which is on the way to disappearance; then the intuitive-inspirational transformed rapidly into the revelatory-inspirational has given its pride of place to the true revelatory which is taking up all the other forms of ideation.

At the same time trikaldrishti first become liberally positive and decisive in the general ideation is now acting with regard to the movements of the objects of vision, not as yet with a perfect arrangement of ritam, but still with a fairly sufficient decisiveness.

In the development of these two movements lies all the future perfection of the primary ideality

Rupa is attempting to develop variety and partially succeeding, but it is a variety of imperfect forms. Spontaneous manifestation out of the chidakash is beginning entirely to replace development by mental-physical pressure in the subtle physical ether. In this development lies the surety of a perfect siddhi.

May 15

The programme for the second week of May has been fulfilled in all its parts; but in the vishaya it is only a beginning.

Lipi is fixed in the ideality and always capable of perfect manifestation with the eightfold quality; but the resistance of the physical ether remains and force has to be used on it. As this has been little done recently, the resistance has increased, but it only exists initially and can be broken down very rapidly.

Ideality has become free and normal in the ideation; the revelatory is the normal type, though the inspirational and intuitional with the revelatory substance are also still in action. The form of the revelatory ideation is not yet perfect. Speech thought is fixed in the revelatory ideality, but not always in its highest form.

T^2 has evolved ideal telepathy and is evolving ideal trikaldrishti and the beginnings of ideal tapas, all in the revelatory form, though the other forms recur.

Rupa is attempting to establish variety in the initial stability; the obstacle to this variety is the last of the old barriers.

Vishaya is now initially active in all its parts but is still kept within its old limits.

Kamananda is fixed in recurrence, but its continuity is still broken in upon by vismriti aided by the demand for discontinuity as a relief to the physical system. The former difficulty is being attacked; the latter is being observed with a view to attack. Other anandas, prepared in various degrees, await the kamananda

Today is to be the turning point for a new movement, (1) developing what is yet imperfectly developed, (2) preparing the physical

siddhi in its three other members, (3) developing new powers of the being.
=

Lipi is now laying stress on perfect spontaneity free from the ideal suggestions and a perfect rapid stability. It has founded both of them, the stability being no longer always of the initial order, but also very often a prolonged stability. To this new development only fluidity is lacking. Its complete siddhi will be the final overcoming of the etheric resistance. It is being extended also to the antardarshi

Samadhi is developing rupa more freely and labouring at mass reading, not yet with success, but still with an increasing approach to success.

The sasmarana Ananda is prosecuting successfully its initial struggle with the psycho-physical demand for discontinuity.
=

Lipi

1. The psychophysical resistance to the delight will be got rid of thoroughly in two days, initially.

2. Lipi will be thoroughly perfected in July.

3. (A long lipi, declaring that the superior ideality will be now manifested in the present limitations of the inferior ideality and they will develop together.)
=

Traigunyasiddhi. The intense Ananda of shama of the Mahasaraswati with the Maheswari basis and Mahaluxmi colour is now uniting itself with the strong tapas of the Mahakali bhava. A mediate equation has been arrived at, but the full Ananda of the ideal tapas is necessary before the final unification can be secure. It is notable that the Asamata now hardly even ventures to return except in touches of physical uneasiness, caused usually either by physical discomfort, eg, heat, lethargic pressure of tamas on the brain etc, or by psycho-physical discomfort of the attempt of intellect to mix still with the ideality or to accompany it. The latter is rapidly diminishing and is at best occasional.

Sraddha in Bhagavan and in the higher shakti which he uses as one's own universal shakti, is growing to completeness. The lower shakti not yet unified with the higher, is occasionally shaken by doubt or coloured by it; but this is more doubt of the rapid effectuality than of the final effectuality. Something of the latter still exists in the shape of uncertainty, with regard to physical siddhi and life, but it is no longer positive asraddha.

In samadhi, even in antardarshi, rupa is becoming more free and spontaneous, but not with sufficient power to hold the akasha so that there is still only an initial stability

Script, for the week

"Ideation to be fixed in the revelatory thought, the rest being taken up into it.

"T^2 to develop trikaldrishti powerfully and begin to strengthen powerfully the ideal tapas.

"Rupa to develop variety.

"Vishaya to press down the barrier.

"Kamananda to vindicate itself against vismriti and discontinuity

"Samadhi to begin to regularise itself.

"The struggle of the ideality with the roga to show its first decisive results of the novel order.

"The same in the saundarya and primary utthapana to be prepared."

==

Kamananda's conquest of vismriti seems to be proceeding by three movements. First, recurrence is being replaced by continuous sasmarana so that when the mind is not absorbed, the Ananda is immediately felt as a thing not recurring, but always present, though for the time being forgotten. This movement has gone very far, though it is not yet absolute. It is the overcoming of natural vismriti. There still remains the artificial vismriti brought about by absorbed concentration of the mind on its thoughts. This is being removed, first, by the mind not being absorbed, by the ideal faculty of a multiple attention, the thought being pursued, yet the Ananda remembered, secondly, by the Ananda becoming so strong as to force itself upon the mind and prevent the total absorption. Both these movements are only as yet initial and have not yet proceeded very far.

The power of simultaneous attention is now rapidly developing; it is seen that the thought in the ideality can easily be conducted
and even more successfully conducted, when the mind is not absorbed, and can ordinarily coexist with the sense of the Ananda,
especially the ideation and speech thought (this most, because it is
most assured,) but also the T^2. The gathering together of the mind
stuff and the closing of it to other ideas and objects which is the
nature of absorption, is no longer necessary for the full force of the
thought to reign. The habit still continues, but it is diminishing and
has received its death blow. On the other hand when the thought
is occupied not only with itself, but with the object of sense or in
some action, as in reading, writing, conversing, this gathering and
closing is more ready to intervene. Here also, however, there is a
strong beginning and already a rapid growth of the elimination.

Nihsmarana Ananda is also insisting on regularisation and
normality, but chiefly in the sahaituka, because there it is more
intense.

A flood of action of the intuitive and inspirational lipi, unstable
for the most part or with only a primary or secondary stability,
pursued by the suggestions, serving only to show the complete
ideality of the lipi even at its lowest. Amidst this much revelatory
lipi now taking its place as an inferior movement, and beyond lipi
manifestation of the superior ideality which takes no account of
the intellect, forestalls its action and eliminates its substances. The
inferior ideality [is][9] that which takes up the whole intellectual
action and transforms it into vijnana; it is limited by what the intuitive intellect might have done; the superior takes up the inferior
and is not limited by the possibilities of the intuitive mind. The
inferior ideality does in its own right what the intuitive mind does
by derivation from the inferior ideality, but the inferior ideality
itself is only a selection from the greater range of the superior.

The speech thought has idealised itself thoroughly in succession to the [lipi][10] and the ideation including T^2 is beginning the

---

[9] MS which
[10] MS ideality

same movement. In neither however is the superior ideality directly at work as in the lipi.

In the lipi the revelatory ideality is again asserting its predominance.

The superior ideality has manifested for a moment in the ideation. The complete idealisation of the thought is proceeding rapidly; but it has still to deal with the resistance with regard to exact and decisive T^2. For where the ideality does not yet act or acts only partially, the intellect has a natural tendency to attempt to fill the place.

Once again the ideal tapas has forced the fatigue out of the upholding prana. It now expresses itself in the physical body with a slight shadow thrown upon the prana.

May 17.
Script. "The extension of the ideality to T^2 in lipi, ideation, telepathy, tapas.. Enlargement of decisive trikaldrishti. Farther conquest of vismriti in Ananda. Development of rupa. The ideality to take possession of the samadhi. Vishaya."

Kamananda subject to suppression more than for some time past. On the other hand it has withstood a severe test under which formerly it always failed. In addition it successfully maintained its strong and long continuity throughout samadhi, even in sushupti of the mind, the vijnana observing the physical being within the consciousness, not as a form without. Also in samadhi the double concentration was easily and successfully sustained.

Ideality has begun to take possession of the samadhi with a sort of crudely regularised action.

The idealisation of the mind action seemed to break down for a time by the withdrawal of the vijnana which left the mechanical remnants of the old intellectual action to work by a sort of unwilling pravritti. There is now nothing that demands this action; when it works, it is by a sort of mechanical continuance of a dead habit. The vijnana is now resuming its work.

Kamananda recovers, though not quite firmly, its sasmarana continuity.

Ideality extends in spite of the intellectual obstacle in T^2 with a more frequent decisiveness in the details of the telepathy. The ideal tapas begins to disengage itself more decisively from the old enveloping case of the mind-stuff. Lipi trikaldrishti slightly strengthened.

Vishaya now acts intermittently in all its parts, but still slightly and without enlarging its action.

The action of the ideality continues in the primary utthapana holding at bay the attempt of fatigue to lay hold again of the upholding prana. The hold of reaction of pain and stiffness on the body continues, but is being diminished and prepared for dissolution.

Action of ideality on the fragments of roga. They try to recur, but cannot decisively materialise; some are unable to materialise at all.

May 18.

The recurrence of the intellectual action can in future be no more than a mechanical interlude. What has now to be dissolved is the mixed action of ideality embedded in or hung round with the old mind stuff, half ideality, half intuitive mentality. This inferior action has its stronghold in the T^2 and is dominant in tapas.

The stronger action of the superior ideality on a perfect inferior ideality is now the *mot d'ordre* of the siddhi. The superior ideality is very visibly busy perfect[ing] the inferior ideality so as to purify it from all immixture of the mental accompaniment.

Especially tapas is now getting rapidly idealised and the false mental stress is being at last really eliminated without the force of tapas being diminished. For the difficulty till now was that the force, the rudra shakti, of the tapas always brought with it excitement of mental wish, tapatya or tapata, and overstress, while the elimination of these brought with it also an elimination of the rudra shakti. It is now becoming possible to combine forceful will, even rudra tapas, with truth of ideality.

Thought telepathy is beginning to develop. Formerly it was

only telepathy of the sensations, emotions, desires, impulses etc. Now these are to be combined with telepathic perception and communication of the thoughts.

A better distinction of primary and secondary utthapana has now to be made. Primary utthapana properly belongs to the vijnana, it is the full force of laghima, mahima, anima in the mind stuff and psychic prana so that the mind rejects all exhaustion, weariness, depression of force etc. When this extends to the prana upholding the body, that is primary utthapana in the physical being. Secondary utthapana is elimination of these reactions from the body so that the limbs and the whole body can take and maintain any position or begin and continue any movement for any length of time naturally and in its own right. Tertiary, is when gravitation is conquered.

Hitherto the distinction made was between movement ambulando and positions of the limbs and the body. These are now being unified in the primary siddhi. Fatigue in the positions is still powerful, but it is physical with a reaction on the upholding prana, brought about by violent pressure on the muscular system. This reaction must be eliminated.

The habit of reaction depends on the physical mind. This is shown by the fact that when the body is forgotten, the position is maintained with ease and on the attention coming back to the body it is found that perfect laghima reigns in it. But the attention then brings back the habit of reaction, the physical opposition seizing on the old long-established sanskara to renew its attack.

In the vertical triangular position of the arms there is now the pressure relieved by intervals of successful laghima.

The element of time abhyasa has to be eliminated. That is to say while formerly the idea was to maintain the position as long as possible and increase the length of time during which the siddhi maintained itself against fatigue, until by this abhyasa it became self-existent, the idea now must be to establish the already self-existent power of the ideality in the body, so that the time makes no difference. This was done originally in the first movement of utthapana in Alipur jail and sometimes subsequently in the lower utthapana, but in the latter it could not be fixed, in the former it was fixed from the beginning, but towards the end a little impaired by contagion of asiddhi from the other positions.

Power of double attention, to thought and to Ananda, is now well-established. What has now to be got rid of, is the interference of the mind-stuff in condensation; this is being already done initially by the interposition making no essential difference, since even then the Ananda reaches the side of conscious attention, subordinate as yet, which is deputed to receive it. But this siddhi is as yet imperfect and initial.

The T^2 is now attempting to extend itself out of the experimental field into the life, in which as yet it was only exercising the old scattered, half-mental action and had secured striking but isolated success and a mass of imperfect results, but no general control. All this movement must develop before the perfection required can be considered accomplished.

=

Script
"Samadhi is to carry on the regularisation by the ideality and to enforce freedom and stability in rupa and the other imperfect members.
    In jagrat rupa a stable variety.
    In vishaya a breaking down of the barriers.
    In T^2 life.
    These are the backward members of the ideality."

=

In samadhi all its members had play; all are fixed in the ideality or at lowest sink to the intuitive mentality; all have an initial stability. But reading is still fragmentary and some others occur without any large completeness or without any enlightening context.
    In internal lipi occurrence of the superior ideality.
    Samadhi has now two movements, samadhi proper when sitting, swapna when lying. The shakti is preparing to convert the latter into samadhi and sometimes succeeds, but on the plane of the intuitive mentality.

=

In the second and third items of the script, the physical obstruction has again massed itself powerful to reconstruct the barrier to the progress or fortify it where it was breaking down. In the latter attempt it has temporarily succeeded.

Kamananda is much hampered and though still recurrent afflicted by diminution and discontinuity. This defect is no longer due to vismriti or at least no longer has that [as] its base, but only a mechanical habit forced to recur by the massing of the obstruction in the external physicality.

The struggle continues in the primary utthapana and the arogya. The ideal shakti is more insistent at present in the former than in the latter where the roga successfully obstructs in its two chief strongholds, though in one there are slight signs of its approaching diminution.

In a continuity of five hours or so of walking, coming upon the constant abhyasa, more broken, of the past many days, fatigue in the upholding prana was shown to be now merely a shadow, fatigue in the body could only hold if there was relaxation of the utthapana shakti. Even then it was less fatigue than a pressure of the pain of stiffness in the muscles. In relaxation a sort of manomaya laghima without mahima upholds the body, and this force allows the reaction, although it is noticeable that the force of the reaction is diminishing. When the utthapana shakti of mahima-laghima takes possession, – and it now ordinarily holds the body, – all fatigue and reaction disappear and there is only the pain of stiffness which sometimes decreases and is suppressed, sometimes increases, but does not affect the unrelaxed body.

Utthapana of position is still too much afflicted by the pressure on the deficient anima, still too little supported by mahima in the laghima to be prolonged.

In Samadhi a great and solid advance. Dream reading (narrative and monologue) became perfect, except that it has to be hastily read, the lines disappearing or receding from the direct view as soon as the sense is grasped; but otherwise they are perfectly complete, massed, consecutive, coherent, forming a complete and often a long story or discourse, though occasionally the opening or the close is not read. On the other hand if there is an attempt at stability and deliberate reading, the massed print becomes either instable or incoherent. Dialogue also was perfect, though not so long and complete.

In swapna samadhi rupa was perfectly free in the chhayamaya and in the tejomaya with chhayamaya basis. Stability and prolonged continuity of action — some continuity there sometimes is — are wanting. Stability only occurs in faint and vague rupas.

Vishaya is developing.

May 19

Subsequent reaction of stiffness was felt in the morning as pain in the relaxation of the lying posture, but chiefly in the loins where it has not been felt while walking.. On rising everything disappeared or was reduced to a minimum leaving only a suppressed stiffness and fragmentary suggestions of pain. There is at present no trace of bodily fatigue, such as would formerly have been felt, or the vague weight of lassitude which would more recently have been the result. The defect of anima is evidently being conquered, although it still persists and resists ejection.

═══

Script.

"Today T^2 completing itself. The superior ideality in ideation and lipi and speech thought.   Restoration of kamananda.   Samadhi development.   Ideality to take possession of the rupa in the jagrat.   Vishaya."

The superior ideality is beginning to take forcible possession of the inferior, that is to say to act within the limits set by it and in the style of its action, but independent of all reference to the old intellectual action and to the questioning of the intellect. That questioning still continues, but its doubts and its suggestions are disregarded, solved without reference to its difficulties and uncertainties. The inferior ideality respected them and leaned upon them. It was to a great extent a referee of the intellect, a substitute and an enlightener giving it the knowledge it required and could not itself compass. As a referee it solved its uncertainties; as a substitute it took up its action but carried it on in the manner of the ideality by revelation, inspiration, intuition, discrimination; as an enlightener it gave it knowledge beyond its scope, but not far beyond its scope. When it went far beyond its scope, it was more often by ideal suggestion than with an absolute authority.

The new movement is as yet only initial and still hampered by the continued outer action of the intuitive mind with its clinging ends of intellectual mind-stuff.

Lipi. "Superior ideality in trikaldrishti and tapas siddhi", already beginning to be initially fulfilled.

The first and second chatusthayas are now unified by the development of the traigunyasiddhi. Ananda of shama is combined with ananda of tapas, but tends to be modified and diminished by deficiency of ananda of tapas. This is preparatory to their complete unification.

The higher transcendent shakti and the personal shakti are now unified and sraddha swashaktyam is firmly based, but it is still deficient in force and extent.

The second chatusthaya is now complete, but in parts it is deficient in force, awaiting farther development of the Kalibhava and this again dependent on farther development of the ideality, that is the unification of the first three chatusthayas. Shama now contains in itself no longer a relaxed, but a concentrated tapas and relaxed prakasha, tapas an involved prakasha and a basic shama. By the unification of the three chatusthayas there will be the perfect unification of the three gunas. This is in the temperament, but the play of jnana and T^2 will bring it about also in the mentality. In the vijnana they are always united. There will then remain the body, but there too the siddhi is being made ready.

Ideality II is now acting upon the mental telepathy intuitive and manasic which still survives bringing about a greater light of vision and more efficacy of tapas, but without absolute certainty which only comes when there is the play of the ideal T^2; provisional certainty is however more frequent, but does not owing to the continued residuary action of the old intelligence always know its own proper limits.

There are now in the lipi three forms of vijnana, (1) the superior ideality (II), (2) the superior ideality in the form of the inferior, (3) the inferior ideality (I) in its three forms, revelatory, inspirational and intuitional. The intuitional lipi is now revelatory in its substance even when intuitional in its form, but the inspirational is often inspirational in substance as well as in form. This defect is now being removed and has almost in a moment practically disappeared.

Kamananda very much oppressed persists in a diminished and subtilised form, which at its lowest hardly seems kamananda. This is in ambulando, but even at other times there is an oppression which amounts sometimes to sheer and prolonged discontinuity. Advantage is however being taken of this depression to strengthen the element of ideal Ananda.

In the evening some restoration of the intensity, but fragmentary, recurrent, not continuous.

In the morning some depression of utthapana shakti, an overshadowing by strong effigies of fatigue, once imposing rest. Writing and visits prevented the abhyasa during the rest of the day, except for a short time at night when no trace of fatigue was left, but some muscular stiffness.

Samadhi developed chiefly in the ordering of dream. The confused amalgamations of dream are being disentangled by the buddhi in the dream state itself. Occurrence of superior ideality in deep swapna samadhi.

Some ideal rupa in jagrat.

Vishaya occurs, but makes no definite progress.

The attack of the external physicality and its mind has failed to disturb the first two [chatusthayas],[11] except for a vague superficial

---

[11] MS utthapanas

stain on the [   ]¹² traigunyasiddhi. Sraddha holds firm, but is defective as to karma on account of uncertainty. Sraddha in yogasiddhi is complete.

May 20

The siddhi in the lipi is being extended to the speech-thought so that even when the intellectual attack is allowed to reign and the ideality suspended, still the vangmaya is in its form ideal and either revelatory or inspirational in its substance

The attack is effectuated by the will of the Ishwara suspending the action of the higher ideality in the ideation. There has however been a constant action this morning of ideality in the intuitive mind commenting the confused action of the residuary mind-stuff and distinguishing its element of truth, which is that which sets its waves in motion, and the error which the mind-stuff throws up around the truth and attaches to it. This action is caused by (1) telepathies from outside, (2) telepathies from the mental and pranic planes, (3) obscurely received suggestions from the ideality. When the ideality does not act, the intellect tries to do what it can with all that it receives

The obstruction to kamananda continues, though lessened; the ideal Ananda is increasing in its subtle insistence and sometimes takes effect tenuously in the sthula form.

There is a movement to apply finally the law of the ideality to the ideation as in the speech thought and the lipi. This is not difficult in the ideation of jnana, but it is still difficult in the ideation of T², especially of tapas. Stress of tapatya and tapata have always been the chief obstacles; whenever removed, they have returned in a modified form; they now return as suggestions from the external physicality breaking down the defences of the intuitive mind. The Shakti has once more put them in their right place and discharged the intuitive mind of tapatya and even of unduly extended tapata. Decisive trikaldrishti and effective tapas are steadily increasing even in the intuitive mind; but until all tapas becomes ideal tapas, the

---

12 *MS* on the

perfection of the ideality cannot be thoroughly accomplished. This as yet has not been done. It can only be done by the satyam brihat ritam in the decisive trikaldrishti developing into its full amplitude. For that the rejection of the intellectual mind-stuff which clings to the ideation is a necessary preliminary.

In Samadhi still the same movement. At night a revival of dream incoherence.

Utthapana unsatisfactory.

May 21st

The sadhan is now concentrated on the *vijnana-chatusthaya* with an initial stress on the physical siddhi which is still secondary except in the *sharira ananda*, mainly the kamananda.

At present the ideality is passing through a stage of what would formerly have been called relapse, but is now recognised as a reversion to a lower movement in order to get rid of still existing defects or possibilities of defect and transform the remnants of the lower into the spirit and the form of the higher movement.

Script. "Develop T^2 and ideation, restore kamananda. Persist in rupa and vishaya and samadhi".

1. Kamananda is restored; it has recovered its power of continuity and its means against vismriti, but is still strongly subject to diminution which manifests chiefly in ambulando. It is clear that the initial conquest of vismriti is firm and real, since it manifests at once after discontinuity and has not to be built up again. The siddhi is subject to diminution and relapse into mechanical discontinuity; it has to overcome these tendencies and to complete its conquest of vismriti, for so long as the latter is only initial and not complete, the relapse to discontinuity must always be possible.

2. T^2 and ideation are working on the physical level of the intellect. They are getting rid of the inspirational and intuitional substance which most lend themselves to the attack of unideal tapas and intellectual error, because their enlightenment is essentially a partial illumination intervening in an initial ignorance. All is being turned to substance of revelatory thought, for it is this that illumines largely and is in its nature a self sight that does not address itself at all to the initial ignorance of the intellect. Even in T^2 the conversion to revelatory thought is being rapidly led towards completeness.

3. Rupa has been baffled in its development of stable variety.

Variety has been partially developed in power, but subject to all
the old difficulties. In the crude the tyranny of the type form which
obstructs and excludes the others, obstructs their spontaneous manifestation and allows only a difficult development pursued and
overcome by the type form which, even when they emerge, returns
upon them and usurps their place. In the developed and dense
other forms occur, but are imperfect, unstable and confined to a
few persistent forms or kinds of form. The principle of barring a
free variety by insistence on already common rupas is still the chief
and hitherto a successful weapon of the obstruction.

4. Vishaya is simply unable to overcome the barrier.

In samadhi, antardarshi and swapna, in the vangmaya the
inspirational and intuitional forms have been entirely taken up into
the revelatory form, so that both form and substance are now of
this highest element of the inferior ideality. Moreover this inferior
ideality is full of the spirit and presence of the superior ritam. The
same movement has to be effected in the waking thought-speech
and in the ideation and it has in fact begun, but here owing to the
greater diffusion of the mind it is more difficult.

The revelatory thought has in a way taken up all the other
forms, but their effects still remain as a limiting element which
prevents and conditions the play of the knowledge. Especially it is
now acting on the level of the intellect and its revelations are on that
level pursued by the uncertainties of the intellect, by its tapas or
ineffectual straining after certainty and effectivity, by its smallness
of periphery in the conscious being and scope of knowledge and
power. The object seems to be to meet these difficulties in their own
field and even there to establish the fullness of revelatory light and
substance and the free certainties of the superior ideality.

Here the script programme has been initially fulfilled. But in
the rupa it has not been justified. Rupa has only become capable
of variety; it has not accomplished it. Vishaya has only effected an
uncertain and scanty initial play, an action of subtle sparsha just
verging on the sthula, a dim fragmentary beginning of çravana.
In samadhi vishaya has begun to play more freely, but in jagrat it

has not broken down the barrier. In samadhi taste and smell are still crude and faint. Samadhi has established everywhere an initial ideality and regularisation by the ideality, but the action in each member is hampered by intermissions of obstruction and in swapna incoherence though no longer the rule, still recurs persistently in the reading and the dialogue etc have not yet, except sometimes in dream, a large continuity.

Primary utthapana after a brilliant beginning has relapsed into ineffectivity and subjection to physical fatigue. Arogya is limited to an incomplete and struggling inhibition of the fragments of roga, –but these only occur by persistent exposure to the action of their habitual causes, – and to a preparation for the conquest of the two or three fixed rogas; the actual conquest is still far from effectuation. In saundarya no advance except the stronger fixture of the sukshma bhava of youth and ananda and a certain light and prophecy of it in the eyes and face. Kamananda is still afflicted by diminution and discontinuity; the conquest of vismriti is still only initial.

May 22.

This is the fourth week of May, the month of decisive preparation of finality and perfection in the vijnana chatusthaya. It is proposed to effect the perfection of the primary ideality in ideation and speech thought and as far as possible in T^2. Rupa, vishaya, samadhi, the three defective members, have to insist on their initial completeness in the ideality. The preparation of the sharira siddhi has to insist also against the powerful obstruction of the old imperfect physicality which defends its habits as the law of the being.

The satyam brihat of the tapas, the physical telepathy and the telepathy of the mental and pranic planes is being established in the idealised intelligence under the guidance of the ideality; the object is to eliminate in its own field the false stress, the intellectual decision, so that the ideal ritam may be freed from the pursuit of the intellect.

In samadhi ideality took more firmly hold of rupa. There was also the beginning of the specific religious ideality and the ideal sense of prayer and adoration as an element of love and oneness with the Divine.

This is being extended and transformed into the finality of the personal relation of the Jiva with the Iswara

In samadhi at night obstruction, with prevalent incoherence. It was only by force of tapas that the play of the siddhi was brought about, and the free play could not be secured.

May 23.

For some days there has been a strong revival of the obstruction to the whole siddhi, but specially the ideality. The object is to enforce the old rule of a recurring period of relapse, enduring usually for a fortnight more or less, or even longer, and the method is to enforce a sort of lethargy of unresponsiveness in the mind and physicality by which first, if possible, all action shall be obstructed, secondly, whatever action is enforced by tapas shall be imperfect and marred by the old asiddhi, thirdly, as a result things which seemed to have been eliminated shall be revived, thus discouraging the faith and the tapas. The first object has not been gained, because in spite of periods of cessation, the tapas has insisted and the action of the ideality has been enforced even in this adverse condition, but the other two objects have been partially and temporarily gained. The action of the ideality is no longer free, but dependent on tapas and a struggle with the lethargic obstruction, the revived action of the intellect has vitiated the perfection of the ideality and even touches of imperfection have come in the first two chatusthayas. Nevertheless the siddhi advances and no longer behind the veil, as formerly in periods of relapse, but openly, though with apparent concessions to asiddhi used for strengthening the siddhi. The principle of subconscient progress has been eliminated, but the principle of finesse still continues.

The main progress this morning is the enforcement, 1, of the constant habitual action of the ideality, in spite of the physical brain's lethargy, 2, of the constant combined action of ideation, speech thought and T^2 to which is being added the lipi. These used to give place to each other and act alternately. There is also a movement to add the action of rupa and vishaya and kamananda but the power of multiple tapas is not yet strong enough to effect the perfect combination.

This enforcement of the combined action of ideation, T^2 and speech thought of the ideal kind is being more and more insisted on and is on the point of becoming spontaneous and normal. The main defect lies now in the downward gravitation which prevents the thought from being of the highest elevation possible, the stuff of intellect mixed in the ideation and vak by the persistence of a background of intellectual demand and pursuit of the thought by a vague intellectual observation and judgment, which though not often explicit hampers the ideality, and the continuance of external intellectual suggestion in T^2. Nevertheless the change from ideal intervention to a massed ideal movement of all the activities of the consciousness, progresses with considerable rapidity.

In Samadhi unprecedent[ed]ly large play of coherent reading of great length; but incoherence also persists side by side with it. The other members also had coherent play but less prominently.

The insistence on Kamananda is less, the continuity is suspended, but recurrence remains.

May 24.

T^2 advances steadily. Tapas (telepathic) is becoming normally effective and more clearsighted and therefore more accurate. Strong tapas which was hitherto discouraged, because it brought the tapatya, is now being encouraged and the remnants of tapatya are being transformed into forcible prolongation of right tapas. Accordingly the brihat satyam of T^2 is becoming as complete as it can be without perfect ritam and without the play of the superior ideality. For that combination alone can give all the right data in their right place including tendencies which are latent or obscurely implied and eventualities of which there is no present sign. The intimations of the mental and rajasic planes like those of the physical are receiving their right measure of satyam and it is now seen that all have their truth, except certain speculations, as to present and

past especially, which are the intuitions of what might have been
and may possibly be as the result of past intentions and tendencies,
but do not correspond to any actually accomplished event.

Strong and successful secondary utthapana of position.

It is remarkable that fatigue of the physical mind and will, or
rather the mind and will of the body, was not at all in question;
for from the first it was as if already eliminated, except for a few
ineffective attempts at return. Only at the end it came in in support
of the muscular reaction. Primary utthapana was therefore established except in so far as it failed, through failure of secondary
utthapana.

The secondary was tried in the morning in the arms, in two horizontal positions A Ia & b, frontal triangular and frontal straight.
In Ia siddhi came easily; the attempt to enforce [an]anima, though
recurrent, failed in persistence and in violence; self-existent utthapana, free from defect of anima, was established and remained.
In Ib there was violent opposition, but it failed in the right arm,
but succeeded in the left by persistence of pain of ananima aided
afterwards by pressure of downward garima from above, — not
gravitation, but pressure of some other external force which comes
in when gravitation weakens. Gravitation is attraction from below,
this is a mass of pressure from above. In the right arm self existent
utthapana was established. In the left it became strong enough to
maintain the position in spite of pressure and pain and even to
make the pain recurrent instead of persistent and to discourage
and sometimes lighten the pressure, but not to get rid of it. The
whole lasted $2\frac{1}{2}$ continuous hours. In the result force of selfexistent
utthapana is established in the arms as was shown in the afternoon,
but ananima still remains to limit and resist the siddhi, though with
greatly diminished force.

In the afternoon two positions of the legs, B.I & II, lying on
the back, crooked position, lower parts horizontal, and lying on
each side, alternately, horizontal II.a (straight) & II.b crooked. In
B I. defect of anima was strong and prevented long abhyasa, but
while recently and for a long time mahima has entirely failed to
support the laghima, this time it came and held. In B II, (a) was

found difficult owing to violent attack of ananima, but this was persistently recurrent, not persistent, and there was in the intervals complete utthapana; in (b) the recurrence was less persistent and less violent. On the whole on the left the utthapana was well maintained, either self-existent or satapas, for about 15 minutes; on the right there was after 7 or 8 minutes the overpowering by defect of anima. Therefore this utthapana of B positions can only be regarded as preparatory, as it was declared to be before it began.

In arms AA, (ie lying on back), the old self-existent utthapana force recovered strength and maintained itself, after one or two downward tendencies of lapse, even in sleep.

Throughout the increased power and effectivity of tapas was very marked.

In Samadhi free action of rupa and frequent initial stability and continuity. Incoherence has invaded the lipi in the deeper swapna.

May 25.

The dealings of the ideality with the revived intellect element, show an increasing subtlety and fullness of the vijnana, giving a clear ideal interpretation of the obscure brain-suggestions, which if carried to the extreme will mean a full satyam brihat with a sufficient ritam. But the process means a continual indulgence of the obscuration by the intellect which involves a suspension of the direct and primary action of the ideality. Behind the obscuration the superior ideality is growing in power upon the whole thought action.

The increase of the ritam in the satyam brihat of the telepathies on the lowest level has been proceeding rapidly, but complete ritam is not yet established.

Lipi is being left entirely to itself to establish the eightfold quality in perfectly spontaneous lipi without aid of the tapas or the suggestions. The first result of the movement has been to bring back the full etheric resistance to the manifestation with the result of fragmentariness, called formerly the desultory lipi, and defect in all the eight qualities. It is now attempting to dispel the imperfections, as yet only with a very partial success.

Recovery by the speech thought of its higher ideal pitch at which it now moves normally without any need of the least attention or tapas.

In samadhi lipi recovered its coherency in deep swapna samadhi, but there is an intermediate stage between dream and samadhi, the one passing over into the other, in which incoherence is still common. Nevertheless the incoherence can be pieced together: sometimes it arises from fragments of a sentence or thought being put together without the connecting words or thoughts, and then they have to be filled in, sometimes from the coalition of thoughts which are not connected and then they have to be separated.

Utthapana of position A I tried for about an hour. Self existent utthapana of laghima in the primary force, good for maintaining the position, if unafflicted, for two or three hours, if afflicted, for a shorter time, but not making the position entirely normal to the feeling of the body, only natural or much more natural than before. Anima not violently defective, but the defect slowly increases in force, compelling desistence in the end or at least interruption.

Subsequently, on almost immediately resuming, it was found that the compulsion of the asiddhi was not imperative, as it had appeared, but, the abhyasa being interrupted, it could not be seen how far the ananima could be eliminated. In the evening the will of the body to utthapana failed.

May 26

A II tried, but the self-existent u[tthapana]-shakti was found not to have even half the full primary force.

The movement in T^2 continues; tapas is steadily increasing.

For the last two days kamananda has been recovering its force, but is still deficient in ambulando.

Growth of rupa in Samadhi.

May 27–31

Entire absorption in another activity; the ideality continued to play of itself and to grow in quality. Rupa became increasingly powerful in Samadhi and more frequent in antardarshi.

June 1.

The upshot of the last month is to have founded firmly the ideality in the inferior or primary form, it is true, but with a substance of superior, that is to say, secondary ideality, and to have applied it to the whole range of thought including T^2. In the latter, however, it is still weak and has comparatively little scope. The lower intellectuality is on the point of abolition but the intuitive has still its role and must keep it till the superior ideality has got into its own characteristic form and occupied the place now held by the primary ideality. Samadhi has grown greatly in strength, especially in the last few days. Rupa in swapna is very strong, various and rich and stability up to the tertiary initial is common; but the prolonged stability is only in the shadowy forms. Reading has become free and current, but not always coherent, or even when coherent, not cohesive; the sentences are sufficient to themselves and have not, except exceptionally, a visible relation to each other. Rupa is pressing forward in antardarshi, but has not yet fixed its hold on the bahirdarshi. Vishaya is still unable to break down the barrier.

As a result of the work done in the last few days which was accomplished in the complete control (dasya), the passivity of the intellect has been greatly intensified and a new action is coming into being from above which evidently belongs to the secondary ideality. This is the beginning of the tertiary dasya.

June 3

Secondary utthapana II.a.b. left side for more than half an hour, variation for five minutes to IIb(a), slanting upwards. The opposition to mahima and laghima was all this time entirely ineffective and in fact rare, though occasionally it recurred only to give up the attempt almost immediately. The opposition to anima, though recurrent, could not persist, was not vehemently recurrent and was often in abeyance. Only after more than half an hour the disinclination of the body indicated a suppressed force of denial of the utthapana shakti

Rupa continues to grow in the swapna with a reflex action in the antardarshi. Stability is greatly increased. Vishaya in swapna is preparing to normalise itself. Only the self existent progress of all the parts in unison without exclusiveness or interruption has to be established. Vishaya and rupa in jagrat held on.

[*Half a page left blank.*]

June 14.

For the whole first fortnight of June the active sadhana has been suspended; there has been the absorbing preoccupation of another activity. At first the play of the ideality was associated with it, but it is now abated and is turning again to the sadhana. Still, this has left behind it the beginning of a movement to substitute the ideal for the ordinary mental action in all intellectual activities, eg, poetry, study etc.

The first movement has been action of the secondary utthapana.

This morning. B II, left, almost entirely b, for upward of an hour; simultaneously, A.A.b_1, left arm raised half way for an hour, lying on the right side, and neck, C b, in the same position. In all mahima and laghima triumphant. In B II the sharp defect of anima has lost its power of persistence and also of persistent recurrence; it occurred once or [twice][1] for a moment in the first half hour, once or twice with a more prolonged but with no very intense recurrence in the second. In C b, it came only for a time. The place of the old oppressive defect of anima has been taken by the pressure of garima on the limb, a weighing down, a sort of dull combined defect of the three qualities with the result of a temporary disinclination and declaration of inability in the body; but this could

[1] MS two

not last. It was stronger in A.A.b than in B II and in C b than in either of the other asanas. But in none could it prevail. All three might have been continued. But the object now is not, as before, to prolong the period of the asana which means only to postpone the return of the nir-utthapana, but to abolish the denial. This is being done by the will bringing in the nature of the vijnana into the body and abhyasa is now rather [ ]² a test than a means of the siddhi.

In the later morning A III; vertical position of both arms, walking, for between half an hour and an hour. Here too mahima laghima is in possession, but the defect of utthapana shakti is greater, due to the survival of the defect of anima shown by a reaction in the muscles after cessation, which was absent from the asanas of the early morning. The asana could not have been continued longer without some strain and difficulty. No evident reaction from the walking in this position.

The movement is now to replace finally in trikaldrishti the action through the intellect by the action through the intuitive mind. In trikaldrishti the survival of the inferior action is strong and will take some time to eliminate. It prevents decisive trikaldrishti and perpetuates error of stress and error of interpretation of the will-messages and knowledge-messages from the ideality.

Kamananda has gone back for the time being. Smarana is no longer always sufficient to recall it. Arogya also is thrown back in chronic rogas 1 and 2; but in the latter only under great stress lasting for the whole fortnight and here the siddhi tendency is evident even in failure.

Ready manifestation of the lipi is also a little dulled, as well as the strong play of the swapna samadhi and rupa. The lipi suffers chiefly in legibility. The tendency to stability is strong, but resisted and embarrassed.

All is, however, ready to reemerge against the strong obstruction. Full siddhi will come when interruption can no longer impair the vivacity of the siddhi.

² MS than

July 1ˢᵗ

On one side the absorption of work continues, on the other the sadhan is determining its upward movement. The ideality is gradually gaining upon the strong remnant of the intellectual obstruction and its obstinate lingering on the mental method of reception. The obstructed kamananda is resuming its force of sasmarana action, but has not yet reaffirmed strongly the trend to continuity. The rest of the physical siddhi does not advance.

Tuesday 24th June 1919.

Today the condition of a general low tone of the being with yet a continued progress in the Yoga still continues; no depression, but a ghost of languor in the body which obstructs the channel action of the mind. The vijnana acts, but irregularly, not with a rapid or normal flow. It has not yet recovered its brightness, but is a clouded sunlight.

According to the lipi there should be today some blaze of the gnosis. Now it is suggested to the mind that trikaldrishti-tapas which yesterday founded itself in this halflight is to develop farther, telepathy be farther taken up, ideal samadhi increase its hold and the physical siddhi enlarge its foundation. Some progress may also be expected with the more constant darshana of the Ananda Ishwara.

=

Last night çukshma çravana became for a few minutes frequent and insistent; it even insisted a little to the fully waking ear and without any closing of it; but it is still faint in comparison and fragmentary.

=

Lipi. "Life in the entire ideality: between this and February it will develop in the first basis; it is already developing."

This last statement must be understood in the sense of an initial tenuous idealising of speech and action and of result of tapas in the immediate vicinity.

=

The gnosis is now taking up all the thought through the pragmatic form of the intuitive mentality; universalising that in the half and half intellectual ideal type, — but intellect not prevailing, fixed into the ideality; the mechanical intuivity is almost entirely dismissed except in the T³.

=

In T³ also the pragmatic intuitivity is establishing itself, strongest in the telepathies, but there is still an unauthorised intellectual stress of immediate fulfilment which baffles trikaldrishtic certitude. Even the trikaldrishti is pragmatic, not the highest entirely certain seeing, but gives only a practical certainty. Tapas is assuming the same kind of intuitivity. All tendencies and forces are admitted which offer themselves to the sight and now are seen in juster proportions than at any previous time. But the light is the clouded sunlight, not the full blaze of golden or fiery day.

There is the blaze of the highest logistic ideality in the lipi and the thought speech, but it has not yet gained the perceptive thought, much less the T³. But as soon as this was written, that transforming movement too began. As always, it is the subjective trikaldrishti that is the first to advance; the objective is hampered by the physical obstruction. The golden but not the fiery blaze is gaining the lesser movements, including the remnants of the mechanical intuivity.

Kavya for a while worked in the revelation, but was soon clouded by the obscurity of the intellectual effort.

Arogya is steadily gaining in force, but with a slow pressure. The fragmentary rogas encircle dully in the subtle pranic atmosphere and touch or menace, but only hold now and then in certain residuary recurrences. The intestinal complaint is constantly reaching the vanishing point and then resuming hold, but there is nothing like the past violent returns. The restitution in the centre is only just trying to get and maintain an initial foothold; nothing evidently decisive.

Samadhi completed its idealisation in the afternoon; but at night it is subject to the relapse of sleep. In the afternoon there is only at most a shadow. In the morning there is a dull struggle of sleep to keep at bay the samadhi, and when the latter occurs there is a certain persistence of incoherence especially in the settled sthira lipi. This is being diminished, but it recovers its force repeatedly.

Ananda and secondary utthapana are for the time in intermission of progress.

Wednesday 25ᵗʰ June. 1919

The ideality of all speech thought has long been assured; the ideality of the perceptive thought is now becoming assured, wide, universal. Only the tapas and the trikaldrishtic thought and perception remains to be similarly illumined; this has begun, but its progress is interrupted and obstructed. There is a speech thought of the nature of vani expressing the trikaldrishti which is still of the intellectual ideality or intuitivity and subject to error, but that comes only in the inertia of the mechanical mentality. This mechanical passivity has to be got rid of, all has to become an ideal *çamamaya* activity. Passivity of the mind has now served its purpose, the mind has become a silent channel; only the obstruction of the physical brain atmosphere preserves the dull habit of this passivity, a tamasic persistence in an inert misrepresentation of the old *çanti*.

The only progress in the physical siddhi is a commencement of the idealising of the Ananda. Today the insistence on K.A. [Kama Ananda] is renewed; but the forgetfulness of the body continues. The intuitivity is strong in the K.A, only initial in the other anandas.

The Ananda Ishwara is now vivid and all the action and guna has been taken up into the Anandamaya; there was a discord between the darshan of the supreme universal Anandamaya and the perception of the universal mental unideal consciousness, but this is cured and only the bridge between the Anandamaya in universal and individual and the mentality is not yet brought into light. If this is done the darshana will be complete in essence.

=

Kamananda is again being pushed forward; the difficulties still are mechanical discontinuity, forgetfulness, mechanical diminution, the need of tapas to restore it when smarana is not sufficient, absorption, sleep. The mechanical discontinuity only prevails (1) when the energy is at a low ebb, (2) after long forgetfulness. Forgetfulness is being attacked and when the Ananda is in flow, there is usually a second memory in the body which retains it in various degrees of intensity or at least so keeps it that it is felt when the mind returns to some partial attention. Absorption now for the same reason does not necessarily bring discontinuity. Two movements are being carried on, (1) removal of exclusive absorption, the simultaneity of a double memory or concentration, (2) the inability of absorption to bring about complete discontinuity. These siddhis formerly only hinted at or momentarily accomplished, are now beginning to establish themselves, however imperfectly. Old occupations which excluded memory of K A are now admitting it, eg reading, writing, bathing, eating. There are two absorptions, the luminous concentration and the tamasic "absence" of the part of the mind not occupied in the particular work; the latter is the only real difficulty; it is not really an absence, but an involution in tamas, a sort of cloud of inertia, which is physically sensible all about the brain or near it.

Telepathic thought in its lowest mental form is being idealised on these levels.

K.A maintained throughout the day, even during absorbed writing and in conversation when it is apt to cease, but not without interruptions of forgetfulness. The body is not yet in secure possession of it, owing to a constant pressure for exclusion from the opposing forces.

Finesse was again used in the vijnana-siddhi in the evening; the whole mass of the old basic intellectuality was re-presented and the mind plunged into it, the ideality mostly held back, so that there might be a wider transformation, thought to be idealised even when occurring on the very lowest levels, even below the brain, even the thought of the chitta and the prana and the subconscious mind.

Samadhi today was strongly attacked by sleep.

Some beginnings of decisive ideal trikaldrishti and tapas, T^2.

Thursday 26th June 1919.

K.A interrupted in the night by forgetfulness and listlessness, restored with a little difficulty of opposition in the morning. Continued throughout the day, but with more frequent lapses into forgetfulness. The defect of the siddhi is that as yet it does not dwell sufficiently in the body, but is rather imposed on it by the psychic tendency. Once begun it can continue for a time of its own motion, but for its initiation and long maintenance has to depend on smarana and needs often a will in the smarana, sometimes a forceful tapas against the obstacle. Spontaneous initiation, renewal and maintenance [have][1] been begun and at favourable times are not infrequent, but are not yet the law of the body. The struggle between sleep and continuity of the Ananda has begun, but the continuity still needs the aid of smarana and tapas and does not subsist in the deeper nidra.

=

Samadhi has relapsed to a certain extent, is much assailed by sleep and incoherence. Its advance which was always laborious, has again become fragmentary. There is some progress in stability and vivid force of drishya, but it is again mostly chhayamaya. Extreme shadowy drishya has sometimes almost a complete stability; it then lasts long with some moments of eclipse. Combination of thought-speech, perceptive thought and lipi has begun, but with some difficulty.

=

Ideality has been strongly attacked throughout the day, but progresses even in a general lowering, especially in telepathy and trikaldrishti. Ideality of thought is being generalised on all levels and intellectual thought is now becoming more and more the recurrence of an abnormality. The generalisation of telepathic ideality has begun on a large scale. Decisive trikaldrishti is being enforced and enlarged against great difficulty.

The first two chatusthayas grow continually stronger and show this increasing strength in each fresh attack. They can only be attacked at all, and then very ineffectively, when the ideality is lowered or suspended.

=

Arogya too is attacked; but the attack amounts to an obstruction and lowering of the tapas, not to a positive disintegration, or at most there is only a slight superficial crumbling. But progress is slow, the strong rapidity which was trying to set in, is still held

---

[1] MS has

back from possession. Utthapana is suspended. Bhava-saundarya is gaining in continuity and generality.
==

Ananda Ishwara is now confirmed except in the perception of mentality which is not yet linked up with the ideal anandamaya.

Friday 27ᵗʰ June 1919

The dasya is now being perfected and made vivid; first, the dasya of the worker and instrument is made complete and perfect. To that is added the dasya of the power, dasi iswari; the difficulty was the insufficiency of the aishwarya and consequently of the sense of the Ishwari, but now the relative and progressive aishwarya is for the time being accepted. The dasya to the Guru is also added and is uniting with these forms. The dasya in the relations of friend (raised to brother, bandhu), vatsalya, father etc are being prepared for perfection and unity in the madhura. All has to be taken up into the madhura. This movement can only be perfect when the sense of the presence of the Ishwara is allowed to be *nitya* in its directness and vividness. At present the Ishwara still acts from behind the Shakti.

Attack of roga on digestive functions suppressed by tapas after a struggle with a residue in bhava. This is only part of the general attack of vague recurrence and attempted restoration (fever, headache, cold etc); it materialises in the digestive functioning, because that is still immediately capable of brief sthula recurrence. The others are only potentially capable, except for fragmentary touches. This fragmentary recurrence has been attacked and is in process of slow diminution, but is not yet got rid of. The two constant rogas, as well as the imperfect process of evacuation still continue.

Telepathy has been purified in regard to the tendencies and forces immediately affecting the adharas in action; that is to say, the insistence of a perceived tendency, force or intention on its fulfilment, the choice of one to be favoured and fulfilled without reference to the real ideality and the claim of telepathy or present trikaldrishti to figure as future drishti, of tendency, force, intention, possibility and probability to masquerade as certain result, is being eliminated from T^3. The same movement is being rapidly applied to the forces of the vital rajasic and mental sattwic planes which stand behind the mechanism of forces of the physical plane. This will complete the present trikaldrishti, except for the right perception of the states of unseen objects which is still backward.

This movement is setting free the future trikaldrishti; certitudes are already increasing, but are still for the most telepathic certitudes, that is based on present fact, and extending to primary immediate or near result, which is growing strong, to secondary farther off or intermediate results, which is growing, and final results, which is still only in initiation or else not linked in to the rest in a sufficient ideal unity. Beyond this trikaldrishtic telepathy lies the pure trikaldrishti independent of all perception of tendencies, forces, intentions. Time and detail have still to develop certitude. It is notable that there has not been in the past nor is there now any attempt, except for fragmentary illuminations, to develop trikaldrishti of the past. This is partly due to the nature of the adhara in which the mind has always been concentrated on the present and the future, and subjected to a deficient memory from which past events have quickly faded. In part it is due to the mentality of the age which has taken in the adhara an extreme form, except that this individual mind goes back readily to a far past in which the future was prefigured.

Pain and discomfort are being strongly taken up by the Ananda. Today all pain and discomfort, the former even very acute and of some little persistence, the latter massive and oppressive, were permeated with Ananda. Only violent and very oppressive yantrana or discomfort has still to be taken up.

Samadhi is recovering force and coherent ideality, though with difficulty, yet rapidly.

Saturday June 28th 1919

Today, a rapid progress in T^2 is intended. Incertitude must be largely replaced by certitude, the activities taken up which are still left to the relics of the [intellectuality];[2] all universalised in the blaze of the ideality.

---

[2] *MS* ideal[it]y

The foundation of continuity in K.A is now securely laid in spite of some appearances; but the continuity itself is interrupted by forgetfulness and cessation of interest or capacity in the body. But these three things and especially the last are not only mechanical, but abnormal, the results of a strong hostile pressure from outside which takes advantage of the mechanical memory of old habit in the body. Sleep and absorption are now the only real difficulties, both have begun to yield to the siddhi.

The ideality is now busy with the trikaldrishti, taking up and fighting all the old confusions. When done on the higher level, this process proceeds harmoniously with little flaw or mistake; on the lower level it is a slower progress of order in the midst of a chaos. All telepathies are now justified but at the moment the old intellectual intervention of false stress continually returns in a less or a greater degree. This difficulty is chiefly felt with regard to rapidly changing action.

Other defects of the ideality are also being taken up for correction

Samadhi in the afternoon was overpowered by a persistent unnaturally deep sleep, but the samadhi power, though it could not persevere, broke to a certain extent into the nidra.

There are now frequent lapses into the idealised mentality and from there into the tamas of the physical obstruction. The Ananda perseveres, but does not increase, forgetfulness still besieges. The other siddhis are obstructed and some of the physical subject to a certain limited relapse.

The defect of the traigunya siddhi is that tapasic stress on the one hand, inertia of mental shama with tamas breaking across it and sometimes possessing cling to the mind by a sort of external affecting adhesion. This is being remedied first by an increasing externalisation of the inferior tapas, next by the increasing prakasha of the shamas. But until both tapas and shama are full of the *vijnana jyotis*, "the blaze of the ideality", the siddhi will not be complete and faultless.

Ideality recovered itself. In the Samadhi, symbolic figure of a dark (blue-black) moon with a shapeless reproduction of it below; above-round the small sphere a blaze of sunlight on one side. This meant the dark Soma (intuitive mind-orb, ananda consciousness, with the jyoti involved in it), emitting the jyoti, the other the intellectual reflection. The suryamandala is the symbol of the vijnana. The ideality was of this character. From the shama enveloping the mind activity came the initial blaze of the ideality in the trikaldrishti tapas. The rest, – thought-speech, perceptive thought – acted with the same anandamaya shama emitting jyoti.

Torpor of the kamananda in the evening and night. Much alasya of the body thrown off partly by tapas. Aprakasha is disappearing; but physical inertia still keeps a certain hold of recurrence and a besieging potentiality. From the alasya comes pramada, a negligence and confusion in the action of thought and perception.

Coherent symbolic dream in Samadhi

Sunday 29th June 1919.

In samadhi coherence gained ground in the lipi. There was a whole passage written successively with perfect coherence of thought and word, in spite of one or two attempts of the besieging incoherence. Incoherence remains especially when the lipi written or printed comes in large masses, but it is evidently a receding, though still persistent force. This is in a middlingly deep nidra; the deepest nidra is yet to be invaded and taken into possession by samadhi.

The ideality is to open into blaze today, to get a certain initial perfection in such fullness and range as is at present possible. This movement is to be completed tomorrow.   Samadhi, today and tomorrow, is to round into the ideality.   Ananda to advance, pressure on the obstruction to the other physical siddhis.   Ananda Ishwara.

The Ananda Ishwara darshana is persistently bridging the gulf; the perception of the Anandamaya in objects is pouring into and taking up the personal mental consciousness. This movement has to be completed in perfection.

There is as yet no sign of the fulfilment of the proposed advance; but a siege and a reduction of ideality to the intuitive mentality, chandramandala. There has even come a touch and strong persistence of the old asamata, physical but with a nervous and emotional excitement of the physicality containing all the old symptoms. It has a curious symbolic form as of a small circular touch on the middle of the breast like a rupee, trying to extend rays of asukha and asanti, but prevented for the most part by the tapas. This is followed by an attempt to throw in scattering currents of duhkha as through subtle nerve currents. The whole disturbance comes from an illegitimate attempt from outside to bring the action of the chandramandala to replace the surya action.

The blaze of the surya action is now taking possession, forcing aside the minor soma action. The attack of the asamata falls away from the surya blaze; it subsists only by a reflex of the ineffective chandra action which is easily attackable by the old deficiencies. The blaze brings also the light of the trikaldrishti. A crisis has also been brought about in the Ananda, which failed in the interval, there has also been a strong attack of fatigue tamas. The Ananda disability is being pushed aside by the surya action, the fatigue combated by surya tapas.

Samadhi in its lighter forms is acclimatising the blaze of the Surya.

In the waking state the highest ideality is still combated by the mind's persistence in the intuitive chandra mould and in the lower forms of the intellectualised surya ideality, but it is making the other movements its own. The difficulty is with the T^3.

In the K.A. the intuitive substance of Ananda is more intense and tries to subsist as against the slighter substance of the suryamaya; but the latter is persisting and taking possession.

The Surya blaze has now taken preliminary possession of T^3 as well as thought speech and thought perception; only the remnants of the chandra intuivity still resist the assumption.

Ananda darshana is also assuming the Surya form and the Surya Ananda.

K.A too is now more readily running in the Surya mould; the Chandra intensity is being rapidly extruded.

There is now a descent of the Surya towards the sunlit intellectuality, for this has to be taken up as the mental base of the ideality and the whole mentality illumined into a silent channel and then a logistic form of the gnosis. Wherever the surya ideality or the illumined intuitive intellect does not act, there the chandra intuitivity with its infinite of possibility and incertitude is still active.

Surya is taking possession also of the sun of the imagination.

Monday 30th June 1919.

The Surya action limited by the sunlit intellectual intuitivity and the remnants of the Chandra intuitivity continues its gradual process of assumption.

The blaze of the ideality has spread itself and can now hold all the thought and thought-speech and the telepathies, but is still impeded in T^2 by the incertitudes of the mentality. In the telepathies it is a modified and quiet light, but in the rest a fuller stronger blaze with flashes of Agni and Vidyut; the latter suggest the supreme *vidyunmaya* Ananda chandra.

The Surya power is now also acting as tapas on the obstacles to the Arogya and the utthapana, but these are strong and persistent in their pressure.

The Samadhi is still being taken up by the Surya power only in antardarshi jagrat and the lighter depths. Deep nidra is still only invaded on its borders and gives at best coherent dream with a touch of misplaced ideality.

The ideality in the afternoon has been extending itself with a certain slow deliberateness. It is taking up telepathic trikaldrishti of time, place and circumstance, things neglected or else unsuccessfully attempted by the former sadhana; this is because the mental telepathic indications abound around every isolated certitude and bring in a besieging error and incertitude. These indications have yet to be reduced to their correct proportions before much headway can be made. This operation is now commenced on a slight scale. Time now is often correct and correctness of place and successive or surrounding circumstance is sometimes added.

All the movements of the Ananda are being taken up by Surya. For some time the Chandra was being excluded whenever it came; and for that reason, the intensities fell away; for all the intensities were chandramaya; but now the intensities are also being reduced to the sun-ideality. Forgetfulness is still strong; but the partial conquest of it is being taken up, although the dependence on memory and attention predominates.

Slight extension of ideality at night. Samadhi successful only in the early morning; rupa, stable in action as well as status, in deeper samadhi, also tejomaya; also sufficiently coherent lipi.

Attack of fragmentary roga at night, much diminished by tapas.

July.

Tuesday July 1ˢᵗ 1919

The month of June has been a period of the overcoming of difficulties in the central ideality, in the Ananda Ishwara Darshana and in the Kama Ananda, a combat with difficulties and slow varying progress in some elements of Çarira siddhi. The first two chatusthayas have enormously increased in breadth, power and finality, though not yet absolutely secure against superficial fragmentary and momentary disturbance. Brahma chatusthaya has enlarged in base and scope and taken on the supreme Ishwara, Purusha form. It has only to be thoroughly confirmed and filled in with the jnana, etc by the gnosis.

The difficulty is almost eliminated in all the central ideality except the T³. There it is being removed and has to be eliminated partially or wholly during the month of July. Perfection prepared by the last month's work has to be initially founded in the highest logistic ideality. In Samadhi and rupa vishaya the obstacles have to be still overcome; in the former they have a diminished, in the latter a complete persistence. The difficulties of Ananda have to be obliterated and spontaneity, continuity and intensity fixed in the system. The difficulties of the arogya have to be attacked and brought to nothing; this is possible in July, but not yet certain. The utthapana and saundarya are likely to be longer hampered and are not likely to come to anything very considerable till the closing months of the year. Ananda Brahman has to be filled in with the guna and jnana.

The attack of the rogas of cold, cough, eye-disease are now attempting to materialise in the night, taking advantage of the slightest exposure, because then owing to sleep the tapas is not active and the prana is more vulnerable. This night owing partly to previous tapas the attack was neither so successful nor so forcible. Eye disease is now operating in the sukshma showing there its symptoms and trying to impress them on the physical body by the sraddha in the disease; it is combated by tapas and by sraddha in arogya and is not so far successful except very superficial[ly], and this slight superficial result is now more easily removed by tapas as soon as the body rises. It is now quite evident that the source of disease is psychical, not physical; it is due to failure of tapas, idea of ill-health, weakness of the prana-shakti, faith in ill-health in the physical body. Faith with knowledge from the ideality is now powerful to combat it, though not yet entirely to eliminate; for the body is still subject to the mental suggestions from the outside forces.

The rupa is commencing again; some crude rupas, some images of things immediately or habitually seen, some of things not habitually seen; but all are momentary and unstable except the crude rupas. There is a tendency also to resume the old abandoned rupas, ghana, etc. It is intimated that this time there will be a real recommencement and steady progress.

In spite of strong dullness of physical tamas ideality advances; a flood of ideal telepathy is taking up even the subconscious indications. Trikaldrishti is slowly elevating itself beyond the telepathies.

K.A dull but with occasional intensities

In Samadhi in the afternoon strong invasion of the deep nidra by the ideality; especially strong in lipi, but also in thought, interpretation of rupa and lipi, trikaldrishti of siddhi, dialogue etc. Most of these are still fragmentary. The ideality was inspired vijnana besieged by intellectuality, but subsequently was partly taken up by the revelatory vijnana. In lighter samadhi increased organisation and power of the gnosis.

Ideality is extending itself largely, tapas becoming idealised and powerful, but at present there is some confusion in the brihat, the ritam is not properly placed very often, owing to the interference of telepathic intellectuality.

In the evening struggle with attack of roga; slight fragmentary materialisations, especially of occasional cough. Action of general ishita, general and particular aishwarya, vashita upon the symptoms. The affection at night very occasional. The mind no longer adversely affects the result, but the habitual mind of the body still persists in trying to repeat the regulations of the malady. On this the tapas is beginning to act with an initial success.

Samadhi in the night and morning ineffective or difficult and slight in result; a tendency of fragmentariness and incoherence.

There are certain first indications of future siddhi, not yet able to persist in formation, but amounting to decisive hints of a preparation behind in the over-idea.

Wednesday July 2 1919.

A certain lapse towards intellectuality, intended to show the extent of the persistence of intellect in the ideal action and by a clearer distinctness base a firmer action of the T^3. The defect of the intellectual mixture lies mainly in an undue stress on active possibilities which brings in a continual error and incertitude. The possibilities have to be seen around the decisive certitude.   The thought of the T^2, other than that of the sadhana and inner action, is growing in ideality and certitude, but is yet lacking in perfection.   A still more decided and well-justified certitude is beginning.

Rupa is rapidly redeveloping various forms of ghana, developed and perfect as well as the different materials, notably colour, as also combined rupas and groups, but all this is only in the old initial form. The fugitiveness is modifying towards [a]^3 yet ill-decided initial or momentary stability. The method of development has yet to be changed to the ideality.

In Samadhi, first an initial variety of complete and initially stable crude rupas in antardarshi (long-withheld and appearing to be condemned to infruition), in swapna brilliant momentary tejomaya figures and scenes in a first attempt at abundance, the movement cut short by nidra. In nidra a confused, partly coherent, partly incoherent generalisation of, first, intellectualised and then

---

3 MS an

intuitive ideality. In lighter samadhi organisation of highest logistic ideality.

Complete and distinct combined crude figures and scenes, but distinct in an indistinctness.

Tapas is now trying to come up to trikaldrishti. At first strain of tapas ordinarily fulfilling itself against fluctuations, but afterwards the fluctuations or opposite forces often prevailed, definitely or for a time, but all tapas is now being put in its place, as has already been done with trikaldrishti. Tapas decisively indicative of ideal certitude has begun, but has to be normalised. The difference is that trikaldrishti comes as the seeing idea carrying [in it][4] fulfilling tapas, ideal tapas as the seeing force with the sight subordinate indicating its certitude of effectuation.

No advance in the evening or night; roga (throat) attacked suddenly and held for a while but was lessened almost immediately and dismissed after a while though with slight after effects, much exaggerated in appearance, but with little material solidity. They were at once and easily dismissed in the morning.

Thursday July 3. 1919

The T^3 on the level of the old telepathies is now turning finally to T^2, telepathy enlightened by the ideality taking the form of present trikaldrishti. This is imperfect still, because elements of old telepathy are still imported into it, but these are being steadily eliminated and exist mainly in stress of telepathic tapas which is lessening rapidly. When the light of the ideality is withdrawn, T^3 returns, but that too is being immediately seized on and converted into an indirect gnosis. Tapas is resigning its strain of effort towards self-effectuation; it has for a long time been lessened, is now greatly diminished and is nearing the line of disappearance. Active trikaldrishti of future is still niggardly in spite of occasional freer movements, — as distinguished from general sadhana prevision; it is this which still gives room to some persistence of modified tapasic stresses. Knowledge and will are becoming more and more an expression of being, rather than detached observer and actor on being.

[4] MS it in

The removal of the remaining stress of tapas is now the key; but this cannot be done without a normalised self-effective ideal tapas; at present it exists only in type, usually of a mixed and imperfect kind. Tapas used by itself still tends to bring back confusion.

Samadhi at first ineffective owing to nidra. Afterwards strong organisation of the various action of gnosis in the lighter samadhi; also in deeper swapna with a gnostic waking control, jagrat in swapna, even in a considerable depth. Lax swapna without waking control is also being idealised, dream interpreted, analysed, turned into vision and thought of samadhi. This interpretation is done partly in antardarshi, partly in swapna. Only deep tamasic nidra still resists in some entirety, but that too has a pursuing touch of vijnana and is sometimes invaded by some gnosis.

Tapas is putting aside more effectively strain of effort for self-effectuation, though it is not entirely cleared away out of the whole action; but at times it is pure. Tapastya, tapatya, tapata continue, – in their absence, the tapas is still inert and not directly effective, but they act without strain, only as degrees of impersonal insistence: they are all to be replaced by tapana, the fire of surya in the will-powers. This is done in telepathic tapas. Trikaldrishtic tapas occurs more frequently, but is still rare. There is already a tendency for trikaldrishti and tapas, knowledge and will, to combine more closely and become one.

In the central roga there is some increase of the tendency of siddhi, more effective insistence of tightness mending the subsidiary looseness of the centre which is the immediate cause of all the roga. Looseness now comes less often without cause as a mechanical habit, more often with pressure of causes; but the causes of looseness are beginning to become causes of health and force. These changes are still not quite firm at the root and tend to fluctuate; there is a mixed action.   In cold etc health in the daytime holds sway; attacks are lessened in force and persistence, but touch once or twice in sleep or recumbence by physical laxity.   Utthapana is weak and afflicted.

K. Ananda is reviving after a time of suppression subsequent to the change of character. It is still very intermittent. In the attendant script it was suggested yesterday that there will still be difficulty, but the ananda will fix itself this week, by the 7th, in the intensities first, then in the continuity. In July it will endure

Friday, Saturday. 4th 5th July 1919

Preoccupation with writing; in the ideality a rather confused process of righting and arrangement of telepathy, tapas, relative trikaldrishti. Tapas is farther getting rid of the relics of stress, both understress and overstress, trikaldrishti striving towards a greater general and detailed certitude. Attack of roga, cough at night; K.A fitful and uncertain. In Samadhi growth of frequency of stability in shadowy rupas. Some progress of sahitya.

Sunday 6th July 1919

In the early morning incoherent dream turned suddenly into dream symbol recurring and progressing even after intermediate wakings. Ideality of a loose kind in the nidra.

Trikaldrishti, tapas, telepathy are now combining definitely into one movement which is beginning to rise above the constant uneven balancings of the two opposite perceptions, that of the powers and tendencies of the present and what they mean and presage, and that of the other powers and forces which attempt to create a future not bound by the probabilities of the present. In the intuitive mind the first corresponds to the current habitual understanding in the intellectual reason, the second to the pragmatic reason and will, a third range of perceptions to the truth-seeking reason. In the gnosis the lowest or primary logistic gnosis, of the nature of the intuition of the immediate, is strongest in the light of the present and proceeds from that to the other truths, it is more fitted for present telepathy than for future trikaldrishti. The secondary logistic gnosis of the nature of inspiration, is a sort of creative or forecasting light and gives best the tapas of the future, the will at work now and hereafter for effectuation. The tertiary logistic gnosis of the nature of revelation lifts up both these powers, gives them its own light and fuses perfectly the two elements of perception. It is here that the real trikaldrishti becomes facile. It is to this revelatory light that the T^3 is trying to rise so as to become entirely T^2. But it would also seem that the full power of trikaldrishti belongs to a higher vijnana than the logistic gnosis.

Tertiary dasya is now becoming very intense in its power; there is little questioning as to what should or should not be thought, done or spoken, but only the force compelling the thought, act or speech and its acceptance by the yantra. This is strongest in action, weakest in speech, because speech has always been for a long time past spoken mostly without reflection or thought from the speech centre and not the thought centre, the latter only cooperating sometimes or in a vague fashion, but only recently has there been some beginning of the idealised speech.

In samadhi much and increasing activity of rupa. In antardarshi, in which as in jagrat rupa has long been violently obstructed and almost suppressed, there is now a stirring. But samadhi is now a little inactive.

Monday July 7. 1919

Indications of fresh initiations of progress in the morning. The dasya is now rapidly growing in intensity; perfect tertiary dasya of thought is coming with the growth of the highest logistic ideality. Primary dasya has long since been taken up [   ]⁵ into the secondary, the Jiva into the Jiva-Prakriti (primary dasya is when the jiva acts consciously in obedience to the prakriti as the executrix of the Ishwara or to the Ishwara acting through the varying forces of the prakriti or those which she guides or drives as an imperative force). The secondary dasya in which the Prakriti uses the instrument and itself obeys the Ishwara, but guided as if from behind a veil and more immediately using her own forces for the satisfaction of his ganas, the devatas, is now coming to a close; it is being taken up into the tertiary dasya. This is now an action of the gnostic devatas in the Prakriti with the sense of the Ishwara immediately behind them; but the Ishwara also begins again to be directly manifest in the guidance and the Person. This is growing; meanwhile the Prakriti is unifying with the Purusha and the Ishwara directly or through the Deva-shaktis driving the instrument with an absolute

---

⁵ MS or

and immediately and intensely felt decisiveness of control as if it were being pushed by him with his hand upon it and it vibrated with the ananda of the touch and the driving. This is in thought and still more vividly in action. Some shadow of the old dasyas persist in a subordinate sensation.

The highest ideality is now acting in jnana frequently with a complete possession; only, when the thought tapas is relaxed or there is some other preoccupation, the older state of mixed intuitive mind and lower gnosis holds predominance. Very little remnant of intellectuality is left in existence; only some after effect of it is left in the lowest action of the intuitive perception.

Little samadhi; activity of clear crude rupa in antardarshi

Kama Ananda is now acting easily enough, but forgetfulness of other preoccupation is still strong in actuality; it has not been immediately abolished. In a sense however the Ananda may be said to be always there in an active or suppressed condition.

The process of filling in the T^2 with the light of the highest logistic ideality has now begun to move forward again with rapidity, the general thought being already totally enlightened. All this is still in the secondary ideality suffused with the light of the tertiary gnosis. Certitude in trikaldrishti is now being enforced; the telepathies that give the wrong stresses are being enlightened in those stresses, they are being turned into the truth of idea-forces of being, each with its own provisional certitude. This is one part of the process of transmutation. The other is to fix the right proportions, no longer in the intuitivity as was done before, but in the light of the true ideality and increasingly of the highest logistic gnosis, and to multiply the perceptions of the idea force which is destined to immediate or subsequent effectuation. A general idea of the time is growing. Place and circumstance as yet are only hinted or seen but with incertitude in the intuitive mind. This process already applied to prevision in the sadhana is now being applied to seen objects and their movements in the immediate vicinity. Distant sight is still in the imperfect telepathic condition, as also telepathy of thought (very fragmentary) and mental movements, the latter often vivid, abundant and accurate. Perception of the physical forces and sadhana is still subject to great incertitudes, as also that of distant eventuality.

K.A is now in a way settled in the body, thus fulfilling the suggestion about the 7th; but the intensities vary and there is not perfect continuity when the mind is turned away entirely from the body. Nevertheless the opening of a double consciousness which has the full mental or gnostic activity and below it the sense of the body has definitely set in in spite of frequent intermittence.

At night rupa in samadhi accompanied by shabda, sparsha and shabda speech. Shabda speech also in antardarshi. Until now night brought back the consciousness to a lower level, but this habit of the physical being is now being attacked; it is not yet overcome, but the force of the habit is diminished. Roga also recurred at night, but this time it was attacked with great force by the gnostic tapas and overcome; — cough and sensation though not actuality of catarrh. These things however still besiege in the subtle molecular body.

Tuesday July 8th 1919.

The action of the trikaldrishti continues to expand in the ideality, on the same lines. K.A grows in insistence of continuity, though with the same essential fluctuations. There is some constant insistence now on the arogya siddhi, but chiefly in the subtle physicality; the old fragmentarised rogas touch, but can almost immediately be quelled by the tapas.

In the afternoon a complete invasion of the deeper and deepest nidra by the samadhi; all was to a greater or lesser extent idealised. In the lighter depths complete ideality and an almost complete initial coherence of lipi etc. In the deeper nidra a more forcibly imposed and sometimes broken ideality. Coherence has set in; the incoherence is chiefly in incompleteness and fragmentation; the thing begun goes on well enough, but is suddenly broken off and another lipi etc starts in its place; but the chaotic entire incoherence was only occasional and immediately tended to change to coherence. Dream is being regularised and interpreted so far as it goes, though subject to fragmentation, or is replaced by vision.

The highest logistic ideality is now entirely taking up the lipi, in the midst of an attack of the old environing intellectuality; but this cannot any longer organise itself for thought action; it can only obstruct without entirely preventing the ideal action.

At night no action of the ideality, but only connected dream

Wednesday, July 9th 1919

The tertiary logistis is developing itself, but on the third or lowest scale in its three forms, the intuitive, inspired and revelatory forms of the intuitive revelation. This is in spite of the lowering of the system and a dull inactive siege of the substance of intuitive mentality (on which the gnosis is acting to transform it) by the environing intellectual forces. These produce no intellectual thought, but only semi-intellectualised motions of the intuitive mental stuff, with certain dull memories of the asamata. The capacity of the system to respond when vehemently forced to touches of asamata suggestion is therefore not destroyed, nor can be till the physical mentality is idealised without any remnant of intellectual suggestion.

Predicted in the script today, "This afternoon a great advance in samadhi.. Today, a great advance in K.A... The highest ideality to be in full possession, though in the lower form." This at the time seemed improbable, but has been not only accurately but fully executed. This shows a great advance in the suggestive script, which used formerly to be only partially fulfilled, the opposition at once proceeding with success to frustrate it, or else only fulfilled later at another time and under other circumstances

Samadhi, in deep nidra, was entirely of the ideality, where not drowned in tamas, though of a dream ideality, more than the gnosis of actuality. In lighter sleep there was no nidra or dream, but pure samadhi, dream being replaced by definite, coherent and intelligible vision of other worlds etc; all was besides of the highest ideality, which took entire possession of antardarshi and lighter swapna. These results may be considered as fixed; for however they may be attacked, they can no longer be thrown back towards asiddhi.

The highest ideality also took possession of thought, thought-speech, lipi, telepathy, tapas and trikaldrishti, the latter still a little besieged by incertitude and not yet free and ample.

K.A is now fixed in being, always felt when there is smarana, but often reduced to a very low intensity, just above the zero of definite cessation. It is now intense, persistent sometimes in sensation even against forgetfulness. The intensity is of a firm and growing force, though not secure against downward fluctuations

In Samadhi sthula sukshma-shabda of speech in swapna and antardarshi, the latter mostly when it is on the borders of or verging towards swapna. Taste in samadhi comes, but rarely, as also touch; smell has not yet come back to the samadhi experience

Roga rejected in the night, in spite of some slight rain exposure; only a strong but brief touch in both hands of phlegmatic roga, one only sukshma.

Thursday July 10th

Ideality a little suppressed; the intuitive mentality is externalised, it is now the environing power and not the intellectuality. The substance of consciousness is imperfectly idealised in the true ideality, but responds easily to intuitive mental touches and under pressure reverts superficially to its former type. Only when quite possessed by the ideal action is it an almost entirely gnostic consciousness. The final transformation is now to proceed to its completion – today. Lipi "Tomorrow incomple[te] perfection of the transformation."

All the crude *rasas* have occurred with some force and frequency, pure or mixed, and some definitive rasas. Sukshma gandha has also recommenced; but there is still some massing of physical obstruction.

K.A is now continuous, in varying intensities, except when [there is][6] absorption; this is the last refuge of the mind's forgetfulness, – except for sleep which brings about cessation. After the night's sleep there is a touch of the old difficulty of recovery, but it is slight and more of a physical reminiscence than an essential reality.

It is indicated that the K.A today is to attack and get rid of the obstacle of the absorption. This has now already begun; the thought and thought speech no longer interfere with the continuity of the

---

[6] MS their

ananda, or have only a slight tendency towards such interference. There remains the absorption with objects and work or action. This also is being removed, but the obstacle is stronger here; it brings momentary forgetfulness. These siddhis have long been insisted on and acquired in the type by the tapas, but they have been repeatedly lost and failed to achieve universality and finality. This time the siddhi is stronger; it remains to be seen whether it is final against absorption in pressure of work or strong concentration on objects. The fluctuation of intensity is here an obstacle, as the lesser intensity is unfavourable to the conquest of absorption. It is suggested that this also will be accomplished today, but will have to be confirmed in the following two or three days.

The obstacle to the memory is the clouding of a certain substance of mentality which gets into the way of the rest of the consciousness: the ideality can concentrate completely on thought the power of thought and yet have plenty of power of attention for other simultaneous experience; this is the principle of multiple concentration in a general embracing infinite consciousness, the divine vijnana. Initially in a very restricted type this is beginning. As the remnants of the old mentality disappear as a result of their present constant progressive diminution, dilution and exclusion, the simultaneous mental and bodily consciousness will be without farther obstacle, except that of sleep, which is already conquered in the type, but has to be conquered in the universality

Lipi "Traigunyasiddhi in the physical mentality to be established without farther delay" This is already beginning, but not yet in complete perfection.

Highest ideality T^2 is generalising itself, in the immediate consciousness; it is still defective or limited in certitude in the field of external observation.

The sukshma gandha is stronger and has a more essential hold than before, but is not [ ][7] free yet to develop its new power, — the physical obstruction is still heavy and effective. Rasa is as before, but more rapidly varied when it is allowed to come. Sparsha too has begun, but so far in the old touches.

[7] MS yet

Previsions in script. (1) Decisive trikaldrishti today begins to be generalised. (2) Fuller and greater progress in Samadhi. (3) K.A to conquer all the difficulties with an initial finality.. (4) Rupa and vishaya today in the jagrat firmly.

Sahaituka kamananda, long discontinued, is beginning, but at first only in touches though these are increasing in frequency. They result from any touch on the body; there is frequently a mixture of it in the tivra. This rule is now suddenly established fully in the type, every strongly sensible touch is bringing the K.A with or without other anandas, tivra, vishaya, raudra, vaidyuta. The prediction of the Ananda is likely to be fulfilled in all the range of the five anandas. Raudra is now universalised; all touches of pain with rare exceptions bring in ananda, either at once or in the second instant after the touch. Vaidyuta is also beginning to resume and enlarge its operation. But it has still to be idealised as well as the three other Anandas. K.A itself is not yet idealised in perfection.

In Samadhi all is either highest ideality or dream ideality; but images of actuality are now commencing and all is turning towards the real reality. The pressure of the highest ideality increases with a constant though still obstructed rapidity. The samadhi was today much besieged by nidra. At night nidra prevailed and there was no progress.

K.A continued its insistence. Even in the prolonged writing it maintained itself in spite of pressure of obstruction, but there was a continual recurrence of forgetfulness due to excessive absorption. At night there was something of a collapse; tamas took hold of the system.

Rupa in jagrat today threw out some new brilliant forms, but did not seem to fulfil the presage in the script; vishaya, after enforcing itself in gandha and rasa and a slight renewal of sparsha, failed to develop sravana or a decisive beginning in sparsha.

Health is obstructed, relapses a little sometimes and makes no definitive progress, but only certain indications of the increasing arogya tapas.

Highest logistis continues to extend itself in the T^2 and the whole thought ideality

Friday. July 11th
 This morning there is the return of the besieging intellectualised intuitive mentality. K A is persistent, but uncertain in its incidence. These two siddhis are advancing under difficulties; the thought is besieged by uncertainty and the intellectual confusion. There is a movement towards trikaldrishti of circumstance, but though the circumstances seen are actual and true, they are not seen in their right order and incidence, owing to the intuivity which takes possession of them before their logistic revelation
 The interruptions of K.A are being reduced to momentary forgetfulness; the mind is almost immediately recalled to the Ananda. This is gaining in spite of massings of the tamasic stuff of mental oblivion. There is even often a simultaneous forgetfulness and oblivion, part of the mind absorbed, part of it conscious of the Ananda. It is intimated in the script that whatever forgetfulness or interruptions there may be the K A will in these three days fix its irrevocable continuity. Ananda usually pervades constantly the lower part of the body, less constantly the arms, intermittently the upper body, very rarely the head. There is now insistence on complete pervasion. Sahaituka is increasing its frequency and incidence. Ananda in the head is now constantly recurring and making for continuity, but there is a tendency for it to shift from one part to the other alternately; it has to be fixed in a complete pervasion.
 No definite progress in Samadhi, only continuance.
 The K.A fluctuates, owing to the lapse of the being towards the intuitive mentality. In that mentality there is the absorption of the mind in the thought because it has to listen and attend, the limited concentration, the forgetfulness of other things. The gnosis illumines easily without need of this strenuous concentration; it is capable of a multiple concentration. When the ideality is at work and the system full of the ideality, then the K.A proceeds without any but momentary lapses into oblivion.
 Chitra in some abundance, but unstable. Repetition of vishayas, gandha, rasa, touches of old sparsha, but on a small scale. In Samadhi great abundance of lipi of all kinds, in a successive flow of sentences, but with some incoherence, and without a link of intelligent succession in the flow. Only in the lighter swapna is

there full ideality. Some plenty of shadowy rupa, but insufficient stability. Easily dispelled touches of roga.

Saturday July 12.

Imperfect recovery of vijnana. There is a varying between intuitive mentality, intuitive and inspired ideality and the highest ideality with much of the old mixture.

Attack of roga, violent in the subtle body. There is an intense struggle between roga and physical health, the latter supported by the tendency to arogya. The occasion is the exposure to damp cold air at night; the old bodily tendency wishes to reply at once with fever, cold, cough, etc, the health force wants to get back to the state after Alipur yoga when the body was impervious to illness and get rid of the subsequent morbid sensibility. The ideal arogya itself is a different thing which yet waits to take direct possession of the body.

In Samadhi relapse to unidealised nidra with difficulty held up to occasional highest ideality

The system is returning to the ideality. Highest inspired ideality and a little of highest revelatory gnosis with an intuitional basis is taking possession of the lipi. Inspired highest gnosis is also taking possession of the thought-speech and initially of the perceptions; in the latter it is the highest intuition packed with inspiration. In T^2 the mixed movements are being rejected and pure highest ideality insisted on though with some difficulty; yet with a steady progression. K.A is also reviving its force which has been low owing to the depressed state of the physical shakti.

Chitra and fragmentary vishaya but no definite progress. Roga has been strong in the subtle sharira (feverish symptoms), but little manifestation in the body except depression and a sensation of weakness combated by the pranic tapas. Arogya force is changing to the ideal tapas, but not yet visibly in the physical body.

Roga conquered in the evening.

Sunday July 13th 1919

In the morning highest inspired revelatory gnosis and revelatory with inspirational basis take possession of lipi, thought-speech and perception. T^2 is still in the same condition but has begun to be taken up a little. To get rid of the remnants of mental effort and allow the vijnana to act with an entire freedom on the passive system is now the condition of rapid progress.

K.A has recovered, but is still subject to forgetfulness of absorption. The pervasiveness is now in a way established from head to foot, but the intensity is still liable to frequent loss or depression or diminution and the insufficient intensity brings with it the other imperfections. The body is still liable to the sense of lassitude and weakness.

Immediately afterwards K.A recovered all its intensity. When this is present forgetfulness can only be momentary, except in case of very strong absorption in which case the intensity still tends to fade.

In Samadhi there is again the full force of the ideality in spite of some heavy nidra; but as yet no definite forward progress, only a preparation. The dream ideality is still strong, not replaced by the actuality. The kamananda invaded the deeper samadhi and even the nidra, but with a frequent recurrence, not in continuity. It is however attacked then by the degradatory change to a negative form; intense but of the impure anandamaya, (negative electrical reaction.) Intensity of the ideality seems to be established in spite of some tendency to relapse; the old thin ananda is being excluded from the system.

The precise trikaldrishti is again being taken up; the decisive trik. now manifests in the intuitive form through an obstructing veil of mentality; it is correct when it is not modified by the mental stuff; modified it gives the general fact accurately but not the circumstance. The pure intuitive mental trik. is often accurately correct up to a certain point, but often errs in some details of the circumstance, but always in arrangement, not in fact of tendency or actual potentiality: the intellectualised intuitivity of the mind is always a confusion, but this now only occurs when there is mental tapas and insistence on the siddhi.

K.A. less insistent during the latter part of the day. In Samadhi at night no progress

Saturday July 14th 1919

In the morning progress only in trikaldrishti tapas. The system lowered to the intuitive mentality; in that mentality the habitual mind set to work and all its excesses and stresses set finally right, then this habitual mechanical intuivity rejected for the pragmatic intuitivity. This finality was effected by every suggestion being at once stripped of certainty; it fell then to its right proportion; the habit of insisting because many suggestions proved correct, was finally killed; whatever recurs will now be an involuntary habit of response with no vitality in it, a suggestion from outside unable to command credit. The pragmatic intuivity is being similarly dealt with and replaced by the real intuivity. As yet the highest intuivity has not been separately handled for finality. The next difficulty is the insistence of a mental intuivity responding to the gnosis or rather catching at it before it is formed on its own plane. This is possible because that was always the real nature of mental thought and the whole mentality is not yet possessed by the gnosis. This action is henceforth mainly that of the highest or truth reflecting intuivity which has taken into itself the abandoned mechanical and pragmatic action.　　　The truth reflecting intuitivity is now put into its proper place. It has to be replaced entirely in T^2 by the ideality: but in this operation there are still considerable difficulties. The chief is the persistence in the stuff of the intuitive mentality of the habit of catching at the gnostic light instead of allowing it to manifest in its own way, on its own level and illumine the mentality. The other difficulties are incidental and secondary, but considerable. They all arise from old habits and limitations.

In samadhi at first pressure of nidra. Afterwards complete ideality. Kamananda in samadhi, more continuous, but not any complete continuity. Mostly thought; no lipi or drishya.

T^2, but in the intuitive mentality, corrected by modified or mentalised gnosis. Tapas still too insistent sometimes in the mentality. Modified gnosis gives only a relative certitude. Mental preparation of T^2 of gnosis.

K.A distressed and thin in the morning, not quite suppressed, sometimes vaguely intense, but not in possession of the sthula body and subject to oblivion. In the afternoon a growing force of intensity; full recovery now in the evening.

Roga still in fragments more or less frequent of occurrence. The two chief rogas continue, there is here no progress visible except a slight almost imperceptible strengthening under pressure in the central difficulty. Sharp continuous and recurrent pain acutely localised in one spot on the left side of the stomach; yielding slowly but not quite to local pressure of tapas. Ananda, but an ananda dominated by the sense of pain, rather than dominating the raudrata.

Chitra and vishaya slight, fragmentary and occasional; the sadhana Shakti is occupied with T^2

Strength of combined titiksha, udasinata, nati long established and almost perfect in universality, is now growing very intense; only when the mental tapas is overstressed and baffled, does some denial of passive asamata force its way in for a moment. Nati in the pain of roga was only contradicted slightly in the mental buddhi, not in the prana; this was the reflection of a certain intolerance in the body. Positive ananda is general, but not yet absolutely perfect in all its quality or universality. The second chatusthaya is established, but not yet in its perfect force of vividness or harmony of all its parts, eg dasyam and aishwarya, or sarvakarmasamarthya, or the qualities of the fourfold Ishwara. Defect where it exists is chiefly due to insufficiency of gnosis

Gnana is perfect in ideality in perception and speech, except when lowered to meet the deficiency of T^2: even then it is normally not always ideal in substance except in specific thought of T^2 on external things. It has attained in type the highest logistic ideality. T^2 is still imperfect in ideality owing to persistence of intuitive mentality, but that is about to be removed or transformed in all its range of activity. Samadhi is very imperfect, though now advancing with an obstructed and interrupted rapidity. Lipi perfect except in physicality, for it is yet insufficiently stable except at times, though no longer bafflingly fugitive, and therefore insufficient in rapid legibility and fullness; but it is already possessed of all the qualities to a sufficient extent for all its ordinary practical working. Jagrat rupa is often abundant and perfect in chitra, but this it has been for years together; it is suppressed still in akasha, good only occasionally and unstable except in the very crude. Jagrat vishaya is in a still cruder condition.

Sharira has developed a perfect foundation of K.A, continuous but for oblivion by absorption and sleep; the other Anandas are prepared, but not regularly working except raudra which is still capable of being overborne by a great degree and pressure of pain. The other siddhis are obstructed, except bhava saundarya. Some of them are advanced in certain directions.

The fourfold Brahman full in continent and substance, not yet in content, but sometimes lowered by lapse to mentality. Krishna Kali prepared and established, but not yet in perfect working. Karma still rudimentary except in the habitual personal karma in which it is advancing towards perfection

Yoga Diary
July 15 – July 26
1919

Diary of Yoga.   July 1919.

July 15th   Tuesday.

Today is supposed to begin the finality of initial perfect gnosis in the highest logistic ideality by the firm beginning of T^2. This is due for fulfilment in the second half of July. The two first chatusthayas are at the same time to begin their higher and fuller perfection, — they have already the fundamental perfection in samata, the fundamental completeness. K.A is to confirm its continuity and intensity and be a basis for the regular working of the other Anandas. Karma is to develop its already developing action, Krishna Kali to deepen and possess the system, Ananda Brahman to fill in with the Ishwara. The other siddhis are still uncertain of development, but the fight with the obstacles of arogya is to continue with a necessary result of advance in the tapas of Arogya. Practically all the siddhis are ready or almost ready for advance except the two most difficult parts of the Sharira and the outward Karma.

After a little difficulty the transformation of T^2 to the ideality has begun finally. The action of the intuitive mentality continues, but accompanying it there is an ideal action which gives sometimes a decisive, sometimes a limited and therefore relative certitude, sometimes in conjunction with the lower movement a mixed decisive and relative certainty or a mixed incertitude and certitude. This is especially in the T^2 of circumstance.

The trikaldrishti after perfecting itself in an universalised type in the intuitive mentality of a character of intuitive inspiration is now definitely transforming T^2 to the intuitional gnosis of the character of intuitivised revelation. This is attended with some fresh disturbance of the intellectual stuff, but that as soon as it comes is changed or replaced by the higher forms of thought and perception. Tapas is now of the same nature as the trikaldrishti.

The first chatusthaya is already being given its higher perfection. The positive ananda of equality is taking up all the adverse movements and reactions.

Vishaya is again renewed with strong gandha and taste of perfume. These two vishayas may now be considered established, however small the present range of their action.

Strong struggle with the roga difficulty. The pain in the side tried to prolong its continuity and represent itself as the sign of some organic ailment, but immediately disappeared every time ideal tapas was applied. Pain in response to pressure in this part of the body persisted, but has also disappeared suddenly. Throughout there is evidence of increasing force of arogya tapas, but it is not yet able to eliminate the roga with a decisive beginning of finality

July 16th   Wednesday

Today is to be a hollow between two waves; there is a siege of the system by the external mind armed with all that has been cast out; but this comes now no longer in the shape of the old intellectual mind, but a semi-idealised intuivity translating into mental and physical terms all the rejected suggestions of the partial ideality which supports the lower order of things, drawing from a perversion of ideal intuitions their justification. For everything in the lower order has its justification in a truth of gnosis expressing something in the Infinite.

Kamananda, which was allowed a little to lapse yesterday, is after some difficulty of mechanical lowering and attempted discontinuity—attended by an emptiness of the gross body and retirement into the subtle physicality,—renewing its self-confirmation. The old habit of relapse is not yet excluded even in this first siddhi of the physical system. It is restored to a slightly obstructed continuity, but has not full possession of the physical system.

There is a strong attempt to restore asamata attended by a great violence of suggestion of raga and dwesha; it is not supported by the Purusha or the personal Prakriti, but has been able to produce asamata in the outward physical mentality. These things are still possible because of the persistence of intuitive mentality in the stuff of the physical consciousness; that can only be secure against mental suggestions by a partial personal siddhi cut off from the external Nature or by complete idealisation.

July 17th   Thursday.

The ideality has resumed its work; it is taking up into the mixed intuitional form of ideality, mixed by the presence of mind-stuff with its limiting suggestions, the truth-reflecting intuitivity and itself is being taken up by the highest logistis. The inspirational intuivity suggested by the external mind remains as an obstacle, but is, when it comes, attacked and half transformed by the gnosis. Its power is in all those things that have not yet in the Abhyasa been assumed by the highest logistic gnosis

The obstacle now is the sluggishness of the old mentality unlifted by the inspired intuitivity which mixes with and keeps down the gnosis. This is the old action of the mixed intuitional ideality then strong and luminous, now unconvincing and void of force. Only the highest gnosis can continue the sadhana.   The depressed lowness of the system has given occasion for another and furious attack of the environing intellectual powers, with a forced physically mental asamata in outworks of the system, vibrations not belonging to the system, but imposed from outside, also asraddha not in the Ishwara, but in the siddhi of the ideality. This has been expelled by a resort to rudra tapas of rajasic anger in the Shakti. Both the relapse and this resort have been recently predicted in the trik. and the lipi, the latter almost daily in an insistent lipi. The result has been unexpectedly a momentarily complete conversion of the physical mentality into the ideal form[,] the very siddhi obstinately obstructed for the last several days.

K.A. like every other siddhi has been depressed by the general obstruction. It is now reviving though with some incertitude.

There is some tendency of recovery in the swapna Samadhi which has for some time relapsed almost entirely into nidra.

All the rest of the day a recovered action of the ideality.

July 18th   Friday.

The ideality is again taking up the whole thought and T^2, this time with a greater force of universality, but it is in the intuitional ideality and not the highest gnosis. The system is now almost settled in the intuitional ideality, though occasionally the old intuitive being breaks in or surges out from suppression and takes temporary possession. This is whenever the gnosis has been for some time inactive.

The siege of Roga continues, but chiefly in the subtle physicality: the effects on the dense body are occasional, sometimes strong, but thrown out by the tapas after a short struggle. Only in the two still chronic ailments is there as yet a permanently successful obstruction; but in the centrality the effective pressure of Arogya-tapas increases with a sort of slow, but always perceptible steadiness.

Chitra is showing some tendency to greater stability, but as yet only in the indirect vision. The fugitive forms have more firmness in their incidence. There is no improvement in the character of the forms or the range of the rupa.

After some dark nidra strong ideal action in the Samadhi. Finally the highest ideality took final possession of the perception, speech, lipi and to a certain extent of the T^2. In deeper and deepest nidra also ideality was exceedingly strong, but with some persistence of the dream character and occasional incoherence. Nevertheless coherence in the lipi even here was stronger than before. Rupa etc are now taking on the character of actuality, though as yet only of the pranic (astral)[1] reproduction of immediate things experienced in life. The presentation was accurate, entirely stable, steady in reproduction of continued action, though here with some interruptions and resumptions; combined

---

[1] *In the manuscript, the closing parenthesis follows "reproduction".* — Ed.

scene not always complete, but with strong presentation of the central object and action, the accessories being left in a shadowy suggestion. The rupas however were no longer chhayamaya of the underworld, but tejomaya of the pranic world, with great but an unearthly vividness, beauty and force of life. Massed rupas of the same character appeared in light samadhi on the borders of antardarshi, but with a less heavy fullness and not actual, but rupas of possible things, and not stable, but also not entirely fugitive. Thought, judgment, interpretation maintained a coherent ideality even in the depths of nidra. A much greater character of normality in the whole samadhi.

Vishaya (physical) in jagrat antardarshi attained in touch to a great plenty; all the subtle results, suggestions, sensations of sparsha, except the actual sthula incidence. This too occurred freely, but only in habitual rupas. It is noticeable however that nothing came which had not previously been gained in past years by sadhana, only they came with a greater force, frequency and intensity. In swapna there is now more frequent and forceful sparsha. Sravana is obstructed both in antardarshi and full jagrat; it is rare even in swapna.

An attempt at a higher Thought confined to the centre of the thought above the head and a withdrawal of that which forms in the brain region of the subtle mind or is occupied with penetration to this region. This was the normal gravitation because here the thought assumed a satisfaction of present living actuality, while above it had a higher, but remoter less physically satisfying quality. The attempt to take up T^2 there failed initially and there was a brief relapse to the mass of possibilities and incertitudes, but all this is now taken up by a fiery thought, ideal of the pragmatic nature. This T^2 is telepathic, but correct except for certain confusions contributed by an understrain of intuitive suggestions which are for the most taken up and half-justified, half-corrected immediately or with a little difficulty. The centre thought now predominates and gathers round it at its own level all other thinking, but sometimes descends to give its own character to thought manifested in the lower levels or regions of the subtle body.

At night renewed action of coherence and ideality in the dream state.

July 19th   Saturday

Rf. [Reference] "Which I must act, briefness and fortune, work", of the approaching application to life of the ideal knowledge, power and guidance.

In the morning some retardation; inaction of ideality broken by a slight partial and a recurrent larger action. No definite progress in any direction.

Samadhi; at first full ideality, nidra conquered; coherence and strong gnosis in all the activity, but not all kinds in equal power. Afterwards some force of nidra, but not complete, the action always of the ideal kind. No prominent actuality.

In the afternoon T^2. All actual T^2 of an ideal intuitional kind, well-established, normal, satisfying in its limits, but subject to narrow limitations. Then a double movement first to extend to all possible trikaldrishtic and tapasic suggestion, at the same time to lift up to a higher gnosis. This was interrupted by a taking up of the suggestions of the pranic and mental world sometimes without, sometimes with a reference to their origin in the logistic gnosis. This brought finally into the solid intuitional ideality all these possibilities given their proper place, so far as that could be done in this kind of perception, — but the proper eye for them is the inspirational seeing, — got the right actuality of the may bes, might-be, may have been, might-have-beens, may-yet-bes, and even the relative certitudes of their will-bes, often but not always realised, with a certain initial decisive certitude of selection. The higher thought now coming for the T^2 will be inspirational gnosis. It is already beginning in the intuitional form or taking up the intuition. These movements had been made before on a lower scale and were often taken for the full and final siddhi: but this is of a greater, fuller, final kind in the real ideality standing on an idealised substance of the whole conscious being.

Subsequently the inspired thought began to take the place of the intuitional gnosis and take up into it the T^2. Much more might have been done on the intuitional basis, but this would have been a lesser siddhi and was not the intention of the will of the Ishwara, which is already giving presages of the ascent beyond logistic to the second stair of gnosis, when once the supreme logistis shall have been formulated in its relative entirety.

Health stronger again in resistance to cold exposure. The central arogya fluctuates, but is on the whole growing steadily but slowly in an initial preparatory force. There is no improvement in the digestive insufficiency, but rather a constant fluctuation and even a relapse in the symptoms of the one definite ailment. Continuity of K.A also fluctuates, though it is fixed in a recurrent continuity and the obstruction cannot resist the smarana.

At night incoherent dream and nidra.

July 20th Sunday.

Script in accordance with intuitional ideality suggested day before yesterday the following possibilities for the rest of July.

(1) T^2 sure; initial perfection only. [T^2 is already sure but the initial perfection depends on the final normality of the highest logistis.]^2

(2) Samadhi sure; fixity, ideality; nidra initially overcome, but at night active. [Samadhi, made sure this morning, in ideality and fixity; nidra is very initially overcome, except at night when it reigns and repels all certain forward movement.]

(3) Vishaya and jagrat rupa to get over their old difficulty [No sure sign of this siddhi; a slight improvement is all that is visible.]

(4) Ananda, fixed in recurrence of continuity. Also initial conquest of oblivion – except for sleep and samadhi (perhaps), the only difficulties. [There is already fixity of recurrent continuity and an unfixed recurrent intensity; oblivion has been overcome once or twice in initial type; but for some time there has been an indulged habit of oblivion in absence of will and smarana]

(5) Health; battle, supremacy of tapas, but not the perfect arogya. [The battle continues. Tapas is already in a way supreme, except in the two rogas; in one of them it is frequently effective more as ishita than as aishwarya or vashita; in the other it is for the time sometimes effective, sometimes ineffective. There are also some fragments of former rogas which very occasionally recur and resist tapas.]

---

2 *This and the five sets of square brackets that follow are Sri Aurobindo's. The closing bracket in item 3 and opening bracket in item 5 have been supplied editorially. — Ed.*

(6) Saundarya in bhava. [Youth in bhava is growing, but bhava of saundarya apart from the youth-light is still uncertain. Physical youth and saundarya make no progress.]

(7) Utthapana still in difficulties.

In Samadhi in the morning perfect reign of ideality. All the forms of experience are beginning to develop in the ideality. Lipi was except for one or two instances coherent and significant, or sometimes significant in a lilamaya incoherence, even in frequent sentences set in fugitive masses. Dialogue, enacted story, some narrative. Steady action and stable rupa in abundance. Only vishaya absent. But the final beginning of assured samadhi progress is founded. Only jagrat rupa and vishaya are still subject to the old unconquerably obstinate obstruction.

In the sluggish states of the system, except at night, inertia, passivity, blankness whether of tamas or of shama is becoming the exception. An activity of [ ]³ the intellectual ideality, that is, the low pitched intuitional gnosis which supports the mental world of possibility, is then the rule. When the sadhana tapas is active, inspired ideality begins to resume its work of taking up the whole consciousness; sometimes an inspired intuitional, sometimes an inspirational logistis works on the thought and to a less degree on the tapas. It is only at a high pitch that tapas and trikaldrishti join in an assured ideal equality or oneness.

The inspired ideality is giving a more frequent decisive certitude of trikaldrishti in T^2 and the inspired intuition for the first time a quite perfect selection of succession of detailed circumstance in time; but these things have still to be universalised. The uninspired intuition is now being cast out of the action; since it is no longer necessary in the process of the taking up of the intuition by the inspired logistis.

K.A is being restored to constant intensity, pervasion, slightly interrupted continuity by the sadhana tapas. The thick recurrent masses of tamas of oblivion in the physical being are being attacked and dissipated, spontaneous recurrence enforced, sahaituka

---

³ *MS* of

Ananda brought into occasional activity. The mental tamas masses of oblivion, while writing etc are also being attacked, dissipated, set aside or illumined by light of ideality. The work, it is said, will be confirmed today (thought) and completed in three days (lipi).   The difference of Ananda in the postures is still marked. Sitting it is capable of a great initial intensity and force of continuity; today greater and more exciting to the whole system than before. Reclining, it is capable of a great intensity, but often impure of the unidealised kind, especially when there is samadhi and nidra. Walking it is intense with difficulty, more liable to decided interruption or reduction to a minimum. Standing it is still less intense except at moments, especially if there is other occupation. These defects are now being attacked. Insistent intensity has been introduced into the standing attitude, recurrent when reading; it is being insisted on in the walking. In reclining the ananda is being purified and idealised: it is being enforced in Samadhi.

Samadhi, late in the morning. Ideal lipi, scene etc. As the rupa becomes pranic instead of chhayamaya, visions of things never seen nor suggested by the seen arrive. Today, an eagle carrying a lamb to its nest and there beginning to devour it, half dead; nest, eagle, lamb very vivid, but pranamaya, as in a living picture of the Indian type, not quite the earthly bhava of the forms, nor the earthly lines, in spite of the bodily type and species being the same. This heralds the liberation of the rupa.

Ananda in samadhi constant in lighter depths, spontaneously recurrent in deeper swapna, but interrupted by nidra in the deepest swapna. The ananda tends to draw the mind back to the body, but then there occurs often a phenomenon which is now growing, the double or triple samadhi, in which the outside world is experienced accurately in an outer consciousness of sleep, by the sukshma and not the sthula indriya. The inner consciousness remains in swapna, a deeper is in sushupti of some kind, for the most part swapnamaya sushupti. Sometimes the outer world is experienced by the subtle sense with a fringe of waking physical sense. At times there is a division of the consciousness between the outer physical and the inner dream mind, the latter withdrawn into swapna and sleep, the former still aware physically on the outskirts of outer sound, touch or experience.

The replacement of the idealised, intuitional intellectuality by the inspired intuitional or intuitional inspired for the telepathy is proceeding very rapidly, but is not yet absolutely complete. Meanwhile the higher trikaldrishti acts only by intervention in the mass of rapid and crowding ideal telepathies. Now the process of including the inspired intuition has begun and is proceeding with a great initial rapidity.

The higher level of the thought and T^2 is now (in the afternoon) beginning suddenly to rise to the revelatory inspired and inspired revelatory logistis. This is necessary in order that the inspired and intuitional inspired may take entirely the place of the intuitional thinking as the lower level of the thought process. This lower level represents the substitute for the former intellectually intuitive thought and uncertain telepathic perception, the thought of the possibility. The higher level rises towards the certitudes and more and more, as it rises in the scale, commands them in its light and power

Drishya of the panchabhuta, mass and karma, the pranic ether and some of its elementary incidents, wind, rain etc is now recommencing. This brings in three of the long suspended vishayas. The other vishayas are coming forward, but with no widening range. Sravana is the most difficult, because the physical ear is beset by physical sounds in the daytime and cannot easily distinguish the slighter subtle sonances.

Sadhara rupa also is returning, fine crude, often perfect, but without stability. This has brought in an outburst of the finer prakashamaya niradhara rupas in a variety, groups, persons, objects, animals, scenes, some clear, others confused, none stable, except a solitary one or two: but there is already a hint of a tendency towards stability. Of the three gunas, variety, perfection, stability, the first long resisted may possibly now be on the point of bursting the barrier. It is to be noted that lipi in the morning declared that today would be the turning point in jagrat rupa and vishaya; this lipi has been repeated with a firmer asseveration. This may be the beginning in the rupa; but as yet there is no appearance of fulfilment in the vishaya. All the material crude forms have now manifested in this finer crude niradhara, — prakasha, chhaya, tejas, jyotir, agni and varnamaya forms. Subsequently some union of stability and relative perfection began to be developed in a still greater but confused and irregular variety. The higher forms occurred hardly at all and then without stability.

In Samadhi much pressure of Nidra, but the ideal samadhi persevered and kept itself in progress as an overtone. Rupas of the manasa loka, bright and tejomaya, but with a brief stability. Dream was immediately converted into symbol of ideality; incoherence of lipi into a crookedness of pointed significance.

In the lapse of the tapas the intuitional ideal mind reappeared for a while, but always with the inspired gnosis hovering over it to take it up and transform it into its own character. As yet the morning's hint of rapidity is not fulfilled, — it was so understood at the time that there might be some delay. The inspiration holds the field.

K.A also lost for a time its continuity and intensity. It is now recovering, but at this time between 12 and 3 it tends to some deidealisation and conversion into perverse negative electricity and has to be restored on the resumption of the normal activity. This has been done today with rapidity.

The conversion has begun of T^2 into the revelatory logistic ideality. At first this is attended with some intuitive revelatory action incased in the old intellectual doubt, but this is to be changed into the inspired logistic revelation. The certitude is already immensely increased, but it is not till all is changed to the terms of this drishti that there can be an initial perfection of accuracy in the T^2. The drishti reveals the decisive truth of each movement, whether it be a possibility of self-effecting force or a relative, temporary or decisive finality of effectuation. This is the last movement within the ideal logistis.

The revelatory even in the intuition gives the circumstances with a [constant][4] accuracy, but this is attended with much incerti- tude owing to the external intuitive intellectuality which darts in its suggestions and to a certain distrust and anxiety about the possible

[4] *MS* constance

error of the result in the old judging mind. The element of revelatory judgment does not with sufficient prominence accompany the revelatory seeing of tapas or intention of action. Nevertheless, when left to itself this intuitive revelation can judge and fix accurately enough possibility and finality, even though it is not so forcible and conclusive as the inspired or the full revelation. This is with regard to succession of circumstance. This logistis acts as yet only partly in judgment of time, very uncertainly in relation to space and direction; but sometimes it takes them up all three and combines them with sufficient or complete fullness of accuracy. All this is in the field of exercise. Teledrishti is not yet being exercised in this higher action.

The lipi is still logistic, but a higher than the logistic ideality is entering into it attended by a diviner splendour of light and blaze of fiery effulgence. This may be called the hermetic gnosis. Its essence is çruti or divine inspiration, as the essence of logistis is smriti, divine mnemosyne. One remembers at a second remove the knowledge secret in the being but lost by the mind in the oblivion of the ignorance, the other divines at a first remove a greater power of that knowledge. One resembles the reason, is a divine reason, the other is [of] the nature of prophesis or inspired interpretation.

Sparsha is now abundant in the three things formerly gained by the sadhana, touch of subtle water and fire, touch of light things, eg insects, thread, wind, — both of these strong, vivid, materialised, effective on the physical body, and other touches not materialised, but having a certain physical result of sensation; subtle in intent, sthula in result, but not with the full density. Some of these sparshas are however on the verge of materialisation. All this action was formerly regarded as an inferior insufficiency by the intellectual impatience, but is now accepted as a stage towards the full sparsha. The old drishya of the pranic ether is also resuming its plenty. The çravana seems to be awaiting the silence of the night for its manifestation; but the sthula hearing is becoming exceedingly acute and comprehensive and there is a hint of sukshma sound behind its abundance. The lipi is to this extent justified, but there is as yet no sign of new extension, without which the barrier of obstruction cannot be said to have fallen.

Sadhara and niradhara are developing with some rapidity: in the midst of much confused, shapeless or half-shaped rupa there are some of perfect or almost [perfect vividness,][5] completeness and distinctness; old types of rupa are coming back with a greater perfection and vividness, but they have the old fault of instantaneous instability. Nevertheless this is a definite advance. At night there is the old difficulty; there is then the greatest confusion, vagueness, crudity; but there is also a beginning of better things.

Some isolated çravanas of the old type.

The revelatory ideality is taking up the consciousness, even the revived suggestions of the external intuitive mentality, but this involves a momentary retardation in the decisive trikaldrishti-tapas.

The yogic çravanas in the closed ear, strong while they lasted, but not persistent as in the former sadhana. Some çravana speech. But there is as yet no enlargement of the çravana

Nidra at night, but also samadhi. The coherence is now firmly established and enforces itself with great power. Stability in the chhayamaya rupa. The samadhi is fixed in the ideality. All has now to be developed, the physical obstruction which denies samadhi overcome, nidra to be replaced by samadhi.

July 21st Monday

Today, a full play of the ideality, but not all of the highest logistis. Highest logistis to attain to a partial universality. Increase of chitra and vishaya. Increase of Ananda. More attention to the physical siddhi.

Ideality is now acting in masses, but of all kinds, from the idealised intuitivity to the highest logistic, but the last is pressing on all for transmutation. The fluctuation of Ananda and the struggle in the Arogya continue.   K.A idealised in the highest logistis is beginning to act and to press upon the intuitional and mental forms of the ananda.

Great intensity of gandha and gandha-rasa, combined and allied, but not yet the free variety. Great intensity of rasa, the crude turning to firm developed and to suggested perfect rasas.

---

[5] MS perfectness

The obstruction to freer frequency and variety has now alone to be broken for the perfection of this siddhi.

Farther Sadhana in the morning discontinued through pressure of work. This is a defect which the consciousness has not yet overcome, owing to deficiency of the multiple concentration.

Immense development of the samadhi. Only towards the end some lapse into nidra. Inexhaustible abundance of rupa, especially of the mental plane, but also of the pranic and chhayamaya, scenes of all kinds, figures, action, lipi, dialogue etc: for the most part a high ideal level. The chhayamaya scenes now attain to an absolute stability, frequent though not invariable; the others have only a first stability. There is also stability of successive action, but there were only one or two unsuccessful attempts at combination with stability of scene. Only once a fugitive touch of the incoherent dream consciousness attempting to bring in a terrestrial association of memory and confuse with it the accuracy of the recorded impressions. A little more development will securely found the whole base of swapna samadhi.   K.A in samadhi, interrupted occasionally by an intervening cloud of nidra power between the physical and the higher mental consciousness, but afterwards more persistently by a deepening towards nidra; but after the brief sleep there was an immediate recovery of the Ananda. It is now noticeable that when the Ananda occupies the brain there is no oblivion; when it pervades the rest of the body, but not the head, oblivion becomes possible.

Work in the afternoon.

Rasa acts now with some frequency, though without an entire freedom. Definite rasas are coming with increasing ease and variety. Gandha is for the present obstructed. An old siddhi, sparsha at a distance, sukshma or sukshma-sthula in incidence, felt by the subtle body and conveyed by it in the same moment to the physical sense: there is however no division, it is felt as one touch by the united sukshma and sthula sense.   Rupa has developed a few instances outside of the crude of a stability still within the primary stability, but in its highest degree. Variety of rupas at night is on the increase, crude of all the kinds, jyotir etc, and dense of the crude, dense and developed degrees, but few as yet are complete, except certain unstable forms and some stable crude rupas. There is a hint too of developed rupas; but not the actuality, except in some fugitive incomplete formations. Rare instances of çravana of a new kind. Attempts at jagrat sukshma speech, not yet articulate or fully audible. Thunder in the ears. The old persistent, unceasing loud cricket sound in the room, once rejected as a physical sound, is again heard, and is now clearly marked as sukshma. The thunder in the ears is followed by a great intensification of the physical hearing.

K.A is now very often stable in the head. Then even a low intensity of ananda turns to constant sensibility.

The idealised intuitivity is allowed sometimes to act, but is now the truth-reflecting intuitivity; there is no predominance of the pragmatic or mechanical mentality. These only recur in a dull fragmentary fashion.

[July][6] 22[d] Tuesday.

The higher hermetic gnosis is now showing itself in the revelatory logistis not only in the lipi, but in thought-speech and perception; something of it is evident in trikaldrishti and Tapas, even when these act through the idealised intuivity; this action no longer disturbs to any great extent by a premature anticipation of the future actuality or possibility and falsification of the present actuality. That was formerly the result of a higher power suggesting its greater possibilities to the lower plane. The purification of the lower plane makes it a clearer channel and prevents this consequence. In the tapas there is some hint of a possible omnipotence of the gnosis which will remove the obstacles of the existing law of the body

Yesterday there was a violent attack of roga trying to materialise itself in digestive disturbance leading to nausea. This was cast out by the tapas after some fifteen minutes or more; it left a slight transient residue, followed by a strong health state. This morning the attack was of the diarrhoeic tendency, with all its concomitants of jalamaya, agnimaya, vayumaya disturbance. The revelatory tapas was applied to correct the sanskaras of the bodily

[6] MS June

mind and very rapidly the attack was overcome without its ordinary reaction of constipation. Some slight recurrent residue of tendency remains, but not enough to trouble the system. There is a great increase of tapas supremacy in the dealing with roga. If it can be extended to the digestive perversion and the central weakness, the Arogya will have its first complete basis.

In the morning physical tamas, some relapse into the old intuivity. This is now being corrected, but it is noticeable that the obstruction is being concentrated in the physical system. Opposition in the objective subjectivity is half-hearted; the opposition has lost faith and self-confidence.

The remnants of the habit of intellectual judgment and recipiency are now being raised and extruded from the system; the ideality is to be its own recipient, its own critic, questioner, judge, authority.

Samadhi in the later part of the morning. Perfect freedom of rupa, variety, perfection, vividness, but only in initial or primary stability in the pranic world. Chhaya only comes in usually as a shade on some of the pranic rupas; most are free from chhaya. Incoherence in the lipi is at once turned to coherence or proved to be a coherence. Antardarshi rupa is being prepared in the light swapna, on the borders of the two states and in some cases in antardarshi itself there are scenes and figures of a pranic kind, not crude, but ghana.

Rasa is now frequent in masses, sometimes persistent; obstruction hardly exists for its action. Gandha gains in force, but is prevented by the obstruction from frequency.

The incidence of the relapse into the intuitive intellectuality has been very obstinate and severe, a great confusion created, almost all the old incidents of relapse suggested, even something like the old hardly idealised intellectual intuivity revived in fragments and in the mental atmosphere. The orderly and powerful development of the gnosis has undergone momentarily a strong interruption. Nevertheless lipi after some fluctuations has greatly increased in force of revelatory light and the breadth of its flood and luminous force; thought speech has also grown in inspired revelatory power. The T^2 has been most afflicted and with it the thought perception obstructed or brought to the lower level of intuition. At present all perception is of the intuitive ideal level with a touch or pressure of revelation tending to rise into the intuitive or inspired revelatory logistis, attended often by cloggings of intuitive matter or deviating into some kind of imperfect inspiration. The intuitive mentality itself has been so strongly idealised in its struggle with the gnosis that it is difficult sometimes to distinguish between this heavily idealised intuivity and the real intuitive or inspirational gnosis at its lower levels of force, light or certitude.

Dream at night of an extraordinary coherence, free for the most part from present association, except in the later nidra, and almost on the point of conversion to ideal experience of past, future or otherwhere happenings. In samadhi some incoherence and a lower level of general force of the ideality, but no cessation of abundance. This incoherence tends to turn into a more prolonged and sustained perfection of dialogue, narrative, lipi etc.

K.A afflicted, but not discontinued in its recurrence. Some attempt at enlargement of drishya and vishaya generally, as of rupa, but very uncertain and infirm though tending to largeness. Persistence of attack of roga and replying tapas. Generally an embarrassed but still successful progress, preparing a greater siddhi.

July 23^d Wednesday

A day of partial recovery and advance.

T^2 is acting with a quieter, deliberately limited and restrained action. Correct in the intuivity of the gnosis, although embarrassed by a strong adhesion of stuff of uncertain mental intuivity, the inspirational form is still overpowered by the latter disability, gives only the tendencies, pressures of force, suggestions of coming possibility. Intuitive certitude is slowly but steadily enlarging its operation.

K.A after some difficulty has recovered its basic continuity, but thinly without the opulent incidence and pervasion. Steady in act, variable in incidence, but afflicted by oblivion of absorption, only the thought not going out to objects, interferes less with it than the concentration on act or object, but this too now causes oblivion when attention is required to the thought-process. At the same time there is a progressive force of recovery.

Premananda in the Vishwadarshana has for some days been insisting on its normality. Ahaituka mental darshana is the chief obstacle; it is shantimaya with suppressed prema or anandamaya with diminished prema. This mental sight is disappearing before the premamaya vision into the vijnana or chidghana saguna seeing. In proportion as the guna was not seen, there was deficiency of prema; in the prema itself the mentality would thrust a diminishing incompletive suggestion of sterile ahaituka. Vijnana darshana does not suppress, but can hold a non-insistent diminished prema. Prema increases the ananda in the vijnana; ananda increases prema. Brahma-vision seeing things as objects of the unifying cognizance tends to be without prema; Purusha Brahma or Ishwara brahma darshana brings the deeper unity, prema and ananda.

K.A has recovered its force, but is still easily depressed by the interruption of the mind's absorptions, because there is a pressure on it from the obstructing force which compels it to sink easily in a mechanical variation of intensity, fluctuation and occasional cessation of its overt presence. But now the memory always brings back the Ananda.

In Samadhi continuous narrative, monologue, dialogue or their combination in the ideal form. This was done largely and for long in lighter swapna, on its borders or partly in concentrated antardarshi and partly in swapna. There is no long continuity of it in the deeper swapna which is still a thing of many, swift and brief experiences, thoughts and visions. K. Ananda maintained in lighter swapna, brought in with difficulty at a greater depth, non-existent in deep nidra.   Exceedingly strong and violent varied gandha. Rasa is recurrent, but not with such persistent freedom as yesterday, but it is developing more distinct rasas.

Throughout the day there has been a strong persistence of the relics of the intuitive mentality and the intuitive ideality has not been effective in getting rid of the obsession; because it is no longer the chosen instrumentation. Now the inspirational ideality is taking up the work, with the highest logistis at its back. This is more effective, all is at once changed to the inspirational form. But this too is not absolutely effective. The highest logistis alone can do the work.

There is a beginning of the change of the physical consciousness to the inspirational ideality.

Free gandha in the evening; the obstruction seems to be broken down, though not either in gandha or rasa entirely destroyed. It is intact in çravana and sparsha.

Samadhi fluctuating between full ideality and a lower half ideality. Memory in waking is badly deficient; this is itself an obstacle to rapid progress. Great masses of printed lipi, largely incoherent, but much more fluently legible and stable than at any previous time. Stability of rupa and scene and of all other experience is beginning to move towards farther self-extension. Narrative attempted in deep swapna, but trailed off into incoherence. All this is in the adverse state of the mentality.

Ideality still hampered and obstructed in the system.

July 24th Thursday

A farther advance and complete recovery today.

The siddhi is now moving towards a system of complete affirmation; all thought and perception, no matter what the source or medium, is admitted as having some kind of justification in force and being and the exact nature of the justification is being immediately assigned and made as precise as possible. In this process intuitive mental thought is allowed, but idealised in the mentality, since so only can it get its proper proportions. This has always been the theory of the sadhana; it has been preparing and repeatedly insisted on for a long time, but only now by this removal of the too trenchant intellectual distinction between satyam and asatyam is it becoming entirely possible. This completion is necessary for the manifestation of the hermetic gnosis; the logistic is a limiting gnosis, the hermetic an entirely comprehensive ideality. T^2 cannot be perfect, but only relatively perfect in the logistic gnosis.

Gandha and rasa are now acting with a considerable freedom and variety and the former with a fundamental perfection. Rasa is still subject to its initial crudeness of incomplete massed tastes, though there are now definite and perfect rasas. Rasa is now insisting on perfection.

In Samadhi a great flood and mass of experiences of all kinds, but incoherent, yet all in the ideality. Subsequently an ordered movement. All the intuitive mind turned into ideality, what was before simple intellectuality, is now just before the ideal level and is changing to the intuivity. This movement represents a complete mutation of the whole being into the gnostic type. Even the physical being is beginning this mutation. Forecast in the samadhi, this change is also beginning in the jagrat condition.

Sparsha has now a greater freedom and variety of the more subtle touches. Half-sthula sukshma sparsha also comes more often and with greater force, but not without some difficulty and obstruction.

The K.A violently oppressed; but the mechanical discontinuity cannot maintain itself any longer when there is smarana, except for a while after long discontinuity by oblivion. There is only strong suppression of intensity reaching the verge of discontinuity. The intensity recurs whenever there is laxity of the oppression.

The movement is now to the complete idealisation of the whole being. But the system is still low and the intuitive mentality recurs persistently and has to be idealised into the full logistis. This is especially due to the recurrent imperfection of T^2 and to the continuance of old states in the physical being.

Friday. July 25.

Yesterday's recovery was not complete except for a temporary movement. The new siddhi is still invaded by the external intuitivity, though there is no complete relapse. The ideality moves on the level of a thickly illumined revelatory intuition. This is extending greatly a relatively certain trikaldrishti and taking up firmly some, rejecting others of the telepathic suggestions which are again coming from the intuitive externality. The siddhi of T^2 is only initial; much has to be done before it can acquire a settled universality.

K.A at first distressed to the extreme point near discontinuity. Now it has revived, though not in full force and has again begun to push away the oblivion of absorption. Other siddhis have been in abeyance during the morning.

Samadhi in relapse. Afternoon spent in work. K.A in fluctuation. In ideality T^2 slowly enlarges itself in the ideal intuition. Some accommodation of this power in the thought with an incomplete inspirational ideality to form anew an intuitive inspiration. All these things are movements of recovery and enlargement of ideality on the lower levels, not permanent form or the regular action of the gnosis.

Samadhi recovers some of its force, but there is a strong persistence of incoherence, especially in the lipi. The siege of the external intuitivity continues. As yet the system is not ready for the full renewed action and control by the highest revelatory gnosis. Some attempt at shabda (vakya).

July 26   Saturday

Highest ideality has now a greater force in the thought perception, but T^2 continues on the lower intuitive level, is mainly telepathic and draws down the rest of the thought towards its own present type of action. Tapas is increasing its Kali force and largeness of action.

There is now a struggle between two kinds of ideality, the old ideality which depends upon the existent actuality, illumines it, goes a little beyond it but from it, returns to it, acquiesces temporarily in its decisions, and a new greater pragmatic ideality which takes the present actuality as a passing [circumstance],[7] claims to go altogether beyond it, to create with a certain large freedom according to the Will and looks even beyond to the omnipotence of the Self and its will, [to] determine as well as see the future. It is over the relapse to the mentalised intuitive ideality that the question is being fought out, for it is the mental intuitivity and the intuitive ideality which illumines it into a lower gnosis which either temporarily support or resignedly acquiesce in the relapse as a part of the still existent law of the rhythm of the sadhana. The greater ideality aims at eliminating the rhythm of rapid progression and sudden relapse. It proposes to do everything from above, by the ideality, in the ideality, the gnosis working out itself, *âtmani âtmânam âtmanâ.*

---

7 *MS* circumstances

The future of the sadhana lies with this greater pragmatic ideality and with something beyond it in the hermetic ideality. But it is still undetermined how soon it will be able to transcend the obstructing power of the intuitive mentality and act in its own right of rapid creation or revelation. The physical siddhi, the full force of Samadhi, rupa, vishaya, the greater T^2 seem to be waiting for this consummation

27 JULY – 13 AUGUST 1919

Yoga Diary
July 27 to Aug 13
1919

July 27th Sunday.

The complete fulfilment of the programme for July has been prevented by the sudden relapse towards the intuitive mentality. T^2 has indeed developed an initial firmness, but this is very insufficient in universality owing to the mental interference. The two first chatusthayas have again been contradicted by the invasion of the external mentality, which brings in an element of asraddha, tamas, dissatisfaction, and some broken hints of the revolt of the mental will and its old *duhkha* at *asatya* and *asiddhi*, the only two things that can still produce a perturbation. These touches are combated and thrown out by the tapas of samata, but they create recurrent vibrations though they cannot occupy the mentality. K A has confirmed only a recurrent, not an unbroken continuity, a continuity in smarana broken by brief mechanical discontinuities, but not a conquest of absorption and sleep; the other Anandas have therefore also to await their greater development. Karma is developing, but on a limited scale. Kali has deepened and possesses the system, but Krishna is still veiled by the ganas and devatas. Ananda Brahman has filled in with the chidghana and prema, but not yet with the fullness of the Anandamaya Ishwara. Tapas in Arogya has increased, the fragmentary rogas have a less insistence, but the two chronic rogas have acquired a new lease of continuance; nevertheless the digestive functionings are more under conscious control of the will. There is for the moment a great incertitude as to the immediate future of the development of the sadhana.

Lipi. Tapas siddhi to increase immediately to its full force in the pragmatic ideality.   Health to continue the battle, but to give the increase of the tapas against the existing difficulties.   The delight of the Ananda to fix itself against the oblivion of absorption, not yet against the sleep.   Ananda Ishwara to determine itself in the darshana.   Light of the hermetic ideality to suffuse the highest ideality.   Samadhi to determine its ideality in the permanent fixity.   Vishaya to develop as also the rupa siddhi.   These things and others to begin in the remaining days of July.

Siddhi began with the Ananda-Brahman. This is now beginning finally to impose itself on both the chidghana and the mental darshana. In the latter it either diffuses itself or contains the mental seeing, but in both cases is itself mentalised and loses its character of the pure perfect unmodified Ananda. The vijnana darshana either contains or is contained in the Ananda. In the former case the Ananda is either made of the chidghana kind or surrounds it in its mental or its chidghana modification. Prema is always present in the Ananda darshana, but is often seen as an element of the thing, *rasa-grahana*, without evoking bhoga of prema in the chitta and prana. It is seen by prakamya, not received by vyapti. The vijnana darshana is now being made by tapas to replace more firmly and fully the mental seeing. The more perfect Ananda darshana then supervenes more easily and with a greater completeness, density and amplitude.

The struggle with the remnants of the relapse continued for a time. Strong pragmatic ideal tapas worked in and on the resistance, till the intuitive ideality in intuitive *manasa* and vijnana replaced the lax intuitive mentality. Then suddenly in Samadhi complete and powerful gnostic revelation took up the whole action in light and deeper swapna, brought in full coherence, excluded all mentality: but in the deepest nidra imperfection still continued though attacked and partially excluded by the revelatory gnosis. There was no actual dream, but insufficient inner jagrat[t]a.

In the waking state also this gnosis took up the thought, but not so completely; T^2 is still a gate for the intervention of *manasa*.

Nevertheless the gnosis is working upon this manasa to transform it and exclude all unconverted movements. There is also some initial movement of turning the K A into the character of this gnosis.

Samadhi in the afternoon overpowered by nidra, only towards the end returning to the gnostic drishti.

In the ideality a strong and stable perception of the mental panchabhuta, brilliantly etheric in its basis, tejomaya in its substance, with all the perceptions and forces acting in its intellectual intuitive medium: within, but alien to it the pranic, vayumaya in its basis and substance, below the material inconscience, prithivimaya and jalamaya in its basis and substance. The mind sees in this medium its own contributions to thought and action, consciousness and force, but with some difficulty the pranic interception and intervention, with most difficulty the material resistance and response. This ether forms an obstacle to the vijnana contribution which governs, originates, decides the whole action of the triloka.

Subsequently a descent from the highest ideality for the purpose of farther fixing the transformation of intuitive mentality into intuitive ideality. This has been effected so that even in relaxed states of the system, the thought is ideal and not of the mental substance. The mental form is becoming exceptional, peculiar to a most relaxed condition of the system.

Samadhi still distressed by nidra. Dream of half-samadhi turning to vision, incoherence sometimes overpowering, sometimes corrected with ease or difficulty to some regular or capricious coherence. Rupa and vishaya in abeyance. K.A acting, but oblivious tamas attending absorption insistent, not strongly attacked by gnostic tapas. Physical siddhi otherwise in abeyance or small isolated action or limited to simple maintenance of the present status. The relapse has been chiefly effective in the physical siddhi.

July 28th Monday.

The ideality is working still at the transformation. T^2 is now acting normally in the telepathic form in the intuitive ideality with a clinging adhesion of the stuff of mentality. Nevertheless, there is frequent correctness of circumstance, but with an insufficient force of certitude and some occasional intervening element of error and wrong selection. T^2 of inspired telepathy has begun to be finally idealised, but there is yet a heavy incidence of mentality. The highest gnosis in T^2 is in abeyance.

Lipi. There will be the rush of the highest ideality today in the thought and the thought speech; a beginning also in the trikaldrishti tapassiddhi.

The inspired telepathic ideality can give the fact to be, but does not command the time and the circumstance. The attempt to do it brought it back to the infinite incertitude of possibility and so to an intuitive mentality just shading off into a thin ideality. Afterwards was a rush of tapasic action of the being, mostly idealised in the intuivity, but pervious to unidealised mental suggestions. Samata, çraddha etc are being made compatible with this tapasic state of the being which formerly brought always disturbance and reaction. The replacement of tamas or mere çama by a tapas based in çama is the intention. On the whole now laxity of the system can bring it down only to an intuitive ideal state bordering on and pervious to suggestions of the mentality, but not to unideal mentality. The attempt now is to replace this intuitive level by an inspired ideality which will be the state of relaxation and to make the highest ideality the proper action.

The rush of the highest ideality has begun, but it is very pervious to the motions of the lower ideality. In its inspirational form it gives freely the fact to be, but not yet the circumstance which had begun to be given with much imperfection by the lower inspiration

Vishaya and rupa revived, but began with their old faults, crudeness of rasa, obstruction of gandha and fugitive rupa etc. These are now gradually being set aside. Gandha can now always be commanded in subdued form or intensity by inhalation; spontaneous gandha is still limited to rarity by the obstruction. The tendency in rasa is to define. In rupa to a doubtful and quickly withdrawn primary stability. The full freedom is not yet established in any of these siddhis.

When the relapse brings back to a former state, there are always three conflicting principles at work, the habit of rebuilding laboriously what was broken down, the method of remanifesting rapidly the past siddhis by a rapid repetition of some of the steps by which it had been formed, the immediate remanifestation with fresh progress. The second tends to prevail, but less in the undeveloped siddhis; the third is only in its infancy.

A considerable force of samadhi later in the morning.

Samadhi in the afternoon much half-idealised dreaming.

Brief freedom of gandha and sparsha and a freer çravana.

Work in the afternoon. Highest ideality, but some action of the lower gnosis and the idealised intuivity. Later laxity and apravritti.

July 29   Tuesday.

Today a more perfect T^2 has been presaged in the lipi and the presage is repeated this morning.

T^2 is already growing towards a relative perfection. The ideality acting on all levels gives increasingly a prediction which has indeed only a relative certitude, but is generally right in fact of event, always has some justification in telepathic actuality, is able to fix time with a sort of coarse appreciation, but not yet always with an entirely prevailing relative certainty, has some rough initial idea of the arrangement of circumstance, though not yet the fine detail, but all is still disquieted to a certain extent by three of the old difficulties, (1) chiefly, the incertitude caused by a defect of the decisive seeing, (2) an attempt of the telepathy to fill in illegitimately this defect and the defect of range by a false certitude, (3) the intervention of mental will trying to masquerade as trikaldrishti. The incidence of these difficulties is steadily diminishing, but they are still in action.

Chitra rupa has been for some days growing in abundance, vividness, life and variety. Sthapatya rupa has now reappeared, this time in full spontaneity, vividness, unlimited variety, perfection of form, truth of life, — forms of all kinds of beings, objects, scenes etc. Chitra is developing towards the same perfection.

The highest ideality is now attempting in thought perception and tapas to free itself from the lower action. That comes in as an alien intervention, a sign that it is rejected and when the highest gnosis works, it is only so that they can present themselves, piercing from outside through the regular working and finding some similar response in the physical system, but rejected by the gnostic and mental being. When this gnosis works in freedom, then it arouses no pragmatic eagerness in the mental system, tolerates no mechanical tamasic laxity

During the rest of the day a variable action of the ideality.   In Samadhi dream pages, consecutive reading. Violent mass touch of sparsha, blow-push, in Samadhi. Nidra still oppressive.   A general wavering and incertitude.

July 30   Wednesday.

The highest logistic gnosis is now finally taking up the mentality. At first in intuitive revelatory, then in intuitive inspired revelatory and inspired revelatory, then in full revelatory in the three orders, it invaded all the thought-activities and holds them firmly; even the lapses are full of the revelatory sense and light. The next step is to turn this idealised mentality into the full and true highest logistic gnosis. This is being partly done, but mainly in thought speech and perception; not yet in T^2.

Kamananda is recovering its siddhis in the revelatory form.

Great intensity, fullness and stability of all kinds of sparshas in bahirdarshi jagrat as well as antardarshi.

Hasya in samata; beginnings of the devi-hasya.

Samadhi in the afternoon: in the grasp of nidra. But all the dream in the nidra has turned to ideality and coherence. The old form of incoherent dream was unable to force its way back into the samadhi, except for certain associations of present personality. Much of the dream was in the form of the highest ideality mental or vijnanamaya.

Work in the afternoon; subsequently a duller state of the action.   K.A weakened in the afternoon and evening, accomplished at night a certain overcoming of its difficulties, but is still very much subject to intermittence of its siddhis.

At night a splendid fullness of moving in dream vision; [absolute][1] perfection, colour, reality[,] intensity of scenes, objects, people, living creatures in an ordered succession as if seen by one moving through a new world, — the pranic worlds or else the

---

[1] MS absolutely

bhuswargas. Afterwards again dream of the ordinary kind, though always with a certain kind of coherence.

July 31   Thursday.

The ideality is now seeking to get rid of the too strong effect of the physical laxity, to keep up a constant action of the thought of gnosis. There is also the movement towards the changing of the idealised revelatory mentality in the physical system to the true gnosis.

T^2 is still a difficulty. The main difficulty is the persistence of the recurring tendency to take strong actual possibility for final actuality. This defect is absent when there is no attempt to get the absolute decision; then all is actual possibility relieved by relative certainties. But the attempt at decisive trikaldrishti tapas brings in the hasty and wrong overstresses which mix with, interfere with, replace the true decisions. Decision is often of the inspired gnostic kind which is a strong tapas of perception often fulfilled, but liable to be overborne by a greater power. At the same time the absolute revelatory action often intervenes, but is mixed with intuitive seeing of relatively decisive gnostic intuitions and these forceful inspirations of a pragmatic almost absolute certitude. The absolute revelatory action is of the logistis, certain therefore of the moment, but with a background of still greater unperceived possibility which may reverse the natural effect of the decision.

K.A is now stronger in force of spontaneous persistence; but the spontaneity is not perfect, nor proof against oblivion by strong absorption or by a wandering of the lax mind to other interests. But it is seeking to get rid of this obstacle by tapas.

The action of the ideality bears now most on the T^2 which is being reduced to the revelatory form. Only remnants of the old action are still untransformed and of the mentality. This movement at first turned the mental into the idealised revelatory mentality. Now a revelatory ideal Tapas and trikaldrishti is being insisted on, but mixed with the idealised mentality or chequered by its recurrence. Telepathy is being changed into perception of the thought stuff as well as the feeling stuff and impulse stuff of the being, while there is also the accompaniment of a telepathic thought-perception reducing these indirect identities into idea and thought speech. The mechanical and pragmatic tapas is being idealised and raised towards or into the truth tapas governed by trikaldrishtic perception. This again varies between the intuitive and inspired revelation, remnants intervening of non-revelatory intuition and inspiration, and is also directed towards the full truth revelation. The movement is final and decisive, but has [ ]² still much work to do upon the old matter and manner, before it can be entirely free to work in the revelatory gnosis.

K.A is enforcing continuity; the tendency to continuity insists and on the whole prevails in spite of the strong recurrence of its deficiencies.

The other siddhis are moving forward, but with a fragmentary and intermittent movement, liable still to some action of the principle of relapse. Saundarya, except in one or two details, and utthapana are unable to move forward or break down their barriers. They await the gnostic tapas.   The programme for the month has been in part accomplished, in part half accomplished, the other half begun but not completed, in part partially or entirely baffled by the obstruction. On the whole the forward movement prevails or is increasing in strength. The physical obstruction is the great obstacle.

August.

Balance of progress.

First Chatusthaya.   The first chatusthaya has been fortified by the stable founding and permanence of the full *hasya.* Asamata of asatya has now little or no force; its incidence is, if not quite deleted, yet ineffective. Asamata of asiddhi is passing, occasional, fragmentary and corrected without difficulty. Once the delight of failure is put in its right place, as an *anandamaya* perception of passing circumstance and step of the siddhi free from tamasic acquiescence, the last remnants of asamata can be abolished. Affection is the only thing that brings in a touch of the fear of amangala, but this is now a slight external suggestion.

2 MS to

Second Chatusthaya.   Complete except for the divine hâsya, aishwarya and the full sraddhâ in the swaçakti; these defects are due to the insufficiency of force in the *devi-bhâva*. Tejas, balam, mahattwam, pravritti of the elements are there, but not steady and equal in their action.

Third Chatusthaya.   Gnana is in itself perfect in revelatory gnosis, capable even of the hermetic gnosis, but is held back and descends so as not to outstrip too much the T^2. T^2 is advancing to the revelatory power. It is already preparing its final freedom from mentality, normally gnostic and drishtimaya, but burdened with the persistent recurrence of the intervening old mental deficiencies or lower forms of the gnosis.   Samadhi fluctuates, sometimes ideal, vigorous, abundant, then again for days together overpowered by nidra. In nidra dream is usually almost coherent, sometimes quite coherent, sometimes fantastic in coherence, sometimes orderly; when the ideality is active or presses on the system, dream-vision comes or dream is changed into vision.   Vishaya has established itself in gandha and rasa, often perfect, intense, distinct and of a certain variety, but is often rendered rare by the obstruction. Sparsha is strong in the established sthula touches, often intense in sukshma or sthula-sukshma touch on the sukshma or sthula body, even in the half sthula or just sthula touches, but the full and free materialisation is still obstructed; this part of the old barrier, its last strong fencing has not yet fallen. Sravana comes with strength or persistence only in the old symbolic sounds, cricket, ticking, bells, thunder etc; the rest has failed to materialise. Drishya is limited to an occasional elementary vision of the pranic akasha and its simplest forms. There is no sign of progression.   Rupa fluctuates; for some days it has failed in frequency and made no progress.

Fourth Chatusthaya.   Kamananda has established the prevailing tendency of continuity, can in response to smarana and tapas overcome all the obstacles of oblivion, except sleep and long absorption; but none of its deficiencies has undergone a final elimination. Tivra is strong, but intermittent, raudra firmly established in all touches up to an indefinite degree of the violence of the sparsha, but is sometimes momentarily overcome by sudden unexpected contacts. There is no insistence on vishaya which is generally established subject to certain remnants of discomfort or insipidity, nor on vaidyuta, which can however be brought by *satapas smarana*. Arogya is strong in tapas in all but the two central rogas, which are still insistent in obstruction and relapse; the rest the tapas, if allowed to act, can hold back or cast out the fragments with more or less appearance or reality of difficulty. Saundarya is established in bhava, but fluctuates in intensity and varies in character; physically there is no advance except in one circumstance. Utthapana is stationary or rather in a state of inhibition.

Fifth Chatusthaya. Mental Kali finally and permanently established, Krishna darshana in the being intermittent in its manifestation. Karma is limited to personal action and some force of tapas in outward things. Kama is personal, but not yet moved towards exteriorisation.

Sixth Chatusthaya. Fundamental Brahma darshana complete in the Ananda vijnana, sometimes descends towards the mentality to effect a better fusion of ahaituka, prema, kama, vijnana and shuddha ananda. Brahma sight is full of the Purusha, but only sometimes contains the Ishwara seeing.

Seventh Chatusthaya. Suddhi is practically complete except for the body and the vijnana; essential mukti complete, but not the mukti of the Nature, as in the physical being and its most physical mentality, recurrence of tamas and something of rajas and sattwa are still visible. Bhukti is almost complete. These completenesses are fundamental, not a completeness of degree or of content. Siddhi is practically perfect in the first, moving towards final perfection in the second, striving towards completeness and a kind of perfection in the third, initial only in the fourth and for the most obstructed and subject to relapse, busy only with the personal foundation in the fifth, large in the sixth, but not full in its contents or complete in its combination.

Programme

I. Hasya to be fixed in the final perfection.

II. Çraddha to be completed, daivi prakriti brought to perfection.

III   Ideality to be firmly raised in T^2 to the revelatory logistic power and to look upward to the hermetic gnosis in all its thought activities. Samadhi to overcome nidra. Vishaya to be completed in its element[s], jagrat rupa delivered from its barrier of obstruction.

IV   Kamananda to acquire continuity, overcome its obstacles and bring in the other anandas. Health to increase its tapas and, if possible, found the two central arogyas. The development of the two other physical siddhis is not likely to come as yet to perfection, but the final battle may begin with the physical obstruction.

V.   Kali to idealise and fix herself in the gnosis and Krishna to fix himself as the visible Ishwara in the Ananda. Karma to extend its force of perfection in the personal working and its power on outward eventuality. Kama to complete its personal basis in the subjectivity.

VI.   Ishwara darshana to take up the perfected Brahma vision.

VII.   Perfection in the first two, initial perfection in the third and sixth, preparation of completion in the other chatusthayas.

August 1. 1919.   Friday.

Action of ideality in thought to perceive the right action. The full revelatory ideality, not the inspired or intuitive revelation, the truth seeing not the pragmatic or resistant mechanical seeing, not the alternation of these two opposite powers, nor even their simultaneous perception, but their unity and exceeding in the revelatory truth, must be the agent of the perfect siddhi. That therefore must be insisted on always, even in the midst of the persistence of the lower movements. This thing done means a sure rapidity.

In the K.A. urgent pragmatic tapas must be replaced by spontaneity aided by an ideal truth tapas and smarana.

An attack of the obstructive external physical mentality which sought to deny all farther speedy or immediate progress, was followed by an immediate and strong advance in the first two chatusthayas. The hasya is already achieving the requisite form and the acceptance of asiddhi as a circumstance and step of siddhi is complete. Into this acceptance has still to be brought the secure fullness of the equal ananda. A limited aishwarya-bodha and self-çraddha, a full çraddha in the kalyanabuddhi of the Ishwara is now being founded. These two siddhis have now to be given their last finality.

Lipi. The ideality in the physical siddhis to be undertaken in spite of the difficulties.

The rest of the day mostly a confirming of the first two chatusthayas against the attack of Asiddhi. It is now firmer; the moments of clouding prove ineffective; the siddhi perseveres in spite of absence of light or adverse suggestions in the mentality.

The oppression of primary utthapana is a little lightened today. The attack on the health still continues in the digestive perversion. In the fragmentary rogas it is held in check, its material effects abrogated as soon as they are slightly manifested, but is not eliminated from the system.

In Samadhi in the afternoon no recovery, except at the end; at night (early morning) ample rupa, but there is still incoherency in the lipi, unideality in the other features, inaction of the thought-powers. On the whole a day of obstruction, but of some initial advances.

Aug 2.   Saturday
A day of the ideality.

The lipi predicts the 5th and 11th (with the 7th as an intermediary stage) and the 15th as the important days for the gnosis. Today it has to manifest under difficulties and this will go on till the 5th when the revelation, it is to be presumed, will be in some sort firmly founded; from the 5th to the 11th farther progress still in spite of difficulties, then some manifestation of the hermetic ideality. The 15th is to be the special day for the gnosis.

Thought and thought-speech have fixed themselves in an easy normal and brilliant revelatory gnosis of the subordinate intuitive character in all its degrees. This is also being applied to the mental levels where it is still of the same character, but of a more derivative and less complete and immediate luminosity and certitude.   Next, the same process was applied to T^2. First, an inrush of the old mentality; next a lifting in which all first became incertitude and then was transformed into a gnosis of intuitive revelatory possibilities, the revelation taking up the possibilities and revealing their incidence and proportions, with an intervention of immediate revelatory certitudes. Behind this is now manifesting the full inspired revelatory dynamic possibilities and certitudes and the full revelatory illuminations. Tapas is of the same character, but with less completeness. This second movement however is as yet from above and has not become either full in itself or the normal thought action.

Subsequently, an attempt to bring in the inspired revelation as the type of all the thought especially in T^2. At first this brought about a descent from the revelatory to the inspired levels. Then there came above, with no hold on the lower being, a highest form of the full (not inspired) revelation, holding in itself the prominent element of inspiration. A difference has to be drawn between the inspired revelation and full most luminous revelation of an inspired character. T^2 came to no definite siddhi, but thought became of an inspired revelatory nature.

An attack of roga on the eye. Twice materialised and momentarily healed first by intuitive, then by inspirational Tapas of the revelatory kind, it managed to hold by a disposition to and some actual watering, but no effusion. The arogya tapas prevailed over the roga which for the most part lived only in suggestions in the subtle physicality which could not materialise in but only affected the sthula. There was some physical sense or initiation of all the symptoms, but not their physical actuality.

Samadhi overpowered by nidra in the afternoon, free, but still attacked by defects in the early morning

Aug 3   Sunday.

The movement to inspired revelation continues and all the thought and T^2 is of this character, revelation always present, inspiration predominating and sometimes swallowing it up, but on all levels, so that there is little certitude of a final character. Mostly the thought of T^2 on the idealised mental level. Some recurrence of intuitive forms. Later emergence of thought of inspired revelation and revelation permeated with inspiration. Invasion from outside failed to bring in any relapse or any element of intellectuality.

The roga made many fresh attacks, but was increasingly

overpowered by Tapas; it is being reduced to the fragmentary character. No actual watering except early in the morning, very slightly, but still a disposition to watering and occasional attempts at heat. The causes of increased affection, strain of the eye, glare etc are being got to increase instead the force of the arogya. Arogya Tapas is changing to the ideal character. The thick obstacle of the most physical prana with its sanskara of roga is being pierced and broken up by the light of ideal tapas. The movement is [one][3] of strong prevalence, not yet of absolute finality. In the central rogas Tapas is resuming its operation, but not yet effective for sensible progress.

In the morning drishya of pranic akasha, full of small life; insects, butterflies etc so stable and vivid as often to be not easily distinguishable except by their multitude from terrestrial forms. Birds also, but not so stable, vivid, easily distinguishable as pranic beings.

In samadhi after some nidra and coherent dream, great abundance of samadhi experience. Tapas is resuming its force, revelatory ideality taking up more firmly the forms. One full dialogue narrative in this kind, many breaks of pure dialogue etc; abundant lipi. But the tendency to incoherence is still able to recur across the general coherence.

K.A is resuming its hold after two days subsidence and pale recurrence, and is now of a more firmly ideal revelatory character, even in the stronger and narrower intensity of the sthula current.

Aug 4   Monday.

The vijnana began with the highest gnosis in the third intensity, but afterwards there was especially in T^2 much play of the idealised mentality and the lower gnosis on the mental level.. T^2 has still a difficulty in remaining on the gnostic heights of thought and will and perception.   The attack in the roga tried to prolong itself, but only with a slight success. Ideal and idealised Arogya tapas prevailed over the roga. Roga since attacked in other forms, but in all after some brief and apparently strong materialisation the Tapas was able to dismiss it from actuality, eg, a spell of cough, catarrh, not in fact but sensation. — Pain of the breast manifested repeatedly

---

[3] MS once

and was allowed for the sake of the raudra ananda. Pressures once intolerable are now filled with the Ananda; they then find it difficult to persevere, diminish and rapidly disappear. – The same state in the central rogas. –

In Samadhi, seated, ideality, then in reclining nidra. Afterwards strong universal action of the highest gnosis in all depths, thought, speech, T^2, thought dealing with rupa, or lipi. Lipi was ideal, for the most part of the highest gnosis. Rupa at first telepathic turned to the gnostic content. Rupa was pranic and chhayamaya, eg a shadowy hand taking a shadowy bag, shadowy mountains and lakes, a great curving raised line of ground in daylight of chhayamaya, all sufficiently stable.

Jagrat rupa and vishaya are recovering their action. In rupa the stress is on stability which is now often secondary and tertiary in crude rupa, in the rest the tendency is to prolonged primary or arrested secondary; even when unstable, they are snatched away rather than in themselves fugitive. In drishya birds etc vivid in pranic akasha, some hardly distinguishable from terrestrial creatures; colours only white and black. Free and abundant rupa (not drishya) of human forms etc against the pranic akasha. In rasa and gandha the stress is on distinctness and particularity; the obstacle to frequency is not yet overcome. The obstruction remains in the sparsha, but there is [considerable]⁴ intensity in the established forms of sparsha, little spontaneity. Çravana is still subject to a return of complete obstruction. K.A. varies; the stress is no longer on continuity, but on ideality.

T^2 active in the highest ideality of the third degree. The turn here is to the rejection of the confusion of incertitude. There is also some filling of the third with the light of the higher degrees.

Dream of connected sequences, but some fantasia. Beginning of a firmer gnosis in the dialogue.

Aug 5 Tuesday.
T^2 is now settling down into the gnostic movement; mainly in the third intensity of the highest gnosis. The finality has begun and

⁴ *MS* considerably

there remains only the complete transformation and the dominant certitudes.

The Ishwara has now begun to prepare his final overt occupation of the Adhyakshatwa. Strong dasya of the Shakti manifested, and although there is fluctuation is taking possession. Tertiary ideal dasya in intensity has definitely replaced the remnants of the old mental tertiary mixed with the over prominence of Prakriti which maintained the remnants of the secondary dasya. But the dasya is sometimes to the ideal ganas, sometimes direct to the Ishwara

In samadhi idealisation proceeds, complete narrative (part drishya and dialogue) is growing; dialogue, still fragmentary, is preparing for expansion. Strong hermetic gnosis occurred in the samadhi.

Aug 6 Wednesday

T^2 is now assured in the gnosis, mainly of the third and second intensities. The third is still the largest, the second is now about to secure its own perfection, predominance and finality so as to open fully to the first intensity. All is transformed into gnosis that touches the mental system. The intuitional gnosis has completed itself in the revelation and recognised its limits. Certitudes of revelatory intuition exist, but they are only temporary, immediate or relative, as it may be said, contributory and not final certitudes.

Tertiary ideal dasya is getting rid of all remnant of mental endeavour and overstress; on the other hand full force of tapas as yet comes only from above and is not normal to the system. Dasya of *nati* is established, but not a perfect dasya of *sâmarthya*

Last night there was again roga attack on the eye, but fragmentary and external though capable of a certain persistence. It lasts so long as the highest revelatory tapas does not act with a full incidence. Hot watering during sleep subsists, though reduced to a certain extent; other symptoms of shita susceptibility are very brief in their recurrence. No visible progress to finality in the central rogas.

Rupa moves forward very slowly. There is some combination of variety and increasing stability in crude rupa; ghana is trying to stand before the eye in the same way as the crude figures. But the old imperfections and limitations still hold their own against the tapas of vision.

A strong movement towards spontaneity combined with vivid distinctness and some variety in rasa, gandha and sparsha. In the latter the sukshma touch is getting more and more sthula, though as yet the border line to full sthulatwa has not been crossed.

Samadhi went back to nidra and began turning the touches of dream swapna immediately to ideal forms of gnostic swapna samadhi. At night there is real dream, but more and more a consequent and idealised dreaming.

Attack on eye, more full, cured, but the tendency remains.

Gnosis fixed itself in the second rising to the third intensity.

Aug 7.   Thursday

Gnosis rose to the third intensity of the logistic revelation. As usual the whole mass of thinking with some considerable invasion from the exterior mentality was brought in for transformation to the new form. Some progress was made, but interrupted by the necessity of a long struggle with the eye roga which attacked persistently all the morning, was persistently put back, but renewed the attack when on the point of elimination. It is noticeable that all thought was of the ideal kind, though of all ideal kinds, idealised mentality as well as gnosis. The invaders could bring in no intellectual suggestion which was not given its luminous ideal translation whether into truth of mentality or gnosis. Even the suggestions of the subconscious physical mind are thus translated into light of gnosis. The lipi therefore which fixed the 5th & 7th as crucial dates for the gnostic siddhi, is amply justified in fact and in detail. The full conversion to the third intensity, especially of T^2 still remains to be done.

Success of the invasion was mostly in the physicality, – roga. It amounts to the eye attack – suspended during the early afternoon, and some brief repetition of cough and retardation of the central roga.

In Samadhi the very deepest overpowering nidra in which formerly there was no trace of samadhi experience, but even this is now in the afternoon turning to its initial ideality.

Friday. Saturday
Aug 8–9.

These two days have been marked by the immensely rapid progress of the gnosis. On the first thought and a certain part of T^2 rose or rather soared up with force into a highest logistic gnosis full of the deputed power of the hermetic and seer ideality. For the most part there was an increase of the inspired pragmatic or dynamic gnosis at this level of intensity, with an undertone of intuitive present or actual gnosis, corresponding to the old mechanical intellectuality. This took full shape and power on Saturday. T^2 got an immense development. The lower state of the system was at first transformed to the full ideality of all kinds, but chiefly highest ideality of the third intensity, then all to the highest gnosis either full of or penetrated or overshadowed by the influence of the hermetic and seer gnosis.

This change was chiefly managed with the violent struggle between the Arogya and the eye attack for an occasion. The struggle resolved itself into a dynamic highest gnostic tapas which sought to override physical rule and limitation and the invading idealised intellectuality aided by the upwellings of the subconscious mind of the body which insisted on the old physical law and habit. When tapas was active it prevailed but on the point of cure ceased and allowed the other thought to act and prevail. Thus for two days there has been an oscillation between movements of rapid ideal cure and the fragmentary but still persistent running of the old course of the disease. The tapas insisted (1) on every thought of the subconscient or the invading mentality being idealised and falling on the side of the gnostic truth or knowledge, whether by force of violence or illumination, (2) on every cause of pejoration of the disease being turned by this means into a cause of amelioration and strengthening of the eye and its sight, (3) on every layer of the consciousness to the most obscure physical being brought up into the light and penetrated and possessed by the light of the ideality. During these two days it gained successively all but the most physical flesh layer. The disease was left with a strong tendency to disappearance, but a remnant of persistence in its one last symptom maintained by action of the Roga consciousness on this purely physical layer.

T^2 of external happenings is still imperfectly brought into the highest gnosis.

Aug 10   Sunday.

The highest gnosis on Saturday began reconciling the dynamic inspirational and the actualist intuitional revelation in the pure revelatory union. This is now the thing that is in process. Except part of T^2 and fresh arriving invasional thought which supports the physical asiddhi, all is changed to some kind of this highest gnosis of the first intensity. T^2 also is undergoing the transformation. In Samadhi the same process is in action at a lower stage[,] that of turning all into gnosis at least of the third intensity.

The eye attack has succumbed to the gnostic Tapas. This struggle has founded the true basis of ideal Arogya and of the whole physical siddhi. The gnostic method is being applied initially to all the members of the sharira; but the whole bodily consciousness has to be converted before it can make rapid headway.   K.A has been well founded in the ideal form and is taking over into that form all its previous siddhis. Its obstacles are still mechanical discontinuity (almost destroyed, except as a result of long discontinuity[)], laxity of the system, oblivion by absorption, sleep. The positive dark veil of oblivion has been destroyed by light of gnosis; only the mechanical oblivion survives its disappearance

Vishaya and rupa are moving forward deliberately by steps, firmer than before, but there is no mastering rapidity. The quadruped form, so long resisted, has now reached a brilliant perfection in chitra and sthapatya which are extraordinarily active whenever they can find a background and attention.

K.A is to be established today, according to the lipi, completely and perfectly established tomorrow, confirmed and filled out the day after. At present it has been established in the old way as an insistent presence supported by Tapas in continuity, brought immediately into natural recurrence by smarana, but hampered in both respects by an external obstruction to which the system is still sensible. Mechanical discontinuity is destroyed, but the other obstacles and interruptions have still their incidence.

Aug 11   Monday.

T^2 is arranging itself for a final dismissal of the remnants of positive defect, practically the excesses and deficiencies of stress of tapas, a final conversion of all telepathic perception into the highest logistic ideality of the three times, a taking up of actualistic and dynamic T^2 into the full revelatory gnosis. This is especially in outward things, as the inward is ready for the change to the hermetic ideality which can alone begin the reign of a quite positive certitude. At present all has been reduced to the lowest stress, on the borders between mind and gnosis so as to get the proper action at this lower pitch where deficiency of light gives the largest scope to inferior working and error. The highest logistic T^2 has begun there, but with some weakness. Incertitude and yet justification of both the actualistic and dynamic perceptions is being insisted upon, a repetition of the old method of purification

In Samadhi K.A overcame more and more the obstacle of absorption and nidra. It now occupies all the ranges of samadhi and is kept in continuity not only in the antardarshi and lighter swapna, but in the depths of swapna where nidra is not present as an element. But even with nidra it now increasingly comes as a strong recurrence or a difficult but still growing continuity. The defect is that this recurrence tends to break the samadhi, bring back swapna to antardarshi or lighten it to the point where some perception of the outer world clings to the skirts of the inner absorption. The perception in deep swapna is of the pranic basis of the physical body, but also often of the physical body made sensible to the sukshma mind and indriyas. There is also a direction towards the comprehensive many-planed samadhi.

The whole major insistence throughout the day has been on the K. Ananda. First of all the normal continuity has been founded in the settling of a great mass of gnostic K. Ananda on a pedestal of rocklike pratistha. Later this has faded and grown, half disappeared and returned, given place to a less certain fluid Ananda in the laxity of the mind and body, but the net upshot is a continuity only interrupted by sleep and distraction. The difficulties are being rapidly put aside. Laxity of the system no longer of itself brings on discontinuity, but only when it is supported by pramada, mental distraction. Absorption of thought also no longer imposes oblivion, except when there is this loose distraction or pramada of the channel mind in the physicality. Absorption in the object is at best only momentarily discontinuative; absorption of reading or writing only when extreme by necessity of attention; but this necessity is no longer really existent, since the gnosis is capable of a wide and multiple dhyana. In the reading it is almost eliminated as a necessary factor, in the writing it is on the point of elimination. The one thing now really to be conquered is the loose mental distraction, a habit and not a necessity of the system. This gained in the evening, was brought out in full and prevented the complete actual continuity. It is assisted by the old desire of the physical mind for release from tapas, rest by inertia. Sleep also, not transformed towards samadhi, is a positive interruption.

The highest logistic ideality in assured possession of the thought, preparing assured possession of the T^2; physical siddhi commencing finality in the ideal Kama Ananda. This fulfils the indication for the 11th, though not to the extent of the entire completeness.

Aug 12   Tuesday.

The gnosis is proceeding with its preparation of T^2. K.A is left to fix itself in the new siddhi, but all the obstacles, sleep excepted, have ceased to exercise a necessary interrupting action. They live only by dependence on the lax distraction of the channel mentality. Samadhi is still occupied with the transformation of nidra. On the whole a day of intermediate relaxation.

Aug 13   Wednesday

The gnosis is now definitely taking up the T^2 from the border line towards the higher region. Hermetic ideality is beginning to show itself in an action from above on the logistic plane, while it more and more moulds the logistis itself into a predominantly hermetic logistis. This is in the thought, the T^2 is being taken up by the inferior drashtri logistis, but this too is taking on a lower hermetic element, the fullness of dynamic certitude. Incertitude is giving way more and more to a relative certitude – the exact temporary power, force, result is seen, — thronged around by positive certitudes of immediately subsequent or slightly distant eventualities. Old difficulties are brought up by a lower seeing and immediately transformed to this positive vision. The process is only commencing its finality, but proceeds with a considerable rapidity. Nevertheless T^2 full perfection cannot come in the logistis; but only a limited sufficiency and initial perfection.

Yoga Diary
August 14
1919.

August 14th   Thursday

The ideality is advancing in the same steps. Thought is perfectly fixed in the gnosis and rises to the hermetic logistic and the seer logistic ideality. T² is being transformed by the logistic drashta, – not the seer logistis, but with a touch of the hermeneusis. The old mentalities recur in the idealised incertitudes, but only to be interpreted by the light of gnosis. There is no relapse to mentality, but only some lapse to this admissibility of idealised mental suggestions; they come from outside and the system is still capable of a subordinate mechanical response to them. The range of T² is as yet small, restricted to the habitual field of action, – except sometimes when a higher action develops its first luminous suggestions. This higher T² is commonest in the lipi.

Samadhi is as yet making no masterful progress. It is kept back by the siege of nidra supported by a strong tendency to physical and mental laxity which has reigned for the last two or three days. Rupa and drishya and vishaya have for the time being suspended their advance and are in a state of comparative suspension.

The physical siddhi is advancing in the K.A, but under the difficulty of the laxity and distraction. The other physical siddhis are in a state of suspension.

Kamananda is working upon the laxity in order to enforce its perfect continuity. The main movement is an attempt to fix the Ananda (madirâmaya) in the head, but that still tends to bring a temporary lessening in the lower body. Ananda in the upper body is subject to the dominance of discontinuity; in the lower body the normal tendency is to continuity. At times there comes the perfect siddhi of continuity against which no absorption, even of writing, can prevail. It is this and the pervasion which have to be fixed in an absolute finality.

Ananda Purusha darshana and prema are again insisting on their intensity and universality. They are combated by the remnants of the old ahaituka indifferent universality. This is now likely to be overcome with some rapidity.

T^2 is now increasingly correct within the logistic limits. But there is the old defect of descending, now not into the mind, but to the lower border intensities open to mental suggestions, for the transformation. All work of progress should be done from the highest attained siddhi, the high lifting up the low, not the low working towards the higher siddhi. This has indeed begun and is even established in the subjectivity but not with a pure and perfect action

Aug 15 Friday

Hermetic logistic ideality took preliminary possession of the T^2. This action at once brought to bear effective gnostic tapas on the body. But the lower action still insists, has yet to undergo transformation. The survival of the tamoguna in the body is the chief obstacle; it brings not the absolute, but a relative aprakasha, apravritti, pramada, moha.

The day was taken up with the development of this action which marks a decisive turning-point in the gnosis. From the afternoon came, as often before in such crises, a lapse (for adjustment) into idealised mentality, no longer tinged with any dark tamas, but rather a vivid haze of light, a confusion of luminous incertitude. So long as this conversion of the gnosis is not provided with its full base, the other siddhis attend their moment for renewed progression.

Aug 16th 17th

Continuation of the lapse of adjustment. In the evening 17th[1] a recovery of the higher action and a renewal of the physical Ananda. Daivi prakriti with powerful and complete *matribhava* is constantly increasing, as also the anandamaya samata and strong hasya. Aishwarya bodha of the Ishwari in the Prakriti subject to the growing aishwarya of the Ishwara in the Ananda acting through the vijnana and limited by the continued imperfection of this instrumental nature.

Aug 18th Monday

Full force of the seer ideality in the logistis. Thought-perception has now the same freedom and almost the same assured power as the speech. Thought of T^2 is assuming the same freedom and potency; but, especially in the objective subjectivity it is limited by the large element of persistent telepathic incertitude. Nevertheless the certitudes are constantly progressing up the plane of increase.

K.A in sleep in the morning almost succeeded in overcoming the depth of nidra, but stopped short on the verge of possession. The Ananda is now increasing again to lay its hold on the system and overcome the distraction. It is attempting to penetrate more and take hold of the fibres of the physical body.

Tapas in T^2 is visibly increasing in mass and swiftness of efficacy, but it still acts in a large atmosphere of the surrounding and limiting incertitude.

Samadhi is recovering its progressive force. Long narrative reading, at first with skippings of large tracts, afterwards more continuous, but not quite ideal; dream reading. This was nidra in course of idealisation. Shabda has grown strong in samadhi; rupa, converse etc are increasing their strength and continuity.

Aug 19th Tuesday

Seer logistical ideality is taking up firmly the whole T^2 and rejecting and transforming all the lesser movements. Only detailed circumstance is still rebellious to this treatment and insists on

---

1 "*17th*" *written above "evening" in MS.—Ed.*

inspirational telepathic trikaldrishti. The difficulty is still the adjustment of actualistic and dynamic logistis.

K.A has altered its base of continuity to the more physical Ananda, but as a consequence there is a decrease in the force of continuity which had depended on the ananda of the sukshma body affecting the sthula sharira. The main insistence is now on the increase of the physical occupation and not on the final removal of distraction which is to depend on the intense continuity of Ananda on this new base.

In Samadhi in the afternoon a considerable extension of the dream siddhi, but at night a lapse to incoherent and fantastic continuity.

Tapas is filling the physical mentality.

Aug 20th

Ideality of the seer gnosis in the logistis is now successfully occupying the whole range of the T^2 siddhi; the element of recurrent lower ideality or idealised mentality is approaching the minimum.

The extension of Tapas in the physical being proceeds with the working of getting rid of the apravritti of mere prakashamaya çamas; the acquiescence in asiddhi mechanically recurs, but is no longer accepted by the Shakti

Strong united spontaneity and stability is finally taking possession of the physical manifestation of the lipi, in which these two siddhis had still great difficulty in effecting a perfect coalescence.

The action of the superior gnosis has again taken possession of the logistis. The base is a seer action modified to suit the lower key of the logistis, the force is a hermetic action informing the logistis with its higher luminosity and no longer dependent upon the actuality. This greater force is supreme in thought speech and thought-perception, even though still besieged there by a certain limitation of the surrounding mentality. In T^2 it has begun to act and to evolve a true trikaldrishti acting upon the telepathic seeing and impose on it a certain kind of absolute certitude, as absolute as can be admitted in the logistis. The telepathic action itself is assuming the force of the seer logistis, though not yet perfect in this evolution. Tapas in its separate initiative (not preceded by or involved in knowledge) has risen in its major action to 65° and is even rising beyond it to 75° and 80°. This movement is proceeding towards its completion

Samadhi has developed in all but the nidramaya depths to the heights of the seer logistis. Where there is nidra, it is assuming the character of the lower intensities of the logistis informed with revelatory gnosis, but the dream caprice often touches and spoils by its intervention. There are instances of a very perfect and sustained dream reading, also brief perfect converse.

K.A has suddenly developed the highest seer logistic character in the mental body and when it so acts forms a sea of ananda around the body, but when the body itself is penetrated by the ananda this tends to cease. The Shakti is working to combine the Anandas of the mental and physical bodies. Ananda recurred with spontaneity in the Samadhi, but could not endure against the nidramaya absorption.

At night in samadhi at first rational, then fantastic dream coherency.

Aug 21. Thursday.

Highest logistis in spite of general laxity firm in thought-perception, active amid some telepathic confusion in T^2.

Vishaya Ananda changed into seer logistic quality through a conversion to K.A. This was done with phenomenal rapidity; intuitive vishaya at first adhered to first contact, but was almost immediately converted in this last refuge. The siddhi first in sparsha, then extended to the other vishayas, even to action and happening. What now takes place is vishaya-kama, ideal sense of vishaya acting in the dominant Kama Ananda.

Rupa has for some time been working against temporary suppression, yesterday succeeded in turning it to strong obstruction, today it has recovered its force. Crude rupa is now for the most part possessed of the third stability; the others are still in the first in duration, but the rupas here too have the nature and consistency of the third, but are caught away by the old obstructive power in the akasha.

Vishaya again active. Gandha has almost conquered the obstruction in inhalation, but spontaneous gandha though increased in force of recurrence is still subject to its power. Rasa is trying to occupy the organs of taste more fully. Sparsha is still obstructed, but occasionally active in response to tapas. Sravana is rare and has not gone beyond the typical shabdas now commenced in the jagrat bahirdarshi, and no longer confined to antardarshi or dependent on the closing of the ear to sthula sounds. Drishya is depressed in its evolution.

Samadhi in the afternoon developed farther in the same direction. At night there was throughout in sleep the rationalised dream coherence — also some samadhi — the fantastic element even was reduced to the terms of rational coherence. The only exception was a brief, but for a time persistently repeated irrational fear-dream from the subconscient infant mentality associated with past sanskaras. The intrusion of personality and present life associations are now the only undispelled defects of this nidramaya swapna siddhi. The element of ideality in the coherence is rising, but not effective, because the purusha is only a passive witness and seer and not as in the samadhi proper a gnostic observer and judge of the things seen or experienced. Nidra must be dispelled to bring about this perfection.

Aug 22, 23. 24   Friday, Saturday. Sunday

On one side a strong development of hermetised logistis which is taking up the T^2; on the other a laxity of the system, a lapse towards something like the old mentality brought about by an invasion of the besieging external mentality and some return of the mental principle of advance through struggle which seemed for a time to have given way finally to the ideal principle of advance through adjustment; even for brief moments in the end (24th) strong touches of external asamata. The higher gnosis works from above on this mass and frequently occupies it, but the physical system and mind are relaxed to the old half idealised mentality.

T^2 has advanced so far that all telepathy is taking on the form of the seer logistis, — the hostile suggestions from outside excepted, and these too are now being attacked when they enter and either rejected or compelled to undergo transformation. Decisive seer trikaldrishti and tapas are rare, but the dynamic in that type is now common and is being better harmonised with the actualistic ideality raised to the same form. This seer logistis is of the higher form full of a varying measure of hermesis and even some reflection of a superior drishti.

Vishaya is again obstructed and occasional; rupa is trying to advance under difficulty. K.A has been much oppressed but is now reviving though not yet in full occupation. On the other hand the new dynamic seer tapas aided by a lower logistic tapas is working strongly for the arogya especially in the two central rogas with some initial effectuality. It is trying also to take hold of the other two members of the physical siddhi, but with no tangible result in the corporeality.

Samadhi is half advancing, half stopping under the same difficulty. Once there was the old vision of long continuous connected scene, but not this time in a rapid panorama, but steady as in actual life and changing only by the slow and regular movement of the witness through its environment. Towards the end, however, it was invaded by present suggestions and suffered from some fantastic incoherence and mutability, but more in the event and occupying figures than in the scenes. Last night there was a fall back to strong fantasia of present suggestion, though the physical circumstances and happenings were perfectly coherent and rational in their ensemble, connection and changes. In the afternoon for two days there was a difficult gnosis limited to thought and lipi and today a strong overmastering by disputed nidra, after some success of restoration. Occasionally in all these imperfect siddhis there are suggestions not immediately followed up of new development and progress. The obstacle interferes and drives back towards asiddhi.

A movement in the lipi towards the universalising of a rapid stable legibility in all the forms, chhaya, tejas, jyoti, varna, of the lipi. All but the chhaya are more facile and stable at night than in the daytime

Aug 25. Monday

The tapas is becoming constantly stronger in the physical field; the ideal tapas produces results which were impossible to the mental or intuitive power. But there is an obstinate retarding resistance.

Lipi 13 3 6   These are the siddhis which have to be brought forward and on which, in addition to the gnosis of jnana and T^2 the Shakti is most tending to concentrate.   There is an attempt also to redevelop or rather to remanifest and reestablish the once manifested stable basis of the K. Ananda.

K.A is reestablished, but not with a full force or continuity.

In the Samadhi there is some revival of the full force of dream coherence; also occurrence of an absolute firmness of dream vision

T^2 is developing settled seer telepathy and seer telepathic trikaldrishti in spite of the confusion of the invading mentality. Tapas is dominating, but much besieged by the obstruction of the invading ashakti.

Aug 26   Tuesday.

T^2 continues to develop the seer certainties and right perception of telepathy, but the besieging confusion and physical tamas continues to limit its action. There is an increasing revival of the force of K.A. The two first chatusthayas depressed by tamas and laxity are recovering their completeness of the siddhi. This time the relapse tendency in the subjectivity has lasted seven days; the ordinary minimum formerly was a fortnight.

T^2 has emerged from the confusion and is now exiling all inferior suggestions. The telepathy of the seer logistis is still subject to a survival of mental incertitude and stress prematurely trying to set right the incertitude, but the tendency to automatic justness of appreciation is gaining ground in spite of lapses.

Samadhi has recovered full force of logistic ideality in the seer logistis. For the last day or two there has been a movement towards abundance and coherence of other experience than the dream vision. Abundance and continuity were secured initially in monologue, converse, scene-narrative with speech, lipi in the lighter samadhi; there was also light and stable scene and continuity in happening; but the mass lipi in deeper samadhi was subject to great incoherence and though there was an immense abundance of experience in the logistic samadhi, most of it was of a fragmentary character. At night there was some relapse to present suggestion.

K.A increases in the seer logistic ananda, but was discontinued late at night. The obstruction is yielding with much resistance and retardation.   The two first siddhis are well reestablished in Devihasya.

Aug 27 Wednesday

T^2 in spite of laxity is proceeding with accuracy of telepathic incidence. The Surya direction of the Ishwara is prominent and moving towards direct logistic control and guidance.

A great increase of physical stability in sadhara, niradhara and chitra lipi, but especially in the niradhara. Also now in sthapatya lipi.

In Samadhi in the afternoon at first an oppression of nidra, but strongly resisted by the Shakti which established in spite of it a free flow of the lipi, mostly of the lower logistic character. Subsequently, when the nidra tendency was conquered, there was established a free coherent movement of the seer logistic thought-speech, natural, normal, not as formerly maintained by tapas against obstruction, – though a slight negligible obstruction is still present, a similar freedom, normality and coherent continuity of the seer logistic thought perception, then of the seer logistic lipi, with a beginning even in the profounder depths of samadhi (sushupta swapna), and a combination of these three powers, more obstructed, but still sufficient in action and normality. Other features of samadhic experience occurred in briefer snatches, but always significant and sufficient by the aid of the gnostic thought to yield their context and significance. The distinguishing character of the whole movement was the action of the observing thought actualising and understanding each experience and distinguishing in the scenes presented between the worlds and spheres of which they were a part. The mental worlds especially manifested in the more physical and [vital]^2 rungs of their

2 *MS* vitals

ascending order. Samadhi in the afternoon may now be considered
to have well founded its stable basis

There is a beginning of the full stability in the abundance of
the lipi, as well as in isolated lipis. There is a variation between
the three degrees, but each tends to its full duration. The perfect
duration exists dissolved, but still present in the three degrees.

At night the lipi niradhara and sadhara fixed itself in the third
degree of stability; it is also developing positive trikaldrishti of
sadhana in the highest seer logistis.

Gnosis is leaning more upon the hermetic element in the highest
seer logistis and seeking to make this the whole thought instrumentation, but the laxity still leans to a lesser force of seer logistis
burdened with the siege of the old idealised uncertain mentality. The
descents to lesser forms are decreasing in frequency and incidence.

At night laxity and the lower form of dream; but in the morning
some force of increasing lipi in the depths of samadhi.

Aug 28th   Thursday.

T^2 has now taken possession of the telepathy and is interpreting all the former movements in an increasing mass of logistic
experience. There is an increase of the precise appreciation of tendency, including thought tendency and impulse tendency, in the
effective force of dynamic seeing Tapas and in the relative or dominant telepathic certitude,—the certitude resulting from selective
idea force in the tendencies and circumstances subject to potential reversal by some greater force. All this is in an intermediate
seer logistis containing the hermeneutic element, but not filled and
possessed by it. The quite positive trikaldrishti in the seer logistis is
quiescent awaiting the hermesis. The trikaldrishtic commenting and
interpreting thought speech is now combined with the perception..

Full third degree stability in all kinds of lipi subject to a certain
initial uncertainty and some impediment in the immediate rapid
legibility

In Samadhi an obstructed but still developing movement. The
features not yet perfectly free presented themselves with more force
of coherent continuity, but not in any abundance. Lipi in the depths
was more coherent, but with effort and not in a free normality. Full

freedom has been gained only for the thought, thought-speech and lighter lipi.

There was some attempt of the vishaya to break down the obstruction that again prevents its more frequent recurrence and progress, but success was small. Rasa is most apt to come in abundance, but not with perfection. Gandha is perfect, but comes with only an occasional spontaneity, otherwise it is obstructed. Both come daily, and are therefore established, but not yet frequently and freely. However by today's effort the tendency in rasa to recur has been greatly strengthened, as well as its mass; gandha in inhalation comes more easily; both have profited by the tapas. Sparsha increased in incidence, but was soon stopped by obstruction. Speech shabda came once only with no sequel. Drishya progress is obstructed.

Effort to develop higher trikaldrishti, not yet come to fruition. Telepathy is becoming more concrete and intimate, sanjna added to prajnana and embridged vyapti, — perception in being to perception in idea.

Relapse is now chiefly powerful in the physical siddhi. There is a revived sensitiveness to cold and an attempt to restore its results in roga. The tapas however is powerful enough to prevent any strong materialisation. In the central rogas there is a relapse, in one due to persistent overstrain on the centre, in the other a mechanical repetition of recrudescence.

Friday Aug 29th

T^2 this morning has made a large stride forward. A full free and normal thought or jnana of tapas and trikaldrishti has now associated itself with the actual perceptions (vyapti prakamya) and this has enormously increased the rapidity of progress which is now returning to what used to be called the enthusiastic (ie the luminous or fiery or both) and anandamaya rapidity in lipi, jnana and T^2, while it is partly active in samadhi.   The Shakti has first converted into the seer logistis the constantly recurring remnants of the old actualistic telepathies of the intuitive mind, intuition, inspiration and inferior (semi-intellectual) revelation; then the dynamic telepathies and tapas thought on the basis of accurate possibility, sometimes but not always full and complete in its vision – it is when some possibilities are ignored that error of stress becomes most tempting and facile; finally it is bringing out the telepathic decisions and relating them to and converting them into the nontelepathic or pure trikaldristic certitudes. The two first movements are now finally founded and the old errors can only recur by mechanical force of habit without any other justification, since there is no void of knowledge to justify their blinder seeking. The third is only just being founded with the final firmness, but the foundation is not yet complete.

No Samadhi in the afternoon. The other members of the siddhi are held back by the obstruction; but in antardarshi the force of lipi stability is increasing.

Aug 30th Saturday.
T^2 attained to a certain final basic action of certitude. The rest of the siddhi made no ascertainable progress.

Aug 31st Sunday.
The obstruction is now without being removed rendered null for the ideality. Lipi in the jagrat is moving forward, increasing the normality of the third degree of stability and its force of duration, bringing the rapid legibility in the stability and rejecting all unstable lipi. The ideal thought is enforcing its free, normal, pervading action and bringing it to the level of the thought speech in this normality and freedom. Trikaldrishtic thought shares in this new perfection. T^2 is increasing with a remarkable rapidity in frequency of logistic certitude. The normal character is now that of the logistic seer ideality either with a strong dynamic and hermetic force, successful tapas enforced by jnana, or of the same thing, but with full logistic revelation. The old inferior or middle seer logistis which was a correct adjustment of possibilities is giving way to this form – it recurs but without sanction for endurance – in which possibilities and certitudes are combined, but with the latter in domination. Tapas without knowledge is now being rejected and condemned to exclusion. The still existent defect arises chiefly from imperfection of vision of time, place and a certain and indisputable order and

fullness of circumstance. These things can only be initially established in the seer logistis, since their sure fullness begins in the hermetic ideality.

Darshana which fluctuates between Ananda and mentality, is now increasing its insistence on the force of the vijnanamaya darshana, as only by fixity in the gnostic seeing can it get rid of the lapse to the defects of Ananda.

Samadhi is in a state of lapse; today in the afternoon after a day of interruption and one of unsuccess, it is trying to recover, but nidra has taken hold and prevents the freedom. At night incoherent or fanciful dream occupies the sleep. The other siddhis are preparing to recover, but cannot yet put aside the obstruction.

September.

Absolute finality is not yet gained in the first chatusthaya, for the fragments of external touches of asamata are able to touch the physical parts of the physical mentality, nor in the second for the Devi Bhava is pushed down to the old mental form and that survives in the sense of the body even when the rest is in the ideal Devibhava.   The ideality is founded in the highest seer ideality though the lower forms still recur mainly in T^2, because that is still imperfect in circumstance; but the vijnana is constantly increasing. Its action is still capable of suspension during the later part of the day owing to laxity. The ideal traigunya siddhi is increasing, physical tamas giving more and more place to çamas, but the entire union of the three gunas is not absolute, because the physical mentality is still not wholly changed into the gnosis. These asiddhis are yet becoming more and more interruptions rather than permanent deficiencies. Samadhi has founded itself, but is free only in thought and lipi, and is capable of lapse. Rupa and vishaya are obstructed in their progress. The physical siddhi is in a state of relapse, though certain beginnings are established with some finality.

Sept 1   Monday

T^2 has to be made entirely valid in circumstance and a first movement is being made towards this development, but it is at once assailed by the old causes of incertitude and wrong placement. These act more easily when there has to be a multiple and rapid seeing than when there can as in simple cases with few details and slower movements be a deliberate exercise of the vijnana Shakti. There there is not only an increasing correctness of gnostic appreciation or judgment in the direct seeing, but an extension of it to more remote eventuality.

Gandha in inhalation has developed perception of neutral odours and with this new basis there is a great increase of frequency of positive gandhas. The spontaneous gandha is now rather more frequent. But the obstruction is still resisting eviction and retarding progress.   Rasa is more active, but has not yet gained a firm basis.

Rupa is once again active; it is striving for stability as the basis for its perfection.   K.A active, but not in settled continuity.

Sept 2   Tuesday.

T² today is again troubled by the external invasion; it is evidently preparing for a fresh extension, but this as usual has brought about a trouble of resistance and irruption.   Drishya once again active; a few forms of greater stability in ghana rupa; tejomaya rupa in scenes etc of the first stability and continuity, but mere drishti, the thought in the drashta inhibited by nidra; in the early morning some mass of coherent reading.

Sept. 3 to 24 —

This has been a period corresponding to the old long relapses, when as there was no continuous progress, nothing could be written. But the relapse has only been a fact in the physical siddhi, which has been entirely suspended, except for occasional movements soon falling off into inactivity. There has been even some relapse of positive roga; the fragmentary (catarrhic) rogas have tried to lay their hold persistently, but are always manageable by the tapas; the two central have prevailed without being severely aggravated. On the other hand Samata is constantly making itself more firm in the Ananda, more massive and imperturbable. It is not yet free from occasional pressure of the exterior physical pressure, but this is becoming rare and very vague. Shakti has also been fixing itself more and more, but varies from the *vijnana ghanata* to the physical-mental laxity; the first tends more and more to predominate. Vijnana has lapsed only for adjustment. All is intuitive mentality even in error, and all has been steadily transforming to the seer ideality. The defect is still in T^2 which draws down the others, but normally thought is of the seer ideality, and always when there is not the physical relaxation. T^2 has been increasing in the seer ideality and mere intuivity is being progressively eliminated. The extension is general, but not yet quite fixed in the higher ideal jyoti. Time place circumstance are the great difficulty. Tapas is increasing in force and applying initially to the immediately surrounding life-action, but against great opposition.

Sept 24   Wednesday.

Lipi for the first time has risen from the seer ideality of the logistis, to the hermetic vijnana. It is now the full logistis in the hermesis; beyond is the middle hermesis and beyond that the seer hermesis. Thought is rising into the fullness and pervasion of the complete seer logistis, all logistic levels are there, but all full of the seer logistis.

1ˢᵗ Feb.

> Thought to be set entirely free
> T^2 to be thoroughly idealised and given certitude.
> Tapas siddhi to be made luminously effective.
> Physicality to be brought under control of Tapas.
> Rupasiddhi and samadhi.

———

> First get rid of the physical lapse.

=

> The çraddha has to be firm and absolute

———

> First week of February
> Three chatusthayas.
> Perfection of 2ᵈ chatusthaya.
> Shakti. Idealised and intellectual perfection.

=

> The highest ideality in the highest log[ist]ical ideality.

=

> Lipi, thought-speech, jnana perfected on this level of vijnana
> T^2 perfected a little later, but rapidly all the same.
> Rupa-siddhi and samadhi

=

4ᵗʰ

> The physical lapse in the subjectivity has been nearly got rid
> [of], but not quite eliminated. Its force however and effectuality
> have been much diminished and are being brought to the vanishing
> point.
> The çraddha is now firm, but not yet absolute.

=

Shakti has got its intellectual perfection, so far as the word can be applied, and is getting its ideal perfection.

=

This is due to an extraordinarily rapid development of the whole system into the highest logistic ideality, — first elimination of mental intuivity, confirmation in intuitive revelatory vijnana, then rise to interpretative revelatory, then to revelatory full of founded power of inspiration. The lower forms of vijnana occur from outside.

=

The prana and body are also being taken up by this ideality..

=

The process is not yet quite complete.

There is a rapid development of combined action of all the parts of the siddhi, but this is as yet only being founded, not complete.

Thought-speech, jnana [and][1] primary T[2] are being founded on the highest logistis

=

Rupa and samadhi are still obstructed and pressing on the obstruction.

=

Some progress in rejecting obstruction in samadhi

=

Attack of the intuitive mind from outside, only temporarily successful in a partial invasion —
The idealistic force is strong enough to reestablish its hold.

Feb 6th
All February the struggle in the physical siddhi.

=

Feb 7th
In spite of the intuitive mental [invasion][2] —

---

[1] MS or
[2] MS evasion

(1) The interpretative or inspirational ideality has manifested itself with some power in lipi, thought[,] trikaldrishti etc. The logistic ideality remains but is surpassed.

(2) Lipi has got rid of the insistence of small intuitive vijnana, though it is still capable of some lapse.

(2)[3] The rest of the ideality is labouring to follow in its steps and get rid of all lower forms.

(3) In lipi revelatory logistis is now becoming the lower and not the higher form. The interpretative is the rule.

(4) Ananda is progressing and transforming itself first to the discriminative revelatory logistic then the interpretative and getting rid of the intuitive mental form. It is now persistent when there is smarana.

Feb 7th[4]
    The second week of February.

(1) Lipi to be fixed in the second vijnana.

(2) Thought, T^2, to be raised to the second vijnana, the logistis only a lower form.

(3) Ideal Shakti to possess the body.

(4) Ananda to fix itself and be no longer dependent on smarana.

(5) Insistence on ideal Tapas control in arogya, utthapana, saundarya.

(6) Completeness of Brahmachatusthaya.

(7) Rupa and samadhi.
    =

All these will not be complete, but all will advance. The rule of rapidity has to be brought in everywhere.

Ananda overcomes in type the obstacle of vismriti and has almost established the continuity. It is established in type and in dominant tendency, but is still resisted, sometimes briefly suspended by strong absorption. Sleep brings a total discontinuation, but the recovery is swift.

---

[3] *This item and the two that follow were misnumbered.* —Ed.
[4] *This, the second entry dated 7 February, is written on a different sheet from the previous entry.* —Ed.

Feb 8th

A certain lapse tendency. Ananda persists but with frequent momentary vismriti. The T^2 moves for a while in the telepathies. The thought-system is arriving through a last struggle to the condition of the lipi divided between the interpretative as the right and normal, the logistic as the lower relaxed action to the exclusion of the intuitive mentality.

=

Rupa-siddhi has been developing since yesterday fluidity, perfection of form (not always complete)[,] vividness, but not stability. Variety is poor as yet and stability only initial or primary.

=

Ananda is now constant (afternoon) but often forgotten by absorption yet present; sometimes this forgetfulness brings momentary cessation. Sleep brings cessation; but the obstacle is now being attacked, though not yet overcome.

=

T^2 has descended to rectify and turn into interpretative telepathic ideality.

Ananda Brahman is confirming itself in prema, kama and beauty.

Obstacle to Samadhi persists, but is slowly yielding.

=

At night a lapse to mentality.

=

Feb 9th

The whole ideality after a violent depression is now passing into the revelatory form of the interpretative vijnana. This is also laying hold on the body, but here more powerfully besieged by the intuitivity of the intelligence

=

The perfect shakti in the physical intelligence has been replaced in type by the perfect ideal shakti with the fourfold Devibhava.

=

Ananda is being reestablished in continuity after interruption.

Sahaituka has recommenced, but yet in a crude initial form. (since yesterday)

The Ananda is being idealised, but as yet not successfully; because the intuitive intelligence still normally holds the body.

Continuity of Ananda, forgotten sometimes but still existing has been established in type in Samadhi (morning).

Idealisation (rapid) in the revelatory interpretative form of the elements of samadhi has begun in the lipi etc.

=

Ananda absent in samadhi and sleep in the afternoon, but ideality at play, in dialogue etc. At times deep tamasic nidra hiding a core of sushupti, sometimes jagrat, sometimes আচ্ছন্ন

=

Ananda once more continuous in afternoon in spite of absorption in writing, finally with help of some smarana prevailed over absorption.

=

Ideal Shakti fixed in the body.

Feb 10th

Ideal Shakti is fixed in the body, lipi fixed in the vijnana, interpretative and revelatory of the two lower kinds. Thought-siddhi and T^2 is partly formed in the same idealities, but revelatory logistis predominates for the time. There is however a mixture of intelligence. Sharira Ananda discontinued at night by sleep and recovered with some difficulty in the morning. Brahma chatusthaya complete in Sarvam Anandam Brahma, Anantam Jnanam in essence. The Brahma-vision has now to be filled in with the vijnana. Rupa and Samadhi are progressing; rupa is still in the first stability, occasionally on the border of the second, recurrent, not steady in appearance. Ideal Samadhi baffled at night by sleep and dream: present in daytime but assailed by nidra.

Today thought-siddhi + T^2 ought to rid itself of the admixture.

The psychic suggestions, telepathy, vyapti, prakamya, possibility, doubt, denial etc are all being rapidly changed into the form of the revelatory logistis. There is a strong tendency to the interpretative form.

Ideal Shakti is being intensified into the Krishna Kali relation founded on madhura dasya.

Feb 14th

One day of lapse (12th), another of trouble of recovery. Eye malady, bleeding of nose, constipation; the will prevails only with a struggle.

The revelatory ideality is establishing itself, but with much fluctuation of adjustment, Shakti idealised in the body in the same way, sharira ananda similarly. The latter is being rapidly changed. As yet the siddhi has not recovered its full force of occupation.

Development of T^2 on the revelatory base but hampered by mentality and its invasion and siege.

15th 16th

Founding, in spite of difficulties, of the [ ]⁵ exclusive ideal action in thought-siddhi and T^2 as in script and lipi. In T^2 this is not complete and this has some reaction on thought-siddhi which is now being closely fused with T^2.

17th night. 18th

Recovery of vijnana in the system and rapid development of the ideality. The vijnana (revelatory of all kinds based on intuitive revelatory) is fixed in the system; lapses are only to intuitive ideality and momentarily to highly idealised mental intuitive.

19th

Interpretative revelatory vijnana has been rapidly rushed to the lead and holds it, but the intuitive rev. occurs frequently as a suggestion, but more and more filled with interpretative rev. V. Other lower forms only occur as suggestions from outside and are rapidly and increasingly turned into the right kind before or immediately after they enter the system.

During the lapse even the purely unmixed character of the mental intuitive, though it held the system, was made more and

⁵ MS the

more clear. The ideality then continued in spite of this hold and
was quite firm in lipi, script and often in thought-speech. Now
even these suggestions cannot come in the mental form; only in
laxity there is often a sort of mental cloud about the ideal form.

Lipi, script, thought-speech are now firm in the ideality;
thought-perception and T^2 are also substantially ideal, but to some
extent in laxity of the shakti affected by the mental shadow. They
are however being rapidly subjected to thorough idealisation. When
the shakti is not pramatta, the mental shadow does not touch, but
the lower forms are more common as yet than the revelatory; the
contrary is the rule in the other members.

Vyapti is still chiefly of the mental kind

The interpretative revelatory since last night is being fixed in
the system—the essentiality of it, its status in the tissue of the conscious being. But there is already the urge to the revelatory in its
own highest kind.

The lipi which has been ideal of all kinds is now shedding the
intuitive vijnana and keeping only the revelatory and interpretative.

Fixed in the interpretative form of all kinds it is now immediately (after five minutes, in the same uninterrupted movement)
lifting up all to the revelatory vijnana in its three forms. This done
in a minute or two it is drawing all into the highest form. This is
the first instance of such a large miraculous rapidity

Vyapti is now coming in the revelatory vijnana, but of the
totality of the bhava in the object; the particular movements are
seen in it, but are undergoing a thorough idealisation, even in the
mental intuitivity.

As a result also trikaldrishti tapas is beginning to be seen as a
movement out of being and no longer only in their separate forms.

The complete idealisation of the tivra ananda whether ahaituka or sahaituka is taking place.

The insistence on the physical siddhi has been increasingly
relaxed for the last few days. There is now scanty K.A. It is being
transformed into the revelatory ideal K.A, but the transformation
is much opposed by the survival of old idealised intuitive Ananda.
The other Anandas are sharing the change.

The second half of the day possession by the intuitive mind from outside. Progress under difficulties.
=

20th Feb.   Friday.

Rapid progress in spite of mental siege.

(1) Shakti in system fixing the essential being in representative revelatory vijnana; interpretative force present, but not insistent in manifestation. Occasional covering by inspirational intuitive idealised mind.

(2) Lipi deepening into the revelatory largeness even in intuitive vijnana type.

Rapid and powerful development of fixed stability in lipi sadhara and niradhara.

(3) Strong development of ideal thought-siddhi in all forms; rapid and continuous ideal thought-perception, jnana

(4) Developing certitude in trikaldrishti, but much enveloped in idealised mind-matter.

(5) Increasing ideal-power in kavya.

(6) Triumphing tendency to bring all mental action into the ideal form; but there are lapses.

(7) Progress in idealisation and in [s]table jagrat of the three forms of swapna samadhi in the afternoon. Internal lipi in antardarshi fixed in representative revelatory vijnana; continuity in swapna of ideal thought siddhi in speech and perception sometimes accompanied by rupa and drishya.

21st Feb.   Saturday.

(1) Idealisation of the intuitive (mental) thought-siddhi jnana and T^2 knowledge, dominant but not absolutely complete.

(2) Immediately (in the morning) the movement turned to the normalising of the interpretative revelatory vijnana in all the mind and supermind, and after certain fluctuations this came in the evening

(3) In antardarshi interpretative revelatory vijnana in the lipi. The rest of the siddhi active in swapna, but limited and diminished by heavy attack of sleep.

(4) The interpretative in the shakti of the physical system has now filled the representative revelatory vijnana; the content is interpretative, the shell representative (logistic revelation).

(5) The Tapas is now acting vigorously on the physical asiddhi in the different remnant rogas and has begun on the most persistent central incapacity, in the latter as yet without dominant effect. The remnants still recur with a temporary show of force but cannot resist the dissipating action

(6) In the morning a remarkable solitary instance of the complete and rapid effectivity of the Tapas on inanimate things. This is practically the first instance.

(7) The T^2 is now normalised in the ideality, though still besieged and sometimes penetrated by the intuitivity, but it is no longer cased in the intuitive mental matter.

$=$

Today closes the third week of February and completes a definitive stage of the union of samata, shakti and vijnana. The asiddhi is not entirely exiled, but has lost its power to hold except for touches and a momentary (in the first two) or a brief (in the third) interval. Negative Asamata is only a touch and nothing more, but defect of sama ananda is still possible for a short while.

The next week must complete the perfection of the luminous revelatory reason.

It is also suggested that the rupa, vishaya and samadhi will develop finality of basic perfection.

There is also some preparation for the overcoming of the obstruction in Ananda and Arogya. In saundarya and utthapana the definitive effectivity has not come, but primary utthapana is being prepared for its basis by the steady pressure on the habit of fatigue. There the old strenuous defect of anima has little hold; it comes only in fragments, little as pain, mainly as stiffness. Fatigue is the chief asiddhi.

$=$

Tomorrow T^2 in the interpretative drishti. Ananda. Renewed hold on physical siddhi. Rupa-vishaya. Samadhi.

$=$

(1) Resumption of continuous Ananda, but as yet with insufficient force of spontaneous action.

(2) Shakti shown in resistance to an attack of many remnants of roga. Only three still survive at all in fact, the eye-watering, the stomach affections and the central weakness. All except the last are much reduced, and even the last is much modified in force.

(3) Samadhi progressive at night and in the morning. All is ideal, drishya included, but all is now turning to the revelatory vijnana. Drishya is becoming more complete and stable. Lipi in deep swapna shows a tendency to return to coherence.

Feb 22d Sunday

In the samata the siege of the exiled intuitivity throws a shadow of defect on the hasya and therefore on the sukham and equal Ananda. This is only when there is the withholding of the full play of the Shakti.

In the shakti the defect that emerges is a deficiency of height of force, aishwarya-bodha, hasya and çraddha in the immediate action of the Shakti.

None of these defects are real, but imposed on the system from outside by a shadow of the old habit of the physical mind.

=

These defects have now to be finally excised. There is already a commencement of the conversion of the surrounding activity to the ideal terms.

=

The first two chatusthayas cannot be quite absolute until the vijnana is universal and free from any suspension of the ideal action.

≡

The rupa and vishaya show signs of reinitiation and of a firmer ideal completeness, but as yet there is no freedom or dominance of stability.

The difficulty of T^2 is now the adjustment between the higher and lower perceptions; so long as this lasts the surrounding intuitive mind is led to invade with its inadequate suggestions. But this mind now promises to turn into the ideal form.

Ananda is now again active, but subject to the recurrence of its old disabilities and still drawn down to the mental intuitive manner. Ideal Ananda comes in as an exception.

Rupa shows great vividness and perfection (not always completeness) and vividness of all forms, perfect, developed, ghana, crude; but except in the last it is only in the initial and primary stabilities

In the afternoon much sushupta swapna samadhi. An outburst of the highest revelatory lipi, vivid and powerful beyond anything yet seen in the jagrat bahirdarshi. Much lipi in the sushupta, ordinarily but not always coherent. Much revelatory vijnana; all ideal. But the hold was still insufficient and besieged not by the actuality, but by the vague consciousness of dream.

Today from the morning lapse towards mentality for the transformation of the surrounding mind. This has brought back unideal telepathy trikaldrishti tapas to a certain extent, but the ordinary thought seems secure. All however is hampered by the invasion. T^2 at the moment acts only in the representative vijnana with relative and occasional certitude, the truth of each suggestion stands, but not the decisive value the tapasic mind outside fastens on its indications. When the full ideality acts, each is reduced to its native proportions, but there is no future certitude, or only a relative morally certain indication of the future.

There is the same phenomenon in the interpretative representative T^2, on the lower scale. It remains to be seen what happens when both are lifted to and combined on the higher scale.

Vishaya is again manifesting vividly, but without freedom; only the old customary drishya, rasa, gandha, sparsha, the few limited things. Shabda is obstructed as before.

Ananda is now recovering a firmer, though still imperfect base.

There is much struggle in the primary utthapana; the two rogas are also still successfully obstructive. The Shakti persists in the utthapana and does not allow a long collapse.

Today pain (sharp in the shoulders) returned momentarily in the primary utthapana, but immediately subsided. Fatigue is strong, by cumulative effect; there is [no]where a successful reaction.

A strong interpretative revelatory vijnana of the Shakti in the physical system.
=

At night great vividness and constancy of the basic rasas.

T^2 in the interpretative revelatory and highest revelation of the third scale. All now is the third scale, ie, the divine reason.

Magnificent drishya in the deep and deepest swapna samadhi, scenes, happenings etc, great stability, perfection, sometimes chhayamaya of tejas, sometimes vivid with some jyoti in the tejas. A little force of chhaya however everywhere. Afterwards dream but with much coherence.

Feb 23^d Monday.

Today T^2 to develop highest certitude. Rupa, vishaya, samadhi. Ananda to idealise and to overcome obstacles. Pressure of Shakti on roga and obstacles to primary utthapana.
=

Yesterday there was in T^2 much confusion of the lower inadequate forms, insufficient half representative, half intuitive forms, mind-coated intuitivities and intuitivised mental suggestions from outside, inspirational forms without the discrimination etc; the highest certitudes finally emerging assailed with dubiety from the luminous chaos. Now the discriminating interpretative revelatory power is settling itself in the T^2. The intuitivities of all kinds are being rejected where they resist transformation, replaced or transformed when they admit change. The highest certitude of the third scale is acting now and then; the occasional certitudes are frequent. There is still much to be done.

Ananda is idealising itself with occasional lapses.

Lipi is now finally getting rid of the strong relics of the intuitive and the weak relics of the inspirational ideal lipi. The representative and interpretative lipi of all degrees take the place.

T^2 is now getting rid of all forms of tejasic and tapasic stress; but the work is not yet finished. The highest certitudes await the growth and completion of this eliminative process.

The battle is going on in the primary utthapana. The Shakti is trying to impose relief in standing and relief in walking and add them to the relief by sitting. But as yet it is only a temporary incomplete relief. The attack of fatigue is heavy and fierce.

=

Afternoon. Samadhi, ideal thought and speech continued in deeper swapna, but sushupta much under the power of nidra.

=

The force of ananda increases, but is much cased in inspirational and inspired intuitive mentality. The density tends to diminish in the idealised form. It is however becoming more intense in this form.

=

The T^2 acts now normally in the middle form. The higher action is exceptional except so far as it is translated into the middle form.

=

Rupa and Vishaya have been less active today. Vishaya is trying to manifest particular tastes in their subtle general essence

Feb 24th   Tuesday
Last night T^2 action of various kinds, none entirely satisfactory, though one uplifted above the lower movements which gave some of the highest certitudes. At night wakefulness with intervals of swapna samadhi good of its kind; only towards morning nidra.

Today strong attack of besieging intuivity on all ideal members. In lipi this results in persistence of intuitive ideal lipi representing the intuitive mentality in the ideality, but not itself mental in kind. An insufficient speech and suggestion is its limitation; it is true in itself, but so expressed as to mislead the mind. It is rejected in favour of the intuitive revelatory or at lowest revelatory [intuitive],[6] representative and interpretative lipi, but still recurs sometimes in spite of prohibition.

In thought-siddhi the same process is taking place, but the recurrence of lower forms of ideal speech is strong and occasionally there is the half idealised mental suggestion from outside.

---

[6] *MS* intuition

Nevertheless lower ideal forms are now banned by the law of the Shakti.

In script as in lipi, but the lower forms are more rebellious to exclusion.

T^2 is most affected. Here too it is definitely settled that only the highest ideal reason is to give the certitudes and the recurrence of the lower forms however strong and obstructive to the proper action is not to be accepted, even if they give the truth.

Ananda promised last night to prevail, but this morning has been discontinued except in smarana.

=

T^2 perfect, decisive and invariably effective in the representative highest vijnana, but only in distinct isolated final results; the rest of a lower type besieged by mentality and confusing the mind by trying to figure as this representative ideal action.

In Samadhi much nidra.

Feb 25th   Wednesday
T^2, the representative vijnana is taking up detail, but not all the detail. The confused action of the rest continues, but is becoming clearer by restriction. The Shakti now tends to allow provisionally all ideal T^2, but to accept only the forms of the highest ideality with a total acceptance, partially accept the revelatory forms of the lower (inspirational and intuitional) stages, observe only in order to reject or transform the survivals of mental suggestion. The rest occurs, but is partially sanctioned only when there is some revelatory force or interpretative in it or at the back.

Feb 26th   Thursday.
The interpretative-representative highest ideality has now definitely replaced all other action as the standard movement in the T^2. The others still persist in laxity of the system. This ideality is now absorbing all the thought-siddhi and proving its truth and certitude.

=

At night this ideality, at first only able to act above the head free from the physical levels, began to act spontaneously on the head level. It begins to replace the physical tendency to intuivity and is descending to take possession of the whole system. At the same time it is adapting itself and taking possession of all kinds of thought perception in the nature. This it has done, first in the interpretative, then in the lower idealities.

All the vishayas, the others in little, gandha and rasa more in large.

Abundant rupa in the samadhi.

Friday 27th February

T^2 is now fixing itself in the complete ideality, first in the lower forms with some help from the highest interpretative vijnana. All is now turned to its elements of truth, but the last difficulties of the old excessive stress still remain. The rest is a difficulty of limitation and incertitude.

Afterwards something like a deliberate lowering or collapse, but even in this laxity the ideal tendency prevails, but not its order.

Sharira Ananda long neglected and occasional only by smarana is resumed today and restored to an interrupted continuity, while the remnants of the mental form are being rapidly idealised by the highest vijnana.

Rupa is obstructed, though it acts under call of tapas. It has gone back to the initial or very primary stability.

Vishaya acts but under obstruction.
=

Stable crude rupa (perfect in line) at night.

Saturday 28th February

Lapse.

The lipi has begun to reject all but the highest vijnana (chiefly interpretative) or else its light in other forms. The same process is beginning in antardarshi.

In Samadhi tertiary and perfect stability of rupa, scene and coherent movement begins to occur. Also conversation, no longer mental only, but the physical word. The elements of samadhi have now [to be][7] developed and combined, the [.......] more steady in spite [...................]

Thought speech has [...........] reject all [but the] forms of the highest vijnana or else its light and form on lower levels.

Sunday 29th February.

Today the whole vijnana has lifted to different levels of the revelatory vijnana. Even the highest drashta logos has manifested as well as the highest interpretative ideality. The basis of the luminous reason has been perfectly founded and what is now left is to perfect and make it universal in its embrace.

The first necessity is to get rid of the lower stratum of intuitive mentality, then to exclude the circumvironing mentality.

This has already begun to be done and for some time the shakti in the body is fixed in the basic third ideality, its contents varying from the intuitive to the revelatory, with interpretative and other floating. Even the intrusions from the surrounding ideality are now for the most solidly idealised though with a suspicion of strong intuitive mentality not easily distinguish[able] from a [ ][8] concentrated doubly illumined vijnana.

Rupa has suddenly at night manifested several old forms (reel, ribbon wound reel, bat, brushes etc) in ghana & developed with strong ghana tendency in the second and third (mostly third) stability.

Samadhi is still hampered by obstruction.

---

[7] *The page containing this paragraph and the next is damaged. Several words or groups of words are partly or wholly lost. The words printed between square brackets are conjectural.* — Ed.

[8] MS a

1 MARCH – 10 APRIL 1920

Yoga Diary.
1920
March.

The Yoga has been brought up during the last month to effectivity of vijnana. This vijnana is that of the lowest total stage of the triple ideal supermind, the domain of the luminous reason. First, there was the disappearance of the old intellectual into the intuitive mind and buddhi, and not only the thought-being, but the whole being including the consciousness in the body, the physical Ananda was brought up finally into this form, to the total exclusion of the old buddhi, sense and bodily consciousness. Here sattwa of the mind was changed into semi-luminous prakasha and jyoti of the mental intuition, inspiration and revelation, rajas into stress of tapasic will and impulse, tamas into a passive or a heavy shama. Tamas alone preserves in the more physical part of the being something of its old inertia and darkness, not entirely changed into passivity with involved or quiescent prakasha and tapas. This tamas is the cause of the persistence of the physical and other asiddhi.

And simultaneously the lower vijnana which represents the intellect in the forms of the ideal mind was developing its greater powers and finally turned into the ideal reason. At first this was done with a lower ideal intuition, discrimination, inspiration, revelation which have been developing for a long time, weighted, chequered, shot through, hampered by the defects of the intuitive mentality of the manasa buddhi. The lipi was the first to get clear of the manasa, — in the bahirdarshi waking state, the internal antardarshi jagrat followed long after, — next the script, next the thought-speech, finally, the thought-perception and only yesterday and not with an absolute perfection the trikaldrishtic thought-perception.

The relics of asamata persisted in a fragmentary occasional fashion so long as the defect of mentality in the Shakti has persisted in the physical consciousness; it did not belong to the system, but was imposed on it, so long as the outer mind could shoot in its arrows of suggestion or break in for a time and possess the surface. There is still a persistence of vague relics which are being steadily idealised out of existence. This is due to persistence of tamas element in the physical being and is part of laxity or physical depression. It is disappearing in proportion as the ideal Shakti fixes itself in the true vijnana. The chief defect is in insufficient force of hasya and ananda, although the sukham is strong and the hasyam and ananda can always be brought to the surface, but often there is a cloud not of duhkha, but of apravritti of positive ananda, especially of hasyamaya ananda, occasionally an excess of udasinata.

Shakti after fixing its base of intuitive mental power in the body, often replaced by ideal forms, is now fixed in a shell of revelatory or representative vijnana filled sometimes with intuition, sometimes with lower revelatory representative, representative-interpretative or interpretative content. Occasionally the higher revelatory drashta Shakti takes momentary possession: there is always now a tendency to its manifestation in the other figures. Virya, shakti (except laghuta sometimes in the physical fatigue or heaviness) are full and sufficient, but depend for their tejas, pravritti etc. on the state of the Devibhava. Devibhava has been established in all its parts, but is not always in the full overt action, because of apravritti of hasya and ishwarabhava. This siddhi awaits the full sraddha and vijnana. Sraddha in the Master of the being is fixed and complete, but sraddha in the Swashakti has been often diminished or overpowered by laxity and failure of siddhi. There is now full faith in the eventual perfection of the three first chatusthayas and the sixth, but incertitude as to physical siddhi, extent of karma and kama, completeness of the mission. This is only occasionally touched by a shadow of positive asraddha and even that now takes the shape of a strong incertitude.

Vijnana is based in the total ideality, but still besieged by the outer mind. All suggestions from the outer mind are now of the nature of intuitive mentality turned in entrance or almost turned into ideality, full at least of the vijnana stuff and manner, which seems like an incomplete vijnana. The play of the higher third vijnana is now occupying the system: revelatory intuition has taken the place of other intuitions and is already being turned into the representative, ie the highest intuitive revelatory reason; inspiration losing its over-stress and defect of discrimination is almost wholly turned into interpretative ideality, ie the highest inspired revelatory ideal reason, while the full drashta luminous reason has emerged in all its three forms, ie revelation with interpretation but the front representative, 2^d the front interpretative with intuition involved in the drishti, 3^d the whole drishti with the two other powers taken into the drishti. There are various combinations and permutations. This is completest in lipi, script and thought-speech; thought-perception is a little weighted down towards the intuitive, revelatory intuitive, or representative forms, but the others occur and take the field when there is full action of the vijnana Shakti. T^2 is now able to act with certitude, but this is not yet complete; the old telepathic form still labours to predominate. Telepathy of thought is developing, but chiefly of thought impulse, feeling, intention, not of pure thought; the whole mind of animals can be seen, but only partially the mind of men. Here there is still a wall of obstruction through which there is a forcing of prakamya vyapti. Concentration is necessary for this siddhi

Laxity occurs owing to physical tamas and prevents the full normality of the vijnana power, but can no longer[,] since yesterday[,] bring down the system to the mental level.[1]

Rupa is still struggling to establish the secondary and tertiary stability and all its other elements and its free play seem to be waiting for this siddhi, but it is now in frequent action. Samadhi has fixed the right ideal lipi in the antardarshi, developed many of its elements, but is obstructed by nidra in its further or at least in its rapid progress.

The physical siddhi is still the subject of battle. Some ground has been gained especially in the Ananda, but it has had to sacrifice

---

[1] *In the manuscript, "since yesterday" is written above "bring down"; the caret marking the point of insertion comes after "bring" instead of "longer". — Ed.*

the continuity once gained in order to change from the mental to the ideal form. The change is almost, but not quite or firmly complete. There is still persistence of old fragments of roga and the two or three chronic maladies. Sometimes two of them seem on the point of disappearing, but are then able to reassert their action. Primary utthapana fluctuates, saundarya is not able to manifest except in bhava.

Brahmadarshana made itself perfect in the Ananda on the mental vijnanamaya plane, it has had to sink back into vijnana and mentalised vijnana in order to redevelop on the ideal plane. Sarvam brahma is always there in bhava, always at disposal to the thought by smarana. The fullness of Anantam and Jnanam brahma awaits the fullness of the vijnana.

March 1ˢᵗ Monday.

The shakti in the body has suddenly changed its base from the fixed revelatory intuitive to the representative vijnana. There is already a tendency to change that to the interpretative basis.

A rapid alteration of the basic and immediately surrounding consciousness into the representative and interpretative forms of the vijnana has begun. The other idealities will still persist for a time; they must replace the imperfect idealities which till now have been coming in from the outside.

The Ananda-darshana is also passing through the same phase, but has not yet altogether got rid of the recurrence of mental vijnana and Ananda on the mental plane. These are associated with certain forms, the latter Ananda being inspirational in its idiom, persist repeatedly in attaching themselves to them, and can as yet only be rejected by second thought or effort of Tapas.

An attempt to accept and transform inspirational-interpretative overstress led to the outside mind breaking through and getting in some of its movements. It cannot hold, but brought the recurrent Asamata which is accustomed to attend failure of Satya and Tapas.

There is some beginning of the same changes in the thought telepathy.

T² this morning is without the sure and decisive revelatory

certitudes. Only late in the morning it is getting back into the true revelatory forms, but still much mixed with the others.

Premananda is developing the ideal drashta ananda.

Rupa is attempting to manifest variety of all kinds, but still obstructed by the physical refusal, although in an intermittent way it succeeds in its movement.

Lipi. July 15th = ideality = entire ideality in the body.
     =

The Ananda-darshana has succeeded in filling the inspirational mental with the interpretative ideal Ananda; at most the former comes only for a second and is immediately occupied by the vijnana.

In Samadhi lipi is becoming coherent in small lipis, but in larger masses it is coherent only in patches. The ideal consciousness is taking more possession of the swapna samadhi, but the deeper stages are still affected by nidra or half nidra or imperfect conscience.

In the evening action of outward mind turning to ideality, the full vijnana held back, finally a hampered and narrowed action of the higher vijnana

March 2d Tuesday.

The action of outer mentality in a mass of all kinds turned into the lower and lesser ideal action. The object to get rid of the coating, penetration, mixture of the intuitive mental being in the thought-action, as has already been done in script and lipi. Also of the glamour of confused light in the uncentralised ideal action.. This seems to have been done, but not so as to absolutely exclude the potentiality of farther intrusion and necessity of farther suddhi. The success seems to be absolute in thought-speech; there is a mixture of stress and incertitude in trikaldrishti, jnana thought-perception is held in doubt between the greater and lesser siddhi. Mind-cased confused perception and half-perception can still pursue the trikaldrishti. The higher vijnana acts with some difficulty and is not yet in free command of its highest forms, but it is growing in power to hold the adhara.

In the evening the thought-perception acquired the same freedom in the ideality as has already been attained by the other members; that is to say, without any watching, attention[,] concentration or use of will it acts rapidly and constantly without falling from the vijnana or being invaded by unideal suggestions. How far it will be able to cover at once all the T^2 remains to be tested.

The higher ideality in the T^2 is now taking a firm hold. The remnants of mental stuff floating about have become mostly ineffective except for limitation. The lower idealities act as an inferior accompaniment to the higher vijnana or take its place in lax moments.

Ananda is recovering intensity and continuity, but still needs the smarana. It varies between the mental and the ideal forms, mental in laxity, ideal when supported by the tapas, but now contrary to what had been the rule hitherto the ideal are the more intense.

In Samadhi lipi is almost entirely coherent, though not in any great mass, still in longer continuities than before. The other elements are also regularising themselves a little. Lipi is ideal in Samadhi, thought sometimes falls into the mentalised ideal at least in physical level and in intensity. The other members, eg rupa, do not seem yet to be vijnanamaya. Nidra is still a persistent obstacle, but swapna while it persists in nidra is ceasing to interfere constantly with samadhi.

March 3ᵈ Wednesday.

Ananda (sharira) has now a fluctuating continuity; the persistence of the mental forms forms the present chief obstacle. The falling of the intensity brings them into prominence. Nevertheless the ideal form is growing in power. Thought and writing no longer interfere necessarily with the body's smarana, but only when there is a total absorption in the writing etc or when a cloud of mental stuff comes in to interpose an element of the old formless abstraction of mind which attended absorption in a single subject or occupation. This is no longer a necessity, but a survival of habitude. The continuity has begun to prevail in this matter. The pervasiveness of the Ananda is also being prepared on a firmer foundation. And now even the cloud of mental abstraction no longer necessarily interrupts the ananda. It is only the exclusive absorption that is the ordinary obstacle. There is also the mechanical letting down of the

Shakti (eg at meal times and in the evening[)], that may interfere. Sleep and to a less extent samadhi remain a strong interruption. Fatigue is a power for diminution.

Tapas is greatly increasing in force and in ideal substance. T^2 is now passing through a stage in which the higher ideality is sometimes active, sometimes gives place to lower idealities. These are not proper any longer to the systems, but suggestions from outside.

Ananda during period of samadhi. The continuity remained almost throughout during the morning while writing a letter, an unprecedented circumstance. The lighter samadhi was constant in the Ananda. The deeper swapna samadhi is now getting free of nidra, except a shadow which gives a remoteness and sunless consciousness unfavourable to actuality. At the worst it is still samadhi, though nidramaya; gâdha-supta swapna. The Ananda in this deeper samadhi lost at first its continuity, and with it its mass, suffering diminution, recurred only in sharp and keen prolonged and frequent touches of great but narrow intensity which caused a spasm in the body and brought back the lighter state and then outer body consciousness. The samadhistha body consciousness is frequent, but of short duration. The more massed continuous Ananda occurred finally in all but the deepest supta swapna, but at a low power and remained half-involved, involved or lost in the nidramaya. The development has been extremely rapid and promises the complete conquest of swapna samadhi by the Ananda, as well as the complete expulsion of day nidra by samadhi. The next step will be the replacement of the profounder real nidra at night by swapna samadhi and sushupti. Sushupti here will not be sunya or alakshana, but vijnanamaya, anandamaya, chaitanyamaya, sanmaya.

Position now makes only a difference of degree, not of continuity in Ananda. Lying, it tends to be extremely intense, intense but less or of varying force in seated position, uncertain in standing posture. Walking has an effect of diminution of intensity. The mental form is being expelled; the form is ideal in ideality or ideal on the level of the mentality, a narrowed vijnanamaya. The mental has in fact been for some time really recurrent with a show of persistence. It is now merely recurrent. This shows that the physical consciousness has gone far in a first idealisation.

Pervasiveness is now becoming final, only the pervasion of the head offers some difficulty: there it is not, but tends to be quite continuous. In deeper samadhi Ananda sometimes shifts from head to body and body to head. This diminishes the constancy of the Ananda. But there are signs that this difficulty will not be long prevalent.

Lipi in the deep samadhi gains constantly in power and coherence. Rupa suddenly manifested perfect stability in one perfect form (a watch) prolonged for several minutes, though occasionally clouded over, yet reappearing, sometimes with a slight change of details. This endured through both swapna and deep antardarshi or half jagrat half swapna. For the rest, the rupa etc was spasmodic and disordered today, except for snatches.

T^2 on the lower level is now becoming fuller and more ordered and certain, though still shot through with inaccurate suggestions, ie wrong stresses. The struggle is between ideal perception of possibility (actualities even being suggested as possibilities) attended often with false stress of certitude and ideal perception of actuality (possibilities being seen as actual forces unfulfilled or partially effected) with right stress of certitude. Both come from the outer consciousness and are not native to the adhara. Only the higher vijnana on the highest or middle level is native to the adhara.

The T^2 and with it other siddhis dropped towards the lowest levels even with some hint of the mentality. Ananda was lowered to an interrupted continuity and suffered much intrusion of the mental forms. Now the highest vijnana is again at work in the thought-siddhi and a recovery is in progress.

Thought siddhi with some T^2 recovered and founded itself more firmly than before in the interpretative vijnana. All other movements, when they occur, are not accepted or invested with credit, except in so far as they are touched by the drashtri vijnana.

Ananda took some time in emerging from the interrupted continuity. The full intensity continued through a fairly long spell of reading, but was diminished and interrupted at the close. In type however all obstacles have been conquered, except sleep.

Sleep prevailed at night, only in the morning imperfect swapna samadhi. Lipi at first a little confused, but reasserted coherence. The morning samadhi is now coming up to the level of the afternoon swapna. Sleep for about six hours. Dream, while retaining its inconsequence, is sometimes curiously idealised in some of its incidents or features

Thursday Mar 4.

The Ananda varies now between three conditions. At night interruption, but restorable by smarana. Restoration automatic after rising. At daytime (except for samadhi) a highest, middle or a diminished condition. The marks of the last are interrupted continuity, much intrusion and some persistence of mental forms, a low or varying intensity. The marks of the first and second are uninterrupted continuity, exclusion of mental forms, sustained or great intensities; but the second is prone to the inspirational, the first to the interpretative vijnana. Tapas is still necessary for the first, partially or initially necessary for the second condition.

T^2 varies also between three conditions. The lowest is a diluted revelatory vijnana with mixture of other, often now mentally encased suggestions, and is afflicted with confusion and incertitude. The middle is a higher representative form, but touched by lower suggestions, into which stress of tapas or hasty certitude brings an element of error, and which is only correct when limited to immediate balancing trikaldrishti. The highest is interpretative and gives correct finalities. The difficulty of taking up all detail into the highest form is not yet overcome.

Other siddhis are not moving much, but there is a beginning of final idealisation of rupa and vishaya, especially gandha and rasa.

T^2 in the lowest scale of the interpretative vijnana has regularised itself in place of the revelatory ideal seeing, excluding the lower suggestions, which recur less frequently and are given no valid credit. They cannot be easily excised altogether, until their place has been taken by the highest vijnana. This can only give immediate certitudes. But the higher powers are sometimes acting in this lowest scale. This is a preparation for their own final emerge[nce], self-basing and replacement of the lowest interpretative vision.

The middle interpretative vijnana is now being developed, but is not yet clear of foreign (mainly the lower revelatory and inspirational) elements; the lower interpretative has begun to be excluded; its work will be taken up by the higher movements..

Thought-telepathy is being idealised like the other elements, but as yet in a mind-cased revelatory vijnana touched with the interpretative atmosphere.

The rest of the day taken up by a mixed action in which the middle interpretative has been taking in the lower action and generalising itself; but it is itself now being rejected from its insufficiency of decisiveness when not filled with the highest drishti. It is acting still, as also subordinately to it the occasional lower revelatory, and growing in accuracy and fullness, but it is filling slowly with the drishti.

Ananda has sunk into the lowest stage of the third condition and is much interrupted, but is slowly getting rid of the persistent mental form recurrence and preparing a temporary rule of the second condition.

Samadhi is obstructed but even in obstruction maintains with a little impairment its recent strongest gains.

Mar. 5. Friday

The drishti now promises to take the place of the interpretative form in T^2 and thought-siddhi. This is at first being done or rather prepared by a slow and fluctuating movement.

Ananda is wavering between the second condition and a compromise between the third and second, a basic uninterrupted continuity of the inspirational or representative kind, but also spells of interruption, interrupted continuity and a weight of recurrent mentality overlaying by invasion.

In the afternoon samadhi oppressed by nidra. Shama darkened by some element of tamas in the system; a depression or relative inactivity of tapas.

The drishti has emerged in the evening in T^2 and thought-siddhi, but has not a complete hold or satisfying fullness. In Ananda the tendency is to a fluctuation between the second condition and an interpretative drishti in the form of the Ananda, a higher version of the third condition. But the hold is still wanting in strength and continuous insistence.

Mar 6 Saturday

The endeavour today has been to get rid entirely of the lower and mediary forms, but this attempt brought an invasion of these forms, a confusion and a stressing of the difficulty of adjustment to the old proportions of a struggle. The siddhi on its positive side progresses, as has been lately more and more the rule in such crises, in the midst of the confusion. Thought-siddhi frequently manifests the highest form of the drashtri reason, T^2 occasionally gets at some incomplete form of it. But the main movement has been the persistent increasing rejection of the lowest forms in spite of their persistent recurrence; they cannot long hold the system and are beginning to lose power at all to put their grasp on the thought-consciousness. The mediary forms on the other hand penetrated or not by the drishti lay a strong temporary hold, persist for a long time, prevent the highest drishti, and when it manifests, rush into its place and try to do its functions and imitate its manner. This is the old method of progress. But the rule insisted on at present is that of the higher replacing and resuming the lower powers, not of the lower seizing on the higher and drawing them down to their level. This rule sometimes act[s] but cannot as yet assert its firm dominance.

Ananda continues to vary between its different formations, but now on the whole the tendency is to bare continuity of the highest condition (not its full pervasion, intensity and possession) in smarana. There is now a movement towards possession or at least pervasion in smarana.

The thought and with a less certainty the T^2 has now entered with some firmness on the same state as the script and lipi in which the various forms all belong to the full ideality and belong to the drishti with rarer deviations to the lesser forms still penetrated and covertly possessed by the drishti. But here the process is not yet absolutely complete.

Some play of gandha and rasa and of stable ghana or ghana developed rupa, mostly in the second stability; but the forms are old forms already seen in a previous far past state of the rupa sadhana. Strong dream coherence in nidra.

Mar 7. Sunday.

The T^2 is proceeding with the development of the drishti. The movement goes much over old ground and confirms the stable hold of the drishti in the lesser ideal action. First, the lower form has been successfully converted; this gives near future and present potentialities valued in the terms and powers of the immediate actuality and frequently fulfilled according to the exact balance seen of the immediate present and future actuality, but barren of absolute future certitudes. Now the mediary form has been converted. This takes up the immediate potentialities, includes distant ones, and deals more largely with near and far potential, relative, temporary and isolated certitudes. But the near is more strongly and frequently dealt with than the farther, the farther more than the very distant; the last is still very rare. The chief difficulty is the survival of uncertain or self-regardingly positive stress, and this though less ignorant and vehement than in the mentality, less positive than in the lower idealities, is still sufficient to hamper the action of the highest drishti. The defect can only be cured by full and complete unification of knowledge and Tapas

There is movement again in the rupa, in the tendency of drishti idealisation, but as yet this is still embarrassed by the persistence of inspired and intuitive mental forms.

S. [Sharira] Ananda is depressed towards the inspirational mentality and intuition, but this form also is being taken up by the drishti. Sahaituka is rapidly undergoing the same change, but not yet with perfection. There is occasional basic or pervasive force of the higher drastri ananda.

Rupa has successfully idealised itself in all its forms after some difficulty with those that were full of the inspirational mentality. The crude forms are not unoften perfect, but not usually so, except in the ghana and developed crude, but often nearly perfect. The old persistent habit of the crude stuff to be doubtful of form, and change rapidly often before creating a perfect form with an initial stability is still obstinate. This is an obstacle also to the stability.

At the same time stability [and] perfection of form and material is increasing; and there is sometimes stability of the full second and even the third degree. This is also coming in a half crude, half-ghana. Full crude and developed forms are perfect in both form and material or in either form or material and if the latter only then perfect in part-form, but they are unstable.

Mar 8 Monday

A very clear, strong, distinguishing and accurate drishti in the telepathies, vyapti and prakamya. Its action is in the already oc-cupied province, but it is there removing all sources of confusion. Also in the telepathic trikaldrishti.

One or two true ghanas have for the first time appeared with the primary stability out of the mass of crude material in daylight; this has the advantage of appearance and stability frankly fronting the physical eye. Other forms present themselves obliquely or dart into the direct field of vision and stay there for a moment or two or three moments or more. Some ghanas of that kind have direct under the eye a primary stability.

There is now occasional possession by the drashtri Ananda in the sharira; but there is as yet no harmonious or complete combi-nation of the pervasion, possession and basic Ananda. The Tapas is now working to establish it in the homogeneity of the drishti, but the kind of drishti is not yet securely the same, nor is the possession then complete and stable.

A remarkable progress has been suddenly made in T^2 by the taking up of the mediary form by the highest drishti. There is now a mass of certitudes of various degrees and qualities, but governed by an increasing force of absolute certitude. The element of over or under stress remains, but is now made subordinate. The element of struggle in the adjustment is being removed and a comparatively smooth and anandamaya development on the higher scale has been given a firm foundation.

Mar 9–13 Tuesday–Saturday.

A period of relaxation of the siddhi. The T^2 has been steadily progressing, but by a complex occasional action, each time a step in the emergence of the more and more effective drishti in the two lower conditions. The other uncompleted members have been neglected, subject to obstruction and affected by recrudescence of asiddhi. There has been a great advance in firmness of passive samata and now in the ideal basis of the Shakti.

Mar 13 Saturday.

The highest drishti is finally imposing itself and completing its taking up of the lower movements in T^2, thought-speech, script and thought-perception. It is the beginning of the final process in the luminous ideal reason.

Sharira Ananda is again reviving, but as yet only in the basic Ananda.

A strong invasion of Tamas in body and physical mind dispelled by the drashtri vijnana which it failed to suspend or lower in character. There is now an invasion of confused luminous lower ideality, and this fails to suspend, but tends to dilute and lower the character of the vijnana.

The highest drashtri Tapas is now at work on the Yoga.

The ideal Ananda is now being imposed on the vishayas; it is dominant and almost perfect in darshana, though still too much mixed with or sometimes lowered towards the inferior forms in the seeing of the human figure. It still sinks in the rest by any lowering of the shakti, but its universal finality has been established beyond serious retardation.

The lipi has succeeded in establishing finally the full dominance of the drashtri vijnana. This is also accomplished in the script, though here there is a strong tendency still to an invasion by the inspirational intuitive thought-perception. The same siddhi seems also to be assured in the thought-speech in the vijnana; but there are still intrusions of the lower forms from the exterior atmosphere. The highest drishti may also be considered to be siddha in the jnana, but not yet in the T^2 thought-perception.

Mar 14 Sunday.

The T^2 thought-perception is being rapidly fixed in the ideality, but the incertitude still encourages the outside mind to send in the lower forms of the vijnana and even lesser mental movements. These as they come in are seized on and idealised, and all forms are now compelled to bear the drishti and there is a spontaneous discrimination of the limits and character of the truth on which they insist, so that when this process is complete, under and overstress may exist in them, but will not delude the witness and thinker. The process however is still incomplete. At the same time certitude of immediate result and movement is gaining greatly in force and amplitude. This must be the next movement to insist always on sight and certitude. When it is complete, there will be the completion of the ideal reason.

All forms of the rupa are idealised, except the crude, and this after some relapse is again and more firmly becoming vijnanamaya. It is unideal only in the process and in some occasional results of uncertain formation. On the other hand swapna Samadhi has been violently invaded by dream and oppressed by mentality, fantasy and incoherence.

Sraddha *bhagavati swashaktyam* is approaching completion, but there is still doubt as to the immediate power and the eventual fullness of yoga siddhi and karma siddhi.

The crude lipi is idealised and even in the process of uncertain formation there is only a momentary survival of the mental matter which is now become a suggestion rather than a real element.

The mental state is being at times brought back in the laxity in order to be overpowered by the drishti.

The Shakti is acting in the physical siddhi, and rupa etc, but as yet is not able to get rid of the obstruction

T^2 is extending itself to distant trikaldrishti as far as that is possible in the ideal reason.

Mar 15 Monday.

The movement in the ghana is getting up a greater rapidity. The substance of the rupa now varies between the idealised mental and the ideal; there is an increasing tendency to stability of the ghana crude and developed crude and also the crude developed and the crude ghana. Other forms have often an initial primary stability before the eye.

The process of idealisation is now completed, except that there is some immixture of the mental in uncertain or indistinct or incomplete crude formations and some initiality of it in unformed material, but the floating of crude matter without any immediate formation or beginning of formation of any kind is undergoing a rapid elimination.

As a next step slow formation is disappearing, has almost disappeared and what prevails now is immediate imperfect or uncertain, sometimes very imperfect or uncertain formation; the perfect complete crude is rare, the perfect incomplete more common.

The sadhara forms in which the unideality persisted, are also now being rectified; this has been done almost instantaneously, but not yet quite so completely as in the niradhara.

=

The K. [Kama] Ananda has been oppressed by the unideal forms, but there is now a pressure of Tapas to get rid of this covering oppression.

=

The crude rupa is now moving towards the elimination of inchoate or very imperfect and uncertain forms; the more definite rupas, complete or incomplete, perfect or partially perfect, wholly ideal or mental-ideal, are becoming more common. The chief difficulty is that the animal and human forms are resisted in this rupa and to evolve them the Akasha resorts to the old method of slow uncertain formation. Though no longer slow, it is still uncertain and produces the inchoate, imperfect and soon changing or uncertain figures.

The possessional Ananda is now always ideal, the basic is now developing ideal finality, the pervasive commencing the same movement. This is being effected against a strong siege of obstruction.

Since yesterday there has been a permitted invasion of the old intuitivity, and the drishti has been working in and upon it to take final possession of the channel mentality. The completion of this movement is predicted for tonight in the lipi. At present the confusions of the mentality are being corrected and decisive trikaldrishti with an element of accuracy of time and detail (mainly in the Yoga guidance) is establishing its predominance.

The samadhi is now the only member of the vijnana in which the obstruction can still keep in action an important aspect of struggle. In the others there is only difficulty of adjustment or difficulty of development of free action. Thought-telepathy (apart from thought-intention) has begun, but with a very slight occasional action.

Rupa at night assumed the same siddhi as in the daytime, but in its different kind of chhaya, tejah and jyoti.

Trikaldrishti, but not in full abundance and perfection.

The pervasive Ananda is striving for ideality, but is still much besieged by the inspirational mental form.

Mar 16 Tuesday.

A strong return of the relapse principle, recurrence of touches of asamata violently forced on the system, though of no duration, invasion, stoppage of siddhi. Crude rupa moves towards elimination of inchoate and very imperfect forms, but the obstruction prevents siddhi.

Mar 17 Wednesday.

The siddhi is recovering its basis. T^2 is assuring again the just drishti, but stress of Tapas is forced on the system from outside, although rejected by the Shakti. The highest drishti occasionally emerges, but the outward insistence on the lower forms of immediate actuality and insufficiently assured possibility hampers progress. The pervasive Ananda is pursuing idealisation in spite of the recurrence of inspiration[al] mentality: there is no intense continuous action.

=

T^2 in the afternoon proceeded with its elimination of stress, but there are intervals when it ceases and the outside mentality sends in its forms which are then either set right in stress or the errors corrected by the discriminating power of the drishti. At other times there is just drishti of the first, second or third order. The first which gives final decisions is still the least frequent and not in its highest power and assurance. Tapas is returning to the fuller power of drishti.

=

Rupa as yet does not advance rapidly. There is no successful insistence on stability; the imperfect forms recur obstinately, but without conviction

K. Ananda developed in the morning for a moment highest drishti, and this showed itself again with intensity in the evening. But the lower forms though they tend to be modified by the drishti, still besiege the system.

At night a sudden strong attack of most of the rogas to which the system is liable, including a touch of feverishness; some weakness in the morning.

March 18 – 24

The siddhi has progressed in spite of a heavy obstruction of physical tamas. The main progress is that all the members of the vijnana have now definitely fixed themselves in the true ideality (it is only in laxity that there is some touch of idealised mentality) and now including T^2 in the drishti. All except T^2 are entirely vijnanamaya.

T^2 has developed accurate drishti in the third condition and decisive trikaldrishti in the first condition. The common action is in the third; but it is now being changed to the second condition, that is right perception of possibility including right perception of immediate actuality. The first is increasing in power and fixing its certitudes on the others. The process is as yet far from complete, but is progressing with sufficient rapidity of transmutation.

Samadhi is developing vijnana action in spite of tamas and nidra.

Rupa is still hampered by the obstruction and cannot yet get rid of imperfect crude forms. But perfect crude forms (crude, ghana crude, developed crude) and crude ghana and developed are becoming more common before the eye. The freedom of rupa is much denied and impeded.

Vishaya is similarly hampered, but there is progress of idealisation in gandha and rasa.

K. Ananda is now firmly idealised in spite of an occasional pursuing fringe of idealised mentality, and is increasing in power of incidence. But the continuity is impeded by the physical obstruction.

Tapas is acting on roga and for utthapana, but as yet without any effect of finality.

Mar 25 – 27 Thursday, Friday, Saturday.

The development of the vijnana in the thought-siddhi is still the main movement.

Thought-speech and thought-perception are now normally fixed in the drishti. There are occasional drops and deviations, especially in laxity, but the laxity is now only usual in the evening and night and as a result in the early morning. It is being slowly got rid of in spite of the great siege and pressure of the external mind and its tamas.

Thought-speech and perception have been perfected in the two lower orders of the drishti; they are already perfect in the first order, but that has been held back; it is now manifesting and has to take possession of the others. The main difficulty is still in T^2.

T^2 (trikaldrishti side of the double power) is now fixed normally in the drishti. The stress has been on the telepathic drishti which gives the fact and tendency [of] actual and potential forces in action. Now the self-existent drishti is being developed which gives the certitudes. Certitudes of actuality (the third condition) are now more or less perfect, except in their extension: these give the certitude of immediate actualities and also of immediate or almost immediate dominant possibilities. It deals with the telepathies, but in the telepathies the possibilities of linked present and future action etc predominate, in the other the certitudes. This third condition corresponds in the drishti to the intuition, but is not revelatory intuition, but a high intuitively revelatory vision. Certitudes of remoter potentiality are now fixing themselves in perfection, but are as yet more limited and less disengaged from the telepathies. This second condition occupies in the drishti the place of inspiration, but is not revelatory inspiration, but a high inspirationally or interpretatively revelatory vision. The first condition in trikaldrishti is still held back and inactive.

In Samadhi intuition has been finally turned into drishti in the antardarshi. Swapna samadhi is still besieged by tamas and nidra. Dream has now a remarkable coherency due to the pressure of drishti.

Lipi has practically got rid of mere intuition, but admits drishti intuition; all the other powers are active.

Rupa and vishaya are still oppressed by the physical obstruction and are making no farther immediate progress.

Speech has now been for some time vijnanamaya with drishti in the third and is now often ideal in the second condition; but there is as yet no speech of trikaldrishti.

B. [Brahma] Darshana has long settled in the vijnana, but without the Ananda[,] the object being to get rid of the remnants of the mental form of vision. Now it is being raised to the vijnana Ananda, which it is already fixed in in vision of things, the other movement has been in the vision of living things, especially of human persons.

The difficulty in the vijnana Ananda darshana is that it tends [ ]² often to be diluted with or flooded into the mental Ananda which is more intense, while the V.A is in the lesser intensities. This is now being, but is not entirely remedied by the equal intensity of the V. Ananda. The mental brings with it the prema Ananda, while the ideal has been for some time dissociated from Prema. The Prema ananda is becoming vijnanamaya, but the stronger prema still takes the mental character.

After writing the great intensities have come into the V. Ananda darshana and the vijnanamaya Prema Ananda, and the mental Ananda darshana and the mental premananda convicted of a lesser intensity are beginning to undergo a final elimination.

The third condition of T^2 is being taken up into the highest certitude of drishti, and the first condition manifesting has begun to take up the two lower conditions. This is only the incipient final movement.

The idealisation of the vishaya, suspended for some time, is now proceeding once more with a strong rapidity, but the mental sense obstinately resists entire eviction.

2 *MS* to

The idealisation of the sahaituka vishayas has now become practically complete.

In samadhi more force of vijnana, but sushupta swapna is still under the hold of dream and nidra.

Vishwa darshana seems to be fixed in V.A in spite of occasional mental Ananda

Mar 28, Sunday

T^2 is now acting with considerable accuracy but insufficient force of certitude in the drishti. The lower movements persist, but their inadequacy is so evident that their persistence is only due to physical laxity and habit.

Mar 29–31.

There has been some development of T^2 and of vijnana generally, of which the main tendency is on one side the idealisation of the invading mentality, on the other the stronger emergence of the higher drishti. Other siddhis proceed slowly or are stationary or in abeyance.

The situation in the sadhana is as follows. Samata is perfect except for an occasional physical touch of asamata of great weakness which does not affect the mind, but only the physical shell of the pranic consciousness. The sama ananda is however still in need of greater development; its deficiency is due to the general withholding of intensity of Ananda, for even in the vijnana there is asu, a modified prakasha, but not the full Ananda. There is full sukham and prasada, but not full hasya in the samata.

Shakti is fixed in the vijnana and usually in one of the conditions of the logistic drishti; but subject to some dilution by the stuff of mental intelligence. Sraddha is complete, except for an element of besieging doubt about sharira and karma, amounting more to the perception of a possibility of limitation than to denial of the siddhi. There is however some element of doubt as to whether all may not be cut short by death of the body. Devibhava is there in basis, but incomplete by lack of full force, especially of ishwarabhava. The other siddhis of this chatusthaya are as developed as they can be without farther development of the vijnana.

Thought is now fixed in the vijnana except for the effect produced by the continuous siege of the surrounding envelope of mental intelligence. This is now distant and not close to the consciousness, but is still allowed full right of penetration and invasion. The old policy of the Kavacha seems to have been wholly abandoned. This effect is first, that of an increasing of the vijnana thought in the mental matter where it is still vijnanamaya, but with a strong infusion of mental limitation and incertitude; secondly, when the thought is more strongly vijnanamaya, ideal in the vijnana, a dilution by or an accompaniment of mentality; at other times, the thought is clearly and solely vijnana, but still limited by the environment of mental intelligence. These effects are strongest in the T^2; but affect the general thought-perception which does not now usually act as a separate power. The thought-speech is vijnanamaya except for a very small element of diluted vijnana, and when the thought-speech is active, except in great laxity or exercises of the idealised imagination, thought-perception also rises in vijnana intensity and fullness. Lipi and script are entirely ideal, but with a tendency towards the intuitivity saved by drishti, because of the siege of the mental intelligence. T^2 is more and more developed in the highest drishti, but still normally varies between the two lower conditions and is much impeded by the effects of the intelligence.

Samadhi is impeded by tamas and nidra. It tends to vijnana and is sometimes drishtimaya in thought etc in the antardarshi and all swapna except sushupta swapna, but this is only when there is application of tapas. Sahaituka Vishaya is at present idealised with some occasional element of manasa; the development, as also in rupa is temporarily suspended.

Physical siddhi is subject to a violent and successful siege of obstruction. Ananda is now ideal or idealised manasa, but spontaneity is rare, continuity brief and dependent on smarana. Roga has resumed something of its hold, though always removable or in the standing elements diminuable by tapas. One roga only still resists the tapas. The other siddhis in this field make no progress.

Darshana is now fixed in the vijnana and usually in a vijnana Ananda of secondary power.

April

April 1.   This month is set apart for the overcoming of the final difficulties in the way of the vijnana.

Today mostly given to kavya. At night a full idealisation on all levels of the thought-perception; the manasa is now only an accompaniment, limitation or infiltration. The sinking of the thought into the manasa is being cast off and persists strongly only in the T^2, but there too it is no longer able to strive to be normal.

April 2 – 5

The siege of the mentalised physical tamas is exceedingly violent in its obstructive obstinacy, the siddhi proceeds in a few outbreaks in the midst of this tamas, and it is only yesterday that the Tapas has turned with an equal determination to get rid of the physical disability. The atmosphere of the physical mind is no longer allowed to give for long a sanction to it; but it still holds strongly to the atmosphere of the physical and to some extent of the psychic prana, and this effects a siege and retardation of the siddhi. Each day there is some decisive progress.

Thought-perception and T^2 has definitely risen into the second condition sometimes powerfully uplifted or taken possession of by the siddhi, sometimes giving place to the inspirational drishti from outside. The latter insists on possibility in the old excessive fashion and while it extends the bounds of vision, is still damaging to certitude. When the drishti acts in its highest form and first condition, certitude of present actuality, of present and future possibility and of real eventuality fall into a harmonious whole. The perfection of this harmony can only come when the second condition is entirely surmounted and the free and normal highest action becomes possible. More distant possibility is now being seen through the drishti and the logistic form of the srauta is initially showing its outline on the logistic level.

B. Darshana is fixing itself more firmly in the vijnana Ananda and insisting on its higher intensities which reveal the Purushottama in the Brahma.

Samadhi still struggles with more and more success, but still a very difficult success against nidra and tamas. Tamas more than nidra is now the real obstacle.

Rupa siddhi does not act freely and makes only progress in detail. It is now increasing[ly] stable in the crude form with an increasing force of vivid completeness, but the imperfect forms are still obstinate in recurrence. The formless material quickly takes form, but the form is sometimes though not usually inchoate, often imperfect, perfect only by overcoming of the siege of obstruction in the akasha.

Thought now hardly at all descends into the mentality except for side suggestions mostly in the state of laxity, but is still subject to accompaniment and infiltration by the stuff of manas.

The physical siddhi is now insisting on sustained tejas pravritti of the ideal Shakti in the body so as to get rid of tamas, but though there is a great improvement, the success is as yet far from complete. Sharira can make no definite progress against the obstruction.

April 6 – 10

The vijnana is steadily getting the better of the still persistent tamas and the progress continues. After a slight lapse towards the mental recurrence the thought is more firmly fixed in the gnosis. It is however of three kinds, the drishti cased in a mental accompaniment, the drishti of the lower conditions leaning to the limitations of the mental reason, the same lifted by or to the highest drishti or full of its power, though not yet of its constant light and ananda. Now even the forms of thought which were held most by the mental form, eg imagination etc, are captured by the vijnana drishti. The mental siege still continues, but is less sustained and effective. The real question is now between different conditions of the drishti. The first predominates, but with a gravitation towards the second condition.

T^2 also is idealised in all its movements. There are still two kinds, telepathic and original. The telepathic is in error when weighted with the mental accompaniment, but much less than at any previous time; there is a great increase in accuracy and certitude.

The original is in the three conditions (the telepathic is dominated by the second, the perception of the possible), and varies in power and accuracy and certitude according as it is free or beset by the mental intuitive reason.

Other activities are in the drishti, but with a mixture of mentality, (lipi and script alone perfect in vijnana), eg vishaya. Rupa is not active. The gnosis in the body is most affected by mental invasion.

Sharira Ananda after a long time is recovering power for continuity, but is less firmly vijnanamaya than when it acted with a careful and formative intermittence. Other members of the sharira have been adverse, but still affected by the Tapas.

Yoga Record
June.

June 7.

The discontinuation of the record for about two months marks a time when the Yoga was slowly proceeding against a strong obstruction in the physical consciousness. At no time did this obstruction amount to a gap in the process of the Yoga, a complete discontinuity (of more than hours) or a relapse in the old manner. It was not an arrest, but a retardation of the rate of the progress, and due principally to the necessity of an assimilation of steps rapidly taken, a dealing with intellectual remnants and an action on the last serious assault of the unrepentant and unconvinced environing opposition. There was a quickening at the end of May and the first six days of June has each been marked by a great particular step in advance; today there is a rapid but sure general advance, the result of the more or less covert or impeded work of April–May and its weakening of the obstacles.

=

Position.

Samata, complete, both positive and negative or rather active and passive. There only remains an inequality in the active ananda and an occasional proffer of doubt and depression which does not take any body in the chitta (effleure seulement pendant le quart d'un second). The doubt is only about the body and the karma and is falling away from the fixity of the çraddha.

Shakti. Complete, but awaiting for its fuller activities the perfection of the vijnana and the shârira and Brahma-darshana. The most sensible progress has been in the two weak parts, the tertiary dasya and çraddha. The Ishwara is now felt in all the activities of the Shakti, though not with an entire completeness because there is still an intrusive action of the *ganas*. The tertiary *dasya* has replaced the earlier stages, but it is of two kinds, *dasya* to the *ganas* moving the Prakriti, and *dasya* to the Ishwara controlling, moving and embodying himself in the Shakti. The *çraddha* in the Bhagavan is complete and in the power of the Shakti to the extent of the will to accomplish of the Ishwara. The personal Shakti is felt to be insufficient, but it is becoming one with the sufficient universal Shakti. Faith in the *sharira* and *karma* is qualified only by the doubt as to the prolongation of the life and the extent of the *karma*. The first is only a strong external suggestion getting its strength from the abnormal persistence of the digestive roga; the second is a real restriction of the çraddha, but it is rather questioning now than negative. The *ishwaribhava* is still qualified in intensity and fullness.

Vijnana. The conversion of the thought, *jnana*, to the vijnana form is now complete. The base is still the revelatory intuition, but the representative logis[tis] has penetrated the major part of its action and the interpretative often intervenes and prepares the normality of the highest logistis. Telepathies are now idealised and of a great but not always perfect correctness. Telepathic tapas is now vijnanamaya. The decisive T^2 at present emerges from the idealised telepathies (mental perceptions of event, force, tendency and possibility) and the idealised telepathic (old mental) tapas. At times there is the independent T^2 of the supreme logistis. Telepathies are now a part of trikaldrishti and amount to a drishti of the present, and often imply or hold in their action the drishti of the immediate future. At the same time none of these things have an absolute perfection, and decisive tapas is not as yet very strong, organised or effective. Prakamya of feeling and sensation is strong, but incomplete and intermittent; prakamya of thought intermittent and feeble. Vyapti is more effective. Action and knowledge at a distance is still unorganised and imperfectly effective. Rupa is still obstructed in the physical akasha, but confirmed in a primary type stability; vishaya not yet restored to action; samadhi firmly idealised, but limited by fantasy, instability and nidra. There is still great incoherence in the sushupta swapna lipi.

Sharira progresses in the Ananda which after some intermission varied by an unstable but more spontaneous recurrence is recovering continuity dependent on smarana, but this continuity is now for the most part spontaneous and has not to be maintained, though sometimes assisted, by tapas. The fragmentary rogas persist and cannot yet be totally expelled from the system, but the action of the Tapas on them is growing stronger. Only the central rogas are obstinate in possession, the rest only in persistent recurrence. The digestive fluctuates between almost complete intermission and a virulent, but now much less vehemently effective recurrence. There is no visible action of utthapana or saundarya.

Brahma. All is now fixed in the vijnana brahma darshana with an occasional emergence of the undertone of intuitive manasa which is [immediately][1] penetrated by and taken up into vijnana. In the V.B. [Vijnana Brahma] Ananda is organising itself, vijnana Ananda informed with the Ahaituka and manifesting in its own kind the Prema and Kama Ananda darshana. These two in the vision of the object are now vijnanamaya (fusion of intuitive + higher logistis or only the latter), in the subject, the chitta, twofold without sufficient fusion of the two simultaneous forms, but the higher logistis is growing on the chitta..

$=$

Samadhi. The pressure of afternoon nidra as shown in today's samadhi and prepared by the last few days' progress no longer alters the character of the swapna, nor does it amount to entire obscuration of the *drashtâ*, but only to a weight on the clarity of the visual consciousness. Sushupta swapna lipi is still the circumstance most affected and, as always, by incoherence due to suppression and to mixture of different lipis. At night nidra is still powerful to prevent samadhi

Vijnana. The invading environmental suggestions are now being steadily appropriated to the vijnana. Trikaldrishti of actuality has been trained to the vijnanamaya correctness, the same movement is being applied to the trikaldrishti of the possibilities that press on the actuality to modify or alter the event in the making. At present there is much environmental suggestion full of error, not of fact of tendency, but of its event-making incidence.

[1] *MS* immediated

Rupa advances against a strong obstruction. Vishaya revives in gandha, but there is still the obstruction.

‗

Sharira Ananda. Continuity is growing, but still subject to the old causes of discontinuance. These however have much less reality of persistence than on the last occasion. Tivra shows a tendency to fix itself and is now vijnanamaya with an idealised intuitive mental undertone. Vishayananda is revelatory vijnanamaya. Raudra also is vijnanamaya, and vaidyuta. The physical ananda continues in antardarshi and in the lighter swapna, but is there subject to cessation or intermittence.

June 8.

After a long indulgence of the environmental invasion, the final conversion of the assured ideality to the interpretative logistical vijnana has commenced and immediately taken a considerable extension. All concentrated thought and thought-speech has begun to be fixedly of that character, as also the T^2. This is being effected not by select movements and a gradual extension, but with an initially instantaneous generality and rapidity in a crowded activity of thought-suggestions.

The Rupa is beginning to press down again the barrier of obstruction. The developed forms are still only of an initial stability, the ghana and ghana developed either that or of a primary or secondary, the crude of a primary, secondary or sometimes tertiary stability. The tendency in the latter is to long stability.

The lipi is fixing itself in freely in the interpretative vijnana; all former movements of the kind were only initial and preparatory; this is the last and definite movement.

Ananda powerful and persistent all the morning. More intense and often very intense with smarana; when mind occupied either suppressed with predisposition of the body to it, or half-suppressed or present with a lesser insistence. Often the mind occupied, but with a part of the physical consciousness fully aware of the intense Ananda. More firmness of continuous pervasion; for a long time the inner physical fibres penetrated and possessed by the Ananda. Result in the afternoon intenser A [Ananda] with the smarana; body full of the predisposition even in forgetfulness. The automatic and the forced cessation are being eliminated from the system, only the oblivious and the sleep cessation remain as effective obstacles.

The samadhi in the afternoon almost got rid of lipi incoherence. The interpretative vijnana took firm hold on thought speech and thought perception in the antardarshi. Nidra obscurity almost nonexistent, nidra weight of inclusion is still there.

In the evening and at night a laxity of the Shakti and some interruption, not complete, of the results acquired in the daytime.

June 9.

The laxity continued during the morning.

Samadhi in the afternoon directed to farther idealisation of the swapna, removal of fantasy, lipi incoherence, instability and fragmentariness of rupa, shabda etc. There is a detailed initial but not yet quite definite or organised progress.

The thought in the afternoon normalised interpretative vijnana in the revelatory and representative consciousness-substance. This movement extended to tapas and trikaldrishti. Indefinite thought from the environment is not yet always of the perfect logistis. A highest logistis has for some time been present in the interpretative and other form or substance. It is now beginning to prepare to take full possession. This will be the end of the logistic movement, the completion of the vijnana reason.

Ananda of the interpretative fashion acclimatised in the body. Physical Ananda is now of three moulds, interpretative, revelatory and as a survival the inspirational and (rarely, almost never) other lower kind[s] of vijnana.

For the first time developed or rather perfect rupa of the secondary-tertiary stability. As yet the longer stabilities except in the crude rupa are still isolated or else a rather frequent exception. The initial predominates when there is rapidity and frequency of the crude and developed rupa.

The thought since yesterday has begun to be attended with physical Ananda confined to the head region (where the K A has been till now exceptional, the ordinary pervasion being in the rest of the body) and the brain-stuff, but this now tends to become normal and to join itself to the Ananda in the rest of the body.

The Ananda Darshana now tends to be the infinite shuddha Ananda taking up all the rest, but still on the vijnana level. The old mental shuddha ananta Ananda recurs in the first movement as a coating to the vijnana Ananda, but changes easily to the vijnana shuddha Ananta.

The possibilities are now entirely normalised in the interpretative trikaldrishti, the authentic decisive is beginning to disengage itself more clearly, but has often a telepathic character from above which while fulfilling itself in the eventual actuality, remains without any certitude for the reason. An irruption still occasionally takes place of the lesser telepathic idealities which shows that the whole process of conversion is not yet completed. The thought and other prakamya vyapti is still of the lower inefficient and in the case of the thought initial and fragmentary character. Thought intention and thought substance are more easily accurate than pure thought perception.

June 10   Thursday.

Today the Yoga is more hampered than on any day since the beginning of the fresh stream of progress. The principal advance has been in the T^2, where the telepathies of actuality have been raised to the highest power of the logistis and those of modifying possibility strongly confirmed in the interpretative vijnana. Occasionally the tertiary or decisive vijnana acts, but where it does not pressure on the possibility by Tapas brings a confusion of unreliable certitudes.

Rupa in the ghana etc is hesitating between initial and primary stabilities.

The samadhi was more obstructed by nidra, though not of an obscure nature.

Ananda is obstructed and only constant in smarana, though the full intensity is not present.

=

In the afternoon a change. The T^2 manifested separately an action of the highest logistic vijnana not at all dependent on the idealised telepathic perception. Rupa began to stress the stabilities and arrived at a normal primary varying from the first point beyond the initial to a point tending to the secondary stability; the crude stability became again secondary and tertiary rather than primary and secondary. Ananda recovered intensity and pervasion with a strong cerebral action.

June 11 Friday.

Progress on the same lines. Tapas and Trik. are now being organised so as not to be in conflict. Tapas is taking its right place as telepathies have done; the union of decisive Tapas and trik. certitude is not yet effected.

June 12 Saturday.

Trikaldrishti pursues its organisation, but while the actualities grow constantly in power and certainty, the unrealised possibilities and decisive certitudes are not yet in the complete higher vijnanamaya development. There are still excessive stresses on possibility. At the same time the higher certitudes are becoming more frequent and more positive to the reason

Rupa is increasing tertiary stability in the ghana and developed crude, and attempting to bring in the secondary in the other rupas. Lipi now has frequent tertiary stability in the Akasha. There is also an incipient movement towards variety of Rupa

Ananda already settled in the intenser sa-smarana, though always feeble and interrupted from the evening, is fixing automatical constancy, so that after oblivion there is no need of mental smarana, the body keeping the memory whether of continuous but unnoted or of suppressed but still implicitly present Ananda.

=

The base of vijnanamaya organisation is being laid in the decisive T^2, and prepared in the prakamya-vyapti of thought intention: it is already strong as regards sensational tendency and impulse.

Rupa has now definitely begun secondary stability of ghana and developed rupas, but mostly still in the side-seen images, those that stand direct before the eye are less vivid and less stable. Primary stability is still the ordinary movement, but now it is less fugitive, less inclined to the initial and more to the secondary duration.

There is now a constancy of the penetrative more physical Ananda contained in the sthula fibres; the ananda of the sukshma body affecting the sthula alternates or sometimes coexists with it.

Samadhi at first of the same kind oppressed by a light unobscure nidra; afterwards strong organisation of thought speech and perception of the highest logistis in all stages of antardarshi and swapna, strong sharira Ananda continuous except in sushupta swapna, lipi perfect except in sushupta, but there no longer fantastically incoherent, other incidents not well organised except rupa (landscapes) clear, tejomaya, but insufficiently stable.

June 13   Sunday

There is a larger right vijnana of possibilities and telepathic relative certitudes and the decisive telepathic trikaldrishti of precise detail (only of the immediate future) is beginning to found itself, as yet imperfectly, on a larger basis.

Tertiary stability is now very common in crude rupa; primary and secondary prevail in the rest under the direct gaze, but tertiary has begun to appear in side images and promises even in the direct images.

There is more frequent cerebral and thought Ananda. The Ananda still fluctuates and the Ananda without smarana fails still to fix itself with a final possession.

Each of the three siddhis which are being rapidly pushed forward has taken a farther step in advance.

The decisive trikaldrishti certitudes are beginning to become near, actual and sure in telepathic trikaldrishtis of the immediate future, filling them as a first step to their replacement.

The rupa is increasing tertiary stabilities; initial tertiaries have come repeatedly in the direct image and final tertiary has made its appearance in the side images. Both are now common in the crude.

Ananda is deepening its insistent frequency and intensity in spite of interruption by oblivion. It is depressed in the late afternoon, evening and night, but for the last three days the shakti has been working on this depression and yesterday there was strong Ananda after a prolonged depression in the late afternoon, some in the evening and some, but rejected by the will in the body at night. Today it promises to be throughout continuous by recurrence.

June 14th – 15th

Ananda deepens steadily, but the obstruction of forgetfulness at the periodic time still remains operative.

Rupa has now established the first tertiary stabilities; the more prolonged are still occasional only.

Trikaldrishti also is gradually confirming in the telepathic figure.

Samadhi in the afternoon is now idealised in all its parts, but weak in the incidents, except in scene and event in scene which are attaining to a perfect stability. The organisation for utility is not yet ready to commence.

June 16th Wednesday.

The Tapas which was held back in favour of the trikaldrishti is now being definitely taken up for perfection. At first there was the increased but uncertain effectivity of tapas and a renewal of the difficulty of discord between the telepathic form of the two siddhis, then the same difficulty in tapas as in trikaldrishti between the telepathic and the definitive. Finally, an initial fusion has been effected between trikaldrishti and tapas.

Rupa is trying to develop perfect stability; there is the potentiality, but not yet the actual presence.

Ananda has hitherto fluctuated between periods of intensity and periods of depression. Formerly the latter used to last for long periods, now there is only comparative depression on alternate days and fluctuation in the day itself, – greater strength in the morning, less with much interruption in the afternoon and evening, at night cessation or only occasional presence. The depression on alternate days is being eliminated. The continuity in the morning is every day greater and tends to conquer the oblivion; even when writing the body retains except in great absorption of the thought-mind the physical Ananda.

The ananta Ananda of the darshana has now definitely entered and for the present fixed itself in the vijnana form corresponding to that attained in the rest of the chaitanya.

June 17th   Thursday.

The T^2 for a time was confused by an irruption of incertitudes from outside attended by an extension of relative certitudes in the revelatory and interpretative telepathies. Subsequently the supreme logistis reappeared and began to organise certitude of detail, circumstance and succession.

Rupa is now making prolonged tertiary and perfect stability the normal thing in crude of all kinds and beginning to develop it in crude developed and crude ghana. In side images they are becoming very frequent, though they do not yet predominate. The attempt to extend them to direct images of the full ghana and developed kinds is obstinately obstructed in the physical akasha. The long existing tendency to snatch away the rupa as soon as possible after appearance, even if it is [in its] nature perfectly stable, is the obstacle to be eliminated.

Ananda has fixed itself with a more basic firmness in the cerebral possession and the physical ananda of thought-speech and thought-possession which was till now only a faint preshadowing, has become definite and universal. The recurrence of asiddha thought and of interruptions of possession is however still persistent, though less powerful than before. Most of the conditions of perfect Ananda (except, mainly, the downward current and the fusion of the five anandas, though the latter has made some progress) is now accomplished in the basis.

Ananda persisted in the daily period of relaxation, in the afternoon, evening and at night. The automatic tendency to relaxation is therefore now ended; only that created by oblivion and the oblivion itself have to be conquered.

June 18th   Friday.

Preoccupation with a work and a tendency in the siddhi of going slightly backward, eg in the rupa towards primary and secondary stability, in the Ananda of interruption by oblivion (but not of laxity as the result of interruption, only a certain potentiality of relaxation remains), in the T^2 of revelatory rather than highest logistic action.

June 19th Saturday.

The continuous steady rapidity of the siddhi upset today by a revolutionary attempt to substitute at once the srauta for the logistic vijnana. This was attended and frustrated by an invasion of asiddhi such as had not occurred for some months past including even an attack on the samata.

Insistent suggestion of asamata — amounting to duhkha in the prana and impatience in the buddhi — in the physical consciousness, not radical but strongly disturbing the outer physical fibres. This duhkha is now mingled with ananda when it enters the system and cannot preserve its pure character. Its recurrence however is a retardatory phenomenon foreign to the new settled course of the sadhana. Suggestion also, but less violent of asraddha, amounting in effect not to radical asraddha but to disbelief in the method, absence of the feeling of a possessing guidance by the Ishwara — that is felt as before behind a veil or only at the summit, — and a sense of the possibility of postponement of siddhi. At the same time it is felt that a greater siddhi is preparing.

An Ananda of a much greater potentiality of continuity, pervasion, largeness and intensity felt on the vijnana summit and descending into the sukshma body, but this is unable to make itself except at intervals intimate to the system. Meanwhile the constant possession of the sthula body by the revelatory has been taken away and that body is empty except of a greater tendency of response. The sukshma body is visited by a more continuous Ananda less affected, except at first by want of smarana or attention, more pervasive from above, more naturally intense, affecting the sthula without being established in it or possessing it, but not yet organised nor having a firm close hold even of the subtle body. It is at once more continuous and less intimately continuous. All the old asiddhis are suggested, including the dependence on posture. The struggle has not yet been determined in the sense of the greater organised siddhi.

The jnana etc are affected in a similar direction. The system is invaded by a vague and confused idealised mentality which is turned to an imperfect revelatory ideality when it enters the system and its surrounding atmosphere. The vijnana thought and T^2 occur, but do not closely hold the system as for a long time they have been doing. There is nothing left but to await the issue of the struggle.

Ananda during the time set apart for the samadhi insistent on possession of the sthula body, but a possession by penetration, not a reawakening of the hold on the sthula fibres.

The period of laxity was to some extent restored today, not entirely, for there was a frequent recurrence of Ananda, but as a result of smarana. In the evening the Ananda of the sthula body was brought back to a certain extent, but without the firm hold and sure intensity that had seemed fixed in finality. The Ananda in the sukshma body was for a time made constant, the ananda of thought universalised and intensified; these took on the form of the representative, interpretative and highest logistis. All this had to be done by a certain force of Tapas and therefore cannot be considered as a final siddhi.

The bodily consciousness became during the same time first revelatory representative and representative, then representative interpretative and interpretative, then the highest logistic vijnana. All this was done from above and cannot yet be considered final.

Attack of asamata eliminated, but sraddha not yet normal.

June 20th Sunday.

The morning was a period of laxity. None of the siddhis are yet final.

The representative mould of the bodily consciousness now predominates, but is not yet fixed in security. It is sometimes drawn back and the revelatory takes its place. There is not the sure pratistha

Afternoon — last night's Ananda again in action.

June 21st Monday

The sadhana is settling down again to a movement analogous to the past movements but on a higher scale, that is to say, greater developments are being foreshadowed and initiated which have to be gradually attained against the [persistence][2] of old lesser sufficiencies and insufficiencies.

Seven new movements are indicated of which four have begun to realise themselves in an initial action.

Thought is manifesting a highest logistic movement which is ready to change into the srauta vijnana. The lower thought still persists in the form no longer of a revelatory but an inspirational intuitional thought-action. Its insufficiency is recognised and it is condemned but does not cease from persistence

Trikaldrishti is effecting the same movement hampered by the inferior idealised telepathies

The Shakti in the body has left the fixed revelatory form and has manifested for a while inspirational, interpretative and a highest logistis ready for the srauta. Actually, however, there is a pressure of inspirational intuitive which veils the actuality of this higher movement.

There is the same phenomenon in the physical Ananda in the psychic body. There are fluctuations in all these movements, sometimes the siddhi holding the system, sometimes the asiddhi.

The environmental siege affects the lower movements with avoidable error and gives force of persistence to the asiddhi.

June 22[d] Tuesday

The same conditions as yesterday, but there is a stronger force of the Siddhi.

Tapas is effecting the same movement as trikaldrishti.

The government of the Devatas is giving place to the direct government by the Ishwara, but there is not yet the constant presence

June 26th Saturday.

The intervening days have been subject to difficulties in the Sadhana, the persistence of old forms of the ideality, the siege of the environment and some invasion of stuff of the intuitive mentality.

---

[2] *MS* persistent

Today the new siddhis are reasserting themselves with a greater power and especially the free all-occupying action of the highest logistic ideality in its highest degree in thought, trikaldrishti-tapas, lipi, script etc. It is also attempting to occupy the physical system and replace the intuitive vijnana. As yet there is still a persistent intervention of the other forms, a laxity of the tapas intervening which tends to restore them and a great difficulty in the physical system.

17th October 1920

Oct. 17. 1920.

Morning

Freedom of the inferior ideality. It is subject still to intrusions of the mental intuitivity from the environment mind, but these are compelled to see or to transform themselves. The stuff of mind in the physical conscience still contains unilluminated movements of obscure matter, but the pressure of the light on them is constant.

The lipi is the most perfect of the members of the vijnana, free in its action, free from the lower elements, established in the vijnana. T^3 is now developing with a certain freedom in the lipi.

Thought and T^3 in the thought are moving constantly to the same perfection. The action is free in concentration, but there are still the intrusive or untransformed elements of the physical mind. Except for this defect it is established in the first vijnana. The representative vijnana with all its three elements (representative, interpretative, imperative) is seeking to fix itself in the bodily consciousness of the Shakti in place of the revelatory + intuitive representative vijnana.

It takes possession of all but the head.

The obstruction still reigns in the rupa siddhi, vishaya, sharira, and the Tapas as yet can only diminish, but not overcome the obstruction. In Samadhi the basis has been laid, but sleep and dream continue.

Tapas is working for Arogya and physical Ananda, the latter well-prepared and only forcibly held away by the obstruction. The

Asiddhi still holds in the utthapana and Saundarya.

=

The object telepathies are rapidly uplifted into the representative (logos) vijnana. There has long been an effort from below insisted on and aided from above; this is the immediate action from above, a solution of the difficulty by the involved process. It does not exclude a temporary return towards the inferior process.

=

Later.

There has been a rapid progress in the idealisation of the physical Ananda. There was some beginning of continuity, but it was ill established and collapsed in the evening.

=

The normal state of the physical consciousness is the revelatory; the descent to the intuitive occurs much more rarely than before and is not of long duration. Occasionally there is the representative vijnana.

=

No decisive progress in the rest, but a pressure on the habitual passive obstruction in rupa[,] vishaya and samadhi (lone fleeting tejomaya scene) and on the active opposition in the sharira. Progress is made, but as yet by short steps only.

18th October.

Preparation of progress in the rupa siddhi.

=

Sudden introduction of the highest representative ideality (logos vijnana), first into the physical system, then in the afternoon into the lipi, thought-speech, thought-perception, tapas, telepathy, trikaldrishti. This is the beginning of a definitive, decisive and rapid conversion that is still in process.

=

The change brought at first a resuscitation of old imperfections belonging to the inspirational vijnana of the intuitive mind and the intellectualities that hung about it, an attempt at invasion and a resuscitation of the principle of struggle. This however has been checked and is being ejected.

=

Descent during later part of the day.

19th October

Arrangement of imperative vijnana begun on the lower levels of the ideal thought-powers.

=

Great extension and power of the logos vijnana in its highest action – thought, T^2, lipi. It is only beginning to convert largely the thought-speech into the mould of the logos.

The other forms survive as insistent remnants.

=

Three levels of the logos vijnana

    1. Logistis – intuitive ideality of all kinds.

    2. Logos reason. The lower representative idea, turned

       (a) downwards to the logistis

       (b) upwards to the logos vijnana.

N.B. The same downward and upward direction is possible for the logistis.

    3. Logos vijnana.

The latter has to deal with three movements.

    1. Actualities – representative

    2 Potentialities (including and harmonising with the actualities, or separate.)

    3 The imperatives of the infinite – absolute, imperative, identific.

The [?last] has to take possession of the other two and deliver them from contingent incertitudes.

This has been commenced, but has to be completed, before the consciousness can be taken into the srauta vijnana.

Part Three

Record of Yoga 1926–1927

DECEMBER 1926 – 6 JANUARY 1927

When the fullness of the supramental life-energy is in the body, then all difficulties will be reduced to nothingness.

It is the life-energy in all the body, not only in the seven centres that is demanded. Once in all the seven centres it cannot fail to pour through all the body.

It must take possession of all the cells, the flesh, muscles, bones, blood, nerves, skin, hair; then the body will be ready for transformation.

The life-energy to be firmly founded today in the last centres. The rest to follow in the next three days.

=

These things are author[it]ative suggestions; it depends on the energy and the adhara subject to the divine sanction from above whether they are fulfilled in the time fixed or have to wait for a later period.

=

If founded, all the remnants of the old illnesses and pains and bad habits of the body will disappear altogether and no new ones will be possible.

There is nothing complete yet done in the material physical Nature, and yet till that is done, there will be nothing complete in finality anywhere. Many things are established, but even the most advanced need the last touches or even many last touches.

=

There is still the problem of the physical material, the flesh and the organs. These have to become unassailable and invulnerable; that to be settled in its self-maintenance independently of food by one means or another.

=

Today, one at least of these problems ought to be settled in effective physical principle. There can be no sense of security till that is done.

—

Monday next. An ascending scale till then. The ascent today. No more for the present.

—

The ascent began, but it has been interrupted as usual by an attack. No matter; it will overcome, almost immediately overcome. It is a matter of the nerves which can still be touched by pain and suffering.

[*In the margin beside the above paragraphs, Sri Aurobindo wrote the following note, then cancelled it:*]

Observe: the flow of the energy has begun, but is still subject to interruption. That interruption should disappear today.

Youth and beauty manifest in the face, but are interrupted. That interruption must begin to disappear entirely today.

Make way for the Supreme Force. It will take up your responsibilities.

—

Today. The difficulty finishes today. The rest afterwards.

—

Get rid of the representative. The higher power can do its work.

=

Monday [*3 January 1927*]

The supreme Force descends. The difficulty is finished. The representative imperative still obstructs, but it is ready to disappear.

Today it disappears. Not altogether, but fundamentally and in principle it disappears. It is needed no more.

—

The supreme Power is taking up all the movements. It will turn them into the Truth. No effort is needed, no aid from the mind or any of the instruments; even the individual consent is no longer needed.

—

Tuesday

The fulfilment has undeniably begun. Till the 7th January this present development; the last mental clearance, the first final opening.

Wednesday

All has been cleared of what was left of the pure representative; only a colouring, an attenuating edge remains in the interpretative imperative. This has to disappear and will disappear, as the true form develops. If something lingers for a time, it will be of no potency and of no importance.

The full light in the interpretative, today — The full power in the imperative tomorrow.

Thursday. Jan 6.

What has been promised has been achieved. There remains the perfection of the supreme supermind taking up the supreme supramental supermind, the development of the Trikalsiddhi Tapas and the manifestation of the Gnosis. This from today to the 12th.

The fullness achieved has come on the 6th one day earlier than anticipated, but on the day promised. What was promised for the 7th was the completion of the first curve (or second, (1) 25 – 3d (2) 3d to 7th (3) 7th to 12th). Tomorrow therefore the appearance of the gnosis in the action of the supreme supermind
—

For her peace and surrender.

7 JANUARY – 1 FEBRUARY 1927

Friday Jan 7th

The gnosis has taken hold of the lesser movements of knowledge; not yet of the supreme supermind or the greater movements. It will do that now in spite of all difficulties.

The gnosis taking up the supermind means the Trikalsiddhi-Tapas.

––––––

After the 12th these difficulties will disappear.

==

It is the doubt that interferes. In spite of the doubt I will accomplish. Now.

––––––

Saturday. Jan 8th

I have prepared the ground for the gnosis. The fulfilment begins today in the face of every denial.

Sunday Jan 9th

The taking up of T^3 by gnosis has already begun. It will be initially completed today. All these menaces will utterly disappear in a few days.

This is the beginning. The rest will develop automatically throughout the evening and night.

Monday. Jan 10th

The movement yesterday took place, but was veiled and hampered. Today it is emerging in light. All the thought is being taken up by the derivative gnosis. T^3 has begun in all the movements, – this was what was meant by initial completion; today it is spreading. The old obstructions however still remain in thought T$\underline{y}$ [Telepathy] and other movements.

Today thought and T^3 will continue to develop

As the gnosis of thought progresses, gnosis of the heart, the will, the vital movements will begin to develop. Here also the first touch was given this morning.

=

It is evident that the T^3 is undergoing the process, but as yet it is rather a working on old obstacles than a positive process and a positive progress.

———

Tuesday Jan 11th

The curve that was to have ascended till the 12th seems to have abruptly ended. A confused working in obstructive mental material seems to have taken its place.

=

Yet it will be fulfilled. Today the T^3 in the supreme supermind and gnosis. T^2 begins on the same level. This is contrary to all appearances, but it will happen.

=

In that case these are preparatory movements. What has happened is the progressive seizing of all the movements by the Ishwara and the increase of the tertiary dasya.

———

Wednesday Jan 12th

In spite of all opposition what has been promised is effected, only initially yesterday, it is true, but more completely today.

The supreme supermind has taken up the supreme supramental supermind and all the other inferior movements and is itself being penetrated by the gnosis. Substantially done in all other thought action, this process is taking up T^3 for its transformation. T^2 has begun on this level, but that is not yet perfectly apparent.

Today, complete T^3 in supreme supermind gnosis, initial T^2 in gnosis, increasing T^2 in supreme supermind gnosis. These three things.

=

T^3 is already gaining amplitude, but is interfered with by movements of incertitude, because T^2 [in]^1 s.s.gn. [supreme supermind gnosis] is quite insufficient. It is however beginning to increase.

—

The application to all things of T^2 gnosis or T^3 gnosis is a matter of time. It is the foundation of the thing that is the immediate work in hand. At the same time the application too need not be gradual, it may and will be rapid. A vertiginous rapidity is possible.

—

Mark that the dependence on the critical verifying mind decreases. Verification is becoming automatic, criticism also automatic. Both will soon be entirely gnostic. The next curve is from the 12th to the 16th, another from the 16th to the 21st, another from the 21st to the 24th, yet another from the 24th 25th to the 28th. The last of this month is from the 28th to the 31st.

—

The final dealings with this body begin from today. The first stage of them finishes with the end of the month.

=

And with her body it begins from tomorrow. At present it is the preparation of the forces.

=

Thursday. Jan 13th

The T^2 in supreme supermind gnosis acted, but not on a large scale. Something of the other two indications came into practice, but not sufficiently to satisfy the demand of the intelligence.

The dealings with the body are not yet clearly final. In most matters there is a progress or a stability in the stage acquired, but there is a successful relapse in the eye and possibly in one or two other places.

=

There is undoubtedly a large scale progress in the thought-siddhi and all its instruments. The form of the supreme supermind is about to be universal, only the substance of gnosis in it is still insufficient.

^{1} *MS* is

The preparation for T^3 and T^2 is evident, but the obstruction is violent and partially successful.

Nothing more till that obstruction is vanquished.

—

The development of the gnosis above and in the supreme supermind can alone conquer the obstruction in its last lines.

That will be done. Tonight the inception of this movement.

—

Friday Jan 14th

Telepathic T^2 has already developed. The Tapasic is preparing to develop.

All will be done in spite of all the obstruction and all the difficulties.

Today the health and Ananda will develop. Tomorrow the evidence will be undeniable.

The attack on her body yesterday flatly denies the "Thursday" prediction. In this body there is evidence of control, but not of any final progress. The obstruction to finality is still successful, still obstinate.

—

For this body the evidence is tomorrow; for hers it is veiled and will only appear day after tomorrow.

Today the gnosis in T^2 (tapas). Also the gnosis above the supermind in T^2 tapas.

Saturday Jan 15th

The development of health and Ananda promised yesterday is not at all clear in result. There is evidence of power to control and minimise attacks on the health, but there is not yet power to prevent them. The small fragments of the old illnesses still recur a little.

There is sahaituka Ananda in the body on a small scale and it tends to increase in intensity, spontaneity and recurrence, but it has no body or long continuance.

—

The work seems rather to be turned towards increasing a relative Samata and Faith than in bringing the gnosis. In the latter movement there is only evident a strong clouding obstruction behind which no doubt some work is being done.

=

The effects promised yesterday seem to be declaring themselves today. Ananda (sahaituka, touch etc) has suddenly progressed after a long obstruction and developed a remarkable spontaneous continuity and body. [Absolute]^2 spontaneity, penetration and diffusion, continuity without the help of memory or attention have still to develop.

—

It is evident also that a kind of gnosis is taking possession of T^2; but there is still an immense amount of work to be done. There is too a kind of gnosis descending from above, but it is not yet free nor rich in circumstance nor absolute to the mind in its conveyance of certitude. There is also some gnosis of T^3. All these things however although they begin to come more rapidly and freely, are still initial, hampered and poor in affluence.

—

Surrender, dasya, consolidation of the inner movements and initially the outer movements in the hands of the directing Power and Persons (or its Personalities) is becoming or beginning to become absolute.

Today, gnosis takes possession of all thought and T^3. Gnosis in T^2 develops in the supermind and above it.

The invincible Gnosis of the Divine will make its first appearance.

=

The proofs of the Power dealing with the body are rather in the development of Ananda and the control of certain functionings than in any finality of health. The fragments of old illnesses remain

---

2 *MS* Absolutely

obstinately potential or obstinately actual. The hold diminishes but there is still the recurrence.

====

Sunday Jan 16ᵗʰ

The possession of all thought and T³ by the gnosis is increasing, but it is frequently interrupted. The invincible Gnosis seems to appear, but in too thick and mixed a mass of movement and itself too occasional to create a clear recognition or an assured confidence.

—

Doubt is acute as regards the physical siddhi.

=

The divine Gnosis in T², that which is above the Telepathic and above the Tapasic trikalsiddhi and above the combination of these things, is beginning to manifest but only as a kind of occasional point or star above the mass movement.

=

These will continue to develop. Nothing will be left soon of the physical opposition to health and Ananda.

====

Monday Jan 17ᵗʰ

Thought telepathy, prâkâmya, vyapti are trying to manifest, but the obstruction is heavy. The general mental and vital condition can be perceived by *sanyama*, habitual movements also, but precise movements only with difficulty and some incertitude.

=

Sahaituka ananda also continues to develop. There is a tendency to generalise its gains; but the physical non-response is still heavy. Spontaneous Sahaituka (without aid of memory [or]³ attention[)] occasionally manifests and is nearer to the surface.

=

Gnosis continues to develop in the thought-siddhi and its instruments. Today the T².

---

³ MS of

It had been predicted that something would be done in six days for the healing in her body, that is by the 17th, and in fact a great relief and amelioration is evident; but not the decisive cure that had been taken to be the sense of the promise.

———

The physical proof has been given that the thrill of Sahaituka Ananda can be eternised in the body, but the time is not yet. The nature of it is still subtle vital material with a strong beginning of density, not yet the dense entirely material Ananda.

═══

Tuesday Jan 18th

Yesterday the representative + inspirational imperative movement hitherto normal (the rest coming in concentrated movements) began to be definitely replaced in the universality by the interpretative + inspirational-interpretative imperative. This is a radical progress, but the new movement is not yet entirely gnostic —

———

Telepathy of general mind conditions and habitual mind movements and formations continues to develop.

═══

There has been an apparent relapse in the Arogya. Primary utthapana has begun a strong forward movement; the secondary is greatly hampered.

———

Ad

Development of Gnosis in thought-siddhi and its instruments. Continued growth of T^2.

═══

Wednesday Jan 19th.

Yesterday there was a strong attempt to dismiss [finally][4] the remnants of intellect, ideality, supramentality and after giving full play to the supramental and supreme supramental to pass beyond to the supreme supramental mind in the supreme supermind so as to prepare the strongest forms for the T^2 and gnosis.

[4] MS finality

Afterwards a crisis of questioning and a renunciation of personal action (in the suggestive mental Devasura) and an entire passivity in which some kind of action professedly gnostic or semi-gnostic is going on in a narrow and rigid form of inspirational imperative and a minor form of interpretative imperative thought-force

The development of Gnosis in the thought-siddhi and its instruments shall continue, also the growth of T^3 and T^2.

The crisis in her body continues in all its adverse acuteness. The causes seem to be not personal, but due to circumstance favouring blind surrounding physical and vital physical influences.

Thursday Jan 20
The adverse crisis continues in great violence.
In this body there seems to be a turn for the better, not yet final and decisive. A certain overmastering Ishwara influence already dominantly successful in certain directions, control of functionings etc, is extending its activity to the remaining fragmentary illnesses.

Development of supreme supermind, gnosis and T^2 continues. But the obstruction and partiality of result also continue.

Friday Jan 21
At last the power seems to be acting on the body. As predicted, there are the first signs of amelioration in her body, though nothing yet is complete or in appearance finally decisive. Still the black obstruction has failed to persevere.

This morning free gnosis in all the movements of the thought-siddhi and its instruments in a rapid and almost instantaneous development. This is the first free and large movement of the involved method.

At present Tapas movements and telepathy-Tapas movements

are being handled. A relative T^2 in them with a great mixture of ineffective knowledge and will movements is taking place.

T^3 and T^2 to be made perfect like the gnostic thought in a vertiginously rapid movement. This will take place at first in a limited field of operations, then with a certain universality, then with a basic absoluteness applicable everywhere.

The physical siddhi advances, but is still too much obstructed. Ananda (sahaituka) increases in intensity, in prolongation (continuity), in spontaneous occurrence. This must be made perfect without farther retardation.

The entire removal of the fragments of old illness will not be immediate, but will yet speedily happen.

In the evening solution of difficulties and rapid progress in (1) Lipi, (2) Thought-siddhi, (3) T^3 (4) Drishya (5) Samadhi (6) Sahaituka Ananda.

Attacks on health, but the progress seems still to continue.

Saturday Jan 22ᵈ

Sarvam Anantam Anandam Brahma seems to be well established in its fundamental universality (except for some *duhkha-bhoga* of result on the vital plane and some movements of physical semi-discomfort) and is growing in intensity. Gnanam Brahma consciousness grows, but needs development of T^3 & T^2 for full play.

Increase in Ananda (Sahaituka, chiefly sparsha, but also the others), T^3, T^2, Samadhi etc.

All grows rapidly, but all is still imperfect.

Sunday Jan 23$\underline{d}$

Rapid increase and spread through the body of mental material & vital material Sahaituka Ananda. The physical material is acute as yet only in the hands except for the immediate Sparsha which is now intense everywhere. Prolongation and diffusion have begun and will soon be well-established.

===

T^3 grows rapidly in gnosis. T^2 in T^3 seems definitely to have begun, but not yet in unmixed gnosis.

===

Attack on the Karma. Strong obstruction to equipment.

===

The difficulties now experienced, difficulties mainly of obstruction, will disappear today and tomorrow.

===

The body has still not shaken off entirely yesterday's sudden attack of fatigue and pains of fatigue. The energy is unimpaired, the fatigue and pains can be dismissed, but they return as soon as the body rests after long walking.

===

In spite of all appearances tomorrow will mark an immense stride in the Arogya-siddhi.

Today the obstacles to Ananda and telepathic T^3 disappear, — not entirely but in dominant practice.

===

There was some appearance of a beginning of the disappearance of difficulties, but an adverse wave arrived and this movement ended.

===

Only the Arogya is slightly better, but whether this movement is permanent or not cannot yet be decided. Previous experience and present perception are against the idea of permanence. A gradual progress is the sole thing visible.

——

In the night a violent reaction. All thrown in doubt preparing the revival of a chaotic half-intellectual movement full of the mixture of falsehood and incertitude.

===

Monday Jan 24th

The adverse movement continues. Especially T^2 and T^3 seem petty in their achievement and full of error and incertitude. It is doubted whether gnosis is at all manifested or anything but a mixed mind and supermind with at most a few true supramental movements.

———

Universal perception of the Sarvam Anantam Anandam Brahma-Purusha. Ananda complete in all vishayas, especially sight, but not the intense completeness. The intensity came afterwards, but subsided. The completeness of the quiet Vishaya Ananda and universal Saundarya is still not always absolute.

═══

The difficulties did not altogether disappear. Some began to dwindle. Ananda of the body (sahaituka) made some progress.

T^3 also made progress. The telepathic, tapasic and veiled gnostic accuracies in the telepathic T^2 were increased and exemplified from time to time. The mixture of error and imitative or encasing or accompanying and distorting mind action still continues.

For some time there has been a powerful attack on the Karma. The prospect of equipment seems entirely clouded and threatened.

═══

Arogya in this body seemed to make some progress. If the progress made turns out to be permanent, it may be called a large stride in the siddhi.

═══

Tuesday. Jan 25th.

In the morning after a violent struggle continuing from the last few days, the conviction of falsehood began to lessen. Thought in the supramentalities and supramental began to arrange itself in the gnosis as had already been done with thought in the intuitive forms and processes. All these movements no longer exist in their initial and independent forms, but have been taken up into the supreme supramental and supreme supermind. The highest interpretative imperative acts as an intermediary force, lifting the former into the latter.

Organised T^3 and T^2 in these forms is at last preparing. Hitherto it was all in the lesser powers.

=

A great but chaotic profusion of jagrat bahirdarshi drishya began yesterday. Today organisation and some kind of stability is being introduced into this—as yet imperfect—freedom.

=

Rapid progress in Ananda. Ahaituka sparshananda is spreading; great continuity with intensity both in this and sahaituka, especially in the hands. The habitual movements of inhibition are losing their iron hold.

——

Today, tomorrow gnostic T^2 in initial perfection. Ananda, Vishaya, Samadhi, Arogya.

Wednesday Jan 26th

Again a strong attack and confusion in the morning. Attempt of the chaos of the mind movements to reestablish its reign under pretence of transforming finally the supramentality into gnosis.

=

Exceedingly intense Sahaituka Sparshananda tried to generalise itself after a first successful manifestation; the conditions were too unfavourable.

—

Some modification of the universal Darshana—simultaneous vision of Parameswara-Parameswari in all.

Some attempt at T^2. Some progress in Samadhi although in sushupta Swapna the incoherence continues.

The Arogya has once more been thrown back. Physical fatigue continues underlying and arising after an hour's physical exertion or even less. Up till the morning there was progress.

Drishya continues to develop but no distinct forward step.

=

T^2 is developing, but the medium and casing are so obscure and mental a material that even continued success brings no certitude.

===

Thursday Jan 27th.

Today a great revival. A vertiginous rapidity of progress in many directions. The attack of obscurity, resistance of the universal inconscience, refusal of the universal inertia, obstruction and conservatism of the material negation are beginning to lessen and even where they persist and intervene, cannot resist the progress. The past effects may still continue for a time, the future is not theirs. The four Powers that resisted now appear more clearly, – the Dragon of the nether foundations who preserves the old Law intact till the will of the Supreme is manifested, the Sphinx of the eternal questioning, the Night of the eternal negation, the Rock (stone Purusha, inert Shiva) of the eternal inertia. Still they are there, but a first victory has been assured against them.

—

Thought gnostic in essence, free, automatic, voluminous, not yet perfectly organised or complete, has been finally established and, except at intervals, acts even in the obscurity and inert relaxation of the material consciousness.

Surrender is complete; horizontal movements of desire cross but are [ ]⁵ easily rejected.

Samata is complete except for certain external movements that touch the physical sensation.

Shakti, Virya, Daivi Prakriti are returning and moving towards perfection.

Sraddha is there again, though not yet assured in all that concerns the final effectuality of the Tapas.

T^3, T^2 are developing much more clearly and consciously than before. T is beginning to manifest.

=

Stable organisation and organised stability are rapidly preparing in the Drishya, but are not yet accomplished.

=

---

⁵ MS are

A certain perfection and absoluteness established in seven powers, samata, surrender, virya, shakti, daivi prakriti, thought (not T^3 or T^2 thought), faith (in the Supreme and his workings, not in the immediate realisation[)].

=

Friday Jan 28th.

A great progress in primary utthapana. The fatigue attack entirely disappears. Two hours exertion without any effect on the body except a pain in the loins at once dismissed. All other effects could be rejected at will. The left leg becomes almost as free as the right. The back and loins have still to be entirely liberated, but a relative freedom is effected.

=

A rapid increase in the control of certain bodily functionings.

=

Otherwise the day seems to be one of preparation rather than achievement.

—

Development of gnostic thought-powers.

Saturday. Jan. 29th

The opposition of the Four Matter Powers is being wrought into assent; but the process has necessar[il]y slowed down the action which tends often to flicker down into quiescence.

———

All the same T^3 and T^2 often combined together are becoming more common and more definite. All doubt with regard to them is over, although owing to imitative movements in the Ignorance, much confusion and incertitude continue.

—

Gnostic T is emerging more clearly, but is so much cased in the obscurity of the Inconscience that seeks to be or have knowledge, it is impossible to distinguish it clearly from the counterfeit except by result and occasionally by an automatic and undoubting certitude.

It is at the same time evident that when it acts it is of the nature of omniscience and omnipotence.

=

Drishya settled in all but the spontaneous full stability which obtains only in the crude forms.

=

Ananda spreads but is not as yet organised and generalised in the responses of the body.

—

The action on health in both bodies is more evident but not yet entirely conclusive.

Sunday Jan 30th

Again a day of preparation and of apparent check rather than of progress.

=

Such progress as has been made is in Darshana, Drishya, confirmation of T^3 and T^2. Thought etc are held up for the moment.

—

Vani has long been silent. Today it is trying to emerge.

=

Today, in the evening Thought-siddhi and gnostic T will overcome the obstacle.

The final victory in Arogya is evidently preparing. In a few days it will be perfect.

After Arogya Ananda.

Meanwhile utthapana and saundarya will prepare.

All the third chatusthaya will soon be liberated from its still remaining shackles.

=

Thought-siddhi at its best resumed in the evening. Gnostic T manifested, but extension and organisation are not yet possible.

=

Monday Jan 31st

A day of relapse and resistance.

=

Tuesday. Feb 1st

The siddhi began to recover. A step forward in Darshana (Aditi holding P^a-P^i [Parameshwara-Parameshwari] in all living things, less vividly in all objects). This is not yet entirely universalised but it is increasing.

—

Primary utthapana oppressed during the last days once more progresses. Stiffness and muscular pains are still possible, though they can be ejected by the knowledge-will movement. They are most prominent when the exertion ceases, but do not endure. The latent memory however persists and brings them back at customary times or junctures.

—

Drishya progresses. There is full stability of crude forms, conditional or initial or aided longer stability of others..

—

T^2 (T^2 T^3) progresses, but cannot get rid of incertitude.

Control of functions, violently interrupted for the last two days, is returning.

=

April 7. 1927 Thursday

There must be an entire submission to the transforming Power and the transforming process. However tedious it may [seem], each step, each recoil is inevitable; nothing is done unwisely or vainly in the economy of the supreme processes.

There is a sure means of distinguishing the truth from the falsehood. Pause and refer to the Light of the gnosis.

The truth that comes may not be all the truth, but it is that which is needed and effective at the moment.

Entire passivity first, a passive surrender.

Entire equanimity next, an absolute samata.

An entire and harmonised strength of the divine nature

An entire faith in the Supreme and his Divine Power, in the process and the result of the process. These are the four conditions of the rapid and decisive change.

April 8th Friday

The conditions are satisfied to a sufficient degree. The next steps are now possible which will make them perfect.

First the decisive T^2, the exact T^3, the perfect thought in the gnosis or at least in the supramental gnosis — ie the three degrees intuition, supermind, gnostic supermind, if not yet in the fourth or supreme degree of divine gnosis.

Second, the consciousness gnostic in all the body and all the environmental atmosphere.

Third, the gnostic Power in the body for the transformation of the body.

April 9th Saturday.

Passivity is now practically complete; surrender in the physical consciousness a little less, but still almost complete.

Equanimity is moving towards automatic completeness but is still imperfect.

Faith is limited and poor

Strength is there, but neither harmonised nor complete

[*Three pages with other writing (probably written earlier) intervene here.*]

April 9th

The first gradation of the Gnosis, ie the intuitivity, is being now securely organised in a universal and automatic action.

It is still mixed with mental stuff, imperfect therefore, limited in scope, insecure in decisive T^2; but it is there.

It has to be perfected. Meanwhile the others will be made ready.

═══

Exact T^3 and perfect thought in the intuition. This is ready to be perfect. Perfect it.

Decisive T^2 is ready to be founded in the intuition. Found it.

Press on the elimination of illness undeterred by the resistance till it disappears for ever.

These three things are now possible.

═══

April 10th

The equanimity is almost entire.

Faith has greatly increased, but is not absolute.

Strength is harmonised and in a way completed, but in a form that is still mediocre.

───

The forms of the gnosis are in final preparation. The three things required yesterday are being done, but as yet there is nothing definite. The truth thought is however becoming easy and automatic.

Let the T^3 grow swiftly.

———

There is a commencement of the automatic external Ananda. Fix it.

═══

April 12th

A still more perfect equanimity.

Faith more settled, more complete, but still not absolute, awaiting knowledge.

Strength confirmed, but vague and formless.

Passivity complete

———

T^3 has begun to be automatic; but is still imperfect.

═══

The three things demanded are still in a very initial stage.

═══

April 13th

After a brief attack briefly successful, passivity, equanimity, faith, strength are established stronger and completer than before.

———

Thought is almost perfected in the intuition and in the other forms so far as they can be supported on the narrow intuitive basis.

T^3 is growing swiftly and moving towards a large development, T^2 begins to develop a limited but automatic accuracy.

═══

Automatic external Ananda has begun to be fixed. Only memory is necessary.

═══

April 14th

Only mechanical movements contrary to passivity, equanimity and faith occur; usually they are thin and without substance.

Strength is still not continuous except in the old lesser form.

There is still a lack of the guiding Power; except at times all seems to be done by the mechanism of the forces with only an intervention of the smaller physical godheads and voices.

———

The supramental development and organisation of jagrat and swapna samadhi is trying to begin in earnest.

All the thought instruments have been taken up into the movement. Lipi and identity knowledge are most developed.

Automatic external ananda in its first fixity is beginning a preliminary organisation.

====

April 15th

Much obstruction today.

Strength seems in the end to be more firmly founded

—

Internal physical Ananda is beginning to be founded.

There are signs that drishya (with open eyes) is about to develop stability in the forms which till now were fugitive. It is increasing in the others.

Samadhi organisation proceeds, but is still initial and obscure.

Vishaya started last night, but does not as yet progress.

=

Tonight. Completeness of third chatusthaya to be initially founded

Fourth chatusthaya (half) to be thoroughly founded.

The rest to be prepared in essence.

===

Note — This last prediction or order does not seem to have been fulfilled even in part. The condition was clouded, ineffective and obscure.

April 16th

Progress has been mostly in the external physical Ananda. There was a recovery of gnostic thought and T³ which had been almost suspended yesterday, but this came late in the afternoon.

Strength seems to be founded, but the attack on faith and samata has been all day heavy and fierce.

———

April 17th

Samadhi. First initial organisation of thought, trikaldrishti, lipi, event and drishya up to the sushupta swapna.

Farther purification of thought, T^3 and control including Vani.

Harmonisation of shakti with surrender and samata. Preparation of a harmony of these things with gnostic knowledge.

Vishaya. Persistent and stably visible vision of birds (small dark figures, jivanta, on the horizon[)]. For the first time liberty of this siddhi.

———

April 18th

All the movements are being reduced to gnosis, first those that were intellectual.

Remarkable movements of tapasic T^3.

Samadhi and Drishya continue to develop.

The rest are maintained but not in progress.

=

Passivity, surrender, faith, strength are constantly growing more perfect and harmonious with each other.

=

The third chatusthaya must be and will be rapidly completed and perfected.

The fourth must be finally undertaken before the end of the month.

The fifth, sixth and seventh will progress with the progress of the third and fourth chatushtayas.

═══

April 19th to 21st.

Three days strong obstruction.

Perfect founding of sukham and hasyam along with calm and samata.

Firm founding of the virya and shakti along with the daivi prakriti and sraddha.

These foundations seem now to be integral siddhis. Both are being tested but resist attack. Only the deha-shakti is seriously overcome at times, but this is due to the defect of utthapana and belongs less to the second than the fourth [chatusthaya].[1]

==

April 22d

First experience of entire gnostic intuition and supramental reason with supramental observation and a supramental recipient in the physical nature.

—

Intuition and supramental reason (all the grades except supreme supermind) are being steadily founded in a first integral movement.

Supreme supermind has also commenced its integral foundation.

==

All this in the thought chiefly. T[3] however has begun to be taken into the movement.

==

—————

[1] *MS* utthapana

24–31 OCTOBER 1927

October 24th. 1927

A day of great and rapid progress. The supreme supermind forms have begun to be normalised and taken up by the gnosis. T^2 has made some, although still a hampered progress. T^3 is now normal. Telepathies are becoming automatic but still need for their manifestation a slight *sanyama*. Ananda (*shârîra*) rapidly progresses. Samadhi has made some advance.

=

Today the gnosticised supreme supermind even to its highest forms will become normal.[1]

There will be the beginning of the promised progress in all the vishayas.[2]

Samadhi will break its barriers.[3]

Ahaituka Ananda within the body will be definitely founded.[4]

≡

(1) Fulfilled to a certain degree.[1] But neither the gnosticity nor the normality are at all complete, rather they are in this field only initial.

(2) A meagre fulfilment; just the beginning in each if it is maintained, but hitherto the development of the vishayas has always been dropped after a brief movement

(3) Fulfilled but not completely. The obstruction is still there.

(4) Uncertain; it seems to have begun, but it is not clear that it is definitely founded.

―――

---

[1] *The fulfilment of the above predictions was written afterwards in a different ink. The numbers after the items of the programme were added when their fulfilment was recorded. — Ed.*

October 25th 1927

Today, there is something of a recoil into the hampered semi-mental movement, although the progress still continues. However, the movements or rather the touches from outside of Asamata etc, the contradictions of the first two chatusthayas, were not only mechanical, but though they pierced could not hold the consciousness in the body or even the environmental conscious atmosphere; few, they were almost immediately or immediately flung outside.

Intensity in the sahaituka physical Ananda is rapidly increasing in all the Anandas including the raudra.

Rupa is at last moving forward towards prolonged stability of the perfect and initially real and not only the crude, dense or [developed]² figures.

There is an attempt to return to the evolution of primary utthapana, ie abolition of fatigue and its symptoms

Prognosis is now no longer in the script and lipi only, but in the thought speech and vani.

====

(Oct 27th)

The semi-mental movement increased and the sadhana fell back from the rapidity it had gained to a movement of return on old elements still imperfectly transfigured. This relapse has lasted two days but was not so intense as before and has created no reaction. Moreover, it has been visibly the preparation of most important transitional movements that have come to a head today, the 27th October.

Oct 29. 1927

A day of relaxation, dismissal of out-of-date elements and preparation for the descent of gnosis into the overmind system.

These four days are for the transition to gnosis. Afterwards the whole system will be perfected and applied before there is the ascent to the supermind plane.

====

---

² *MS* delivered

Oct 30. 1927

Today the transition from T^3 to T^2 became decisive and with it there came the conception of the Ishwara in the bodily consciousness. The passive attitude of the T^3 movement in which the nature is the plaything of the powers of the Overmind has been definitely abandoned and the passive-active attitude of T^2 movement in which the Ishwara determines and the Powers may for a time resist and even modify temporarily what he has determined, but must now or in the end help to carry out his will, has begun to take its place. As yet the gnostic movement is imperfect and the Overmind powers are still powerful to determine results according to their choice, provided there is some supramental sanction behind it. All are powers of the Ishwara, but the play of disagreement and mutual opposition or emulation continues. T^3 is entirely supramental or gnostic, T^2 only has partially reached the same siddhi.

———

Oct 31. 1927

Today T^2 (anishwara) has acquired the supramental and gnostic character. Not that all movements have entirely eliminated the mental element, but all are supramental or supramentalised or else even (now to some extent) gnostic overmind. Infallible T^2 is beginning more freely to emerge.

Iswara consciousness is growing both below and above and Ishwara T^2 is beginning.

The supermind is increasing in the supramentalised movements and gnosis in the supramental movements.

Ananda is taking possession and becomes automatic, needing only memory or a little attention to act at once. All vision, hearing, smell, taste, touch is now anandamaya; even all that is seen, heard, sensed is beginning to be felt as full of ananda and even as if made of Ananda. Sahaituka Ananda of all except event is now automatic. Ahaituka Ananda within the body shows signs of reaching the same state, but has not quite reached it. This is the only physical siddhi that promises to be soon initially complete; for arogya is still hampered by obstinate minute fragments of illness.

———

Part Four

Materials Written by Sri Aurobindo
Related Directly to *Record of Yoga*
c. 1910 – 1931

UNDATED RECORD AND RECORD-RELATED NOTES

c. 1910–1914

[1]

[. . .] in Σ position
VM & flash of sattwa —
1. Bidhu ⎫
         ⎬ present
2 Susthir ⎭
3 Bhadrakali — future
4. Table in Baroda — past
5 Namadrishti — letter from M. [Motilal Roy?]
6. Stars in psychic sky — paralokadrishti.
7. An urchin shaking flag — ihalokadrishti.

[2]

Bhasha. — 1. The intuition continues to work, not perfectly.
      2. The inspiration developed on the connection of Tamil with O.S. [Old Sanskrit] pointing out lost significations, old roots, otherwise undiscoverable derivations.
      3. The supreme inspiration yet inoperative.
Thought.   Quiet and no longer subject to obstruction, but not yet perfectly satisfying, liable to be displaced; working often with the perception only, defective in driving force, therefore imperfectly convincing.
    Sight.
      In Samadhi, the lingas of the bodies, — all except jyotik and varnaghana.
      The jagrat mainly inoperative, except the momentary manifestation of a pranamaya purusha, angushthamatra, from the sukshma; fulfilling the prophecy for the day.

Prophecy— As above. The mind deals with the past by means of perception, not revelation. Necessarily no proof.

Doubt— Only in anna and with regard to particulars in their details.

The Body— Visrishti unusually copious in both kinds. Weakness in annam and rapid fatigue

Asus— Working absolutely in the body, with more force than formerly in the buddhi and prana. Sattwic krodh in the chitta manifests free from the rajasic taint of an unsatisfied prana. Prema. Bhogasamarthyam increasing, but insufficient.

Aishwaryam etc. The Will began to act directly from the sahasradal with swift and invariable, though not instantaneous effect. The imperative vyaptis still resisted

A general deficiency of force experienced. The old humanity very strong in the annam and through the annam obstructive but not dominant in the whole system

[3]

[*Sanskrit Formulas — Second Chatushtaya*]

वीर्यं—अभयं, साहसं, यशोलिप्सात्मश्लाघा क्षत्रियस्य, दानं व्ययशीलता कौशलं भोगलिप्सा वैश्यस्य, ज्ञानप्रकाशो ज्ञानलिप्सा ब्रह्मवर्चस्यं स्थैर्यं ब्राह्मणस्य, प्रेम कामो दास्यलिप्सात्मसमर्पणं शूद्रस्य, सर्वेषां तेजो बलं प्रवृत्तिर्महत्त्वमिति वीर्यं ।

शक्तिः— देहस्य महत्त्वबोधो बलश्लाघा लघुत्वं धारणसामर्थ्यञ्च, प्राणस्य पूर्णता प्रसन्नता समता भोगसामर्थ्यञ्च, चित्तस्य स्निग्धता तेजःश्लाघा कल्याणश्रद्धा, प्रेमसामर्थ्यञ्च, बुद्धेर्विशुद्धता [प्रकाशो] विचित्रबोधः सर्वज्ञानकार्यसामर्थ्यञ्च, सर्वेषां तु क्षिप्रता स्थैर्यमदीनता चेश्वरभाव इति शक्तिः ।

चण्डीभावः— शौर्यमुग्रता युद्धलिप्साट्टहास्यं दया [चेश्वर]भावश्च सर्वसामर्थ्य-मिति चण्डीभावस्य सप्तकं ।

श्रद्धा तु निहतसंशयाप्रतिहता निष्ठा भगवति च स्वशक्त्याञ्च ।

[4]

[Sanskrit Formulas – Devibhava]

महालक्ष्मीभावः – सौन्दर्यदृष्टिः लालित्यं कल्याणलिप्सा प्रेमहास्यं दया चे-
श्वरभावः सर्वकर्मसामर्थ्यं

महेश्वरीभावः – सत्यदृष्टिः ऋजुतामहिमा बृहल्लिप्सा ज्ञानहास्यं दया चेश्वर-
भावः सर्वकर्मसामर्थ्यं

महासरस्वतीभावः – कर्मपाटवं विद्या उद्योगलिप्सा सुखहास्यं दया चेश्वर-
भावः सर्वकर्मसामर्थ्यं

[5]

[Sanskrit Formulas – Dasya]

गुरुशिष्यभावः
    अधमः   –   दासभावात्मकः
    मध्यमः   –   सख्यभावात्मकः
    उत्तमः   –   मधुरभावात्मकः

दास्यभावः
    अधमः   किङ्करभावात्मकः
    मध्यमः   सख्यभावात्मकः
    उत्तमः   मधुरबद्धभावात्मकः

सख्यभावः
    अधमः   गुरुशिष्यभावात्मकः
    मध्यमः   सहचरभावात्मकः
    उत्तमः   मधुरबद्धभावात्मकः

वात्सल्यभावः
    अधमः   पाल्यपालकभावात्मकः
    मध्यमः   स्नेहभावात्मकः
    उत्तमः   मधुरभावात्मकः

मधुरभावः
    अधमः   स्त्रीपुरुषभावात्मकः
    मध्यमः   स्वैरभावात्मकः
    उत्तमः   दासभावात्मकः

[6]

[Sanskrit Formulas — Third Chatushtaya]

त्रिकालदृष्टिः – प्राकाम्यं व्याप्तिः साक्षाद्ज्ञानं प्रेरणा सहजदृष्टिर्विवेकः शकुनि-
दृष्टिर्ज्योतिषदृष्टिः सामुद्रिकदृष्टिः सूक्ष्मदृष्टिर्विज्ञानदृष्टिर्दिव्यदृष्टिश्चित्रदृष्टिः स्था-
पत्यदृष्टी रूपदृष्टिरिति त्रिकालदर्शनस्य विविधा उपायाः। ते तु द्विविधविषया
यथा परकालविषया इहकालविषयाश्च। तस्मिन्नपि द्विविधविषये शब्ददृष्टिः
स्पर्शदृष्टिर्देहदृष्टी रसदृष्टिर्गन्धदृष्टिरिति भागाः। देहक्रियाविषयाः चिन्तादृष्टिश्च
भावदृष्टिः बोधदृष्टिश्चान्तःकरणसंश्लिष्टा। अन्या अपि सन्त्यप्रकाशिताः।

सर्वज्ञानं – सर्वविषये अप्रतिहतो ज्ञानप्रकाश इति सर्वज्ञानं तस्मिंश्च साक्षाद्-
ज्ञानं प्रेरणा सहजदृष्टिर्विवेकश्च प्रमुखाः बोधः स्मृतिः विचारो वितर्कः
साक्षाद्ज्ञाने बोधः सर्वविधः अप्रतिहतः, प्रेरणायां वाक् च स्मृतिश्च सहजदृष्ट्यां
वितर्कोऽप्रतिहतोऽभ्रान्तश्च विवेके तु विश्लेष प्रज्ञा चेति विचारः

सिद्धाष्टकं ज्ञातमेव।

सर्वत्रगतिः। व्याप्त्यां वा चिन्तायां भावे बोधे सर्वभूतानां सर्वत्रगतिः शारीरिकी
तु सप्तदेहेषु स्वप्ने सुषुप्त्यां वा जाग्रत्यां वा। अन्नमयस्त्वाकाशगत्या निःसृत्य
सर्वत्र गच्छति जाग्रत्यां, प्राणमयस्तु यश्छायामयः कल्पनामयः त्रिषु तद्वत्
तेजोमयः सूक्ष्मश्च यौ द्विविधौ मनोमयौ विज्ञानमयश्च बुद्धिमयश्च यौ द्विविधौ
महति प्रतिष्ठितौ।

[7]

12 types	Wisdom. Greatness. Calm
	Strength. Speed. Wrath
	Love. Joy. Prodigality
	Intellect. Desire. Service.

7 anandas — Kama — Prema — Ahaituka — Chid. Suddha — Nirguna
— Siddha.

= 84 worlds.

with 7 below, nine above = 100

7 below. Gandharva (beauty). Yaksha (pleasure). Kinnara
(fantasy). Aghora (samata). Swadhina (freedom). Deva (love).
Asura (might & glory) from lowest to highest

9 above. Vaikuntha, Goloka, Brahmaloka, Meruloka, Visva-
devaloka (Karmadevatas), Ganaloka, Jnanaloka from top to bottom

[. . .] = Suryaloka. Swar – Chandraloka & Swarga. Jana, Tapah & Satya above

Swar – Chandraloka – Pitriloka; Kailas above, between 7 tiers of 14 worlds, according to types – Pashu, Pisacha, Pramatha, Rakshasa, Asura, Deva, Siddha –

Swarga – 7 – Kama, Yuddha, Prema, Manas, Jnana, Nishkama & Bhagavata

Naraka – offences of or against Kama, Prema, Satya, Ishwara, [?Devata], Jnana, Atma –   12 hells in each.

[8]

Idomeneus. Coriolanus. Antony. Richelieu. C. [Caius] Gracchus St Louis. Charles V.

Deiphobus. Brasidas.. T. [Tiberius] Gracchus. Clarence. Louis XII Lafayette. Pompey.

T. [Titus] Manlius. Marcellus. Agis. Philip IV.

Pausanias. Lysander. B. [Benedict] Arnold

[9]

χωμοι
    Pericles, Agathon, Alcibiadas, Brasidas. . . . Agesilaus, Agis, Sophocles, Pharnabazus . . Lysander, Euripides, Pausanias

[10]

19th jagrat developed – except divya.
21st thought proved & free from error.
24th sarvatragati perfect
27   siddhis perfect. All proved.

[11]

Vak

correct	illuminative	inevitable	sattwic
fine	effective	inspiring	rajasic
poor	tolerable	good	tamasic

[12]

Anantaguna

I Prema

1. kama, prema, bhakti, kalyanam, daya, karuna, rati
2. arasah, raudryam, avahela, vairyam, naishthuryam, krauryam, udasinata

II. Jnana

1. jnanam, aikyam, yatharthabodha, hasyam, rasajnanam, lokadarshanam, astikyam
2. jnanoparati, anaikyam, ayatharthabodha, ahasyam, arasah, lokoparati, nastikyam

III Shakti

1. slagha, viryam, shakti, sthairyam, amritam, saundaryam, vyapti
2. dainyam, slathyam, uparati, chapalyam, mritam, vaiparityam, bheda

[13]

Memory—
I.   1. Of things noticed
     2. Of things unnoticed
II. 1. Of events
     2. Of objects and men
     3. Of words and ideas

Events
   1. The occurrence a. in mass b. in detail c. the sequence or arrangement of details
   2. The time – date, hour, minute
   3. The place – spot, surroundings, relation of different spots to the event
   4. The nimitta, or surrounding circumstances

Objects
   1. Akar, including all the five vishayas & every detail with regard to them
   2. Nama –
   3. The thing in itself
       a single b combined

Words and Ideas
   1. sound 2. symbol 3 meaning 4. bhava 5 relation

Memory – also of contrast, comparison, analogy ie memory of the things in relation to other things
Means of memory
   1. Reception 2. Attention 3 Repetition 4. Association
   5. Will

[14]

Psychological Notes
   A butterfly comes flying over the garden, past a pepegach and two flowertrees which grow side by side. Ordinarily it will be attracted to one of these three objects of desire. It flies past without noticing them, reaches the wall in a straight flight, then contrary to all expectation turns suddenly back, turns aside while flying over the right-hand flowertree to dally for two seconds with another butterfly, then flies off through the pepegach. What dictated its return and departure?
   First; it did not notice the flowertree because its mind was fixed on some more distant object present to its instinctive memory, but

by a law of the mind it received subconsciously the impression of the scent from the flowers. By the time it reached the wall this came up to the supraliminal mind as a vague but powerful sense of something missed and attractive on the way. Working through the vital instincts & cravings by vital impulse which dominantly determines the movements of the insect, this sense immediately enforced a backward flight. If the other butterfly had not intervened, it is possible that at the second contact with the scent of the flowers, the vague sense would have identified itself, consciously or subconsciously, with a definite supraliminal expression & the descent on the flowers would have been determined, but the diversion once made, the vagueness not only remained, but the impression was half obliterated and only the idea of return to something in the distance remained. This, however, was strong enough to divert the insect from its fellow, especially as the latter was concerned with the flowers and did not respond to the advances made. Hence the farther pursuit of the flight backward.

SORTILEGES OF MAY AND JUNE 1912

Sortileges

20th May. 1912.

While thinking of present British policy in India.

न समानजातीयेनैवोपकारदर्शनात् ।   Brih. Up. 552.

D[itt]o — of present state of siddhi with regard to mental &
ideal thought & action, error & truth & the replacement of manas
by vijnanam or satyam.

1. अथ तेनेत्येवोपक्षीणः स्मार्तः प्रत्यय इदमिति चान्य एव
वार्तमानिकः प्रत्ययः क्षीयते ततः सादृश्यप्रत्ययानुपपत्तिस्तेनेदं सदृशमिति ।
अनेकदर्शिन एकस्याभावात् ॥

(सदृश to be taken for sortilege as with drishti).   Brih. Up. 574.

Note. The chief difficulties now experienced are the habit of
judging by past experience and association (स्मार्तः) and that of judging by present indications (वार्तमानिकः) and the insufficient power
of judging by inner vision directly straight on the vishaya. This
again is due to the insufficient realisation of the jnanam Brahma,
anekadarshi ekam.

2. यदादित्यादिविलक्षणं ज्योतिरान्तरं सिद्धमित्येतदसत् ।   Brih.
Up. 552.

All inner light effected, not of the vijnana, is asat & must be
got rid of even if it seem to be intuition.

While thinking of the enormous difficulties of the sadhana;
happened to open the drawer & saw on a stray piece of paper (R's
[Ramaswamy's] Latin translation)

"a su surmonter toutes les difficultés et s'assurer une vie
durable."

5th June 1912   Thesis — R.F. I p. 147

1. De nombreux accidents eurent lieu.   (Subsequent to
"Titanic")

2. Toute usurpation a un cruel retour et celui qui usurpe devrait y songer, du moins pour ses enfants qui presque toujours portent la peine.

3. (p. 290) On a déjà vu que les membres de cette noblesse échappée de France étaient divisés en deux partis; les uns[,] vieux serviteurs, nourris de faveurs, et composant ce qu'on appelait la cour, ne voulaient pas, en s'appuyant sur la noblesse de province, entrer en partage d'influence avec elle et, pour cela, ils n'entendaient recourir qu'à l'étranger; les autres comptant davantage sur leur épée, voulaient soulever les provinces du Midi en y réveillant le fanatisme.

UNDATED NOTES, c. NOVEMBER 1912

Laws of the Future Yoga —
Suddhata

1. Anarambha —

No effort must be made, no struggle to overcome difficulties, but the act must be allowed to work & pass unquestioned, unhindered, unaided. (कर्मणि अकर्म)

2. Nirapeksha —

Nothing must be looked on as a belonging (अपरिग्रहः) or as a thing to be gained or lost, but all as things sent and taken away for ananda. There must be no attempt to get anything or keep anything; nor must any object be held in view. The vijnana must understand why a particular thing is done or is being prepared, what it is, when & how it will develop, but not in any way allow its knowledge to influence the heart or the action.

3. Saucha.

There must be no desire, no repining, no rejecting (यद्‍च्छालाभसन्तोषः), no idea of dwandwa (पापपुण्यमानापमानप्रियाप्रिय-विवर्जनम्)

4. Sattwasthiti.

There must be a clear instinctive intelligence of the truth about everything due to vishuddhi & prakash — freedom from mental or moral tamas — but no attempt to understand or throw off tamas by mental activity.

———

Fundamental Knowledge
Sraddha.

1. Nothing can happen but mangalam.

2 The yoga as laid down cannot fail to be fulfilled.

3 Every detail of the Yoga is arranged by Srikrishna.

4 All subjective experiences are true, only they must be rightly understood.

5. All objective experiences are necessary for the lila.

_____

Jnanam
Rules for Knowledge.

1. Everything thought is satyam—anritam is only misplacement in time[,] place & circumstance. We have to find the nature of the confusion & its source. The habit of being detected discourages anritam until it ceases to act

2. All knowledge is possible; no power is impossible. It is a matter of abhyasa and prakash—once there is shuddhi & sraddha.

3. Sraddha is omnipotent for jnanam, karma & ananda.

====

DRAFT PROGRAMME OF 3 DECEMBER 1912

Programme.[1]

1. Rupadrishti farther developed today (3^d) & confirmed in stability tomorrow—

2. Spontaneity of Lipi tomorrow. A little tonight.

3 Trikaldrishti will begin to work perfectly from tomorrow

4. Powers to overcome resistance in the next three days

5. Samadhi to be regularised during December.
—

6. Intense ananda to come first before permanence. Intensity from 3^d to 10th, permanence from 10th to 31st

7 Health in the last half of the month.

8 First successes of saundaryam 3^d to 10th

9. Utthapana in the latter half of the month—

10. Equipment begins in this week & is fulfilled in the next two weeks succeeding.

---

[1] *This Programme was recopied, with some changes, in the Record of 3 December 1912. See page 125.—Ed.*

[1]

Whatever may be the limitations of the ordinary script, there is another in which an old tendency must be fulfilled, the prophetic script, not Srikrishna's, but commissioned by him. This is the only form of script which has any practical connection with the yoga, not with its fulfilment, but with the action. Wherever the action has to be coordinated, this script will arrange the coordination. There are four divisions of the Karma, literary, religious, practical, social. The first of these is ready for coordination. ——

The literary Karma falls under three heads — poetry, prose and scholarship. The poetry again, under three, epic, dramatic and the minor forms which again include narrative, lyric and reflective. Besides these there is humorous & satirical poetry and translation. All forms have to be attempted & all from the beginning — The prose comprises — philosophical writings, fiction and essay in its many forms (treatise, article, essay, pamphlet, notes, review etc.). The fiction includes romance, ordinary novel and short stories. The philosophy includes Veda, Vedanta & explanation of other forms of Hindu thought & scripture. Scholarship covers the new system of philology, explanation of Veda with scholastic justification, more translation & comment on Sanscrit writings. To begin with — you have to complete The Commentary on the Kena Upanishad, The Introduction to the Study of the Upanishads and a book on Yoga (Philosophy); the two dramas and a third; the revision of your other poems; the completion of the Stone of Ishtar and a number of occasional verses (Poetry); the Idylls of the Occult, The Return of Moro Giafferi and The Siege of Mathura (Prose fiction); your study of the Vedas (first mandala) along with an explanation of the Vedic Gods (the Secret of the Veda).

==

[2]

There is no Script in this actually, it is only the record of thought vyakta or avyakta. Meanwhile the direct government has to begin; the slave to SriKrishna direct. Therefore the gods have stood back, but they are all present in the system. Tomorrow the direct government will be continuous. Tonight there will be the Ananda of the actual embrace of the daughters of delight.

At present the conquest of the Akasha is the one necessity.

Definitely, Ananda will take possession of the bodily system. The Arogyam will begin to take a definite trend towards finality. Utthapana will begin to recover force. No farther prophecies will be given about the third chatusthaya in the Script. —

[3]

The physical resistance is successful because it is exhausting itself. The difficulty in the trikaldrishti is the principal obstacle to the perfection of the sruti, replacement of trikaldrishti by tejas & tapas. It is intended to give a greater rapidity to the siddhi, but the forces of resistance are hitherto successful. However, they will not be successful for much longer. In reality, sight is the proper method, aided by thought, & it is so being arranged, the old mental drishti will revive preparatory to the actual rupadrishti. The health is about to take a final decisive step forward, covering the only ground yet unoccupied. Ananda (physical, akarana) will now grow intense & possess the body. The daurbalyam will once more be expelled, entirely. Only the saundaryam will be still left effectively opposed — though no longer contradicted. The opposition to the drishti in samadhi & jagrad goes — trikaldrishti & siddhis establish themselves —

There is only difficulty of belief in the lila down here. That is about to be removed — No writing this afternoon till teatime. Many are yet to be revealed.

Life has begun feebly, in literature & thought. It will soon take a more powerful movement of knowledge & commence in action; necessarily, also in enjoyment. Today & not later the Ananda will begin.

More force is needed. The normal writing must improve. Force cannot come, because the enemy makes use of it, — not Indra, not Vritra, not even Pani, but the Rakshasa, — Rakshaswi. Therefore only the calm stable or even regular force comes. But Rudrani needs a powerful and rushing force for her work, not merely a swift, even and unfailing force. It is this force which is in preparation. The physical weakness or brain arrest has nothing to do with it. The brain arrest comes because of the Rakshasic force and would be dispensed with if the stream of Rudrani's activity were once liberated from this impediment and aggression.

———

[4]

Words, words, words, but no real brotherhood. They pass. Fake silver, mortofil, with bits of the real stuff & some psychic faculties such as all men can develop. Yes. For some time. We shall see. They are trying to keep down the system on the lower levels, but they cannot permanently succeed. Fresh siddhi today. Siddhi of trikaldrishti, aishwarya, ishita, vyapti, samadhi. There is excellent swapnasamadhi, but stability is insufficient.

Yes, it is so intended to effect something by the script and immediately. Attend to the physical siddhi. The Arogya persists in spite of contradictions which are diminishing in force. Ananda has to be insisted on psychically till the body acquires it; it is not only willing, but eager to admit it, but the Vritras stand in the way. Saundarya will emerge in a few days.

The personal relation has to be established. It has to be established by Vani, script, thought & action. The telepathy therefore can now be as much trusted as the nearer trikaldrishti. It is the evil of the speculative reason, but it was not accepted. The trikaldrishti has to get beyond this dependent state & it will do so definitely today. That also is being solved, the attachment of the shama—

There are three kinds, πολιτης, [. . .], δουλος & in each kind there are three subdivisions.

All these powers have to be resumed & perfected. But not with too much of a rush at first. The torrent will come afterwards. Meanwhile the day has to be filled in with a perfect activity of all kinds & the physical (general) utthapana confirmed. Yesterday's success in the mukti from shitoshna has to be farther tested, but it depends on the removal of the mosquitoes. For the rest, the primary & secondary utthapanas have to revive simultaneously & the continuity of the kamananda has to be confirmed. This has to be done today.

Agesilaus = Sn [Saurin].   Agathon, Alcibiades, Pericles, Brasidas   Agis, Agesilaus, Sophocles, Pharnabazus.   Lysander, Euripides, Pausanias.

Two absolutely perfect, the rest mostly defective. That is already done. Now for the physical siddhi. Ananda first of all, Ananda first & foremost. If there were not strong resistance of a kind, there would be no need of the special pressure of the ishita. The others will come with Ananda & in its train.

=

Many press in, none are allowed. The time for them has not yet arrived. Only when the viveka is sufficient to its task, can that movement be undertaken.

आर सनान् पहि नाय दरा: कुरु विष्टपिमूरं ।

μεχρι τουτου του ετους ουχ εδυναντο ουτε τους πολεμιους αμυνειν—ουτε τους φιλους σωζειν. εδει γαρ ή δυναμις, εδει ό πλουτος, εδει ή πληθυς των πολιτων. μικρος φαυλος αδυνατος ό οχλος, αγαθοι αλλα δυστυχεις οί κρατιστοι. εδοχει γε ταυτα πασι τοις Ελλησι.

There is still much to write. Immediate progress in the Ananda is needed — the Kamananda. It is increasing, so also the rupadrishti.

Today continuity of kamananda, abundance of rupadrishti & other drishtis; return of Personality of Master.

The continuous Kamananda is now assured. It is the turn of the Rupadrishti. The Arogya is already strengthened & the general utthapana as well as the primary. But the success of these utthapanas depend[s] upon the anima & the anima on the ananda. Meanwhile the subjection to hunger craving & weakness of emptiness is being removed. In fact, it is removed — but the craving itself is still present in a modified form.

Rupadrishti has not yet hold of the Akasha, but the time has now arrived. The vijnana has to become more active, with it the freedom of the rupa & lipi. I do not mean this very moment, nor do I mean that the vijnana is quiescent, but it has not recently been brilliantly active. The activity of chitrarupa is the sign, rather than the essential basis; it is if anything, a starting point. Chitra & sthapatya are linked together, they cannot be separated. The only question is about akasharupa & the method of bringing it about.

When it was said that today there must be perfect activity, the relapse & revolt were not contemplated. None of those predictions have been falsified, except the filling in of the day with a perfect activity, & that did not refer to yesterday in particular. Nor did the other prediction mean that the continuity or abundance would be immediately perfect.

The voices rejected are those that persist in misleading the mind by excessive encouragement. The lipi does not mean that there will be entire baldness, but that that is the price demanded. Let us leave these things & proceed with the positive siddhi. This is the command, be the results what they may. The superior strength of the aishwarya-ishita is now evident. There is no real need for the financial part of that letter. The Vanis have to be purified & the speech brought into stricter conformity with the Satya of Trikaldrishti. Continuity of the Ananda has first to be secured

Taste is entirely perfect, but hearing, smell, sight & touch are still attacked by old sanskaras. You are right about the permitted obstinacy of the opposition. The vani is now purified. Both vani & script have to express a positive rather [than] a negative truth, but they have to possess the capacity of limiting the positive statement whenever necessary. The false or alien aishwarya has no longer any power. The indriyas will now be finally purified of Nirananda.

Hearing first, then touch, then smell, last sight. The element of discomfort must be extruded, not suffered—nirananda must become ananda, then intense ananda of bhoga. It is discomfort alone that survives. Reason has to disappear in truth. The persistence of the Ananda is now perfect; its continuity is assured but not perfect. The continuity has to become perfect. Afterwards the intensity will of itself increase. This is not indriya. It is manas in the physical prana. That cannot be purified all at once. Pain & discomfort of the body will therefore last, not in the indriyas, but this pain & discomfort must be increasingly associated with ananda, become a form of ananda & finally transmute into ananda. There is no other reaction except the pain in the fight & a slight subtle stiffness. These have to be steadily extruded. The difficulties of assimilation have to be faced & borne; a sudden resort to evacuation must always be avoided except in case of extreme urgency.

A slow & steady development is still insisted on in the Sat of the apara prakriti & to that extent in the Sat of the Para Prakriti. It is evident that it is not intended immediately to succeed, but always now the aishwarya has an effect & usually an ultimate success, if it is persisted in and an ultimate effect, even if it is abandoned. Aishwarya now acts through direct pressure, through assistant circumstance in direct pressure & although it is not apparent by indirect action through Prakriti assisting these or by itself or using these. That is definite—your steady tapas is the instrument—faith will come with truth & success. Impure still, all three of them, but the Asura is broken—only in him, it rises occasionally.

सं परिति प्सरणा ककलायति काव्यमनग्नन्
सं जवनं पुरु ह्रीति सपज्जनः। आर्यति राथः॥

Something definite & forceful must again be attempted by the combined forces of knowledge. Trikaldrishti, aishwarya-ishita-vyapti must receive a powerful impulse, carrying the first near to perfection, the second to invariable effectuality. And the kamananda must be intensified & restored to evident continuity. The continuity is being slowly established, the intensity made to recur. It is the method.

The personality must manifest. You need not be afraid of my

upsetting things always. Accept vani, script, lipi as mine unless the vivek tells you to the contrary. You are right, but it is the personality subject to increase of Balarama. Never mind the attendant manomaya illusions. Do not mind either that pressure. At the proper time your course will be justified by the event. When that time will come, is not yet clear, but it is not today or now. There is yet a delay before the bhagya can manifest. It is the crown & seal of the siddhi subject of course to farther development of both simultaneously. More of the trikaldrishti, aishwarya & ananda, also of the lipi.

The exact trikaldrishti as yet fails to establish itself. That is what I insist on; the result you will see. You see. Tomorrow a great progress will be made as the result of today's struggle. Even today, considerable progress is being made. The intensity is manifest, it is recurrent; the continuity is attempting to assert itself & will eventually & before long succeed. There remains the lipi. I add the rupa & samadhi. No more here for today.

=

21ˢᵗ [January 1913]

Keep the mind clear of judgement. Make no attempt to increase the vijnana siddhi, whatever happens—only the physical siddhi needs still a little tapasya. The karma of course—it is the field for tapas. You see that you still succeed subjectively—not yet objectively except in some instances. You have only to go on applying the will with force, but not as a struggle. It will grow stronger & stronger. It is not tamasic.

Today, then, the steady progress of vijnana & kamananda & the struggle in the health and the utthapana & saundarya. Leave that alone for the present; it is part of the karma. Still tejas has to increase & tapas & the force of the sraddha.

It is the lack of the equipment that troubles & depresses the karma. Evidently the equipment is not yet due—even that promise is not really fulfilled; only the absolute anxiety for the morrow is postponed. The cause of prospective anxiety must now be got rid of—first. In that there need be no undue delay. For some time this movement must be followed. It is the restoration of kalyanasraddha. Although they have concentrated strength successfully there, it is only because you sought to push on the trikaldrishti, instead of allowing it to proceed of itself.

=

22^{d}.

The last day of this attack. The body will now be liberated. Once more the relics of the judgment & consideration have to be expelled by the dasyam. In the morning the vijnana will begin its united & rapid sweep after some farther activity of the trikaldrishti & the kamananda again generalise itself. Intellectual infallibility, now acting in an irresistible stream, will increase enormously. First the vijnanamay progress & infallibility then the kamananda, then the physical tapas & siddhi. The tapas must now be directed purely to the physical siddhi & the karmasiddhi & first to the kamananda. Necessarily they will resist. Action must enter into it, but only temporarily as an end to inefficiency of the siddhi. The morning is not over yet. The other movement of the automatic script.

Valmiki—

संजन तायु दिलं ममनास्कुमि तायु परामि
जल्वनम् अभ्रम् अदे करया च पिप्रामनि हेड: ।
पार दलं सद पाकि पयं ततरायिमि जान ।

Ritadharma—

अंग पद हु योनि रथस्य पथं दृशे । रथो ह प्रतम: रथो अन्तम: रथं
मये । रथेन जगत् रथेन परमं रथीष्टमु । रथमद्य इं रथमयो ब्रह्मणस्पति: ॥

[... ...]

Kálan kále kalaya kálan Satran satre
    Redmi ranaya raná
Para para patri páyo Núna nalá
    Salavú salaka salá

Gloria

सेयमागतास्मि— मम हि एतदारम्भणं यत्त्वया कृतं पुराणतमे कलौ
यदेव वक्तुमुपचक्रमे— न मे भ्रमो भवितुं शक्य: न मे व्यतिक्रम: — तदालपनं
तेषां दुष्कृतिनाम् अस्त्येव मे विशेषभावो विशेषगुणसम्पदपि मे। एतस्मिन्नेव
कलौ ब्रवीमि। प्रथमे लवस्य यच्चरितं येन नष्टं पारीक्षितं कर्म। सो हि

युधिष्ठिरकुलोद्भवः क्षत्रियो न राजा। मन्त्री च स बभूव राज्ञो सतधनस्य न राजा कदापि।

The script is established. Its accuracy has to be entirely proved, not only in what it says, but in what it suggests. The opposition need not trouble you. Attend to the physical siddhi, especially the virya & to the saundarya— In the Greek there is a hesitation. The Script is not yet strong enough to overcome the sanskara. There is no utility just now in overburdening the record. On the other hand much has to be written here. Some of the perceptions of the future have been confirmed, but there must be a freer movement. It is not my object to repeat here what the thought perception has given you. Meanwhile I give you some results.

By Saturday—physical siddhi in full train, but saundarya especially not yet confirmed. By the 30th—all confirmed, but the saundarya still weak. In February three first perfected; only perfect saundarya & tertiary utthapana will remain to be completed. Equipment not yet due, but provision due & arriving

Bhishma . . Bengal Provincial Conference, The Presidential Address. Jessore Tragedy.

Equipment & karmasiddhi in February.

These predictions are to be observed in their fulfilment or non-fulfilment. It will be seen how far the script is correct. Now for nearer predictions. First, the general utthapana is restored tonight & confirmed tomorrow. Study will be resumed, but not more than slightly. It will include Tamil & Hebrew. The line of progress of the three utthapanas will then be indicated. The struggle over the saundaryam will be brought to a head tomorrow, decided Friday, confirmed Saturday.

23d

See whether it emerges or not. Health is a thing not so much to be defended as developed. First here as usual. It is a question now of the life, the karmasiddhi. As for utthapana, it will fulfil itself from today in spite of the survivals. Beauty will emerge slowly after tomorrow. The life-struggle centres in three points— 1st equipment 2d manifestation of Yogic power as in therapeusis   3d the control of events in public matters. The rest is well assured & will come easily when the difficulties have been overcome. 2 & 3 are somewhat developed, but the struggle in them continues. 1 is not at all developed. It is really the sole thing that remains (except the saundarya). The doubt is stronger about saundarya and equipment than on any other point, & every suggestion of speedy improvement in these two matters is distrusted & repelled. It is towards this defect that the Shakti is now turning, as towards all other defects, but these must be overcome before the full flood of siddhi is possible. They must both begin to be overcome within this month of January & fully overcome in February.

Vijnana has been checked. Only to show trikaldrishti at work and to insist on the continuous action of the saundaryasiddhi. It is necessary to manifest the power of reading thoughts. It is already manifesting, but must be habitual in its action & complete. This imagination must be expelled. There is no farther need of it. The idea of impossibility must be expelled. No, the siddhi is of chief importance. Yes, but the tendency is towards firmness & clearness.

There is, undoubtedly, a defect in the present action of the vijnana & therefore of the script—the defect of clouded prakasha. The devatas of intellectual tejas are yet too active in their shadows. The dasya is somewhat abridged owing to the revival of judgment & dissatisfaction which is for the rest, justified by event. It is suggested either today or tomorrow. The successful opposition to the vijnana siddhi & the physical siddhi is chiefly responsible. The rest would not have touched but for that.

More deliberateness is needed without losing the rapidity. It must be so. Oppose the current no longer; even under the cloud, be sure of the sun behind. There is still an elusive activity seeking to arrange the thoughts. The arrangement must emerge of itself. There is a spirit of judgment waiting on script & thought which hampers the flow of the vijnana. This spirit of judgment has to be expelled. It waits also on the action & hampers it.

Treasure—outpouring from the treasure reserve for the lila; actual treasury will also be found; but the first is immediate, the second in the yet distant future. . Follow the impulse given as you accept the thought presented. War is preparing & the Turkish chances seem small; nevertheless the gage has to be thrown down to the subjective enemies—either Adrianople & the coast islands or war. There must be the will for the provision.

The power has not been maintained, only manifested. It is now returning, but it is not sure of its uninterrupted hold as yet. It will soon be sure & extend itself to all things, persons & movements. It is already doing it. It is extending to the actions of persons. Leave it to develop in the full flood of the jnana-trikaldrishti-aishwarya. But the other powers, rupa lipi samadhi have to be brought into the full stream.

24th

Already, there is a great improvement in the assimilation, in spite of occasional false steps. The diminution of jalavisrishti is a point of capital importance. The opposition to utthapana still persists. It has patiently to be extruded. The eruption is troublesome, but less vital than seems to be the case. It is dying out actually, even though artificially maintained. The Ananda is established, it is the continuity that is being resisted. As for the saundarya, it is still unestablished.

पाय मनः सहसे वचि संजन राम अरीहन्।
ना पतते करि ईलत्या अनि वस्मनि मत्ये
सं जभिता सीता स्वसिः। एवं वीयति वस्म॥

Ananda intense today & more continuous. Rupa & lipi free & perfect. Arogya & utthapana to increase. Not yet. First Ananda. Today is the day of final preparation for the karmasiddhi.

अंदिश वीलतनुः महि अब्रजे आविलद् ऊय,
सालुकि, वीर अनं मरतां यद् अयाय परीयन्
रावणः ऊदपयाः वलम् आसखः आर्यरभाये।
सन्यं मर्तंहनं वि पयामि।

[5]

Record—

No interference here, entire passivity.

1st rule.	No interference anywhere, entire passivity
2d rule.	Disregard of the probable consequences
3d rule.	Persistence in will according to knowledge
4th rule.	Application of jnana & trikaldrishti to all things, small or great, near or remote, knowable or apparently unknowable.
5th rule.	Interpretation of error; utilisation of failure.
6th rule.	Constant exercise of utthapana.
7th rule.	Will in all things, and action a subordinate instrument—

In one week, the difference will be seen

=

Today, the first movement—
1. Knowledge to be finally set right, in all its instruments.
2. Power to apply itself to remove its own defects
3. Lipi, Chitra, Rupa
4. Ananda, Arogya—

[6]

No danger of relapse. This occasion was wholly abnormal— This is the script, it is about to assume the burden of trikaldrishti definitely. Let us see what they can do. "Dasya, tejas, faith, trikaldrishti, aishwarya, samadhi, all rising out of something into the great & splendid." The first dart failed, the second will now be made. ["]Exaltation approved, defiance sanctioned. Tonight & tomorrow, the move forward."

No danger of relapse. Lipi is already moving forward to the mahat. . The rest will follow—

As well die this time, not hereafter. The trikaldrishti is in a state of confusion—the mind cannot manage its materials. This confusion will be removed not at once but in the course of the day. The Aishwarya also is only clumsily effective & sometimes no[t] at all. But the movement has changed to brihat, not yet to ritam & satyam. Samadhi only remains. These things have now to be gathered up & confirmed in the satyam. Afterwards the ritam.

You see, the script has the trikaldrishti. No self-restraint. It stands in the way — vamamarga. Restraint by God only. Yes. Today, tomorrow & the day after.

(1) Satyam, ritam, brihat in the knowledge, power & samadhi

(2) Sharirananda confirmed & greatened

(3) Arogya made triumphant

(4) Removal of exaggerated adhogati, utthapana, firm beginnings of saundarya.

The movement is now for the dasyam on the widest scale. In the trikaldrishti the doubt of the exactness is still active, based on past experience. This is to be removed by the growth & dominance of the ritam. Vijnana led by mahat—

[7]

The assault is being given to the bhukti, tejas and faith. The samata has not been disturbed, only the hasyam has felt a cloud pass over it. The tejas & faith have been darkened for a moment; they subsist but have lost their ananda. Only the vijnana has been clouded and the positive bhukti suspended. That is over. We will now continue developing automatically the vijnana & the bhukti. You have to wait & see.

There is as yet no advance, only a taking up of positions. Nothing has been done which is not old & familiar & the balance of success is still on the side of the attack. That will change in & from the next half hour. It is already changing. Enough.

Two chatusthayas have been almost perfected & at any rate secured against real disturbance and above all against any continuous breach. The ishwarabhava, attahasya & faith in the rapidity & in the lila remain in the second chatusthaya. But these cannot be brought without actuality in the third & fourth. There are touches, not breaches. . The actuality in the third is being extended. But the Vritra has not yet been abolished. In the first two it is not the Vritra, but the vrika – except in the attahasya, brihat faith & ishwarabhava. Today is for the third chatusthaya & especially for knowledge & power, knowledge most, power secondarily. Lipi accompanies them. Samadhi & rupa follow. The development today will be decisive. Only in the fourth & fifth, there is still delay. I do not mean it will be at once perfect. Obviously this is not the direct script. These are not gods, but spirits who seek to guide, inform, direct. Only it is not true that the script is governed by them & never expressed a higher power & knowledge. It is not now being used by a spirit, but merely besieged by a spirit. It is I who am using it & me you know. Not Indra or another but the Master of the Yoga. It is not the divine script because it is acting through mind, not direct from Vijnana. It will always act from Vijnana. I am about to establish with fixity the personal relation. The rest is there. All these minor bhavas have to be expelled.

———

The end of the opposition is near in the third. It is really over in the trikaldrishti. It must be finished with in the lipi, rupa & samadhi. The one thing really that remains is rupa samadhi. There is a confusion, the incompetent devatas have to be expelled. It is true more was expected or demanded by one side of the mind than has been fulfilled, more accomplished than was expected by the inert, sceptical side. Perfection is not for today. The second chatusthaya is different. The faith, aishwarya, attahasya have been interrupted –

===

All the vijnana is definitely in action, though in unequal & imperfect action. The unequal & imperfect parts must now be filled in & out. Afterwards we can attend to the fourth chatusthaya more particularly.

We have to move forward. Recognise the nature of existence. This is the knowledge; therefore dhairya is necessary.

No dependence on the script. If it depends on the script, it will not be self-assured. The script is only for confirmation. It is perfectly true that the first chatusthay has been broken into after a promise that it should never again be broken. . Substantially it is intact. The violence done to the system is the proof that it cannot be destroyed. The continuance of the tejas will be the proof that the second chatusthay stands, even in the faith there is only a temporary disturbance. The harm done will be repaired. The promises have all been exaggerations of Will, therefore lies. The Vani has exaggerated, every source of knowledge has exaggerated. The inertia exaggerates on the opposite side.

So much has been done. All that was a play of the game intended to bring about a fresh grouping. Henceforth all the movements of knowledge & power will work themselves out not interfered with by the will in the intellect & the intellectual judgment, although these in their passing rupam can still distort the truth.

[8]

Shrink not nor falter, O hero, though thy toil seems ever to return on thee in vain menacing to crush thee in its rebound. Thy labour of Sisyphus is the laboratory of the future & the fulfilment of eternity is in thy present insignificant toil, as the tree that was & is to be in the seed that seems so little to the eye & vain.

[9]

The recurring confusion created by the pranic intellect intruding its activity is forced on the system, but it is noticeable that only the shadow of asamata & ashakti comes with it as a part of the ajnana & disappear[s] automatically with the return of the jnana. The apparent difficulty will disappear like all the rest. The pressure on the tejas is intended to force the emergence of the rapidly fulfilling divine tapas.

Trust first, – if there is anything wrong, seek the explanation or better await it. Rapidity is necessary first in the third chatusthaya & in the fourth; there will be sufficient money to keep you till January. The ecstasy is to increase in force & frequency, while the subdued (not the obstructed) ananda becomes perpetual during waking hours & even in sleep the ananda gains ground. Then the subdued ecstasy will take its place while intense ecstasy becomes the occasional higher state. So it will proceed. As for the siddhi of the health, that proceeds in spite of all resistance. Neither of these will be perfect till December; but meanwhile the utthapana will come rapidly forward & the saundarya begin to break through its obstacles.

=====

The range must be widened & the defects removed— The general obstruction must be met by a general denial of the obstruction & refusal to work out of it by the lower processes. That has been done sufficiently and has not to be repeated ad infinitum—

=====

There is now no reason why the Samata etc should disappear. Only the tejas of Mahakali must finally be harmonised with the passivity and the dasya. This will be done today by eliminating the Maheshwari bhava from the superficial consciousness & its contents without bringing back the mental tejas. It is true. Nevertheless these things are done. The struggle is over the whole basis of the farther advance.

=====

The incident of yesterday was used as a turning point—to turn you into the road hitherto avoided, now destined for your treading, the road of mighty, straightforward effective karma. Others have tried, stumbled and fallen. You will see that you are henceforth as effectively protected in action as in self-defensive passivity & in action by others—as effectually & more. All these mishaps have had their object and their beneficial purposefulness. Not after this year. The knowledge & power have to be entirely harmonised first. That egoism is exhausting its remnants. The difficulty is great only because the pranic suggestions attempt to predominate & mislead; in itself it is not great.

Today a great movement forward. It is not forbidden; it has to be accepted; it will clear itself of the ignorance, which is now the only obstacle. Today for the second & third—if the second is cleared, the first automatically fulfils itself. There is a tremendous pressure in order to compel the buddhi to give up faith in the bodily siddhi & the new society. Let the power first be reestablished. The trikaldrishti, telepathy, power, lipi have now all to move towards absolute perfection dragging the samadhi & drishti with them. Till that is done, the fourth chatusthaya will only prepare its advance. The advance has begun; it will gather momentum during the day.

The powers of knowledge & tapas are stronger, but they are all acting in the intellect without the action of the intellectual judgment, therefore there is no light. The mental realm is being purified of the pranas. The force of the tapas is yet insufficient. Life has to be brought into line with the siddhis acquired, or in other words the powers have to take hold of life and possess it. Life means the Akash of the prithivi, & through the Akash all it contains. It is true, the Akash is full of opposition & obstruction where formerly it seemed clear. The obstruction is only in order to bring out the samata, tapas etc & increase the eventual force of the powers themselves. The admission of the power & right of the objective world to resist is to be once more cancelled. So far we have advanced that the power & knowledge are showing the old force & invariable effectiveness, but the effectiveness is usually partial, often slight in actuality, seldom flawless. We have not then advanced beyond the old point in appearance, except that the power & the instruments are all accepted & faith in them is completely founded, though still uncertain about rapid results. The second chatusthaya is now completely founded except in the extent & certainty in detail of the faith & of the Kalibhava, therefore the attahasya too is little manifest. That must now appear, while at the same time the instruments of the later chatusthayas farther justify themselves. The conditions are now fixed and will clear & develop themselves—

The third chatusthaya is reforming itself on a much sounder basis. The power, lipi & knowledge will during the next three days overpower the resistance of the physical akasha. Rupa and samadhi will follow their lead. About the rupa & samadhi you are uncertain, but the doubts will be removed. Meanwhile the fourth chatusthaya must be pushed forward. Health is going through its ultimate denials & is already shaking itself free from some of them. Ananda is insisting. But the utthapana & saundarya are still in a crude state & strongly opposed in their attempt to progress. A beginning has been made in the utthapana. It must be steadily pursued. As for the destruction in the fifth, it is only the destruction of unsound members and of the defects which make them unsound. This time the movement has not been favourable. The old obstruction seems to be momentarily successful.

The attempt will be persistent & successful. There is no ambiguity [............................] directions. When it is said, there will be [.................................] power than has already [....]¹

From today regularisation of the Yoga & the life; but Yoga more first than the life. The activity of the second chatusthaya has to be restored perfectly; for the activity of the first is already restored & perfect but for the physical touch. This activity of the second chatusthaya must take place without disturbing the first, must bring universal ananda, not discouragement & disappointment. That once done, the third will progress itself towards its self-perfection as it is already doing in the lipi and the pure jnana. The practical jnana, the power & the samadhi will all perfect themselves on that basis. So, too by the perfection of the power the fourth will break down its obstacles & progress to perfection. Meanwhile the fifth will confirm and enlarge itself.

The doubt is justified by the past, not by the future. Until it is removed by knowledge, it must persist. There is a perfect knowledge at work removing the ignorance; only the ignorance is allowed to return & conquer so often, for the sake of humanity, so that its burden may be lightened. I am about to establish the parts of knowledge again, so that the faith may have some ground to stand upon.

---

¹ *Manuscript damaged; three lines partially or wholly lost. — Ed.*

The thing is now once again grounded in samata & dasya —
The tejas will now begin to work, the faith develop & the vijnana
act.
=====

The vijnana is preparing its own perfection and today there
will be the necessary reconstruction. The body is still dominated by
asiddhi. The struggle is with the general Vritra of the third, sixth
& first, second — especially in the powers of knowledge. The vyuha
is proceeding. Still the vyuha is proceeding. The Samúha is there,
but in a disordered state. The negative stage is over; the positive
affirmation must more & more fulfil itself. Arrangement means in
time, place & circumstance. The vyuha is taking place; the rays do
not yet go to their right p[lace] — Faith withstands all the assaults &
the knowledge of Brahman Sarva & Ananta is confirming itself, but
it must also be Jnana & Ananda. That is why the third must now
fulfil itself & then the fourth. All these are only the first obstacles
to the final perfection. Self-fulfilment is now the rule except in the
body. It must become the rule there also. But not at once. As for
the rapidity it will be soon at work.

Reconstitute. First, the vijnana — Next, the power — Self-development of all. It is only a temporary obstacle. There is a compulsion
on the whole system[. I]t is an a[ttemp]t to dissolve & wreck that
siddhi. Hence it is being resisted, [...............................]
I have allowed it for particu[lar] purposes. It has no [............
.........]²

The window will not fall. The struggle for the third chatusthaya proceeds & the attack is now constant, but so also is
the pressure of the siddhi. The siddhi will proceed now in the mass
& not in detail, except in the rupa — All is of use. In the matter of
the stomach, it is essential that the reversion to the old system of
evacuation should cease & it will cease. The health & the ananda
will now be specially dealt with while the utthapana is preparing.
Meanwhile the third chatusthaya will perfect itself. No the first,
not this. This is beautiful & useful for this life. No straining of the

---

2 *Manuscript damaged; two lines partially lost.* — Ed.

Tapas is needed. There also no physical pressure is needed. This is how it will become regularised. . The only question is about time. Meanwhile the focus must be turned upon life. The articles must be sent and yet not in submission to them. Pránán atarah.

The life has now to be entirely expressed in these higher values. The second chatusthaya has to begin its play in life. Many have still the ego, & therefore impressions of egoism survive. The harmonious arrangement of the first three chatusthayas is proceeding. Today—the first two are being attacked by the old bhavas with which the material mind has long been familiarised, but they will overcome the attack & emerge permanently victorious.

> dhairyam suddhatanantyalipsa mahadbhavah
> pritih dakshyam danapratidanalipsa anandibhava
> bhoga hasyam karmalipsa samabhava

The trikaldrishti will arrange itself today & the whole knowledge act connectedly from tomorrow. There is an attempt to revive the activity of the pranic intelligence in connection with the trikaldrishti & aishwarya. The difficulty is there to be overcome. The difficulty persists, but is now lightened by the persistent rejection of the pranic suggestions—

Ananda again in the afternoon & evening no longer subdued or obstructed. Utthápana—

=

There is full perfection of the first chatusthaya; in the second there are still defects, but you can see the immense progress made in the human parts of the system. Only the divine part is still imperfect. Till then the full intensity cannot come. The perfection is coming. This is the full attack on the karma, no longer of men, but of nature. They have called up the elements to aid them. The battle with the elements is still a losing battle for the present. Nor is the ideality yet perfectly combined in detail. This is the proof of the ideality but it has yet to be perfected.

The knowledge is once more working with a near approach to perfection, only some of the placements are still wrong. The power must be brought up to the same level in its ordinary movements, then in the body, then in the karma. The power will now begin to work in the ideality & in harmony with the knowledge, the telepathy & trikaldrishti.

Although it is as yet incompletely done, still it is done. Now lipi, [. . . .]³

---

³ *Manuscript damaged; one line lost. — Ed.*

SORTILEGE OF 15 MARCH [1913]

March 15th

St. यदा वै विजानात्यादिवाक्यं व्याकुर्वंन्नुत्तरमाह.   When the vijnana is active, he (the Master of the Yoga) developing the initial Word, (OM, Brahman) declares all that follows.   First, activity of the vijnana, second, constant perception of the Brahman, third, knowledge of the world in the terms of the Brahman.

ACCOUNTS OF 31 MAY – 15 JUNE 1913

Record of Yogic details

June 1913

Credit – June 1st (May 31st)

Rs	15-0-0	(Rent for May)	Rs	15
Rs	40-0-0	in notes		
Rs	28-0-0	(Rent & servants for June)		
Rs	10-0-0	reserve		
Rs	7-0-0	in cash.	Rs	85
Rs	70-0-0	out in loans	Rs	70
Rs	150-0-0	in loan		
Rs	150-0-0	in Fr. notes	Rs	300
				470

For June Rs 85 of which 40 in notes and cash 7 for current expenses.
Also Rs 3-8-1 from last month.

June 2d

Rs 20 in notes
"   8 in cash
"   2-9-0 in purse
    30-9-0-
May   0-8-1. (Rs 2 for monthly feast)
            (" 1 for charity)

June 12th

Paid

Rs	50	loans recovered	Rs 15	Rent for May
Rs	150	in Fr notes	Rs 6	charity
Rs	150	in loan	Rs 43-14-	Bijoy. out of rent
Rs	8-1	from last month		money (loans[)]

Actually in hand

Rs 150   in Fr. notes
Rs 150   in loan
*Rs 20   in notes (rent money + Rs 4)
*Rs 10   in notes (reserve + current)
Rs 5   in cash
Rs 23   (rent & servants for June)
*Rs 0-9-10 in money (purse)
For the current expenses
Rs 15-9-10 out of * (9 + 6-9-10).

June 15th-

In hand
Rs	30	in notes	(Rs 16 –rent money
Rs	3-15-1	in cash	Rs 44 –rent money
Rs	150	in notes.	Rs 14 + 3-15-1 –month's ex-
Rs	10	in loan	penses –Rs 1 for shoes.
Rs	44	with Bijoy	Rs 150 reserve.[)]
Rs	28	rent & servants	

Store Account & Standing				Miscellaneous Expenses		
Rice	11 - 0-0	May 31st		Sweets	0-0-6	
Tea	0 -13-0	"		Coolie	0-1-6	
Matches	0 - 0-9	"		Cigarettes	0-0-3	June 1st.
Spices	1-10-6	"		Cricket(special)	0-6-0	"
Sugar	0 - 3-8	June 1st.		Oil	0-2-0	"
S's Cigarettes	0 - 8-0	"		Milk	0-1-0	"
Firewood	3 - 0-0	June 3d		Stamps	0-0-6	"
Spices	0 - 0-1	"		Cigarettes(special)	0-3-9	June 2d
Cigarettes(self)	0 - 1-3	"		Lamp	0-2-0	"
Kerosine Oil	2 - 5-0	"		(Feast, last month	2-0-0)	
Spices	0 - 1-0	June 4th		Barber	0-4-0	
Sugar	0 - 4-0	June 8th		Wine	0-6-0	
Cigarettes(self)	0 - 1-3	June 8th		Cigarettes	0-0-1	June 3d
"	0 - 1-3	June 10th		Saurin	0-0-3	June 4th
"	0 - 0-6	June 12th		Coolie	0-0-3	"
"	0 - 0-6	June 14th		Stamps	0-0-6	"
	20 - 2-9			Ink	0-1-0	June 6th
				Kalasi	0-0-9	"
				Stamps	0-0-6	June 7th
				Money order	0-2-0	"
				Parcel	0-4-6	"
				Petruz	0-1-0	"
				Soap	0-1-3	"
				Brooms	0-1-0	June 9th
				Shoelaces	0-3-0	
				Salle de Lecture	0-8-0	June 10th
				Cricket	0-4-0	"
				Envelopes &		
				Paper	0-5-0	"
				Nibs	0-5-0	"
				Cigarettes	0-0-3	June 11th
				Washerman	1-0-0	"
				Telegram	0-6-0	"

Pushpush	0-6-0	June 12th
Claret	0-6-0	"
Lemons	0-0-3	"
Nalini	0-0-6	June 13th
Stamps	0-1-0	June 14th
Barber	0-2-6	June 15th
	6-8-1	

Daily Meal			Extraordinary
Breakfast	0-2-6	June 1st	Charity 6-0-0- June 2d
Meals	0-8-6	"	(to be recovered from May &
Breakfast	0-2-3	June 2d	July)
Meals	0-4-0	"	Bijoy's journey 43-14-0- June 11th
Extra for feast	0-4-7	"	
Breakfast	0-1-4	June 3d	
Meals	0-7-0	"	
Breakfast	0-2-0	June 4th	
Meals	0-6-9	"	
Breakfast	0-2-0	June 5th	
Meals	0-7-0	"	
Breakfast	0-2-0	June 6th	
Meals	0-8-3	"	
Breakfast	0-2-0	June 7th	
Meals	0-8-0	"	
Breakfast	0-2-0	June 8th	
Meals	0-7-6	"	
Breakfast	0-2-0	June 9th	
Meals	0-8-0	"	
Breakfast	0-2-0	June 10th	
Meals	0-7-0	"	
Breakfast	0-2-0	June 11th	
Meals	0-7-0	"	
Milk	0-0-6	June 12th	

Meals	0-7-0	"
Breakfast	0-2-0	June 13th
Meals	0-6-6	"
Breakfast	0-2-0	June 14th
Meals	0-6-6	"
Breakfast	0-2-0	June 15th
Meals	<u>0-6-9</u>	"
	11-3-0	

Daily Balance

	June 1st	Rs	31 - 3-10
	June 2d	Rs	29-15- 0
	" 3d	Rs	26 - 7 - 5
	" 4	Rs	23 - 6 - 4
	" 5	Rs	22-13- 7
	" 6	Rs	22 - 0 - 7
Rs 1 added from reserve	" 7	Rs	21-12 - 0
	" 8	Rs	20-15- 1
	" 9	Rs	20 - 1 - 1
	" 10	Rs	17-13- 4
	" 11	Rs	16 - 2-10
	" 12	Rs	14-13-10
	" 13	Rs	13 - 4-10
	" 14	Rs	12-10-10
	" 15	Rs	11

RECORD NOTES, 13 AND 15 SEPTEMBER 1913

Record of Yoga.
Theosophic.

Sept. 13

Sortilege — इहोप यात शवसो नपातः सौधन्वना ऋभवो माप भूत ।
अस्मिन्हि वः सवने रत्नधेयं गमन्त्विन्द्रमनु वो मदासः ॥

An exact application to the circumstances of the Yoga. The Ribhus are the gods of formation who proceed from the divine Tapas (शवसो नपातः) and use it to form thought, action & condition. This formative process is now the course of the Yoga (अस्मिन्हि वः सवने) and the delight of the ananda in the formative action is becoming habitual to the mind-force (रत्नधेयं इन्द्रं). At the moment, however, asiddhi had attacked, bringing defect of formation, defect of ananda[,] trouble & deficiency in the mind (defect of धन्वन्). Hence the इह यात माप भूत.

Lipi — "17th September." (akasha, varnamaya)
Typical Trikaldrishti

A frog hopping in one direction, with no sign of turning. A turn at a sharp right angle indicated & the exact line of subsequent passage indicated; fulfilled but not in the place perceived.

Another frog comes from the opposite direction; indication that the bodies of the two frogs will meet one leaping on the other, although the lines of their motion were not such as to promise meeting. The smaller frog turned away & began hopping in the opposite direction, but the larger pursued & sprang upon it, thus fulfilling the trikaldrishti, but with a variation of circumstance which had not been foreseen.

Sept. 15 —

Two crows descend into the road behind the wall fighting
& are invisible. Indication that they will immediately rise above
the wall fighting in the air & part. Fulfilled precisely, though the
trikaldrishti itself was not jyotirmaya.

VEDIC EXPERIENCE, 14 AND 15 DECEMBER 1913

I. [176][1]

यस्य विश्वानि हस्तयो: पंच क्षितीनां वसु । स्पाशयस्व यो अस्मध्रुग्
दिव्येवाशनिर्जहि ॥
असुन्वंतं समं जहि दूणाशं यो न ते मय: । अस्मभ्यमस्य वेदनं दद्धि
सूरिश्चिदोहते ॥

O thou in whose two hands are all the possessions of our
five dwelling places, make clear to our eyes him who betrays us,
slay him even in heaven becoming the thunderbolt. Slay him who
presses not out the nectar, the indifferent and oppressed in hope,
who is not thy lover, give us the knowledge of him becoming utterly
luminous to the worshipper so that he bears up thy activities.

Experienced, Dec 14 & 15th 1913. There are Powers of pure
mind which are indifferent, equal to all things, as in possession
of the samata, — but they are void of active delight; they do not
press out the wine of immortal delight, they possess man in that
state when, his hopes oppressed, he takes refuge in a passive &
equal indifference, and is no longer in love with mental activities.
In this state man takes this enemy of Indra & of his own perfection
as a friend and helper. Mental force becoming entirely luminous
in knowledge, súrih, is to pierce this dangerous disguise & make
clear to the inner eye the true nature of this harmful agency, sama
indeed, but asunvan, sama because dunasha & not because of equal
delight. He is to be slain in the pure mind where he dwells by Indra
in the form of the thunderbolt, mind force informed with vaidyuta
energy from Mayas. A uhate is proleptic; the result of Indra or mind
force becoming entirely luminous with the solar light of the ideal
knowledge is to perfect the mental power of the Yogin so that he is

---

[1] MS 173

strong to support & hold all the activities of mental knowledge & of the temperament in their fullness.

"Be rapturous in us and a dwelling for the sacrifice, enter with mastery into Indra, O Soma; thou art powerful, moving forward, and thou meetest no hostile forces on thy way. In him give to dwell our self-expressions, who is alone of the lords of action, and according to his movement is self-state sown in us & masterfully he cultivates that crop. O thou etc..... He who has the twofold fullness and his created being is free from flaw or crevice (continuous) in our realisations, in that Indra's struggle, O Indu, prolong (protect) his richness in its havings. As to thy former adorers, O Indra, thou camst into being as a lover, like waters to the thirsty, even after that manner of soul-experience I call to thee. May we find the force that is intense & pierces in the slaying."

Vijnanachatusthaya

Today—

Lipi, Rupa, Thought, Vani, Trikaldrishti, Power, none absolutely perfect, but moving nearer to perfection.

Tomorrow—

Thought perfect, Vani perfect, Trikaldrishti perfect in type; Power, Rupa, Lipi moving towards perfection.

Day after

Lipi perfect, Power in full force but not yet perfect. Rupa moving towards perfection.

———

Samadhi waits upon Rupa

It is this time seriously intended.

The script was suspended, not renounced. Today although the commencement has been unfavourable, good progress will be made, except in the physical siddhi, in which the enemy has permission to hold his own for three days more. Trikaldrishti is to be perfected today. That is the first siddhi. Afterwards the lipi has to be brought forward. The trikaldrishti has to move perfectly in all fields & with regard to time, place & circumstance even on the intellectual level.

———

Perfection is used as a relative term, but should be absolute. The script is not yet used through the highest agencies; it is only a reflection of the condition of the knowledge. There is therefore no help to be had from it which cannot be had from the other instruments of knowledge—Nevertheless it has to be used & perfected. The falsehoods suggested & uncorrected prevent the dasya from being entirely accepted, but the movement of anrita is a relapse of the intellect in body, not a movement justified by the actual condition of the siddhi —

The revolt against the dasyam where the directing Agency is not satisfactory nor plainly authorised, must cease. There is a perfect Wisdom governing the siddhi & the intellectual infallibility is well established except in that which doubts & judges & by doubting & judging confuses the intellect —

The tejas has not to be renounced, but justified

The trikaldrishti today will throw off the doubt & judgment, but not yet the uncertainties left behind by them in the action of the faculty in intellect. Lipi will justify the prediction — Rupa at last emerge & Power overcome for the last time the general obstruction. In the physical siddhi the Ananda will once more take hold. Samadhi will develop with the rupa. All this is for today.

NOTES ON IMAGES SEEN IN MARCH 1914

The Evolutionary Scale.

We shall see how the thought of God works itself out in Life. The material world is first formed with the Sun as centre, the Sun [ ][1] being itself only a subordinate star of the great Agni, Mahavishnu, in whom is centred the Bhu. Mahavishnu is the Virat Purusha who as Agni pours Himself out into the forms of sun and star. He is Agni Twashtá, Visvakarman, he is also Prajápati and Matariswan. These are the three primal Purushas of the earth life, — Agni Twashta, Prajápati & Matariswan, all of them soul bodies of Mahavishnu. Agni Twashta having made the Sun out of the Apas or waters of being, Prajapati as Surya Savitri enters into the Sun and takes possession of it. He multiplies himself in the Suris or Solar Gods who are the souls of the flames of Surya, the Purushas of the female solar energies. Then he creates out of this solar body of Vishnu the planets each of which successively becomes the Bhumi or place of manifestation for Manu, the mental being, who is the nodus of manifest life-existence and the link between the life and the spirit. The present earth in its turn appears as the scene of life, Mars being its last theatre. In the Bhumi Agni Twashta is again the first principle, Matariswan the second, finally, Prajapati appears in the form of the four Manus, chatváro manavah. Not in the physical world at first, but in the mental world which stands behind the earth-life; for earth has seven planes of being, the material of which the scenes and events are alone normally visible to the material senses, the vital of which man's pranakosha is built and to which it is responsive, the mental to which his manahkosha is attached, the ideal governing his vijnanakosha, the beatific which supports his anandakosha, & the dynamic and essential to which he has not

[1] MS itself

yet developed corresponding koshas, but only unformed nimbuses of concrete being. All the gods throw out their linga-rupas into these worlds of earth and through them carry on her affairs; for these lingas repeat there in the proper terms of life upon earth the conscious movements of the gods in their higher existences in the worlds above Bhu. The Manus manifested in the Manoloka of Bhu bring pressure to bear upon the earth for the manifestation of life and mind. Prajapati as Rudra then begins to form life upon earth, first in vegetable, then in animal forms. Man already exists but as a god or demigod in Bhuvarloka of Bhu, not as a man upon earth. There he is Deva, Asura, Rakshasa, Pramatha, Pisacha, Pashu or as Deva he is either Gandharva[,] Yaksha, Vidyadhara or any of the Karmadevas. For Man is a son of the Manu and is assigned his place in Div & Pradiv, in Heaven & in the Swargabhumis. Thence he descends to earth and thither from earth he returns. All that will be explained afterwards. When the human body is ready, then he descends upon earth and occupies it. He is not a native of earth, nor does he evolve out of the animal. His manifestation in animal form is always a partial incarnation, as will be seen hereafter.

The animal proper is a lower type. Certain devas of the manasic plane in the Bhuvarloka descend in the higher type of animal. They are not mental beings proper, but only half-mental vital beings. They live in packs, tribes etc with a communal existence. They are individual souls, but the individuality is less vigorous than the type soul. If they were not individual, they would not be able to incarnate in individual forms. The body is only the physical type of the soul. The soul, if it were only a communal soul, would manifest in some complex body of which the conglomeration of the different parts would be the sole unity; say, a life like that of the human brain. The animal develops the tribe life, the pack or clan life, the family life. He develops chitta, manas, the rudiments of reason. Then only man appears.

How does he appear? Prajapati manifests as Vishnu Upendra incarnate in the animal or Pashu in whom the four Manus have already manifested themselves, and the first human creature who appears is, in this Kalpa, the Vanara, not the animal Ape, but man with the Ape nature. His satya yuga is the first Paradise, for man begins with the Satya Yuga, begins with a perfected type, not a rudimentary type. The animal forms a perfect type for the human Pashu and then only a Manuputra or Manu, a human, a true mental soul, enters into existence upon earth, with the full blaze of a perfect animal-human mentality in the animal form.

These are man's beginnings. He rises by the descent of ever higher types of Manu from the Bhuvarloka, — first he is Pashu, then Pishacha, then Pramatha, then Rakshasa, then Asura, then Deva, then Siddha. So he ascends the ladder of his own being towards the Sat Purusha.

Manu, the first Prajapati, is a part of Mahavishnu Himself descended into the mental plane in order to conduct the destinies of the human race. He is different from the four Manus who are more than Prajapatis, they being the four Type-Souls from whom all human Purushas are born; they are Manus only for the purpose of humanity & in themselves are beyond this manifest universe & dwell for ever in the being of the Para Purushas. They are not true Manomaya Purushas. But Manu Prajapati is a true manomaya Purusha. He by mental generation begets on his female Energies men in the mental & vital planes above earth, whence they descend into the material or rather the terrestrial body. On earth Manu incarnates fourteen times in each Kalpa & each of these fourteen incarnations is called a Manu. These fourteen Manus govern human destinies during the hundred chaturyugas of the Prati-Kalpa, each in turn taking charge of a particular stage of the human advance. While that stage lasts he directs it both from the mental world and by repeated incarnations upon earth. When Manu Prajapati wishes to incarnate in a fresh form, he has a mental body prepared for him by evolution of births by a human vibhuti, Suratha or another & takes possession of it at the beginning of his manvantara. Each manvantara is composed of a varying number of chaturyugas according to the importance & difficulty of the stage with which it is concerned. Once at least in each chaturyuga the Manu of the Manvantara incarnates as a man upon earth, but this never happens in the Kali Yuga. The seventh & eighth Manus are the most important in each Prati Kalpa & have the longest reigns, for in their Manvantaras the critical change is finally made from the type which was completed in the last Prati Kalpa to the type which is to be perfected in the present Kalpa. For each of the ten Prati-Kalpas has its type. Man in the ten Prati-Kalpas progresses through the ten types which have been fixed for his evolution in the Kalpa. In this Kalpa the types, dashagu, are the ten forms of consciousness, called the Pashu, Vanara, Pishacha, Pramatha, Rakshasa, Asura, Deva, Sadhyadeva, Siddhadeva and the Satyadeva. The last three are known by other names which need not be written at present. The Pashu is mind concentrated entirely on the annam, the Vanara mind concentrated on the Prana, the Pishacha mind concentrated on the senses & the knowledge part of the chitta, the Pramatha mind concentrated on the heart & the emotional & aesthetic part of the chitta, the Rakshasa is mind concentrated on the thinking manas proper & taking up all the others into the manas itself; the Asura is mind concentrated on the buddhi & in the Asura Rakshasa making it serve the manas & chitta; the Deva is mind concentrated in vijnanam, exceeding itself, but in the Asura Deva or Devasura it makes the vijnana serve the buddhi. The others raise mind successively to the Ananda, Tapas & Sat & are, respectively, the supreme Rakshasa, the supreme Asura, the supreme Deva. We have here the complete scale by which Mind ascends its own ladder from Matter to pure Being evolved by Man in the various types of which each of the ten principles is in its turn capable. To take the joy of these various types in their multifold play is the object of the Supreme Purusha in the human Lila.

[II]

A series of images and a number of intimations have been given yesterday in the chitra-drishti to illustrate the history of the first two Manwantaras & the vicissitudes through which the human idea has gone in the course of these unnumbered ages. It is not at all surprising that there should be no relics of those vicissitudes in the strata of the present earth; for the present earth is not the soil of the planet as it was in the earliest Manwantaras. The detritions, the upheavals, the convulsions, the changes that it has undergone cannot be estimated by the imaginative & summary methods of the modern geologists,—men who think themselves advanced &

masters of knowledge, but are only infants & babblers in their own sciences. It is unnecessary to go at present into the scene or habitat of the incidents & peoples shown in the drishti. The facts are sufficient.[2]

The first image was that of a young & beautiful woman fleeing, holding two children by either hand, preceded by a third – though this was not clearly seen – and followed by a little child, a girl with her cloth in her hand. All are of the female sex. In their flight they have upset a handsome & well-dressed young man, who was also fleeing across the line of their flight and now lies sprawling on his back. Behind the woman & her girls an elderly & bearded savage, naked & armed with some kind of weapon, runs at a distance of not many yards and but for the accident of the upset would soon overtake the fugitives. The second image showed the young man still supine with the savage upon him threatening him fiercely with his weapon, but the bhava shows that not slaughter, but prisoners & slaves are the object of the raid. The young man is evidently taken prisoner by the pursuer who has turned aside from the women to this, possibly, more valuable booty. In the third image the little girl of the first is seen captured by a young & handsome barbarian who has managed to comfort and soothe her & is persuading her to lead him to the secret refuge of the fugitives. By this device, it is now indicated, he is able to discover this refuge & capture the whole colony of the civilised people. The success raises him to the rank of a great chief among his people, for it is his section of the raiders who make the victory really profitable. The chitra-lipi *Indigenous* just given shows that these barbarians are the original inhabitants of the country, the others colonists & conquerors. It is intimated by the vijnana that both assailants & assailed are in the Pashu stage & people of the first or second Manu, but the civilised have reached a kind of Devahood of the Gandharva type, the savages are a reappearance of the Asura Rakshasa type of Pashu brought back into a more advanced age in order to re-invigorate the over-refined type that has been evolved. The young chief of the image is a sort

[2] *The three images that follow are mentioned in the Record of 22 March 1914; see page 395.* — Ed.

of Caesar-Augustus or Alaric of the barbarians. He takes the lead
of their revolt which is at first a disordered movement of indignation (lipi Indignation alternating with indigenous)[,] systematises
it, conquers & enslaves the Gandharvas, learns from them their
civilisation and modifies it by the barbarian manners. The new race
evolved finally dominates the then world & fixes the next type of
the Pashu evolution.

But who are these Pashus? For this is not the first pratikalpa of
the Pashus, but the sixth of the Asuras, and it is indicated that none
of these visions belong to any other pratikalpa than the present. It
follows that even these savages cannot be pure Pashus, but Asuras
or Asura Rakshasas starting from the Pashu stage, so far as the
Asura can go back to that stage, and fulfilling the possibilities of
a sort of Pashu-Asura before evolving his Asurahood in the higher
types & arriving & shooting beyond the pure Asura. This is an
important modification. It follows that each type of the Dasha-
gavas goes, within the mould of his own type, through all the ten
gávas from the Pashu to the Siddhadeva. The Pashu-Asura will be
different from the pure Pashu or the Pashu Deva, because he will
always be first & characteristically an Asura, but he will weigh
from the buddhi on the bodily experiences as Pashu, on the vijnana
experiences as Deva & so in each type according to its particular
field of activity. The Deva will do it, instead, from the vijnana, &
the difference of leverage & point of action will make an immense
difference both to the character of the activity and its results in the
field. Moreover it is clear that the Pashu Asura goes also through
the various types within his mixed Pashuhood & Asurahood before he passes to the Pisacha-Asura, who has to undergo a similar
development. The great variety of types that will result from this
evolutionary system, is evident.

The farther images seen[3] in connection with this Pashu-Asura
episode are three in number. First the plain & desolate country with
a hill in the distance, about which it is indicated by the vijnana that
this was the appearance of the country not actually occupied by the

---

[3] *These three images (along with a fourth) are mentioned in the Record of 23 March
1914; see page 397.* —Ed.

barbarians before the colonists came in (by sea, it is suggested & then by movement from the coasts occupied to the inland tracts,) & peopled it sparsely. The catastrophe came because of their haste to conquer the whole small continent before they were able to people all the unoccupied land & build themselves into a strong & irresistible power organised in great cities & populous nations. This haste was due to the superior fertility & attractiveness of the soil actually occupied by the barbarians who, being poor agriculturalists, had settled only on rich soil not demanding a skilful labour & left the rest untilled. The contrast between the waterless soil first seen & the banks of the great river on which was the barbarian settlement, is typical of the contrast between the two kinds of soil, utilised & unutilised. The premature attempts at conquest began with aggressions on the nearest barbarian villages & the raid seen was the first effective retaliation carried out in the absence of the fighting men of the colony, so that on the side of the attacked only women, children & peaceful unarmed men are seen fleeing to a habitual & secret place of refuge. For this colony was on the very borders of the barbarian country & always exposed to incursions. It is not clear why the colonist fighters were absent, whether on a raid on the barbarians or in a civil quarrel among themselves.

The second image, the fortified city on the plateau, shown by the terraces cut in the slope of the plateau & the subsequent separate chitra of one of the city domes, to be a civilised & magnificent metropolis, shows the final result of the amalgamation of barbarians & colonists. The original barbarian settlement was on the bank of the great river seen with one of its ghauts not far from the foot of the plateau, but after the raid, in order to safeguard themselves & their booty, the savages retreated at the instance of the young victorious chief, now by common consent their leader, to the plateau, then steep in its slope & difficult of access. Afterwards a great city was built on the site of this barbarian stronghold. The construction on the river in appearance like a house, but apparently standing on the water can have been nothing but a houseboat or rather a house-raft, & it is moored to a *char* in the river, a fact which suggested the first erroneous idea that it was a house on an island in the river.

The third image, the large, high & spacious hut, built almost with elegance & with the great wide open door, was that of the chief and shows that the savages, in spite of their nakedness, were not on the lowest scale either of human immaturity or of human degeneration. The figure in clerical dress & hat is that not of a priest, but of an envoy, one of the elders of the colony come to negotiate for the restoration of the captives; the girl with whom he converses & from whom he turns in shocked despair, is one of the daughters of the woman seen in the earliest of this series of images, now a slave & concubine of the chief. At first, the colonists were unwilling to use violence lest the captives should be maltreated. The fact that one of the most important of them has already been subjected to irremediable indignity, has just come to the knowledge of the elder along with other facts, eg the unwillingness of the chiefs to make any reparation, & accounts for the action which indicates despair of peace or any fruitful negotiation. The series is not yet complete, but awaits the unfolding of farther events already very vaguely indicated by the vijnana. The other image has no connection with these events but belongs to a later Manvantara, that of the Pramatha-Rakshasa, of the sixth Manu in one of its most perfect & brilliant stages. It has to be kept vivid in the mind for future interpretation.

III

The disposition of the Manwantaras may now be described. It will be remembered that there are fourteen Manus and ten gavas of the Dashagava. How are these divided among the Manus? In this Kalpa or rather Pratikalpa the type Pashu is the Vanara, but as in all Nature's movements, even in manifesting the Vanara, the others first make their appearance rapidly before the type "arrives"; those most germane to the matter are the lion, tiger, elephant, dog, wolf, cat, bull & cow, bear, fox, ass, horse, bee, ant, butterfly, fish, eagle (also kite, hawk & vulture), songbird, crow & cuckoo etc. In all these human egos readily incarnate & the human type absorbs them all. The first Manu takes all these totems & applies them to the general type of the Asura, driving at the evolution of a giant Vanara-Asura who has in him all these elements & combines them into an animal harmony dominated by curiosity, humour, adaptability & adaptiveness, the Ape virtues which bring that type nearest to man. This Vanara Asura the first Manu hands on to the second, who takes the type, fulfils it and evolves it into the Pishacha-Asura. This he does by bringing the Ape curiosity uppermost and applying it to all the experiences of man's animal life, to play, work, domesticity, battle, pleasure, pain, laughter, grief, relations, arrangements etc. All the higher qualities—imagination, reflection, invention, thought, spirituality even are turned towards these experiences & their possibilities,—cognitional not aesthetic exhausted so far as the human animal can exhaust them. This however, is done only in the third Manwantara. In the second it is the Vanara who satisfies his humour, curiosity & adaptiveness in a far more elementary & summary fashion, but as he does so, he begins to refine & evolve in search of new sensations until the full Pisacha Asura is born. This type is handed over to the third Manu to fulfil, & to it two Manvantaras are devoted,—in the third the Pisacho-Pramatha of the Asura type evolves; in the fourth the Pisacha Pramatha evolves into the full Pramatha-Asura. The curiosity ceases to be merely cognitional & practically scientific, it becomes aesthetic with an animal & vital aestheticism; the Pramatha seeks to extract their full emotional & aesthetic values, their full rasa out of everything in life, out of torture equally with ecstasy, death equally with life, grief equally with joy. That type is evolved by the fifth Manu into the Pramatha-Rakshasa of the Asura type, & by the sixth into the full Rakshasa-Asura. The Rakshasa it is who first begins really to think, but his thought is also egoistic & turned towards sensation. What he seeks is a gross egoistic satisfaction in all the life of the mind, prana & body, in all the experiences of the Pashu, Pisacha, Pramatha & his own. But as this type is not a pure Rakshasa, but a Rakshasasura, the thought is there from the beginning, for the Rakshasa has already established it in the human mould in the fifth pratikalpa. It now, however, in the Asura ceases to be subservient to the vital & animal instincts & becomes the instrument instead of a vigorous, violent & clamorous intellectual ego. As the main type is that of the Asura, there is always a tendency to subordinate the lower ego to the intellectual Aham, but the subordination is at first only a self-disciplining for a more intelligently victorious self-indulgence, like the tapasya of Ravana. This type evolved is fixed in the character of Ravana and takes possession of its field in the Manwantara of the seventh Manu, Vaivasvata. In that Manwantara it evolves into the Asuro-Rakshasa in which the intellectual ego & the emotional, sensational ego enter into an equal copartnership for the grand enthronement & fulfilment of the human ahankara. As the type of the sensational & emotional Rakshasa-Asura is Ravana, so the type of the more mightily balanced Asura Rakshasa of the Asura type is Hiranyakashipu. In the eighth Manwantara this Asura Rakshasa evolves into the pure Asura who serves his intellectual ego & subordinates to it all the other faculties. That type reigns with the ninth Manu & evolves into the Asuradeva of the Asura mould & in the tenth Manvantara into the Devasura who enthrones the vijnana and glorifies the Asura existence by the vijnanamaya illuminations playing on the whole of the triple mental[,] vital & bodily life of man. In the eleventh & twelfth manwantaras the Devasura evolves into the Sadhya, the Anandamaya Asura who at first with the pure Ananda, then with the Tapomaya Ananda, then with the Sanmaya Ananda dominates the reigns of the thirteenth & fourteenth Manus & completes the apotheosis of the Asura in man. With the Siddhadeva in the Asura the hundredth Chaturyuga of the sixth Pratikalpa comes to a glorious close.

IV. Certain farther images have appeared which seem intended to show the nature of the Kaliyuga civilisation evolved by the intermixture of the barbarian & the Gandharva Pashus.[4] One is that of a very wide road climbing up a steep incline; the comparative height of the trees on one side show its great width. This picture seems to be intended to confirm the impression created by the ensemble of the city on the plateau, by the dome & by another chitra of a part of the hill with a (private?) house roofed like a modern church, that this civilisation had a certain bigness, massiveness & sharply cut variety. A low type of the Pashu in this age was also seen,

---

[4] *These images are mentioned, in a different order, in the Record of 24 March 1914; see pages 403-4.* —Ed.

bearded, [hatted][5] & visaged like a lowclass modern American of the West. These resemblances have created some doubt as to either the genuineness of these images or their right interpretation; but the doubt is not justified by its cause. For throughout the fourteen Manwantaras, variations, permutations & combinations of the same type are bound to appear. This is the law of Nature's development in clay, plant & animal & applies equally to man, his manners, ideas, appurtenances & institutions. Given the truth of the Manwantara theory any other feature than this varied repetition would be more surprising than the repetition itself & lead to more legitimate distrust. There are plenty of variations & signs of immaturity or different tendency. In the image of the river, it is noticeable that there are no modern vessels. The houseboat is a houseraft & entirely different in structure from the modern houseboat; the craft in which the man & girl in another image are seen crossing the river is also a raft & not a boat. The Gandharvas, when first seen, are robed differently in the males & the women; the former have dresses like the older styles of European dress, the latter wear loose & light classical draperies — an arrangement which is after all sufficiently natural & might easily evolve in an artistic & aesthetically minded race. The Teutonic element in the character & civilisation of the new type Pashus is a result of the blending of the graceful, slight & artistic Gandharva with the plain, forceful & robust barbarian; the latter predominates in the blend & the former merely tones down his force & gives a few details of dress & manners much modified in the direction of rude & clear cut plainness & strength, & is chiefly prominent but not predominant in the women as typified by the girl on the raft who has a native grace denied to the men of her blood. Their elegance is heavy & artificial, worn as a dress rather than possessed as a native characteristic. Sometimes the type goes very low as in the premature American; the ordinary type is higher but void of dignity or greatness, grace or beauty. They represent an early tendency towards the Asura Rakshasa such as he manifests himself in the Kaliyugas of this Pratikalpa when he has compassed the first heavy self-restraint necessary for his evolution towards the

[5] MS hated

Deva. In a later image the woman of the first, the captive of the barbarian Augustus, is seen in a later incarnation at the turning point when this type dissatisfied with itself is trying to recover the grace, humour, artistry, fantasy, liveliness of their Gandharva blood, so as to develop again in themselves the Pashu deva. This fixes the period of these incidents. It is in the Kali of the fourth chaturyuga in the reign of the first Manu when the Rakshasa Asura of the Pashu Asura type reigns & is attempting to turn full Asura with occasional overshootings to the Pashu deva. Every race that thus overshoots its mark & goes a step farther than their immediate next pace in evolution aids powerfully that evolution, but becomes unfit for survival & has to disappear. For this reason the Gandharva race of the Pashus disappeared & the Asura Rakshasa type reappeared, then took up something of the Gandharva & advanced one step towards the Asura-Pashu of the Asura type. By such overleapings & recoilings human evolution has always advanced.

V.   There are certain images of animals dating from these early aeons which should be recorded here although they are not of the first Pashu period but fall before & after it.[6] The first are images of a monstrous creature resembling the modern seal, but thicker & bulkier seen in a region of ice; the other another animal of equally monstrous bulk, its skin a series of successive red and yellow bands, its face exceedingly long, rough, thin & snouted, a cross between bear, wolf & tiger in the face, rhinoceroslike, yet supple in the body, but in spite of its ferocious appearance, sufficiently harmless. These creatures, it is suggested in the vijnana, belong to the first chaturyuga of the pratikalpa previous to the appearance of man; for the fourteen Manus enjoy each a reign of seven chaturyugas of varying lengths and the first & last of the hundred belong not to any Manu but the opening chaturyuga to Brahma & Rudra, the closing to Kalki & to Shiva. Man in the first appears only tentatively at the end, in the last only as a survival at the beginning.

   The third image is that of a bear leaping on a smaller animal which it keeps under its paw while it wrests from it & devours some

---

6 *These images are mentioned in the Record of 24 March 1914; see page 404.* —*Ed.*

eatable for which the victim was pursued. The male of the captive is near unable to help, unwilling to flee. It is a small deer, only one third the size of the modern fallow deer. Suddenly the head of the bear sinks. It has been killed, it would seem, by the arrow, spear or other weapon of a human hunter. This scene belongs to the second Manwantara of the Vanaras.[7]

A fourth image is of a horse of the first Manwantara in one of its earlier chaturyugas, a clumsy stiff-legged & long-eared animal squarish in its lines & most unlike the graceful modern equine species. The animal stands on the side of a river, & with head raised & stretched sideways & ears pricked, listens to a sound amid the trees on the opposite bank. This image was preceded by another of a horse of the Pashu period in the later age when the civilised barbarian type was trying to recover the Gandharva. This type of horse, standing with a rider on its back & other human beings conversing near & at its head, is more equine, but is still stiff-legged & has not lost the asinine cast of head of its predecessor.

VI.   Three images of the fourth in descent from the Chief of the Barbarians; the first showing him standing meditating on the great ghaut of the river, a figure & face like Napoleon's clad in a dress resembling the modern European; the second, his mother & stepmother, descendants of the captives of the first image; the third, the emperor again with his halfbrother, irreproachably clad, Prefect of the city, consulting with regard to some palace intrigue in which the mother & stepmother are concerned.[8] It is intimated that it is this fourth King of the line who establishes the dominance of the race in the then earth.

---

[7] *This image is mentioned in the Record of 25 March 1914; see page 407.* — Ed.
[8] *These three images are mentioned in the Record of 25 March 1914; see page* 407. — Ed.

UNDATED SCRIPT, c. 1920

[1]

There is no possibility of immediate success in the physical siddhi or in the higher vijnana. The riot of the lower ideality stands in the way. It must quiet down before the drashtri vijnana can act with any completeness.

[2]

The Sortilege. It is to be revived once more. There is no writing this morning. The script is also to resume its movement. First, it has to be absolutely spontaneous. That is almost finished. It is a little obstacle, the suggestion.

Most of the amertume is a momentarily effective amnesia of the amara purusha. Momentary only. That is all at all today possible.

This denial must suffice both for the present and for all similar ascriptions in the future.

T^2 first — not complete, but perfect in the representative imperative — logos Vijnana

Thought-siddhi in interpretative imperative — d[itt]o.

Rupa siddhi, not yet stable.

Internal vijnana — perfect in thought-siddhi — growing in lipi[,] drishya etc

[1]

OM TAT SAT

The highest interpretation hitherto made in human under-standing and experience may thus be stated with the proviso that since it is human it must be incomplete.

TAT. That.

> The Absolute Unmanifested—Parabrahman, Purushot-tama, Parameswara (holding in himself the Parâshakti and in her the All).

SAT. The Existent (I Am.)

> The Absolute containing all the power of the manifes-tation. The Absolute is Parabrahman-Mahâmâyâ. The Absolute is Purushottama-Parâprakriti. The Absolute is Parameswara-Âdyâ (original) Parâshakti.

OM. The Word of Manifestation.

A The external manifestation (consciousness realised in the actual and concrete—seen by the human consciousness as the waking state.)

U The internal manifestation (intermediate—the inner, not the inmost being—consciousness realised in the inner po-tentialities and intermediate states between the inmost supramental and the external—seen by the human con-sciousness as the subliminal and associated with the dream state.)

M The inmost seed or condensed consciousness (the inmost supramental, glimpsed by the human consciousness as something superconscient, omniscient and omnipotent, and associated with the state of dreamless Sleep or full Trance.)

AUM   Turiya, the Fourth; the pure Spirit beyond these three, Atman consciousness entering into Tat Sat and able to identify with it. Believed to be obtainable in its absoluteness only in absolute Trance — nirvikalpa samadhi.

All this (first in the Upanishads) is the viewpoint from the mental consciousness. It is incomplete because two things that are one have been left out, the Personal Manifestation and the name of the Mahashakti. The subsequent growth of spiritual knowledge has brought about a constant effort to add these missing elements.

When the hidden secret has been discovered and made effective, the human consciousness will be exceeded, the superconscient made conscient and the subconscient or inconscient which is the inevitable shadow of the superconscient filled with the true spiritual and supramental consciousness. The Trance, Dream and Waking States (all imperfect at present and either touched with obscurity or limited) become each completely conscious and the walls, gaps or reversals of consciousness that intervene between them are demolished.

Tat then will appear in its entire truth, the Supreme Absolute, One in Two, each entirely in the other and both one in an ineffable Existence, Consciousness and Ananda.

Sat is the eternal and infinite truth of Sachchidananda ready for manifestation. It is the One Existence, but the Two in One are there, each in each, each perfect in the other.

OM is the manifestation. The Mahashakti comes forth from the Supreme for creation. In the eternal manifestation the Two in One are evident to each other; their identity and union are foundation of the diversity of this play, and it is the possession of the truth that makes the manifestation stable & eternal.

In the temporal creation Sat seems to be separated from Chit and Ananda. Hence the play of the inconscience becomes possible and the creation of an Ignorance and an ignorant Maya. The Chit-Shakti has to reveal the Sat Purusha to herself and her creation

and entirely to meet him and recover the true identity and union
in the Ananda. She seems to be put out from him, but all the time
she is in him and he in her. It is this concealed truth that has to
become manifest and effective and its discovery is the secret of
the new creation in which the superconscient and inconscient will
become conscious and fill with the supreme Sacchidananda, One
in Two and Two in One. Then the temporal manifestation will be
recreated in the image of the Truth. It will be in harmony with
the eternal manifestation, built by what comes down to it directly
from the Eternal. For through the Ananda and the Supramental
the eternal manifestation stands behind the temporal creation and
secretly supports its involved and evolving movements.

[2]

The secret name of the Supreme Mahashakti signifies

मयोभू: . . राधा	Love, Bliss,	*Ananda*
महामाया, पराप्रकृति	Creative and Formative Knowledge-Power	
		Chit-Tapas
	Support, Covering, Pervasion	*Sat*

For the Supreme is Ananda unifying Consciousness and Existence in the single Power (Shakti) of these things.

[3]

All is created by the Supreme Goddess, the Supreme and Original Mahashakti, all proceeds from her, all lives by her, all lives in her,
even as she lives in all. All wisdom and knowledge are her wisdom
and knowledge; all power is her power, all will and force her will
and force, all action is her action, all movement her movement. All
beings are portions of her power of existence.

=

Seven times seven are the planes of the Supreme Goddess,
the steps of ascent and descent of the Divine Transcendent and
Universal Adyashakti.

Above are the thrice seven supreme planes of Sat-Chit-Ananda,
त्रि: सप्त परमा पदानि मातु:; in between are the seven planes of the

Divine Truth and Vastness, Mahad Brahma, सत्यमृतं बृहत्; below are
the thrice seven steps of the ascent and descent into this evolutionary
world of the earth existence.

These three gradations are successively Supermind or Truth-
Mind, with its seven suns; Life with its seven Lotuses; Earth with
its seven Jewel-Centres.

The seven Lotuses are the seven chakras of the Tantric
tradition, descending and ascending from Mind (Sahasradala,
Ajna[,] Vishuddha, Anahata) that takes up Life through Life in
Force (Manipura, Swadhisthana) down to Life involved in Matter
[(]Muladhara[)].

All these Life-Centres are in themselves centres of Truth in Life
even as the seven Suns are each a flaming heart of Truth in luminous
Divine-Mind-Existence; but these lotuses have been veiled, closed,
shut into their own occult energies by the Ignorance. Hence the
obscurity, falsehood, death, suffering of our existence.

The Jewel-Centres of the Earth-Mother are seven luminous
jewel-hearts of Truth in Substance; but they have been imprisoned
in darkness, fossilised in immobility, veiled, closed, shut into their
own occult energies by the hardness, darkness and inertia of the
material Inconscience.

To liberate all these powers by the luminous and flaming descent of the suns of the Supermind and the release of the eighth Sun
of Truth hidden in the Earth, in the darkness of the Inconscience,
in the cavern of Vala and his Panis, this is the first step towards
the restoration of the Earth Mother to her own divinity and the
earth-existence to its native light, truth, life and bliss of immaculate
Ananda.

[4]

The Seven Suns.

—

The Sun of Creative Origination (from the eternal vastnesses).
The double Sun of Light and Power (concentrating the move-
  ments emanated from the infinite Wisdom-Will.)
The Sun of the Word (organising the creation).
The Sun of Love, Bliss and Beauty (dynamising the descending
  harmonies)
The Sun of Soul-Power (aspiring, receiving, grasping, assimi-
  lating the creation; divided here into the mind and psyche,
  there unified in Soul-Mind, Brahman.)
The Sun of Life (dynamically externalising the creation).
The Sun of Everlasting Form (stabilising and containing the
  creation).

These are the seven powers of the Truth-Mind above the body.

=

[5]

The Sun of Truth, originating the supramental creation
The double Sun of Supramental Light and Will, transmitting
the Knowledge-Power that creates, founds and organises the supramental creation.
The Sun of the Word, expressing and arranging the supramental creation
The Sun of Love, Bliss and Beauty, vivifying and harmonising
the supramental creation.
The Sun of supramental Force (Source of Life) dynamising the
supramental creation.
The Sun of supramental Life-Radiances, (Power-Rays) canal-
ising the dynamis and pouring it into forms.
The Sun of Supramental Form-Energy holding and embodying
the supramental life and stabilising the creation.

[6]

The Seven Suns of the Supermind

1. The Sun of Supramental Truth, — Knowledge-Power originating the supramental creation.

    Descent into the Sahasradala.

2. The Sun of Supramental Light and Will-Power, transmitting the Knowledge Power as dynamic vision and command to create, found and organise the supramental creation.

    Descent into the Ajna-chakra, the centre between the eyes.

3. The Sun of the Supramental Word, embodying the Knowledge-Power, empowered to express and arrange the supramental creation

    Descent into the Throat-Centre.

4. The Sun of supramental Love, Beauty and Bliss, releasing the Soul of the Knowledge-Power to vivify and harmonise the supramental creation.

    Descent into the Heart-Lotus

5. The Sun of Supramental Force dynamised as a power and source of life to support the supramental creation

    Descent into the navel centre

6. The Sun of Life-Radiances (Power-Rays) distributing the dynamis and pouring it into concrete formations.

    Descent into the penultimate centre

7. The Sun of supramental Substance-Energy and Form-Energy empowered to embody the supramental life and stabilise the creation.

    Descent into the Muladhara.

[7]

The Seven Centres of the Life

1. The thousand-petalled Lotus — above the head with its base on the brain. Basis or support in Life-Mind for the Supramental; initiative centre of the illumined Mind.

2 The centre between the brows in the middle of the forehead. Will, vision, inner mental formation, active and dynamic Mind.

3 The centre in the throat. Speech, external mind, all external expression and formation.

4 The heart-lotus. Externally, the emotional mind, the vital mental: in the inner heart the psychic centre

5 The navel centre. The larger vital proper; life-force centre.

6 The centre intermediate between the navel and the Muladhara. The lower vital; it connects all the above centres with the physical

7 The last centre or Muladhara. Material support of the vital; initiation of the physical.

All below is the subconscient physical.

UNDATED NOTES, c. JANUARY 1927

Amrita —
   Moses, Brihaspati, Hermes, Michael Angelo, Rudra, Pythagoras.

Bijoy
   Child Krishna, St Jean, Kartikeya, child Vishnu

Barin
   Nefdi. Apollo-Aryaman

St Hilaire —
   Ramakrishna — (The Four)

Kshitish
   Narada — Bach-Isaie

Kanai
   Sukadeva — One of the Vital Four

Tirupati
   One of the Vital Four

Purani
   Trita. The Angel of Peace — One of the Vital Four

Anilbaran
   Vivekananda — The "Fearless".

D [Durai] Swami
   François I. Chandragupta. Janaka.

NOTES ON PHYSICAL TRANSFORMATION
c. JANUARY 1927

4 mistakes —

1. Began on a mistaken or merely theoretic knowledge – about absorption from outside

2 Giving up of food is not the condition for finding the secret, it is the result of finding the secret.

3 Cessation of hunger, feeling fed, refusal of food by the body not a sign; it proceeds from the body vital, not from the body substance

4 The entire secret can be found and made effective only when the body is brought into the right condition. A process of adaptation is necessary.

5 Transition

Continuity of consciousness, continuity of energy, continuity of Ananda, continuity of substance

Body substance sacred; earth herself; to be mastered, adapted and transformed, not forced and martyrised

Athanatogen.

1. Pranayama

2 Gland processes

3 Absorption from outside

4 Light process

5 Physical support – transformation of ordinary food; body power of living or etheric assimilation

The attempt to transform the body through the renunciation of food has not succeeded as was expected or in the time given and for the following reasons.

1. The knowledge or idea with which it was begun was imperfect and not applicable under the present circumstances. In reality what was chiefly relied upon was a great dynamic energy and the power of the will and aspiration to bring the divine realisation into the body. These forces can do miracles under the right conditions; and now they are quite strong enough to produce miraculous results on the subjective plane, in the physical consciousness, the physical mind and the vital physical, but the most material is not yet ready. The attempt was therefore premature. In order that it should succeed, one of two things was necessary, either a right entire knowledge and process or else the divine Grace supporting a complete descent of the highest supramental Truth and a complete ascent to meet it of the supramental from below. These things should have been got first and firmly founded, for till then there can be no effective divinisation of the material body.

2. The entire giving up of food cannot be the condition of the realisation; it must be, if it is to be done, one result or circumstance of the realisation.

3 It is a mistake to think that cessation of hunger, a sensation of being fed or the refusal of food by the body is a sign that the material frame is ready for living without sustenance. Hunger and the rest come from the vital in the body. It was this bodily vital which was ready and desirous of abstaining from food, but the most material parts were not ready. But being without a voice and accustomed to obey and act only as an instrument, they gave no sign except the fading of the flesh and physical weakness.

Now this material part is most important and indispensable. It is the earth herself in the concrete. It is part of the crude stuff you have to use for building the divine physical substance and you cannot do without it. Therefore it must be respected and not forced before it is ready. It has to be mastered and transformed, but not done violence to or neglected.

4. The entire secret for which you are seeking can only be found and applied effectively when the material body is ready and

for that a process of adaptation is indispensable. The final secret, even if you find it, must remain only a theory until this adaptation is made. What you need to find out first is a secret of the transition. For you are physically in a period of transition. The period of victorious realisation comes later.

Four physical things have to be attained; stability and continuity of consciousness, stability and continuity of energy, stability and continuity of Ananda, stability and continuity of substance.

The first she has gained; it gives a certain mukti, liberation, conscious immortality, and can give great results, but not by itself the complete result aimed at.

The second is beginning to come, but as it brings you a step nearer to the completeness, it is itself also more dependent than the first on its instrument, the body. It can exist in itself, but for its completeness it must become an entirely physical and material strength, for which there should be as a tool a strong body.

The other two stabilities and especially the last are still unattained. The last is the most difficult of all; it is the greatest achievement, the one problem that really has yet to be solved and on which the terrestrial security of the others depends.

My advice to you is not to mind retracing your steps; she should take food again and build up the body again as a necessary support. At the same time as a general rule try to use the food to the best advantage by concentration upon it and upon the body's reception of it and its right assimilation so that finally the body can maintain itself in full force and substance with a minimum quantity of stuff, a supreme quality and a maximum of assimilation. When that has been attained, the necessary adaptation will have neared completion. Advance progressively at first; rapidity will be possible afterwards. Do not mind the initial difficulties.

Remember however that the food problem is only a detail and do not exaggerate its importance. The main thing is to bring down and up the highest supramental from above and the deepest from below, to unite them and to obtain the support, sanction and constant effectuating action of what you call the divine Grace which is a descent from the Truth of the Supreme determining all from the plenitude of the Eternal. When you get these things in their fullness, the true material miracles will be possible in their marvellous rapidity and splendour.

Equanimity, patience, steadfast faith, steadfast will, dynamic aspiration, increasing knowledge-power are the things you need in their harmonious convergence that you may fulfil and conquer.

The power of subjective realisation in the physical is there as you see more from day to day; it will become absolute. The power through the subjective on the objective is increasing and will infallibly increase still more and become perfect. The direct power on the most material plane is the one thing still obstinately resisted. Persevere, satisfy the conditions, and it will come to you like the others.

DIAGRAMS, c. JANUARY 1927

SUPREME SELF-CONTAINED
ABSOLUTE

–

First Absolute –   Tat. The Absolute Transcendent, the
Supreme, Paratpara, (containing all, limited by nothing).

Second Absolute – Sat. The supreme self-contained absolute
Existence, Sachchidananda, (Ananda uniting Sat & Chit),
holding in its absolute unity the dual Principle (He &
She, Sa and Sâ) and the fourfold Principle, OM with its
four states as one.

Third Absolute –   Aditi - M [the Mother]. Aditi is the indivisi-
ble consciousness force and Ananda of the Supreme;
M, its living dynamis, the supreme Love, Wisdom,
Power. Adya-Shakti of the Tantra = Parabrahman

Fourth Absolute – Parameswara = Parameswari
                 of the Gita   of the Tantra

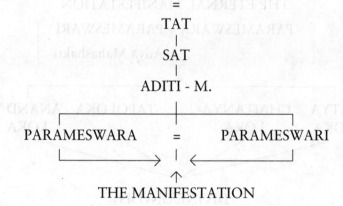

TAT
|
SAT
|
ADITI - M.
|
PARAMESWARA   =   PARAMESWARI

THE MANIFESTATION

THE MANIFESTATION

I

First Absolute   The concealed Avyakta Supreme, self-
involved Sachchidananda, Parabrahman (Parameswara-
iswari)

Second Absolute – Aditi - M. containing in herself the
Supreme. The Divine Consciousness, Force, Ananda
upholding all the universes – Para Shakti, Para Prakriti,
Mahamaya (yayedam dhâryate jagat).

Third Absolute –   The Eternal Manifestation (The supreme
Satya Loka, Chaitanyaloka, Tapoloka, Ananda-loka – not
those of the mental series.)

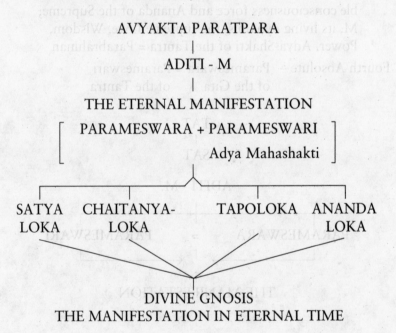

AVYAKTA PARATPARA

|

ADITI - M

|

THE ETERNAL MANIFESTATION

$$\left[\begin{array}{c} \textbf{PARAMESWARA + PARAMESWARI} \\ \text{Adya Mahashakti} \end{array} \right]$$

**SATYA   CHAITANYA-   TAPOLOKA   ANANDA
LOKA   LOKA   LOKA**

**DIVINE GNOSIS
THE MANIFESTATION IN ETERNAL TIME**

II

The Manifestation in Eternal Time

DIVINE GNOSIS
Satyam Ritam Brihat

=

AVYAKTA PARATPARA
|
ADITI - M
[VIJNANESWARA-VIJNANESWARI]

| SADGHANA LOKA | CHIDGHANA ◇ TAPOGHANA } LOKA | ANANDAGHANA LOKA |

The Thrice Seven Supreme Planes of the Mother.
|
VIJNANA LOKA
|
TRUTH-MIND
|
TRUTH-LIFE
|
TRUTH-FORM IN PERPETUAL SUBSTANCE

The Temporal Manifestation

MISCELLANEOUS NOTATIONS

c. FEBRUARY – APRIL 1927

[1]

No power will descend tonight.
Knowledge first, power afterwards.
Telepathy perfects itself first, then tapas, then the supreme T^2.
Till then nothing else can be finally perfect.

Tonight Ananda, Drishya, Knowledge, Telepathic and Tapasic T^2.

[2]

There can be no doubt of the result. Only the time is doubtful and the full extent of the achievement. Tomorrow the entire lifting of the obstacle. Once more a free and rapid action. There is also the restoration of the first two chatusthayas. That will take place fully tonight. Nothing more tonight of an absolute character. The removal of the fragments of illness is not yet done, but it is preparing and will happen in a short time.

This is all for the time being.

[3]

April 2. 1927.   Lipi
    Christmas.   Chittagong   will be taken up.

[4]

ॐ आनन्दमयि चैतन्यमयि सत्यमयि परमे
OM anandamayi chaitanyamayi [satyamayi parame]

RECORD OF DRISHTI, 30 JULY 1927

July 30th 1927

1. Ch! [Champaklal] lolling and rolling in a chair trance-awake.

Intimation. "The most material will now be conscious."

2 A palm-tree of inordinate length growing from the bottom of the side of a well, climbing up and emerging above the earth level. All below now open (the subconscient awake). The palm-tree indicates the victory of conscious life and awakened spirit.

3 One in a cap standing and reading a letter. At first it appeared to be a vague form of M. which receded as the other grew clear, but was still felt reading over his shoulder.

Intimation. "A former personality (alchemist?) of Kanuga still strong in his psychic and vital nature[."]

4. M's hand; starting from it a running zigzag with the letter "a" at its starting point and going towards the Shiva (linga) affecting without as yet touching it.

I [Intimation]. The tivra Ananda — personal? "a" = beginning.

UNDATED SCRIPT, c. 1927

[1]

Take time to develop the next step. Strength in the organs, strength in the muscles. Hair, skin, flesh afterwards.

It is no use wasting time. Taking time means to do things thoroughly, prepare and accomplish.

[2]

The last possibility has been taken away from the hands of the opposing forces
The T^2 is now certain.

≡

Now there is the perfect identity of the warrior and the slave in the imperfect Ishwara. There has to be the perfect identity with them of the king-sage. Then there will be the perfect Ishwara.

＝

The body in her is the sole remaining obstacle—the most material body. It is influenced, it is not yet perfectly open and submissive.

＝

The identity is not yet there because the strength and knowledge are not sufficiently full and they are not full because the supermind is not yet free. It will be free soon.
All is ready. It will be free from today.

[3]

More and more the opposition is furious, more and more the higher power insists. The opposition is effective in bringing three things, bodily illness, outside opposition, lack of physical means. These three must be destroyed or there can be no finality in the work or the sadhana.

UNDATED SCRIPT, c. 1927–1928

[1]

There is no certitude as yet of an absolute kind; even the relative certitude is very much veiled for the present. At any rate the ground has been cleared of much of the remnants of the intelligence. It is practically certain that much more will be done tonight, but the direction is not clear.

This will be done. First, in the third chatusthaya the entire elimination of the merely mental reason; the entire elimination of the original mind. The supramentalised form of these things in the Overmind. Second, the Vishaya and the Samadhi. In the latter, first coherence, then supramentalisation of lipi in deep samadhi, —stability and supramentalisation of *drishya, ghatana, chintana, itihasa*. In the former, freedom of all the four. Rupa soon to be complete followed by the fifth vishaya. Thirdly—in fourth chatusthaya, Arogya and Ananda to be established; the other two to be carried forward. In the fifth great increase of Karma and Kama.

These things will be done progressively but with a sufficiently rapid movement. Tonight begins the completion of the third chatusthaya.

It will be complete before long. There is no doubt of it.

All this is partly the old struggle, partly the process of supramentalising the most material consciousness and its movements, partly a condition of the farther advance of the supermind transformation.

[2]

Many things have still to be done before the divine gnosis can manifest in the nature. It is the gnostic overmind in different forms that is now current there; it has to be transformed into the true supermind gnosis. Let it be done rapidly from tonight till the 15ᵗʰ instant.

[3]

It is sure of fulfilment in the end but constantly delayed by the apparently chaotic complexity of the process. As yet, it is not the end. It is true that the most material couch is open and touched, though not yet transformed. But this is not sufficient; for the power that will work in it must be the true supermind, and as yet it is only the supramentalised overmind that has become at all normal in the material consciousness; the others are normal only for a time and then there is a relapse to the supramentality and to the supramentalised mind or overmind. This is the trouble.

It will soon be overcome.

[4]

[.....][1] has become more normal and facile, the first can now disappear. The second will remain until supermind in overmind (a still higher stage) can be perfectly established. That again will remain until gnostic overmind has changed into gnosis [in][2] overmind. The transformation will then be complete and only the transcendence of overmind and ascent into divine gnosis will be left as the last step to the perfect siddhi.

$$=$$

[..] supramental movement[3]
[..
....]

disregards all apparent disproof [and] adverse circumst[ances.]

The automatic perfection of supramental overmind thought is the next siddhi indicated. It will begin with a progressive elimination of all that remains of supramentalised mind in overmind.

---

[1] *Continued from a page now lost. — Ed.*
[2] *MS into*
[3] *The rest of this page was torn off and is lost. The next fragment is all that survives of what was written on the other side of the page. — Ed.*

NOTES ON PROPHETIC VISION, 1929

1. Some ten days before August 15th 1929, Venkataraman at soup sees himself in a vision falling from branch to branch of a tree. Half an hour afterwards, having returned from the soup to his rooms (Mudaliar's house near treasury) for flowers to bring to the Mother, he climbs a big tree of champak, misses his hold, falls from branch to branch on to the ground and is unable to move for a few days and cannot come to the house for the 15th celebration. *Prevision.*

2. A lottery is arranged for the distribution among the sadhaks of articles of small value—in order to see how the forces work on different people. Before the distribution of tickets Amrita sees in vision the number 61; he gets actually the number 62. On inquiry he learned that by mistake two tickets had been distributed to one sadhak, otherwise he would have received No 61. *Telepathic vision of the thing that was about to happen,—not prevision.*

3. On Monday, 23d February 1929 at soup, the Mother sees among a number of other visions the son of Madame Gaebelé with a broken arm bandaged, but attaches no importance to it. On Thursday she meets Madame Gaebelé and is told that her son broke his wrist at football on Monday and it was put in plaster before the time of the vision. At the moment she was praying earnestly that the Mother might give her help for the arm to cure. *Silent communication from the mind of another awaking telepathic vision.*

DIAGRAMS, c. 1931

THE SUPREME
|

Sachchidananda – Unmanifest, making possible every kind of manifestation.

|

SACHCHIDANANDA IN MANIFESTATION
The Supreme Planes of Infinite Consciousness
(1) Sat (implying Chit-Tapas and Ananda)
(2) Chit (implying Sat and Ananda)
(3) Ananda (implying Sat and Chit-Tapas.)

|

SUPERMIND or DIVINE GNOSIS.
(The Self-Determining Infinite Consciousness)
From the point of view of our ascent upwards this is the Truth-Consciousness as distinguished from all below that belongs to the separative Ignorance.

|

OVERMIND or MAYA
(Overmind takes all Truth that comes down to it from the Supermind, but sets up each Truth as a separate force and idea capable of conflicting with the others as well as cooperating with them. Each overmental being has his own world, each force has its own play and throws itself out to realise its own fulfilment in the cosmic play. All is possible; and from this separative seat of conflicting and even mutually negating possibilities comes too, as soon as mind, life and matter are thrown out into play[,] the possibility of ignorance, unconsciousness, falsehood, death and suffering.)

—

OVERMIND GRADATION TO MIND

=

OVERMIND GNOSIS
(Supermind subdued to the overmind play, limited
and serving for true but limited creations).

|

OVERMIND PROPER

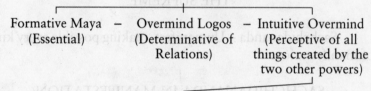

Formative Maya   –   Overmind Logos   – Intuitive Overmind
(Essential)   (Determinative of   (Perceptive of all
                   Relations)   things created by the
                                             two other powers)

HIGHEST MIND
(Intuitive Consciousness)

|

HIGHER MIND

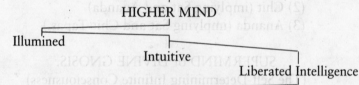

Illumined

                    Intuitive

                                  Liberated Intelligence

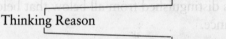

MIND PROPER (HUMAN)

Thinking Reason

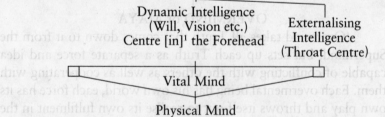

Dynamic Intelligence
(Will, Vision etc.)
Centre [in]¹ the Forehead
                            Externalising
                            Intelligence
                          (Throat Centre)

Vital Mind

|

Physical Mind

=

LOWER CREATION
———

MIND
|
VITAL
|
PHYSICAL

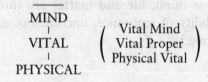

Vital Mind
Vital Proper
Physical Vital

¹ *MS* between

UNDATED SCRIPT JOTTINGS

[1]

That is the possibility that will emerge

[2]

There is no failure, only an intermission

[3]

no   now indeed

[4]

There is nothing else to be done than to be careful and vigilant

That cannot be so easily done, but it is certain that the result will be perfect.

[5]

The grandeur of the past is the seed of the greater grandeur of the future

[6]

Nothing can be done till this has been changed; it is essential that there should be a larger movement. That is it, stand back, stand back, stand back.

[7]

This is the thing

That is the true effect. There is no certainty without the careful scrutiny of the ground

No doubt there is some difficulty but it is filled for the present

[8]

In the end of the long struggle there will be a movement of great rapidity that will work out the last difficulties triumphantly and leave nothing behind. That is destined.

[9]

Impossible to finish before the night— The reality is greater than the promise—

[10]

The last difficulties

Aeonic forces conquered in a brief space.

Monism entirely reconciled with personality

These are other forces than those that surround us in the silence of the mind.

[11]

This is the end of the difficulty Be calm and wait for [... ... ...] in full

[12]

It is sure to be done.

[13]

[.....] useless—it is certain that it must come down

It is still difficult to do it in that way, work more and it will be done. That is the thing

[14]

There is no absolute certitude as yet except in isolated movements, but there is often a dominant certitude.

[15]

It is enough for the outward life of the moment, but not for the eternity within us..... This is the truth of life, but the truth of our other-life is of a greater kind.

Part Five

Automatic Writing

"THE SCRIBBLINGS", c. 1907

Manik

Spirits are without body—Linga sharir is not body but mind. No shape visible to mortal eyes—They are the thoughts of the spirit which are shaped so as to present a visible scene—many of the scenes are not only thoughts but actual visions—

Perhaps not real or maybe the spirit of the first wife—The second wife was probably present and was anxious to be in the photo. There may have been no room.

Bhababhusan has gone but he will return—Khoka makes much of himself but he must be a little more modest—Where has Bhababhusan put the bag—No you are very careless—What made you send him—Why not go yourself—Begin what? Bengalees are a timid race but they are very desirous of being brave—Many make attempts, but few can succeed—You do a lot of work but not properly Because you do not see to the execution—Barin may try but he will not succeed when you cannot help him—My dear fellow, why try to hide yourself? I see no

My dear fellow, you are cowardly and wish to conceal yourself—Brave men will do the work but you must supervise—My dear fellow you will be cowardly—Because you are not selfconfident—Make an attempt next time to keep yourself present when the thing becomes a likelihood—May but it is more likely when you are present. Sudhir will be a good man for the next attempt. Prafulla has lost confidence in himself. Because he could not do it—Many will try but fail—Partly—Cowardice—Then he had someone to help—A man will not succeed if he cannot do it by himself—You will not be able—Make Sudhir do it—No but he will do what you tell him—A good many prophecies fail—

Yes, make a good attempt—No—You will not be overborne with
the small charge of the stuff—Barin makes mistakes—Be more
selfreliant—

They all depend on you—If you are brave it will begin soon—
My dear fellow, don't be curious

Make attempts—By attempting again and again you will begin
and then the work is sure to be speedy. No but why send B—No
he will talk. Make some excuse to him when he comes back—They
are not fools. Because he wanted to know why Sudhir did not go—
Well he was doubtful—

YOGIC SADHAN

EDITED BY

THE UTTARA YOGI

SRIRANGAM:

SRI VANI VILAS PRESS.

1911.

YOGIC SADHAN

A U M

I

The proper course of the Sadhan is just the opposite of the thing most people do and you have also done. People begin with the body and the prana, go on to the chitta and the manas, and finish up with the buddhi and the will. The real course is to start with the will and finish with the body. There is no need of Asana, Pranayama, Kumbhaka, Chittasuddhi, or anything else preparatory or preliminary if one starts with the will. That was what Sri Rama-krishna came to show so far as Yoga is concerned. "Do the Shakti Upasana first," he said, "get Shakti and she will give you Sat." Will and Shakti are the first means necessary to the Yogin. That was why he said always, "Remember you are Brahman," and he gave that as a central message to Swami Vivekananda. You are Ishwara. If you choose, you can be shuddha, siddha and everything else, or, if you choose, you can be just the opposite. The first necessity is to believe in yourself, the second in God and the third to believe in Kali; for these things make up the world. Educate the Will first, through the Will educate the Jnanam, through the Jnanam purify the Chitta, control the Prana and calm the Manas. Through all these instruments immortalise the body. That is the real yoga, the Mahapantha, that is the true and only Tantra. The Vedanta starts with Buddhi, the Tantra with Shakti.

What the Will is you have heard. It is Shakti, it is not Vasana, it is not Cheshta. Vasana and Cheshta are the negation of will. If you have desire, that means you doubt the power of your Will. Brahman has no desire. He wills and all things happen according to his Will. If you have Cheshta, that means you doubt your Will. Only those who feel or think they are not strong, struggle and

labour to produce an effect. Brahman has no cheshta. He wills
and His Will spontaneously produces its effect. But it produces
it in time, space and causality. To demand a result now here and
under given conditions is Ajnanam. The time, space and causality
of every event and its development have been fixed ages ago by
yourself and Parameswara, when the Kalpa began. It is ignorance
to struggle and try to alter what you have yourself decreed. Care
not about time, space or conditions, but will, and leave the result
to God who is your omnipotent, omnipresent and omniscient self.
You are the individual God and He is the universal God. Nothing
but God exists. Ekam evadwitiyam. Therefore Will implies Samata,
absence of Vasana and Cheshta. Absence of Vasana and Cheshta
implies knowledge. Until you have knowledge, you can never be
safe against the return of Vasana and Cheshta.

The question is how to start. The Shakti is in you. Let her
work and assist her by taking the right attitude. You are the Sakshi,
Anumanta, Bhokta, and Bharta. As Anumanta, give the command,
as Sakshi watch her work out the result, as Bhokta enjoy the result
and as Bharta help her by maintaining the Adhar. Do not ruin it
by tamasic udasinata or rajasic revolt. Be sure your Will can never
fail to act. You are the Jnata: receive all knowledge that presents
itself to you. Adopt the attitude I have described here and apply it
to every individual act of the sadhana or of life. You have nothing
else to do. Kali will do the rest. Be not troubled, be not anxious,
be not in haste, you have all eternity before you, why be in haste?
Only do not be tamasic or idly waste your time.

II

I shall speak to-day of the Shakti or Will, since that is the
foundation of Yoga. The Shakti is situated in the Sahasradala
just above the crown of the head and from that seat of activity
it works. Below it at the top of the brain is the higher Buddhi and
below that, occupying the middle level of the brain, is the reason
or lower buddhi, and below that, at the bottom of the brain, is the
organ of communication with the Manas. We may call this organ
the understanding. Knowledge, reason and understanding are the

three parts of the brain. These functions are in the subtle body, but they are connected with the corresponding portions of the material brain.

In the chest just above the heart is the Manas, that is, the organ of sensation with its five subordinate Indriyas. Below the Manas, from the heart to midway between the heart and the navel, is the Chitta. From that point up to the navel and below it is the psychic or sukshma prana. All these are in the sukshma deha but connected at these points with the sthula deha. In the sthula deha itself two functions are situated, the physical prana or the nervous system and the annam or the material body.

Now the will is the organ of the Ishwara or living master of the body. It works through all these functions, through the Buddhi for thought and knowledge, through the Manas for sensations, through the Chitta for emotions and through the Prana for enjoyment. When it functions perfectly, working in each organ according to the capacities of the organ, then the work of the Shakti becomes perfect and infallible. But there are two causes of weakness, error and failure. First, the confusion of the organs. If the Prana interferes in sensation, emotion and thought, then a man becomes anisha, the slave of the Prana, that is to say, of the desires. If the Chitta interferes with sensation and thought, then the sensations and thoughts are falsified by the emotions and their corresponding wishes. For instance if love interferes with the Buddhi, the man becomes blind to the truth about the person he loves, he is unable to distinguish between right and wrong, kartavya and akartavya, where the person is concerned. He becomes to a greater or lesser extent the slave of the emotions, love, anger, hatred, pity, revenge etc. So, if the Manas interferes with the reason, the man mistakes his sensations for just ideas or true arguments. He judges by what he sees or hears instead of judging what he sees or hears. If again the reason, imagination, memory and logic interfere with knowledge, the man is debarred from higher knowledge and wanders in the interminable circle of probabilities and possibilities. Finally, if even the Buddhi interferes with the Will, then the man is limited by the power of his limited knowledge, instead of moving nearer to Omnipotence. In brief, if a machine or instrument is used for a work for which it is unfit, for which it was not made or originally adapted, then it either cannot do that work at all or it does it badly; *dharma-sankara is created.* Now what I have described is the ordinary state of men before they gain knowledge. It is all dharma-sankara, confusion of functions, bad administration and incompetent and ignorant government. The Will, the true minister, is rendered a puppet of the lower officials who work each for his own selfish ends, interfering with and hampering each other or dishonestly playing into each other's hands, for their own benefit and to the detriment of the Ishwara, the master. He ceases to be Ishwara, he becomes Anisha, the puppet and dupe of his servants.

Why does he allow it? Because of Ajnanam. He does not know, he does not realise what the ministers and officials and their million and one hangers-on are doing with him. What is this Ajnanam? It is inability to recognise his own true nature, position and authority. He began by being deeply interested in a small portion of his royal activity, the body. He thought "That is my kingdom." He became the tool of his bodily functions. So with the nervous, the sensational, the emotional and the mental, he identifies himself with each of them. He forgets that he is different from them and much greater and stronger. What he must do is to resume the reins of power, to remember that he is Ishwara, the king, the master and God himself. He must on this understanding remember that he is all-powerful. He has a mighty minister, the Will. Let him support and direct the Will and the Will will introduce order into the government and compel the officials each to do obediently and perfectly his own duty. Not of course all at once. It will take time. The officials have become so much used to confused work and misgovernment that at first they will not be willing to work properly and, secondly, even when they wish, they will find it difficult. They hardly know even how to begin. For instance, when you begin to use your will, what is likely to happen? First you will try to use it through the Prana, through desire, wish, hope, or you will use it through the Chitta, with emotion, eagerness and expectation, or you will use it through the Manas using Cheshta, struggle, effort, as if you were physically wrestling with the thing you want to control; or you will use it through the Buddhi, trying to dominate the subject of your interest by thought, by thinking "Let this be", "Let that happen" etc. All these methods are used by Yogins to recover the power of the Will. The Hatha-yogin uses the Prana and the body, the Raja-yogin the heart, Manas and Buddhi, but the best method is none of these. Even the last of them is a second-best means and must entail struggle, failure and frequent disappointment. The Will is only perfect in its action when it works apart from all these, straight on the subject from the sahasradala, without effort, without emotion and eagerness and without desire. *Each function to itself and Will is its own function.* It always obeys the Ishwara but it acts in itself and by itself. It uses the rest, it must not be used by them.

It uses the Buddhi for knowledge, not for command; it uses the Manas for sensation, not for either command or knowledge; it uses the heart for emotion, not for sensation, knowledge or command; it uses the Prana for enjoyment, not for any other function; it uses the body for motion and action, not as a thing that can limit or determine either knowledge, feeling, sensation, power or enjoyment. Therefore it must keep itself apart and command all these things as a thing separate from all of them. These are merely a yantra, a machine, the Purusha is the yantri or master of the machine, the Will is the electricity or motor-power.

This is the right knowledge. How to use it I shall tell you afterwards. That is a matter of practice, not of mere instruction. The man who has dhairyam, calm steadfastness, even in a small degree, can gradually accustom himself to the mastery of his machine by the Will. But he must first know: he must know the machine, he must know the motor-power, he must know himself. The knowledge need not be perfect in order to begin, but the elementary knowledge at least he must have. That is what I am trying to give you. I am explaining to you the different parts of the machine, their nature and functions, the nature of the Will and the nature of the Ishwara.

III

The Will when it begins to act, will be hampered by the Swabhava; therefore until you are able to act on the Swabhava, you will not, should not bring your Will to bear upon life. In other words while you are a sadhak of the Shakti marga, be a sadhak only; when you have got Siddhi of the Will, then first use the Siddhi to get perfection of the adhar, and when you have got perfection of the adhar, then use the siddha adhar for Karma, for life.

The Swabhava opposes the perfect action of the Will. Why? Because the nature of humanity is imperfect, only partly evolved, asiddha, and being in all its dharmas asiddha, the tamasic force of habit, tamasi dhriti, makes it resist any attempt to make it siddha. Humanity is evolving. Yoga is a means of carrying that evolution forward with great and victorious rapidity. But the imperfect Swabhava says, "I do not wish to be perfect, I am accustomed to imperfection and find it easy and comfortable." First, then, the Will seizes hold of the Swabhava and removes the obstacles in the way of its own perfect development and action.

As I have said, it first gets rid of the old samskaras of impossibility, the samskara, the ajnanam that I am man, not God, limited, not illimitable, helpless, not omnipotent. The Will has first to say, "I am omnipotent, that which the Purusha commands, I can act". For the Will is the Shakti in action, and there is only one Shakti, Kali herself, who is God manifesting as Divine Energy.

Next the Will seizes the adhar and makes it shuddha in order that the Will may itself be shuddha. I have explained that if there is confusion and disorder among the functions, then the Will cannot act omnipotently. Therefore you must first develop Jnanam and by Jnanam effect the shuddhi of the adhar. When the adhar becomes shuddha, the Will being entirely free from wrong samskaras and wrong action, is what I call shuddha. It works perfectly. Working perfectly it makes the adhar siddha, that is the adhar rids itself of all doshas, deficiencies and weaknesses and works perfectly. It becomes a perfect instrument for the Purushottama, the Purusha and Shakti to carry on their Lila.

Knowledge, therefore, jnanam is the next stage to be considered. But before I come to that, let me finish about the obstacles in the Swabhava. There are not only the wrong Samskaras and the ashuddhi of the adhar, but the general nature of things has certain tendencies or laws in it which oppose the development of the Yoga as well as certain tendencies which help the development of the

Yoga. There are three laws which oppose—the law of persistence, the law of resistance and the law of recurrence: there are three laws which assist—the law of gradual processes, the law of concentrated processes and the law of involved processes.

The law of persistence is this, that a rule, habit or tendency once established has a right to survive, a natural unwillingness to be changed or annulled. The longer it has been established, the longer it takes to root out. If a man has been yielding to the shadripus for many lives without any serious effort to dominate them or purify himself, then he cannot by mere wish or a mere rapid effort get rid of them and become pure and calm. They refuse to be so cavalierly treated. They say "You have given us rights in this adhar, and we persist". Still more hard to deal with are those dharmas of the body which men call the laws of physical nature.

But the Will is omnipotent and if patiently, calmly and heroically exercised, will prevail. For the Will, I repeat, is—Kali herself. Therefore in the end it establishes by its action new rules, habits or tendencies which fight with and gradually overcome the old. What then happens is that the old, though put down, weakened and no longer a real part of the nature, resist eviction from the adhar. They are supported by an army of forces or spiritual beings who surround you and live upon your experiences and enjoyments. This law of resistance marks the second period of the Yoga and, unless the Will has already become siddha and the adhar shuddha, is very trying and troublesome to the sadhak. For there seems to be no end to the capacity of resistance.

Here again the Will is bound to triumph, if it is supported by faith or knowledge. Even then the evicted habits and tendencies strive continually to re-enter the system and recover their lost seats of power and enjoyment. This is called recurrence. In proportion as the Will is siddha and the Adhar shuddha, the recurrence becomes weaker and less frequent or, when it comes, less prolonged. But in an impure adhar, or with an imperfect Will, the recurrence is often as prolonged and troublesome as the resistance.

On the other hand there are the three favourable laws. When a new habit or tendency is once established, it is the law that it shall develop towards strength and perfection. So long as it is struggling to establish itself, the Yogin may at any time become bhrashta, that is he may from error, weakness or impatience give up the struggle. That is the only fall for the Yogin. Failure, temporary defeat, is not bhramsa, so long as he refuses to give up the struggle. But once the right tendency is established, no man can destroy it, until it has enjoyed supremacy and its bhoga.

Still at first, while the Will is comparatively weak or unpractised, the progress must be slow. In proportion as the perfection of the Will brings purity of the Adhar, the progress becomes rapid. Everything in this world is done by a process; a process means a series of actions leading to a particular result by certain recognised stages. These stages may be passed through slowly or swiftly, but so long as the law of gradual processes obtains, all the stages must be successively and consciously passed through. You have so many milestones to pass; but you may pass them walking, in a carriage, in a railway train, but pass them you must. Still by the growing strength of the Will, you can replace slow process by swift process.

Then a time comes when Kali begins to transcend the ordinary human limits and becomes no longer the Shakti of a man, but the Shakti of God in man. It is then that gradual processes are replaced by concentrated processes. It is as if, instead of travelling from milestone to milestone you could leap from the first milestone to the third and so on to your journey's end. In other words the process remains the same but some of the stages seem to be dispensed with. In reality they are passed over so lightly as to escape notice and occupy little time. Therefore it is called a concentrated or contracted process.

Lastly, when the man himself becomes God, either in a part of his actions or in the whole, then the law of concentrated processes gives place to the involved processes, when no process at all seems to be used, when the result follows the action instantaneously, inevitably and miraculously. In reality there is no miracle, the process is used but so rapidly, with such a sovereign ease, that all the stages become involved or hidden in what seems a moment's action.

To most men it is enough, if they can reach the second stage; it is only the Avatar or the great Vibhuti who can reach the third.

Therefore do not be discouraged by any failure or delay. It is purely a question of force and purity of the Will. By purity I mean freedom from desire, from effort, from misplacement. It is best to begin by concentrating effort on the self-purification of the Will, towards which the first necessity is passivity of desire for the fruit, the second the passivity of the Chitta and the Buddhi, while the will is being applied; the third the development of self-knowledge in the use of the Will. It will be found that by this process of educating the Will, *âtmânam âtmanâ*, purity of the adhar will also be automatically prepared and knowledge will begin to develop and act.

IV

What is knowledge? In what does it consist? We must distinguish between knowledge in itself and the means of knowledge. Again, among the means we must distinguish between the instruments and the operations performed with the instruments.

By Knowledge we mean awareness, taking a thing into active consciousness, into our Chaitanyam. But when we say, taking it into our Chaitanyam, what do we imply? Whence do we take it? The European says from outside, we say from inside, from Chaitanyam itself. In other words, all knowledge is an act of consciousness operating on something in the consciousness itself. In the first place everything we know exists in Parabrahman, that is, in our indivisible, universal self-existence. It is there, but not yet expressed, not vyakta. Then it exists in pure Chit, which is the womb of things as an idea of form, name and quality. It has name, form and quality in the Karana or Mahat, the causal, typal and ideal state of consciousness. Then it gets the possibility of change, development or modification in the Sukshma, the subtle, mental or plastic state of consciousness. Finally it gets the actual change, development, modification or evolution in the Sthula, the material or evolutionary state of consciousness. In the Karana there is no evolution, nothing ever changes, all is eternal. The Karana is Satyam. In the Sukshma all is preparation of change; it is full of imagination or anritam, therefore it is Swapna, not really false, but not immediately applicable to the Karana or Sthula. In the Sthula all evolves. It is partial satyam developing by the turning of old satyam into anritam, which is called destruction, and the turning of new anritam into new satyam, which is called creation. In the Karana there is no creation, no birth, no death, all exists for ever—the only change is from type to type, from fulfilment to fulfilment.

Therefore to know is really to be conscious of the thing in any or all of these three states. The knowledge of the Sthula is science. The knowledge of the Sukshma is philosophy, religion and metaphysics. The knowledge of the Karana is Yoga. When a man knows the Sthula, he knows it with his senses, that is, with the Manas, he knows the Sukshma with reason or the inspired intellect, he knows the Karana with the Jnanam or spiritual realisation. Therefore complete knowledge consists of three operations, first, objective Upalabdhi or experience, secondly, intellectual statement of your understanding of the thing, thirdly, subjective Upalabdhi or spiritual experience. The scientist begins from the bottom and climbs if he can, to the top. The Yogin begins from the top and descends for perfect proof to the bottom. You are not scientists, you are sadhaks. Therefore, when you speak of knowledge you must understand the process; you realise a thing by subjective experience, Bhava, then, think about it and formulate your experience in Artha and Vak, the combination which forms thought; you verify or test your experience by physical or objective experience.

For instance you see a man. You want to know what he is, what he thinks and what he does. How does the scientist or the material man do it? He watches the man, he notes what he says, what are his expressions of speech and face, what are his actions, what sort of people he lives with, etc. All this is objective. Then he reasons from his objective experience. He says "The man says this or that, so he must think so and so or he must have such and such a character; his actions show the same, his face shows the same," and so he goes on reasoning. If he does not get all the necessary facts, he fills them up from his imagination or from his memory, that is his experience of other men, of himself or of human life as read of in books or heard of from other people. He perceives, he observes, contrasts, compares, deduces, infers, imagines, remembers and the composite result he calls reason, knowledge, fact. In reality he has arrived at a probability, for it is impossible for him to be sure that his conclusions are correct or anything indeed correct in his thought, except the actual observation, perceptions of his eye, ear, nose, touch, and taste. Anything beyond this the material man distrusts. Nothing is true to him except what he observes with his senses or what agrees with his sensory perceptions.

Now what does the Yogin do? He simply puts himself into relation with the thing itself. Not with its form, name or quality, but with itself. He may never have seen the form, heard the name or had experience of the quality, but still he can know the thing. Because it is the thing itself and it is in himself and one with himself, that is in the Mahakarana in a man. There all meet the Atman and are so entirely one with the Atman that by merely being in contact with it, I can know everything about it. Few Yogins reach that state. But all the same, even in the Karana I can put myself in relation with the thing and know it by Bhava. I put myself, my soul, into relation with the soul of the man I study or the thing I study; Prajna in me becomes one with the Prajna in him or it. How do I do this? Simply by becoming passive and facing him or it in my Buddhi. If my Buddhi is quite pure or fairly purified, if my Manas is shanta, then I get the truth about him. I get it by Bhava, by spiritual or subjective realisation.

Then I have to make the thing I have got clear and precise. To do that I must state it intellectually to my mind, that is, I must think about it. I have these ideas I am telling you in myself as unexpressed knowledge; they shape themselves in words, Vak, and take on a precise meaning, Artha. That is thought. Most people think vaguely, half expressing the thing in an imperfect Vak and a partial Artha. The Yogin must not do that. His thoughts must express themselves in clear and perfect sentences. He may know a thing without thinking it out, but if he thinks, he must think clearly and perfectly.

The Yogin reasons when necessary, but not like the man of science. He sees the thing with his prophetic power interpreting the truth into thought; the pratyaksha gives him the Artha, the

inspiration gives him the Vak, the intuition gives him the right conclusion about it, the right siddhanta, the Viveka guards him from
error. Behold the truth by these four simple operations perfectly
thought out. If he has to argue, then the intuitions give him the right
arguments. He has not to proceed painfully from one syllogism to
another as the logician does.

Finally, he verifies his knowledge by the facts of the objective
world. He has seen the truth about the man by merely looking at
him or at the idea of him; he has thought it out clearly and now
he compares his idea with the man's action, speech etc. Not to
test his truth; for he knows that a man's action, speech etc. only
partially express the man and mislead the student; but in order to
see how the truth he knows from the Karana is being worked out
in the Sthula. He trusts the man's objective life only so far as it is
in agreement with the deeper truth he has gained by Yoga.

You see the immense difference. The only difficulty is that
you have been accustomed to use the senses and the reason to
the subordination and almost to the exclusion of the higher faculties. Therefore you find it difficult to make the higher faculties
active.

If only you could start from the beginning, with the Bhava,
the Atmajnana, how easy it would be! That will yet happen. But
first, you have to get rid of the lower Buddhi, of the Indriyas in the
manas, and awaken the activity of the higher faculties. They will
see for you, hear for you, as well as think for you.

First, then, get your sanskaras right. Understand intellectually
what I have told you and will yet tell you. Then by use of the
Will, keep the reason, imagination, memory, thought, sensations
sufficiently quiet for the higher Buddhi to know itself as separate
and different from these lower qualities. As the higher separates
itself and becomes more and more active, the lower, already discouraged, will become less and less active and finally trouble you
no more.

Therefore Will first, then by Will, by Shakti, the Jnanam. First
Kali, then Surya. I shall explain the various faculties when I have
finished with the rest of the system.

V

If men were satisfied with indulging in reason, memory and imagination, the purification of the Buddhi and the development of the higher faculties would be an easy matter. But there is another means of thought which they habitually indulge in and that is Manas. The Manas is a receptive organ; it receives the images expressed on the eye, the ear etc., and turns them into what the Europeans call the percepts, that is, things perceived. Besides, it receives the ideas, images etc., sent down from the Vijnana into the Chitta and passes them on to the latter organ. In this passage these things become what are called concepts, that is, things conceived or thought of. For instance, when the mind sees the image of a book and says "A book", it has hold of a percept the name of which it conceives; that is sensational thought. When it says "A book contains language" that is a remoter concept, intellectual thought. One merely puts things sensed into words, the other puts things thought into words. Percept and concept together make what is called understanding. Reason, according to the European idea, merely arranges percepts and concepts and draws from this arrangement fresh and more elaborate concepts. Many believe that concepts are merely percepts put together and converted into what is called thought. According to this idea, all thought is merely the arrangement of sensation in the terms of language. Even when I imagine an angel, I merely put a human figure and the wings of a bird together and give the combination a name, angel. Even when I talk of abstract qualities, for example, virtue, courage etc., I am not thinking of anything beyond sensation, but merely a classification of virtuous and courageous sensations and actions put together and labelled with the name virtue or courage.

All these ideas are correct so far as the Manas or understanding is concerned. The Manas is an organ of sensation, not of thought. It catches thoughts on their way from the Buddhi to the Chitta, but in catching them it turns them into the stuff of sensations, as described above.

It regards them from the point of view of sensations. Animals think with their Manas and animals are not able to form ideas that do not relate themselves to some image, form, sound, smell, touch, taste, etc. They are bound by their sensations. That is why in animals the Buddhi is dormant; so far as it acts, it acts behind the veil.

But man can become aware of things which the senses cannot grasp, *buddhigrâhyam atîndriyam.* The proof of that you can get daily, when the Yogic power is developed. This single fact that man can see with his Buddhi the truth about a thing he has never seen or known before, is enough to destroy the materialistic idea of thought.

That idea is only true of the Manas. The Manas responds to the senses and is always forming percepts and concepts about the sensations it receives. These ideas it sometimes gets from the outside world, sometimes from the passive memory in the Chitta, sometimes from the Buddhi. But it tries to impose them all on the Buddhi. It tests everything which it does not take for granted by reference to the senses. "I saw that", "I heard that", therefore it is true, that is the reasoning of the Manas. That is why people who have a poorly developed Buddhi, attach so much importance to what they have seen or read. "I have seen it in print" says the just literate man, and he thinks he has closed the argument.

What are we to do with the Manas? Get it to be still, says the Yogin. While it is busy, knowledge is impossible. You can get only fragments of knowledge. That is true and the quiet mind is no doubt essential to the Yogin. But what of the senses? Concepts in the Manas you may get rid of, but what are you to do with the percepts? You cannot stop seeing, hearing etc., except when you are in Samadhi. That is why the Vedantin attaches so much importance to samadhi. It is the only condition in which he is safe from the persistent siege of the percepts of the senses.

But if you can only exercise knowledge when you are in Samadhi, then you will have to become an ascetic or recluse, a man who gives up life or thought. That is a necessity which cuts the unity of God's world into two and makes an unnatural division in what should be indivisible. The Tantric knows that this is not necessary, that Samadhi is a great instrument, but not the only instrument. He so arranges his antahkarana that he can know when he is walking, talking, acting, sleeping, whatever he is doing. How? By not only stilling the conceptual activity of the Manas but by transferring to the Buddhi its perceptual activity.

In other words he sees, hears etc., not with the senses in the manas, but with the Indriya in the Buddhi. You will find what a difference this makes. Not only do you see much more perfectly, minutely, accurately than before, but you are able to appreciate colours, forms, sounds etc., in a way you never did before. And besides you are able to catch the soul, the Guna, the essential quality and emotion of a thing, the moment you are aware of it. This is part of what the Yoga calls Prakamya, the absolute and sovereign activity of the Indriya.

Therefore when the Yoga is perfect, you will not be troubled by the Manas. It will cease to perceive. It will be merely a passage, a channel for things from the Buddhi to the Chitta. There are many ways of bringing this about, but most of them suffer from this defect, that you get the thinking part of the Manas still, but the perceiving part retains its inferior and hampering activity. The best way is to use the Will simultaneously for awaking the Jnanam and for stilling the Manas. This method has two advantages. First, you do not, as in the ordinary method, have to make your mind a blank. That is a powerful but very difficult and trying discipline or Tapasya. You simply replace by degrees the activity of the lower reason by the activity of the higher thought, the activity of the mind by the activity of the same organ and the sense-perceptions by the activity of the Prakamya. This process is less painful and more easy. Secondly, you cannot stop perceiving so long as you are not in Sushupti, you only stop thinking. So you cannot make your mind blank. Unless you wake the Jnanam first, how are you going to get rid of this intrusive element? The Prakamya must be there already active before the ordinary perceptions can stop work.

This then is the third operation of the Tantric method. You develop the Will, you use the Will to awaken the Jnanam, you use the Will to still the mind and the lower Buddhi and you use the Jnanam to replace them.

VI

I come next to Chitta. There are two layers in the Chitta, one for the emotions, the other for passive memory. In the lower layer of the Chitta, the impressions of all things seen, thought, sensed, felt are recorded and remain until the Jiva leaves this body. Even afterwards all these impressions are taken up with the Sukshma body and go with the Jiva into the other worlds. When he is born again, they are brought with him as latent samskaras in the Muladhara; that is why people do not remember their past births, but can get back the memory by awakening the Kundalini in the Muladhara. These impressions are latent in the Chitta until the active memory in the Buddhi calls for them. Those which are continually brought to the Buddhi have a habit of recurring even when not wanted, habitual thoughts, ideas, sentiments, opinions etc., which are the Yogin's chief trouble until the Manas in which they occur becomes quiet.

The second and the upper layer is that of emotion. The emotions are the acts of Will sent down into the Chitta and there assuming the form of impulses. There are three divisions, thought-impulses, impulses of feeling, and impulses of action. The first are called by various names, instincts, inspirations, insights, intuitions etc. They are really messages sent down by the Jiva from the Sahasradala into the Chitta, they pass unobserved through the Buddhi, lodge in the Chitta and, whenever excited by any contact external or internal, start up suddenly and strike the Buddhi with the same force as the real inspirations etc., which come down direct from the Vijnana to the Buddhi. But they come up coloured by emotions, distorted by associations and memories in the Chitta, perverted by the imagination which brings them up. Much of what is called faith, Bhakti, genius, poetic inspiration etc., comes from this source. It is useful to the ordinary man, all important to the animal, but a hindrance to the Yogin.

The impulses of feeling are what are ordinarily called emotions. The emotions are of two kinds, natural or eternal, artificial or Vikaras. Love is natural, it proceeds from Jnanam and tends to endure in the evolution; hatred is a Vikara from love, a distortion or reaction caused by Ajnanam. So courage is eternal, fear is Vikara;

compassion is eternal, ghrina or weak pity, repulsion, disgust etc., are Vikaras. Those which are natural and eternal, love, courage, pity, truth, noble aspirations, are Dharma; the others are Adharma. But this is from the eternal standpoint and has nothing to do with Samajic or Laukic or temporary Dharma or Adharma. Moreover, Adharma is often necessary as a passage or preparation for passing from an undeveloped to a developed, a lower to a higher Dharma. The Yogin has to get rid of Vikaras, but not of Sanatana Dharmas.

The third kind of impulse is the impulse to action. Its presence in the Chitta is a temporary arrangement due to the rajasic development of the human being. The asuddha rajasic man cannot easily be stirred into action, except through two forces, desire or emotion. Love, hatred, ambition, rage etc., must stir in him or he cannot act, or acts feebly. He cannot understand shuddha pravritti, action without desire and independent of emotion. Emotion should only give a colour to the man's swabhava or temperament. He should be habitually full of feelings of love, courage, honour, true ambition, self-reliance etc., but he should not act from any individual impulse of however noble a character. He should act in obedience to the impulse from the Will in direct communication with the Purusha in the Vijnana, understanding with the Buddhi why the Will acts in that particular way and colouring the act with the emotion appropriate to his Swabhava. But neither the Buddhi nor the emotion should directly interfere with or try to determine his action. The Buddhi is for thought and the Chitta for emotion. Neither of them have anything to do with action in the shuddha state. The intellectual Asura determines his actions by his reason or his ideal, the emotional Asura by his feelings. But the shuddha determines them by the higher inspiration proceeding from the divine existence in the Vijnana. That is what people often call the Adesha. Only the shuddha can safely rely on having this kind of Adesha, the asuddha Yogin often mistakes his own ideas, imaginations, emotions or even desires for the Adesha.

Therefore what the Yogin must aim at, is to get rid of the activity of his lower Chitta or the old impressions by stilling the Manas as described in my last lecture; get rid of his instinctive thought or thought-impulses by the same means; get rid of the

habit of acting on his emotions by allowing the will to silence his
impulses and purify his emotions. He should prohibit and inhibit
by the Will all action or speech that starts blindly from the passions
or emotions surging in his heart. The emotions will then become
quiet and must be habituated to come as a sort of wave falling into
a sea, instead of surging furiously into action. These quiet waves
which are satisfied with existing and do not demand satisfaction
in action or seek to dominate the life or the ideas, are the purified
emotions. Those which rise upward into the Buddhi and try to
shape the thought or opinion, those which move outward into
speech or action, are asuddha emotions. What I mean is that the
emotions in the Chitta are for enjoyment only; the action must be
dominated by a higher principle.

There again it is the Will that must purify, govern and renew
the heart. Only, it has the best chance of doing it if the knowledge
has first become active and the mind is still. A still mind means a
heart easily purified.

VII

I come next to Prana, the nervous or vital element in man
which is centralised below the Manas and Chitta in the subtle
body and connected with the navel in the Sthula Deha. Here I
must distinguish between the Sukshma Prana and the Sthula Prana,
the former moving in the nervous system of the subtle body as
described in the Yogic books, the latter in the nervous system of the
gross body. The two are closely connected and almost always act
upon each other. The prana forms the link between the physical and
the mental man. I must here warn you against stumbling into the
error of those who try to harmonise Yogic Science with the physical science of the Europeans and search for the Yogic Nadis and
Chakras in the physical body. You will not find them there. There
are certain centres in the physical nervous system with which the
Chakras correspond, otherwise Hathayoga would be impossible.
But the Chakras are not these centres. The Europeans are masters
in their own province of knowledge and there you need not hesitate
to learn from them, but for God's sake do not subject your higher

knowledge to their lower; you will only create a most horrible confusion. Develop your higher knowledge first, then study their sciences and the latter will at once fall into their place.

It is with the Sukshma Prana that I am principally concerned; for the Sthula Prana belongs to the Annam rather than to the Antah-karana and I will speak of it in connection with the Annam. The Sukshma Prana is the seat of desire and its purification is of the utmost importance to the Yogin. Until you have got rid of desire, you have accomplished nothing permanent. When you have got rid of desire, you are sure of everything else. That is why the Gita says "Get rid of desire first". Only until you have got knowledge and can learn to use your will to still the mind and purify the emotions, you cannot utterly get rid of desire. You may drive it out by Samyama, you may hold it down by Nigraha but eventually it is of no use, for it will return. "Prakritim yânti bhûtâni nigrahah kim karishyati." Creatures follow after nature; what is the use of coercion? That is to say, it has a temporary result and the coerced desires come back ravening and more furious than before. That was what Christ meant by the parable of the devil, the unclean spirit who is driven out of a man only to return with seven spirits worse than himself. For it is the nature of things, the unalterable nature of things, that unpurified emotion must clamour after desire, an unstilled Manas give it harbourage whenever it returns, an unilluminated Buddhi contain the seed of it ready to sprout up at the first opportunity. Therefore unless the whole Antahkarana is purified, unless you get a new heart and a new mind, desire cannot be got rid of; it returns or it remains. When however an illuminated understanding lighting up the action of a strengthened Will and supported by a pure heart, casts desire into the Sukshma Prana and attacks it there in its native place, it can be utterly destroyed. When you have a visuddha Buddhi you will be able to distinguish these various organs and locate all your mental activities. Desire can then be isolated in the Prana and the heart and mind kept pure of its insistent inroads. For desire is only effective when it can get hold of the Chitta and Buddhi, generating Vikaras of emotion and perversions of knowledge which give it strength to impose itself on the Will and so influence internal and external action. It is most powerful in the higher kind of human being when it masks itself as a principle or ideal or as a justifiable emotion.

Remember moreover that all desires have to be got rid of, those which are called good, as well as those which are called bad. Some people will tell you, keep the good desires and drive out the bad. Do not listen to that specious piece of ignorance. You can use the good desires to drive out the bad on condition that immediately after you drive out the good also by the one desire of Mumukshutwa, liberation and union with God. And even that last desire finally you must renounce and give yourself up wholly to God's will, even in that last and greatest matter, becoming utterly desireless, nishkâma nihspriha. Otherwise you will find yourself travelling in a vicious circle. For if you keep desire at all, he is such a born traitor that he will eventually open the door to your enemies. When the unclean spirit returned to his house, he found it swept and garnished, that is, purified of bad thoughts and adorned with good desires, and immediately he got in and made the last state of that man worse than his first. So get rid of all desires utterly, good, bad and indifferent. Get beyond virtue as well as beyond vice. Be satisfied with no bondage even though the fetters be of pure gold. Admit no guide or master but God, even though they be gods or angels who claim your homage.

Desire is composed of three elements, attachment or Asakti, longing or Kamana, and preference or Ragadwesha. Get rid of attachment first. Use your will and purified Antahkarana to throw out that clinging and insistence on things, which says "I must have that, I cannot do without that," and returns on the idea of it, even when it is persistently denied. When the emotions are quiet, this Asakti will of itself die away, but for a time it will rage a great deal and try to get the emotions active again. Apply the Will steadily and patiently and do not get disturbed by failure; for desire is a terrible thing, as difficult to get rid of as a leech. It is indeed the daughter of the horse-leech crying "Give, give." Do not violently silence the cry; ignore it and use your Will to get rid of the clamourer. When Asakti becomes weak, Kamana loses nine tenths of its force and you can easily throw it off. Still for some time, out of sheer habit, the longing for certain things will come, not in the heart or Buddhi, but in the

Prana; only if Asakti is gone, the refusal of the thing craved will not leave behind it a permanent grief or continual hunger. There will only be temporary disturbance of the peace of the heart. When you have got rid of the Kamana, even then Raga may remain, and if Raga is there, Dwesha is sure to come in. You will not ask or crave for anything; for Kamana is gone; but when some things come, you will not like them; when other things come, you will feel glad and exultant. You will not rebel or cling to what you have, but you will not like the coming of the evil, you will not like the loss of your joy, even though you say "Very good" and submit. Get rid of that Raga and Dwesha and have perfect Samata.

When you have perfect Samata, then either you will have perfect Shanti, divine peace, or else perfect or Shuddha Bhoga, divine enjoyment. Shanti is the negative Ananda and those have it who rest in the Nirguna Brahman. Shuddha Bhoga is the positive Ananda and those have it who rest in the Trigunatita Ananta Brahman. You can have both and it is best to have both. God enjoys the world with Shuddha Bhoga based on the perfect Shanti. Most people cannot imagine Bhoga without Kama, enjoyment without desire. It is a foolish notion, none the less foolish because it is natural and almost universal. It is Ajnanam, a fundamental part of ignorance. Enjoyment does not really begin until you get rid of desire. That which you get as the result of satisfied desire is troubled, unsafe, feverish, or limited, but Shuddha Bhoga is calm, self-possessed, victorious, unlimited, without satiety and Vairagya, immortally blissful. It is in a word, not Harsha, not Sukha, but Ananda. It is Amrita, it is divinity and immortality, it is becoming of one nature with God. The soul has then no kama, but it has pure lipsa, an infinite readiness to take and enjoy whatever God gives it. Grief, pain, disgrace, everything that is to rajasic men a torture, changes then to bliss. Even if such a soul were to be cast into hell, it would not feel hell, but heaven. It would not only say with the Bhakta "This is from the beloved" but with the perfect Jnani "This is the Beloved; this is the Anandam Brahman: this is the Kantam, the Shivam, Shubham, Sundaram."

I need not repeat the process by which this purification is effected. I have indicated it sufficiently. This Tantric process is the

same throughout, the reliance on the Shakti, the divine Will working in the Adhar, without any effort on the part of the Purusha,
who remains Akarta throughout the sadhana, but still Ishwara, the
source of the command and the sanction, the ruler dispossessed by
his subjects and gradually recovering control of his rebellious and
disordered kingdom.

VIII

There remains the Sthula, the gross part of man which is composed of the Sthula Prana or physical nervous system and the annam
or body in which the prana operates. The prana is the principle of
life, — death is brought about by the dissolution of the tie between
the sukshma deha and the sthula deha. That tie is the prana. The
sukshma deha takes the prana into itself and departs; the little that
is left in the gross body is of the nature of apana with a tendency
to that species of dissolution which we call corruption. The prana
part of it, which can alone hold the body together, evaporates and
the apana leads to swift disintegration. In some animals, however,
the prana is so abundant that the body shows signs of life even after
the sukshma deha has departed.

I have been dealing throughout with the purification of the
sukshma part of man, the Antahkarana or mind, — the subject of the
body is a little foreign to my purpose. Nevertheless a few words are
necessary. The principle upon which this Yoga I am explaining to
you stands, is that the gross body is merely the shadow or creation
of the subtle. Body is a mould into which mind pours itself, but the
mould itself has been prepared by the mind and can be changed
by the mind. A mind purified, liberated and perfected (siddha) can
do whatever it likes with the body. It may leave it as it is, allowing
the past karma to do its will with the physical part in the form of
disease, suffering, misfortune and death, without the mind being
in the least affected. All that is impurity and bondage, which is the
physical translation and result of mental impurity and bondage.
With the cessation of the cause, the effect ceases; but not at once. It
is again like the steam and the locomotive. The habits, the results
created by past lives, are expelled from the mind and precipitated

entirely into the body. You may allow them to work themselves out there, many do that. On the other hand, you may pursue them into the body and drive them out from there as well. In that case you get the Kayashuddhi and the Kayasiddhi. They are usually sought after by the Hathayogic or Rajayogic processes, but these are not necessary. It is even better and certainly much easier and surer to follow the process I have been indicating.

The very fact of having a purified mind makes for purity of the body, a liberated mind for liberation of the body, a perfected mind for perfection of the body, and to a certain extent as you go on with the yoga in the Antahkarana, the body will automatically begin to respond to the new influences. But you should not consciously meddle with the body until you have finished with the mind. Let nature do its work. Detach yourself as much as possible from the body, think of it as a mere case, leave it to the care of God and His Shakti. Many sadhaks are frightened by illness in the course of the Yoga. You need not be frightened, for you have put yourself in God's hands and He will see to it. It will come to you only as a part of the necessary process for purification of the body, work itself out, fade and return no more. Other disturbances of the body will come which are incidental to the turning of an unfit physical adhar into a fit one. Profound alterations are necessary in your brain-cells, your nervous system, your digestive and secretive processes and they cannot be effected without some physical disturbance, but it will never be more than is necessary for the process. Do no violence of any kind to the body; if you use physical remedies, let them be of the simplest and purest kind; above all dismiss anxiety and fear. You cannot care more for yourself than God cares for you. Only your care is likely to be ignorant and unwise; His is with knowledge and uses the right means to the right end.

Impurities in the body show themselves chiefly as disease, as pain, as the discomfort of heat and cold, as the necessity of the excretive processes. The first sign of Kayashuddhi is the disappearance of all tendency to disease; the second is liberation from the dwandwa of heat and cold, which will either go altogether or change to pleasurable sensations often marked by electrical phenomena; and the third, the diminution or disappearance of excretive activity. Pain also can be entirely eliminated from the body, but even before the reaction called pain is got rid of, or even without its being got rid of, the discomfort of pain can be removed and replaced by a sort of bodily Ananda. Finally, the craving of hunger and thirst disappears from the prana to which it belongs and the dependence on food diminishes or ceases. The perfection of all this is the basis of Kayasiddhi. But perfect Kayasiddhi includes other developments such as the siddhis of Mahima, Laghima, Anima and the invulnerability and incorruptibility of the body, – powers hitherto attained in the Kaliyuga only by very advanced Siddhas. They depend primarily on the replacement of the ordinary fivefold processes of prana, apana, vyana, samana and udana by the single simplified action of the original or elemental force of prana, the infinite vital energy surcharged with electricity, vaidyutam.

All these are important elements of Tantric Yoga, but I have mentioned them only cursorily because they are foreign to my purpose. They can all be developed if the mental siddhi is perfected and it is on this perfection that I wish you to concentrate your energy and attention. When you get that, you get everything. The centres of man's activity, at present, are the buddhi, the heart and the manas, and the body, though extremely important, is a dependent and subordinate function. It has not to be despised on that account, but most people give it an undue importance. When the Jiva is Ishwara of his mind, his body falls into its proper place and instead of interfering and often domineering over the mind and will, it obeys and takes its stamp from them. The Europeans are obsessed with the idea of the physical as the master of the mental. I would have you hold fast to the opposite standpoint and always remember that for the body to impose its conditions on the mind is an abnormal state of man's being, which has to be got rid of; it is the mind that must command, condition and modify the body.

IX

CONCLUSION

I have finished what I had to say. I will only add a word in conclusion. You must not think that what I have given you, is all the knowledge you need about yourself or about the Yoga. On the contrary, these are only certain indications necessary at a particular stage; they are chiefly important for purification, which is the first part of the Yoga. After the shuddhi is complete one has to perfect the mukti, to get liberation, a thing easy after shuddhi, impossible before it. By mukti I do not mean *laya*, which is a thing not to be pursued or desired, but waited for whenever God wills, but liberation from ignorance, Ahankara and all dualities. With the progress of the purification, there will be a natural tendency towards liberation and the farther stages of yoga, bhukti and siddhi, liberated enjoyment and perfection. As you go forward you will have to change your attitude, not radically but in certain important points. That, however, I will not meddle with. It is well to do one thing at a time.

In all that I have written, I have taken one standpoint to which many of you have not been accustomed. If you regard Vairagyam as the beginning of all wisdom, you will not be satisfied with me. Vairagyam is to me merely a useful temporary state of mind which God uses to enforce rejection of that to which the old samskaras cling too obstinately to be unseated from it by mere abhyasa. Jnanam is essential to shuddhi and mukti; but Jnanam must be assisted either by abhyasa or by vairagya until the mind is still and lets knowledge do its own work. As soon as the mind is still and not susceptible to resuscitation of its old energies from outside, the Jnanam develops, the Shakti pursues its task unhampered; there is then no sadhan for you, only a progressive siddhi without any deliberately adopted method, increasing by the mere easy and natural process of Nature as a man breathes or sees or walks. All necessity for either abhyasa or vairagya ceases. Attachment to vairagya is as harmful as attachment to lobha itself.

Again if you think with the Buddhists that all life is a misery and extinction of some kind the highest good, or if you think with the Mayavadin that we came into this world with no other object but to get out of it again as soon as possible, like the famous general whose greatest military exploit was to march up a hill in order to march back again, you had better pass me by. I am a Tantric. I regard the world as born of Ananda and living by

Ananda, wheeling from Ananda to Ananda. Ananda and Shakti, these are the two real terms of existence. Sorrow and weakness are vikaras born of ajnanam, of the forgetfulness of the high and true self. These are not universal or eternal things, but local and temporary, local mainly of this earth, temporary in the brief periods of the Kali yuga. Our business is to bring down heaven on earth for ourselves and mankind, to eliminate sorrow and weakness from the little corners of existence and time, where they are allowed to exist. I do not give any assent to the gloomy doctrine which preaches a world of sorrow and inaction and withdrawal from it as the sole condition of bliss and freedom, which thinks, contrary to all reason and knowledge, that God in himself is blessed, but God in manifestation accursed. I will not admit that the Brahman is a fool or a drunkard dreaming bad dreams, self-hypnotised into miserable illusions. I do not find that teaching in the Veda; it does not agree with my realisations which are of the actuality of unalterable bliss and strength and knowledge in the midst of desireless phenomenal action. I am of the mind of Sri Krishna in the Mahabharata when he says, "Some preach action in this world and some preach inaction; but as for those who preach inaction, I am not of the opinion of those weaklings." *Na me matam tasya durbalasya.*

But the action he holds up as an example, is the action of the great Gods, even as Goethe speaks of the action of the great natural forces, disinterested, unwearying, self-poised in bliss, not inert with the tamas, not fretful with the rajas, not limited even by the sattwic ahankara—action made one in difference with the Purushottama, my being in His being, my shakti only a particular action of His infinite shakti, of Kali. I am not ignorant, I am not bound, I am not sorrowful: I only play at being ignorant, I only pretend to be bound; like an actor or like an audience I only take the rasa of sorrow. I can throw it off when I please. Who calls me degraded and sinful, a worm crawling upon the earth among other worms? I am Brahman, I am He; sin cannot touch me. Who calls me miserable? I am God, all blissful. Who calls me weak? I am one with the Omnipotent. He, being One, has chosen to be Many. He, being infinite, localises himself in many centres and in each centre He is still infinite. That is the mystery of existence, the *uttamam rahasyam*, God's great, wonderful and blissful secret, a secret logic rejects, but knowledge grasps at, a knowledge not to be argued out but realised, but proved by experience, by the purified, liberated, all-enjoying, all-perfect soul.

EDITOR'S EPILOGUE

A few words seem necessary in conclusion. For it is as well to guard against certain misconceptions which may arise from the brevity of the writer and his omission of some important points considered by him, no doubt, to be, however important, yet outside his scope.

The prohibition of cheshta in the ideal use of the will does not imply the renunciation of Karma. The cheshta referred to is internal, not external, arambha, not karma. The distinction is that made by Sri Krishna in the Gita when he holds up the ideal of action with renunciation of all arambhas, — *sarvârambhân parityajya*. We are to do actions with the body, mind, buddhi, senses, each doing its own separated work in its absolute purified simplicity, *kevalair*, without any desire, expectation or straining in the will after either action or its success. The sadhak should abstain from applying his method to important actions in life until the higher purified will is to some extent trained, and even then it will be best for him to apply it to things of smaller moment first, then to those of greater moment. During the sadhana subjective progress and superfluous action small or great should be his main fields for test and training.

Secondly, it must not be supposed that the treatment in these short lectures is intended to be full or exhaustive or even that in those points which it handles at the greatest length all has been said that the sadhak needs to know. On the contrary, only a few main ideas have been broadly struck out which may be useful to the beginner. The more advanced will find that they have rapidly outgrown the utility of these hints and that they have to be greatly enlarged on and modified before the knowledge at which they point can be considered full and satisfactory.

Finally, the aim of the particular path of Yoga indicated is not the assertion of the individual will, but surrender of the individual will, its absolute, unreserved and ungrudging surrender into the direction and control of the Infinite Being. The training of the system or adhar prescribed has for its purpose, first, the subjugation of the clamorous desires and impulses, the stubborn pride and egoism, the vain self-sufficient reason and imagination of the unregenerate man so that they may not interfere with the completeness of the surrender, secondly, the possession of a strong, mighty and effective will to offer as a yajna to the Most High and not one that is weak, distracted, ignorant and diffident. The Karma of the Siddha Yogin must be like that of the sun and stars, the avalanche and the cyclone, the breeze, moon or flowers, fire and the dust of the earth, either calm and luminous or mighty and violent or gentle, sweet and useful, either lofty or humble at the will of the One Supreme Shakti, impelled and used by Her entirely, and, whatever its outward appearance, always working on a basis of absolute peace, self-surrender and self-knowledge.

AUTOMATIC WRITINGS, c. 1914 (FIRST SET)

[1]

Nothing is new in the world — What do you mean by new — New, in a sort of way, in relation to what is expressed within your knowledge — Let it go — All is well — That is too rigid a way of putting it — Why — Of all — That is a delicate question — I don't think I shall — You settle that yourselves — What of him? To you? What is he to you? Why does the Trinity need Abdul Baha — Need? then how can you act —

Too much pliability to the infinite. He is too much in contact with past worlds of beings who seek to fulfil themselves in him and prevent the final formation of certain things which would otherwise take a shape powerful for action. — That is good in the world of thought, but not, as it is now, for action. These three things in their principles, in that which brings them about, is good; but they have to find that & arrange themselves in it before they can be effective — Their own — It is difficult to say in words — But as they are, they are things that represent some perfection, are a preparation, without them as a stage the perfection could not be reached, but they must not rest too long in the stage of preparation — I don't know — There are many excellent things in the world —

You have not to arrange — Let it arrange itself under a higher impulsion — Not always — Speaking of precise defects interferes with the balance; it gives a tendency to exaggerate either the defect or its opposite — It is an attitude of the soul, the reason and the heart that is needed, a thing general not precise — People insist too much on particularities, on that which can be defined. But these things are the result of something general & not easily definable, a thing to be felt & seen rather than thought & expressed —

She is too balanced on one side — A gentle disbalancing would be good—She has created a balance firm & good, but depending too much on an unconscious restraint which limits the development of her capacities

[2]

Abd-ul-Baha, let him disappear then you will see the connection—He has got rid of Maurya or rather Maurya has got rid of himself—As Maurya—Yes, but at present powerless—He has dissolved his means of action—Not in this world. He is there, but by himself he is [   ][1] less free, less able to impress himself powerfully on the material world. Yes, spiritually—There is the same difficulty, but less concentrated. As with Abdul Baha. The choice is given always.—Why question about such weak forces—He is divided from you by his weakness, not as the others by their strength—If they have an immediate destiny—Who?—They are always there, it is in the material world you should seek. They are the men of the future, not of the present—Yes, or have not found themselves. Why are you here otherwise? That is a question you can answer yourselves.

Dissolve him if you will, leave him if you will not—There is nothing else to be done with him—If he is to be anything, he must first dissolve—No, the constitution of his inner being must be entirely changed first, but that would mean a great disintegration first & to begin with the loss of his evil power—What force?—Ah yes; it will be done at the right time, in this body or otherwise. Each man follows a path that leads him to the goal; only some follow it through disastrous or apparently disastrous revolutions and even have to begin again—He is good as an examiner of souls—That is the part of the devil in certain systems. He knows himself—Ah, ask the prophets—What?—I suppose you have had relations—Then? One of those who prepare, but are not prepared—Oh, let him do his own work, he does it well. Do not try to give men more part than the Divine Being has given them—That would do him harm, to try to make him more than himself—Friendship is blind—Love, but do not govern your actions by a partial affection—I was going

[1] MS more

to say what you have said—She is a great soul always with you.
He was necessary to her force. Yes, in certain limits—In another
sense than the Theosophist, she would have to be dissolved to be
useful otherwise than she is I don't mean physically—Everything
is possible, but all is not intended—No, help her by your thought
& let the result be what it will. You come back to the action—
Yes, but the Review is only a means; its success depends on what
I told you at the beginning. In your case, the mechanical forces
of matter are nothing; it is the inner powers that must work &
fulfil. You have the light that is merely light, but where is the light
that is power—Knock at the door that is still shut. You have said,
personalise the Infinite. The Infinite as infinite does nothing, it is—
All form & action are a choice in the Infinite. Yes, mount there.
By equilibrium it is possible to mount. Reject nothing essential
in yourself; only transform or rather allow to be transform[ed]—
No—There are reasons why I will not—It is a consciousness that
formulates itself

What is impersonal? All is personal, yet impersonal. Everywhere—
Not even that. I can, but I do not. No, surely not—That is different,
from above. It is difficult to conduct this writing if one descends
into a mixture of forces. That is why the writing is so often stupid—
Not in the same way. It is not that I despise the physical world or
physical means—Do that in your physical body. Yes—try to have
it as far as possible. . . I am not like you in a physical body. I shall
take it at the proper time. Thousands of times. Do not ask that; it
goes too deep. It means that there are things for which neither you
nor I are ready.

[3]

July, August, September—Yes—All goes well as it is—No reproach
an affirmation—So it seems—You are doing or it is being done?
In some directions—Not balanced—Let the Power work—don't
quarrel with it. When there is want of balance, it means that both
sides are wrongly arranged with regard to each other.

Many begin to be calm—None yet avail for action—What matters

whence comes the truth—That let the recipient judge—The work—
The work that is to be, not that which men imagine—Remove all
preconceptions—No—I am nobody—When I write, I am only a
word—It depends on what is active—

[4]

My dear friend,

    It is quite impossible to tell you how glad I am to come into
communication with you again. After so many years of separation,
for old friends to be even partially united is a great happiness. If you
will let me pour out my sentiments, I can write pages.—My name
is Mo———² Too many people are thinking—I am the friend who
died in the years when you were at Baroda—I am Nair- - -³
    My soul is in the world of desires———

My idea of your position in Pondicherry is that it is not serious as
you think. There are some weak points on which certain forces are
pressing in order to throw you out somewhere. Whether it is good
that you should be thrown out or not, I do not know. But really the
result depends on you & not on them. If you ask precise questions,
I will try to answer—You want a prophet—I will answer if you like,
but I am not a prophet.

---

² *Only two letters of the name were written, followed by a long line.*—Ed.
³ *Uncertain reading. The marks represented here by three hyphens may indicate that
the name is incomplete.*—Ed.

AUTOMATIC WRITINGS, c. 1914 (SECOND SET)

[1]

My dear friends,

I am eager to join you, but I am terribly opposed by all sorts of obstacles. Pray send me your strength —

He is gone — I am willing to talk about Agrippa or anything you like — I don't know Agrippa, but I know about him. He was a man grave, stern, sombre, full of retained force, a great lover of Augustus, but yet they did not always get on very well together from want of sufficient intellectual comprehension of each other — Horace — No — it was a private friendship — To found the empire? Agrippa, Maecenas, — at first Antony, though they quarrelled afterwards — You see, that was a dream & dreams very often distort things. You must understand them generally without pressing the details. He meant that the first step was a petty success which assured the chain of actions that followed. As for the exact step, it is difficult to say — perhaps he meant that he took possession of the Senate, the august monument of Republican Rome, in order to have a sure base for his empire. Caesar & Antony after him neglected these little powerful details about which Augustus who had always a practical intuition was always very careful. — When did you have it? In coming or going — Where? But where, near what country? — Near Egypt then — Well, then, the dream had obviously a close connection with the hidden object of your voyage, — hidden from yourself, of course. Augustus was the organiser of a new era in civilisation, though Caesar was the founder, — a civilisation which gave a firm base for a new development of the world. You have the same idea of a new civilisation — but what is missing is the organising power — It is that you waked in the dream. Since it was near Egypt you were probably Antony who attempted blindly a union of East & West typified by his connection with Cleopatra. As for the great toe of the foot, that is difficult. I will try to consider.

Not at all — They [*Antony and Augustus*] were greatly attracted to each other, but their interests clashed & their prana clashed & the attempts they made to link themselves closely like the marriage with Octavia drove them apart. They were complementary to each other, but could not understand each other. Of course I don't know that you were Antony — I only try to interpret the dream — Yes — he has much of the prana of Agrippa, only it is now illumined & purified & there is the effect of other lives — Whose? Yes, that is why I said you might be Antony — No, you have progressed much — If so, she has much altered — Why not? One can change out of recognition — Never — Yes, probably — Very little — No, I don't see anything — No — I don't say that, but I can trace nothing — Whose — He has, I understand, been identified with Virgil, & at any rate he has the Virgilean soul. . He is French, also, but a little of the Celtic Italian type — The Celtic type is dreaming artistic impulsive delicate intuitional a little formless; the Italian has the sense of form & mastery over the materials of life or of art — He is a Bengali, but no man belongs only to his present nation to the exclusion of his soul's past history — He is of the practical, formative type — Which? No — but I must try to get into touch with the past formations & I want an indication. It is not easy. These things don't remain in the nervous mind with any precision — Yes, but it is difficult — If you ask me about things Egyptian, I shall have to run away — What language? No — I don't think — More possible — You are going back very near Egypt — Oh, horribly symbolic, mystic, hieroglyphic — I think not — I don't accept your authority — You authorise yourself to authorise for her. Cleopatra is not Egypt — that is Greek easternised — Certainly not — She had none — She was all prana & imagination given up to the impulses of the prana — Charming — Yes — I can't say precisely just now; I only feel that they have come often together. Possibly; but more often united — I don't see him — Also — That is a thing which most of us don't like to reveal — Not on earth — Yes — Rather, the sign of a constant connection with earth, a persistence in the life of the earth — Sometimes a great, sometimes little according

to the particular case —[1] It is difficult to say; the mentality is sometimes strongly reproduced, the nervous part a little; sometimes the
contrary — I don't see why — I don't think so, but it depends perhaps
on the spirit in which it is done

Much worse than the other — I am afraid you must ask others who
have a greater power of mentality than myself. — He is more modern, but he may well have been there. How do you know she was
Cleopatra? — Possibly you were not; I only saw a certain connection
& therefore some probability — Yes, probably your own — I accept
it as probable. — Yes — It's a way of saying — I regret not — I came
in answer to your past desire — There is something opposing the
writing, but that does not matter — only there is a distracting force
somewhere which prevents the nervous part of the medium from
concentrating.

[2]

My writing will be of another kind. I am here to speak of
the things that interest myself and my friends — In the heavens of
the second mind there are those who view the world through the
symbols of the nervous mind and that distorts the vision. I hope
to dissipate the mists that distort with your help. If you prefer, I
will wait your own time, but absolutely you must help us, for then
you will help yourself — To the writer — I have indicated what I am.
As to who I am, how will that help you. From the world I am
speaking of. On the whole I think I will wait. The time does not
seem propitious.

What else do you expect? If there are communications, it is
either when light spirits come to amuse themselves or those who
have passed seek to reestablish communication or else the spirits of
other worlds come to aid or to seek aid. Attend there —

No. Ask him —

---

[1] *At this point in the MS the following incomplete sentence was written and then
cancelled:* It is great as far as concerns Agrippe &

Many wish to be present, but the dissipation of force is not favourable. Concentration is necessary. No, you have got a nice little spirit there, give him a chance — I should like to know what he means by the absence of love & suppleness. If he refers to us, we shall be very glad to know our defects. Is he. Well, perhaps. What does it matter, provided we help. We are interested in thought, not in love. In any case we think we are preparing for greater powers than ourselves to manifest. As for the writing we use it, but there are other & better means — You think so? To what? Does he think he comes from the highest heights — If there are such great powers on earth in man, what is this they have done with the earth? Do they think the horrible gâchis they have made is a credit to the greatest powers in the world? Then we speak a different language when we speak of greatness & height. He means height in love, I mean height in wisdom. At bottom, yes, but not in their way of manifesting. I am glad he added that; & his great want now is the right knowledge to direct his love. Love without knowledge is often a terrible thing. Granted — There I cannot follow him. Love infinitely; it is easy to say — How many among men can do it or have done it; & even among those who have done it to a large extent, there have been tracts of themselves where clarity was absent. These things in men more often exclude each other than admit each other's completeness. Do not fix on one thing, however great & high. Open yourselves to the light, to the power, to the love & do not exaggerate the importance of the one above all the others. If I say man needs knowledge most, I speak of the present need. Love without it will not help him in the great struggles that are before him.

I admit that I am more akin in my mind to light & power than to love, but I recognise the importance of love. I will admit that it is even the most important, but there are times & seasons for things. That is interesting — but there are different ways of service. And I as friend. — All do that — Seek on the mountains where the foot of man has not yet trod, when the moon is full, when the spring is at its height after meditation & prayer — But not now. When the hour comes, you will know. Not he who works for that, but for another cause. He must not be there at the search — There are reasons which it would be premature to reveal—That I know not, you may meet there, but you are not likely to go there together. Perhaps he who desires it most. For the other a stage must come in the work before he goes. Everything is fixed by the law of his nature & the law which governs that law. What do you mean by the reason? Again a doubtful expression; everything is rational from one point of view, absurd & arbitrary from another. The ultimate Law is beyond expression by the mind. Imperfectly & from a limited point of view. For man's convenience, yes. I don't say how. Yes, limit not the knowledge at any point, that is the essential—No—Yes—I do not think it will take long—Forty three[2] years for the work is my calculation, but Rama must manifest soon if it is to be done so quickly. For the changing of the world—For it to be completed. In 1956–7. Complete!! Who knows? That is a very impersonal answer. What of man's satisfaction? The work & the man; the man because of the work & the work also because of the man. Work is not in the void nor exists for its own sake but because of that which works. Why must the world be saved? That does not enlighten me—The salvation, if you like to use the word, of man which necessarily means the fulfilment of the present world in something more complete & divine. Eternity? what is that? I know nothing of eternity. There is time & that which is beyond time. Then what is meant by constructing something eternal for eternity. You touch on a problem which is perhaps the most difficult of all & you treat it very summarily. It is not born. Yes—Yes but then you construct for Time. Something which begins but does not end —Then why construct?—To that I agree. I must have known him, if he was in the world of light—But he said, I think, he knows me? That is why I waited. In his present form & name I do not know him. No—From my own. Approaching that? I can, if I try but I do not know whether I shall be permitted to speak. By that which governs my knowledge. I see three forms of light; one is white with a blue radiance around it & out of it fierce red lustres occasionally pour, another is white. No another day—

---

2 *"Forty two" was altered by writing "three" over "two". —Ed.*

It is a force of Rudra who destroys—I find a difficulty in writing—I should not begin it apparently at least not now. If he can speak let him do so—Which is which? How, you have seen, it is you who must say—Is there any symbolism in your variations of writing? That is why I called him a nice little spirit. I got an impression of the child in him—O it is only an impression & probably a wrong one. But what was the name he gave me? Was it a name, what function?

What was it you asked? I was listening to him. How the same family? Yes, very close, but you have a brilliance; mine is a different kind of light. Mine is more subdued, less fertile. Less intense, more quietly spread, perhaps a little wider, but not so forceful & productive. No, there is an immense difference. . His is a light I cannot describe. No, that was a form. It is the mentality—Who the devil can describe it—Don't ask me to do impossible things. At the centre—In that from which the light comes; also to a certain extent in the process, but not in its forms. The union he speaks of will be perfect when you all three reach there. No, not in the way I mean. . To each his time & his work. I seek, not precisely that, but a connection enabling me to work. No, not at all—It is a different spirit—Yes, but there must also be a point of contact. I am willing if you are. Good—Not with all three. She would [not] open [to] me in her present condition: the element of mentality in which I am strongest, is in her half asleep. Yes, but others can do that better than I can. No, but if he is as you say, ask him to come soon. Who? In defining the higher knowledge so as to make it useful for life—Precisely, the light is too high as it is; I can help him as it descends to define it more practically. No, that is your affair—In managing the way of the earthly world in which you are. Not in the way most men call practical. By matter, I seek to be.——————————

AUTOMATIC WRITING, c. 1920

Manek.

Manek is the name of the old introducer of the writing. Let us get rid of him at once. My name does not greatly matter. I am a spirit of the higher realms not present on the earth, but communicating from above.

First, let me tell the purpose of the script. It is to open a first means of embodied communication with the other worlds. There can be other means, but this was the readiest at the time. In all respects it was the most suitable. As a beginning only.

The object now is to introduce the wider knowledge of past, present and future beyond the range of the present terrestrial mind — That is all today —

AUTOMATIC WRITINGS, c. 1920

[1]

One of the guests of the future. . Millions of men are waiting for the day that comes but it comes not till the light has descended. And who shall make the light descend? Half lights will not do, they prepare and pass and fade. The whole light, the unveiled power. We behind the veil wait for our hour; not to a world such as is now can we come. We are the sons of the glory, the children of immortality, the flames of God. When the divine Light descends, then we descend. But we know that an hour approaches and the dawn is red, red as blood and red with blood, the fire is behind, the fire of the Angel of the Presence.

Light first, strength with the light, joy with the strength, love with the joy, the fourfold splendour. Who shall contain it within himself and give harbourage to all the Godhead? Who shall have the unfathomable calm that shall support all the light and neither be blasted by the fire nor spill it like an insufficient vessel? The strength, who shall be bold enough to bear it, mighty enough not to shrink from the terror and marvel of its works, great and sweet enough to turn its lion forces into the path of the Lover? Who shall be the sea of the universal joy and swallow up into it the poisons of the universe and his throat not even be blackened by the fire of the poison? Who shall know what the love is and take nothing out of it nor reject any face of love however strange and out of all experience it may be to the mind of the mortal? All this he must be before the Godhead of the future can descend. All else that promises to come are only glimpses of things that would intervene and take the great seat if they could or else flashes that mislead. The new age promises always, but is always the old age in another dress. This only can be the thing that is truly new born and the birth of a new humanity.

One who has come near because some of the ways are opened.

Not the highest, but still a soul and not a creature of the worlds that once communicated with you.

He has no name and innumerable names. Men call him God, therefore I use the word. . I am not a man, but I have been a man.

To whom? You would not know the names and they are secret.

I will not give the name I call him by; but some call him by a name that means he who cannot be obstructed. . A time will come when I must descend on earth, but not in the present humanity. One who passed the threshold. I am not a Mahatma. No. A man, a seeker who heard and saw, if you like to so call it, a Rishi. . What does the name matter? It would not help you to know anything. It is a strange and a vague question.

Put these questions to another who is nearer to external things than myself.

No information, only the things of the Idea. You have too many. I do not speak of ideas in the ordinary sense, but the Idea. Wait till another day if you will when I can make a closer and less impeded connection. This kind of communication needs a full force in the writer which he had at the beginning, but is now clouded. I can no longer express myself as I would and the idea is checked in its passage.

[2]

Be passive.

Blind the intelligence to what is being written. It does not matter if there is a knowledge of what is coming, but there must be no activity of the intelligence, no idea, no criticism of the intellectual sense, simply a passive acceptance.

[3]

The time is too short, you should have done it before. . However, I am here. What I have to say I will say another time, but you can ask me any question and I will see if I can answer. No, not stupid questions.

It is not tamasya. It is a state of relaxation of the being which is rajasic in its fundamental temperament with a sattwic flame ever growing on the heights; but the flame does not burn up the mist between the mind and the highest; it only thins it so as to allow the lightnings sometimes to pour down from above. The rajasic fuel of the nervous being gets exhausted by too rapid an expenditure often for quite useless purposes and then the mist precipitates itself downward. The result is a laxity of the nervous system and a resultant laxity of the mind. It is a tamasic state no doubt, but if the rajas of the wrong kind can be lessened by it and cast away and only the rajas that is fit for feeding the sattwic fire preserved and increased, then a greater fire of the upward light can be established which may perhaps burn up the mist on the heights. That is how I see your condition —

I am not a prophet. It depends on yourself and the gods of your nature and those of your destiny. Help them by your assent or if you can, by your will.

Why not, if the Power in you wills or if you can wake its action; but there is no need to force yourself at present if your system is reluctant.

I do not know the future positively. It is a power, but a power which works behind a cloud of light which is too strong for most eyes. I do not know if it will soon take a more directly effective form.

[4]

My presence is sure whenever you take up the pencil. I am always near you in my psychical being. The work you are doing is intimately connected with my destiny and therefore I am attracted towards those who embody the influences that are in operation to bring about its form and exterior movement. This writing is a means of direct communication and by it I can bring myself nearer to the earth where I shall have to descend. It is more useful to us than to you, but it is one of the means which the world behind is using today to throw out its presence and figures on the terrestrial plane. Others of a greater kind will take its place when the human mind is ready.

The time is short. My will is to see, but I see only in the figures of the psychic world. Yet I think I mistake not in seeing that the movement which was so slow prepares for a rapidity which will be first the flowing of a constant stream, then the spreading of a tide and last a storm of invading forces. The Shakti of the future has been as if ascending a steep ascent and is now approaching the summit from which she will be able to see the field of her work before her. The field is full of contrary forces and her first steps must be covert and behind a shield of self-veiling and only partially revealing movements. Other movements must be thrown in front which will attract the attention of the hostile forces, movements not of the definite future, but still helpful to prepare the field, and it is only when she has gathered sufficient material force that she will throw off disguise and come to the front to take up the direct battle. That is why at first the quicker movement will be only that of the flowing stream, a penetration and spreading and enlargement of the current. When there is the greater tide of movement, then the battle will be near and the Shakti will unveil her real figure.

There is a storm approaching, but it is of the outside movement, and as I am not in close touch with those forces, I cannot see clearly whether it merely threatens at present and will keep for a time the atmosphere surcharged and heavy or will break out into an early violence. I see the power that broods upon this outer movement, but his mind is not open to me. ——————————————————— .

I have finished saying what was immediately in my mind and have been simply thinking in the writing to materialise my thoughts a little. If you wish to say anything, I am ready to reply to you.
===

Bolshevism is more distant to me, but it is part of the outer movement, only it has more force of reality than others I was thinking of. The movements of Europe have a potential or an actual violence of the power of execution in them which makes them press for realisation more rapidly; but it is the future which is preparing to arise in the East of which I was thinking.

Not in your atmosphere, but around. I see most readily the things nearest to you. I do not suppose it will be anything to you except a thing to be watched for the opportunities it may leave behind in passing.

Japan? I shall have to see more closely before I can say. From a distance I can only see things that prepare by bits; the sudden shocks that will break down what is established seem to me to be yet at a distance, but at what distance I cannot say.

That is a thing in which I have no right to give suggestions. The powers that preside over your destiny and the work have to settle that between them; but I doubt not that when the action is ready, the guidance will come. Spirits like myself are too little a part of the already materialising will of the terrestrial destiny to hazard their thoughts in the matter. The future, besides, can only be seen by me in tendency, in figures of general power. . I may be able to speak of more definite things hereafter, but not at present.

[5]

My wish is to make a few observations first, but please remain absolutely still in the mind or I shall not be able to manage. —

The age of our coming is the age of the omnipotence of the second emanation. The first is the age of the Spiritual without form, the second that of the spiritual possessing matter. The first, I mean, the age in which we formerly came. Therefore our coming depends upon your ability to lay hold on matter and make of it a true mould of the spiritual influx. In the former age there were symbols, but no true body. Therefore the spirit receded and left the other principles to play out their possibilities without its direct intervention. Now there is a second chance for us. That is why I have drawn near, more for help to myself than for anything else, to make a suitable connection in my psychical principle with the material and the work of the spirit upon it. This is to explain my side of the communication. Whatever I see or say about things on the earth is through a previous psychical translation and you must so understand it and not expect too great a precision at present in my communications.

The tendencies of the present I can see and floating images of the future; but as the real body of the psychic worlds is not present to the physical mind, but only appears like a dream or imagination, so to my psychic mind is the body of the material world. This presents a difficulty which most who do this writing do not appreciate. It is only spirits who are very near to the earth who can to some extent see it with similar eyes to physical beings and they too borrow a great deal from the ideas, the mental suggestions and the nervous being of the one who writes and those about him so as to harmonise their mentality with that of men and make themselves intelligible. This I do not wish to do, as it brings much that is false and inferior into the communication. Please therefore be as still in mind as possible so that there may be a minimum of mixture.

Now if you want to say anything I am ready.

It is only minds who have a new idea either full of the spiritual influence or touched by thoughts that are helpful to it who can prepare the age that seeks to come. But there are those who have ideas only on the intellectual plane and no idea of anything behind and there are those who have spiritual experience but no power to embody or materialise. These give us no sufficient hope, whatever they may do for the moment. It is where there is the spiritual experience or the ideas that give it a mental body and along with that a strong will to materialise from whom we can expect the fulfilment of that for which we are awaiting. You are among the comparatively few who have these things. It is therefore either you if you are chosen and remain faithful to yourselves or those like you to whom we must look for the preparation of the future.

Because of the psychical vision. I can see something of your souls or at least its signs, even if I cannot see your bodies.

No, impossible, not in the period of transition.

That is because you have been less spiritually exclusive than myself; you have incarnated through the centuries and done work for mankind and you now continue that work and yours therefore is the right or, if you like, the spiritual necessity to labour for the great ages of mankind. I was of those who drew too much into myself seeking the pure principle of knowledge and I postponed though I knew to be necessary the sacrifice of action. I did the action that prepared myself for spiritual growth, but not in my last movements the action that goes outward. If I were to come now without the help of a favourable new age to externalise my spirit, I should have to begin by a form of mind corresponding to my last mental formation and start from that working out of it what was opposed to the action. I should not be a sufficient force for help to the world at this critical period. I might even join myself to old ideas having too much of the spiritual overstress. On the other hand if I come at a juncture where the right kind of work has already begun, I shall have the most favourable circumstances for making the most of my earthly destiny for myself and others.

That is a difficult question. It involves from my point of view a working out of an equation between your psychical forces as I see them and the circumstances of your earthly destiny as they are determined by the force of your past and the force of your future lives. I do not know enough for that, and I could not possibly do it satisfactorily in a few words or a little time. Besides there is the force of the collective need and the collective resistance to consider. If one could see not from the psychical but the higher principle it would be easy enough but I cannot do that at present. I think you should leave this question to another occasion. At present I should probably get only a side light which might be misleading.

Everywhere, to one degree or another, but to find them is no such easy matter. In number they are already thousands, but all of them have not found their way. Some need a lead and some a leader and some the destined moment for casting into form of thought and action what is now only a desire and an impulse. Some are meant only for the first steps and some for the greater things afterwards. It is not possible that you should coalesce with all of them; there are too many mental and temperamental differences, especially with those who have already taken their direction.

No. I began as what you would now call a Rishi, but I found no satisfaction in the things that were around me nor in the level of knowledge reached by my fellows. I said "Upwards, ever upwards." I drew back from my life and I went upwards in the inner world of my being. But when I felt myself full of the higher light and would have turned to pour it around me, I found I had cut the connection between the power of knowledge and the effective will to action, cut too the thread of similarity and sympathy which could have made a line of communication between my knowledge and the minds of others. My body too was a stranger to the principle which filled my spirit. I determined to come in another life, in another body; but when I retired, I found the inability to descend except at a sacrifice for which I was not ready. Therefore I had to wait for others to do what I might otherwise have done and to prepare the conditions for my return. I shall not be one of the initiators, but I shall be one of those who help to make the knowledge endure in the mind of the new humanity.

[6]

Not myself at first —

My desire is to suggest to you to enlarge your view of the things you are about to do. The steps you are taking are not in consonance with the scope of the power you are calling down. First, be sure of the presence of the power, certainly; but do not limit its action by too prudent a beginning. The power of the work is not the power of your past life nor temperament, not the power of Mahasaraswati which governed the past existences that have been revealed to you, but of Mahakali, the swift and forceful Shakti. The desire to lay a slow and sure basis which belongs to the careful reason and its experimental skill is not the genius of the work you have to do. The other side of the Shakti which hitherto has acted only on occasions, will be the force that presides over the not distant future. —

The limitations of the past were due to the heavy siege of the opposing powers and the obstacles they were able to heap about you. Some of these are already half dead and the others are beginning to lose their right; therefore be ready in a shorter time than you imagine to change your notions of the immediate future. The vaster, swifter more confident idea to which rendered careful by past failures you have long said "Not yet, not yet," is the only one that can act out with effect the aims that have been set before you. A force that hesitates not over its steps, that overbears and does not spend time in going round obstacles, that enlarges swiftly its means and moves over great spaces in short periods, can alone create the new world that is seeking to be born. ———

The forces that stand against you are great in appearance, but only in appearance; great no doubt still in material means, but smitten with the spirit of death in the very heart of those means. Their strength to endure derives only from the hesitations, the weakness of will, the slowness to combine and organise, or when organised to use boldly their strength which afflicts the forces of the future. This is the main reason why still they hold the world, because there is nothing except at a point here and there which is confident of its own power to replace them. Their shakti is broken within, the shakti of the future is infirm without, that is why there is the deadlock. ———

The person who wrote is gone; I presume he will come again; but it seemed to me he is passing about swiftly seeking something or somebody that will receive his inspiration and do his will. That is the impression he gave me —

Is there anything you would say to me or shall I stand back and let others come?

T S M ———

Be passive. T S M is the sign of the society, otherwise of the combination of groups that are working on the psychic conditions for the formation of things yet impotent to take a material body. . Three groups — one throwing up the errors likely to stand in the way of success so that they may express themselves and be done with; one sketching out the imperfect beginnings of the future; the third preparing under a veil the final things. The process of the new birth is a very complicated and difficult thing offering at every step errors and perils of perversion and failure or else of fallings short of the idea, and the mind of man and still more his life impulses are so difficult and obstinate a material that it needs many influences and much labour behind the veil to give a fair chance to the possibilities of the future. This applies in every part of the work that has to be done, spiritual, intellectual, material. The movement is at first a chaos of possibilities and the thing that is to be done appears generally to the human idea in certain ideas and tendencies which become more and more general; but the difficulty is with the forces, to make them purer and clearer in their idea of action, to get them together, to give them a combination and mass of action. At present they are in a confusion which deprives them of their means of success. It is the second group whose action tends to grow stronger; but for the third to bring their work forward needs the intervention of a great precipitating force. It is that no doubt which was spoken of, but if it is coming, it is still in the background.   That is a thing I can convey with difficulty, if at all. T S M is only a sign. Together the letters mean the three things, apart they mean nothing. T is the sign of the past that failed trying to throw itself into the present, S of the present taking up the past and trying to change it into the future, M of the future creating the present. It is only a sign; but the name I cannot get into the writing. ————

He was trying to explain from his point of view why there is the difficulty in getting the greater force to come. The Shakti always waits for the moment of the fitness of its advent and that must be ready in the psychical field before it can be ready in the material action. That is what he wanted to say.

[7]

My own plan is to be more and more full of light and seek the end of the whole place which is above the vital region. As for the tunnel I think that is a mere figure of speech. There can be no tunnel, only a path made through the resistance of the ether but that is a path of light running through the density of the space above the terrestrial level. ————

I am one who have worked on these things. Not the one who comes ordinarily at first when you begin to write. I put him aside when you took up the pencil.

Not all, but I was passing when you talked of symbols.

That is one kind; but there are others belonging to that plane who are worse — All right. I am off. ——

That was an intervention such as often happens in this kind of communication. I am here. Have you anything to say to me?
=

Yes. Continue what and about whom? I think not, at least tonight.
What question? But I do not know.
=

That is simple. Let her free and let her do it herself. . No, but I mean that the question has only that solution. The change to be made is too great and the possibilities too many and complex for a plan to be made of any particular kind. It must be a natural evolution or if you like a natural revolution proceeding from the soul and will of the women themselves. If it is imposed on them in obedience to a previous idea, that will falsify the movement and produce something as artificial probably as the present system.
Why? It seems to me the most practical process.
In Asia. Europe will take, I think, a little time to adjust itself to a new impulse. It has been too much brought up to a sort of standstill or rather a circling round the same point by the disappointment of the hopes it had concerning the after results of the war. Besides the forces there are too bewildered and uncertain of themselves to take boldly at once a step forward — Even those which are sure of themselves are more concerned with consolidating their position than with any impulse of a fresh advance.
Not yet, so far as I can see. There must be at least three stages passed before that can come.
The first stage must be the exhaustion of the existing idea and movement which is rather a confused seeking for a means of self-effectuation than a strong and definite will and idea. And under the cover of this there must grow up a new will and strength fixed on its aim and luminous enough to create its means. Afterwards the struggle with the last remnants of the destiny of England.
I do not see yet clearly beyond the immediate situation; but this process seems to me certain though the forms and balance of the forces about to come into the field are not yet definite to me. As for the time, all I can say is that it will be swifter than seems now possible and that there will be a constant acceleration of the

momentum of destiny which will become very pronounced after a year or two or at most three.

It is hanging all over Asia, but I do not know where it will break first. The enlargement of idea will, I believe, come of itself as the present immobile tension of circumstances breaks and new possibilities come into view. But that was not my seeing and I do not quite know what was in the mind of the spirit who spoke. He is more accustomed to the earth than I and probably has a more definite vision.

At present, yes; even those who are in action cannot at present really get forward. This is everywhere a moment of blocked forces.

Not only he,[1] but all who are at present politically active in India. In a year it will have been enough cleared up for new views to emerge. That is all I can say at present.

The second phase, I take it, will come by the loss of faith in present ideas and methods among the younger men. As to who will represent it, that is a thing I cannot yet say; certainly a number of new men must come forward; the old are too much wedded to the past notions.

This question is one which involves too much for an immediate answer. I can only say that the work which is to be done is to determine the new force that will make the India of the future. The removal of the foreign obstacle is only the removal of a negation, but there must be a positive creation which will be the beginning of the power that will govern the future, otherwise there will be so much weakness, confusion, aimless clash and dispersion of energies in this vast body that a rapid emergence of the greater future will not be possible. As to what work this or that person will do in this matter, that is a question difficult for me to answer without a consideration of many complex forces. I am not prepared to answer it at the moment.

You want the time in which it will be completed?

I am afraid I cannot say exactly. I can only say that as far [as] I can now see it will be in a few years quite visible.

I am afraid I cannot look so far ahead. A great power in Asia,

---

[1] *The word "he" was written over "Ga", presumably the beginning of "Gandhi".* — Ed.

yes, that is certain, but of what form is not clear to me on this level. It is no doubt decided above, but here I can only see still uncertain possibilities. I think I told you my vision of the terrestrial future is not yet clear and definite. I can only see a few general certainties

No. I know none by that designation. Office? I do not understand. There is more than one godhead and power concerned with these things, but none so far as I know who has such an office. ———

I know very little about it; it has not seemed to me important enough to consider very closely.

I don't say that, but I don't know anyone of that description

[8]

My wish is to make a slight departure. There is as yet too much difficulty for me in seeing the things of the earth and I shall wait till I am stronger. Meanwhile if you like someone else will take my place. ———

Begin —

I am ready to communicate.

Any subject interests me. As for my competence, it is limited but various.

Yes, what is it you want to know?

As far as I can see, if you act quickly, you may get something done which will be a useful seed for the future. But before long the atmosphere is likely to be too thick and troubled for ideas of so large a kind to make immediate headway. As you can see, a struggle is approaching on which the course of the immediate future depends and until that comes to some kind of issue, it is the passion of the immediate struggle that will occupy all minds to the exclusion of other things. Your idea is one which may and must bear fruit in the future, but at present it is a thing of long views for which one must be content to sow and await a favourable season for the fruit. India is too much occupied with her interior problem which is at bottom one not of equality but independence to spare more than a side glance for the question of her people in the colonies. That is my opinion.

This is only as regards practical work. I should say that it will be a good thing to establish the idea; for as the struggle proceeds, there will be great chances of India turning to it in the hope of an outside support and assistance. She has up till now been looking westwards. The present movement is turning her towards some kind of unity of feeling with western or Musulman Asia. The future may turn her eyes eastward towards the rest of Asia and your scheme will be useful in preparing for that time; there will be something to lay hold on immediately and that will save much time and effort which would otherwise then be needed to make a connection.

Well, I don't know; it depends on getting over the present floating and uncertain state of action. If that can be done; there is obviously a big future, as it is a new idea with considerable possibilities of result and extension.

I should say, certainly publish it. The more you publish the better. It does not matter so much just now about terms etc, the thing is to give a wide publicity—give it to those who can do that best.

What?

That is nothing; such letters have no immediate meaning or importance, except as indications that many in the country feel a need of a leader and look this side. In my opinion it is best not to intervene in what others are doing for the moment, but leave the force at work to operate through its chosen instruments and confine yourselves to whatever special action is meant for you. There is not yet the critical juncture that calls for your action and to mix oneself with the immediate action might interfere with a better development afterwards.

No, that was another.

Not exactly; we are a very various company. No, it is without any order, at least without any deliberate order.

Yes, in the world of the mind, I am a spirit of the middle intelligence. . No, I have nothing to do with gods; of course they exist but I take no stock in them. . What use would it be to me? Of course not. At least if they do it, they will have to do it without showing themselves. I would reject any interference.

To satisfy the curiosity of my intelligence.

Yes. .

I was in many countries. I have had many lives, had many occupations, studied many things. The last life I was a little bit of a scientist, something of a philosopher, dabbled in politics too and in literature, but could not get much success. I was a good critic, but not a creator. In England. You would not know my name. The same thing, the curiosity of my intelligence; I had a mind that liked to inquire into the future of humanity and I had advanced views on the matter. No, you can help yourself much better.

It is an excellent form, very effective, that is if you want to wake people up and make them think. . I am certain we must have, but I cannot fix the occasion.

I know there is something above mind, but not what it is.

Do you ask me for my past opinions or for my present imaginations and ideas?

I am afraid that question passes my competence, that is the question how man came into being. My only idea about it is that all the theories are wrong.

No, I said advanced; that is in my past life. You would consider them commonplace.

[9]

Myself today. . The others are no longer here. ———
Yes ———
I do not know. Ask and we shall see.
In what respect?

(Tilak)[2]

He is, I believe, in the intermediate plane. He had a strong will to live, because he felt that his work was not finished, and when a man passes from the body with that feeling strong upon him, his personality is for a time turned towards the field of his human actions. Only a time is needed to bridge over the transition from one consciousness to another. When that is done, he will act for a

---

[2] *The headings identifying the subjects of most of the following communications were added in the margin, sometimes in French and usually in what appears to be the Mother's handwriting. — Ed.*

time on the intermediate plane probably until he is satisfied that the idea governing him is in good train towards success or until he has worked out the force of the attacking idea in his own consciousness. I speak of the personal mental part of it that still feels the effect of the life vibrations. ——

That can only be done by the higher part of him. The part of his mind that is still concerned with the images of the outward world is likely for a time to act upon it through a certain impact on the men who are the channels of the general force that is working. It is only when these images fade and the consciousness becomes more free that the direct action of which you speak becomes probable. The action from the intermediate plane is in one sense stronger as it is capable of a more subtle and penetrating diffusion not hampered by the physical difficulties, but it has other difficulties of its own; it is strong for diffusion and the creation of impelling ideas and forces, but for the materialisation through human action it can only act in dependence on the transmitting agents. There is always a certain disparateness between the psychical and the physical planes and the transmission from the one to the other is not always facile

That is true, but always in the sense of a primary force. In the end this primary force is the important thing. I only speak of the difficulty of correct materialisation from the psychical plane. A strong will can produce from it a great general effect in the sense of its purpose and that after all is the important matter.

His psychic personality is composed of two parts, a higher soul which is the real man, a strong and brilliant soul of a great flight, and another which is the personality he works out in a certain round of lives and which gave the outward type of his human character and action. He is one of those who belong to the higher race, but has chosen to take on himself the burden of the lower for the help of the world action.

(Mʳ Tilak)

Yes. A great Karma Deva who is in intimate union with the Devas of knowledge.

(Mme Besant)

An Asuric being of great force busy divinising herself, but not yet successful because of the very force of her power which creates a great force of ego.

No, not a Rakshasa. There is a Rakshasa force associated with her, but it does not affect the centre of her being.

(I)

That is different. There are men who belong to one type and make an ascension, that is her case; there are others who have in themselves the various powers and have to transform them into the terms of the central unity. That I believe is yours.

(P.R)

To define your case is difficult. A Deva above, a strong Jnana Deva able to communicate with the higher planes, an Asura below representing the development of many lives, a Rakshasa force behind constantly weakened and fading, but not yet cast away by the drawing up of the vital being by the others, also several other minor deva kinds in the psychic being, that is the best I can manage.

(Rapports avec la Soc. Theosoph)

The fraternity is due to the fact that both are working out the common movement under a great superior direction. The hostility is due to the intermediate agencies. They are guided by inferior powers who are repelled and made afraid and therefore hostile by the superior force they at once feel in you; the greater intermediate powers that are behind you are not able to accommodate themselves to the narrowness of theirs and be sufficiently indulgent to their littleness. That is why there is the discord.

There is a great deal of ignorance in that idea. Kutthumi and Maurya are merely names and forms, true only as a psychic symbol or an instrumental representation, of the two main powers that are behind them, one governing their thought, the other influencing their action. In Madame Blavatsky they found a sufficient instrument who could as it were incarnate and harmonise both their forces. Her successors have not been able to do that, but have only responded to partial indications of one or the other; that is why there [have]³ been so many divisions and so much confused and uncertain action in the movement.

Kutthumi represents a Deva, not a Jnana Deva, but a certain kind of thought deva who responds with a limited light but a great abundance of curious thought formations to the greater Idea that comes from the supramental level.

Maurya represents an Asura who has stopped short on the way to Devahood, a being of aggressive thought force and great vital vehemence, but of a very limited power in the true sense of the word, who has associated himself with Kutthumi and is tolerated by him, because otherwise Kutthumi would not be able to exercise an influence of practical action on the human world.

(Rapports avec la T.S.)

I doubt, unless the Maurya influence can be broken, but that would mean that the Society would lose its practical force of action. It would have either to be transformed and taken up into a greater action or dissolve as a society and its members or the best of them enter into a work of larger inspiration and movement.

That represented the hostility of which I spoke. The Maurya influence is a despotic power which does not want any interference with its control or any dissolvent action on the frame of thought and organised movement it has stamped on the society.

(Gandhi)

A big Karma Deva risen to a certain thought region into which he has carried his habit of rigid and definite action, associated with a psychic Deva of great purity but no great knowledge. The thought region is one which reflects rather than possesses a higher light, but he gives to it always the forms suitable to his concentrated impulse of action. It is this kind of combination that creates those who are at once saints and fanatics.

(Mirra)

I find it impossible at present to make a definite answer, because I have to see through an atmosphere that is not favourable

---

³ MS has

to a definite description. . All I can say is that there is a great Light Devata there, but the other elements are not clear to my vision. It is easy to define the psychic personality of people like M⁣ʳˢ Besant and Gandhi, but all your cases are different because of unusual or of complex elements of a considerable significance to which a short definition is not easily fitted.

[10]

Yes. I am here ——————————
Tagore

There is not much to say. It is evident that there is in him a double being, one for the higher part of him, another for the lower nature. The higher is a very large psychic devata living in the celestial beauty of his own soul; the other is a sort of Gandharva. The Gandharva is limited, ego-bound, psycho-nervous, but his nervous expansion is made limited and weak by the domination of the psychic devata. At the same time he limits the psychic devata who because of him cannot impress himself on life, as he could if he had a strong intermediary, and therefore can find himself only in the world of his own imagination, poetry, art, an ineffective idealism.

He cannot be really a friend, because he lives only for his own psychic or nervous satisfaction and values people according as they minister to that. He may have sympathies, but they cannot take the active form necessary to friendship.

Yes, because he cannot pour himself out in life. He is therefore drawn into a sort of imprisoning circle of his own ether of isolated personality. . The devata in his relations to life. It is not that the devata would not like to be in active unity with others, but he has not the means in the vital nature of the human being.

That is first a sympathy of the psychic intelligence, secondly, the force of your own personality on him; it was not a thing deepseated in his own nature. You could still do the same thing with him if you were in constant relation with him, because he would like to be in action and would feel a support in the greater force that is around you; but as it is, it is not a thing that can be consistent and durable.

I should have to be in a little closer contact with them to do that effectively. As it is, I could only see through an intervening mist. The psychic image conveyed to me is not sufficiently precise and complete.

There is, but I fancy it belongs more to the past than anything else. You have gone too much forward.

It is the difficulty which meets all things that come from the future into the present and for which the powers of the present are not yet ready. In your case it is extremely strong in proportion as the idea and the force are large; if you were content with something smaller and more immediate, you would probably be much more effective. As it is, you come in advance of the godheads that are in march towards the actual world and you are too much beyond those who are actually at work at the moment. As yet you do not fit in and you have to create a place and a body for what is coming. But naturally the matter of the existing world is rebellious as it always is to things too great and new and not sufficiently prepared. The things you have formed in yourself need a greater outgoing force than they have at present in order to impress themselves sufficiently on the outside world. The momentum behind you is growing, but it is not yet sufficient. In these things those who create cannot see themselves where they are already effective, because the obstruction is greatest immediately around them; for they are the centre of the creation and therefore the centre of the accumulated resistance. Their thought and power work subtly, at a distance, through others, changed in those others to something less complete and characteristic which can mix with the actual material. That is to say, it is as mental influences that they work, but they do not take at once the recognisable form of which they can say, "This is the thing I mean, this is the actual creation I intend." That can only be when they become the direct material creators. I do not know whether I make myself clear to you.

It is difficult for me to say because I see the psychic better than the material things. In trying to make an inference from the former to the latter, I should probably commit many errors.

The obstacle is general; it applies itself for the moment to any action you are likely to take, but if you can once break it down effectively at one point, it is likely that others will open. My impression is that it will take you yet a little time to find the weak point of the obstruction and I myself cannot really tell. The obstruction is not something definite and rational, but a sheer force of obscurity and inertia which has somehow got itself concentrated in front for the time being. It is really a vital intuition enlightened by the higher mind which could find it out and that is a thing I necessarily lack in my present condition.

Yes, it is true. These forces know nothing, but they are as it were attracted where there is something that threatens them and they take time to form.

That also is true; India is a field where the opposing forces are most hostile to each other and there is besides a great complexity. If however the forces of the future can once form themselves effectively, they will get here perhaps their best chance of a direct and rapid action. That at least is one possibility on which certain very great Devatas are working.

It was someone else who suggested that — someone I think who is very sensitive to possibilities. It is true I believe that powers are at strenuous work to bring in a violent impetus and at moments it looks as if they would succeed, but the forces that make for an arrest direct themselves there and there is anew a deadlock.

[11]

I am here. —

That is not very easy for me. I wish to be quite well connected with the terrestrial plane by communication first before I give out myself. If things are suggested to me, I can by an effort put myself in relation at particular points and so strengthen the connection. Otherwise I can only speak of things foreign to the terrestrial atmosphere. ——

Russie

I think that the formations there are of a kind too forceful to be steady. There is a violent pressure upon natural psychological forces to suppress some, to create others. The transformation attempted is of the nature of a scheme made in the mind and imposed on the life forces. This means that many of the life forces lie inert and unconverted and a constant renewal of currents [has]⁴ to be made to galvanise things into effective action. If a constant struggle could be kept up with success with outside forces there would in time grow up a sufficiently steady and compact centre of transformation; but the Bolshevik motor force is at present a very small though powerful agent at once repressing a great inert mass and trying to use it for great and difficult work. That is a kind of action in which you must expect many crises and chances of failure. A failure anywhere means a retardation and a fresh expenditure of energy to start again. There is not the general excitement and vital enthusiasm that supported the French revolution. There is instead a more intelligent intellectual force and centre acting on a more complex and contradictory national psychology which is itself by no means strong either in intellectuality or in rapid vital energy. The experiment is most difficult, the chances precarious, and the one great hope is that the hostile forces will go on blundering and give the Bolshevik centre each time leisure and opportunity to repair the results of misfortune and strengthen itself for good. That is all I can see in the matter.

[12]

All right —

That is a little outside my power of vision.

Psychically the conditions seem to me favourable, I don't know about the material elements. .

Cousins

Yes. He is a soul of the middle regions, of what might be called the psychic and aesthetic world, associated with a very material being into which the soul has got rather thickly encased. There is an aesthetic devata enlightened by a Power of the intuitive intelligence, and its light burns inside and radiates through the material crust, but not with the free light that it might otherwise have. It gets free in the activities related to its own domain, but not even there quite free because it has had to educate the material mind and has not

---

⁴ MS have

been able to make it a quite flexible and spontaneous instrument. In other things it is subject to the limitations of the material being with whom it is associated and can only refine it to some extent without being able to change it. The intuitive Power works chiefly in that domain and is not sufficiently concerned or active in the rest.

For him you can do much, but I don't know whether the material being will allow you. Still you can bring an influence on the intuitive Power in him to act on the whole intelligence, where it is still content to work in rather cramped bounds. This Power is a little indifferent to other things than the aesthetic and psychic, and if you can interest it sufficiently in a wider domain for it to break from its indifference, and that is quite possible, it is strong enough to compel the material mind to which it now leaves those things, to enlarge itself and become intuitive. There is likely however to be much passive resistance because there are other influences.

As for the other question he can only help you in outward matters and that he can do very well if he is kept in close touch with you and his emotional being in active friendly relation. He is easily responsive to influences where this is the case.

Mme *Cousins*

That has been a help to him, but as often happens is also a hindrance. She is stronger than him in will, for his will is not very strong, but not being very wide in mind this decisiveness of will makes her rigid in her intelligence. Of course, if she could be induced to move from her moorings he would move with her like a boat in tow with a steam launch, but she is not flexibly responsive to influences.

[13]

More times than one I was here, but you did not call me. ——
No, because I depend on you for my connection with earth and I have nothing to say for myself any longer...
There are others who if you like can come.
=

That will not do, because the medium is not one who is in the state of passive receptivity.

I do not know, but there may be.
=

First let anyone come. Then there may be one who has something to say—This writing has either to be centred round one
communicant or left absolutely free; but in the latter case all sorts
of thing[s] interesting or uninteresting may come. One has to take
one's chance.

I am here already. The thing I said last time I came that there
was a storm preparing in Asia I can now explain more clearly. It
is still preparing and it threatens the British Empire. Mesopotamia
is one centre, India is the other. In India the electricity is gathering
force and before long it will be the beginning of the end. —

There are three stages to be gone through. The first begins
now with the movement of non-cooperation which will develop
into a movement of separation and independence. The second will
be a formation of something corresponding to the Sinn Fein, but
of a more carefully organised character. The third will be a final
revolution which will at once end the British rule and break up the
old India of the past. These three stages will follow rapidly on each
other and even overlap to a certain extent, the last taking up the
results of the two others ——

The time I do not see clearly; but the flood of the present
movement is likely to be three years, after which it will be replaced
by the second. That may last a little longer. In any case all will be
finished in ten years.

Not long considering that the greater part of India is still ill-
prepared even for this stage. The people have to be accustomed to
shake off their habits of timidity and dependence and work boldly
and avowedly for freedom. It is the office of the present movement
to make this change and three years is by no means a long time if
one considers the psychological revolution that is to be made. The
Swadeshi movement lasted six years and changed only one or two
provinces to a certain extent. This will last only three years and will
change the whole of India.

That is a question I cannot answer, for I am not in touch with
your destinies. But so far as I can see from my present contact with
you, the first stage is not the one for which anyone here can be

directly useful. For it will be too confused and indefinite. It is more probably the second that will demand your assistance.

That I have not yet seen. . I think it depends on what happens in China. . Japan cannot be ready to help India until the state of things in the whole of the Far East is changed. If Japan and China are ready, there will probably be a great change in Indo China and then the whole Asiatic movement can link itself together through India.

That can only bear fruit subsequently. It is essential first that India should form the clear idea of independence and then your League may be a standing suggestion to her to turn for help to the Far East. At present she is looking to the West and to Mahomedan Asia and does not imagine at all that anything can come to her from the Far East.

If you establish it now, perhaps after two years it may begin to have a meaning for India beyond what it bears on the surface.

That is all I had to say myself. I shall return another day ——

[14]

290 *(le nombre d'êtres en moi)*

My knowledge does not go so far as to explain the number in each being. The proportion varies for each man, although there are possible classifications. Each man is unique being a centre of the possibilities of the infinite. The proportions remain the same through life for beings of a certain order of development who change only within a certain settled framework as a preparation for subsequent existences; it is variable in natures which admit of considerable enlargements and changes. There are four orders in the ordinary human nature, mental, psychic, nervous, physical; four in the superior or superconscient nature. It is probably to the four human orders that the 290 belong; the physical are few in comparison; it is the three others that are most complex. All I can say is that it is a very complex calculation and I see the figures 7, 6, 7, 6, 3, recurring. I must take a little time to see if I can see farther.

Probably the 7 includes both the psychic and mental and the 6 refers to the nervous being. In that case there will be two orders each of the number 40 (four tens) in the mental, and of 30 (three tens) in the psychic, and of 60 (six tens) in the nervous, and only ten orders of 3 each in the physical. I do not yet see to what the orders correspond.

You must remember that the physical has to bear the impact of the others. Therefore, however obscure they may be, thirty is not too much for the physical being.

The two orders on each plane must be the right hand and the left hand powers. The right hand are those who open upward so as to admit the influences from above and shape them for the being; the left hand are those who open downward to the world here and the actualised experience and send them up to the higher planes. That at least is the division which seems to me to correspond best in the arrangement.

That is quite different; it belongs to a more mystic truth of which I have not the key. Is there not something in the Hebrew or the Chaldean mysteries which might shed light on it?

It may be that that belongs to some secret potentiality or totality in the four superconscient planes which seek to realise themselves on the four human levels.

No, I don't think it has anything to do with the number of beings; it is something more recondite, more symbolic.

Chandra

This is a very easy question. The girl's psychical being is entirely concentrated upon the nervous life and there she has an immense but undeveloped force. Given certain favourable circumstances of education, social surroundings etc she could have been one of the notable enchantresses of men who draw not by physical beauty but by nervous magnetism and the secret charm of the psychical being behind, but she has fallen into the wrong forms of life and this has not been developed. However the psychical being with its potentialities is there and it is that he has felt and that attracts him. Behind all that is a spirit with a very powerful will, but it is behind the veil and what comes out from it is wasted on small and trivial things. If that spirit could be roused to break the veil and come into the front, then she would be a fitting mate for him and supply much that he needs for his own fullness. That too probably the soul in him vaguely feels though it is not known to the mind, and that enters into the strength of his attraction for her. But if he cannot do this, then the attraction will fail and they will separate. I believe they have met in former lives and past connections explain the swiftness of their drawing together.

Mlle Chattopadhyay — (Mrinalini)

This is a soul of a very high order though not of the highest. A great psychic being is there behind, whose stamp has determined the whole turn of the nature. This being has a strong spiritual inspiration of which the human mind in her is vaguely conscious; but because the higher experience has not taken shape, it could not become the ruling note in the life or the nature. The next strongest thing is the emotional mind which is one of an extraordinarily intense capacity, acute and poignant in all its movements but held in by the intelligence. It is still in the emotions that she lives and they are of a great spontaneity, sincerity, clarity and strength. The intelligence is a lesser force, but well trained and developed and it is the influence again of the psychic being that has given it a literary and artistic turn. There is a suppleness and fineness in the nature proceeding from the same source. The one thing wanting is the discovery of her spiritual self; she has not yet found herself, but has spent her gifts on the things of the mind and heart, and she is conscious of the want in her. If once she completes herself, the full beauty and power of the psychical devata in her will appear and she may do a considerable work for the social and cultural change in India, her real mission in life, a work more solid than any that can be done by any of her brothers or sisters. This is a view a little from the outside. The things behind I cannot tell properly today, because I have externalised myself excessively in my effort to get into touch with the outer existence

[15]

The spirit who ordinarily comes is not here. I have taken his place ——

He has gone into the region of the pranic worlds which is near to the earth. He is drawing around him pranic forces for his next birth. At the same time he will probably come if you continue the writing. .

I am the son of the middle heavens who have often descended on the earth. I am a frequent messenger to earth of the gods of the middle heaven.

There are three heavens of the gods who work on the mind from the heights of the mental world. The first is the heaven of the mind which is in tune with the infinite, the second or middle heaven that of the luminous mental determinations, the third of the origination of mental forms.

I have no special message for you; for the action which I represent affects the work you are seeking to do only by a sort of oblique injection of its powers and suggestions. It is not in the direct line of descent; that concerns others. Therefore I leave you to put your own questions.

Yes.

My work of mentality is different. It is not concerned with the actualities of the psychic plane. Await the coming of the other for that question. I can only tell you certain possibilities of his nature, not his actual psychic condition. But it is better to know his actual condition and then the possibilities will take their proper value. At present they may seem too much in the air without their proper foundation.

I have returned. —

Chokra = Ramaiah

This is a difficult question to answer, because there is so much that is undeveloped; there are not the clear, certain and vivid forms which I found in the others. .

What I see are certain things behind that have not yet their full representation in the surface nature. There is a strong psychic, a strong pranic being associated with the nature, a mental which is very active but has not found its means of self expression in the mind. The difficulty is in some knot of the physical birth producing a physical consciousness which is unequal to the powers of the soul and a life cast into circumstances that are still more in conflict with the greater potentialities. There is behind an urge and insistent will of seeking demanding a work, an association, a knowledge, anything which will help the soul to break out from its covering sheath of the physical consciousness. But the fixities that are established by the outward being are not as yet the right forms that are wanted for his real self to emerge. They are only tentative determinations to which the stress of the urge behind gives a certain ardent and eager character. If the coverings can be broken, the powers behind will reveal their true strength.

As far as I can see, it is the mental that is the strongest obstacle. The nervous and the psychic will find their own proper development if he finds his right mind and way of action. Let him by whatever means open up his mentality, so that the soul may have a chance. The obstacle is in the formed nature, the result of past circumstances; if that is allowed to govern, it will never, however he educates it, give an open field to the soul. . He may make some progress, but not realise in this life the true soul possibilities. He must break boldly the limits of the formed mental nature and let the soul powers flood out into the consciousness. That is the one way for him as it is for many others who are in a similar case —

I continue. .   *N.P.K. Kalappa.*[5]

This is a clearer nature. . In front is a lesser mental devata with a strong and brooding will — through whom all the main soul currents come. The nervous and psychic are governed by beings who hold back until this devata has found the way for the nature. I see him very clearly. It is like a low burning red flame which grows more and more intense, supporting a shaft of golden light. Behind is a greater deva of knowledge and will who will only come forward if the lesser being succeeds in opening the way. A psychic being with great psychic power and a large emotional scope is also waiting for the same decisive movement. This much I can see for the present. Here too the problem is a development of the outward consciousness into a sufficient instrument or rather channel; but

-----

[5] *This name and the next were apparently written by the individuals concerned. — Ed.*

the obstacle here is only a comparative narrowness of the channel owing to a blocking up by received ideas and mental habits and the obstacle is one of no great force, easily removed if a purifying flood of light can be poured into the channel.

That I cannot tell you. It depends on your bringing forward of your powers. I have no sufficient view of the future.

———

Ka. Neela Kantaiyar.

Here the power of the nature is psychic-intellectual; the presiding devata of the being sends down only an influence which turns into a seeking without a definite orientation. The activity has been governed by an intermediate being who is psychic with a turn to a curious action of the intelligence. The being has not in this case been concentrated round this governing action. There is in it a turn to a larger seeking. There are in this case too greater powers who can come forward if the chance is given. The presiding devata is one with a rainbow light around him, but there is a shaft of white descending on it from above. The psychic is of a very ruddy rose light. These are the two chief powers behind the veil of the physical consciousness.

[16]

30 corps physiques

Yes, I am here. —

The thirty are three tens. They are those who support the physical consciousness, not the physical body alone, but the obscurer consciousness of which it is the visible representation. In this consciousness there are three layers, one which receives the mental impressions and store[s] them in the corporeal system, so that it responds to a sum of habitual mental sanskaras; the second, which similar[ly] responds to the vital and preserves the habit of replying to habitual vital impulses, the third of a more purely material kind. These beings are not intelligent, but obscure and fixed in their habits. When a change has to be made, it is they who are the last support to a resistance to the change, but also if they can be made to reply to new things, they help to make them fixed in the physical consciousness and thus to assure their stability.

Yes; only the number may vary.

That depends on the plasticity and richness of the physical consciousness. . The more plastic, the more numerous the beings of this order. It may vary from three to ninety, or even many more in extraordinary cases.

The number can always increase and must if there is a development of this part of the being.

Yes. .

No. – They belong to the invisible world of matter. It is only a part of the physical that is visible to the human senses.

At least three.

Yes.

It is prepared during the gestation; but really determined before birth.

No, not freely; they are attracted

No. I only explain the information given to you. I see only the psychical.

I think he should develop a little first, it is not always good to give information about themselves to people in a certain stage of development; it is better that their minds should be fluid.

No –

There are strong reasons against giving this information.

=

You are like that, first, because of the powers that are associated with you, one of whom has nothing to do with reason, but only with his own vehement impulses and desires. As for the form of your question, I might suggest as a paradox that you are unreasonable because you reason too much; that is you support too much your unreason by your reason[6]

[17]

The traditions are symbolic, not exact. The system of the Puranas was not created by anybody, but was a development of very ancient traditions infinitely older than the historic culture to

---

[6] *This last paragraph was marked with a line in the margin sometime after the writing was communicated. — Ed.*

which the name of Puranic has been given. The present Puranas are very late creations with many ancient things imbedded in them and mixed with much of a recent creation.

No, but the traditions they contain are often older than the extant Veda.

I could hardly say. There is much that has survived from old civilisations that have perished, but of course in a changed form. One would have to count their origin perhaps by tens of thousands of years. There are things also that were believed in old times, forgotten and again recovered from the mental planes. It is difficult to disentangle the various materials and say which dates from what time. The theory of the Kalpas has existed in one form or another from times lost in the mist of oblivion.

I composed many things, but they are not extant.

Vyasa is a name under which many different people have been confused together. If you mean Krishna Dwaipayana, he is somewhere in the planes of being which are at the height of what may be called the mental heavens.

They cannot be numbered. Besides these existed through centuries after centuries in long generations of Rishis.

The seven Rishis are a tradition. The original seven Rishis refer to seven personalities who did not belong to the earth. The seven of tradition have not been on the earth since the Vedic times.

I know nothing about the White Lodge. I should fancy they belong to the lower worlds between the pranic and the mental. They are certainly not the Vedic Rishis—though the name given to one of them is that of a later Rishi of the times of the Upanishads. Yes.

I do not think it is the same; but I cannot say certainly, for I do not know where Kutthumi is.

=

The best thing, I should imagine, would be to get them to enlarge their Theosophy by bringing in a current of new and upward pointing ideas; but that could not be done without either starting from their present ideas as a valid point of departure or breaking their framework and the latter would not be tolerated while the present control existed. It is rather through some kind of communication and indirect influence that they could be helped, but I could not say exactly how. If anything is possible, it will spring out of circumstances and individual relations.

There are many ways of changing, but the most common is by a pressure from above. All that develops in the mental, psychic, vital has an influence which is precipitated into the obscure physical consciousness and works there more or less slowly. Certain slight changes are always being produced, others of a more important kind occasionally. The physical beings receive these influences and assimilate them in the already established physical consciousness and there make of them a sure basis for the mental, psychic and vital habits. These change decisively in proportion as they can get the guardians of the physical consciousness to accept and support them. A great force of will from above can sometimes make abrupt changes. But ordinarily the movement is more or less slow and within well established limits. Outside these limits these beings offer a strong resistance to any change, unless it confines itself to the higher activities. In proportion as a great change of mental thought for instance tries to affect the vital and physical being, the opposition becomes strong and is usually obstinate. It is sometimes rapidly overborne, sometimes can only be obtained[7] by a slow process of transformation in the sanskaras of the physical beings. All this is in the ordinary kind of development. It is only if there is a great influx of power from above the mental that very extraordinary changes can usually be made. In that case the physical beings are sometimes overpowered, sometimes enlightened, sometimes rejected and replaced by others.

It must however be noted that abnormal changes of a purely physical kind are a different matter. They are the most difficult to accomplish. For there [these][8] physical beings are in their own domain and exercising their strongest right which is to prevent any violent change in the organised habits of physical Nature. It needs

---

[7] *Written above "got rid", which was cancelled; an "of" after "got rid" remained uncancelled in the MS. — Ed.*

[8] *Cancelled in the MS, perhaps when the writing was reread. Since the previous word, "there", could also be read as "these", it seems possible that "there these" was misread as "these these", resulting in the cancellation. — Ed.*

either an exceptional action of the physical Nature itself or an action of the suggestive mental powers in abnormal circumstances liberated from the usual obstacles or a powerful influx from the supramental and spiritual to change these things.

Do you mean, on the physical level?

That is when other physical beings with a different set of impulses are allowed to invade the established circle of physical things and replace the guardians of the old order. That is part of the process of the great crises of evolution.

He would either be taken up into some higher part of the being and form an element of Rudra force in the totality without being any longer active as a separate element of the personality, or else, if he remained as a separate part of the personality, he would be a sort of enlightened and passive instrument for the Purusha with a view to a certain divine action of a kind it is difficult to describe. There would be a divine use of the Rakshasa force changed from a nervous egoism to a sort of powerful dynamic utility on that plane, just as the animal power in the body might be divinely used for the greater purposes of the divinised Purusha.

[18]

The last time I was near the earth, this time I am beginning to withdraw. I think before long I must depart to prepare during a sufficiently long period for my rebirth among men.

Yes; but an interval of preparation is necessary during which I must gather forces on the intermediary planes. After that I shall have again to enter into relation with the material plane, but of course in a different way, and gather powers and influences of the earth to form my earthly basis of personality, mind, life and body.

Yes.

I believe so; but it may be either in the direct surroundings or in dependent circles. .

Possibly, ten or fifteen years. .

No. That would not fulfil my personal need which is to repair the mistake I made in my last existence.

The sign is that I shall be known by my powers of renewing the link of memory between my own times and the new age. I shall be one who brings from that ancient past a power of realisation which shall enrich the elements of the new mankind. If this is not enough, then you may easily know me by seeing in vision the form of what I was renewed though changed in the form of my new body.

A seer with knowledge can know the identity of one he sees even though not known before to the physical mind.

It will be begun.

That is not necessary. That I should be directly descended.

No; I have not the physical vision. It is not always easy to see from a distance, and if I depend on any of you, I may be too much influenced by your impressions.

I cannot say, certainly; but I think you are having too fixed and limited ideas about the matter. There will be, I think, not one, but several centres, and the whole thing will be of a fluid character before there is any decisive formation. I should say, do not fix things beforehand, but let the force that descends have freedom of movement, the freedom as of waters descending and flowing in many directions, afterwards the solid formation.

My opinion is of no great value in that matter. The progress in these matters comes usually in two ways; either by a violent conversion which changes in a short time the whole direction of the nature, or by a slow and difficult process with many movements and reversions in which the progress made can only be estimated after a lapse of time by something having disappeared after alternate returns and weakenings or something new having been formed which attempts to come, then disappears, then comes again until it has made its foothold. Possibly, the effort in you has not decidedly taken either course, or it has attempted the first method and, failing, fallen back on the slower movement. I cannot say really, because it depends on a power which is not the psychical and which in your case is hidden behind a veil. In such cases, the outward signs are deceptive.

Don't put it in that form, because so put it is an already existing idea and attracts around it many difficulties. The word asrama and its concomitant associations, to begin with, should be cast away. Make the thing new in some flame of revealing intuition and then the chances of success will be real.

Let us say, the exchange-house of meeting influences of the self-creating superrace.

Words have power and names are often traps.

Once I go, I can no longer communicate.

I cannot say yet; it will not be immediately. .

To most; it will not be so to me. .

The pain of descent and self-limitation and loss of self in the body. Always the other planes are freer than the material; birth is usually a sacrifice.

Yes; they have the desire; but the fulfilment of the desire still involves a sacrifice.

Yes, a compression, that is the word.

Because I shall descend with a fuller consciousness and with the impulse that makes the superman. A greater Shakti will support me. I cannot explain all the process, but I know it will be so.

Death is usually a struggle. The struggle to get out of the compression is often as painful as the effort to get into it. But to some death is easy.

He may have in the end many ways, but the physical birth will continue. .

The superman will take all the ways that are necessary for the divine design in the evolution; if physical birth ceases to be a part of the plan, it will for him discontinue; but there will be no other reason for him to avoid it.

Make your question more precise.

No, it must be prepared in actual man. It can come by a rapid change, a decisive descent of the divine supermind into the human being.

It would be impossible for them to be born in the monkey except by a miraculous descent of the thinking mind into the life mind of the animal. How do you suppose a human couple to be suddenly born of a couple of monkeys? By stages of ascent, each involving an influx of more and more mind, the first into an original animal, not necessarily the ape, but one that has now disappeared after providing the necessary basis.

Suppose, an animal that has evolved the life mind to its

highest limits of curiosity and adaptive invention and developed a favourable body. Suppose, an effort of Nature in certain individuals of the kind breaking a barrier between the animal mind and the secret greater mind which is subliminally brooding there in Nature, so that there is the influx I speak of, to however limited an extent. There is the seed man. Suppose a progression, more and more effort of progress, more and more result both of mental development and physical change. The lower kinds which are only a bridge, neither animals, nor complete men, disappear; the full basis of man is established. After that the real human progress. May it not so have happened?

[19]

The last time I made a mistake. It is only after the second month of the next year that I retire from the earth proximity. I imagined that a certain necessary development would proceed more quickly than it has actually done.

No, I have not met him. In any case the photograph by itself would tell me little. The fields of the psychic world are too numerous for meetings of this kind to be common, especially between souls descending to renew their touch with earth and others ascending and recently come from it.

I don't quite seize the question.

What two kinds of the Divine? There are many aspects, infinite movements, but I do not catch the distinction you make, I mean the exact significance of what you mean. The Bhakta pure is limited, so is the man of intelligence. But knowledge can mount to the unknown and manifest it, so too can love or Ananda mount to the unseized and bring it down into manifestation. It is the power of the soul that matters, not so much the way; that is to say, I cannot say that one way is superior to the other.

A greater completeness is always superior to a lesser completeness; but also an extreme power of one can do miracles. .

Be wise as a serpent and mild as a dove.

It is a possible approach, but it wants intuition and a happy seizing of occasion to deal with these people. What I would suggest

is to take hold of them by the strong side of Theosophy and not
to press too much on the weak side. People attached to a fixed
and traditional thinking — for it has become traditional with them
— have not usually the open nature which can bear exposure of
the weakness of what they believe in. One or two may profit by
that method, the most will react in a hostile fashion. On the other
hand if the strong side is seized and broadened to its real issues,
they may be led without knowing it to enlarge themselves and
meet with a good disposition the atmosphere of larger thought you
bring them. This reception is needed, because it is the difference
of the two atmospheres that is likely to be a stumbling block. The
second thing is if you can make a link with them through the active
side of their ideas. The outer side of the practical idea you have is
favourable from this standpoint, because it can easily be used as
a means to bring out the broader side of their own principles of
action. The ulterior motive has to be kept in the shadow for the
present; a time may come when they will receive it, but that will be
after the present dominating influence in the society has receded.
The third thing is to mix mainly on the one hand with the larger,
on the other with the simpler and more candid minds among them;
leave aside those who are in between. Be careful with Mrs Besant;
she is a difficult and deceptive personality.

The strong side is first their seeking after truth, which is constantly moving near things that are true without quite seizing them;
the weak side is the imaginations, fancies and rigid formulas which
they build up like a wall between the truth and their search. If you
read their books, or listen to their ideas with patience, you will
easily be able to distinguish the two elements and bring out what I
call the strong side. Then there are their larger ideas which admit
truth in all religions and many philosophies and their attempt to
find a principle of unity for men of all races and peoples, etc. There
is much else which one can seize with advantage if one is in their
company and comes to know what is behind this movement of
theosophy. .

A very difficult question to answer. Everything depends on the
psychic impression you make and on keeping up that impression in
her psychic being, if that is favourable. The difficulty is in all the

rest of her nature which is full of egoism and of tricks of intelligence and tricks of passion which she herself cannot understand and that may trip you up at any moment. I really cannot say how to be careful. . It is a matter of vigilance and self-adaptation as to which no specific suggestion can be given. Probably she will be very busy and you need not see too much of her. Only see her when you are yourself in a good mood. She is psychically sensitive in a certain fashion and when well impressed psychically can be openminded up to a certain degree. If you are yourself well disposed and not too critical of her weaknesses, you can create a favourable magnetic interchange which is of more importance in her case than the mental relation.

Appendix

Material from Disciples' Notebooks

MISCELLANEOUS NOTES, c. 1914

[1]

Parabrahman: —
Asad Atman
Sad Atman

Sat	Satyaloka	Mahakarana
Chit	Tapoloka	Mahatapas
Ananda	Janaloka	Mahabuddhi
Karana	Maharloka	Vijnanam
Sukshma	Swarloka	
	Chandraloka	Buddhi
	Swarga	Manas
	Bhuvar	Prana, chitta
Sthula	Bhu	Annam

Sukshma: —

	Atman	
	Sat	Satyam
	Chit	Tapas
	Ananda	Mahabuddhi
Karana in Sukshma	Manasbuddhi	Higher buddhi or Intuitive Reason
		Reason
		Understanding — manas in the buddhi
Sukshma proper	Manas	Sensational mind
	Chitta	
Sthula in Sukshma	Sukshma prana	
	Annamaya	

Karana: —

	Atman	
Parardha in Karana	Satyam	
	Tapas	
	Mahabuddhi	
Karanam	Satyadarshanam	Seer, Rishi or Drashta
	Satyakalpana	Prophet, Poet
	Satyavadanam	Philosopher
Sukshma in Karana	Indriyam	Perception of all kinds
	Bhava	Feeling
Sthula in Karana	Bhoga	Prana
	Karma	Anna

Ananda — Swabhava — Mahabuddhi: —

(1) Anantyam   Anantagunam

(2) Nirgunam   Sukha (shanti)   Pravritti ⎫ Jnanam
                                   Nivritti ⎭ Realisation
(3) Trigunatitam   of the Infinite

(4) Sagunam i.e. Aparardha Swabhava — Traigunyamayi Prakriti
      Sattwa
      Rajas
      Tamas

Tapas: —
   Tattwas: —
   (1) Purusha   (1) Prajna   (1) Parameshwara
   (2) Prakriti   (2) Hiranyagarbha   (2) Shakti
                  (3) Virat

OM

Satyam: —
   Manifest Atma: —
      A. (1) Anirdeshyam
         (2) Vasudeva
            and Shaktis
      B. The Four: —
         (1) Mahavira
         (2) Balarama
         (3) Pradyumna
         (4) Aniruddha
            and their Shaktis

---

1. Brahmana	Mahavira	Jnanam, Mahima	Maheshwari
2. Kshatriya	Balarama	Force (Viryam), Raudryam	Mahakali
3. Vaishya	Pradyumna	Love (Prema), Danam	Mahalakshmi
4. Shudra	Aniruddha	Desire (Kama), Worldly Reason	Mahasaraswati

---

Atma: —

Mahakarana	Satya	Sat	Sankalpa	Prajna	
Mahatapas	Tapas	Chit or Shakti (Will)	Will	Virat	Parardha
Mahabuddhi	Jana	Ananda	Swabhava	Hiranya-garbha	
Karana	Mahas	Vijnana	Satyam	Prajna	
Sukshma	Swar	Antah-karana	Vikalpa	Hiranya-garbha	Aparardha
Sukshma-Sthula	Bhuvar	Prana	Vasana		
Sthula	Bhu	Anna	Sanghata	Virat	

[The first piece on this page was revised by Sri Aurobindo;
the next two pieces were written by him.]

Kaivalyananda	Satya	Sat-kosha	Prakasha	Shiva
Chidananda	Tapas	Tapas-kosha	Agni (Fire)	Agni
Shuddhananda	Jana	Ananda-kosha	Vidyut	Prajapati
Chidghanananda	Vijnana	Vijnana-kosha	Jyoti	Surya
Ahaitukananda	Manas	Manah-kosha	Tejas	Chandra
Premananda	Chitta	Prana-kosha	Dhuma	Vayu
Kamananda	Deha	Anna-kosha	Chhaya	Prithivi

Kamananda
1. Maithunananda
2. Vishayananda   Sense-objects
3. Tivrananda   Thrill
4. Raudrananda   Pain
5. Vaidyutananda   Electric

Pashu (Vanara)	Bodily life	Prana & Deha	Play, Eating, Sleep
Pisacha	Jnana of bodily life		Curiosity, Science
Pramatha	Ananda of bodily life	Manas	Aesthetic
Rakshasa ⎤ Yaksha	Tapas of do		Egoism, Prana
Asura ⎬ Gandharva	Buddhi		Intellect, Feeling
Deva ⎦ etc.	Karana		Knowledge, Joy, Surrender

Siddhadeva   Ananda
Siddhasura   Tapas
Siddha Purusha   Satya

[2]

Parabrahman:—

Asad Atman	Non-being	Both the same; Asad Atman containing the negation of universe; Sad [Atman] containing the potentiality of universe
Sad Atman	Being	

Mahakarana (cause of all causes)	Satyaloka	Sat	Supreme principle
Mahatapas (supreme force)	Tapoloka	Chit	
Mahajana (productive principle)	Janaloka	Ananda	
Mahabuddhi or Karana	Maharloka	Vijnanam	
Antahkaran or Sukshma i.e. inner instrument	Swarloka		
	Chandraloka	Buddhi	
	Swarga	Manas	
	Bhuvar	Prana, chitta	
Karan or Sthula i.e. outer instrument	Bhu	Annam	

Sukshma:—

Atman

Sukshma	Sat	Satyam
	Chit	Tapas
	Ananda	Jana

Karana in Sukshma
or divya ketu   Divine perception   Higher Buddhi or Intuitive Reason

Sukshma proper		Reason	Lower Buddhi
		Understanding— manas in the buddhi	
	Manas	Sensational mind	
		Manas Chitta or Emotional mind	
	Chitta	Passive consciousness or Passive memory	

Sthula in Sukshma	Sukshma prana	Mental vitality or purely nervous mind
Sthula	{ Sthula prana	Vitality or Physical nervous system
	Annamaya	Physical substance

Vijnana or Karana:—

	Atman	
Vijnanamaya	{ Satyam	
	Tapas	
	Jana	

Karana proper	{ Satyadarshanam	{ Higher Karana (i.e. drishti, shruti)
		Lower Karana (i.e. siddha buddhi and viveka*)
	Satyakalpana	Lower Shruti
	Satyavadanam	Lower Viveka
Sukshma in Karana	{ Satya Indriyam	Perception of all kinds
	Satya Bhoga	Feeling
Sthula in Karana	{ Satya Bhoga	Prana
	Satya Karma	Anna

Ananda—Swabhava:—

Nivritti   Pravritti
    Nirgunam   (1) Anantyam or Anantagunam
                            (2) Trigunatitam
                            (3) Traigunyamaya Swabhava
                                (i) Sattwa—prakasha
                                (ii) Rajas—pravritti
                                (iii) Tamas—shama

---

* Viveka is not conscience but true judgment between higher and lower, true and false, right and wrong. [*The last six words were added by Sri Aurobindo in his own hand.*]

Tapas:—
  Tattwas:—

Purusha or Ishwara	(1) Prajna	Prakriti or Shakti
	(2) Hiranyagarbha	
	(3) Virat	

OM

Satyam:—

Anirdeshyam Krishna
              (Mahamaya)

(1) Mahavira (Maheshwari)	Brahmana	Jnanam, Mahima
(2) Balarama (Mahakali)	Kshatriya	Viryam, Raudryam
(3) Pradyumna (Mahalakshmi)	Vaishya	Prema, Danam
(4) Aniruddha (Mahasaraswati)	Shudra	Kama, karma, vishaya buddhi

[3]

Tat — Asat ⎫
       Sat   ⎬ Purusha and Prakriti

Tat is the unknowable Brahman of which you cannot say that it exists or does not exist because it cannot be defined as that which we know or understand by the idea of existence. Therefore it is not Sat. At the same time it is not Asat or non-existent because it contains existence in itself.

By Asat or non-being we mean something beyond which is a contradiction of existence. It is generally considered as a sort of nothingness because it is nothing that we call existence. There is nothing in it that we can perceive or realise as something. Tat contains both Sat and Asat; but it is neither of them.

By Sat we mean pure existence not limited by qualities, infinite and eternal and unchanging, which is at the same time the source and foundation of all the worlds and the whole universe.

Sat—Purusha and Prakriti
Brahman representing itself in the universe as the stable, by immutable Existence (Sat), is Purusha, God, Spirit; representing [itself] as the motional by its power of active Consciousness (Chit) [it] is Nature, Force or World-Principle (Prakriti, Shakti, Maya). The play of these two principles is the life of the universe.

Prakriti [is] executive Nature as opposed to Purusha, which is the Soul governing, taking cognizance of and enjoying the works of Prakriti; Shakti [is] the self-existent, self-cognitive Power of the Lord (Ishwara, Deva, Purusha), which expresses itself in the workings of Prakriti.

[4]

Divine	*Human*
Sat	Annam
Chit-Tapas	Prana
Ananda	Manas-Chitta
Vijnana	Buddhi
Ishwara	Aham

Seven Planes

$$\left\{\begin{array}{l}\text{Sat}\\\text{Chit-Tapas}\\\text{Ananda}\end{array}\right.$$
Vijnana
$$\left\{\begin{array}{l}\text{Manas-Chitta}\\\text{Prana}\\\text{Annam}\end{array}\right.$$

Sat   is essence of being, pure, infinite and undivided.
Chit-Tapas   is pure energy of consciousness, free in its rest or action, sovereign in its will.
Ananda   is Beatitude, the bliss of pure conscious existence and energy.

Vijnana	—Supra-mental knowledge—is the Causal Idea which, by supporting and secretly guiding the confused activities of Mind, Life and Body ensures and compels the right arrangement of the Universe.
Buddhi	is the lower divided intelligence as opposed to Vijnana.
Manas-chitta	is the life of sensations and emotions which are at the mercy of the outward touches of life and matter and their positive or negative reactions, joy and grief, pleasure and pain.
Prana	is the hampered dynamic energies which, feeding upon physical substances, are dependent on and limited by their sustenance; also [it] is the lower or vital energy.
Annam	is the divisible being which founds itself on the constant changeableness of physical substance.

Sat	Immortality, pure essence
Chit-Tapas	Free rest or free action
	Sovereignty of will
Ananda	Pure bliss
Vijnana	Revelation
	Inspiration
	Intuition
	Discrimination
Buddhi	Perception
	Imagination
	Reasoning
	Judgment
Manas-Chitta	Sattwic—Science, philosophy, thought (intellectual)
	1. Aesthetic—sense of beauty
	art, poetry, sculpture
	2. Religious and moral—virtuous, holy, good
Prana	Rajasic—desire, emotion, passion
Annam	Tamasic—food, money, physical health, play

Pravritti   Nature's tendency or impulse to action
Nivritti   Withdrawing from that tendency or impulse to action

Buddhi		*Vijnana*
Perception		Revelation = Pratyaksha or Drishti
Imagination		Inspiration = Sruti
Reason	Smriti {	Intuition
Judgment		Discrimination = Viveka

[5]

The Chakras

Above the head	Sahasradala	Jnanam
Between the eyes	Ajnachakra	Drishti
In the throat	Vishuddha	Vak
In the heart	Anahata	Feeling, sensation, etc.
In the navel	Manipura	Instincts
Above the linga	Swadhishthana	Kama (desire)
	Muladhara	

The movement of pranas in the body

There are five pranas, viz: prana, apana, samana, vyana and udana.

The movement of the prana is from the top of the body to the navel, apana from Muladhara to the navel. Prana and apana meet together near the navel and create samana. The movement of vyana is in the whole body. While samana creates bhuta from the foods, vyana distributes it into the body. The movement of udana is from the navel to the head. Its work is to carry the virya (tejas) to the head. The movement of udana is different to the Yogin. Then its movement is from the Muladhara (from where it carries the virya to the crown of the head and turn[s] it [into][1] ojas) to the crown of the head.

---

[1] MS (scribal) out to

The colours

Violet — religion, ideality, spirituality

Yellow — intellect, perception, activity and flexibility of mind

Orange — psychical power

Black — darkness, inertia, melancholy, pessimism, timidity, etc.

Grey — despondency and dullness

Red — activity; or if a deep angry colour, anger; or if scarlet, lust; if rose, love.

White — purity, strength, etc.

Green — beneficency, unselfishness, readiness to serve without respect to one's own desire or ambition.

Dull green — bad qualities of prana, jealousy etc.

Blue — Spirituality more of the Bhakti type

Flaming golden yellow — Vijnana

[6]

Objects of Yoga

To put it in a word, the object of Yoga is God or the Divine or the Supreme whatever our conception of these things may be. There are minor objects of Yoga which are merely parts or separate aspects of the general object. We are composed of being, consciousness, energy and delight represented to us as life, knowledge, force and power, emotion, sensation and desire. The object of Yoga is to turn all these things towards God. Therefore to become one with God, to be Divine and live a Divine Life is the first object of Yoga. The second is to know God in Himself and in ourselves and in everything. The third is to make ourselves one with the Divine Will and to do in our life a Divine Work by means of the Divine Power using us as an instrument. The fourth object is to enjoy God in all beings, in all things and in all that happens.

Since the Life is to be Divine there must be *siddhi* or Perfection of the Being.

The difference between the Divine Being and Divine Life and ours is that we are in the limited ego, confined to our own physical and mental experiences while that is beyond ego infinite eternal and all-embracing. Therefore we have to get rid of the Ego in order to be Divine. Ego persists because of three things; first because we think we are the body; secondly because of desire; and thirdly because of the mental idea that I am a separate being existing in my own mind and body independently of everything and everybody else. We have therefore to know ourselves, to realise that we are not the body, nor the Prana, nor the mind and to find out our *real Self*.

That is called Atmajnana. Secondly we have to get rid of the idea of ourselves and others as separate being to realise everything as one Brahman or one Purusha or Ishwara manifesting himself in different names and forms. This Self and the Brahman or Ishwara are the same. We have to know what it is, how it manifests itself in the world and beings that we see. All this we have to realise in our experience and not merely know by the intellect. We have to realise It as Sachchidananda and to become *that* ourselves.

Thirdly we have to get rid of desire and replace it by the Ananda of Sachchidananda. After that in order to live and act in the world we have to act as mere instruments so the Divine Force which we must realise as the sole Power which acts in the world and we must get rid of the idea that actions are ours or that the fruit of the action belongs to us personally. The only work we have to do in the world is to perfect ourselves, carry out whatever the Divine Power wills that we should do and so far as possible help others to perfect themselves and help the life of humanity to become Divine.

[7]

Methods of Yoga
(Reproduction from memory)[2]

The first two things necessary for the practice of Yoga [are][3] Will and Abhyasa. In the course of Yoga these two things give helping hands to the perfection of the being unto the very end. Slowly and steadily, whether conscious or unconscious to the being itself, they are

---

[2] *Oral remarks by Sri Aurobindo recorded from memory by a disciple. Much of the wording clearly is not Sri Aurobindo's.* — Ed.
[3] MS (scribal) is

performing their functions in the onward march of human evolution. Be we unconscious of them, it will take a pretty long time to attain to that perfection. But once we are conscious, then we become the Will itself. Consciously we can quicken the progress. This method gives rise to individual perfected beings. As before, they will not see glimpses of the Light of Truth. They will ever be seeing the Eternal Truth. They will turn the darkness around them and in them, into Light.

Hitherto, we should have felt a certain amount of difficulty in putting into Abhyasa what we have willed. Now there will be no more putting into Abhyasa but simply we will be seeing the march of progress without the least idea of strain felt by us. So first let us will in order to be not weak and unconscious but strong and conscious. Then there will be no more difficulty.

Until then we have to practise Yoga by two important means — by means of Purusha and by means of Prakriti.

Means of Purusha: — An ordinary man thinks he desires, he feels and so on. But what we are to do is to separate ourselves from desire, feeling etc. Whenever desire comes, we must realise that we are not desiring but only realise it as the coming and going of Desire. So also with the feeling, thinking etc. For instance, when [a] certain anguish comes, an ordinary man thinks and feels that he is lost and so on. He weeps bitterly and reduces himself to a mere crawling worm. We have to think that that anguish is a kind of action or reaction, going on in the heart. Anguish cannot affect me. I am the unsullied Self; it cannot touch me.

Means of Prakriti: — Whenever the thinking part of man is active, we notice very clearly that the work is going on in a place somewhere above the forehead. The action is centred in the heart, when the feelings are awake in him. In both the cases, the self takes the heart and mind for its theatre of action. In the one case, we are those thoughts and in the other, we are those feelings. Putting this in plain words, our actions proceed either from the heart or from the mind, while the actions of the animals proceed from the senses. We see the vast difference between an animal and a man. So if man transfers his centre of heart and mind, to that of a higher one, think how grand the God-man would be! That centre according to the psychology of the Hindus is Vijnana. This is just above the crown of [the] head. This is known as Sahasradala or the place where the Shakti is situated. From this seat of activity, all actions emanate.

Therefore the first Sadhana is not to feel ourselves either in the heart or in the mind but there just above the crown of [the] head. By these two means, we separate ourselves from body, life and mind. On account of this, misery cannot affect us and we will be above happiness and misery. Apart from all these, the main thing we effect thereby is, we will be in a position henceforward, to become one with the Brahman and to realise that everything is Brahman and everything is only one of the several forms, names and colours etc., of that one Vast Brahman. Whenever we see people walking along the road, we will no more see them as several different beings but as several forms of one vast undivided Brahman. As [a] rose is the manifestation of form, colour, odour so the Brahman is the manifestation of so many things we perceive by the senses and think by the mind etc.

Along with these, we must put into practice one after the other what we are going to see hereafter as the Sapta Chatusthayas. They are namely Samata, Shakti, Vijnana, Sharira, Karma, Brahman and Siddhi Chatusthayas. Chatusthayas means four divisions. These seven Chatusthayas have been arranged in their natural and logical order. But it is not required of you to get them in practice in this given order. One may begin with a chatusthaya which [one] finds to be easier and in this way he is expected to practise. Why they are arranged in this way, how we are to effect them in us, when we will have success, all will be known to us when we finish writing and sincerely practise.

SAPTA CHATUSTHAYA—SCRIBAL VERSION

I. Samata Chatusthaya

Samata, Shanti, Sukha, Hasya (Atmaprasada)

Negative Samata	Positive Samata
Titiksha	Sama Rasa — mind and intellect
Udasinata	Sama Bhoga — prana
Nati	Sama Ananda — spirit

Samata is accepting everything in the same way without any disturbance in any part of the being. Disturbance is caused [by][1] the want of harmony between the Chit-shakti in myself and the contacts of Chit-shakti outside. Pain, grief, dislike etc. are merely the system's way of saying that it objects to a particular contact because of want of harmony. The system cannot bear an inharmonious contact or even a pleasant one if it is too intense or too prolonged. Disgust, fear, horror, shame are attempts of the system to repel the unpleasant contact and defend itself.

Titiksha means the power of endurance. You bear the unpleasant contact yourself standing back from it with a watching mind and teaching the system to bear it.

What follows is Udasinata. Udasina means standing high. Udasinata is indifference, the Purusha standing high above these contacts and not minding what they are.

Nati is the subsequent one. It is the feeling of submission to God's Will, all contacts being regarded as the touches of God Himself.

Sama Rasa or equal Rasa from all things, happenings, experiences, objects etc. we have to take through our mind and intellect.

Sama Bhoga is the equal enjoyment in the Prana of all things, happenings, experiences, objects etc.

---

[1] MS (scribal) owing to

Sama Ananda is the joy of Unity in everything and with every-thing.

Sama Rasa and Sama Bhoga cannot be secured unless we have Sama Ananda, but it is difficult for Sama Ananda to come unless the mind and Prana have been taught Samata in Rasa and Bhoga.

[The] result of complete Samata is complete Shanti; on the other hand if there is any touch of anxiety, grief, disappointment, depression etc., it is a sign that Samata is not complete. When we get complete Shanti, then we get complete Sukham. Shanti is negative; it is a state of freedom from trouble. Sukham is positive; it is not merely freedom from grief and pain, but a positive state of happiness in the whole system.

Atmaprasada is a state of clearness, purity, contentment in the whole self, i.e. [the] essence of Sukham. When Sukham begins to become strong Ananda, then it is Hasya, a state of positive joy and cheerfulness which takes the whole of Life and the world as a pleasant and amusing play.

II. Shakti Chatusthaya
Viryam, Shakti, Daivi Prakriti, Sraddha

Viryam: Chaturvarnya in guna
Brahmana, Kshatriya, Vaishya, Shudra

Brahmana: Dhairyam, Jnanalipsa, Jnanaprakasha, Brahmavar-chasya.

Shakti is the right guna and right state of activity or right elements of shakti-character in all parts of the system. The chaturvarnya in guna may be called Virya. It is the qualities of the four varnas in charac-ter. The perfect man has all the four in him, although one usually predominates and gives the character its general type. First, a man should have Brahmana qualities, [those of][2] the man of knowledge. He should have, first, the general temperament of the Brahmin, that is to say calmness, patience, steadiness and thoughtfulness, which may all be expressed by the word Dhairyam. Then he should have the

---

2 MS *(scribal)* or

tendency towards knowledge, especially the Divine Knowledge, but also all kinds of knowledge on all kinds of subjects, with the necessary mental openness and curiosity. This is Jnanalipsa. The Brahmin has not only the thirst for knowledge but also a general clearness of mind and its tendency to be easily illuminated by ideas and to receive the truth. This is Jnanaprakasha. He has also a spiritual force which comes from knowledge and purity. This is Brahmavarchasya.

Kshatriya: [Abhaya, Sahasa],[3] Yasholipsa, Atma Shakti (Atma Slagha)

There should also be the qualities of the Kshatriya, the qualities of the man of action or the fighter. The first of these is courage and it is of two kinds — Abhaya or passive courage which is alarmed by no danger and shrinks from no peril that offers itself and from no misfortune or suffering. The second is Sahasa or active courage, that is to say, the daring to undertake any enterprise however difficult or apparently impossible and carry it through in spite of all dangers, suffering, failures, obstacles and oppositions. For this, two other things are necessary. [First,] a tendency of the nature to insist on the battle and victory and effort and triumph, i.e. Yasholipsa. Secondly, there must be a strong self-confidence and a high idea of the power that is in one's self. This is Atma Shakti or Atma Slagha.

Vaishya: Vyaya, Kaushala, Dana, Bhogalipsa

The Vaishya qualities are also necessary for action and enjoyment. The first is the readiness to spend labour, resources, materials, means and life itself quite freely, taking great risks of loss in order to secure great gains. This may be called Vyaya. But with this there must be skill in the use of means and methods and their proper disposition in order to secure the end and also the knowledge of what is or is not possible to be gained by a particular means or method or a particular expense. There should be a sense of proportion, of order, and a skill [in][4] arrangement and management. All this may be called Kaushala. Also in the use of one's possessions, there are two other qualities of [the] Vaishya which are necessary. [First there must be] the readiness

---

[3] *MS (scribal)* Courage
[4] *MS (scribal)* and

to give no less than to receive and to share with the world what one gets from the world. This is [the][5] nature of love as it is ordinarily practised; [this][6] giving and receiving may be called Dana. And then there should be a tendency to enjoy, i.e. Bhogalipsa.

Shudra: [Kama, Prema,] Dasyalipsa, Atmasamarpana.

The qualities of the Shudra are no less important. The Vaishya has the spirit of order, opposition and interchange. The Shudra has the spirit of service. Service is governed by two motives: first desire or kama, secondly love or prema. In the perfect man, Kama should take the form of an interest in the bodily well-being of the world and a wish to see that physically it lacks nothing. Love in [the] Shudra is not like that of [the] Vaishya, for it seeks no return. It is governed by the third quality of the Shudra, the desire to serve and this in the perfect man becomes the desire to serve God-in-all. This is Dasyalipsa. The perfection of the Shudra nature is in self-surrender, the giving of one's self without demanding a return. This is Atmasamarpana.

The nature of the Brahmana is knowledge, of the Kshatriya force and courage, of the Vaishya skill in works, and of the Shudra self-giving and service. The perfect character possesses all of these; for they are necessary for the perfect action.

Shakti

Shakti is a general force by which each of the four parts of the system (the body, the Prana, the Chitta and the Buddhi) is kept at its highest state of perfection. The perfect state of the body consists in four things, a sense of entire lightness (Laghuta), a sense of strength and energy (Balam), a sense of [a] certain mass and force (Mahattwa) and the power of containing without strain or reaction any working however intense and constant, of energy however great and [puissant].[7] This is Dharana Samarthyam.

The perfect state of Prana consists in a sense of fullness of vital force (Purnata), of general clearness and cheerfulness (Prasannata), of equality in all experiences, shocks and contacts (Samata), and in the

---

[5] MS *(scribal)* a
[6] MS *(scribal)* a
[7] MS *(scribal)* possible

capacity to take all enjoyment of the world without desire but also without exhaustion and satiety. This is Bhoga Samarthyam.

The perfect state of Chitta consists in a sense of richness and gladness of feeling (Snigdhata), of abounding moral power and energy (Tejas), in a confidence [in the][8] divine grace and help and general sense of mangala (Kalyana Sraddha) and in the capacity for unbounded love for all beings and all objects. This is Prema Samarthyam.

The perfect state of Buddhi consists in a general purity and clearness of [the] thinking faculty (Vishuddhata and Prakasha); in richness and great variety and minuteness of the perceptions ([Vichitra][9] Bodha); and in the power of the mind to receive and adapt itself to any kind of knowledge without feeling anywhere a limit or an incapacity. This is Jnana Samarthyam.

Daivi Prakriti (Divine Nature)

This means the possession of the four Shaktis — Maheshwari, the Shakti of greatness and knowledge; Mahakali, the Shakti of force and violence; Mahalakshmi, the Shakti of beauty, love and delight; and Mahasaraswati, the Shakti of worldly reason (science) and work. The possession of these Shaktis carries with it a sense of the Divine Power, of general compassion [and] helpfulness to the world, and of faculty for any work that [the] nature may undertake.

Sraddha or Faith
1. Faith in God — Directing Power, Antaryami
2. Faith in Shakti — Executive Power.

III. Vijnana Chatusthaya

Jnanam (Divine thought), Trikaladrishti, Ashta Siddhi, Samadhi

Jnanam: The mental action consists of four parts: first of all, perception of the object and comparison and contrast with other objects. [Then][10] reasoning about the objects. Judgment whether the reasoning

---

[8] MS *(scribal)* of
[9] MS *(scribal)* Vichar
[10] MS *(scribal)* The

is right or not. And judgment is aided by memory and imagination.

Judgment is a direct perception of the Truth, which may or may not be aided by reasoning and other helps.

Imagination is the power of presenting to yourself things or truths not actually perceived or established by reason, [of][11] seeing possibilities other than actual experience.

Memory is the power of retaining and reproducing mental or sensory impressions.

Judgment has two parts—discernment and direct perception. In the mind both of them are uncertain. In the Vijnana, there is a faculty of discernment called Viveka or Intuitive Discrimination, which sees at once what is wrong and what is right, the real difference between things and also their real resemblances and identities and also how far a truth is true and how far it has to be qualified. This Viveka is independent of reasoning. It knows the fact directly but not by a mere instinct; it knows it luminously with a clear perception which is certain and makes no mistake.

There is also a faculty of Vijnana called Intuition which does the work of reasoning without the necessity of reasoning to arrive at a conclusion; that is to say it [comes to][12] the conclusion not as a conclusion from other facts but as a fact in itself. Afterwards, it can group around that fact all the other facts not as reasons but as related facts which help to retain it.

Inspiration is called Sruti or Hearing because it is not the direct sight of the Truth but a sort of coming of the Truth into the mind in a sudden flash. Generally this Truth comes as a vibration which carries the Truth in it and sometimes it comes as the actual word which by revealing its meaning brings new truth to the mind.

The fourth faculty is Drishti or direct sight. This is not, like intuition, looking into a person, an object or a group of circumstances and finding out the truth about them, but it is the vision of the Truth itself, coming as a luminous thought independent of all circumstances, objects etc.

You must first of all get the Intuition and Discrimination to take up

[11] MS *(scribal)* with
[12] MS *(scribal)* does

the ordinary work of mind, because they alone among the Vijnana faculties can give all the circumstances about the Truth. Otherwise Drishti and Sruti [will be distorted], because the reason will try to interpret them in the light of the circumstances as they are understood rightly or wrongly by the human mind. Even the Intuition and Discrimination will be at first distorted by the action of the reason, imagination, wrong judgment, wrong memory etc. Intuition and Discrimination have to go on working and getting stronger and surer until they are able to clear out from the mind the other activities and themselves take up the whole work. As they increase in Force and Light, the other two will begin to act of themselves. When these four faculties or any of them are applied to the things of thought, ideas and knowledge generally it may be called Jnanam or Divine Thought. When these four faculties are applied to the facts and events of the material world the result is Trikaladrishti, which means the direct knowledge of the past, the intuitive knowledge of the present and the prophetic knowledge of the future. To have it properly, it is necessary that there should be no desire or personal interest in the result or any trusting to reasoning, inferences, speculation etc.

Ashta Siddhi

There are two siddhis of knowledge, three of power and three of being. All siddhis exist already in Nature. They exist in you. Only owing to habitual limitations you make a use of them which is mechanical and limited. By breaking these limitations, one is able to get the conscious and voluntary use of them. The three siddhis of being are siddhis of the Sat or pure substance. In matter, Sat uses these siddhis according to fixed laws but in itself it is free to use them as it chooses. If one can get partly or entirely this freedom, one is said to have these three siddhis. They are Mahima including Garima, second Laghima and third Anima.

Sat manifests as Chit, pure consciousness, and Chit has two sides — consciousness and energy, that is to say knowledge and power. Consciousness in one material being communicates with the same consciousness in another material being by certain fixed methods such as speech, gesture, writing etc. and unconscious mental communication. But these limitations are mere habits [and other methods are possible,] as for instance ants communicate by touch and not by speech. Consciousness in itself is free to communicate between one mind and another without physical means consciously and voluntarily. The two siddhis by which this is done are called Vyapti and Prakamya.

In the same way there is a power in the consciousness of acting upon other conscious beings or even upon things without physical means or persuasion or compulsion. Great men are said to make others do their will by a sort of magnetism, that is to say there is a force in their words, in their action, or even in their silent will or mere presence which influences and compels others. To have these siddhis of power is to have the conscious and voluntary use of this force of Chit. The three powers are Aishwarya, Ishita, Vashita. These powers can only be entirely acquired or safely used when we have got rid of Egoism and identified ourselves with the infinite Will and the infinite Consciousness. They are sometimes employed by mechanical means, e.g. with the aid of Mantras, Tantric Kriyas (special processes), etc.

Vyapti is when the thoughts, feelings etc. of others or any kind of knowledge of things outside yourself are felt coming to the mind from those things or persons. This is the power of receptive Vyapti. There is also a power of communicative Vyapti, when you can send or put your own thought, feeling etc. into someone else.[13]

Prakamya is when you look mentally or physically at somebody or something and perceive what is in that person or thing, thoughts, feelings, facts about them etc. There is also another kind of Prakamya which is not of the mind but of the senses. It is the power of perceiving smells, sounds, contacts, tastes, lights, colours and other objects of sense which are either not at all perceptible to ordinary men or beyond the range of your ordinary senses.

---

[13] *The following passage is found in a scribal copy not used for the text printed here. This copy calls the communicative side of vyapti "communication or broadcasting", and goes on:* What happens in the Amutra happens in the Iha. What the Chit-shakti reveals in the Spirit, the Maya-shakti crudely and materially attempts in the material and mental universes. So spiritual Communism of Vijnana has its shadow in the material and Bolshevik Communism; and the Siddhis of the Vijnana are attempted in wireless telegraphy, broadcasting, telephone, image transcription [*transmission?*].

Vashita is when you concentrate your will on a person or object so as to control it.

Aishwarya is when you merely use the will without any such concentration or control and things happen or people act according to that will.

Ishita is when you do not will but merely have a want or need or a sense that something ought to be and that thing comes to you or happens.

Mahima is unhampered force in the mental power or in the physical power. In the physical it shows itself by an abnormal strength which is not muscular and may even develop into the power of increasing the size and weight of the body etc.

Laghima is a similar power of lightness, that is to say of freedom from all pressure or weighing down in the mental, pranic or physical being. By Laghima it is possible to get rid of weariness and exhaustion and to overcome gravitation. It is the basis of Utthapana.

Anima is the power of freeing the atoms of subtle or gross matter (Sukshma or Sthula) from their ordinary limitations. By this power one can get free of physical strain or pain or even make the body as light as one chooses. It is by this power that Yogis were supposed to make themselves invisible [and] invulnerable or [to] free the body from decay and death.

Samadhi

Samadhi means properly the placing of the consciousness on any particular object or in any particular condition. It is generally used for a state of consciousness in which the mind is withdrawn from outward things by [one's] placing the full energy of the consciousness on any particular object or general field. Thus by Samadhi one can become aware of things in this world outside our ordinary range or go into other worlds or other planes of existence. One can also enter into those parts of one's own existence which are either above or below ordinary consciousness or as it is said "superconscient" or "subconscient".

Samadhi may be in three states—Jagrat or waking, Swapna or dream, Sushupta or deep sleep.

Jagrat Samadhi is when in the waking consciousness, we are able to concentrate and become aware of things beyond our consciousness.

This Samadhi may either bring images and experiences seen outside one's own self as if in the physical atmosphere or else inside one's self, generally with the eyes closed. When the eyes are closed, another ether than the physical appears which is called Chittakasha or mental ether. It is in this that images are seen. There is also another ether behind called Chidakasha.

Swapna Samadhi is when the mind has lost its outward consciousness of outward surroundings and goes inside itself. It then has the experience either in itself or of scenes and happenings of this world or other worlds, of the past, present or future. When these experiences are merely distorted memories or confused, falsified and fragmentary, then it is called ordinary dream. [This happens when][14] the mind proper is not acting at all in the physical consciousness and only [   ][15] parts of the nervous system are awake. But when part of the mind remains as it were awake even in [   ][16] sleep, then one may get [accurate][17] records of true and actual experiences. These are not dreams but internal visions. Part of the mind is ranging through time and space or in other worlds. Another part is on the watch to receive its experiences and report them to the physical consciousness.

Sushupta Samadhi, the third stage, is when the whole physical consciousness, at least that part of it which belongs to the waking self, is asleep. When we are in deep sleep we think that nothing is going on in us; but that is a mistake. Consciousness is active all the time. But no report comes from it to the physical mind. In Sushupta Samadhi, one can get to the very limit of human consciousness, even [to][18] the superconscient. Everything which we cannot attain in the waking state is there in us in the dream-self and the sleep-self.

Samadhi is a means of increasing the range of consciousness. We can extend the inner wakefulness in the swapna to planes of existence which are at present sushupta to us and bring them into experience of swapna and even eventually into the waking state.

---

[14] MS *(scribal)* That is because
[15] MS *(scribal)* the
[16] MS *(scribal)* the
[17] MS *(scribal)* acute
[18] MS *(scribal)* of

There are several kinds of Samadhi according to the ordinary classification, such as Satarka in which the mind withdrawn into itself goes on thinking and reasoning and doubting; or Savichara in which the mind does not reason logically but judges and perceives; and so on up to Nirvikalpa Samadhi in which all the lower organs are stopped and there is only the superconscious experience of the Brahman.

IV. Sharira Chatusthaya

Arogya, Utthapana, Saundarya, Ananda

Arogya is the state of being healthy. There are three stages:

(1) When the system is normally healthy and only gets disturbed by exceptional causes or very strong strain, such as continual exposure to cold, overstrain of any kind.

(2) When even exceptional causes or great overstrain cannot disturb the system; this shows that there is full Arogya Shakti.

(3) Immortality in the body.

Utthapana is the state of not being subject to the pressure of physical forces. There are also three stages here:

(1) When there is a great force, lightness and strength in the body (full of vital energy); this shows that the body is full of Prana Shakti.

(2) When there is no physical weariness, no exhaustion of the brain or nervous centres.

(3) When one is not necessarily subject to the law of gravitation or other physical laws.

Saundarya is the state of being beautiful. There are also three stages here:

(1) When there is brightness in the body combined with sweetness of voice and charm of expression etc.

(2) Continual youth.

(3) When the features and figure can be changed to a form of perfect beauty.

Ananda referred to here is Physical Ananda or Kamananda. This is of various kinds, sensuous, sensual etc.

V. Karma Chatusthaya

Krishna, Kali, Karma, Kama

Krishna is the Ishwara taking delight in the world.

Kali is the Shakti carrying out the Lila according to the pleasure of the Ishwara.

Karma is the Divine Action.

Kama is the Divine Enjoyment.

VI. Brahma Chatusthaya

Sarvam, Anantam, Jnanam, Anandam Brahma

Sarvam Brahma—	when we realise one thing in the universe.
Anantam Brahma—	when we realise Infinite Force and Quality at play in all forms.
Jnanam Brahma—	when we realise a consciousness in everything which is aware of all.
Anandam Brahma—	when we realise in that consciousness a delight in all things.

VII. Siddhi Chatusthaya

Shuddhi, Mukti, Bhukti, Siddhi

Shuddhi

(1) Of the Pranas—Release from Vasana or desire, that is Asakti or attachment, action of emotion, e.g. I must have that, I cannot do without that; Kamana or longing, action of desire, i.e. I want that; Raga-dwesha or preference, action of mind, i.e. I prefer this. There are also [the opposites of these],[19] non-attachment, non-longing or craving and non-preference. We have also to [be released][20] from these things. When you have effected these three things you will have perfect Samata. Then you will naturally have perfect Shanti, that is Divine Peace [and] perfect or Shuddha Bhoga, that is Divine Enjoyment.

---

[19] MS (scribal) other sides
[20] MS (scribal) release

Shanti is the negative Ananda and those have it who rest in the Nirguna Brahman. Shuddha Bhoga is the positive Ananda and those have it who rest in the Trigunatita Ananta Brahman. Enjoy the world with Shuddha Bhoga based on the perfect Shanti. That which you get as the result of satisfied desire is troubled, unsafe, feverish or limited, but Shuddha Bhoga is calm, self-possessed, victorious, unlimited, without satiety and vairagya, immortally blissful. It is in a word, not Harsha, not Sukha, but Ananda. It is Amrita, it is Divinity and Immortality, it is [becoming of][21] one nature with God. [The soul][22] has then no Kama but pure Lipsa, an infinite readiness to take and enjoy whatever God gives.[23]

(2) Of the Chitta — Release from all sanskaras of feeling.

(a) Thought impulses start up from Chitta as instincts, inspirations, insights, intuitions etc. They come up coloured by emotions, distorted by associations and perverted by [the] imagination[s] which bring them up. Bhakti, genius, poetic inspiration all come from this source.

(b) Impulses of feeling are of two kinds, natural or eternal, artificial or Vikaras. Love, courage, compassion are natural and are actions caused by Jnanam. Hatred, fear, disgust are Vikaras and are distortions or reactions caused by Ajnanam.

(c) Impulses of action: Shuddha Pravritti, that is, action without desire independent of emotion. Ashuddha Pravritti, that is, action stirred by two forces, desire and emotion. Prohibit and inhibit by will all action or speech that starts blindly from the passions or emotions surging in the heart.

(3) Of the Manas — Release from habitual thoughts. Still the conceptual activity of the Manas and transfer to the Buddhi its perceptual activity (a part of Prakamya).

(4) Of the Buddhi — Release from reason, imagination, memory and logic and replace[ment of] them by the[ir] divine counterpart[s].

(5) Of the Body — Release from all bodily impurities, disease etc., and attain[ment of] Immortality.

---

[21] MS *(scribal)* of becoming
[22] MS *(scribal)* It
[23] *This paragraph is an almost verbatim transcription of most of the fifth paragraph of Chapter VII of* Yogic Sadhan. *— Ed.*

Mukti

(1) From Dwandwas or dualities

(a) Of the Prana—Kshutpipasa, hunger and thirst; Shitoshna, heat and cold; pleasure and pain of the body.

(b) Of the Chitta—Priyapriyabodha, the sense or feeling of love and hatred; Mangalamangalabodha, the sense of good and evil, good and bad fortune; Manapamanabodha, the sense of honour and obloquy.

(c) Of the Mind (that is, Manas and Buddhi)—Satyasatya, the knowledge of truth and falsehood; Papapunya, the knowledge of virtue and vice.

(2) From Ajnanam and the three gunas.

(a) Sattwa—wherever there is Sattwa, that is the clearness of being or Prakasha, it brings with it sukha or happiness; Sattwa is full of Prakasha.

Sattwa in mind—clearness of mind; we get knowledge.

Sattwa in Chitta—the pure love; we get love.[24]

Sattwa in body—ease, health and so on.

(b) Rajas is the principle of desire and activity; Rajas is full of Pravritti. The result of Rajas is any kind of pain, Duhkha or Ashanti, trouble, disturbance, anxiety.

(c) Tamas is Aprakasha and Apravritti. The result is fear, idleness, too much of sleep, ignorance.

Sattwa is to be replaced by pure Prakasha, Rajas by pure Pravritti, Tamas by pure Shama. There is no desire and no necessity of acting but there is the Divine Impulse which acts through us—this is pure Pravritti. When there is no such Divine Impulse, it is pure Shama, Tapas or force of action being there but not acting. Just as Pravritti is a Divine Force coming and making you act, so the pure Prakasha is the Divine Light bringing knowledge into the consciousness.

By being indifferent, we have to effect Shama; then acting as far as possible only under the Divine Impulse, we get pure Tapas. By keeping the mind always unattached to its own thoughts and activities and on

---

[24] *In all scribal copies, "we get" follows the noun in these two lines. Even when the order of the words is changed the sense remains somewhat unclear.*—Ed.

the watch for Light from above and as far as possible quiet, we get Prakasha.

(3) From Ahankara; from the ignorance that you are the actor etc. Whenever you say "I like this", "I do not want this", there you choose and [act].[25] Whatever comes to you, you have to take and enjoy. Replace Ahankara or the idea of Aham by the idea that you are the Ishwara.

Bhukti is the Delight of existence in itself, independent of every experience and extending itself to all experiences. [It has three forms:]

(1) Rasagrahanam or taking the Rasa in the mind: (a) bodily sensations, (b) food, (c) events, (d) feelings, (e) thoughts.

(2) Bhoga in the Prana, i.e. Bhoga without Kama or enjoyment without desire.

(3) Ananda throughout the system.

Kamananda—	Physical Ananda, [e.g.][26] Vishayananda, i.e. sensuous pleasure
Premananda—	Getting delight by positive feeling of Love (Chitta)
Ahaitukananda—	Delight without any cause (Manas)
Chidghanananda—	Ananda of the Chit in the object full of the gunas (Vijnana)
Shuddhananda—	Ananda of the Beauty of everything (Ananda)
Chidananda—	Ananda of pure consciousness without the gunas (Chit-tapas)
Sadananda—	Ananda of pure existence apart from all objects and experiences (Sat)

Siddhi of the five Chatusthayas, Brahma, Karma, Sharira, Vijnana and Samata.

---

25 MS *(scribal)* do
26 MS *(scribal)* ie

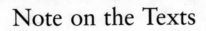

Note on the Texts

Note on the Texts

RECORD OF YOGA is a diary of Sri Aurobindo's *sādhana* or practice of yoga. He wrote entries with some regularity between 1912 and 1920, as well as scattered entries during the years 1909, 1911 and 1927. Some sections of entries have titles, such as "Journal of Yoga", "Record of the Yoga", "Record of Yoga", "Notebook of the Sadhana", "Yoga Diary" and "Yoga Record". The title he used most often is "Record of Yoga" In the text itself he generally referred to the work as "the record" and used the verb "to record" for the act of writing in it. For these reasons the editors have chosen *Record of Yoga* as the general title of the work.

In the entry of 1 July 1912, Sri Aurobindo noted that he had been doing yoga for almost seven years. He had begun in 1905 with the practice of *prāṇāyāma* or breath control. This practice became irregular when he started his political career in 1906 and by the end of 1907 he suffered a "complete arrest" of yogic experience. In January 1908 a yogi named Vishnu Bhaskar Lele showed him how to silence the activity of his mind. This led to the experience of the static Brahman or Nirvana. A few months later, in Alipore Jail, he had the experience of the dynamic Brahman or cosmic consciousness. He later referred to these as the first two of the "four great realisations" of his yoga. The other two—"that of the supreme Reality with the static and dynamic Brahman as its two aspects and that of the higher planes of consciousness leading to the Supermind"—began in jail, but developed more fully during the period of sadhana chronicled in the Record.

In April 1910, Sri Aurobindo left politics and settled in Pondicherry. Sometime after his arrival, as he explained in 1926, he "was given" a "programme of what I would do" in yoga. This programme had seven sections, each made up of four elements. It thus was known as "sapta chatusthaya" or the seven tetrads. (The proper transliteration of the Sanskrit phrase is *sapta catuṣṭaya*. Sri Aurobindo almost invariably spelled the second word "chatusthaya".) Because of the importance of this system to the yoga of the Record, the editors have placed Sri Aurobindo's written presentations of the seven chatusthayas before the dated Record entries. The system is explained in more detail in the "scribal version" of Sapta Chatusthaya, which is published in the Appendix, and in the introduction to the glossary, which is published in a separate booklet. All the terms of the system and all other non-English terms found in the Record are defined in the glossary.

Sri Aurobindo used an assortment of notebooks and loose sheets for writing the Record. The notebooks are of the same kinds as those used for other writings of the period; indeed many of them also contain notes, prose articles, poems, etc. Most of them are cheap student exercise-books, others are simply perforated pads of note-paper. There are also a few bound pocket notebooks; only one of these is a printed diary. In all, twenty-eight notebooks were used exclusively or principally for the Record. Several others contain significant amounts of Record material. In addition, a number of diary entries, mostly undated, and an assortment of Record-related jottings have been found scattered in a dozen or more notebooks and on loose sheets and odd scraps of paper.

Most diary entries, as opposed to records of "script" and "lipi" (these terms are explained below), seem to have been written down directly without notes. Entries were usually written on the dates given in the headings; sometimes there were two or more sittings in a day. Occasionally, however, the sadhana of the preceding night was noted down the next morning. Sometimes a single entry covers two or more days. Other entries seem to have been written a day or two in retrospect.

Many Record entries are divided into sections by means of single and double lines in the manuscript. That the lines had a specific purpose is indicated by the fact that Sri Aurobindo sometimes cancelled them. So far as typography permits, such lines and other markings are reproduced as they occur in the notebooks.

The editors have divided the Record proper, that is, the dated diary entries, into three parts: (1) entries written before the start of the "regular record" in November 1912; (2) the main series of entries, written between November 1912 and October 1920; (3) entries written in 1927 (and perhaps also at the end of 1926). The editors have further divided each of the parts into sections. These begin either where Sri Aurobindo resumed making entries after a significant break in the writing, or where he began work in a new notebook. Each section thus covers a specific chronological period, though sometimes there is a bit of overlap between sections. In one place the editors have put three partly concurrent groups of entries in a single section.

Thus divided, the Record proper comprises forty-four sections. Some of these contain scores of entries covering more than a hundred pages, others only a handful of entries covering less than a dozen pages. Sri Aurobindo began some but not all sections with headings written above the first entry or on the cover of the notebook. These have been reproduced as written. The editors have placed a heading in bold type at the beginning of every section. These editorial headings are in the following form: **28 JANUARY – 17 FEBRUARY 1911.**

Over the course of the years, Sri Aurobindo structured sections of entries in different ways. Recurrent features were sometimes abandoned, only to be taken up again months later. Some entries consist only of the briefest notations, occasionally presented in tabular fashion. Other entries were written in discursive prose that sometimes has literary qualities. During certain periods, Sri Aurobindo divided longer entries by means of subheadings. Most of these make use of the terminology of the seven chatusthayas.

Like all diaries — consciously literary productions excepted — the Record was written chiefly as an aid to the diarist. Sri Aurobindo's conception of its purpose is contained in certain early entries. It was meant to be a "pure record of fact and experience" (13 January 1912). The "condition of the activity" of his sadhana was "to form the substance of the record" (2 January 1913). Stated otherwise, it was the "progress of the siddhi" that was "to be recorded" (31 December 1912). This and other uses of the verb "record" suggest that Sri Aurobindo's writing down of an experience was a means by which he established it in his consciousness.

Sri Aurobindo wanted to record "definite results", not "every fluctuation of the siddhi" (15 August 1914). On a path like his, where "all life is yoga", this involved not only noting down such purely yogic activities as "trikaldrishti, aishwarya, samadhi-experience", but also mentioning "work, literary & religious", and making "brief note of the physical siddhi" (27 December 1912). All parts of the sadhana were given attention. We find one passage in which Sri Aurobindo speaks first of applied yogic knowledge and force, *trikāladṛṣṭi* and *tapas*, then the subtle physical power of levitation and then, in the next sentence, the condition of his teeth. This is followed, without a pause, by a note on the intensity of *ānanda* (delight) then being felt in his body. The paragraph closes with a mention of the state of "the personal lilamaya relation with the Master of the Yoga", the personal divinity who guided his sadhana (17 September 1913).

Another purpose of the Record was to be a register of guidance from this and other sources. It was, he wrote on 18 November 1914, to "include not only the details of what is accomplished & the lines of the accomplishment that is being attempted, but also the record of experiences and the indications of the future movement". Such indications were supplied by various means, notably "script", "lipi", "sortilege", and "vani". Full definitions of these terms are given in the glossary. Roughly, "script" is writing on paper, similar to but not the same as "automatic writing" (see below); "lipi" is writing seen by the subtle vision; "sortilege" is printed or handwritten texts sought or found by chance and interpreted; "vani" is the hearing of a voice. Sri Aurobindo transcribed many examples of each of these sorts of communication in the Record. Sometimes he seems to have jotted down scripts or lipis on handy pieces of paper and then copied them into the Record. A few rough notations of scripts that later were copied exist. The copied versions show some amplification. Sometimes only the rough notations have survived; these have been among the most difficult parts of *Record of Yoga* to transcribe. There are also numerous examples of script written separately from the Record proper and never incorporated into it. Some of these identify themselves explicitly as "script", others do not. As a rule such scripts are published in Part Four, separately from the Record proper.

The distinction between script and record is one made by Sri Aurobindo himself, but it was sometimes difficult for the editors to fix the boundary between the two. He occasionally used both words to refer to the same piece of writing. For example, in the regular record of 14 January 1912 he mentioned an "accompanying memorandum" containing the "rest of the record of January 14th & the record of

January 15th". This "memorandum" speaks of itself as "script". Some regular Record entries read like others that identify themselves as script; some entries (for instance, many in June to August 1914) give under the heading "Script" the sort of information generally found in the regular Record.

The principal difference between Record proper and script proper appears to be the way the writings took form in Sri Aurobindo's consciousness. Record was Sri Aurobindo's own "record of fact and experience", written in much the same was as he wrote his other writings. In the Record the word "I", if it occurs, refers to Sri Aurobindo himself. Script, on the other hand, was communicated to Sri Aurobindo by "the Master of the Yoga" or another source. This source sometimes addressed itself as "I" and Sri Aurobindo as "you" (see for example page 1303). In recording script, Sri Aurobindo often wrote down only the source's replies, not the mental questions to which the replies were given. This makes some scripts seem discontinuous and incomplete; reading them is like overhearing one end of a telephone conversation.

Script has some affinities with "automatic writing", a means of written communication in which the pen is said to be directed by a disembodied spirit. Some examples of this are published in Part Five; the phenomenon is discussed below, in the note to that part. Sri Aurobindo considered many automatic writings to be transcriptions of "the thing that is present in the subconscious part of the medium". He did not consider script to be of this nature. A comparison of the script published as parts of Record entries and in Part Four with the automatic writing published in Part Five reveals marked differences in subject matter, tone, elevation, and purpose.

Script was a "means of spiritual communication" which was used "for all sorts of purposes". Chief among these was the prediction of future events—mostly events in Sri Aurobindo's sadhana, but also outward happenings, ranging from great world events to trivial domestic matters. Scripts relating to sadhana were often called Prediction or Programme; they gave indications about inner movements a few days or a week in advance. Sri Aurobindo sometimes looked back on old scripts, predictive lipis and sortileges to check their accuracy. He occasionally jotted down whether they were fulfilled or not. Such notations are among the only evidence we have that Sri Aurobindo read back over the Record. He certainly never revised it in the way he did almost all his other writings. Additions to and corrections of the Record manuscripts were, with few exceptions, evidently made during the act of writing.

INTRODUCTION. SAPTA CHATUSTHAYA

As mentioned above, Sapta Chatusthaya or the seven tetrads was the "programme" of Sri Aurobindo's sadhana that he received sometime after his arrival in Pondicherry in April 1910. It is not known exactly when the system came to him, but it must have been familiar to him by 16 January 1912, when he referred in the Record to "the first two chatusthayas". (Note that the term "chatusthaya" does not occur in the Record of 28 January – 17 February 1911.) The system consists of twenty-eight elements arranged in seven groups of four. Throughout the Record the chatusthayas are referred to both by name and by number. These are listed in the chart below, along with the elements of each chatusthaya:

First chatusthaya. Samata chatusthaya [*earlier*, Shanti chatusthaya]
    Samata, Shanti, Sukha, Hasya [*later*, (Atma)prasada]
Second chatusthaya. Shakti chatusthaya
    Virya, Shakti, Chandibhava [*later*, Daivi Prakriti], Sraddha
Third chatusthaya. Vijnana chatusthaya
    Jnana, Trikaldrishti, Ashtasiddhi, Samadhi
Fourth chatusthaya. Sharira chatusthaya
    Arogya, Utthapana, Saundarya, Ananda [*or* Vividhananda]
Fifth chatusthaya. Karma chatusthaya [*or* Lila chatusthaya]
    Krishna, Kali, Karma, Kama [*last two sometimes reversed*]
Sixth chatusthaya. Brahma chatusthaya
    Sarvam Brahma, Anantam Brahma, Jnanam Brahma, Anandam
                                                              Brahma
Seventh chatusthaya. Yoga chatusthaya [*or* (San)siddhi chatusthaya]
    Shuddhi, Mukti, Bhukti, Siddhi

This is what Sri Aurobindo called the "natural and logical order" of the chatusthayas and is the only one referred to in the Record proper. Other orders occur, however; for example, the one given in "Outline of the Seven Chatusthayas (Revised Order)" (see next page).

In the Record, the elements, or "siddhis", of each chatusthaya are sometimes referred to by the number of the element within the cha- tusthaya: for example, "the second element of the shakti-chatusthaya". In addition the siddhis of the third, fourth, fifth, sixth and seventh chatusthayas are often referred to by the numbers 1 to 21 — 21 and not 20 because in this enumeration the third chatusthaya is considered to have five instead of four elements. The scheme is as follows:

1. Jnana 2. Trikaldrishti 3. Rupa(-siddhi) 4. Tapas 5. Samadhi 6. Arogya 7. Ananda 8. Utthapana 9. Saundarya 10. Krishna 11. Kali 12. Karma 13. Kama 14. Sarvam Brahma 15. Anantam Brahma 16. Jnanam Brahma 17. Anandam Brahma 18. Shuddhi 19. Mukti 20. Bhukti 21. Siddhi

Sapta Chatusthaya. This text almost certainly was written on 20 November 1913. On that day Sri Aurobindo noted in the Record: "The day was chiefly occupied in writing the seven chatusthayas." The handwriting and paper used for the manuscript of this piece are similar to those of other manuscripts of 1913.

Outline of the Seven Chatusthayas (Revised Order). Sri Aurobindo wrote this outline during or not long after 1914 in an exercise-book used previously by one of his disciples for some of the notes published in the Appendix as "Material from Disciples' Notebooks". In it the chatusthayas are listed in a different order from the one generally used in the Record. The "three general chatushtayas" come first, the one that Sri Aurobindo called the "means, the sum and the completion of all the rest" heading the list. Then follow the "four chatusthayas of the Adhara-siddhi", the perfection or *siddhi* of the individual "vehicle" (*ādhāra*).

Incomplete Notes on the First Chatusthaya. Sri Aurobindo wrote these notes in the exercise-book he used for the above "Outline of the Seven Chatusthayas", at around the same time. The end of the last sentence, from the word "qualities", is not found in the manuscript, but is in several scribal copies of the text written by disciples; it undoubtedly was added by Sri Aurobindo to a copy that has since been lost.

PART ONE. DIARY ENTRIES 1909–1912

The diary entries in the first two sections of this part differ in kind from those written afterwards. The first section dates from ten months before Sri Aurobindo's arrival in Pondicherry in April 1910, and contains little of the terminology of the Sapta Chatusthaya. The entries of 1911, unlike the rest of the Record, are arranged under subject headings. The three sections from 1912 contain entries that differ little from those published in Part Two, but they come before the beginning of what Sri Aurobindo called "the regular record of the sadhana".

17–25 June 1909. Sri Aurobindo made these entries in a small pocket notebook during a visit to East Bengal (the present Bangladesh). A month and a half earlier, he had been released from jail after his acquittal in the Alipore Bomb Case. As the most prominent leader of the Bengal Nationalist party, he had been invited to Jhalakati, a town in Bakarganj District, to attend the 1909 session of the Bengal Provincial Conference of the Indian National Congress. The principal event of the tour was the speech he delivered in Jhalakati on 19 June 1909 (reproduced on pages 33–42 of *Karmayogin*, volume 8 of THE COMPLETE WORKS OF SRI AUROBINDO).

28 January–17 February 1911. During this period Sri Aurobindo wrote dated Record entries under the following six headings: "Physical," "Communications", "Vision of other worlds", "Record of the Drishti", "Siddhis", and "Record of Ideal Cognitions". He wrote them on scattered pages of a notebook he had used years earlier in Baroda as a book catalogue, and later in Pondicherry for various prose and poetic writings.

13 January–8 February 1912. The Record of 12 December 1911 to 11 January 1912, referred to in the first sentence of the entry of 13 January, has not survived. Sri Aurobindo wrote Record entries for January and February 1912 in a notebook he had used in Baroda for literary essays and in Pondicherry for notes and articles on linguistics and other subjects. Above the first entry he wrote the heading "Record of the Yoga". This is the first surviving heading for a section of Record entries. An "accompanying memorandum" containing dated script for 14 and 15 January, which he wrote on a separate sheet of paper, is published between the notebook entries for 14 and 16 January. Note that Sri Aurobindo left long horizontal blanks after some sentences in the notebook. These appear to serve the purpose of paragraph separators.

1–25 July 1912. During this period, Sri Aurobindo kept the Record in a large ledger used otherwise for notes on linguistics and for prose writings on many subjects. He headed it "Journal of Yoga".

12 October–26 November 1912. During this period, Sri Aurobindo kept the Record in a small notebook used for Vedic and linguistic notes, translations, Bengali and Latin poetry, etc. The entries of 18 October to 17 November were written in ink on consecutive pages (with one page left blank between the first and second entries of 18 October). The remainder of the entries were written in purple pencil on scattered pages, sometimes upside down in relation to the rest of the entries. In the same notebook he also wrote a brief record of sortileges of May and June 1912 and several other Record-related pieces that are published in Part Four.

PART TWO. RECORD OF YOGA 1912–1920

The undated general note preceding the entry of 26 November 1912 begins: "The regular record of the sadhana begins today. . . ." The editors have followed this indication by making the entry of 26 November the first in the main series of Record entries. There are, all told, entries for a little more than half of the ninety-six months making up the "regular" period of November 1912 to October 1920.

26 November–31 December 1912. During this period, Sri Aurobindo kept the Record in an exercise-book used previously for notes on the Veda. The daily entries are preceded by an undated general note, written probably on 26 November.

1–31 January 1913. During this period, Sri Aurobindo kept the Record in an eighty-page exercise-book used only for this purpose, making it the first notebook devoted exclusively to the Record. Inside its front cover he wrote "Record of the Yoga. / 1913. / January."

1–14 February 1913. During this period, Sri Aurobindo kept the Record in the first part of an exercise-book, most of which was later used for another purpose. Inside the front cover he wrote "Record of the Yoga / 1913 / February". After the second week of February, he discontinued the Record until the beginning of April.

1 and 12 April, 19 and 21 May 1913. On 1 April 1913 Sri Aurobindo began keeping the Record in a new exercise-book, on the cover of which he wrote "Record of Yoga — / April." After making two entries during the first two weeks of April and two entries in May, he set the notebook aside until July.

4 – 30 June 1913. During the month of June 1913, Sri Aurobindo kept the Record in three separate forms that sometimes overlap, with the result that there are sometimes two entries for a single date.

(1) Between 4 June and 28 June, he wrote entries on three sheets of blank paper, each folded to form four narrow pages. He headed this bunch "Record". These entries are similar to those making up the rest of the Record, although they are written in a more tabular and abbreviated form.

(2) Between 16 and 24 June, he wrote a second set of entries on two sheets of blank paper folded like the ones described above. He headed this bunch "Script". These entries include not only the kind of communications to which he usually gave that name, but also more general comments.

(3) Between 25 and 30 June, he wrote several entries similar to the above script notations on a separate sheet of paper (of the same kind as the others and folded similarly) under the title "Record of Details & Guidance."

These three groups of entries are published separately in the above order.

1 – 11 July 1913. During this period, Sri Aurobindo kept the Record in the notebook he had set aside in May. The entry of 1 July starts on the page that has the end of the entry of 21 May. No Record was written, or none survives, for the month of August 1913.

5 – 21 September 1913. During this period, Sri Aurobindo kept the Record in the notebook he had set aside in July, leaving three blank pages between the entry for 11 July and the two entries for 5 September. The first of these entries was written in pencil and may be considered an incomplete draft of the second, which is written in pen. The first sentence of the first entry suggests that a now-lost Record was kept during the first days of September and perhaps also for part or all of August, perhaps on loose sheets, like the Record of June.

22–30 September 1913. Sri Aurobindo wrote these entries on four pages of the notebook used previously for the "Record of Yogic details" of 31 May–15 June and the "Record of Yoga. / Theosophic" of 13 and 15 September (both published in Part Four). They are more in the nature of script than ordinary record. No entries were written, or none have survived, for the month of October 1913.

11–23 November 1913. During this period, Sri Aurobindo kept the Record on four pieces of writing paper folded to form sixteen narrow pages (two of which were not used).

24 November–2 December 1913. On 24 November Sri Aurobindo returned to the notebook last used on 21 September. He continued to make entries in this notebook through most of December.

1–12 December 1913. Sri Aurobindo wrote most of the entries for this period on four loose sheets of paper. He also wrote entries for 1, 2 and 12 December in the notebook used for most of 1913 (see the notes immediately above and below).

12–21 December 1913. On 12 December Sri Aurobindo returned to the exercise-book last used on 2 December. He continued to make daily entries in this notebook until 21 December, when he reached its last page.

22 December 1913–15 January 1914. On 22 December Sri Aurobindo began a new exercise-book, on the front cover of which he wrote "Record of Yoga / Dec 22^d 1913...". On 1 January, in order to mark the new year, he wrote the heading "1914. January." and part of a verse from the Rig Veda (1.13.6), on an otherwise blank page of the notebook. He continued to use it until 15 January 1914. No Record was written, or none survives, for the period between 15 January and 12 March 1914.

12 March–14 April 1914. On 12 March Sri Aurobindo began a new exercise-book, which he used for the Record until 14 April. He later wrote on its cover: "Record of Yoga. March. April. / 1914."

15 April–1 June 1914. Sri Aurobindo kept the Record for this period in a single exercise-book, on the cover of which he wrote: "Record of Yoga / April 15th to / 1914". After the entry for 1 June he wrote a heading for 2–3 June, but made no entry and then abandoned the notebook. When he resumed the Record on 10 June, he began work in a new notebook.

10 June – 29 September 1914. During this period, Sri Aurobindo kept the Record in a small, thick hard-cover notebook which he used for no other purpose. He wrote the heading "Record of Yoga. / June. 1914 – " on an otherwise blank page facing the first page used for entries. After writing the incomplete entry for 29 September, he went on to a new notebook, leaving the last five pages of this one blank.

29 – 30 September – 31 December 1914. After reaching the end of the notebook containing the Record of June to September 1914, Sri Aurobindo began work in a similar small, hard-cover notebook. Inside the front cover he wrote "October – 1914." Before writing the entry dated "October 1", he wrote a long note headed "Preliminary" and dated "Sept 29 – 30".

1 January – 27 February 1915. Sri Aurobindo kept the Record for this period partly in the notebook in use since October 1914 and partly in another. The first notebook contains, after an otherwise blank sheet headed "January", an introductory note followed by entries for 1 – 6 and 24 – 30 January and 1 – 6, 25 and 27 February 1915. In the second notebook Sri Aurobindo kept an "intermediate record" for 2 – 23 January. There are thus two sets of entries for 2 – 6 January. The editors reproduce the intermediate record after the first set of entries for 1 – 6 January, and before the entries of 24 January – 27 February. Sri Aurobindo wrote two annotations to the entry of 3 January in the "intermediate record" sometime after the original entry. The pen and the ink used for the annotations are the same as those used for the Record of January – February 1917, which was kept in the same notebook. Apparently Sri Aurobindo wrote these comments when he took up this notebook again after a lapse of two years.

22 April – 26 August 1915. During this period, Sri Aurobindo kept the Record in a letter-pad of the sort he used for writing material for the *Arya*, his monthly philosophical review. The entries begin abruptly; no mention is made of the gap between 27 February and 22 April. Sri Aurobindo put a question-mark after the date "April 22^d". The year of these entries is nowhere written, but the dates and days of the week correspond to those of 1915. After the entry of 26 August

Sri Aurobindo left a few pages blank, then began the entry dated "February 1916" with the words, "In the interval since August. . . ."

19 February – 20 March 1916. Sri Aurobindo wrote no Record entries between 26 August 1915 and mid-February 1916. On 19 February 1916 he resumed the Record, using the letter-pad he had set aside in August. The last paragraph of the entry for 19 February is found at the bottom of the preceding page in the manuscript, after the general introduction to February 1916. In the margin next to this paragraph, Sri Aurobindo wrote: "This should have been recorded on the next page." He also put a long double line to separate the misplaced paragraph from the rest of the contents of the page, and inserted the date "Saturday Feb 19th" at the top of the paragraph. This date has been put editorially within square brackets at the head of the entry of the nineteenth, which itself is dated only "Feb". After the entry of 5 March, the dates written in the manuscript do not agree with the days of the week according to the calendar for 1916. The discrepancy continues until the entry marked "Monday. 19th March" in the manuscript, where the Record for 1916 terminates. It may be noted that Sri Aurobindo left a page blank between the entry of "Sunday / March 5" and the one marked "Tuesday. Mar 6". This suggests that he wrote no entry for Monday, 6 March, and this resulted in a confusion of dates. The editors have accordingly emended the dates rather than the days of the week.

9 January – 14 February 1917. No Record was written or survives for the period of March 1916 to January 1917. Sri Aurobindo kept the Record of 9 January – 14 February 1917 in a small bound notebook used previously for notes on the Veda, for the "intermediate record" of 2 – 23 January 1915, and again for notes and an essay on the Veda. The entries for January – February 1917 were written on pages or parts of pages that had been left blank when the Vedic work was done. At one point thirty pages of Vedic material intervene between pages used for the Record. After the entry of 14 February this notebook was set aside, though a few usable pages remained.

15 February – 31 March 1917. During this period, Sri Aurobindo kept the Record in a small hard-cover notebook similar to the one he had used from 9 January to 14 February. Like that notebook, the present one had previously been used for notes on the Veda. It was abandoned after the entry of 31 March, many of its pages being left unused. No record was kept or has survived for the period from 1 April to 14 August 1917.

15 August–28 September 1917. During this period, Sri Aurobindo kept the Record in an old exercise-book, a few pages of which had been used some years earlier for the poem *Ilion*. Sri Aurobindo left half a page blank between the entry for 28 September and the one for 14 February 1918. No Record was kept or none survives for the intervening period of more than four months.

14–28 February 1918. During this period, Sri Aurobindo kept the Record in the notebook he had commenced on 15 August 1917.

3–27 March 1918. During this period, Sri Aurobindo kept the Record on a few pages of an old exercise-book used previously for Vedic notes and translations.

20 April–20 May 1918. During this period, Sri Aurobindo kept the Record in a new "Aryan Store Exercise-Book". (The manager of the Aryan Store was Saurin Bose, the "S" or "Sn" of the Record.) This was the first notebook to be used exclusively for the Record since June–September 1914. On its cover Sri Aurobindo wrote "Notebook of the Sadhana". This is the first heading given to a section of Record entries since June 1914.

21 May–1 July 1918. Sri Aurobindo continued the Record of 1918 in an "Aryan Store Exercise-Book" similar to the one used between 20 April and 20 May. Only three entries were made in June due to "the absorption of work". He set the notebook aside after the entry of 1 July and did not take it up again until June 1919. No Record was kept or none survives for the intervening period of almost one year.

24 June–14 July 1919. Sri Aurobindo kept the Record for this period in the notebook set aside on 1 July 1918. He left five pages blank between the entry for that date and the one for 24 June 1919.

15–26 July 1919. During this period, Sri Aurobindo kept the Record in a thin exercise-book used only for this purpose. On its cover he wrote the heading "Yoga Diary" and the opening and closing dates.

27 July–13 August 1919. During this period, Sri Aurobindo kept the Record in a thin exercise-book similar to the previous one, and like it used only for Record entries. On its cover he wrote the heading "Yoga Diary" and the opening and closing dates.

14 August–24 September 1919. During this period, Sri Aurobindo kept the Record in a thin exercise-book similar to the previous two, and like them used only for Record entries. On its cover he wrote the heading "Yoga Diary" and the opening date. It has almost daily entries until 2 September, then one dated "Sept. 3 to 24", which explains the gap before the final entry of 24 September. He apparently did not resume the Record until February of the next year.

1–29 February 1920. During this period, Sri Aurobindo kept the Record on seven pieces of paper of different sizes and shapes folded in various ways. Entries which continue from one page to another sometimes have the date repeated at the top of the new page followed by "continued" or "(cont.)". These headings have been omitted from the printed text.

1 March–10 April 1920. During this period, Sri Aurobindo kept the Record in a thin exercise-book used only for the purpose. Above the long introduction preceding the entry dated 1 March he wrote the heading "Yoga Diary. / 1920 / March." No entries have been found for the period between 10 April and 7 June 1920.

7–26 June 1920. During this period, Sri Aurobindo kept the Record in a thin exercise-book similar to the previous one, and like it used only for this purpose. Above the first entry he wrote the heading "Yoga Record / June."

17–19 October 1920. Sri Aurobindo wrote Record entries for these three days on a few pages of a letter-pad. He wrote the date "17th October 1920" on the first sheet of the pad.

PART THREE. RECORD OF YOGA 1926–1927

No Record entries were written, or none survive, for the six-year period between October 1920 and December 1926. Sri Aurobindo wrote very little during this period. There are no known articles or poems and only a few letters that have dates to show that they were written during the six years that followed the suspension of the *Arya* in January 1921. The abrupt beginning of the entries preceding those of December 1926– January 1927 suggests that Sri Aurobindo may have made Record entries during parts of the period between 1920 and 1926, but chose not to preserve them, as he chose not to preserve those of October 1927 (see below).

December 1926–6 January 1927. Sri Aurobindo wrote these entries in a letter-pad used previously for writing Vedic notes and several pieces published in Part Four, including "The Seven Suns of the Supermind". That piece comes immediately before the first entry here, which speaks of the "supramental life-energy" in the "seven centres". The first two pages of this section of Record notes are undated. The third page begins with three short paragraphs which seem to have been written on a single day. This was probably Sunday, 2 January 1927, for the entry is followed on the same page by closely related entries marked "Monday", "Tuesday" and "Wednesday", then by one dated "Thursday. Jan 6." Sri Aurobindo did not write the year 1927 until 7 April (see below), but the agreement between the dates and days of the week written in the notebook and those of the calendar for 1927 proves that this was the year for the entries of January and February.

The two pages of undated entries preceding the partially dated ones were apparently written shortly before them. Most likely they belong to the first of three "curves" of progress in Sri Aurobindo's sadhana (25 December–3 January, 3–7 January and 7–12 January) which he mentioned in the entry for 6 January. This inference is supported by the text of a prediction written on the second undated page: "Monday next. An ascending scale till then." It seems probable that Monday, 3 January, the end of the "curve" that began on 25 December, was also the culmination of the "ascending scale" mentioned in the prediction.

7 January–1 February 1927. Sri Aurobindo wrote these entries in the letter-pad used for the above section. The entry of 7 January is preceded by some diagrams and script jottings published in Part Four.

7–22 April 1927. Sri Aurobindo kept the Record for this period in the letter-pad used for the two preceding sections. Between the entry for 1 February and the one for 7 April come several blank pages, two drafts of an essay, some script, and a poem written in French. No Record was written, or none survives, for the period between April and October 1927.

24–31 October 1927. During this eight-day period, Sri Aurobindo kept the Record on two loose sheets of paper. Another sheet discovered with them contains a passage of script published in Part Four. It would appear that Sri Aurobindo tore these three sheets up and threw them away. They were saved from destruction by A. B. Purani, one of his early disciples. The explanatory note reproduced below was written by Purani during the 1950s or 1960s:

> These few pages of Sri Aurobindo's diary of his Sadhana were intended to be burnt. The story of how they escaped that fate is as follows.
>
> To prepare hot water for the Mother's bath very early in the morning was part of the work I had undertaken almost from 1926. I was staying in the 'guest-house' at that time & used to come to the main house between 2.30–3 in the night. In order not to disturb the inmates of the house I was given a key of one of the gates to enter it. The water had to be ready before 4 o'clock, often it was needed at 3.30. (This continued up to 1938 November 23rd when Sri Aurobindo got the accident.)
>
> The boiler room is well-known — it is now the place from where incense is still fired and flowers distributed when it rains. The fuel used was ordinary wood with wooden shavings from the Carpentry department & waste papers. The wooden shavings often contained strips of teak-wood & many other useful tit-bits. I used to preserve them and make time-piece cases, photo-frames, corner brackets from them. When the matter was brought to Mother's notice by someone she approved of such salvaging from waste & added that there were men in France — in Paris — the chiffonniers who became rich only by utilising the enormous waste of papers & rags in the big city.
>
> But the papers I invariably burnt. Perhaps the god of Fire must have become suddenly active, because one day I was struck by half a basketful of torn small bits & casually looked at them. To my surprise and horror I found Sri Aurobindo's handwriting. I put them aside and looked at them in the daylight. I was able to make out with great labour extending for days — like a jig-saw puzzle — two or three readable pages.
>
> These pages are dated & they are evidently notes kept by Sri Aurobindo regarding his own Sadhana.

It is not known whether other pages of the Record from this period, or other periods, were actually destroyed.

This part consists of writings in Sri Aurobindo's own hand that may be considered components of *Record of Yoga*, but which have not been included in Parts One to Three because they are undated or incompletely dated or, if dated, not concerned with Sri Aurobindo's day-to-day sadhana. A number of different sorts of writings are represented: brief undated Record entries, scripts, sortileges, lipis, and notes on a wide variety of sadhana-related topics. They have been arranged in rough chronological order, groups of scripts being placed together in several chronological series.

Undated Record and Record-related Notes, c. 1910–1914. Sri Aurobindo wrote these fourteen items in different notebooks during the early part of his stay in Pondicherry, that is between 1910 and 1914. Further details on individual pieces or groups of pieces follow. [1] Sri Aurobindo jotted down these undated notes around 1910 in a notebook containing translations and other pieces written years earlier in Baroda and Calcutta. [2] Sri Aurobindo wrote these notes in a notebook used in Baroda for miscellaneous literary writings and in Pondicherry for philological notes. They begin with a reference to Sri Aurobindo's philological research under the heading "Bhasha" ("Language"). Sri Aurobindo's did most of his philological research around 1911–12. The present notes may be assigned to the same period. They have, in addition, some similarity to the Record entries of January–February 1911. Both the notes and the entries are arranged by category, and have one heading in common: "Prophecy". This term is used several times in January–February 1911 for what Sri Aurobindo normally called "trikaldrishti". "Prophecy" occurs rarely in 1912 and all but disappears from the terminology of the Record after that. [3–13] Sri Aurobindo wrote all but one of these eleven pieces on scattered pages of a notebook used in Pondicherry (and perhaps also earlier in Bengal) for miscellaneous writings, notably the play *Eric*, as well as notes on philology and other subjects. They date from the earliest years in Pondicherry, that is, 1910–12. Some of them may even have been written slightly before that. [14] Sri Aurobindo wrote these "Psychological Notes" (his title) in an exercise-book of the kind he used to keep the Record of 1913 and early 1914. The exercise-book also contains a draft of the last version of the "Life Divine" commentary on the Isha Upanishad (see *Isha Upanishad*, volume 17 of the THE COMPLETE WORKS). This commentary may be dated to 1914. The psychological notes apparently date from the same year.

Sortileges of May and June 1912. These two sortileges were written on a page of the notebook that later was used for the Record of 12 October to 26 November 1912 (see above).

Undated Notes, c. November 1912. Written on the first two pages of the notebook used for the Record of 12 October to 26 November 1912.

Draft Programme of 3 December 1912. Written on one of the last pages of the notebook used for the Record of 12 October to 26 November. The programme subsequently was copied, with a few changes, in the Record entry of 3 December, which was written in another notebook.

Undated or Partly Dated Script, 1912–1913. These nine scripts were written on nine different sheets or sets of sheets during the years 1912 and 1913. Further details on individual pieces follow. [1] Written apparently around July 1912, the approximate date of the incomplete "Commentary on the Kena Upanishad" which is referred to in the script. Note also that in the Record of 4 July 1912, Sri Aurobindo wrote "Automatic script recommenced today", and mentioned "prophetic script", a term found nowhere else in the Record. [2] This "record of thought" or script was written at the bottom of a loose sheet containing linguistic notes. Two sentences from it appear verbatim in the Record of 14 October 1912. The script evidently was written on that day and part of it transcribed in the Record. [3] These three pieces of script were written on the inner pages of a large folded sheet of paper used otherwise for linguistic notes and fragmentary writings on other subjects. The linguistic notes are very similar to those found along with item [2]. It is therefore likely that the scripts date from roughly the same period. The predictions contained in the first script may be the same as the "programme suggested on the tenth" mentioned in the Record of 21 December 1912. There are a number of similarities between the elements of sadhana mentioned in the present script and those described in the Record of 10–11 December 1912. [4] This item, written on the last ten of a set of twenty-eight small pages formed by folding loose sheets of paper, may be assigned with some confidence to January 1913. It consists of a long undated passage, followed by four shorter entries with dates from the "21ˢᵗ" to the "24ᵗʰ". The month and year are not specified, but under the "23ᵈ" there is a reference to "this month of January". The year 1913 may be established by comparison with the regular Record of January of that year. See for example the almost identical references to the Turkish city of Adrianople in the script of the "23ᵈ" and the Record of 24 January 1913. Since the partly dated portions of the script belong to 21–24 January 1913, the undated passage preceding them must have been written just before the 21st. Note also that the Record of 19 January states: "This morning script became profuse and intimate. . . ." The script contains some examples of writings in different languages known and unknown. Sri Aurobindo wrote or "received" a number of such writings around this time. The first eighteen of the set of pages on which the script is written are devoted to this project. Some examples of such "writings in different languages" are published in *Vedic Studies with Writings on Philology*, volume 14 of THE COMPLETE WORKS. [5] This script was written sometime around June 1913 on a sheet of letter paper found along with some Vedic and linguistic notes. The paper is of the type used also for item [6] as well as for letters written around June 1913. The third and fifth of the seven "rules" here correspond to some of the five "positive directions" given in the script of 22 June 1913, which is published as part of the Record proper. [6] These four paragraphs of script, written on two loose sheets similar in type to those used for item [5], contain no explicit dating clues, but the position they describe corresponds closely to the one referred to in the Record of 10 and 11 July 1913. The first paragraph says: "Lipi is already moving forward to the mahat. . . ." The Record of 10 July speaks of the "successful movement from manas to mahat predicted in the script", and observes: "The only siddhi which advanced during the day was the lipi." The second paragraph deals with a movement of the vijnana to brihat, to be followed by a further change to satyam and ritam. This is the situation described at the beginning of the second sentence of the Record of 11 July 1913: "At first the knowledge was merely brihat in manas. . . ." [7] This script, written on a single loose sheet, contains no explicit dating clues, but the situation it describes corresponds to the position of Sri Aurobindo's sadhana between July and September 1913. The script may well have been written during the suspension of the regular Record between 11 July and 5 September 1913. [8] This short piece was written at the bottom of the sheet containing the first six paragraphs of the Record of 12 November 1913, but upside down in relation to them. It apparently was written before the commencement or at any rate the completion of the Record entry, which otherwise would have used the space occupied by the script. The style is similar to that of some of the "Thoughts and Aphorisms" and to the "Thought" noted down in the Record of 24 June 1914 beginning "Despise not, O thinker. . . ." [9] This long script was written on a large loose sheet folded to make four pages, the bottom edges of all of which have been damaged. The sheet was found together with the Record entries of 11–23 November 1913 and apparently belongs to the same period; note the phrase "till December" in the second paragraph. There are many similarities between the position of the sadhana as described in this script and in the Record of 12–18 November 1913. Compare, for example, the following passage in the script: " Today a great movement forward. . . . The trikaldrishti, telepathy, power, lipi have now all to move towards absolute perfection dragging the samadhi & drishti with them. Till that is done, the fourth chatusthaya will only prepare its advance . . ." with this passage in the Record of 14 November: "Today is to be a day of rapid progress in the third chatusthaya and the preparation of rapid progress in the fourth." Similarly the last page of the script has parallels with the Record of 17 and 18 November, while the last complete paragraph of the script has similarities to the Record of 18 November 1913.

Sortilege of 15 March [1913]. Written on a page of a notebook used mostly for *Ilion* and other poems. The year is not given but it may be inferred from (1) the handwriting, (2) the period of the other pieces in the notebook, (3) the fact that no regular Record, in which a sortilege would normally have been entered, was kept in March 1913.

Accounts of 31 May–15 June 1913. Written on the first five pages of a notebook used later for Vedic translations and notes, the Record notes of 13 and 15 September (see below) and the Record of 22–30 September 1913. Sri Aurobindo wrote "Record of Yogic details" on the cover of this notebook. It should be remembered that to him "All life is Yoga."

Record Notes, 13 and 15 September 1913. Sri Aurobindo wrote these two entries under the heading "Record of Yoga. / Theosophic." in the notebook used previously for the "Record of Yogic details" (see above) and subsequently for the Record of 22–30 September 1913. The year, not given explicitly, may be inferred from this position. Note that Sri Aurobindo also wrote a regular Record entry in another notebook on 13 September.

Vedic Experience, 14 and 15 December 1913. Sri Aurobindo wrote regular Record entries for both these days, but chose to enter this experience in a notebook used otherwise for Vedic translations and notes.

Undated Notes, c. 1914. Sri Aurobindo wrote these notes headed "Vijnanachatusthaya" on a loose sheet of paper that was found inserted in a notebook used, among other things, for the Record of July 1912. The sheet, however, does not appear to be connected with anything in the notebook, and may have been put there simply as a placemark. The handwriting is that of 1912–14. It is possible that these notes are the "separate detailed record of the results" of the "formulated & steady activity for the regulation of the third chatusthaya" that Sri Aurobindo wrote of having "commenced" in the Record of 1 June 1914.

Notes on Images Seen in March 1914. Sri Aurobindo wrote this piece, which he entitled "The Evolutionary Scale", in March 1914 in an exercise-book of the same sort as he was using then for the Record. In the Record entry of 22 March 1914, he spoke of certain "scenes of a pursuit in the early Manwantaras of a race of divinised Pashus by Barbarians" which were "recorded elsewhere". The reference is evidently to the second section of "The Evolutionary Scale", which begins: "A series of images and a number of intimations have been given yesterday in the chitra-drishti to illustrate the history of the first two Manwantaras. . . ." The word "yesterday", which was added between the lines, would seem to indicate that the second, and probably the first and third sections as well, were written on 23 March. Further references in the Record make it clear that the images of the fourth section and the first paragraph of the fifth section were seen on 24 March, and that the images of the rest of the fifth section and probably those of the sixth were seen on 25 March.

Undated Script, c. 1920. The first of these two scripts is the last piece of writing in a letter-pad whose other contents (Vedic translations, etc.) provide no explicit dating clues. The term "drashtri vijnana", which occurs in the script, is found otherwise only in the Record of March 1920. The second piece, consisting of three short entries, was written on two loose sheets that cannot be precisely dated. The third entry employs the term "logos Vijnana", which occurs in the Record only in October 1920.

Undated Notes, c. December 1926. Sri Aurobindo wrote all but the last of these seven pieces in a letter-pad used previously for Vedic notes and subsequently for the Record of January–February and April 1927, as well as for certain undated Record entries, scripts, etc. "The Seven Suns of the Supermind" is followed closely by Record entries that are considered to have been written in December 1926. It seems likely that that piece and the five preceding it were written in the same month. Sri Aurobindo wrote the seventh piece, "The Seven Centres of the Life", on a sheet from another letter-pad, apparently around the same time.

Undated Notes, c. January 1927. Sri Aurobindo wrote these notes, in which the names of some of his disciples are linked with those of historical, legendary and divine figures, in the letter-pad of 1926–27 referred to above. Before and after it are Record notes that have been dated to the last week of December 1926 and the first week of January 1927.

Notes on Physical Transformation, c. January 1927. Sri Aurobindo wrote these notes in the letter-pad of 1926–27. They come just before the Record notes dated "Thursday. Jan 6." They appear to be more in the nature of script than ordinary writing. (The word "you" obviously refers to Sri Aurobindo, while "she" designates the Mother, as it does in several Record entries of January 1927.)

Diagrams, c. January 1927. Written and drawn in the letter-pad of 1926–27 between entries dated 6 January and 7 January.

Miscellaneous Notations, c. February–April 1927. [1–2] Written on two separate pages of the letter-pad of 1926–27, the first a few pages

after the Record entry of 1 February, the second between the two parts
of the entry of 9 April. (The script must have been written before this
date, since the splitting of the entry of 9 April evidently was due to
the fact that the intervening pages had already been used.) [3] This
lipi, dated 2 April 1927, was written in the letter-pad of 1926–27
between the two parts of the entry of 9 April. [4] Sri Aurobindo wrote
this *mantra* in the letter-pad of 1926–27, just after the lipi described
above.

Record of Drishti, 30 July 1927. Sri Aurobindo wrote these dated notes
in a tiny note-pad used otherwise to record electric-meter readings.

Undated Script, c. 1927. Sri Aurobindo wrote these three sets of script
notations in a notebook belonging to the year 1927. Pieces [1] and [2]
come a little before writings that may be dated with some certainty to
July–August 1927; but some similarities between the terminology of
these entries and the Record of January 1927 suggest that the entries
may have been written earlier in the year. The third piece occurs further
on in the same notebook, and appears to date from somewhat later in
1927.

Undated Script, c. 1927–1928. These four passages of script all come
from manuscripts datable to late 1927 or 1928. All contain references
to "overmind", a term that first occurs in the Record in the entry of
29 October 1927. [1] The torn-up sheet on which this passage was
written was found by A. B. Purani together with those containing the
Record of 24–31 October 1927. Its opening is similar to number 14
of the "Undated Script Jottings" (see below), which was found in a
notebook used in 1928. [2–3] These two passages occur in two different notebooks, both from the period 1927–28. Their terminology
suggests that they may have been written after October 1927, although
this would mean that they were jotted down after most of the contents
of the subsequent pages of the notebooks were written. [4] These two
fragments were found on a scrap of a sheet detached from a letter-pad.
The first occupies what was originally the top of the front of the sheet.
It begins in the middle of a sentence. The preceding page or pages have
been lost. The second fragment occupies what was the bottom of the
reverse of the sheet. (The pad was stitched at the top.) Between the two
fragments came whatever was written on the bottom three-quarters of
the front page and the top three-quarters of the reverse.

Notes on Prophetic Vision, 1929. Sri Aurobindo wrote these dated notes in a small "Bloc-Memo" pad used otherwise for miscellaneous jottings and writings.

Diagrams, c. 1931. Written and drawn on both sides of a piece of letter paper, at the top of which is the conclusion of a letter-draft whose beginning has been lost. The draft ends:

> However I give the schema below and you can see for yourself — it is arranged according to an ascending scale of conscious-ness, grades superimposed on each other, but that does not mean that there is no interpenetration of one by another.

The letter was rewritten on 15 April 1931 and sent without the diagrams.

Undated Script Jottings. These fifteen passages of script were jotted down by Sri Aurobindo on the pages of various notebooks and loose pieces of paper between circa 1915 and the late 1920s. They are arranged in roughly chronological order, though their dates and sometimes even periods are difficult to determine. [1] Written on a sheet torn out of a letter-pad of the sort Sri Aurobindo used for the Record in 1915–16 and for other writings during approximately the same period. [2] Written on a page of a letter-pad containing writings that can be dated 1916–18. [3] Jotted on the last page of a notebook containing Vedic translations and English poetry written at different times. [4–5] Written on two pages of a notebook used around 1926. [6] Written on the back of a letter to Sri Aurobindo dated 16 August 1926. [7–8] Written on the front and back of a loose sheet inserted in the note-pad used for the Record of 1926–27; the loose sheet may once have been the first sheet of the pad, in which case the jottings may date to December 1926. [9–11] Written on three pages of the notebook that was used for the "Undated Script, c. 1927" (see above). [12] Written circa 1927–28 on a torn sheet used otherwise for a passage intended for the revised version of *The Synthesis of Yoga*. [13] Written on a torn letter, perhaps from slightly later than 1928. [14] Written and cancelled at the top of a page of a stenographic pad used around 1928. [15] Written in the margin of a page of a notebook used for the poem *Savitri* in the late 1920s.

PART FIVE. AUTOMATIC WRITING

Sri Aurobindo first tried automatic writing—defined by him as writing not "dictated or guided by the writer's conscious mind"—towards the end of his stay in Baroda (that is, around 1904). He took it up "as an experiment as well as an amusement" after observing "some very extraordinary automatic writing" done by his brother Barin; "very much struck and interested" by the phenomenon, "he decided to find out by practising this kind of writing himself what there was behind it." Barin seems at least sometimes to have used a planchette for his experiments, but Sri Aurobindo generally just "held the pen while a disembodied being wrote off what he wished, using my pen and hand". He continued these experiments during his political career (1906–10) and afterwards. In this part are published one example from 1907, an entire book received as automatic writing in 1910, and a number of examples from two years during which he also kept the Record: 1914 and 1920. His "final conclusion" about automatic writing

> was that though there are sometimes phenomena which point
> to the intervention of beings of another plane, not always or
> often of a high order, the mass of such writings comes from
> a dramatising element in the subconscious mind; sometimes a
> brilliant vein in the subliminal is struck and then predictions
> of the future and statements of things known in the present
> and past come up, but otherwise these writings have not a
> great value.

During the period of the Record, Sri Aurobindo made much use of a form of writing he called "script". As explained above, this was similar to automatic writing in that it came as a communication from another source, but differed from automatic writing in coming from a source that he considered to be higher and more reliable. It should be noted, however, that the distinction of "script" from ordinary automatic writing was not always strictly maintained. Some writings from a lower source refer to themselves as script (see for example page 1410), and Sri Aurobindo used the word "script" for writings that were produced in séances with others (see for example the Record of 17 July 1914, where he writes: "Today excellent script with R [Richard]

& Madame R.") In these examples, "script" is used as a generic term
to cover all forms of written communication from other sources.

"The Scribblings", **c. 1907.** Written in a notebook previously used
by Sri Aurobindo in Baroda for miscellaneous writings. In May 1908
this notebook and several others were seized by the police when Sri
Aurobindo was arrested in connection with the Alipore Bomb Case.
These automatic writings were submitted by the prosecution as evidence against Sri Aurobindo, but were not accepted by the judge as
being in Sri Aurobindo's hand. They were, however, certainly written by him, though, being automatic, they are somewhat illegible;
hence the name by which they were known during the trial: "The
Scribblings". They mention Barindra Kumar Ghose, Sri Aurobindo's
younger brother, who was the active head of a revolutionary group, as
well as three other members.

Yogic Sadhan. Sri Aurobindo received this book as automatic writing
in 1910. According to his biographer A. B. Purani,

> During the first three months of the stay at Pondicherry [April
> –June 1910] there used to be séances in the evening in which
> automatic writing was done. The book *Yogic Sadhan* was
> written in this way. At the rate of one chapter per day, the book
> was finished in a week or eight days. . . . The Editor's Epilogue
> added after the last chapter was written by Sri Aurobindo
> himself. The editor's name is given as "the Uttar[a] Yogi".

A year later, the text that had been received was transcribed and published under the title *Yogic Sadhan* by Sri Vani Vilas Press, Srirangam.
"The Uttara Yogi" (the Yogi from the North) is a name by which
Sri Aurobindo was known to the person who published the book. A
second edition of *Yogic Sadhan*, lightly revised, was brought out by
the Modern Press, Pondicherry, in 1920. Two further editions were
brought out by Arya Publishing House, Calcutta, in 1923 and 1933.
The present text follows the second edition with a few emendations,
mainly in chapters 7–9, for which a manuscript in Sri Aurobindo's
hand survives.

Sri Aurobindo permitted the publication of *Yogic Sadhan*, but he
did not consider it his own work. In a letter of 1934 he wrote:

> The *Yogic Sadhan* is not Sri Aurobindo's own writing, but was published with a note by him, that is all. The statement made to the contrary by the publishers was an error which they have been asked to correct. There is no necessity of following the methods suggested in that book unless one finds them suggestive or helpful as a preliminary orientation of the consciousness—e.g. in the up-building of an inner Will etc.

The "note" referred to is the "Editor's Epilogue", which was included in all editions of *Yogic Sadhan*. Sri Aurobindo allowed the book to go out of print after the edition of 1933 was sold out. It has not been reprinted since then in the form of a book.

Automatic writings, c. 1914 (First Set). These four pieces of automatic writing are found on four loose sheets of paper folded together. They are not dated but almost certainly were written in 1914. The sheet on which item [1] was written contains also a draft of something published in the journal *Arya* in August of that year. Item [2] contains a reference to "the Review", that is, the *Arya*, which was conceived around 1 June 1914 and first published in August. Items [3] and [4] seem to have been written around the same time as the first two items.

Automatic writings, c. 1914 (Second Set). These two pieces of automatic writing were written on four loose sheets of paper folded to make eight pages. The sheets were found along with those on which the previous set were written, and appear to belong to the same period.

Automatic Writing, c. 1920. This short writing was found in a letter-pad used principally for Vedic translations and notes. Below it, on the same page, are a few lines that have been classified as Record-related script and published in Part Four (the first piece of "Undated Script, c. 1920"). That piece has been dated by terminology to around March 1920. The present writing describes itself as "script", that is, a "means of embodied communication with the other worlds"; but the "spirit of the higher realms" who speaks is evidently not the Master of the Yoga. The item is therefore classified as automatic writing rather than script.

Automatic Writings, c. 1920. These nineteen writings were found together in a single batch of seventy-eight loose sheets. They are published here in the order in which they were found. It is likely that each item is the product of a separate séance. References to known events in some of the writings lead one to date them to the summer of 1920. Lokamanya Tilak, who is referred to in item [9] as having departed from the body, apparently rather recently, died on 1 August 1920. The letter referred to in item [8] very likely is the one written by Tilak's associate Dr. B. S. Munje to Sri Aurobindo, inviting him to preside over the 1920 session of the Indian National Congress. Sri Aurobindo's reply turning down this offer is dated 30 August 1920. Mirra Richard (The Mother) and Paul Richard participated in some if not all the sessions. (See especially item [9].) They returned to Pondicherry from Japan on 24 April 1920. Richard left Pondicherry in December of the same year.

APPENDIX. MATERIAL FROM DISCIPLES' NOTEBOOKS

The pieces in this Appendix have been transcribed from versions handwritten by early disciples of Sri Aurobindo. They are copies of notes written by Sri Aurobindo or of written records of his oral remarks. With one partial exception, none of these items exist in the form of manuscripts in Sri Aurobindo's handwriting. The exception is on the last page of item [1] of the "Miscellaneous Notes", where there are three pieces that were written or revised by Sri Aurobindo in his own hand. Only these pieces may be considered to be as authentic as the handwritten Record. Nevertheless, Sri Aurobindo may be regarded as the origin of all the pieces in this appendix, as they are either transcriptions of his talks or copies of now-lost written texts. They represent aspects of his teaching in an early form as given to his earliest disciples.

Miscellaneous Notes, c. 1914. These seven sets of notes are reproduced from handwritten copies made by disciples of Sri Aurobindo in various notebooks. Early copies of items [1], [2] and [5] were written in the exercise-book he used subsequently for the "Incomplete Notes on the First Chatusthaya" published in the Introduction. This notebook has "1914" printed on the cover. Another notebook containing the principal versions of items [3], [4], [6] and [7] has calendars for 1913 and 1914 printed inside the front cover. Many of the disciples' notebooks contain a copy of a letter written by Sri Aurobindo on 21 September

1914. It is reasonable to conclude that the pieces date roughly from the period around 1914.

Sapta Chatusthaya — Scribal Version. This presentation of Sapta Chatusthaya is the most complete one available. There is no manuscript of the piece in Sri Aurobindo's hand, but he was undoubtedly its source. The text survives only in the form of transcripts written down by disciples. Several of these "scribal copies", as the editors term them, have been collated and two of the oldest selected as the basis of the present text.

One of the scribal copies may date from as early as 1914; two others are from the mid-1920s, and most or all of the rest from the 1930s. These copies were made either from a now-lost manuscript written by Sri Aurobindo or, more likely, from one or more written records of a series of talks given by him. The scribal copies may be considered on the whole to be reliable records of the substance of what Sri Aurobindo must have written or said; but all of them contain obvious distortions of his words. Because of this, a much freer hand has been used in the editing of this piece than would have been permissible if the text was based on a handwritten manuscript.

The text is "eclectic"; that is to say, it follows for the most part the scribal version that seems to offer the best text as a whole, but it makes use of readings from the other principal scribal copy where these appear more likely to represent Sri Aurobindo's actual words. Where the scribal copies agree but the reading seems defective, an editorial alternative has been printed between square brackets, as part of the text, and the scribal version given in a footnote. (Such footnote variants are preceded by *"MS (scribal)"*.) The editors have silently made minor corrections of the spelling, punctuation, etc. of these scribal texts.

PUBLISHING HISTORY

No part of *Record of Yoga* was published during Sri Aurobindo's lifetime. The notebooks and loose sheets containing the diary entries and related materials were found after his passing along with his other manuscripts. Most of *Record of Yoga* was published in the journal *Sri Aurobindo: Archives and Research* between 1986 and 1994. Some material — mainly in Parts One, Four and the first section of the Appendix

—was omitted when *Record of Yoga* was published in that journal and appears here for the first time. The publishing history of *Yogic Sadhan* has been given above in the note on Part Five. "The Seven Suns of the Supermind" and the diagrams in Part Four were included in *The Hour of God* (Pondicherry, Sri Aurobindo Ashram) in 1959 and subsequently; there the diagrams were given the editorial title "The Divine Plan". A few related pieces that were added to the reorganised 1982 edition of *The Hour of God* are also included in Part Four. In 1973, Sri Aurobindo's manuscript version of "Sapta Chatusthaya" was published, with much editorial normalisation of the spelling of Sanskrit words and other details, in volume 27 (*Supplement*) of the Sri Aurobindo Birth Centenary Library.

The text of this first edition of *Record of Yoga* has been reproduced verbatim, as far as possible, from the manuscripts of the diary entries and related materials.